Roots Music

The Library of Essays on Popular Music
Series Editor: Allan F. Moore

Roots Music

Edited by

Mark F. DeWitt

University of Louisiana at Lafayette, USA

ASHGATE

Wherever possible, these reprints are made from a copy of the original printing, but these can themselves be of very variable quality. Whilst the publisher has made every effort to ensure the quality of the reprint, some variability may inevitably remain.

Published by
Ashgate Publishing Limited
Wey Court East
Union Road
Farnham
Surrey GU9 7PT
England

Ashgate Publishing Company
Suite 420
101 Cherry Street
Burlington
VT 05401-4405
USA

www.ashgate.com

British Library Cataloguing in Publication Data
Roots music. – (The library of essays on popular music)
1. Music and race. 2. Ethnicity in music. 3. Folk music–
History and criticism. 4. World music–History and
criticism.
I. Series II. DeWitt, Mark F.
780.8'9-dc22

Library of Congress Control Number: 2011932119

ISBN 9780754629627

MIX
Paper from
responsible sources
FSC
www.fsc.org
FSC® C013056

Printed and bound in Great Britain by
TJ International Ltd, Padstow, Cornwall.

Contents

Acknowledgements

The editor and publishers wish to thank the following for permission to use copyright material.

American Folklore Society for the essay: David Evans (1974), 'Techniques of Blues Composition among Black Folksingers', *Journal of American Folklore*, **87**, pp. 240–49; David Samuels (1999), 'The Whole and the Sum of the Parts, or, How Cookie and the Cupcakes Told the Story of Apache History in San Carlos', *Journal of American Folklore*, **112**, pp. 464–74. Copyright © 1999, American Folklore Society.

Cambridge University Press for the essays: Alex Stewart (2000), '"Funky Drummer": New Orleans, James Brown and the Rhythmic Transformation of American Popular Music', *Popular Music*, **19**, pp. 293–318. Copyright © 2000 Cambridge University Press; Aaron A. Fox (1992), 'The Jukebox of History: Narratives of Loss and Desire in the Discourse of Country Music', *Popular Music*, **11**, pp. 53–72.

Center for Black Music Research for the essay: Gerhard Kubik (1998), 'Analogies and Differences in African-American Musical Cultures across the Hemisphere: Interpretive Models and Research Strategies, *Black Music Research Journal*, **18**, pp. 203–27; Barry Jean Ancelet (1988), 'Zydeco/Zarico: Beans, Blues and Beyond', *Black Music Research Journal*, **8**, pp. 33–49.

Duke University Press for the essay: Barry Shank (2002), '"That Wild Mercury Sound": Bob Dylan and the Illusion of American Culture', *boundary 2*, **29**, pp. 97–123. Copyright © 2002 by Duke University Press.

English Folk Dance and Song Society for the essay: Hazel Fairbairn (1994), 'Changing Contexts for Traditional Dance Music in Ireland: The Rise of Group Performance Practice', *Folk Music Journal*, **6**, pp. 566–99.

John Wiley & Sons for the essay: Sara Cohen (1995), 'Sounding out the City: Music and the Sensuous Production of Place', *Transactions of the Institute of British Geographers*, New Series **20**, pp. 434–46. Published by Blackwell Publishing on behalf of The Royal Geographical Society (with the Institute of British Geographers). Copyright © 1995 The Royal Geographical Society.

MIT Press for the essay: Michelle Kisliuk (1988), '"A Special Kind of Courtesy": Action at a Bluegrass Festival Jam Session', *The Drama Review*, **32**, pp. 141–55.

Society for Ethnomusicology for the essays: Peter Manuel (2010), 'Composition, Authorship, and Ownership in Flamenco, Past and Present', *Ethnomusicology*, **54**, pp. 106–35. Copyright © 2010 by the Society for Ethnomusicology; Pearl Williams-Jones (1975), 'Afro-American

Series Preface

From its rather modest beginnings in the 1950s, the study of popular music has now developed to such a degree that many academic institutions worldwide employ specialists in the field. Even those that do not will often still make space on crowded higher education curricula for the investigation of what has become not only one of the most lucrative spheres of human activity, but one of the most influential on the identities of individuals and communities. Popular music matters, and it matters to so many people, people we can only partially understand if we do not understand their music. It is for this reason that this series is timely.

This is not the place to try to offer a definition of popular music; that is one of the purposes of the essays collected in the volumes in this series. Through their Popular and Folk Music series of monographs, Ashgate has gained a strong reputation as a publisher of scholarship in the field. This Library of Essays on Popular Music is partly envisioned as a complement to that series, focusing on writing of shorter length. But the series is also intended to develop the volume of Critical Essays in Popular Musicology published in 2007, in that it provides comprehensive coverage of the world's popular musics in eight volumes, each of which has a substantial introductory essay by the volume's editor. It develops the Critical Essays volume in that it makes overt recognition of the fact that the study of popular music is necessarily inter-disciplinary. Thus, within the limits set by the genre coverage of each individual volume, and by the excellence of the essays available for inclusion, each editor has been asked to keep an eye on issues as diverse as: the popular music industry and its institutions; aspects of history of their respective genres; issues in the theories and methodologies of study and practice; questions of the ontologies and hermeneutics of their fields; the varying influence of different waves of technological development; the ways markets and audiences are constructed, reproduced and reached and, last but not least; aspects of the repertory without which there would be no popular music to study. As a result, no disciplinary perspective is privileged. As far as possible, no genre is privileged either. Because the study of rock largely led the growth of popular music study, the genre has produced a very large amount of material; it needs a volume to itself. Much writing on jazz tends to circumscribe the genre clearly arguing that it, too, needs a volume to itself. Other forms of music have been distributed across the remaining volumes: one on electronica; one on forms of mainstream pop (still frequently omitted from academic surveys); one on specific North American forms which lead to hip-hop; one on the appearance of popular music within other (particularly visual) media; and two final volumes covering 'world' and 'roots', musics whose relationship with more obviously industrialized forms is most particularly problematic. While this categorization of the world's popular musics is not perfect (and is variously addressed in individual volumes), it is no worse than any other, and it does enable the inclusion of all those academic essays we feel are worth reproducing.

The field of study has grown to such an extent that there is now a plethora of material available to read, and the growth of the internet makes it increasingly available. Why, then, produce this series of essays? The issue is principally one of evaluation. Where does one start? It is no longer possible to suggest to new entrants in the field that they should read everything, for there is much which is of lesser value. So, what you will find collected in these volumes is a selection of the most important and influential journal articles, essays and previously-published shorter material on the genre area concerned. Editors were given the brief of choosing not only those essays which have already garnered a great degree of influence, but essays which have also, for whatever reason, been overlooked, and which offer perspectives worthy of greater account. The volumes' editors are all experts in their own fields, with strong views about the ways those fields have developed, and might develop in the future. Thus, while the series is necessarily retrospective in its viewpoint, it nonetheless aims to help lay a platform for the broad future study of popular music.

ALLAN F. MOORE
Series Editor
University of Surrey, UK

Introduction

One eminently reasonable approach to the study of any genre of popular music is to begin by accepting it on its own terms: to study the people who self-identify as musicians, fans, critics and industry executives of the genre, as well as their creations and interactions. This approach is well represented elsewhere in this series, with volumes on rock, jazz, electronica and so on. Another approach, however, is to inquire whence came a genre such as rock, or the style of a particular band. Such is the path I personally followed from listening to bands like Led Zeppelin and Lynyrd Skynyrd in the 1970s, to immersing myself in echoes of the 1960s blues revival, to a career in ethnomusicology.

The fascination with the origins of popular music is widespread and stems from a more general search for authenticity in our globally interconnected world (Bendix, 1997; Holt, 2007, pp. 38–41; Redhead and Street, 1989), a hunger that popular music purveyors continually whet using the roots metaphor, among others. Many popular music fans seem endlessly curious to know or imagine what the original forms of their musical passions sounded like, prior to their industrialization. Coming from another direction, individual musicians from traditional cultures who wish to profit by participating in the popular music industry find that it is advantageous, and often even obligatory, to claim 'roots' for their music in the ages-old culture that they can claim as their birthright (Taylor, 1997, pp. 125–45). Yet another pathway is to work with or imitate other musicians who can claim such roots when you yourself cannot: the 'roots by association' approach (Taylor, 1997, pp. 28–52). Ethnomusicologists and folklorists may begin by studying traditional music as practice and find themselves also looking at commercialized offshoots thereof or even participating in its commoditization (wittingly or unwittingly) through the public release of field recordings (Feld, 1996; Zemp, 1996). Scholars are also examining the impact that commercially released recordings have on traditional forms and repertoires. Process and product in our age are inextricably intertwined.

For all these reasons and more, the creators of this series saw fit to include volumes on roots music and world music. Mostly following general usage of these terms in the industry, this roots volume comprises musics whose origins can be traced to North America or Europe, including the broad category of folk music as well as blues, country, gospel and other ethnic and indigenous musics from these continents. The rest of the world, including Latin America and the Caribbean, falls to the world music volume. As Allan Moore has noted in his *Critical Essays in Popular Musicology* (2007), a great deal of the best scholarship on popular music is published in book form, which is by definition not eligible for inclusion in this series focused on journal articles. Still, a comprehensive sampling of roots genres and high-quality scholarship on them published in journals would be impossibly large for this volume. I have had to balance the values of significance, diversity and championing the unjustly overlooked when selecting items for inclusion. I also employed a variety of methods for identifying possible candidates: my own training and experience as an ethnomusicologist and scholar of Louisiana Cajun and Creole music, recommendations from colleagues and citation statistics from the Web of Science indexes using various searches for keywords and selected journals. Only essays published in English were to be considered. Also, since *Roots* was the assigned title for this volume when I joined the project, I have used that rubric as a criterion for relevance, selecting some essays that specifically used or analysed the roots metaphor. For this reason, some dimensions of theoretical breadth mentioned in series editor Allan Moore's preamble received more attention (history, ontologies and hermeneutics) and some less (technologies). I would like to acknowledge an intellectual debt in this project to Olly Wilson, one of my mentors in graduate school at the University of California, Berkeley, and to thank the following colleagues for their helpful guidance as I considered essays for inclusion in this volume: Lee Bidgood, Philip Bohlman, Jeffrey Callen, Loren Chuse, Timothy Cooley, Jacqueline DjeDje, Tony Dumas, David Evans, Kevin Fontenot, Eddie Meadows, John-Carlos Perea, Brenda Romero, Neil Rosenberg, Barbara Taylor and Jeff Todd Titon.

The volume is divided into three sections, roughly following the dialectical thesis-antithesis-synthesis model but with a twist. The roots metaphor is already pervasive in public discourse about music. Witness: the Jamaican subgenre or historical period known as 'roots reggae' (Veal, 2007); a four-part series on 'American Roots Music' produced for the Public Broadcasting System (PBS) in the United States (http://www.pbs.org/americanrootsmusic/) that was further merchandized in CD and book formats (Santelli *et al.*, 2001); the marketing of 'roots music' by record labels large (Columbia's 'Roots N' Blues' series) and small (Arhoolie Records); online entrepreneurs (http://www.cdroots.com/, http://www.rootsworld.com/); and so on ad infinitum. Therefore the thesis for musical roots needs hardly be made; it seems more urgent first to deconstruct the whole notion of roots, then to examine how such botanical and agrarian metaphors still pervade the thoughts and emotions of musicians, music fans and scholars, then finally to look at popular music genres, such as country, that are widely believed to have grown from roots sources. Thus the essays are grouped in the order of antithesis ('Roots, Deconstructed'), thesis reconsidered ('Roots, Experienced') and synthesis ('Offshoots'). The remainder of this introduction gives some background on the roots concept in popular music and provides rationales for the essays included in this volume, including discussion of numerous worthy essays that were unavoidably excluded for reasons of space and format.

Roots, Deconstructed

Benjamin Filene has formulated a definition of roots music useful for scholarly purposes: 'musical genres that, whether themselves commercial or not, have been glorified as the "pure" sources out of which the twentieth century's commercial popular music was created' (2000, p. 4). We can easily extend this working definition to include the current century. Narratives of roots music collapse categories of folk and popular music into reconfigurations that revise history and privilege the authenticity of select genres and individuals. Reminiscent of Hobsbawm and Ranger's *The Invention of Tradition* (1983), some scholars have gone further to suggest that reception of roots music in certain cases is constituent of the genre itself. For example, Marybeth Hamilton suggests that it was there at the Brooklyn YMCA, in a single room some time in the late 1940s, that the Delta blues was born. It was born, that is, in the mind of one of the YMCA's long-term residents, an impassioned record collector named James McKune. Born around 1910, McKune was the driving force behind the cohort of music enthusiasts who powered the blues revival of the 1960s, when white Americans and Europeans rediscovered a music that African Americans were leaving behind. (2002, p. 123; see also Keil, 1985)

Fabian Holt, in his *Genre in Popular Music*, also stresses the socially constituted nature of genres: 'genre is not only "in the music," but also in the minds and bodies of particular groups of people who share certain conventions. These conventions are created in relation to particular musical texts and artists and the contexts in which they are performed and experienced' (2007: 2). He dissects roots music discourse in his chapter on *O Brother, Where Art Thou?*, a film whose associations with roots music have also been noted by Filene (2004) and Richard Middleton (2007). For Holt, '*O Brother* is a larger-than-life Hollywood adventure that glorifies the past in accordance with dominant sensibilities of the present', 'a fantasy of the unmediated' for both the eyes and the ears, in which contemporary artists perform music from six decades past (2007, pp. 34–35). He notes the success of the film's soundtrack as a commodity unto itself; its rejuvenating effect on bluegrass listenership; its stimulation of the marketing of roots and Americana categories in a Tower Records store; its influence on the PBS television series (Santelli *et al.*, 2001) that followed the release of *O Brother* by fifteen months; and even (perhaps) its effect on Filene's decision to recast his dissertation work on vernacular music into his book on roots music (Holt, 2007, pp. 38–49).

In the last chapter of his book, Holt attempts to achieve 'a different anthology of American popular music' by theorizing 'a poetics of music in between genres', by which he appears to mean a consideration of statistically smaller genres that are considered 'foreign' or otherwise outside any discussion of musics representing an American national identity (2007, pp. 151–80). While his examples of 'music in between genres' (from Latin pop, zydeco and Tejano music) mostly fall within existing conceptions of American roots music, notably the PBS series, nonetheless his discussion addresses a real imbalance in public and scholarly discourse about the origins of American popular music, which focuses largely on racial categories of white and black and the interaction between the two. Other ethnicities, be they Afro-French Creole or Native American or Mexican-American, are left out of the discussion or mentioned as an aside.

In this volume, I have striven to avoid replicating the imbalance of considering black–white relations to the exclusion of everything else. Indeed, it may have been the identification of American folk music with whites that spurred on the use of 'roots music' as a more inclusive terminological umbrella covering, in the case of the US public television project, 'blues, country, bluegrass, gospel, Cajun, zydeco, Tejano, and Native American' (http://www.pbs.org/americanrootsmusic/). All of these genres except Cajun are represented in this volume, but I must say it was difficult and I'm not sure that the set of essays included here is satisfactorily diverse on this score. The preponderance of literature on black and white music, which also happens to permeate my research area, frustrated my attempts at being more inclusive. I look with editorial envy at collections of new, original essays that have the luxury of diversity by design, such as Radano and Bohlman's wide-ranging *Music and the*

Racial Imagination (2000). As it is, all of the essays in Part I 'Roots, Deconstructed' deal with white and/or black music. On the other hand, the topics of some of the essays included, especially Kubik's 'interpretive models' (see Chapter 3) and the whole subject of blackface minstrelsy, contain arguments that are not specific to African-American music and that can be applied more generally.

In Chapter 3 Gerhard Kubik, a scholar of both African and African-American music, examines a number of spatial metaphors that appear to govern scholarly approaches to 'African-derived' musics – the 'racial marguerite', 'societal molecule clusters', 'the tree of ontogenesis' (with roots, of course), cultural diffusionism – as well as some more abstract interpretive notions. The relevance of Kubik's indictment of the 'roots' concept as 'pseudo-historical reductionism' to Filene's characterization of roots music as 'pure source' is clear. While others have found 'root music' to have originated as a term in popular music in the 1980s or 1990s, Kubik quite rightly points to a popular culture phenomenon (in both book and television form) of the 1970s, Alex Haley's *Roots*, as a seminal event in the development of the concept. In the end, Kubik reminds us that

> any culture, whether of the present or the past, is multicultural: at every stage of its history, it is the result of forces of invention, borrowing, reinterpretation, and innovation. The very word "hybrid," borrowed from genetics, loses its qualifying capacity from the moment one realizes that all cultures have never been anything else. (p. 69)

Kubik's analysis of interpretive models is quite general and could be handily turned to examine discourse more generally in areas outside of the African diaspora. The twinned development of European nationalism and folkloristics could be deconstructed similarly into strands of biological reductionism ('nature'), socio-psychological determinism ('nurture'), pseudo-historical reductionism ('roots', ahistorical notions of timeless tradition), historical particularism (an atheoretical interest in historical and ethnographic detail for its own sake), cultural materialism (a Marxist insistence on economic causation) and cultural diffusionism (for example the historic-geographic method, see Goldberg, 1984). It could also be applied to other diasporas such as the Jews or the Roma.

While Kubik's interpretive models are quite usefully general, his survey of the literature is silent on some major work on African-American music that had been published a few years prior to his essay. How might he or we characterize the work of Samuel Floyd (1991, 1995), for example, or Paul Gilroy (1991, 1993)? Floyd's *The Power of Black Music* does, on one level, essentialize black music with its very title and his arguments embody elements of Kubik's second ('nurture') and third ('roots') interpretive models. Floyd himself admits to a certain mysticism in his approach (1995, p. 270), nowhere more evidenced than in his application of Gates' black literary theories (1988). Floyd considers African cultural elements that predate the Middle Passage ahistorically ('below ground' for Kubik's tree of ontogenesis) in relation to African-American music which, as Kubik points out, exists '"above ground level," in the clear light of historical consciousness' (p. 58). But Floyd has other fish to fry; his mission is not to interrogate the very notion of black music, but rather to establish an interpretive framework for music by African-Americans that encompasses both vernacular and cultivated traditions. Moreover, the journal that he founded (*Black Music Research*

Journal) published Kubik's very essay, and indeed was one of the most valuable resources in my research for this volume.

The task of problematizing notions of black music is vigorously taken up by Ronald Radano in his *Lying Up a Nation* (2003), largely through an analysis of pre-twentieth-century discourse about music and race: seventeenth- and eighteenth-century missionary accounts; ex-slave Frederick Douglass' 1845 autobiography; the foundational *Slave Songs of the United States* (Allen *et al.*, 1867); and so on. In his campaign against essentialist constructions of black music, including Afrocentrism, Radano unsurprisingly takes issue with Floyd's approach, while he has kinder words for Gilroy, who also challenges Afrocentrism in his account of a *Black Atlantic*. Indeed, it was only for reasons of space and diversity of content that I reluctantly left out Gilroy's 1991 essay (also published, by the way, in the *Black Music Research Journal*). Perhaps the greatest contribution of the essay is that, in the case of the black music/anti-essentialism debate, he tries to find a third path to the truth. 'It is ironic, given the importance accorded to music in the habitus of diaspora blacks, that neither pole in this tense conversation takes the music very seriously. The narcissism that unites both standpoints is revealed by the way that they both forsake discussion of music and its attendant dramaturgy, performance, ritual, and gesture in favor of an obsessive fascination with the bodies of the performers themselves' (Gilroy, 1991, p. 126), such as in debates over Michael Jackson's physical appearance. By contrast, what Gilroy offers is the insight that

> Though [black] identity is often felt to be natural and spontaneous, it remains the outcome of practical activity: language, gesture, bodily significations, desires. These significations are condensed in musical performance, although it does not, of course, monopolize them. In this context, they produce the imaginary effect of an internal racial core or essence by acting on the body through the specific mechanisms of identification and recognition that are produced in the intimate interaction of performer and crowd. (1991, p. 127)

In light of Gilroy's influential work on the Black Atlantic, I would not be the first to ruminate about a White Atlantic (see, for example, Armitage, 2002; Gabaccia, 2004). One candidate example of a White Atlantic in music scholarship is the formation of a canon of English and Scottish ballads by an American scholar, Francis James Child, and the field research and collection of performances of these ballads in the US by an English scholar, Cecil Sharp. The trajectory that folksong scholarship took in the US and Britain had lasting effects on notions of national identity in those two countries, and also on race relations in discourse about folk music. In his historical study of roots music in the US, Filene concerns himself not with genres per se or how they come into being, but rather the activities of people who helped to shape public perceptions of folk music and blues, including scholars Sharp, John and Alan Lomax, Charles Seeger, B.A. Botkin and Richard Dorson; record industry entrepreneurs Leonard Chess and Willie Dixon; and musicians Lead Belly, Muddy Waters, Pete Seeger and Bob Dylan. From Sharp's work on folk song, for example, Filene traces a myth with a 'racial undertone' that 'defined a folk song as an extremely old song, usually a ballad, that had originated from Great Britain and was currently sung by rural, isolated mountain people who were white, Anglo-Saxon Protestants' (2000, p. 26). Furthermore, 'the most significant effect of the myth of the white ballad singer was to help block African-American folk music from gaining a central place in the canon of America's musical heritage' (Filene, 2000, p. 27).

Following from Filene's insights and from my own experiences interviewing folk revivalists (DeWitt, 2008), I wanted to include representative essays on folksong scholarship and on the whitewashing of Appalachian music studies. Representing English ballad scholarship is an essay that came highly recommended by a valued colleague, Dianne Dugaw's research on the reach of antiquarianism in the eighteenth century (Chapter 1). Readers looking for a more ambitious critique of the entire ballad canon will need to look elsewhere, such as Dave Harker's work (1981 [republished elsewhere], 1985) and responses to it (Bearman, 2002; Sykes, 1993). Dugaw offers a more modest but focused corrective to the notion that a revival in interest in English balladry in the eighteenth century, particularly interest in claims to ancient origins, was solely the province of elites. Through close readings of commentary in one antiquarian ballad collection from the 1720s and subsequent plagiarisms by a major London street literature publisher who marketed 'old ballads' in broadside and chapbook form, and in combination with contextual evidence from the historical record, she convincingly shows that antiquarian notions had a broad popular appeal already in the eighteenth century, over a hundred years before Child and the folksong revival that followed him.

On the subject of race and Appalachian music studies, it is by now well established that vernacular music from this region owes its constitution to African-American as well as English and Scottish sources, so much so that these findings are seeping out into popular culture, such as Chris Thomas King's Tommy Johnson character in *O Brother, Where Art Thou?*, rekindled interest in black banjo playing (internet discussion groups, Otis Taylor's *Recapturing the Banjo* project (2008), Béla Fleck's documentary film *Throw Down Your Heart* (2008)) and revival of black Appalachian music performance (for example the Carolina Chocolate Drops, 2010). Almost certainly scholarly work on the African origins of the banjo and banjo playing (Conway, 1995, 2003; Epstein, 1975; Nathan, 1956) and black musicians in Appalachia more generally (see notably Fred Hay's 2003 special issue of *Black Music Research Journal* dedicated to 'Affrilachian Music') has had some influence on these efforts in the public sphere. Allen Farmelo's 2001 essay, included here as Chapter 2, is part of this movement in vernacular music scholarship. Farmelo's remarkably wide-ranging essay, despite its title, limits itself neither to bluegrass music as normally conceived nor to the time period of 1820–1900. He combines contemporary discourse about bluegrass history, historical evidence from the nineteenth century concerning the degree of proximity and cultural contact between poor whites and blacks, and the use of banjos and fiddles by blacks and by white minstrels in blackface, to show that 'Bluegrass music itself incorporates and propagates nostalgic and antiquated sentiments which do not bear out the intricacies of the development of its antecedents' (p. 23). He goes further to offer contemporary ethnographic evidence for the rarity of blacks at bluegrass events.

In the last four decades, there has been a groundswell of appreciation among historians of American popular music and culture that the impact of nineteenth-century blackface minstrelsy can almost not be overestimated. Over forty articles that I considered for this volume at least mention it. As just one example, Farmelo points to the vicious stereotypes in minstrel shows of slaves with their banjos as an obvious motivation for blacks to abandon the instrument (p. 36). The literature on minstrelsy is vast, even if one looks no earlier than

Robert Toll's *Blacking Up* (1974), so the reader looking to catch up would do well to start with Charles Hamm's magisterial 2000 review essay. I can only give examples here; there is no hope of being exhaustive. First of all, there are the studies on the history of minstrelsy itself (Cockerell, 1996, 1997; Dormon, 1969; Lhamon, 1998; Mahar, 1999; Toll, 1974), its connections to parlour music of the period (Dunson, 2002; Linn, 1990) and the legacy of its repertoire of racial stereotypes on twentieth-century American culture and literature (Tuhkanen, 2001; Wynter, 1979). Then there is its impact on performance practice, not only musical performance practice and repertoire (Lightfoot, 2003; Middleton, 2007; Nathan, 1956; Pearson, 2003; Rosenberg, 1995; Sacks and Sacks, 1988; Smith, 1994; Wells, 2003; Wilgus, 1970; Winans, 1976) but also more generally the propensity for whites to imitate blacks (Allen, 2007; Regis, 1999) or other minorities (Deloria, 1998).

From the rich field of blackface minstrelsy studies, the work of Eric Lott stands out for its sophistication and erudition. His 1992 essay, included here as Chapter 4, contains several observations scattered through his oft-cited 1993 book on the subject, and it addresses perhaps the central question concerning the phenomenon: why? Taking a cue from Stuart Hall from the Birmingham School of cultural studies, Lott investigates 'the constitution of white subjectivity by the constant coupling or complex play of racial fear and desire, "othering" and identification, ambivalence and attraction' (p. 79). Grounding his work in eyewitness accounts and images from the period, Lott psychoanalyses the content of minstrel expressions to explore white attitudes towards blacks, especially sexual ones. He connects these deeper longings to the more directly observable behaviour of cultural love and theft, fascination and expropriation of music and other expressions, lending great utility to his work for the study of what Charles Keil famously called the appropriation-revitalization pattern in American popular music, whereby 'each successive appropriation and commercialization of a Negro style by white America through its record industry and mass media has stimulated the Negro community and its musical spokesmen to generate a "new" music that it can call its own' (1966, p. 43). In another essay I would have liked to include in this volume, Richard Middleton (2007) takes a related psychoanalytic approach to nostalgia and the blues.

Lott's mention of Bakhtin suggests a connection to Carnival, which is relevant not only to the analysis of grotesque images but also in light of the fact that blackface performance continues to the current day during the festival of Cajun Mardi Gras (Lindahl, 2001). It is also worth noting, even if the lines of influence are not all that clear, that in the years since Lott's *Love and Theft* book was published Bob Dylan has released a critically acclaimed album using the same title, perhaps taking his cue from Lott (Sheffield, 2001). In 2009 three Nashville vocalists released their first album as a group named Love and Theft (http://www. loveandtheft.com/music.html, accessed 9/1/2010).

Barry Shank must have submitted his 2002 essay on 'That Wild Mercury Sound' (Chapter 5) shortly before Dylan's *Love and Theft* was released, because he cites Lott's work of that title but not the singer's. Shank makes the case for Bob Dylan's use of the conventions of blackface minstrelsy, and for embodying its ideology in ways that resonated with the New Left – that is, whites involved in the civil rights movement of the 1960s. The power of minstrelsy to reconcile artificially the contradictory goals of authenticity and autonomy is repeatedly stressed, using parallels found in the romanticization of blacks by whites active in the civil rights movement and by white fans of black popular music. Starting from Dylan's comments on Little Richard's music, which he had performed as a teenager, Shank analyses the use of register and timbre in Dylan's recording of Blind Lemon Jefferson's 'See That My Grave Is Kept Clean' and his harmonica style to show how the musician transforms the blues according to his aesthetic performance for higher harmonics (the 'wild mercury sound') even as he pays the blues homage. This essay effectively traces 'the simultaneous incorporation and denial of blackness that is the minstrelsy of rock' (p. 127), not to mention the folk music boom of which Dylan was an integral part, and illustrates how blackface minstrelsy had come to pervade the habitus of American popular music listeners a hundred years after the abolition of slavery. In doing so, the author further deconstructs the myth of the white ballad singer in American folk music, whose mantle Dylan once wore. Although there was no room to include it here, Albin Zak's study of Jimi Hendrix's transformation of Dylan's 'All Along the Watchtower' (2004) makes an interesting postscript to Shank's essay by showing a case of the appropriator getting appropriated.

It may be worth a digressive paragraph to note that, outside of the concentrated academic audience to which this volume addresses itself, most readers and writers who concern themselves with roots music do not care a whit to deconstruct their subject, and moreover that some of these writers – Ted Gioia (2006a, 2006b), Peter Guralnick (1971, 1979), Greil Marcus – are worth reading. A case in point is Marcus, a rock journalist-cum-public intellectual who has written quite a bit on Elvis Presley (1975, 1991) and Bob Dylan (1997b, 2005) and topics other than music, but also about roots genres such as balladry (Wilentz and Marcus, 2005) and old-time music (Marcus, 1997a) and always with an eye towards the cultural background of his topic du jour. On the one hand he thoroughly researches his subject matter in the manner that a high-profile writer of non-fiction must, while on the other hand he does not hesitate to romanticize his subject with literary prose such as this: 'Dock Boggs was a singer and a banjo player who sounded as if his bones were coming through his skin every time he opened his mouth; that was the sound that drew people to him' (Marcus, 1997b: 1). Sources like Marcus provide both valuable information from their research and material for further analysis as barometers of public reception of roots music.

Roots, Experienced

Roots music discourse is still firmly ensconced in academic as well as popular arenas. Much excellent scholarship exists that takes the notion of roots for granted, by which I mean to include studies of music and identity (national, racial, ethnic, personal) and of music thought to be closely associated with traditional sources. As the essays in the first part of this book and the discussion above show, the notion of roots music is largely a fiction, and yet it animates and impassions scholars and musicians alike in their pursuits. The essays in Part II 'Roots, Experienced' come from authors who were motivated to investigate the roots of certain popular styles, or who report contexts in which musical roots were at issue, including repertoires (Evans, Manuel), jam sessions (Fairbairn, Kisliuk) and sense of place (Cohen).

The few essays here that directly aim to investigate the musical roots of particular styles and genres (Ancelet, Stewart, Williams-Jones and Wilson) all happen to deal with black music of one kind or another. Worthy foundational studies of other musical styles that almost found their way into this volume include those on salsa (Manuel, 1994; Washburne, 1998), New Mexican music (Lamadrid, 2000), white gospel music (Wolfe, 1983), and klezmer (Kirshenblatt-Gimblett, 1998). Older articles by some well-known figures such as Bela Bartok (Suchoff, 1997), Archie Green (2001) and Alan Lomax (Cohen, 2003) have already been anthologized elsewhere.

Chapter 14, Olly Wilson's influential essay on 'The Significance of the Relationship between Afro-American Music and West African Music', loosens a knotty problem in the study of African-American music: how to talk about its African roots when the direct influences are much more difficult to identify than they are in other parts of the African diaspora such as Cuba or Brazil. Building on previous work of scholars such as Melville Herskovits, Alan Merriam and Richard Waterman (and informed by his own experience in Ghana, where he witnessed the reception of African-American music firsthand), Wilson identifies certain 'conceptual approaches to music making' (p. 308) that are shared by West African and African-American musicians. His key insight is that significant relationships are not to be found in specific melodies or rhythm patterns that had survived the Middle Passage, but rather that

> the particular forms of black music which evolved in America are specific realizations of this shared conceptual framework which reflect the peculiarities of the American black experience. As such, the essence of their Africanness is not a static body of something which can be depleted but rather a conceptual approach, the manifestations of which are infinite. The common core of this Africanness consists of the way of doing something, not simply something that is done. (p. 308)

His discussion of Waterman's five characteristics of sub-Saharan music (1952) and other common traits, along with his analysis of their presence in music like James Brown's 'Super Bad', should be required reading for all students of African-American music. Of course, Wilson's arguments have not stopped scholars since from looking for the survival of specific bits of African cultures in African-American music (for example Kubik, 1999; Meadows, 1979; Rosenbaum, 1998).

Pearl Williams-Jones, in Chapter 13, her essay on the black aesthetics of gospel music, takes as her premise the church as a bastion of conservative cultural practice, in this case African-derived performance practices related to music and worship. Using an approach remarkably similar to Wilson's 'conceptual approaches to music making', Williams-Jones catalogues several musical characteristics and performance practices in gospel music that are both identifiably African in origin and absent from white performance of the same or similar repertoire (see also Boyer, 1979b). While her insights are often keen, such as the integral rhythmic value of breathing in singing, I think that her beginning premise is probably the main reason this essay is so widely cited. It is conceptually convenient to locate authenticity in a place or musical genre, and William-Jones has provided such a locus in her portrayal of 'the black gospel church'. Ignored here are the variations in musical practice across various black church denominations (see Burnim, 1985 for illustrative anecdotes), the presence of Africanisms in some white church denominations (Mosher, 2008) and the countervailing tendency for contemporary gospel music to absorb the latest trends in popular secular music in an attempt to keep young people within the church's sphere of influence (Boyer, 1979a).

Nonetheless, as Bernice Johnson Reagon (1996) has documented and as I have experienced myself in black church settings, there are large grains of truth in what Williams-Jones has set forth.

Gospel music is of interest as roots music not only as a popular music subculture in its own right, but also for its influence on other genres large and small. Its importance in the development of rhythm and blues through such major figures as Ray Charles, Aretha Franklin and Sam Cooke has been much discussed in print and portrayed on film. Recently, Craig Mosher (2008) has extended this line of work to discuss specifically the influence of Pentecostal worship style on rock and roll music, on artists both white (for example the Sun Records stable of Elvis Presley, Jerry Lee Lewis and Johnny Cash) and black (Berry Gordy's Motown studio, among others). In so doing, Mosher usefully pulls together information on these artists and builds on Williams-Jones' earlier work by showing how a particular religious movement (Pentecostalism) has carried West African cultural practices across racial lines and into rock music. A second worthy essay showing the reach of gospel music is Lynn Abbott's 1992 piece on the African-American roots of barbershop singing, prominently gospel quartet singing. By way of Jim Henry, a leading barbershop quartet singer who finished a dissertation on this topic in 2000, as well as Gage Averill's 2003 book on barbershop, Abbott's careful historical work has led to a sea change in perceptions of the form within the barbershop world. Short of including both Mosher's and Abbott's essays here, I can only recommend them both highly to the reader.

Chapter 12, Alex Stewart's 'Funky Drummer' essay, traces some of the roots of funk and acknowledges the influence of gospel on that genre, but his main objective is to show how a New Orleans drumming style came uniquely to influence funk rhythms such as those used by James Brown. While there has been much scholarship devoted to antebellum New Orleans, the musical practices of slaves in that city's Congo Square (Donaldson, 1984) and its role in the early history of jazz, the de rigueur and often romanticized references to the Crescent City in music writing may anaesthetize some to the fact that (even after the disastrous flood following Hurricane Katrina) it is still a musically vital city that has continued as a centre of musical creativity to the present day, due in no small part to the continuation of unique cultural practices such as brass bands and second lines (Regis, 1999; Sakakeeny, 2010). Thus I felt strongly that New Orleans should be represented in this *Roots* volume, and Stewart's work leapt to mind. I had the good fortune to attend a conference many years ago at which Stewart presented an early version of this paper and played audio examples of Johnny Vidacovich's instructional CD and other sources, and I have not listened to popular music the same way since.

Another common misconception centred around New Orleans' reputation as a 'musical birthplace' is that it is also the source for Cajun music and zydeco, two related styles that actually developed in southern Louisiana in rural areas west of New Orleans in a region stretching roughly from Lafayette, Louisiana to Houston, Texas. Folklorist Barry Ancelet has spent his entire career writing about the traditions of the Cajun and Creoles in this region, and he has internalized a vast storehouse of francophone folklore out of which he is able to make frequent and often surprising connections between songs and other folklore items from different places. In Chapter 6, Ancelet traces the etymology of the word 'zydeco', the name by which a certain style of Creole popular music has become known since the time of Clifton

Chenier, and he finds stunning correspondences in song texts and instrumentation between Creole folklore in Louisiana and from islands in the Indian Ocean. What are we to do with this information? Ancelet argues for a common cultural heritage for these items in West Africa, which was historically the source for slaves in both places. Investigating terms for music and dance in West Africa, he concludes that Louisiana Creoles 'took the older sounds, no longer understood, and distorted them into more familiar, intelligible words, thereby changing the denotation while preserving the connotation' (p. 136). In the rest of the essay, Ancelet goes beyond etymology to discuss possible African roots of musical practices (such as Chenier's approach to playing the accordion) and themes in the song texts. As it turns out, his resistance to the spelling of the name 'zydeco' did not gain followers; the genre is still widely and generally known as zydeco and not 'zarico'. While Ancelet was at one time one of the few scholars publishing work on zydeco or the related (white) genre of Cajun music, in recent years this music has attracted greater attention (Brasseaux, 2009; Brasseaux and Fontenot, 2006; DeWitt, 1999, 2003, 2008; Le Menestrel, 2007; Mattern, 1997; Minton, 1996; Olivier and Sandmel, 1999; Sexton and Oster, 2001; Wood, 2006).

The essays here by David Evans on blues and Peter Manuel on flamenco make an interesting pair, in that they both look at processes of folk composition and repertoire and contrast them with the effects that the commercial marketplace has had on defining the very identity of a composition in those genres. While it may now be a commonplace to observe that 'art', 'folk' and 'popular' have proved not to be very useful as overarching categories for music, these two studies made over three decades apart show that the distinction can still make a difference when looking at musical processes.

One of the most cited essays on blues, Evans' study of 'Techniques of Blues Composition among Black Folksingers' (Chapter 8) effectively covers a lot of ground in ten pages: contrasts between white and black folk-singing practice and the resulting white misconceptions concerning blues composition, the effect of commercial recordings on verbal improvisation, examples taken from the author's field research and a proposed categorization matrix for blues repertory. The author addresses the use of formulaic phrases in the blues and finds that it does not always lead to an improvised performance of randomly related verses. Rather, there are songs that tend to be treated as fixed entities, especially if the singer learned them from a commercial recording. Moreover, the commercially recorded numbers tend to contain verses that revolve around a central theme, which nullifies the randomness argument. Evans' two-dimensional matrix thus entails stability (stable/partly stable/improvised) and the existence of a story or central theme (thematic/non-thematic). Since some singers are more given to improvisation than others, it makes good sense to classify blues compositions not only by their lyrical content but also by who is singing them. Mager Johnson sings the first verse of 'Big Road Blues' more or less the same every time and varies the subsequent verses ('semi-stable'), whereas Isaac Youngblood sings a stable version of the whole song as he remembers it from when Tommy Johnson taught it to him. By doing field research and not simply treating blues recordings as authored texts, Evans is able to trace more clearly the workings of a living tradition. Another worthy treatment of blues lyrics came soon after from Jeff Todd Titon (1977). For musical analysis of the blues, Charles Ford (1998) offers an extremely focused look at Robert Johnson's rhythmic practices, especially his insertion and deletion of beats and measures, with occasional consideration of melody and harmony. For a more well-rounded analysis of a blues musician's recorded output with transcriptions of guitar solos, see Evans' work on Blind Lemon Jefferson (2000).

Peter Manuel's study of 'Composition, Authorship, and Ownership in Flamenco, Past and Present' (Chapter 11) compares, as Evans did with the blues, traditional models of musical creation within the genre with practices tailored to the making and selling of commercial recordings, and takes it one step further to consider copyright implications in the context of an actual dispute. His description of the song types called *cantes* and more specific tune types called *estilos* brings to mind analogous systems in other traditions such as Arabic *maqam*, Persian *dastgah* and *raga* from India, and while he does not digress to refer to Harold Powers' remarkable synthesis of these systems in the essay on 'Mode' for the *New Grove Dictionary* (1980), I would argue that such comparisons are worth investigating. Contrast this flexible traditional system of mixing and matching texts and melody types with a scholarly urge to preserve and classify the end products of the system (performances of *estilos*) as fixed repertory items, and with a commercial and legal framework in which authorship must be unambiguously determined in order for copyright to be assigned and through which the copyrighting of traditional materials for decades has been allowed. Enter surviving family members of the Roma (Gypsy) flamenco singer Camarón and their grievance with a family of (non-Roma) musicians who accompanied the singer and arranged and produced the music they recorded together. While Manuel's essay is too recent to be considered a classic, the range and depth of the work warranted its inclusion, and the fact that it appeared only a few months before this writing makes his bibliography a current guide to the state of scholarship on flamenco, one of Europe's quintessential roots genres. Other work on flamenco includes Loren Chuse's on women singers (2003) and Manuel's previously anthologized article on Roma and non-Roma identity aspects of flamenco music (1989).

Chapter 9, Hazel Fairbairn's essay on Irish dance music, likewise looks at the effects of commercial recordings on musical style and repertory, but her main focus is on performance contexts. Not only were regional styles that existed in the first part of the twentieth century collapsed into a national one, but house dances declined precipitously and solo performance practice became replaced with group playing for public dances. When public tastes for dance music moved on, in the 1950s it fell to the government-funded Comhaltas Ceoltoiri Eireann (Henry, 1989) to revive interest in traditional music. Fairbairn credits not the organization's planned programming at its music festivals, however, but rather the unplanned public music sessions that sprang up in bars and pubs around the festival sites for giving rise to the group music sessions that are the hallmark of contemporary traditional music-making in Ireland and elsewhere (see, for example, Miller, 1988). In her tracing of these changing contexts, she takes care also to analyse their effects on the music, such as the impact of the size of the session on the degree of heterophony and melodic detail. The historical perspective, combined with musical analysis and ethnography concerning social protocol and group dynamics of sessions, makes this essay an exemplary contribution.

While Fairbairn addresses the issue of protocol at Irish sessions, in Chapter 10 Michelle Kisliuk takes a more thoroughly ethnographic approach to bluegrass, to the point of recording and transcribing conversation among musicians during jam sessions. While bluegrass started as a commercial subgenre of country music (Rosenberg, 1967), it has been adopted by amateur musicians as their own at bluegrass festivals across the US (Gardner, 2004) and elsewhere. It has acquired a grassroots constituency that immerses itself in live performance of the music, an ideal environment for cultural transmission to take place. This is roots music, experienced at a heightened level in the festival atmosphere. Kisliuk's close description and analysis of a particular jam session illustrates beautifully the intertwined natures of social and musical interaction or, as she puts it, 'The "special kind of courtesy" is as much a musical awareness that reveals social concerns as it is a social awareness that supports musical concerns' (p. 214).

In Chapter 7 Sara Cohen delves yet deeper into the subjective experience of musical roots in her study of one elderly Jewish man's musical memories of growing up in Liverpool. Jack's memories and musical interests run a wide gamut spanning Jewish liturgical song, Yiddish folk music (especially songs about his family's ancestral home in Poland, and not music from the Zionist movement), music of other oppressed diasporas ('They all had their songs ... they've got their roots here, their roots there ... Nobody wants them', p. 152), but most of all popular music as was heard in dance halls when he was a young man. His sense of rootedness in Liverpool has to do with his personal and family history ('My mother and father, my daughter, they're buried here. So where they're buried is my home', p. 151) and his vivid memories of where he danced and whom he knew, made all the more poignant by the passage of time in which dance halls have disappeared and Liverpool Jews have substantially reduced in number. Through focusing on one individual and supplying relevant historical and intellectual context, Cohen captures a complex and nuanced picture of the many sorts of relationships that exist between music and place. Unlike most studies on this topic, the association of particular styles of music with a particular city or region is not stressed – the main nod to 'Liverpool music' is to cast a bit more light on the career of Beatles manager Brian Epstein, as a member of the Liverpool Jewish community. The literature on music and place, if one includes studies of immigrant communities and tourism, is voluminous; some books I have found especially helpful include Feld and Basso (1996), Gibson and Connell (2005), Leyshon *et al.* (1998) and Stokes (1994).

Offshoots

I am aware that by creating this final grouping of 'offshoots' I am ignoring Gerhard Kubik's insight, quoted above, that 'any culture, whether of the present or the past, is multicultural'. The current generation's offshoots become the next generation's roots, and so it continues. The essays here concern themselves with roots music that has been taken and transformed in some way, or with people who belong to racial or ethnic groups considered to be custodians of a roots genre (and who therefore tend to get typecast as expert in 'their' kind of music) and who have elected to branch out into other styles. Some of the transformations covered here have been at the hands of individuals. In other cases, larger forces have been more influential such as the music industries involved with country music and with the accordion, or nation-states that shape folk music to their own purposes.

Roots music's impact on American national identity notwithstanding (see the work of Filene and Holt, discussed above), the ties between certain styles of folk music and nationalist sentiments on the European side of the Atlantic are even stronger. Writing about the relationship between the identity of the researcher and the music that he or she studies,

Svanibor Pettan (Chapter 20) found in the former Yugoslavia 'the conviction that a scholarly contribution is valuable only if it refers to the researcher's national framework' and that 'the emphasis on "Us" did not leave much space for the study of "Others," i.e., "inside" (e.g. musics of minorities) or "outside" (e.g. musics of the world)' (p. 461). The presence of nationalism in folk music is illustrated in this volume's selections by Hazel Fairbairn's essay on Irish traditional music and by Donna Buchanan's account of Bulgarian folk orchestras. Its influence is also noted in Pettan's piece on Romani (Gypsy) musicians and Manuel Peña's on Texas-Mexican music. A bibliographic review of the literature on music and nationalism would be ludicrous to attempt here, as it would span the entire history of folk music studies going back to the eighteenth century. For those who wish to delve further into that subject, the work of Philip Bohlman (1988, 2002) is an excellent place to start.

Layered in between the world music marketing phenomenon of *Le Mystère des Voix Bulgares* that began in the late 1980s and its rural folk basis were the national folk ensembles of the Communist era whose music Swiss engineer Marcel Cellier 'discovered' and compiled (Buchanan, 1997). In Chapter 15 Donna Buchanan's extremely rich account traces the development of these ensembles and the professionalization of musicians in Bulgaria, their cumulative impact on musical practice over time, the replication of state power relations within the ensembles and a glimpse of changes following the 1989 fall of the Communist regime (for more on music post-Communism, see Slobin, 1996). She finds close parallels between the establishment of the folk ensembles in the 1950s and the marketing efforts of the late 1980s in terms of adjusting musical practice to cater to Western tastes. There continues to be keen interest in the US and elsewhere in the music of Bulgaria and other parts of the Balkans, not only among amateur and professional musicians and dancers (Laušević, 2007) but also among academics (Buchanan, 2006, 2007; Rice, 1994).

In Chapter 19, Manuel Peña's essay 'From *Ranchero* to *Jaitón*', music's connection to nationalism is at a remove from the participants' circumstances. Performance of the 'ranchero sound complex' functioned for musicians and audiences to express identification with their nation of origin (Mexico) rather than their nation of residence (the US). The agrarian-themed ranchero repertoire, identified as it was with Mexican romantic nationalism, was ideally suited to this, filtered through musical styles that appealed separately to working-class (conjunto) and upwardly mobile (orquesta) tejanos in the focused time period of 1935–65. Peña's essay weaves the concurrent historical developments of two musical styles in a study that clearly illustrates the distinctness of ethnicity and class in the delineation of identity, music's capacity to express identity and the potential perils of studying one musical genre in isolation. By treating conjunto and orquesta together, the author, who later published entire volumes on each (Peña, 1985, 1999), is able to show how the two musical formations influenced each other in the socioeconomic and cultural environment of Texas over three decades. Other writers have explored gender issues in tejano music (Broyles-González, 2001; Valdez and Halley, 1996).

The romantic nationalism that Peña discusses in the Mexican-American border context is also a prominent feature in American country music writ large, another genre with rural and working-class associations (Malone, 2002). As Bendix (1997) and many others have amply shown, the concepts of romantic nationalism and authenticity are inextricably bound together, and it is the latter that is the subject of Aaron Fox's essay on country music discourse in the US (Chapter 17). Through an analysis of vocal style, Nashville song-writing conventions, and radio formats and technology, Fox deconstructs industry efforts to make country music appear the 'natural' expression of 'real people'. D.K. Wilgus' classic essay on the urban hillbilly (1970) is another that points up the contradictions between the country music industry's representations of its product and how it actually does business, and would have been included but for space. Fox's Derridean analysis of the themes of loss and desire inspired Ron Emoff soon after to produce 'A Cajun Poetics of Loss and Longing' (1998) for Cajun dance music, a genre closely linked to country music since the 1930s. Jocelyn Neal (2007) built on Fox's work to produce a more formal analysis of both text and music in country song-writing.

The perspective of technological impacts on music is represented in this volume by Marion Jacobson's history of accordion reception in the US. In Peña's study of ethnicity and class just discussed, the accordion is a pivotal instrument whose presence served as a class marker, with distinctions made between the diatonic accordion (embraced by the working-class conjunto musicians) and the piano accordion – seen as more sophisticated, occasionally used in orquesta ensembles, avoided by conjuntos. Peña observes, 'The "respectable" class of Mexicans, meanwhile – as well as the Anglo-Americans – have looked with disfavor upon the instrument and the celebrations traditionally associated with it' (p. 434). It is that Anglo-American disfavour, which was hardly limited to the state of Texas, that Jacobson chronicles in Chapter 18 through her detailed description of attempts to legitimize the accordion in the US by associating it with classical music and music education for the masses starting in the 1930s, followed by attempts to enhance the instrument's hipness with youth in the 1960s. These multipronged efforts encompassed technological enhancements to the instrument, along with marketing strategies and institutional innovations, but their success was always limited due to the instrument's enduring associations with working-class immigrants. It was only when 'roots' music became popular, starting in the 1980s, that the accordion gained acceptance. Where instrument manufacturers had failed with their futile declarations to the rock generation that 'Accordions Are In!', ethnic virtuosos like Flaco Jimenez (Scruggs, 2001) and Clifton Chenier succeeded in creating popular syntheses of regional dance music with rock and rhythm and blues that have rehabilitated the instrument in the eyes and ears of the American public.

Based on Jacobson's work, we might say that the presence of an accordion in any popular music ensemble therefore is a pretty good sign of 'roots' ideology somewhere in the immediate semiotic environment, even if the music itself does not indicate such. This is not to say that the accordion is universally viewed as imbued with the authenticity promised by the label 'roots'. In his study of a controversy in Norway between the accordion-based *gammeldans* and the older *folkemusikk*, Chris Goertzen observes that 'while the dance connection for gammeldans is undeniable, fresh, and uninterrupted, both folkemusikk and its associated dance genres required revival ... Gammeldans' music is in continuity of function more literally authentic, but folkemusikk is richer in symbolic historical associations, therefore seeming more authentic' (1998, pp. 108-109; see also Gunkel, 2004 on polka). Likewise in discourse on Cajun music there is some discussion of how the diatonic accordion altered what had previously been a fiddle-based repertoire (DeWitt, 2003), and musicians such as Dewey Balfa and Steve Riley have used a twin-fiddle configuration (sans accordion) for some of their arrangements to evoke an earlier era, but (unlike the Norwegian case) these would be played in the same set with accordion tunes. There is a definite sense in Cajun music, as I daresay there is in most genres where the accordion is a fixture, that there is no going back to musical life without it. A reasonable variety of studies of the accordion now exists concerning various styles that fall under the rubric of this volume, including Irish (O'Keeffe, 2001; Smith, 1997), Scottish (Eydmann, 1999, 2001), klezmer (Horowitz, 2001), Bulgarian (Rabe, 2001), Breton (Perroches, 2001), anglophone African-American (Snyder, 1994, 1997) and Québecois (Begin, 1983).

Remaining to be discussed in this 'Offshoots' section are three essays concerning groups that are typically associated with 'roots' music of some kind – the Roma in Europe and indigenous peoples of North America – whose musical interests obviously range far beyond any boundaries that an ethnic label might indicate. According to Svanibor Pettan in Chapter 20, this is the normal situation for Roma (Gypsy) musicians. The relationship between Romani music and Romani identity is diffuse in the first place, in that the Roma are not one group of people but 'a set of groups' and that what the Roma themselves tend to consider Romani music 'varies from country to country' (p. 464). In a more recent essay, Ursula Hemetek also states that 'there is no Romani music per se' (2009, p. 107) even as she chronicles the lighthearted adoption of a single 'international anthem' by many Roma of different groups. Where folklore ensembles gather to perform, Roma ensembles tend to be far less purist in their presentation than their non-Roma counterparts, eschewing uniform dress and employing synthesizers on occasion. As professional musicians, versatility means more work as they strive 'to accommodate any audience with its own music' (p. 464), even to the point of performing in non-Rom ethnic costume. In support of these general observations, Pettan offers the results of research on the musical tastes of Romani musicians in Kosovo prior to the breakup of the nation of Yugoslavia. He strategically selected the listening samples he played for these musicians according to Rom/non-Rom and local/non-local, and was therefore able to conclude that 'the notion that "we have to appreciate this tune because it is 'our' folk tune," is not of primary relevance to them' (p. 472). His motivation to commemorate Romani musical life in Kosovo and to help surviving musicians in the wake of the 1990s conflicts is commendable. Turning to a critique of folk music research itself as a cultural institution, Pettan sees the Roma as kindred spirits with ethnomusicologists, whose field of study (as I like to tell my students) is simply people making music.

In Chapter 16 Beverley Diamond presents the creativity of women musicians in contemporary Native American music as a manifestation of double consciousness of their traditional music, gender roles and community obligations alongside their roles in modern cosmopolitan society. Widely associated with W.E.B. Du Bois and his 1903 publication *The Souls of Black Folk* (Bruce, 1992), the phrase 'double consciousness' has application here to the experience of indigenous women negotiating their places in today's world, as evidenced by the voices that Diamond presents. The contrast is at times striking between the Roma musicians presented by Pettan, who hold their Romani identity loosely with respect to their own musical tastes and are willing to perform the identity of non-Rom groups, and the women in Diamond's essay who are earnestly and deeply engaged in articulating their identities as women and women musicians within their communities and in negotiating interfaces among their First Nations cultures and 'mainstream' popular culture. As she notes, performers like Buffy Ste. Marie, Joanne Shenandoah and Ulali operate in the context of the popular music industry but on their own terms. Their work can be evaluated neither by some measure of authenticity compared to traditional indigenous music (the influence of which may not be audible) nor by commercial success as measured in Billboard charts or Grammy awards, but rather by how they creatively shoulder the historical and cultural baggage that it is their destiny to carry.

While Diamond is concerned primarily with women who compose and perform their own music, in Chapter 21 David Samuels deals with the creative reception by Apaches of American popular music. This essay was chosen with good reason to conclude a substantial special issue of *Journal of American Folklore* on 'Theorizing the Hybrid' (Kapchan and Strong, 1999). Like Diamond, Samuels is concerned to avoid the authenticity bugaboo, which in discussions of hybridity he identifies as an 'overly archaeological and genealogical' (p. 481) approach to tracing the roots of popular styles. Just as David McAllester (1996) showed how Johnny Cash's 'Folsom Prison Blues' could be reinterpreted as Navajo music in Titon's *Worlds of Music* textbook, Samuels suggests that certain rock songs in circulation on the San Carlos reservation be considered Apache songs, even that bands that recorded them such as Aerosmith and Creedence Clearwater Revival might be considered Apache bands.

Big Bell's heartfelt singing of 'Mathilda' is an extended example of offshoots from roots music. As the author notes in passing, 'Mathilda' was itself a minor hit on the national charts in 1959 for a Lake Charles, Louisiana-based band, Cookie and the Cupcakes (*not* New Orleans-based, as Samuels asserts; see Bernard, 1996). Rock and roll music from this period as made by bands in the Gulf Coast region became retroactively known as 'swamp pop', a term coined by British writer John Broven (1983) that has since become accepted and used in southern Louisiana. It continues to receive radio airplay on public and commercial stations, and in the minds of some it practically has the status of a local traditional music on a par with Cajun French dance music. So a rock and roll song heard nationally when it was first released has since been absorbed into a repertoire that constitutes a regional badge of honour in Louisiana, and at the same time it has become part of the lore of the San Carlos reservation in Arizona 2,000 kilometres away, a song that the legendary departed Apache rock singer Sluggo sang, a song that Big Bell probably performed in his prime with his band the Dominoes. In San Carlos, 'A good song is one that allows listeners to imagine the way things used to be' (p. 485). In a critique of musico-genealogical pedigree tantamount to that of the entire roots music concept, Samuels' crystalline conclusion asks, 'who am I to say this is somebody else's music?' (p. 487). I can think of no better way to end this essay or this volume.

References

Abbott, Lynn (1992), '"Play That Barber Shop Chord": A Case for the African-American Origin of Barbershop Harmony', *American Music*, **10**, 3, pp. 289–325.

Allen, Dave (2007), 'Feelin' Bad This Morning: Why the *British* Blues?', *Popular Music*, **26**, 1, pp. 141–56.

Allen, William Francis, Ware, Charles Pickard and Garrison, Lucy McKim (1867), *Slave Songs of the United States*, New York: A. Simpson.

Armitage, David (2002), 'Three Concepts of Atlantic History', in David Armitage and Michael J. Braddick (eds), *The British Atlantic World, 1500–1800*, New York: Palgrave Macmillan, pp. 11–30.

Averill, Gage (2003), *Four Parts, No Waiting: A Social History of American Barbershop Harmony*, New York: Oxford University Press.

Bearman, C.J. (2002), 'Cecil Sharp in Somerset: Some Reflections on the Work of David Harker', *Folklore*, **113**, pp. 11–34.

Begin, Carmelle (1983), *La Musique Traditionnelle pour Accordion Diatonique Philippe Bruneau*, Ottawa: National Museums of Canada.

Bendix, Regina (1997), *In Search of Authenticity: The Formation of Folklore Studies*, Madison: University of Wisconsin Press.

Bernard, Shane K. (1996), *Swamp Pop: Cajun and Creole Rhythm and Blues*, Jackson: University Press of Mississippi.

Bohlman, Philip V. (1988), *The Study of Folk Music in the Modern World*, Bloomington: Indiana University Press.

Bohlman, Philip V. (2002), 'Landscape-Region-Nation-Reich: German Folk Song in the Nexus of National Identity', in Celia Applegate and Pamela Potter (eds), *Music and German National Identity*, Chicago: University of Chicago Press, pp. 105–27.

Boyer, Horace (1979a), 'Contemporary Gospel Music, Part 1: Sacred or Secular?', *The Black Perspective in Music*, **7**, 1, pp. 5–21.

Boyer, Horace (1979b), 'Contemporary Gospel Music, Part 2: Characteristics and Style', *The Black Perspective in Music*, **7**, 1, pp. 22–58.

Brasseaux, Ryan A. (2009), *Cajun Breakdown: The Emergence of an American-Made Music*, Oxford: Oxford University Press.

Brasseaux, Ryan A. and Fontenot, Kevin S. (eds) (2006), *Accordions, Fiddles, Two Step & Swing: A Cajun Music Reader*, Lafayette: The Center for Louisiana Studies, University of Louisiana at Lafayette.

Broven, John (1983), *South to Louisiana: The Music of the Cajun Bayous*, Gretna, LA: Pelican.

Broyles-González, Yolanda (2001), *Lydia Mendoza's Life in Music: La historia de Lydia Mendoza: Norteño Tejano Legacies*, Oxford and New York: Oxford University Press.

Bruce, Dickson D. Jr. (1992), 'W.E.B. Du Bois and the Idea of Double Consciousness', *American Literature*, **64**, 2, pp. 299–309.

Buchanan, Donna A. (1997), 'Review Essay: Bulgaria's Magical *Mystère* Tour: Postmodernism, World Music Marketing, and Political Change in Eastern Europe', *Ethnomusicology*, **41**, 1, pp. 131–57.

Buchanan, Donna A. (2006), *Performing Democracy: Bulgarian Music and Musicians in Transition*, Chicago: University of Chicago Press.

Buchanan, Donna A. (2007), *Balkan Popular Culture and the Ottoman Ecumene: Music, Image, and Regional Political Discourse*, Lanham, MD: Scarecrow Press.

Burnim, Mellonee (1985), 'Culture Bearer and Tradition Bearer: An Ethnomusicologist's Research on Gospel Music', *Ethnomusicology*, **29**, 3, pp. 432–47.

Carolina Chocolate Drops (2010), *Genuine Negro Jig*, Nonesuch 516995-2.

Chuse, Loren (2003), *The Cantaoras: Music, Gender, and Identity in Flamenco Song*, London: Routledge.

Cockerell, Dale (1996), 'Jim Crow, Demon of Disorder', *American Music*, **14**, 2, pp. 161–84.

Cockerell, Dale (1997), *Demons of Disorder: Early Blackface Minstrels and Their World*, New York and Cambridge: Cambridge University Press.

Cohen, Ronald D. (ed.) (2003), *Alan Lomax: Select Writings, 1934–1997*, New York: Routledge.

Conway, Cecelia (1995), *African Banjo Echoes in Appalachia: A Study of Folk Traditions*, Knoxville: University of Tennessee Press.

Conway, Cecelia (2003), 'Black Banjo Songsters in Appalachia', *Black Music Research Journal*, **23**, 1/2, pp. 149–66.

Deloria, Philip J. (1998), *Playing Indian*, New Haven, CT: Yale University Press.

DeWitt, Mark F. (1999), 'Heritage, Tradition and Travel: Louisiana French Culture Placed on a California Dance Floor', *World of Music*, **41**, 3, pp. 57–83.

DeWitt, Mark F. (2003), 'The Diatonic Button Accordion in Ethnic Context: Idiom and Style in Cajun Dance Music', *Popular Music and Society*, **26**, 3, pp. 305–30.

DeWitt, Mark F. (2008), *Cajun and Zydeco Dance Music in Northern California: Modern Pleasures in a Postmodern World*, Jackson: University Press of Mississippi.

Donaldson, Gary A. (1984), 'A Window on Slave Culture: Dances at Congo Square in New Orleans, 1800–1862', *Journal of Negro History*, **69**, 2, pp. 63–72.

Dormon, James H. (1969), 'The Strange Career of Jim Crow Rice (With Apologies to Professor Woodward)', *Journal of Social History*, **3**, 2, pp. 109–22.

DuBois, W.E.B. (1903), *The Souls of Black Folk*, Chicago: A.C. McClurg.

Dunson, Stephanie (2002), 'The Minstrel in the Parlor: Nineteenth-Century Sheet Music and the Domestification of Blackface Minstrelsy', *American Transcendental Quarterly*, **16**, 4, pp. 241–56.

Dylan, Bob (2001), *Love and Theft*, New York: Columbia CH 90340.

Emoff, Ron (1998), 'A Cajun Poetics of Loss and Longing', *Ethnomusicology*, **42**, 2, pp. 283–301.

Epstein, Dena (1975), 'The Folk Banjo: A Documentary History', *Ethnomusicology*, **19**, 3, pp. 347–71.

Evans, David (2000), 'Musical Innovation in the Blues of Blind Lemon Jefferson', *Black Music Research Journal*, **20**, 1, pp. 83–116.

Eydmann, Stuart (1999), 'As Common as Blackberries: The First Hundred Years of the Accordion in Scotland, 1830–1930', *Folk Music Journal*, **7**, 5, pp. 595–608.

Eydmann, Stuart (2001), 'From the "Wee Melodeon" to the "Big Box": The Accordion in Scotland since 1945', *Musical Performance*, **3**, 2–4, pp. 107–26.

Feld, Steven (1996), 'Pygmy POP: A Genealogy of Schizophonic Mimesis', *Yearbook for Traditional Music*, **28**, pp. 1–35.

Feld, Steven and Basso, Keith H. (eds) (1996), *Senses of Place*, Santa Fe, NM: School of American Research Press; distributed by the University of Washington Press, Seattle.

Filene, Benjamin (2000), *Romancing the Folk: Public Memory and American Roots Music*, Chapel Hill: University of North Carolina Press.

Filene, Benjamin (2004) '*O Brother*, What Next? Making Sense of the Folk Fad', *Southern Cultures*, **10**, pp. 50–69.

Fleck, Béla (producer) (2008), *Throw Down Your Heart* [Film], The Old School, USA.

Floyd, Samuel A. Jr. (1991), 'Ring Shout! Literary Studies, Historical Studies, and Black Music Inquiry', *Black Music Research Journal*, **11**, 2, pp. 265–87.

Floyd, Samuel A. Jr. (1995), *The Power of Black Music: Interpreting Its History from Africa to the United States*, Oxford: Oxford University Press.

Ford, Charles (1998), 'Robert Johnson's Rhythms', *Popular Music*, **17**, 1, pp. 71–93.

Gabaccia, Donna (2004), 'A Long Atlantic in a Wider World', *Atlantic Studies*, **1**, 1, pp. 1–27.

Gardner, Robert Owen (2004), 'The Portable Community: Mobility and Modernization in Bluegrass Festival Life', *Symbolic Interaction*, **27**, 2, pp. 155–78.

Gates, Henry Louis Jr. (1988), *The Signifying Monkey: A Theory of African-American Literary Criticism*, New York: Oxford University Press.

Gibson, Chris and Connell, John (2005), *Music and Tourism: On the Road Again*, Clevedon: Channel View Publications.

Gilroy, Paul (1991), 'Sounds Authentic – Black Music, Ethnicity, and the Challenge of a Changing Same', *Black Music Research Journal*, **11**, 2, pp. 111–36.

Gilroy, Paul (1993), *The Black Atlantic: Modernity and Double-Consciousness*, Cambridge, MA: Harvard University Press.

Gioia, Ted (2006a), *Healing Songs*, Durham, NC: Duke University Press.

Gioia, Ted (2006b), *Work Songs*, Durham, NC: Duke University Press.

Goertzen, Chris (1998), 'The Norwegian Folk Revival and the *Gammeldans* Controversy', *Ethnomusicology*, **42**, 1, pp. 99–127.

Goldberg, Christine (1984), 'The Historic-Geographic Method: Past and Future', *Journal of Folklore Research*, **21**, 1, pp. 1–18.

Green, Archie (2001), *Torching the Fink Books and Other Essays on Vernacular Culture*, Chapel Hill: University of North Carolina Press.

Gunkel, Ann Hetzel (2004), 'The Polka Alternative: Polka as Counterhegemonic Ethnic Practice', *Popular Music and Society*, **27**, 4, pp. 407–27.

Guralnick, Peter (1971), *Feel Like Going Home: Portraits in Blues and Rock 'n' Roll*, New York: Outerbridge & Dienstfrey.

Guralnick, Peter (1979), *Lost Highway: Journeys & Arrivals of American Musicians*, Boston: D.R. Godine.

Hamilton, Marybeth (2002), 'The Voice of the Blues', *History Workshop Journal*, **54**, pp. 123–43.

Hamm, Charles (2000), 'Review of *Demons of Disorder: Early Blackface Minstrels and Their World* by Dale Cockrell; *Raising Cain: Blackface Performance from Jim Crow to Hip Hop* by W.T. Lhamon, Jr.; and *Behind the Burnt Cork Mask: Early Blackface Minstrelsy and Antebellum American Popular Culture* by William J. Mahar', *Journal of the American Musicological Society*, **53**, 1, pp. 165–83.

Harker, Dave (1981), 'Francis James Child and the "Ballad Consensus"', *Folk Music Journal*, **4**, 2, pp. 146–64.

Harker, David (1985), *Fakesong: The Manufacture of British 'Folksong' 1700 to the Present Day*, Milton Keynes: Open University Press.

Hay, Fred J. (2003), 'Black Musicians in Appalachia: An Introduction to Affrilachian Music', *Black Music Research Journal*, **23**, 1/2, pp. 1–19.

Hemetek, Ursula (2009), 'Gelem, Gelem Lungone Dromeja – I Have Walked a Long Way: The International Anthem of the "Travelling People" – Symbol of a Nation?', in Bernd Clausen, Ursula Hemetek and Eva Saether (eds), *Music in Motion: Diversity and Dialogue in Europe*, Bielefeld: Transcript, pp. 103–13.

Henry, Edward O. (1989), 'Institutions for the Promotion of Indigenous Music: The Case for Ireland's Comhaltas Ceoltoiri Eireann', *Ethnomusicology*, **33**, 1, pp. 67–95.

Henry, James Earl (2000), 'The Origins of Barbershop Harmony: A Study of Barbershop's Musical Link to Other African American Musics as Evidenced through Recordings and Arrangements of Early Black and White Quartets', Ph.D. dissertation, Washington University, St. Louis.

Hobsbawm, Eric and Ranger, Terence (eds) (1983), *The Invention of Tradition*, Cambridge: Cambridge University Press.

Holt, Fabian (2007), *Genre in Popular Music*, Chicago: University of Chicago Press.

Horowitz, Joshua (2001), 'The *Klezmer* Accordion: Old New Worlds (1899–2001)', *Musical Performance*, **3**, 2–4, pp. 135–62.

Kapchan, Deborah A. and Strong, Pauline Turner (1999), 'Theorizing the Hybrid', *Journal of American Folklore*, **112**, 445, pp. 239–53.

Keil, Charles (1966), *Urban Blues*, Chicago: University of Chicago Press.

Keil, Charles (1985), 'People's Music Comparatively: Style and Stereotype, Class and Hegemony', *Dialectical Anthropology*, **10**, 1–2, pp. 119–30.

Kirshenblatt-Gimblett, Barbara (1998), 'Sounds of Sensibility', *Judaism*, **47**, 1, pp. 49–78.

Kubik, Gerhard (1999), *Africa and the Blues*, Jackson: University Press of Mississippi.

Lamadrid, Enrique R. (2000), '"Cielos del Norte, Alma del Rio Arriba": Nuevo Mexicano Folk Music Revivals, Recordings 1943–98', *Journal of American Folklore*, **113**, 449, pp. 314–22.

Laušević, Mirjana (2007), *Balkan Fascination: Creating an Alternative Music Culture in America*, New York: Oxford University Press.

Le Menestrel, Sara (2007), 'The Color of Music: Social Boundaries and Stereotypes in Southwest Louisiana French Music', *Southern Cultures*, **13**, 3, pp. 87–105.

Leyshon, Andrew, Matless, David and Revill, George (eds) (1998), *The Place of Music*, New York: Guilford Press.

Lhamon, W.T. Jr. (1998), *Raising Cain: Blackface Performance from Jim Crow to Hip Hop*, Cambridge, MA: Harvard University Press.

Lightfoot, William E. (2003), 'The Three Doc(k)s: White Blues in Appalachia', *Black Music Research Journal*, **23**, 1/2, pp. 167–93.

Lindahl, Carl (2001), 'A Note on Blackface', *Journal of American Folklore*, **114**, 452, pp. 248–54.

Linn, Karen Elizabeth (1990), 'The "Elevation" of the Banjo in Late Nineteenth-Century America', *American Music*, **8**, 4, pp. 441–64.

Lott, Eric (1993), *Love and Theft: Blackface Minstrelsy and the American Working Class*, New York: Oxford University Press.

McAllester, David P. (1996), 'North America/Native America', in Jeff Todd Titon (gen. ed.), *Worlds of Music: An Introduction to the Music of the World's Peoples*, New York: Schirmer Books, pp. 17–70.

Mahar, William J. (1999), *Behind the Burnt Cork Mask: Early Blackface Minstrelsy and Antebellum American Popular Culture*, Urbana: University of Illinois Press.

Malone, Bill C. (2002), *Don't Get Above Your Raisin': Country Music and the Southern Working Class*, Urbana: University of Illinois Press.

Manuel, Peter (1989), 'Andalusian, Gypsy, and Class Identity in the Contemporary Flamenco Complex', *Ethnomusicology*, **33**, 1, pp. 47–65.

Manuel, Peter (1994), 'Puerto-Rican Music and Cultural Identity – Creative Appropriation of Cuban Sources from Danza to Salsa', *Ethnomusicology*, **38**, 2, pp. 249–80.

Marcus, Greil (1975), *Mystery Train: Images of America in Rock 'n' Roll Music*, New York: E.P. Dutton.

Marcus, Greil (1991), *Dead Elvis: A Chronicle of a Cultural Obsession*, New York: Doubleday.

Marcus, Greil (1997a), 'Dock Boggs in Thomas Jefferson's Virginia', *Representations*, **58**, pp. 1–23.

Marcus, Greil (1997b), *Invisible Republic: Bob Dylan's Basement Tapes*, New York: Henry Holt.

Marcus, Greil (2005), *Like a Rolling Stone: Bob Dylan at the Crossroads*, New York: PublicAffairs.

Mattern, Mark (1997), 'Let the Good Times Unroll: Music and Race Relations in Southwest Louisiana', *Black Music Research Journal*, **17**, 2, pp. 159–68.

Meadows, Eddie S. (1979), 'African Retentions in Blues and Jazz', *Western Journal of Black Studies*, **3**, 3, pp. 180–85.

Middleton, Richard (2007), 'O Brother, Let's Go Down Home: Loss, Nostalgia and the Blues', *Popular Music*, **26**, 1, pp. 47–64.

Miller, Rebecca S. (1988), '"Our Own Little Isle": Irish Traditional Music in New York', *New York Folklore*, **14**, 3–4, pp. 101–15.

Minton, John (1996), 'Houston Creoles and Zydeco: The Emergence of an African American Popular Style', *American Music*, **14**, 4, pp. 480–526.

Moore, Allan F. (2007), *Critical Essays in Popular Musicology*, Aldershot: Ashgate.

Mosher, Craig (2008), 'Ecstatic Sounds: The Influence of Pentecostalism on Rock and Roll', *Popular Music and Society*, **31**, 1, pp. 95–112.

Nathan, Hans (1956), 'Early Banjo Tunes and American Syncopation', *Musical Quarterly*, **42**, 4, pp. 455–72.

Neal, Jocelyn R. (2007), 'Narrative Paradigms, Musical Signifiers, and Form as Function in Country Music', *Music Theory Spectrum*, **29**, 1, pp. 41–72.

O'Keeffe, Máire (2001), 'The Irish Button Accordion: An Overview', *Musical Performance*, **3**, 2–4, pp. 95–106.

Olivier, Rick and Sandmel, Ben (photographer/author) (1999), *Zydeco!*, Jackson: University Press of Mississippi.

Pearson, Barry Lee (2003), 'Appalachian Blues', *Black Music Research Journal*, **23**, 1/2, pp. 23–51.

Peña, Manuel (1985), *The Texas-Mexican Conjunto: History of a Working-Class Music*, Austin: University of Texas Press.

Peña, Manuel (1999), *The Mexican American Orquesta: Music, Culture, and the Dialectic of Conflict*, Austin: University of Texas Press.

Perroches, Yann-Fañch (2001), 'Jean Coatéval, the Devil's Box and the Gavotte: The Accordion in Breton Music', *Musical Performance*, **3**, 2–4, pp. 127–34.

Powers, Harold S. (1980), 'Mode', in Stanley Sadie (ed.), *New Grove Dictionary of Music and Musicians*, London: Macmillan.

Rabe, Gee (2001), 'Aspects of Regional Difference and Performance Technique in Bulgarian Accordion Music', *Musical Performance*, **3**, 2–4, pp. 163–84.

Radano, Ronald (2003), *Lying Up a Nation: Race and Black Music*, Chicago: University of Chicago Press.

Radano, Ronald and Bohlman, Philip V. (2000), *Music and the Racial Imagination*, Chicago: University of Chicago Press.

Reagon, Bernice Johnson (1996), 'Volume II: African American Congregational Singing', in *Wade in the Water: African American Sacred Music Traditions*, compiled and annotated Bernice Johnson Reagon, Washington, DC: Smithsonian Folkways.

Redhead, Steve and Street, John (1989), 'Have I the Right? Legitimacy, Authenticity and Community in Folk's Politics', *Popular Music*, **8**, 2, pp. 177–84.

Regis, Helen (1999), 'Second Lines, Minstrelsy, and the Contested Landscapes of New Orleans Afro-Creole Festivals', *Cultural Anthropology*, **14**, 4, pp. 472–504.

Rice, Timothy (1994), *May It Fill Your Soul: Experiencing Bulgarian Music*, Chicago: University of Chicago Press.

Rosenbaum, Art (1998), *Shout Because You're Free: The African American Ring Shout Tradition in Coastal Georgia*, Athens: University of Georgia Press.

Rosenberg, Neil V. (1967), 'From Sound to Style: The Emergence of Bluegrass', *Journal of American Folklore*, **80**, 316, pp. 143–50.

Rosenberg, Neil V. (1995), 'From the Sound Recordings Review Editor: The Classification of Traditional Instrumental Music', *Journal of American Folklore*, **108**, 428, pp. 186–201.

Sacks, Howard L. and Sacks, Judith Rose (1988), 'Way Up North in Dixie: Black–White Musical Interaction in Knox County, Ohio', *American Music*, **6**, 4, pp. 409–27.

Sakakeeny, Matt (2010), '"Under the Bridge": An Orientation to Soundscapes in New Orleans', *Ethnomusicology*, **54**, 1, pp. 1–27.

Santelli, Robert, George-Warren, Holly and Brown, Jim (2001), *American Roots Music*, New York: H.N. Abrams.

Scruggs, T.M. (2001), 'Squeezing the Audience from Both Ends: The *Conjunto* Accordion and the Musical Border Crossings of Flaco Jimenez', *Musical Performance*, **3**, 2–4, pp. 215–28.

Sexton, Rocky L. and Oster, Harry (2001), 'Une 'Tite Poule Grasse ou la Fille Aînée: A Comparative Analysis of Cajun and Creole Mardi Gras Songs', *Journal of American Folklore*, **114**, 452, pp. 204–24.

Sheffield, Rob (2001), 'Dylan's Forty-Third Album Presents the History of American Music', *Rolling Stone*, **878** (September 27, 2001), pp. 65–7.

Slobin, Mark (ed.) (1996), *Retuning Culture: Musical Changes in Central and Eastern Europe*, Durham, NC: Duke University Press.

Smith, Graeme (1994), 'Australian Country Music and the Hillbilly Yodel', *Popular Music*, **13**, 3, pp. 297–311.

Smith, Graeme (1997), 'Modern-Style Irish Accordion Playing: History, Biography, and Class', *Ethnomusicology*, **41**, 3, pp. 433–63.

Snyder, Jared (1994), 'Leadbelly and His Windjammer: Examining the African American Button Accordion Tradition', *American Music*, **12**, 2, pp. 148–66.

Snyder, Jared (1997), 'Squeezebox: The Legacy of the Afro-Mississippi Accordionists', *Black Music Research Journal*, **17**, 1, pp. 37–57.

Stokes, Martin (ed.) (1994), *Ethnicity, Identity, and Music: The Musical Construction of Place*, Oxford: Berg.

Suchoff, Benjamin (ed.) (1997), *Béla Bartók Studies in Ethnomusicology*, Lincoln: University of Nebraska Press.

Sykes, Richard (1993), 'The Evolution of Englishness in the English Folksong Revival, 1890–1914', *Folk Music Journal*, **6**, 4, pp. 446–90.

Taylor, Otis (2008), *Recapturing the Banjo*, Telarc 83667.

Taylor, Timothy D. (1997), *Global Pop: World Music, World Markets*, New York: Routledge.

Titon, Jeff Todd (1977), 'Thematic Pattern in Downhome Blues Lyrics', *Journal of American Folklore*, 90, pp. 316–30.

Toll, Robert C. (1974), *Blacking Up: The Minstrel Show in Nineteenth Century America*, New York: Oxford University Press.

Tuhkanen, Mikko (2001), 'Of Blackface and Paranoid Knowledge: Richard Wright, Jacques Lacan, and the Ambivalence of Black Minstrelsy', *Diacritics*, **31**, 2, pp. 9–34.

Valdez, Avelardo and Halley, Jeffrey A. (1996), 'Gender in the Culture of Mexican American Conjunto Music', *Gender and Society*, **10**, 2, pp. 148–67.

Veal, Michael E. (2007), *Dub: Soundscapes and Shattered Songs in Jamaican Reggae*, Middletown, CT: Wesleyan University Press.

Washburne, Christopher (1998), 'Play It *Con Filin!* The Swing and Expression of Salsa', *Latin American Music Review*, **19**, 2, pp. 160–85.

Waterman, Richard A. (1952), 'African Influence on the Music of the Americas', in Sol Tax (ed.), *Acculturation in the Americas*, Chicago: University of Chicago Press, pp. 207–18.

Wells, Paul F. (2003), 'Fiddling as an Avenue of Black-White Musical Interchange', *Black Music Research Journal*, **23**, 1/2, pp. 135–47.

Wilentz, Sean and Marcus, Greil (2005), *The Rose & the Briar: Death, Love and Liberty in the American Ballad*, New York: W.W. Norton.

Wilgus, D.K. (1970), 'Country-Western Music and the Urban Hillbilly', *Journal of American Folklore*, **83**, 328, pp. 157–79.

Winans, Robert B. (1976), 'The Folk, the Stage, and the Five-String Banjo in the Nineteenth Century', *Journal of American Folklore*, **89**, 354, pp. 407–37.

Wolfe, Charles K. (1983), 'Frank Smith, Andrew Jenkins, and Early Commercial Gospel Music', *American Music*, **1**, 1, pp. 49–59.

Wood, Roger (2006), *Texas Zydeco*, Austin: University of Texas Press.

Wynter, Sylvia (1979), 'Sambos and Minstrels', *Social Text*, **1**, pp. 149–56.

Zak, Albin J. (2004), 'Bob Dylan and Jimi Hendrix: Juxtaposition and Transformation "All along the Watchtower"', *Journal of the American Musicological Society*, **57**, 3, pp. 599–644.

Zemp, Hugo (1996), 'The/An Ethnomusicologist and the Record Business', *Yearbook for Traditional Music*, **28**, pp. 36–56.

Part I
Roots, Deconstructed

[1]

The Popular Marketing of "Old Ballads": The Ballad Revival and Eighteenth-Century Antiquarianism Reconsidered

Dianne Dugaw

As IT IS CURRENTLY UNDERSTOOD, the ballad revival emerged in eighteenth-century England as an activity of the scholarly and literary elite. Writers such as Percy, Ritson, Prior, Goldsmith, and Scott admired, collected, and commented upon old ballads to fulfill an antiquarian agenda. For them, these ballads were remnants of an earlier stage in the nation's literature and history, and exemplified the untainted, untutored genius of the English people. Approached as the exclusive activity of polite circles, antiquarianism—the ballad revival in particular—is not believed to have affected the common people themselves, whose songs and stories continued to circulate in oral tradition, filled the stalls of broadside printers, and provided literary antiquarians with the subjects for their study. Albert Friedman, for example, pointedly excludes the possibility that the ballad revival was felt at the popular level:

By "ballad revival" we usually mean a revival of interest in the ballad similar in nature to the Miltonic, Spenserian, and Elizabethan revivals. ... an openly acknowledged interest in the ballad *on the sophisticated level....* [Friedman's emphasis] Paradoxically, then, the ballad revival did not really affect either the stall or folk ballads, but only the literary world's perception of them, and in no solid sense can this phenomenon be considered a revival.[1]

However, as I will show, the ballad revival was not confined to "the sophisticated level," as Friedman insists, but in fact flourished on the popular level as well. Trained only to view literary culture from the top down, modern scholars have overlooked the significant popularity of "ancient" ballads in the lowbrow street literature sold in eighteenth-century printers' stalls. The fact is, ordinary people, who did not belong to what Friedman calls the "literary world," purchased ballads marketed explicitly for their historical and antiquarian value. Indeed, we can find in eighteenth-century street literature an appreciation for and revival of old songs whose supposed antiquity was their prime selling point. This commercial and popular appreciation for old ballads parallels and actually reciprocates the literary antiquarianism at the polite level, which scholars have always emphasized.

The first antiquarian collection of ballads was an anonymous eighteenth-century work situated midway between the polite and popular audiences—some would say tilted decidedly toward the latter. The first volume of *A Collection of Old Ballads* was published in 1723 by James Roberts, the largest job-printer in London at the time, and the same publisher who printed many of the pamphlets and novels of Daniel Defoe and Eliza Haywood.[2] A compendium of "antique songs written Ages ago," this collection immediately became a bestseller, to all appearances one of the most popular books of the 1720s. Already in the first year, Volume One sold out and went into a second edition only two months after the publication of the first edition. As the full title of Volume One announces, the

[1]Albert Friedman, *The Ballad Revival: Studies in the Influence of Popular on Sophisticated Poetry* (Chicago: Univ. of Chicago Press, 1961), pp. 9–10. For other examples of this approach, see Sigurd B. Hustvedt, *Ballad Criticism in Scandinavia and Great Britain during the Eighteenth Century* (New York: American Scandinavian Foundation, 1916; London: Oxford University Press, 1916), passim.; Henry A. Beers, *A History of English Romanticism in the Eighteenth Century* (New York: Henry Holt, 1898; rpt New York: Gordian, 1966), pp. 265–305; and Bertram H. Davis, *Thomas Percy* (Boston: Twayne, 1981), pp. 72–108 and 125–39.
[2]*A Collection of Old Ballads*, 3 Vols. (London: J. Roberts, 1723–1725). Volumes One and Two of the first edition of this anonymously published work appeared in 1723, Volume Three in 1725. For discussion of Roberts, see Michael Treadwell, "London Trade Publishers 1675–1750," *The Library*, Sixth Series, Vol. 4 (1982): 99–134.

collection was committed from the start to an antiquarian agenda: *A Collection of Old Ballads. Corrected from the best and most Ancient Copies Extant. With Introductions Historical, Critical, or Humorous.* Aware that the ostensible antiquity of his ballads was selling the collection, the anonymous editor, later in the first year, brought out a second volume which contained "Songs, more Antique, and upon far older Subjects" than those in the first. The third volume was added in 1725, a third edition of Volume One in 1727, and, by 1738, the entire three-volume collection appeared in a second edition.[3]

As the commercial success of *A Collection of Old Ballads* attests, already in the 1720s people quite below "the sophisticated level" appreciated a work that drew attention to the antiquity and historical value of ballads, a work manifestly antiquarian in character. The anonymous editor created this antiquarian character in *A Collection of Old Ballads* by writing long and self-consciously learned headnotes to individual ballads. These prefatory remarks supply anecdotes and often elaborate emendations to the ballad stories as well as discussions of their origins, style, and factual authenticity. In his introductions, the editor stresses two principal themes: (1) the supposed antiquity and historicity of the ballads, which are taken for the most part from late seventeenth-century broadsides and garlands; and (2) the pedagogical value of these verse heirlooms which help to preserve the nation's history.

A Collection of Old Ballads presents within its antiquarian framework a variety of seventeenth-century street ballad wares. Long narrative songs depict the trials, tribulations, and occasional victories of historical figures: "A Lamentable Ballad of Fair Rosamund, King Henry the Second's Concubine," "Queen Eleanor's Confession," "The Lamentation of Jane Shore," "King Edward and Jane Shore," "Chevy Chase," "The Seven Champions of Christendom," "Queen Elizabeth's Champion, the Earl of Essex," and other songs on famous and not-so-famous personages in English history. Next, there are ballads of outlaws like Robin Hood and Johnny Armstrong, and paeans to working-class heroes like Dick Whittington and the

---

[3]For a summary of the publishing history of *A Collection of Old Ballads*, see Arthur E. Case, *A Bibliography of English Poetical Miscellanies 1521–1750* (Oxford: Bibliographical Society, 1935 [for 1929]), No. 326. The editor's promise of "Songs more Antique" can be found in *A Collection of Old Ballads*, I, 288.

disadvantaged apprentice who "behaved chivalrously" in Turkey. Finally, the three volumes contain shorter drinking and courtship songs, many of them with a Scottish flavor. In all, *A Collection of Old Ballads* presents 159 song texts with 45 engraved illustrations.

The attitude of the middlebrow editor toward the ballads in his collection is ambivalent and not a little facetious. If he indulges himself fully in the role of antiquarian scholar, commenting at length on the background, style, and significance of the ballads before him, he is also at times utterly disingenuous in this editorial posture, using it humorously and satirically. In his preface, for example, he proclaims slyly that "several fine Historians are indebted to Historical Ballads for all their Learning." Elsewhere, we detect in his remarks humorous and ironic allusions, or we find the solemnity of elaborate and seemingly serious headnotes utterly undercut by ribald or far-fetched ballads.[4]

Much of this facetiousness in *A Collection of Old Ballads* actually plays off highbrow literary debates of the day. In his introductions, for example, the editor alludes to such topics as the pastoral controversy, which prompted the satires of Pope and Gay, and to the quarrel between the Ancients and the Moderns, which is the context for Addison's *Spectator* papers on balladry.[5] The great popularity of *A Collection of Old Ballads* actually shows that "sophisticated" literary disputes, such as the pastoral controversy—and, as I will suggest—the ballad revival, were not beyond the ken of an ordinary readership. But, whatever the significance and reception of the editor's facetiousness and literary references, the advertising announcement for "Songs, more Antique, and upon far older Subjects" makes clear that the editor's antiquarian approach was selling the book. Middlebrow bookbuyers of the 1720s wanted their ballads "Antique": collected together and couched in a ret-

[4]For the reference to historians, see *Collection of Old Ballads*, I, vii. For examples of ironic juxtapositions of headnotes and ballads, see "The Dragon of Wantley," I, 37–42, and "The Scotch Lover's Lamentation: Or, Gilderoy's last Farewell," I, 272–74.

[5]For an example of such literary allusions, see the introduction to "King Alfred and the Shepherd," I, 43–52. For Addison's remarks, see *The Spectator*, No. 70 (May 21, 1711), No. 74 (May 25, 1711), and No. 85 (June 7, 1711). For Pope's unsigned and utterly facetious discussion of the pastoral, see *The Guardian*, No. 40 (April 27, 1713). See also John Gay's satire on the pastoral, *The Shepherd's Week* (London: R. Burleigh, 1714), which throughout makes comical use of popular ballads.

rospective framework of dates, sources, analogues, and learned commentary.

If in the 1720s the publisher James Roberts presented to a mid-level readership England's first antiquarian treatment of "old ballads" as cultural heirlooms, already by the 1730s this antiquarian work was plundered, and its contents and method taken over by unequivocally low-level printers: the broadside and chapbook publishers, William and Cluer Dicey. In the 1720s, William Dicey, joint publisher of *The Northampton Mercury*, began printing broadsides and chapbooks, perhaps to provide his customers with products less expensive than his newspaper. Dicey began this ballad-printing enterprise with an obvious indebtedness to *A Collection of Old Ballads:* he derived a good part of his early ballad stock from the anonymous 1723 collection, whose contents he liberally filched—texts, headnotes, illustrations and all.[6]

Almost as soon as he began publishing ballads, William Dicey expanded his street literature business by taking over the Bow Church Yard printing house in London, which his son Cluer eventually made the chapbook and broadside center of the kingdom. It would be difficult to exaggerate the Diceys' mid-century predominance in ballad printing and street literature in general. They built for themselves a broadside and chapbook empire that dominated the cheap literature market until the last decades of the century. Dicey sheets and chapbooks circulated throughout the entire kingdom, sold by booksellers and copied by printers both in London and elsewhere. By way of Northampton and Bow Church Yard broadsides, the ideas and materials of England's first antiquarian ballad collection reached a wide and apparently receptive lower-class readership. In the eighteenth century the common people in the countryside and in the city purchased songs that were unmistakably proffered as "antiques"

---

[6]For discussion of the Diceys, see Victor E. Neuburg, "The Diceys and the Chapbook Trade," *The Library*, 5th Series, XXIV (1969): 219–31. See also, Robert S. Thomson, "The Development of the Broadside Ballad Trade and Its Influence upon the Transmission of English Folksongs" (Ph.D. diss., Cambridge University, 1974), p. 92ff. Friedman's admirable study briefly acknowledges the fact of the Dicey borrowings (p. 152). However, because he assumes that printed and oral songs are completely separate traditions, Friedman fails to see the implications of the Dicey prints for the Ballad Revival. For discussion of this misleading separation of printed and oral traditions, see Dianne M. Dugaw, "Anglo-American Folksong Reconsidered: The Interface of Oral and Written Forms," *Western Folklore* 43 (1984): 83–103.

in the manner of *A Collection of Old Ballads*. If Friedman's restriction of the ballad revival to the literati were true, we would not
expect to find the Dicey ballads appearing as they do: sometimes
framed by scholarly commentary and advertised for their age and
historicity.

Northampton and Bow Church Yard broadsides not only make
evident the Diceys' indebtedness to *A Collection of Old Ballads*
for their songs, but also show how enthusiastically the broadside
and chapbook publishers took up the antiquarian approach of the
collection. Often the Diceys actually revised and elaborated the
facetious editorial comments of *A Collection of Old Ballads*, purging them of ironic implications and reshaping them for their own
earnest and practical use. In touting the pedagogical and historical
value of his ballads, the editor of *A Collection of Old Ballad* proclaims in his introductory remarks that there are "Children, who
never would have learn'd to read, had they not took a Delight in
poring over *Jane Shore*, or *Fair Rosamond*."[7] In the context of
other remarks in the preface, this observation is, at the least, playful.
However, in its reappearance on Dicey prints, it is not only reshaped
as an earnest recommendation, but expanded as well. In catalogues
and on single sheets, the Diceys prescribe their wares "For Children
to learn to read" in phrases that unmistakably echo those in *A
Collection of Old Ballads*. On their broadside reissue of "Chevy
Chase" we find the following unironic elaboration of the deadpan
remarks on children and reading in the preface to *A Collection of
Old Ballads:*

NOTE: As the Use of these Old Songs is very great, in respect that many
Children never would have learn'd to Read had they not took a delight
in poring over Jane Shore, or Robin Hood, &c. which has insensibly stole
into them a curiosity and Desire of Reading other the like Stories, till
they have improv'd themselves more in a short time than perhaps they
would have done in some Years at School: In order still to make them
more useful, I promise to affix an Introduction, in which I shall point out
what is Fact and what is Fiction in each Song; which will (as may be
readily Suppos'd) give not only children, but Persons of more ripe Years
an insight into the Reality, Intent, and Design, as well as many times the

---

[7]*Collection of Old Ballads*, I, vii.

Author and Time when such a Song was made, which has not hitherto been explain'd.[8]

Obviously indebted to *A Collection of Old Ballads* for their remarks, the Diceys propose, in all seriousness, that their customers appreciate these archaic ballads, and indeed study and interpret them quite as earnestly as Bishop Percy was to study them in the 1760s. In removing from the original remarks all hint of irony, the Diceys transform them into a sincere recommendation. Moreover, in their revision they add to the original passage their promise to discover the "Time when such a Song was made," and to pursue such stylistic matters as "Reality, Intent and Design."[9] Conspicuously purposeful, this expansion of the original remarks actually manifests the same concern with origins and style that guided the literary antiquarians "on the sophisticated level." Indeed, Percy himself made occasional use of the remarks in *A Collection of Old Ballads* in ways not unlike what we find in the Dicey revisions here: he transformed ironic and playful comments into earnest commentary.[10]

Revisions of the headnotes to individual ballads in *A Collection of Old Ballads* further show how the broadside publishers, taking a purposefully antiquarian approach, turned jocular comments into genuine introductions for the ballads. As with their adaptation of the remarks on reading, they supplant the original editor's facetiousness with a tone of sentimental and unequivocal appreciation

---

[8]From "An Unhappy memorable Song of the hunting in Chevy-Chace between Earl Piercy of England, and Earl Douglas of Scotland," in [Percy Collection of Broadside Ballads], Harvard University, Houghton Library, pEB75P4128c, no. 36.

[9]In the comment from which the Dicey remarks are derived, the editor of *A Collection of Old Ballads* makes no claims beyond separating "what is Fact and what Fiction." His complete statement reads: " . . . I have endeavoured to make our old Songs still more useful, by the Introductions which I have prefix'd to 'em; and in which is pointed out what is Fact and what Fiction" (p. vii). For a recent discussion of the journalistic function of earlier broadside ballads, see Lennard Davis, *Factual Fictions: The Origins of the English Novel* (New York: Columbia Univ. Press, 1983). Davis discusses the topical and journalistic nature of street literature of the seventeenth century, when ballads, however old they might have been, were touted as "newe" and "trewe." As my discussion makes clear, this appearance of topicality and journalistic framing of the texts conspicuously disappears in eighteenth-century ballads, replaced by a mode and tone which are, by comparison, sentimental and retrospective.

[10]For discussion of Percy's use of *A Collection of Old Ballads*, see Stephen Vartin, "Thomas Percy's *Reliques*: Its Structure and Organization" (Ph.D. diss., New York University, 1972), pp. 80–94.

of these "old Songs." Headnotes to the ballad "Maudlin, The Merchant's Daughter of Bristol," one from *A Collection of Old Ballads* and the other from a later broadside, illustrate the way the collection's individual introductions were transformed in their broadside and chapbook revisions. The *Collection of Old Ballads* introduction to the ballad reads:

Tho' I do not profess my self an Admirer of the following Song; yet considering its title to Antiquity, it may justly claim a place here; and several of my Readers have earnestly desired to have it inserted. There is one passage in it which petty Cdticks have very much carp'd at, and that is the Time Maudlin's Lover Lay under Condemnation; but if they had consider'd that he was in one of the Inquisition Prisons, where People sometimes lay several Years, they wou'd have found their Cavil very unjust. I must own, I cannot so easily answer another Objection, and that is the Mercy shewn by the Judges to the Three Prisoners, those very Pious Men never having since the first foundation of that Court given another instance of it.[11]

The editor's opening doubts about including the song at all and his final sarcastic quip about "Pious" judges create a disjunction between headnote and ballad: the flippant and ironic headnote clearly directs our attention elsewhere. Only with wry equivocation do these facetious remarks serve the ballad that follows them.

In contrast, the following unironic broadside headnote introduces the ballad of "Maudlin, The Merchant's Daughter of Bristol" without equivocation. It implies an unmistakably more wholehearted acceptance of the historicity and value of the ballad than what we find in the facetious remarks of *A Collection of Old Ballads*. The broadside revision reads:

There is one Passage in this Song much carp'd at, and that is the Time Maudlin's Lover lay under Condemnation, but you may remark that People lie many Years in the Inquisition Prisons. But there is another Objection I cannot so readily answer which is the Mercy shewn by the Judges, since we have not another Instance extant.[12]

If the original remark has been shortened and simplified, it has also been edited in such a way that the broadside commentator actually

---

[11]*A Collection of Old Ballads*, III, 201.
[12]From "Maudlin, The Merchant's Daughter of Bristol," in [A Collection of Broadsides], Houghton Library, 25242.13, Vol. I, p. 13.

treats the ballad with greater seriousness than did the editor of *A Collection of Old Ballads*. The introduction has for its aim illuminating the ballad text. Perhaps the broadside commentator *could* have professed himself, as the earlier editor could not, "an Admirer" of the song. In any case, he was someone who accepted quite consciously and purposefully an antiquarian and revivalist approach to the ballad.

That the Diceys relied upon the 1723 collection both for their song texts and for their approach to these texts is apparent. It is equally apparent, moreover, that this reliance was selective, manifesting an antiquarian agenda to preserve "old ballads." Of the 159 pieces in *A Collection of Old Ballads*, the Dicey presses reprinted in broadside- and chapbook-form more than seventy songs, of which the greater part were the old historical narratives of kings and queens, concubines and outlaws, those songs which the original editor had placed at the front of each volume and had prefaced with long and learned headnotes. The Diceys did not, for the most part, reprint the shorter drinking and courtship songs, and the Scottish ditties, which are placed—almost entirely without commentary—at the back of each volume of *A Collection of Old Ballads*.

From their detailed copying of the illustrations in *A Collection of Old Ballads*, we have additional evidence of the Diceys' indebtedness. Furthermore, these elaborate woodcut illustrations, an advertised attraction, suggest that the Diceys were selling not just old-fashioned ballads, but old-fashioned ballad-sheets as well. A Bow Church-Yard catalogue of 1754 boasts "CUTS more truly adapted to each Story, than elsewhere."[13] This concern with the appropriateness of the illustrations—something of a new development in ballad printing—reflects the publishers' and presumably the customers' interest in the folio ballad sheets that were themselves becoming objects of study. Increasingly toward the end of the century, the folio broadsides were printed so as to accentuate the archaism of the old ballads they contained. Apparently trading on the antiquity of these long, historical ballads, eighteenth-century publishers began to draw attention to their archaism by printing them on heavy, old-fashioned folio paper decorated with woodcuts that were either

---

[13]From a catalogue in the Bodleian Library, Oxford, 258.c.109, reproduced in Thomson, p. 288ff.

markedly antique or elaborate enough to depict details of old-fashioned dress, weaponry, ship design, castles, and so on. (See Figures
1 and 2.)

The Diceys actually seem to have conceptualized their ballad
stock in the same terms used by the ballad revivalists "on the sophisticated level." In 1761 while in the throes of completing his
Reliques, Thomas Percy describes in a letter to William Shenstone
his efforts to ransack "the whole British Empire" for ballad "reliques," which he characterizes as "curious old songs" as opposed
to pieces of "fashion and novelty."[14] Indeed, in the letter Percy
actually states his intention to carry his quest to Bow Church Yard
where Cluer Dicey, "the greatest printer of Ballads in the Kingdom,"
has promised to provide him "copies of all his old Stock Ballads,
and engaged to romage into his Warehouse for every thing curious
that it contains." But the fact is, Dicey seems to have known exactly
what kind of curiosities Percy wanted, for his own catalogues and
advertising squibs reflect a classification very similar to the dichotomy Percy describes: "curious old songs" on the one hand, and
pieces of "fashion and novelty" on the other. Indeed, the Diceys
seem to have been the first ballad printers to separate out and
advertise as "old" a portion of their stock. Dicey catalogues of 1754
and 1764 delineate as a distinct category "Old Ballads." The advertisement for 1754 reads:

A CATALOGUE OF MAPS, PRINTS, COPY-BOOKS, DRAWING-
BOOKS, &c. HISTORIES, OLD BALLADS, Broad-Sheet and other
PATTERS, GARLANDS, &c. PRINTED and SOLD by *WILLIAM* and
CLUER DICEY, at their WAREHOUSE, Opposite the South Door at
Bow-Church in Bow-Church-Yard, LONDON. Printed in the YEAR
M.DCC.LIV.[15]

This distinction between the "Old Ballads" and the other songs in
stock is further emphasized by the variations in broadside format
which the Diceys inaugurated, the first street song printers to do
so: the heirloom "Old Ballads," prized for their length and antiquity,
were printed in the old-fashioned folio format with often elaborate

[14]Thomas Percy, *The Correspondence of Thomas Percy and William Shenstone*,
ed. Cleanth Brooks, Vol. 7 of *The Percy Letters*, eds. Cleanth Brooks and A. F.
Falconer (New Haven and London: Yale Univ. Press, 1977), pp. 108–09.
[15]Bodleian Library, 258.c.109, reproduced in Thomson, p. 288.

FIGURE 1. Engraving from *A Collection of Old Ballads* (London: J. Roberts, 1723), II, opp. p. 191.

FIGURE 2. "The Outlandish Lady's Love to an English Sailor in the Isle of Wight," a broadside in [Percy Collection of Broadside Ballads], Harvard University, Houghton Library, pEB75P4128c, no. 244.

woodcut illustrations; the latest songs of the day—short lyrics, comic ditties, and theatre and pleasure-garden pieces—were printed in the new fashion, on narrow slip sheets. After listing by title many of their other wares, including, as a separate section, items in the "Old-Ballads" category, the Diceys advertise their newer, shorter slip-songs at the end of the catalogue, saying:

There are near Two Thousand different Sorts of SLIPS; of which the New Sorts coming out almost daily render it impossible to make a Complete Catalogue.

The Diceys evidently knew that people were interested in curious and archaic songs and catered to that interest. When the eighteenth-century literary world's "Ballad Revival" was yet at a very early point, they were publishing "Old Ballads" with something of an antiquarian agenda of their own.

If it is clear that the lowbrow printers at Bow Church Yard had, and knew they had, curious "Old Ballad" antiquities, it is also clear from Percy's intention to visit Cluer Dicey that the century's most famous literary antiquarian suspected as much. Indeed, Percy did visit Dicey—whom he described as "an Acquaintance . . . of a much lower stamp"—and from him purchased a sizable collection of broadside ballads.[16] In fact, of the 180 pieces in Percy's *Reliques of Ancient English Poetry* more than sixty are ballads that were already circulating on Dicey broadsides at the time the *Reliques* came out in 1765. Many of these are among the ballads that Percy is known to have purchased at Bow Church Yard.

Of course, the exact relationship of the Dicey broadside ballads to their counterparts in the *Reliques* is impossible to determine. Percy, ever anxious to accentuate the scholarly seriousness of his work and to distance his "reliques" from common streetsong fare, nowhere acknowledges his indebtedness to Dicey. Furthermore, because Dicey got many of his own antique ballads from the 1723 *Collection of Old Ballads*, a work manifestly familiar to Percy, it is extremely difficult to trace the provenance of those ballads in the *Reliques* that were also "Old Ballads" on popular broadsides of the time. But this complexity of provenance and influence is exactly

---

[16]See [Percy Collection of Broadside Ballads], Harvard University, Houghton Library, pEB75P4128c.

the point: it supports the idea of a "ballad revival" well below the sophisticated level. Moreover, the antiquarian interest in "Old Ballads" at the popular level—conscious and purposeful in its own right—actually antedated and intersected with the literary "Ballad Revival" that scholars usually study.

Percy's acknowledged visit to Bow Church Yard shows that Cluer Dicey could not have been oblivious to the sophisticated literary world's increasingly sentimental appreciation of ballads and popular literature. Nor was Percy the only literary figure of the 1760s who is known to have found his way to the Dicey printshop in search of curiosities. On July 10th, 1763, James Boswell records in his journal:

... some days ago I went to the old printing-office in Bow Church-yard kept by Dicey, whose family have kept it fourscore years. There are ushered into the world of literature *Jack and the Giants, The Seven Wise Men of Gotham*, and other story-books which in my dawning years amused me as much as *Rasselas* does now. I saw the whole scheme with a kind of pleasing romantic feeling to find myself really where all my old darlings were printed. I bought two dozen of the story-books and had them bound up with this title, *Curious Productions*. I thought myself like old Lord Somerville or some other man of whim, and wished my whims might be all as quiet.[17]

Boswell's remarks testify to the widespread distribution of Dicey broadsides and chapbooks throughout Britain: after all, Boswell spent his "dawning years" in Scotland. In addition, Boswell's visit to Bow Church Yard supplies further proof of Dicey's acquaintance with persons—and presumably with ideas—from "the literary world." Cluer Dicey, not only in his own revivalist marketing of "Old Ballads," but in his dealings with literary figures like Percy and Boswell as well, had ample familiarity with that "pleasing romantic feeling" about popular songs and stories which underlay mid-eighteenth century literary antiquarianism at all levels: the perception that such ballads and histories were relics, old and valuable.[18]

[17]James Boswell, *Boswell's London Journal 1762–1763*, ed. Frederick A. Pottle (New York: McGraw-Hill, 1950), p. 299.

[18]We find interesting, if tangential, further evidence for Clare Dicey's familiarity with the products and fashions of "polite" culture in a set of "Divers Views ... from Gravesend to Twickenham" which was published (ca. 1755–70) under the imprint of C. Dicey & Co. in Aldermary Church Yard. The twelve broadside "Views" include a woodcut depiction after an engraving by Heckell of Alexander Pope's villa, one of the subjects most celebrated in polite art and society of the

We can assume that Boswell's sentimental collecting intentions were not lost on the savvy businessman, Dicey, particularly when Boswell returned to Bow Church Yard to purchase for his "Curious Productions" some five dozen additional chapbooks, and eventually hundreds more. And, although Boswell's journal entry might lead one to think that only "story-books" make up his "Curious Productions," the fact is that he was an irrepressible singer, and of the chapbooks he purchased from Dicey, a great many contain the lengthy old ballads that had appeared in *A Collection of Old Ballads* and that were beginning to reapear in other literary and antiquarian collections of the last quarter of the century.[19] Indeed, Boswell's chapbook collecting seems to add its own complicating wrinkle to our picture of eighteenth-century literary antiquarianism and the ballad revival, for Boswell is not usually associated in any way with these movements. But the visits of both Percy and Boswell to the Bow Church Yard printshop must have reinforced what Cluer Dicey already knew, and what we should acknowledge: that eighteenth-century Britain was being swept, bottom to top, by a spirit of antiquarianism, a sentimental and revivalist love for old ballads and histories.

Although information is scarce, literary and anecdotal evidence suggests that singers well below the "sophisticated level" of a Boswell also considered these Dicey ballads "old" and also appreciated them as heirlooms. It is clear that among the common people the

---

1760s. The Dicey print is in *London Maps and Views*, Catalogue 23 (July 1980), Robert Douwma Prints & Maps ltd., 93 Great Russelll St., London, item no. 560. The Heckell engraving is No. 7 in Morris R. Brownell, *Alexander Pope's Villa* [Exhibition Catalogue] (London: Greater London Council, 1980).

[19]Boswell's "Curious Productions" contains 83 chapbooks now in Harvard's Houghton Library, 25276.2. Also at Harvard is a much larger collection of "Histories, Ballads, &c." which also seems to have been formed by James Boswell together with Alexander Boswell. The 55 volumes are uniformly bound in half-calf with the name "Boswell" on each volume. A manuscript note on the third flyleaf of Volume 28 reads: "collected by Boswell, the Friend of Dr. Johnson." On the fly-leaf of the first volume of his "Curious Productions" Boswell inscribed: "James Boswell, Inner Temple 1763. Having when a boy, been much entertained with Jack the Giant-Killer, and such little Story Books, I have always retained a kind of affection for them, as they recall my early days. I went to the Printing Office in Bow Churchyard, and bought this collection and had it bound up with the Title of Curious Productions. I shall certainly, some time or other, write a little Story Book in the stile of these. It will not be a very easy task for me; it will require much nature and simplicity, and a great acquaintance with the humours and traditions of the English common people. I shall be happy to succeed for He who pleases the children will be remembered with pleasure by the men."

Dicey "Old Ballads" were sung and sung widely—at least in some sense revived. Virtually all the "old songs" mentioned by authors familiar with popular traditions are "Old Ballad" titles we find in the Bow Church Yard catalogues. Moreover, depictions of lower-class singers like Mr. Burchell in *The Vicar of Wakefield* show that, even at the popular level, at least as Goldsmith portrays it, these songs and stories were perceived as old treasures:

He [Mr. Burchell] sat down to supper among us, and my wife was not sparing of her gooseberry wine. The tale went round; he sung us *old songs* (emphasis mine), and gave the children the story of the Buck of Beverland, with the history of Patient Grissel. The adventures of Catskin next entertained them, and then Fair Rosamond's bower.[20]

We cannot say with certainty that these are broadside ballads. Nevertheless, the Bow Church Yard catalogues contain all the titles (except "the Buck of Beverland") that Goldsmith mentions in the passage quoted here, as well as several others he names elsewhere in this episode of the novel.

This link between popular song traditions and the Dicey prints is further demonstrated by the many ballads and stories mentioned in the prose and poetry of John Clare, himself reared among the lower-class cottagers, apprentices, milkmaids, and laborers who were the broadside and chapbook audience.[21] Clare's descriptions of popular traditions come first hand. Moreover, his comments on the songs and stories of his youth provide an interesting glimpse at the complex trafficking between these two worlds of popular and polite literature to which Clare, celebrated as a "rustic poet," owed some part of his own literary career. Of the popular songs and stories Clare mentions, particularly in his retorspective glances at his early years, a striking proportion were printed by the Diceys. Furthermore, Clare's unpublished song and tune manuscripts, though they consist of songs collected in the 1820s, considerably after the period when the broadside "Old Ballads" flourished, nevertheless contain some variants of the Dicey broadside texts. Clare's remarks leave

[20]Oliver Goldsmith, *The Vicar of Wakefield* (London, 1766), Chapter 6.
[21]For discussion of Clare's life, see John and Anne Tibble, *John Clare: His Life and Poetry* (London: William Heinemann, 1956).

little doubt of the currency of the Dicey "Old Ballads" among lowbrow singers.[22]

But can we find in Clare's anecdotes about these ballads some evidence of a popular antiquarian appreciation separate from yet analogous to the revival on the "sophisticated level"? While it is difficult to unravel fully Clare's complex attitudes toward these popular songs, some of his remarks suggest that the distinction between "old ballads" and "pieces of fashion and novelty" may have operated for him as well. Indeed, on the initial page of the song collection that he had intended to consist of "old Ballads," he laments the "senseless balderdash" that he has found in their place. He says:

I commenced sometime ago with an intention of making a collection of old Ballads but when I had sought after them in places where I expected [to] find them . . . I found that nearly all those old & beautiful reccolections [sic] had vanished as so many old fashions . . . & those who were proud of their knowledge in such things—knew nothing but the sensless [sic] balderdash that is brawled over & sung at County Feasts Statutes & Fairs . . . [23]

Just what Clare meant by "balderdash," we shall never know for sure. However, by the 1820s when he began collecting the songs that people were singing in rural Northamptonshire, a marked change in the content, tone, and format of printed street songs had taken place: shorter, more topical and journalistic ballads and novelty songs—the "New Sorts," one might say—were replacing the "curious old Songs" whose antiquity the Diceys and other eighteenth-century printers had earlier accentuated. It may well be that Clare decries as "balderdash" these new topical and journalistic songs,

---

[22]See for examples of Clare's references, *The Letters of John Clare*, ed. J. W. and Anne Tibble (London: Routledge and Kegan Paul, 1951), pp. 14 and 19. See also *The Prose of John Clare*, ed. J. W. and Anne Tibble (London: Routledge and Kegan Paul, 1951), p. 257. For discussion of Clare's familiarity with Dicey chapbooks and broadsides, see George Deacon, *John Clare and the Folk Tradition* (London: Sinclair Browne, 1983), pp. 35–67 and 210–14. Deacon, like Friedman, rigidly separates songs in print from those in oral tradition as eighteenth-century singers (and collectors too) certainly did not. That he is categorizing songs in ways that Clare was not, is apparent from deacon's surprise and reluctance to accept that Clare considers a broadside version of "The Dragon of Wantley" quite "firmly within the context of a continuing village oral tradition in his poem 'Rural Morning'" (p. 211).

[23]Clare, "Northampton MS. 18, quoted in Deacon, 43.

lamenting the absence of *his* "old Darlings": those retrospective "Old Ballads" of kings and queens, of outlaws and concubines which appeared on the archaic folio broadsides of his youth. Clare certainly mentions such historical ballads repeatedly in his writings—and nearly always sentimentally so.

Clare's song collecting may indeed owe its inspiration to his acquaintance with Percy's *Reliques*, which he first saw in 1820. His delight with Percy's collection clearly was the pleasure of recognition:

D. [Edwin Drury] has sent me 3 vols call'd 'Percy's Relics' there is some sweet Poetry in them & I think it the most pleasing book I ever happend [sic] on the tales are familiar from childhood all the stories of my grandmother & her gossiping neighbours I find versified in these vols—[24]

Clare's avoidance in this letter of the term "ballad" and his reference to the "versifying" of "stories" are confusing: are the Percy ballads verse renderings of narratives his grandmother told in prose? And why the word "tales" for the rhymed and metered reliques? But perhaps in his use of terms Clare is simply imprecise, at least from our vantage point. We might recall that the Diceys, when referring unmistakably to songs, use the terms "stories" and "ballads" interchangeably. Boswell too seems to mean chapbook songs as well as prose histories when he uses the word "story-books."[25]

However unsure we may be about the wording of his letter, we can nevertheless be certain that Clare found in the *Reliques* familiar texts of a good many of the ballads that, elsewhere in his writings, he says that he heard in his childhood: "Chevy Chase," "Jane Shore," "Johnny Armstrong," "The King and the Cobler," "George Barnwell," "The Wandering Jew," "The Dragon of Wantley," and more. These "old ballads" may well have been songs that his grandmother's generation sang in the mid-eighteenth century when the Dicey prints and a fashion for antique historical ballads flourished among the common people. In any case, finding familiar pieces among Percy's reliques clearly reinforced for Clare the sentimental reverence for the old ballads of his childhood that he had voiced many times in

[24]Clare, *Letters*, p. 57.
[25]See the Dicey "Note" appended to the ballad, "Chevy Chase" above (p. 76 and n. 8). See Boswell's remarks from the *London Journal* quoted above (p. 84 and n. 17).

THE POPULAR MARKETING OF OLD BALLADS   89

his poems and prose. This retrospective appreciation, evident already in mid-century broadsides and chapbooks, was still being promoted in the street literature that Clare would have known as a child growing up in the 1790s.

Toward the end of the eighteenth century, the popular appreciation for "Old Ballads," which the Diceys seem to have simultaneously met and fostered, continued even after the Bow Church Yard office no longer dominated the streetsong market. Printers in London and elsewhere followed the lead and duplicated the stock of the Dicey printshop. The London printers Evans, How, and Pitts, and the Tewkesbury printer Harward carried on the marketing of ballads in the archaic folio format. Pitts, in particular, from about 1800 to 1810—the first decade of his career—revived old pieces, publishing them as folios complete with seventeenth-century woodcut illustrations. In the 1790s, just as antiquarian scholars such as Joseph Ritson were busying themselves with ancient "rhymes of Robin Hood," the White Chapel printer Larken How issued a whole series of folio Robin Hood ballads in the style of much earlier broadsides, complete with illustrations made from seventeenth-century woodblocks.[26] And such antiquarian products were not confined to the south of England. Self-consciously retrospective, an eight-page chapbook published early in the nineteenth century by M. Angus in Newcastle ceremoniously announces its contents as:

The laidley worm of Spindelston Heugh . . . A song above 500 years old, made by the old mountain bard, Duncan Frasier, living on Cheviot, A.D. 1270. Printed from an ancient manuscript.[27]

[26]See Joseph Ritson, *Robin Hood: A Collection of all the ancient poems, songs, and ballads, now extant, relative to that celebrated English outlaw: to which are prefixed historical anecdotes of his life* (London: T. Egerton and J. Johnson, 1795). The late eighteenth-century printer T. Sabine prefaced his "Robin Hood's garland" with comments drawn either directly from *A Collection of Old Ballads* or from a derivative Dicey print. See "Robin Hood's garland," Houghton Library, 27257.6.2. For a very brief discussion of conscious archaism in turn-of-the-century broadsides, see Leslie Shepard, *John Pitts: Ballad Printer of Seven Dials, London 1765–1855* (London: Private Libraries Association, 1969), p. 44.
[27]"The laidley worm of Spindleston Heugh," in [109 Chapbooks collected by John Bell, Newcastle], Houghton Library, 25252.19, No. 62. Thomas Evans included this ballad along with almost identical remarks in the 1784 edition of his *Old Ballads, Historical and Narrative, with some of Modern Date,* 4 Vols. (London: T. Evans, 1784). See Vol. III, pp. 171–78. As Evans notes, it was previously published in W. Hutchinson, *The History of the Following Places in Northumberland* (Alnwick: J. Catnach, n.d.), pp. 162–64.

As this bookish little title illustrates, broadside and chapbook readers as far away as Northumberland shared the antiquarian interest that colored English letters in the second half of the eighteenth century. Moreover, lower-class provincial street literature provided at least one further appearance of that curious and remarkably protean antiquarian work, *A Collection of Old Ballads*. In 1839 the Durham printer, George Walker, published for his chapbook customers a song collection of twenty-four pages with the following familiar title:

A Collection of Old Ballads, carefuely [sic] *reprinted from the best and most ancient copies extant. With introductions, historical, critical, and humorous.*[28]

Thus we see that the world of *belles lettres* was not at all unique in the sentimental appreciation of old ballads: already before the middle of the eighteenth century, antiquarian sentiments and methods were in fashion well below the "sophisticated level." William and Cluer Dicey built a prosperous business in street literature by selling to the common people—and eventually to Boswells and Percys as well—"ancient" ballads. Indeed, the eighteenth-century ballad revival was a complex interweaving of influences—traditional, commercial, scholarly, educational, and literary. In it we find the literati not at all in a vacuum, the common people not at all left behind. Amidst a pervasive eighteenth-century fashion for heirloom songs and stories, "Old Ballads" about "Robin Hood," "Rosamund," "Jane Shore," and "The Dragon of Wantley" circulated the kingdom on cheap broadsides and in lowly chapbooks. Meanwhile, gentlemen poets and scholars exalted the past and the common people, indulged themselves in collecting and annotating, and occasionally even found their way to the printshop at Bow Church Yard looking for "Old Ballads."

University of Colorado, Boulder

[28]*A Collection of Old Ballads, carefully re-printed from the best and most ancient copies extant. With introductions, historical, critical, and humorous* (Durham: George Walker, 1839). This chapbook is in the British Library, 012331.g.3.(9.).

[2]

Another History of Bluegrass:
The Segregation of Popular Music
in the United States, 1820-1900[1]

Allen Farmelo

Categories in any case are never watertight, but flow ceaselessly into one another. . . . Musical interactions do not occur at random, but are indicators always of an empathy, even across a social or cultural barrier, which is not necessarily or even usually conscious. That such empathy exists, at levels deeper than those feelings of fear and guilt which lie at the root of racism, is borne out by the history of the musical interaction that occurred in the United States—and, indeed, wherever such encounters occurred.

—Christopher Small, 1987

Introduction

Bluegrass music carries with it two definitive notions: that it is an antiquated style which goes "way back," and that it is, and always has been, a traditional music of white people. Neither notion is entirely true. Recently, historical evidence has been compiled which suggests that in the Southeastern United States before the Civil War, many slaves and poor whites shared an open musical tradition within which they exchanged techniques and repertoires which constitute the musical antecedents of bluegrass. However, after the Civil War, complex social discourses about race and class relationships emerged which mask that open pre-war tradition and produce distinctly white and black musical categories. After the onset of the recording industry around 1900, those postwar categories grew even more rigid. Race records (featuring only black musicians) and hillbilly records (featuring only white musicians) were the most popular, and mutually exclusive, categories.[2] By the early 1950s, race records had become rhythm and blues, while hillbilly music had fissured into bluegrass and other country styles. Bluegrass as a current pop style, however, shows little sign of having traveled this complicated path from the days of slavery to the present. Bluegrass music itself incorporates and propagates nostalgic and antiquated sentiments which do not bear out the intricacies of the development of its antecedents.

This essay assembles another historical narrative that emphasizes interactions between African- and European-Americans between 1820 and 1900. The first half of this narrative is an account of interactions between poor whites and slaves before the Civil War. The second half looks specifically at musical interactions before and after the war. Looking closely at these interactions reveals that popular music in the United States has never been the sole contribution of a homogenous people, but the result of, and a vehicle for, an intricate multicultural fusion. Also revealed are the ways in which this fusion has been wiped clear from view, only to be replaced with notions of strict cultural segregation.

The relevance of the nineteenth century to bluegrass lies partly in elaborating the sociomusicological connections between nineteenth-century popular music and bluegrass today; but what is the relevance of revealing those connections? To what extent do twenty-first century notions of nineteenth-century music affect the trajectory of popular music today? I will argue that historical narratives can play a role in the social politics of today's musical subcultures because historical narratives often form the basis of one's sense of identification with, and inclusion in, a musical scene—much the way a family tree draws one into affiliations with the past and affirms one's place in the present. To initiate this argument, I begin this essay by recounting two current historical narratives of bluegrass which support the notion that it is, and has always been, a "white music." Against the backdrop of these narratives, which help to maintain notions of cultural segregation, this essay's historical narrative, which attempts to reveal the shared musical traditions among blacks and whites, will contrast. I conclude this essay with pieces of my ethnographic research at bluegrass festivals which speculatively point to the role historical narratives play in setting the racial boundaries of the bluegrass subculture. Contextualizing this essay in this way may cast some light on the role of historians of popular music as players in the social politics of the present.

Two Current Histories of Bluegrass

The story of Bill Monroe as The Father of Bluegrass often serves as *the* story about this music, even though, as we will see, its origins are far more complicated. Part of this simplification could be that we often compress U.S. history into stories about the careers of successful white males, leaving others invisible. In *Bluegrass: A History,* Neil Rosenberg focuses on Monroe and the people involved in his career. Robert Cantwell, in *Bluegrass Breakdown: The Making of the Old Southern Sound,* elaborately argues that African-American rhythmic tropes were key ingredients in the bluegrass recipe, but, like Rosenberg, he mostly writes about

Monroe's use of those tropes and his ability to draw on many sources. Mayne Smith, the first to publish an academic essay about bluegrass, succinctly states that bluegrass is "the intimate, personal music of a single man, Bill Monroe" (in Malone 310). In no way do I question or mean to undermine Monroe's centrality to bluegrass or his ingenuity in formatting his broad array of musical abilities into an original, coherent, and beautiful sound. I do, however, agree with Cantwell when he writes that "if we say 'Bill Monroe's music' we are merely repeating what the term bluegrass was intended originally to mean" (60) and, I think, excluding a perspective which situates Monroe and his music within a deeper historical context. Earl Scruggs, the daddy of bluegrass banjo, put forth a similar sentiment more eloquently in a conversation with Sonny Osbourne and Ronnie Reno. As Joe Wilson tells it:

A generation ago some of the founders of bluegrass sat on a touring bus at a festival late at night and discussed the origins of their art. A visiting citizen asked Sonny Osborne an off-hand question about where a particular lick came from and who did it first. Sonny said he didn't know and commented on how fast such things move across the country and between people and how easy it is to be wrong in assigning credit. Ronnie Reno added a philosophical comment noting that credit for other innovations and advances in the music are similarly hard to assign. He noted that credit for some events in history may also be wrong and mentioned the midnight ride of Revolutionary War hero Paul Revere. "Now you really don't know that Paul Revere made that ride," he said. From the darkness at the back of the bus came a droll-voiced comment by Earl Scruggs: "Bill Monroe made that ride!" (54)

Scruggs's comment seems to be both a tribute to Bill Monroe and a critique of the ways some histories can shroud the communal creations of a musical style. The tendency to emphasize one person as the founder of a musical style exists, partly, because star-making machinery (Nashville, Hollywood, Broadway, TV or, generically, "the industry") often focuses its attention on one figure at a time.

Another popular version of bluegrass history looks much like this one currently circulating nationally as part of a primary- and secondary-school education program about bluegrass:

The people who arrived in Jamestown from England in the early 1600s brought with them the instruments and ballads of the times. Songs written from poems of the earliest Greek poets to songs of the gypsies who arrived in Great Britain at the end of the fifteenth century comprised the music these people brought to the new land. People were also arriving from Scotland and Ireland, bringing

their instruments and ballads with similar roots that included Celtic mythology
in the lyrics. [These ballads], considered to be the roots of traditional American
music, [were] the "pop" music of these times. . . . The early Jamestown settlers
gradually began to spread out into the Carolinas, Tennessee, Kentucky and
throughout the Virginias. Traditional country music and string band music flourished in the rural areas and began to gain more popularity in Southern settlements and cities by the 1800s. The invention of the phonograph plus the onset
of radio in the early 1900s brought music of all kinds, including traditional country music, to people all over the United States. One of the most popular duet
teams of the 1920s and 1930s was the Monroe Brothers, Charlie and Bill. . . .
Both Charlie and Bill went on to form their own groups. Bill's new band was
more than just another traditional band; it was the birth of a new form of country music. (*An Overview* 1)

The direct lineage from the Greeks (males) through Western Europeans (also males) and to the Founding Fathers of the United States is part
of a metanarrative which grows out of, and supports, a somewhat white-
supremacist, patriarchal ideology (Eagleton 109-10, Harvey 9, Weatherford 121-31).[3] Bill Monroe never played music with "the Greeks," though
he repeatedly told interviewers that, for at least one memorable and formative night during his teens, he played for dancers with black bluesman
Arnold Schultz until sun up (Rooney 23-24).

Both of these versions of bluegrass history exclude African-Americans and Africans to some degree, if not entirely. This exclusion makes it
easier to assume that bluegrass is part of white, European-American culture in which people of color played no role. In order to more fully
account for the role of African-Americans in the development of blu-
grass's musical antedecents, we now turn to the nineteenth century.

Black-White Relationships in the Antebellum Southeast

As we will see, after the Civil War, a stereotype of rural Southeastern United States musical cultures emerged which both contributed to,
and relied upon, notions of racial segregation: namely, blacks and whites
were so separate and unequal that they rarely played music together, and
their musics were not related. To the contrary, evidence shows that while
segregation was real, it was never absolute. Some sociologists, historians,
and folklorists now suggest that class distinctions often outweighed racial
ones for "poor whites."[4] At times, many blacks and whites interacted not
so much as members of segregated racial groups engaged in cultural imitation or barter but as members of one group sharing class consciousness
vis-à-vis the planter class. I want to follow up on Edward Said's question,
"Do cultural, religious, and racial differences matter more than socio-eco-

nomic categories, or politicohistorical ones?" (325-26)—with evidence
that, in some politicohistorical contexts, in some regions, among some
people, the answer is "no."

Until more recently, historical accounts of nonslaveholding whites
of the antebellum Southeast have focused heavily on yeomen and sharecroppers. Yeomen were small-scale cash-crop farmers who owned land
but not slaves. Sharecroppers were landless, but found steady work
through annual contracts with landed farmers who would pay them a
share of the season's harvest. Another class of whites, which Charles
Bolton calls "a third class of white people" (11), lived more deeply under
the oppressive control of the white elites, or planting class, of the Southeast. These third-class citizens were often tenant farmers who found
themselves in credit debt, a financial situation which left them legally
bound to work without pay for elite land-owners. Others were squatters
eking out subsistence on unclaimed land. Usually these people drifted
from state to state, country to country, job to job. Some found solace
among landed relatives, but a majority of these poor whites were members of uniformly poverty-stricken clans.

In these situations, a white skin held little mentionable privilege. (In
1857 in North Carolina, for example, voting rights in state senate elec-
tions were reserved for those white males who owned more than 50
acres.) As one former slave from Virginia put it: "Did you know poor
whites like slaves had to git a pass? I mean, a remit like as slaves, to sell
anythin' an' to go places an' to do anythin'. Just as we colored people. . . .
Ol' Master was more hard on dem poor white folks den he wuz on us niggers" (Bolton 51). Another former slave of Virginia said that "[y]es de
poor white man ad some dark an' tough days, like us poor niggers; I mean
were lasked an' treated, some of em' jes as pitiful an' umerciful" (30).
Often, indebted whites worked the field side by side with black slaves,
incurred similar punishments, lived in similar quarters, and ate the same
food. Given these shared conditions, at times blacks and whites found
racial differentiation unimportant in the face of overriding class stratification which was keeping both in poverty and bondage. That is, blacks
and whites working together for the same master were at times more
likely to share class consciousness than white labor and white owning-
class were to share race consciousness.

Poor whites were well aware that slavery did not benefit the whole
white race, but only those who could afford slaves. Most poor whites
understood that slavery drove wages down, eliminated jobs, and concentrated wealth in elite pockets. To a certain degree, privilege came with
money and not from lighter pigment. A number of whites worked for free
black land owners, a situation which inverted the notion that, socially and

economically, white skin meant "up" and black skin meant "down." The concept of white skin privilege would have seemed ironic at best to poor whites working land that free blacks owned, as would the idea that slavery helped all white people get ahead.

This is not to suggest that poor whites never tapped into race hatred as fuel for their own superiorist fires. However, the notion that poor whites only hated blacks—and did so as a means to feeling a sense of superiority—fails to account for the multiplicity of poor white social roles and the dynamic ideologies which accompanied each of them. Whites on the verge of class ascent (*e.g.,* yeomen) were more likely to find comfort in racism than were those with little prospect of improving their socioeconomic status (Cecil-Fronsman 90). "Although they lived in a thoroughly racist culture, and although there were enormous social pressures to the contrary, some common whites rejected and others significantly modified the racism that was so pervasive. They found ways to let down the cultural barriers that separated them from black people and forged alliances with slaves" (68).[5]

Sometimes these alliances grew into schemes to liberate profits from the planter-class. An underground trading circuit which depended on open communication and mutual trust between blacks and whites ran through slavery, into the postbellum era, and continues today. Court records document a handful of these alliances. In Savannah, 1838, a free white laborer, Henry Forsyth, and an enslaved black, George [*sic*], stole $118 from their boss/master and ran 135 miles to Augusta. The law caught them. Lockley writes that "[t]he relationships between George and Henry Forsyth as outlined in the trial documents is clearly not one of domination or subordination based on race. Rather two people, who worked together on a daily basis, were able to overcome the obvious status differences between bondsman and freeman to mutual advantage and profit" (63). Throughout North Carolina's Piedmont region, for example, slaves would take from their master and then sell and trade with whites, often for clothes and alcohol. "By trading with slaves, common whites were allowing the boundaries separating them and slaves to become indistinct. Their own self-interest demanded that they see slaves as sharing in a common predicament" (Cecil-Fronsman 94). Perhaps those boundaries were already indistinct. It is easier to imagine that a crime team would have established some interpersonal trust prior even to talking about committing a crime.

Church also frequently served as common ground for poor whites and blacks and as a chance to make music together. The Second Awakening, which began in Kentucky during the early 1800s and spread south to the Carolinas and Georgia, "gave rise to the massive outdoor camp meetings where for the first time black and white met on anything like equal terms" (Small 99). Charles Johnson describes these meetings:

In both slaveholding and non-slaveholding areas the Negroes were allowed to set up their camp behind the preacher's rostrum. Because of the close proximity, their services often merged with those of the whites. . . . As the camp meeting matures, the Negro camp section was sometimes separated from that of the whites by a plank partition. The barrier was torn down on the final days of the meeting when the two peoples joined together in a song festival and "marching ceremony." (46)

This description hints that religious music-making was, from time to time, a shared black and white cultural activity (see also Levine, Black Culture 21-25).

Blacks and whites fell in love. Black men who fell in with white women were often in the most legal danger as the Southeastern states passed laws forbidding black and white interaction, especially intimacy. A white man who fell in with a black woman suffered less under segregation laws. (I've come across no discussion of same-sex relationships between blacks and whites.) Black women often remained anonymous to protect the white man; while white women, if discovered, sometimes pretended to be victims of their black lovers. Because these relationships were illegal, couples tended either to remain underground or distort the truth. This deliberate anonymity explains the lack of documentation. The presence of the children of these intimate relationships, however, challenged racist and segregationist ideologies by making visible the extent to which black and white people were coming together as intimates.

When compiling these contexts (petty crimes, religious services, secret dates) within which poor whites and blacks came together as near equals, a pattern of activity emerges which suggests that people often subverted social norms when the appeal of class alliance outweighed the imposition of racial segregation. However, even with a time machine and full ethnographic training, it would be difficult to know to what extent poor whites and blacks might have shared class consciousness in the antebellum Southeast. We do know that they formed common alliances, conspired against the rich, worked, loved, played, and worshiped together—all in an extremely racist social climate littered with lynchings and riots. Among those who occupy the lowest class strata, in which homelessness, poverty, and bondage mandate a common lifestyle, racist ideologies which would normally divide people can wane.

Similarly, as racist ideologies wane, people who share skin tone may find no racial basis for alliance, allowing class differences to drive a wedge between them. A more detailed analysis of the antebellum South-east shows stratification among nonslaveholding whites. Many, such as the yeomen who owned land and/or maintained good relations with more wealthy relatives, remained relatively stable. They also found comfort in racism as a means of identifying with their socioeconomic superiors, toward whom they aimed to ascend. These are the poor whites who, up until more recently, historians have focused on, giving impressions only of a racial hatred directed from poor white to black slave. Considering poor(er) whites who owned neither land nor slave—and who had previously gone almost unnoticed in history books—gives us different impressions of race relations which, I think, help explain how music has permeated black/white racial barriers in the Southeast of this continent ever since 1615.[6] Considering relationships between poor whites and blacks also suggests that early music of the United States might be best understood as a musical culture shared among blacks and whites rather than bartered between them.

It can be argued that some whites and blacks shared and nurtured a broad cultural reservoir for which division between black and white ownership is questionable at best (see Berlin and Morgan 11-14; Bolton 2-8, 42-53, 65; Cecil-Fronsman 68-96; Conway 15-29, 131, 137, 158; Small 1-5, 117-25; Woodward 3-7, 267-68; Lockley 57-69). As Woodward puts it: "[t]he ironic thing about these two great hyphenate minorities, [white] Southern Americans and Afro-Americans, confronting each other on their native soil for three and a half centuries, is the degree to which they have shaped each other's destiny . . . shared and molded a common culture. It is, in fact, impossible to imagine the one without the other and quite futile to try" (5-6). While I agree wholly with Woodward on this point, I want to shift the sense of irony. That people who often lived, worked, gambled, traded, stole, prayed, danced, and sang together (*e.g.,* see Bolton 42-65; and reference to census reports of 1820 in Lockley 61) "shared and molded a common culture" is not ironic. That, today, many people think that Southeastern blacks and whites did not share and mold together, but merely hated each other, seems more ironic. So does the idea that "black music" and "white music" have nothing to do with each other.

Conceptualizations of the melting pot, on the one hand, and rigid racial separation, on the other, have always been prescriptive, not descriptive. Concepts of segregation are usually social constructs that socially dominant people use toward ideological and political ends, while melting-pot descriptions (the un-writing of difference) have never accounted for the ways autonomous identities have found expression within what can be loosely termed "a shared culture."[7] Grasping at the complexity of black/white race relationships in the US which preceded the recording

industry's construction of strictly black and strictly white musical categories involves reconciling the mutual existence and interpenetration of
segregated and shared culture. Given the historical documentation above,
it is possible to conceptualize "black culture" and "white culture" as
either actual and separate entities, or as socially constructed demarcations
laid over a shared culture. As we will see later, these two conceptualizations share different ideological implications when considering bluegrass
history and why bluegrass still appears as a music whose roots only tap
into European-American groundwaters.

Shared Musical Traditions among Blacks and Whites and Their Disappearances

A history of the antebellum Southeast informs a history of bluegrass
because it was through the relationships among, and the shared culture of,
blacks and whites then and there that some of the key musical elements
which would comprise bluegrass 100 years later were going through significant transformations. Christopher Small writes that "[t]he history of
the American South suggests that there was, and still is, a considerable
number of [white] people who, despite the pervasive racism and the continuing inferior position of blacks, have been able to respond directly to
black culture, and in particular musicking, in ways that other Americans
—and, indeed, Europeans—have not" (137). The preceding discussion of
relationships between blacks and whites in the antebellum South helps
support that claim. Small goes on to propose that the "encounter that
occurred in North America between the two great musical traditions
[African and European] will have made it clear that it occurred principally, and in its most fruitful developments, on the lowest levels of American society, among people who, black or white, were united in one
respect—their dispossession and their alienation from those who [had]
access to power and control of property" (163).

Proximity, as much as, if not more than, shared class consciousness,
lent itself to musical interaction between poor whites and blacks. Shared
class membership brings people together in the same communities,
churches, workplaces, and celebrations. Transmitting musical techniques,
styles, repertoires, and general knowledge usually meant spending time
with people listening to, dancing to, and playing music. The antebellum
Southeast was without electricity, recorded music, television, movies, or
radio. Access to music meant access to a live performance.

In this context, recordings and sheet music did not alienate or reify
musical transmission. Recording technology did not exist yet. Sheet
music remained a tool of wealthy urban musicians. Karen Linn writes that
"[p]laying the banjo 'by note' depended on the availability of notated

banjo music. It was not until the early 1880s that banjo music was commonly published. . . . Before that time buying banjo music took time and money. . . . The music was not published but rather entirely handwritten, making the cost exorbitant" (18). Urban, high-society musicians interested in the banjo, for example, felt that "[p]laying by ear or tablature was for . . . the old-times of the minstrel stage. . . . Notation also allowed musical learning in the privacy of the home, a less intimidating situation for many than spending large amounts of time in places where banjoists congregated to share tunes and techniques" (15). Such congregating was for the poor. The bifurcation between oral transmission and literate transmission paralleled rural/low and urban/high class distinctions—although members of urban high society may have remained ignorant of mountain oral traditions, taking the minstrels as true members of that social stratum. That poor rural people more frequently learned music orally, and less frequently from mediated sources, is apparent.

Oral transmission happens as people interact on equal enough ground that they listen carefully to and imitate each other. Therefore, oral transmission is most common between people who live close together and feel comfortable with each other. The class membership that blacks and poor whites shared was not necessarily a premeditated motivation for oral transmission of musical knowledge. It was, though, grease on the rails of oral transmission because it meant that they would spend time together partying, dancing, singing, and playing instruments. Through this interaction, then, poor whites and blacks might have celebrated and reaffirmed their shared attitudes and assumptions, and class consciousness could have contributed to this reaffirmation. But on this matter we can only speculate. What we can know—and what is more important when considering these relationships as a part of bluegrass history—is the fact that mountain-music traditions, which we may consider the antecedents of bluegrass, were, in many regions, the direct results of mutual black and white participation in a shared oral tradition.

I want to briefly trace a few musical developments which have contributed significantly to the string band format and, consequently, to bluegrass. These include a shared black and white banjo tradition, the disappearance of the black banjo from America's view, the combination of the Scots-Irish-American fiddle and the African-American banjo, and the large-scale commercial introduction of the guitar into Southeastern rural areas. It was these developments, I think, which set the stage for the hillbilly record boom around 1925-26—a boom which branched in the late 1940s and early 1950s into various forms of country music, one of which was bluegrass.

The Black and the White Banjo

Epstein suggests that the earliest black banjo traditions were in the upper South ("The Folk Banjo" 347-59; *Sinful Tunes* 145-47). The banjo as we know it originated from a single-string, gourd-bodied African lute (sometimes called the "hodu") which the Griots of West Africa played to accompany storytelling. Later, banjo makers replaced the gourd with a wooden hoop with a skin stretched over it. A four-string version emerged as early as the late seventeenth century, and the fifth string (usually attributed to Scottish-American Joel Walker Sweeney, 1820) can be seen in paintings of black banjo players from between 1777 and 1800 (Linn 2). The five-string banjo is probably the first distinctly African-American instrument. Details aside, the banjo grew up on the North American continent as part of a resilient African heritage.

Cecilia Conway has compiled detailed documentation of antebellum, postbellum, and twentieth-century black banjo traditions. Solid documentation of these shared traditions is scarce, but Conway has found enough significant clues to upset previous theories of how banjo and banjo-fiddle traditions found their ways into remote white Appalachian communities. Folklorist Robert Winnas argues that minstrelsy introduced banjo and banjo-fiddle traditions into these communities ("The Folk" 407-37). "Archie Green believes that black laborers building the railroads in the mountains provided a source. . . . Tony Russell has examined a third opportunity for black-white exchange—the traveling tent and medicine shows, made up of minstrels and folk performers . . . in the first quarter of the twentieth century" (Conway 121). While any of these sources might have contributed to people's knowledge of songs and different techniques, none account for, or mention, the possibility of ongoing and relatively undocumented oral transmission among blacks and whites in the antebellum Southeast.

Conway's research suggests that whites first acquired and learned the banjo directly from African-Americans in the antebellum Southeast. She notes that "since most of the white mountain settlers tended to be small independent farmers, they were likely to be folk musicians, not too 'classy' to learn banjo by ear and by imitating blacks. These musicians were often Celtic . . . and seemed eager to learn new music from blacks" (137). Families like the Hammonses of the Virginia Piedmont "had access to black musical tradition—including banjo playing—at least sixty-three years before they could have seen a steamboat minstrel [1830]" (135). Conway goes on to document the flow of musical knowledge in what she calls the Sugar Grove Region, a mountainous area about 30 miles in diameter at the conjunction of the Tennessee, North Carolina, and Virginia state borders which contained migration routes for people traveling between Kentucky, North Carolina, Virginia, West Virginia, and Tennessee. Blacks and whites lived in close proximity in this area. Black banjo player Archibald Thompson traveled through the area in the 1850s, and his grandson, Dave, played banjo in this area two generations later. As late as 1915, the Sugar Grove Region saw travelers like Blind Lemon Jefferson who would stop and play music with residents of the area. "[W]ork patterns [of people living in this area] reflect the fact that the mines, like the railroad, accounted for increased contact between local white and black musicians. Moreover, in their home community, frequent string-music gatherings—especially at Christmas—provided the Thompsons opportunities for musical exchange. This exchange sometimes included whites as well as other blacks, for Frank Proffitt, Doc Watson, and others often came to these affairs" (124-25). Conway concludes that "all the Sugar Grove evidence . . . strongly argues that mountain whites acquired their banjo tradition directly from blacks" (146).[8]

It is not clear to what extent we can generalize Conway's findings to other regions of the Southeast. We can, however, document similar social relationships among blacks and whites throughout the South. It may be fair to assume that music played a role in these relationships outside the Sugar Grove region. Bastin's detailed studies of various regions of blues development throughout the Southeast is littered with examples of blacks and whites who played banjo, guitar, fiddle, etc., and also with many examples of black-white musical exchange at all kinds of performances.

Outside localized oral traditions, minstrels, performing up and down the eastern seaboard before and after the Civil War, imitated Southeastern blacks on stages to the delight of huge audiences (on minstrelsy see Blair 52-65; Lott 3-37, 111-35). Because minstrel shows were special events for people living in rural areas, and because promoters of minstrelsy ran many ads, documentation in newspapers, journals, and magazines is extensive. How white performers acquired the knowledge and skills to imitate blacks on the minstrel stage is less apparent, though some information exists. Famous white minstrel Dan Emmet learned to play banjo in 1840 from a white mountaineer named Ferguson. "This man [Ferguson], according to the circus manager, C. J. Rodgers, 'was a very ignorant person, and 'nigger all over' except in color.' He seems to have been a white mountaineer, for he was living in 'western Virginia,' which was then possibly present-day West Virginia, an area where he would have had ample opportunity to learn to play the banjo from African-Americans" (Conway 106). William Whitlock, another famous white minstrel, "would quietly steal off to some Negro hut to hear the darkeys sing and see them dance, taking with him a jug of whisky to make them all the merrier" (Whitlock 1878 cited in Conway). In 1839, Whitlock was ready to perform on stage as P. T. Barnum's banjo player. "[Old Joe] Sweeny's music accomplishments derived from his having been raised among and taught to play as a child by African-American banjo players on his family's Virginia plantation near the old Appomattox Court House," and "Joe Sweeny was not the only member of his Irish family to play music learned from African-American sources" (Conway 108).

Emmet, Whitlock, and Sweeny were the most renowned white minstrels performing before and after the Civil War. It is clear that each of them learned banjo technique and repertoire from African-Americans, or whites who participated in an oral tradition shared among blacks and whites. The nature of their relationships with those from whom they learned was that of apprentice and mentor. As Conway puts it, "[e]ven though a person has a privileged status in a relationship or holds power over another, he may apprentice himself to another with genuine cultural interest" (117). These apprenticeships upset the standard stratification of skin privilege—white over black—in much the same way that labor arrangements in which black land owners hired white workers did. We need to keep in mind that these apprenticeships were based on the assumption that the white person, after mastering some techniques and repertoire, could leave the relationship behind and then go on to use the acquired skills and knowledge toward stereotyping the black mentor for profit. Deviations from the standard stratification of privilege were never permanent or absolute. Conway's research inverts the notion that white banjo traditions grew from minstrel stages. Even if some poor whites of the South got their first tastes of banjo and banjo-fiddle music from minstrels, those performers were the apprentices of black musicians representing a direct thread from blacks to whites to more whites. Evidence suggests, however, that the "African-American banjo tradition—particularly in the Upland South . . . preceded and influenced the minstrel show use of the banjo" (Conway 113). What remains definitive is that whites first learned banjo from blacks via face-to-face oral transmission. This discussion points to a domain in U.S. history which often goes overlooked when considering bluegrass history and the origins of white use of the banjo.

The Disappearance of the Black Banjo

During Reconstruction, a great divergence between black and white use of the banjo was beginning, and this divergence, as it neared completion, was the beginning of an amnesia about shared black and white musical traditions that still permeates our sense of musical history. Great social change during Reconstruction meant a newly defined set of race relationships between blacks and whites. Slavery laws maintained rigid social roles for blacks and whites as bondsmen and freemen. Abolition changed all that, at least on the surface. It was no longer simply legal to oppress blacks so completely, and whites who wanted to feed off of black labor had to come up with new ways of putting free blacks into bondage. Free blacks, similarly, had to find new ways of getting along in the world (see DuBois 13-35). This redefinition of social roles required a redefinition of stereotypes that went with them.

Bastin writes that "[t]he parody of the Negro in minstrelsy could be tolerated by blacks at a time of lesser social change. As social distance grew to physical and psychological distance, intensified beyond all earlier belief after 1896, this stereotyping, once tolerable as crude but harmless humor, became directly offensive. The banjo, ubiquitous instrument of the minstrel stage, embodied this stereotyping, just as later, the watermelon and headscarf would take similar roles. . . . By the turn of the twentieth century, blacks were reacting against the use of the banjo to parody aspects of their lives which were becoming increasingly less tolerable" (14). On the same issue, Linn tells us that "[t]he idea of the Southern black man as banjo player was firmly set by at least the 1840s; in the late nineteenth century the idea was more than just an association. It had become a symbol of a reactionary value system, the import of this symbol hid behind a veil of humor or sentimentality. The figure of the Southern black banjo player stood amid an Old-South mythology, racial stereotypes, and ideas about an instrument that had never been quite accepted into the musical establishment" (41).

With the banjo as a key symbol in the cluster of associations which together constituted a full stereotype of the "plantation darkey," many blacks became aware of the banjo not as a musical instrument great for dancing, but as a humiliating prop that whites used to simultaneously drown out and amplify their virulent racism. As this sense of the banjo emerged more fully, the actual black tradition began to move underground and fade.[9] Linn writes that "[b]ecause the racist imagery connected to the instrument in the national popular culture, the banjo is a problematic cultural symbol for most African Americans. Consequently, few African Americans have communicated about it to the general public" (73). Even though minstrels like Whitlock, Emmet, and Sweeny "were more grounded in the black tradition than their latter-day counterparts . . . that didn't really matter: what generated meaning for the audience was . . . the suggested quality of a banjo in the hands of a make-believe black man" (48).[10]

By the 1890s minstrelsy was loosing its grip on popular interest such that by 1920 it was virtually gone. But minstrels had planted seeds of racist stereotypes in America's ideological soil which sprouted new stereotypes, often focused on urban blacks who had migrated north to industrial towns like Chicago. Images of "horny" jazz musicians with full lips and wide grins took the place of the "plantation darkey," leaving the banjo behind to find a new home in another assemblage of associations which made up the white hillbilly stereotype. It is difficult to pin-point a single cause for the evaporation of the black banjo from popular consciousness. Perhaps the combined energies of blacks rejecting stereotypes, the emergence of new urbanized stereotypes of blacks, and the expanding hillbilly stereotypes of poor white musicians were enough to swing the closet door shut on images of the black banjo player. Whatever the cause, by the mid twentieth century, "the black five-string banjo player, both real and mythical, faded from view" (Linn 76), such that "for most Americans, in the late twentieth century, the African roots of the banjo surprise them" (42).

What are the implications of reframing a history of the origins of the white banjo in this way? On the one hand, the banjo, as a physical object, is often noted as African in origin. The use of the banjo, on the other hand, has too often been mystified as white adaptation to something foreign—a scenario in which white appropriative innovation takes the credit. Three-finger banjo picking has become "Scruggs style," named after Earl Scruggs, who played with Bill Monroe beginning in 1945 at the Grand Ole Opry. Sometimes, this style is attributed to Snuffy Jenkins, another Opry star. Three-finger picking, however, was probably not one person's invention. Its origins are unclear, but it might have grown partially out of rag and blues guitar three-finger picking styles (*e.g.,* Blind Boy Fuller). Metal finger picks, like those Scruggs uses, were common tools of the blues trade. Archie Jackson of South Carolina, for example, "fashionied his finger picks from the metal of sardine cans" (Bastin 168). Perhaps there is a connection here; Scruggs grew up in North Carolina, where the three-finger guitar style was all the rage during his childhood. In my research I have come across a scattering of three-finger banjo pickers who precede Scruggs, and they seem to have connections to the three-finger guitar pickers. Black banjo player Gus Cannon developed a finger-picking technique and performed in medicine shows between 1914 and 1929 (Winnas 424). Perhaps most striking is the banjo playing of Hobart Smith, a descendent of British-Americans who lived in Saltville, Virginia, in the Sugar Grove Region. He has noted that he played with Blind Lemon Jefferson, who influenced his guitar technique and repertoire. Smith also learned fiddle from a black man named Jim Spencer. Residents of this area remember at least three black banjo players from whom, given his introduction to guitar and fiddle, Smith may have learned banjo (Conway 141). His banjo technique has all the trappings of Scruggs's style—high speed, pinched chords, melodic lines woven into a slew of notes, and quarter-note phrases which walk up to the tonic again and again (for recorded example see Lomax, *Southern Journey*.

Fiddle and Banjo Combinations

In order to move closer to bluegrass history, specifically, we need to look at the instrument combinations which preceded, and lent their format to, the string bands which filled record companies' hillbilly catalogs in the 1920s and '30s. We have seen already how the banjo moved from black hands into a mutual cultural status among blacks and whites and then came to be known as a white instrument. This is one of the significant pieces of the string band puzzle. Before and after the Civil War, and into the twentieth century, many instrument combinations which included the banjo could be found all over the Southeast (see Bastin 11-14, 309). It is nearly impossible to specify a rigid format for string bands prior to the onset of the recording industry, perhaps because "bands" were usually informal groups thrown together to play for dances, cornhuskings, auctions, etc. Rigidly formatted instrumentation for bands seems to be the result of commercialization. For example, minstrelsy stages and radio barn dances depended on a well rehearsed and strictly formatted band which promoters could broadly advertise and audiences could expect. Outside these commercial productions, the criteria for a band, regardless of the instrumentation, were probably more along the lines of a good beat and a lively sound suited for set dances, square dances, stepping eight, and more.

Certain instrument combinations which worked well for these dances included the fusion of the African-American banjo and the Scotts-Irish-American fiddle. Some of the earliest accounts of this still resilient combination came out of the Round Peak region of the Blue Ridge Mountains, just east of the Sugar Grove Region in North Carolina. Here, "both Celtic Americans and African Americans highly influenced each other and participated in extensive musical exchange" (Conway 153). "The intense merging of the fiddle and banjo in this region is not too surprising given the information about the early black-white exchange. The old-time string band tradition—an ensemble that honors democratic interaction between the white fiddle and the African-American banjo tradition—is one of the especially important results of blacks bringing the African banjo to this country" (155).

As with locating the origins of the white embrace of the banjo, it is also arguable that minstrels played a role in bringing together the fiddle and the banjo. In 1878, Whitlock claimed that "about 1840 . . . he had 'practiced with Dick Myers, the violinist . . . and on our benefit night, we played the fiddle and the banjo together for the first time in public'" (in Conway 112). Again, there is no hard evidence that blacks and whites had been playing the banjo and fiddle together prior to this date, but this lack of evidence may result from the abundance of documentation of minstrelsy and the ephemerality of oral traditions.

Slaves had been playing fiddle as early as the seventeenth century. By the time of the Civil War, a black fiddle tradition, which still exists in some regions of the Southeast today, was diffuse through that area. The banjo was shared among blacks and whites. Combinations of the two were sprouting up all over the Southeast. There are no distinct roots of the fiddle-banjo combination, but it is clearly a musical child born of nearly equal black and white contribution to its "genetic codes."

Adding the Guitar, Inventing the Blues

The addition of the "Spanish" guitar to the banjo-fiddle combination was important to the development of string bands. "Personal accounts have confirmed that the guitar was added to the fiddle and banjo along the Blue Ridge Mountains of North Carolina soon after the turn of this [the twentieth] century" (Conway 155). Guitars made their way into these regions along the railroads when the Sears Mail-Order Catalog made it available and affordable to rural people in the late 1890s (Bastin 15-18).

As blacks began to drop the banjo for the various reasons hinted at above, they began to pick up the guitar. So did whites. Many players captured on record, such as Maybelle Carter of Southwest Virginia, Elizabeth Cotton of Chapel Hill, North Carolina, and Henry Thomas of northern Texas, found banjo technique and repertoire adaptable to the guitar. The adaptation of claw-hammer banjo technique[11] to the guitar suggests that people who had learned to play the banjo were switching to the guitar, or taking up guitar as another part of their instrumental accomplishments. It was this adaptation, perhaps more than any other musical innovation, which sparked the division of a shared musical culture into what many now think of as "black music" and "white music." The banjo, which would remain a key signifier of Southeastern mountain music, was no longer an African instrument; it belonged to white folks and, apparently, always had.

A Glimpse Beyond 1900:
The Recording Industry, Hillbilly Records, and Bluegrass

At the end of the nineteenth century, many social discourses were gaining currency which supported the notion of a unique and separate white people, known as hillbillies (for accounts of discourses of whiteness see Lopez 191-200; Stepan 20-46; Wray and Newitz 1-8). According to the discourses, these people—like any "folk"—generated, in isolation, their own unique, authentic, exotic culture, and recording company executives drew on and contributed to this notion. Advertising categories, which these executives created to target markets, immediately highlighted the distinction between race records/blues (black music) and hillbilly records (white music). In the form of record sleeves, promotional posters, radio announcements, billboards, mail-order catalogs, and more, the record industry disseminated images of poor, Southern, white people who played hillbilly music and black people who played the blues. Nowhere, to my knowledge, did an image, or even a brief comment, crop up which supported the notion that blacks and whites created music together, ever. It was there, at the onset of mass mediation of recorded music, that the history of mutual black and white musical creations almost entirely slipped the American mind, leaving deep impressions of "musical segregation." Levine explains that "the use of such arbitrary and imprecise cultural categories has helped obscure the dynamic complexity of American culture in the nineteenth century" (*Highbrow* 31).

In the early 1950s, hillbilly music became bluegrass music (for excellent accounts, see Rosenberg, Bluegrass 98-104; Cantwell 41-59). Bill Monroe, dubbed the Father of Bluegrass, had been playing at the top of the hillbilly pop charts for years when his band, the Bluegrass Boys, really hit it big. Around 1951-53, by most accounts, the name "bluegrass" was lifted from its particular association with Monroe to become a modernized version of what was previously known as hillbilly music. Bluegrass, as an autonomous style, is only fifty years old.

Although this essay excludes details of the complex development of country music in the United States during the twentieth century, the detailed analysis of the nineteenth century foregrounds the twentieth century in a way which challenges current historical narratives about the development of bluegrass, such as the story of Bill Monroe as the singular innovator of bluegrass, or of Monroe as repository of an all white-European musical lineage which began among Greek poets. I want now to repeat the question which frames this essay: To what extent do twenty-first century notions of nineteenth century music affect the trajectory of popular music today? What are some of the real-world effects of the circulation of historical narratives?

Hanging-Out at Bluegrass Festivals: An Ethnographic Check-In

Bluegrass is possibly the most exclusively white musical culture in the United States. With the exceptions of a few Japanese bands finding gigs on the U.S. festival circuit, almost all bluegrass performers and audiences are white. Currently Laura Love is the only African-American I'm aware of who performs bluegrass professionally, though only occasionally, on the festival circuit. Neil Rosenberg says that: "[t]he only Black performers I know who are active in bluegrass bands are in Canada" ("Ethnicity and Class" 462). I have only seen a few black people at one bluegrass festival (Winterhawk Bluegrass Festival, 1996). Other people have told me about a few black people's experiences at bluegrass festivals. Yvonne Walbroehl, a San Francisco area flat-picker and chemist, said:

YW: Well, I can relate a story of a friend, a black woman who lives in Santa Cruz. She came up here last year [1996], she plays guitar, and she plays more of the blues kind of stuff, but she loves to come to the bluegrass kinds of events. And in the Santa Cruz area people are very open so she doesn't have to deal with as much of the prejudice as in the Southeast or something like that. She comes to a lot of our festivals, and she was relating a story about Jimmy Martin [*laughing*]. Basically, she wanted him to sign his CD. He was calling over to some friend of his [*gesturing as if to have a person under her arm to whom she is pointing*] and he says "Well, look what I found." I guess he'd never seen a black fan of bluegrass before. (Farmelo 46-47)

Though perhaps insensitive, Martin's sarcasm and sense of irony are appropriate to the degree that his commentary points out his and others' sense of the rarity of black presence at bluegrass events. Given that he has toured as a bluegrass musician for decades, his take on the situation in 1996 is an informed one. Regardless of Martin's intent, at which we can only guess, that woman's exchange with him is a relatively friendly one. That story inspired this less pleasant one from Trisha Tubbs:

TT: I have a friend who is black, and he went to [a] festival with some of his friends. Most of his friends are Caucasian. And he said it was really scary because he thought he was going to be killed.
YW: Well, there's that certain group of people that come hang their Confederate flags out from the camper.
TT: And he really noticed it because he likes the music but he said, "Well, I just don't want to get hurt," which is really sad.
YW: It's a funny thing because we're playing and singing and enjoying something that is essentially a Southern folk art—well, it's not really folk because bluegrass is really a commercial country music that come out of a folk tradition in the Southeast part of the United States—but there was at one time a very racist element to it, as there was to all kinds of entertainment in those days. People were wearing blackface and doing all kind of things that aren't acceptable anymore.

AF: Bill Monroe had people performing in blackface.
YW: Yeah, sure, that was expected even. You couldn't do that now, except maybe at a KKK rally or something. (Farmelo 48-49)

In this brief exchange, a number of associations arise which, when taken together, constitute an improvised and brief history of particularly Southeastern US racism and its iconography: the Confederate flag, banjo players in blackface, the Ku Klux Klan. These associations translate into bluegrass iconography: the Confederate flag still flies at more than a few bluegrass festivals; the blackface banjoist could be Stringbean, Monroe's first banjo player, in blackface; a black person fearing large groups of white people gathered in a rural setting becomes a black person fearing a bluegrass festival.

These stories, drawn from my ethnographic fieldwork, suggest that bluegrass is entangled with a cluster of cultural icons which indicate, and have historically indicated, the racism of poor white Southern people. Bluegrass, along with hillbilly music before it, has always been associated with poor white people—usually Southern, illiterate, unemployed, sometimes inbred and, possibly, mentally challenged (see Green 205; Wray and Newitz 2-3). Hartigan specifies that "[w]hite trash and poor white form a continuum of means of designating 'them.' In between are similar terms with greater regional specificity: 'cracker' in Georgia and Florida; 'linthead' in the Carolinas; 'okie' in the West; 'hillbilly' or 'ridge runner' in West Virginia and the Midwest" (53). The stereotype which people put on poor whites is old, its origins indistinct. The term "white trash" goes back at least 150 years. Former slave Hanna Crasson said "we called 'em pore white trash, we also called patrollers pore white pecks;" and another former slave said that "day wuz called po' white trash" (in Cecil-Fronsman 78). Archie Green suggests that the hillbilly stereotype has its origins in Scotland during the sixteenth and seventeenth centuries. In Scottish dialect, "hill-folk" often meant Presbyterians who had fled, and "billie" meant friend (204). A combination of the two would designate a rural poor white, or a friend of one. Whatever its origins, the hillbilly thread of the white trash stereotype found its way into bluegrass and, while it is losing its grip as bluegrass ascends the pop charts, it remains well embedded in popular consciousness (see Cantwell 41-59; Green 211-23; Lopez 191-200; Rosenberg, *Bluegrass* 18-36; Stepan 20-26; Wray and Newitz 5-6).

Have these stereotypes of poor whites contributed to the nearly exclusive white participation in the bluegrass scene? While noting my tendency to oversimplify social phenomena, I do see connections between any history of bluegrass, the stereotypes which that history supports or denounces, and, ultimately, the social composition of the music's subculture. Presumably, a revised version of the history of black/white relationships in the nineteenth century woven into a history of bluegrass could displace segregationist stereotypes of whiteness which affect the social composition of the subculture. Returning to Christopher Small's comments which open this essay: can historical accounts of shared "empathy, even across a social or cultural barrier, which . . . exists, at levels deeper than those feelings of fear and guilt which lie at the root of racism" help to generate empathy in the present? As historians of popular music concentrate on historical periods like the nineteenth century, new narratives will continue to surface indefinitely. The production of new narratives may help to disturb and uproot stereotypes which depend on certain versions of social history; possibly, the integration of new narratives and the disintegration of stereotypes, over time, will affect the social politics of pop music subcultures. We can, to some extent, play in the social politics of musical subcultures by learning, writing, teaching, and just talking about their histories.

Notes

1. I am deeply indebted to Bill Evans, ethnomusicologist and world-class banjo player, for guidance toward relevant literature and for generously suggesting areas of academic exploration. His academic work, banjo workshops, and musicianship produce a more musicologically grounded account of the material I present in this essay.

2. Referring to the Kentucky-born fiddler Jim Booker, Terry Zwigoff writes that "[h]is eldest son Jim played fiddle on the recordings by Taylor's Kentucky Boys—an otherwise white string band (recorded examples of black fiddlers backed up by white musicians are far from common. The only other example I can think of is 'G Rag,' on which Andrew Baxter plays with the Georgia Yellow Hammers)." Bastin also treats the Yellow Hammers as an anomaly (39). As Zwigoff's tone suggests, this dearth of recorded examples does not mean there was a corresponding lack of black and white musical interaction. Part of the puzzle is that the personnel listings on some of these older recordings contain no names; others list only the main musician while the band members go unmentioned.

3. Especially see Trevor-Roper and Morgan in Hobsbawm and Ranger (15-42, 43-100) on the deliberate invention of false lineages stretching from the Scottish, Welsh, British to the Gauls, Anglos, and Greeks.

4. Both Bolton (4) and Hartigan (51-53) discuss the derogatory connotations of the phrase "poor white," yet both maintain it as a useful, though necessarily qualified, designation. I, too, use it while intending no connotations other than whites who enjoy little to no income. Cecil-Fronsman prefers "common whites."

5. Pierre van den Berghe's *herrenvolk* thesis, which proposes that poor members of the superior race in a racially dichotomized society will ally themselves with the aristocracy and bourgeois in order to maintain a superior status above those of the inferior race, fails to properly account for the role of sub-dominant-class consciousness. Cecil-Fronsman adequately complicates the *herrenvolk* thesis in the context of antebellum North Carolina (82-96).

6. To temper this discussion, I include these comments which run contrary. Samuel Steward, formerly a slave in Wake County, NC, said, "We didn't think much of the poor white man. He was down on us. . . . The rich slave owner wouldn't let his negroes 'sociate with poor white folks." John Smith, also a former slave from Wake County, simply stated, 'People didn't sociate together, poor whites, free niggers, slaves, and de slave owners" (in Cecil-Fronsman 78).

7. John McGowan's sense of "semi-autonomy" is theoretically helpful for thinking about what I call "embedded autonomy." Constructing identity within a social context which aims to homogenize and to differentiate simultaneously is autonomous social action in the sense that one critiques both homogeneity (*i.e.,* saying "I'm different") and heterogeneity (*i.e.,* saying "I'm not different in the way you prescribe"). Considering how such vernacular critiques of class and race categorizations might operate is helpful for imagining a new historical account of class and race relations in the US and elsewhere.

8. This is a very superficial account of Conway's documentation, which includes analysis of population patterns, picking techniques, banjo construction trends, and repertoire exchange.

9. That most black musicians actually shifted away from the banjo toward the guitar is not certain. Enough recordings of black banjo players from the 1920s exist to refute the claim that blacks dropped it al- together, as well as the claim that string bands were white. Bastin's history of the blues, a category which he claims did not exist as such until the twentieth century, is littered with examples of black "bluesmen" who played the fiddle and banjo. We also know that black string bands regularly played for white and black dancers through the Southeast during Reconstruction and into the twentieth century.

10. This stereotyping may have remained irrelevant for poor whites and blacks living in close proximity in rural areas like Sugar Grove and Round Peak. Also, the rising prices of banjos and the falling prices of guitars obviously had something to do with the black rejection of the banjo and adoption of the guitar—though these prices may reflect retailers' ideas about these instruments, too. Linn documents the attempts of white, Northeastern, urban high society to "elevate the banjo," a motivation which confirms its lowly image in musical high society during reconstruction and into the twentieth century.

11. This is a way of playing the banjo. The first or middle fingernail comes down on the strings as the thumb meets the fifth string. Upon lifting the hand back up, the thumb pulls up on the fifth string, sounding it. Claw-hammer is

associated with "old-time" music today—a music which adheres closely to the techniques, repertoire, and instrumentation of the Appalachian mountain music string bands of the nineteenth century—and stands in bold contrast to the bluegrass, three-finger technique.

Works Cited

Bastin, Bruce. *Red River Blues: the Blues Tradition in the Southeast.* Urbana: U of Illinois P, 1995.

Berghe, Pierre van den. *Race and Racism: A Comparative Approach.* New York: Wiley, 1967.

Berlin, Ira, and Philip D. Morgan. *The Slave's Economy: Independent Production by Slaves in the Americas.* London: Frank Cass and Co. Ltd., 1991.

Blair, John G. "Blackface Minstrels in Cross-Cultural Perspective." *American Studies International* 28.2 (1990): 52-65.

Bolton, Charles C. *Poor Whites of the Antebellum South.* Durham, NC: Duke UP, 1994.

Cantwell, Robert. *Bluegrass Breakdown: The Making of the Old Southern Sound.* New York: DaCapo, 1984.

Cecil-Fronsman, Bill. *Common Whites: Class and Culture in Antebellum North Carolina.* Lexington: U of Kentucky P, 1992.

Conway, Cecilia. *African Banjo Echoes in Appalachia.* Knoxville: U of Tennessee P, 1995.

DuBois, W. E. B. *The Souls of Black Folk.* 1903. New York: Penguin, 1989.

Eagleton, Terry. *The Illusions of Postmodernism.* Cambridge: Blackwell, 1996.

Epstein, Deena J. "The Folk Banjo: A Documentary History." *Ethnomusicology* 19 (1975): 347-71.

——. *Sinful Tunes and Spirituals: Black Folk Music to the Civil War.* Urbana: U of Illinois P, 1977.

Farmelo, Allen. "Women's Roles in Bluegrass: A Focus Group Interview with LaVonne Bickle, Jennifer Crum, Allen Farmelo, Trisha Tubbs, Claire Wagner, Yvonne Walbroehl." Unpublished interview transcript, 1997.

Green, Archie. "Hillbilly Music: Source and Symbol." *Journal of American Folklore* 78.309 (1965): 204-56.

Hartigan, John. "Name Calling: Objectifying 'Poor Whites' and 'White Trash' in Detroit." *White Trash: Race and Class in America.* Ed. Matt Wray and Analee Newitz. New York: Routedge, 1997. 41-56.

Harvey, David. *The Condition of Postmodernity.* Cambridge: Blackwell, 1995.

Hobsbawm, Eric J., and Terence Ranger, eds. *The Invention of Tradition.* New York : Cambridge UP, 1983.

202   .   *Popular Music & Society*

Johnson, Charles A. *The Frontier Camp Meeting—Religion's Harvest Time.* Dallas, TX: Southern Methodist UP, 1955.

Levine, Lawrence W. *Black Culture and Black Consciousness: Afro-American Folk Thought from Slavery to Freedom.* New York: Oxford UP, 1977.

——. *Highbrow/Lowbrow: The Emergence of Cultural Hierarchy in America.* Cambridge, MA: Harvard UP, 1988.

Linn, Karen. *That Half-Barbaric Twang: The Banjo in American Popular Culture.* Chicago: U of Chicago P, 1991.

Lockley, Timothy J. "Partners in Crime: African-Americans and Non-Slaveholding Whites in Antebellum Georgia." *White Trash: Race and Class in America.* Ed. Matt Wray and Annalee Newitz. New York: Routledge, 1997. 57-72.

Lopez, Ian F. Hanley. "White by Law." *Critical Race Theory: The Cutting Edge.* Ed. Richard Delgado. Philadelphia: Temple UP, 1995. 542-49.

Lott, Eric. *Love and Theft: Blackface Minstrelsy and the American Working Class.* New York: Oxford UP, 1993.

Malone, Bill C. *Country Music USA.* Austin: U of Texas P, 1991.

McGowan, John. *Postmodernism and Its Critics.* Ithaca: Cornell UP, 1991.

An Overview of Bluegrass Music Presented by the Special Consensus. Buffalo, NY: The Traditional American Music Program (TAM), 1997.

Rooney, Jim. *Bossmen: Bill Monroe and Muddy Waters.* New York: Dial, 1971.

Rosenberg, Neil. *Bluegrass: A History.* Urbana: U of Illinois P, 1985.

——. "Ethnicity and Class: Black Country Musicians in the Maritimes." *Canadian Music: Issues of Hegemony and Identity.* Ed. Robert Witmer and Beverly Diamond. Toronto: Canadian Scholars P, 1994. 415-46.

Said, Edward. *Orientalism.* New York: Vintage, 1979.

Small, Christopher. *Music of the Common Tongue.* London: John Calder, 1987.

Smith, Mayne. "An Introduction to Bluegrass." *Journal of American Folklore* 78 (1965): 245-56.

Southern Journey, Voices from the American South (Rounder CD 1701). Alan Lomax, compiler. Cambridge, MA: Rounder Records, 1997.

Stepan, Nancy. *The Idea of Race in Science.* Hamden, CT: Archon, 1982.

Weatherford, Jack. *Indian Givers: How the Indians of the Americas Transformed the World.* New York: Fawcett Columbine, 1988.

Wilson, Joe. "The Chestnut Grove Quartet." *Bluegrass Unlimited* July 1995: 54-58.

Winnas, Robert. "The Folk, the Stage, and the Five-String Banjo in the Nineteenth Century." *Journal of American Folklore* 89 (1976): 407-37.

Woodward, C. Vann. *The American Counterpoint: Slavery and Racism in the North-South Dialogue.* Boston: Little, Brown and Co., 1971.

Wray, Matt, and Annalee Newitz, eds. *White Trash: Race and Class in America.* New York: Routledge, 1997.

Zwigoff, Terry. Liner Notes to *'String Bands: 1926-1929.'* Document Records (DOCD-5167). 1993.

Allen Farmelo has taught courses on cultural history, fieldwork methodology, and popular music for the Department of Music and the Department of American Studies at the State University of New York at Buffalo.

[3]

ANALOGIES AND DIFFERENCES IN AFRICAN-AMERICAN MUSICAL CULTURES ACROSS THE HEMISPHERE: INTERPRETIVE MODELS AND RESEARCH STRATEGIES

GERHARD KUBIK

Before our eyes, African-American cultures in their various expressions have unfolded a fascinating picture of resilience, transformation, invention, and innovation, revealing analogies, divergences, parallel strands, cohesion, single traits binding certain regions together or separating them, and idiosyncrasies of individual artists. It is a tremendous undertaking to unravel this complexity, spread out over four hundred years. What are the causes of the specifics and generalities? Why are there analogies and differences? What has actually happened during that time span and in all those different places?

Ideological Outlooks and Research Methodologies

While the basic questions are plain, the answers depend not only on our ever-expanding database and individual researchers' methodologies but also on the researchers' ideological outlook. A perusal of the vast literature reveals a recurrence of certain basic assumptions and interpretive models upon which the declared research results depend. In this paper, which is basically theoretical though not devoid of concrete examples, I will outline some of the most influential interpretive models, which I have divided into six categories. My aim is to make us all more conscious of our various modes of thought, even if such consciousness is at times

Gerhard Kubik is a cultural anthropologist, ethnomusicologist, and psycho-analyst. A professor of ethnology and African studies at the Universities of Vienna and Klagenfurt, he also teaches at Sigmund Freud University, Vienna. Professor Kubik is affiliated with the Oral Literature Research Programme, Chileka, Malawi, and is a permanent member of the Center for Black Music Research in Chicago as well as an honorary fellow of the Royal Anthropological Institute of Great Britain and Ireland. His recent books include *Africa and the Blues* and *Tusona – Luchazi Ideographs*.

painful. I will express criticism but without devaluing any individual researcher's methodology or philosophical outlook. Nor do I claim infallible objectivity for myself. And yet, the fact of my almost continuous, thirty-eight–year research in African societies—as well as the legacy of Sigmund Freud in my birthplace, Vienna (see Horgan 1996)—will give this paper a special frame of reference.

The six interpretive schemes to be discussed have influenced research strategies and actual work in African-American studies. All of them, alone and in combination, have been applied to explain analogies and differences not only in African-American music across the hemisphere but in African-derived cultures as a whole. They are the following: (1) biological reductionism, (2) socio-psychological determinism, (3) pseudo-historical reductionism, (4) historical particularism, (5) cultural materialism, and (6) cultural diffusionism. The most elementary schemes are summarized under model (1), while the psychologically most revealing may be those under (2) and (3); the most open-ended schemes are probably (4) and (6).

Biological Reductionism

This model embraces several explanatory schemes. Observers working from this perspective often silently or overtly subscribe to the assumption of a causal link between "race" and "culture."[1] Cultural specifics are imagined to be hereditarily interrelated with "race." "Race" is even thought of as predetermining culture, although it is rarely stated that way explicitly. In their assessment of African-American cultural expressions, this group of observers might therefore begin their treatises with the acknowledgment of racial "identity" markers, implying that African-American cultures are shared and creatively perpetuated only by individuals who can be identified from their physical appearance as African-American. Since physical appearance and heredity-determined behavior are central to the biological-reductionist approach, cultural analogies are emphasized, and differences are interpreted as creative variation within a basic matrix. African-American cultures are generally conceptualized as homogeneous and as demonstrating a kind of innate resilience.

The point of departure and unifying element in this approach is the perception of a set of physiological identity markers serving as a core statement, expanded by the juxtaposition of apparently causally related expressive forms and modes of behavior. Around the core idea of "racial identity," language, art forms, music, literature, dance, etc. are arranged

1. Ironically, neither "race" nor "culture" has ever been successfully defined in anthropology; and yet these concepts remain deeply entrenched in popular *thought styles* (see Douglas 1996 for this term).

Figure 1. The racial Marguerite: expressive culture arranged around the core concept of race

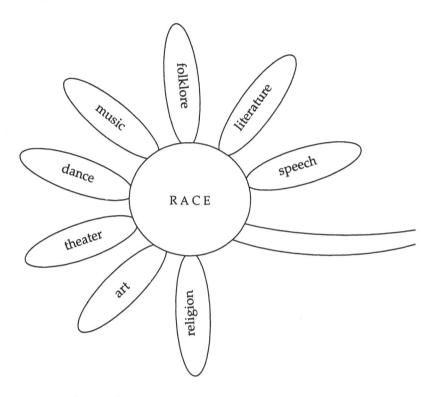

in a manner designed to confirm the identity and innate unity of the population group thereby isolated. I therefore call this model "the racial Marguerite" (see Fig. 1).[2]

Biological reductionism has other forms of expression in the literature. One is manifested in the particular direction taken in behavioral studies identified by the term *ethology*, whose founder was Konrad Lorenz, best remembered by the public for his spectacular communication with grey geese. In his footsteps, other researchers have transferred the methods of Lorenz's work with animals to human beings, thereby launching the branch of *human ethology*. The term "ethology" has been variously defined as "biology of behavior" and "comparative behavioral research," its objective being to understand animal and human behavior from a bio-

---

2. I am alluding here to the well-known "flower societies" of St. Lucia, which divide the larger community into moieties. Individuals can be members either of the group called "La Marguerite" or of that called "La Rose." The members say of one another that they have different characters (Kremser 1993).

logical viewpoint and to analyze "species-specific" behavior (Spindler 1988, 137). A celebrated exponent is Irenäus Eibl-Eibesfeldt, who studied group cohesion and control of aggression in the !Ko Bushman society of Botswana. An analysis of his texts, however, reveals that the ideological basis of his approach lies in unilinear evolutionism. He himself admits that he proceeds from the assumption that his mid-twentieth-century !Ko represent an "antique state of humanity" (Eibl-Eibesfeldt 1972, 21).

Still surviving, although often under surrogate terminology, nineteenth-century unilinear evolutionism has influenced theoretical developments and research strategies throughout the humanities, including African and African-American studies. Authors applying it to music have variously proposed that pentatonic scales are more "primitive" than heptatonic tonal systems, that the history of jazz is an evolutionary sequence from "simple" to "complex" (e.g., in the chords), that on the Guinea Coast the "stage" of anhemitonic pentatonism was passed through by cautiously incorporating two more steps into the scale, with the singers "not yet" certain about their pitch, and that that was the origin of "blue" notes (see Mecklenburg and Scheck 1963). It was even once proposed that musical scales are transmitted by heredity.

Another biological reductionist trend has surfaced more recently, resulting from several breakthrough discoveries in genetics that have raised expectations that a magic key has been found to unlock the causality of gender differences, racial differences, sexual orientation, and the like (see, for example, Begley 1997). In this view, complex human behavior can be reduced to the workings of single genes—a position with the hidden psychological advantage that individuals can thus be acquitted of moral responsibility for their actions.

However, this popular new creed of one-gene/one-behavioral-trait causality is regressive historically, just as much as the fiction of "cultural memory" harks back to eighteenth-century Lamarckism.[3] I anticipate that by 2010, or earlier, when the Human Genome Project is completed, it will become more apparent that the one-gene/one-trait equation cannot be safely used to predict or even retrodict individual behavior, let alone that of large, heterogeneous communities such as African Americans.

Socio-psychological Determinism

In contrast to biological determinists, observers working from the perspective of social or psychological determinism tend to explain analogies and differences in African-American cultural expressions not as manifestations of some innate "nature" of this population group but as a

---

3. Jean-Baptiste Lamarck (1744–1829) was a French biologist who believed that acquired characteristics can be inherited.

result of *nurture* under specific, recurrent circumstances, that is, as behavior that is acquired and developed through processes of enculturation. Researchers working from this model have noticed that a population can be artificially segmented and isolated from the larger context through socio-psychological forces and can be pressed into demonstrating identities that are ultimately ascribed (see Kubik 1994a, 42–43). Put simply, one group ascribes to another group the role it expects it to play; individuals in both groups then come under social pressure to adhere to these stereotypical expectations.

A thorough analysis of this phenomenon was carried out in Burkina Faso by Paul Riesman (1993), who studied social interaction between two groups—the dominant Fulbe and the submissive Riimaaybe, who were subjugated by the Fulbe in the nineteenth century. The Fulbe hold all the political power, and the Riimaaybe are said to "wear imaginary strings round their necks" like goats (i.e., slaves) (172). The groups are said to display certain "ethnic" character differences; but when Riesman examined whether such differences were founded in different modes of child rearing, the result was negative. The groups' different "ethnic characters" were the result of internalized anticipations about the other group. In a stratified society split into oppositional groups, children learn to behave in accordance with the oppositional group's expectations. Enculturation prepares them not only for a life geared to the needs of their specific communities but also for interaction with the opponent. It was observed that, in both ethnic groups, adults pressure their offspring from an early age to learn to behave "like" a Fulbe or "like" a Riimaaybe. Deviant behavior is discouraged. For this reason, suggests Riesman, a Fulbe child will soon develop consciousness that he or she *is* a Fulbe and is *not* a Riimaaybe and will learn to act in conformity with the internalized modes of that group. A Fulbe will appear tone-deaf in contact with Riimaaybe music, and the subjugated people seem incapable of ever understanding the spirited Fulbe court music, with its shrill oboes (*alghaita*), long trumpet (*gagashi*), and military-style *ganga* snare drums.[4] Needless to say, a child of either Fulbe or Riimaaybe parents, raised in a totally different society somewhere else on the globe, would develop quite different behavioral patterns that would have no relation to the Fulbe/Riimaaybe antagonism (see also Kubik 1995, 157–158).

Heterostereotypes do serve a purpose: they guarantee the status quo in social hierarchies. For this reason they also sometimes change rapidly with a change of power. If only minor adjustments are made within the

4. The same applies to other peoples in West Africa whose territories were conquered in a similar way, as I observed myself among the Kutin of northern Cameroon (Kubik 1989, 82–89).

208   BMR Journal

stratified society, the heterostereotypes can be displaced from one area of expression to another—for example, when institutionalized segregation is replaced by economic segregation.

From the perspective of socio-psychological interpretive schemes, it would seem that cultural resilience in minority groups also functions as a defense mechanism against perceived threats to the group. Thus the continuity and resilience of "black" cultures in the Americas into the twenty-first century can be understood as a socio-historical phenomenon resulting from societal splitting mechanisms brought about by a power structure supporting social stratification. To put it simply, if society were not divided, its expressive culture would be equally shared by all. Societal splitting and alienation, with all their attendant in-group/out-group antagonism, often result from prolonged pressure by power groups that have an interest, economically or otherwise, in the split. What initially perhaps are *perceptions* of group differences are then systematically inflated to become *factual* differences in a vicious cycle of self-fulfilling prophecy. The late Alex Haley was painfully aware of this. A week before his death in 1992, he declared that he intended to "take America beyond *Roots* by breaking down what he called the artificial lines of race, lines that too many conclude are walls." These walls were "illusions that had somehow grown into fearsome reality in the American mind" (quoted in Williams 1992, 5).

An early stimulus to systematic research of group interaction based on data collection and observation came from sociolinguistics. Peter Trudgill, in his introduction to *Sociolinguistics* (1974), demonstrates how language usage can define group membership. *Social-class dialects* of English, he says, are indicative of the relative social status of groups in a stratified society (34ff.). His discussion of the formation of social-class dialects suggests analogies with the formation of ethnic groups, as I have shown in an analysis of ethnogenesis in eastern Angola (Kubik 1994b). Inasmuch as language identifies membership in a social class, it also indicates a speaker's membership in other group formations, e.g., ethnic groups. However, speaker recognition tests have also revealed that pseudo-ethnic formations abound on earth, some of the most impressive examples of which are found in the United States. "Blacks" and "Hispanics," for example, are such pseudo-ethnic entities, which can in no way be considered ethnic groups because language and cultural differences cut right across these artificial lines. This has been repeatedly shown by tests in which tape recordings of varieties of American English were played to audiences who were asked to judge whether the speakers were "black" or "white." In one such experiment it was found that the geographical origin of the speakers was much more identifiable than their "race." Another experiment, conducted in Detroit, had an approximately 80 percent success rate for listeners of various backgrounds recognizing "black" or "white" speakers; the 20 percent error rate represents a figure large enough to testify that there is no inherent link between a person's linguistic profile and his or her physiology (Trudgill 1974, 52).

More recently, the musicologist and linguist Benjamin Boone discovered blues-like speech in Jelly Roll Morton's famous 1938 interview with Alan Lomax. His computer analysis of the speech patterns and spectrum suggested "that pitches commonly associated with blues music were being utilized"—not only by Jelly Roll Morton, a New Orleans musician and composer, but *also* by Alan Lomax, a musicologist who grew up in the South, who seemed to have acquired a similar speech template through his own acculturation into the African-American community (Boone 1994, abstract).

These findings might help to temper the emotions that were stirred during the recent discussions in the media about "Ebonics" (a neologism composed of the words "ebony" and "phonic"), referring to what used to be called "black English" or "African-American vernacular English" (see Leland and Nadine 1997; Gibbs 1997). This vernacular, which functions for many as a home language, is grammatically consistent, incorporating phonetic, tonemic, and grammatical characteristics that can be traced structurally to several West African languages. But these features are not "genetically based." Furthermore, the discussion of whether "black English" is a dialect or a language only piles up dead weight. The debate in Africa twenty-five years ago about which African languages should be called "dialects" and which should be called distinct "languages" paralyzed educationists who proceeded from the notion that only "languages" were suitable for teaching in schools. Eventually, Mubanga E. Kashoki of Zambia, some other colleagues, and I exposed the futility of these concepts. We proposed that all variants within a language cluster should be understood as forming a *dialect continuum*. This principle applies equally to European languages. "Schwitzer-Dütsch," "Plattdeutsch," "Wienerisch," and standard High German (Hochdeutsch), the written language, are all part of one and the same dialect continuum that can be called German. Likewise, Oxford English, American Standard English, Guinea-Coast Pidgin, Ebonics, and Australian English are all part of a dialect continuum. Furthermore, each component is a "dialect" of all the other components. Both Ebonics and American Standard English can therefore be considered dialects of English.

It would appear that cultural and linguistic differences that set some African-American communities apart from the American mainstream are enhanced by forces of social marginalization. In reaction to marginaliza-

Figure 2. Aligned societal molecule clusters

Population conglomerate   *Rearrangement in oppositional groups
(with physical appearance and/or lan-
guage serving as identity markers)*

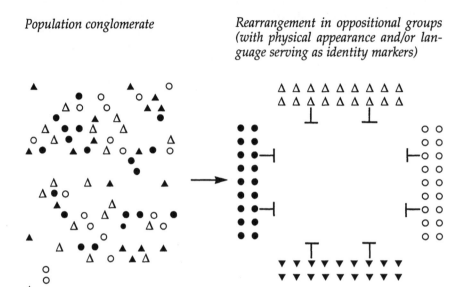

tion and economic deprivation, these communities have developed
defense strategies, emphasizing coherence and separate identities (e.g.,
"black ethnicity") through non-conformist behavior in all sectors of life,
including the arts. Their search for a separate identity goes even to the
point of posterior acquisition of African identity markers that are considered part of a long-standing cultural heritage—the reclaiming of selected
traits from historical sources or archaeology, or traits that are not especially tied to the twentieth century, such as language. Seen from this
angle, society appears to be split artificially into oppositional entities,
each group attempting to bring its members into line. I therefore call this
model "aligned societal molecule clusters" (see Fig. 2). Some authors
working within the socio-psychological interpretive model would also
stress that the marginalized groups' defense strategies ultimately play
into the hands of the very same power structure that has forced them into
marginalization, since they subscribe to the power structure's own biological reductionist ideology.

Pseudo-historical Reductionism

   The central theme of this third model, which gained currency in the
United States especially during the 1970s, is expressed by the idea of

"roots," thereby adding a *diachronic* element to the ideology of (static) biological reductionism. Observers working with the concept of "roots" also ultimately proceed from the notion of "race," vaguely conceptualized as recognizable by certain external anthropologically peripheral physical characteristics, such as skin color, hair texture, etc. However, since the "roots" concept is superimposed on the static concept of biological reductionism, a major cognitional problem emerges: how can a diachronic link possibly be established between Africans, among whom African-American genealogies once started, and the race/culture equation ascribed to African Americans? If the race/culture equation is scientifically valid, African-American and African cultural expressions and their underlying concepts should be identical in kind, but obviously they are not on any conceivable general level.

With the presence now of many African students in the United States, a stunning phenomenon has been observed: mutual distrust. Very few African Americans, particularly within the marginalized social classes, seem to be comfortable in the presence of African individuals or seem to feel any particular bonds of identity with them, in spite of declarations to the contrary. Moreover, the readiness to express this antagonism seems to be inversely proportional to the educational standards of both parties— the least educated tend to express their aversions more openly.[5] Anyone calling attention to this phenomenon will normally provoke a strong negative reaction from the parties concerned. But it is clear from psychoanalytical experience that strong denial reactions always *confirm* the unconscious presence of precisely the ideas or impulses in question. The phenomenon is called *resistance* in the psychoanalytic literature: resistance to a repressed idea that threatens to gain access to Ego's consciousness. One of the tasks of the analyst is to help the client accept the unpleasant idea. The antagonism described can be explained by assuming that Africans are often unconsciously perceived as representing the African American's past—a past long abandoned and immured in the mind. Contrary to all conscious reasoning, Africans symbolize to many African Americans the era of the Atlantic slave trade, or simply slaves (Kubik 1994a, 41). In cross-cultural contact, the encounter with another culture always stimulates unconscious ideas in the individual. It can be a "lost identity" that strives for expression, but that identity is very different from what Ego believes it is. Since it can be negatively charged, Ego is afraid of such knowledge about the self; so Ego projects these contents onto some outside symbol, identifying someone else with the uncon-

5. Any doubts about the reality and intensity of such feelings were quelled by the ample evidence of my own field observations, including symbolic actions, behavioral lapses, and slips of the tongue that regularly occur on both sides during interaction (Kubik 1993a).

scious thoughts. That is also what happens between African Americans and Africans, as it does between adherents to *any* two cultures.

Contemporary African-American self-perception is sometimes symbolically encased in the pseudo-historical concept of "roots." The model of a tree with its roots is so attractive to the mind because its multiple symbolism visualizes deeply entrenched ideas about self. I therefore call this interpretive model the "tree of ontogenesis" (see Fig. 3). Many papers and books have been written on the "roots" of African-American music—the roots of the blues, the roots of jazz. Synchronicity, namely the (belated) twentieth-century encounter between African Americans and their African contemporaries in art and music, as well as in person, is reinterpreted by the "roots" model diachronically, thereby reflecting the unconscious psychological configuration described above. No one talks about "the roots of South African *kwela* music in American swing jazz." Here, researchers prefer to speak of "influences," "adaptations," etc. In self-perception, "African-American culture" appears to stand "above ground level," in the clear light of historical consciousness, while "Africa" is relegated to a position of darkness, an ahistorical existence "below ground level" and yet forming an eternal source of energy that feeds the African-American tree.

Symbolism is always multifaceted and multidimensional. Images have several parallel meanings that neither contradict nor exclude one another. In another dimension, therefore, the "roots" model can also be considered as a disguised version of evolutionism and, as such, pseudo-historical. In a sense, it parallels evolutionistic interpretive schemes developed by nineteenth-century anthropologists that reinterpreted other peoples' cultures as representing earlier stages of their own.

"Roots" as a concept was popularized by Alex Haley's Pulitzer prize–winning book of the same name (1976) and by the television miniseries based on it, which traced Haley's family back to Kunta Kinte, Haley's remote ancestor in Gambia. But by the early 1990s, Haley had largely transcended the concept of "roots" in its original meanings. There have been other signs recently of America's transition "beyond roots" and the breakthrough of a more aggressive, deromanticized perception of Africa by African-American intellectuals visiting the continent. An example is Keith B. Richburg's new book, *Out of America: A Black Man Confronts Africa* (1997), which traces a journalist's ordeal amid racism and ethnicism in Somalia, Kenya, and Rwanda, where the author was mistaken for a Tutsi by Hutu militiamen.

Kubik • Analogies and Differences   213

Figure 3. The tree of ontogenesis

Stem, branches, and
leaves; representing
African-Americans
and their culture (in
self-perception)

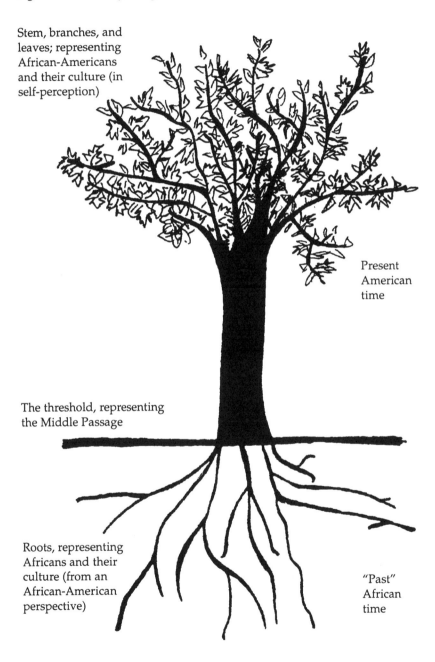

Present
American
time

The threshold, representing
the Middle Passage

Roots, representing
Africans and their
culture (from an
African-American
perspective)

"Past"
African
time

Historical Particularism

This systematic, historically oriented approach, avoiding grand explanatory schemes and working instead from factual data obtained either in the field or in archives, developed in the United States during the 1920s and 1930s. Often described, though not quite accurately, as "historical particularism" (Harris 1968), it was stimulated by the teachings of the anthropologist Franz Boas and has gained momentum in African-American studies. One of Boas's intellectual offspring was the influential Melville J. Herskovits (1895–1963). He rejected nineteenth-century evolutionist ideas about cultural stages and considered the word "primitive" to be invidious and pejorative. Postulating *cultural relativism,* he considered Euro-American culture and lifestyle as just one of the many possible cultural variants, not "higher" or "lower" than any other (see Herskovits 1973). With a new terminology making use of the concepts of *selection, retention, survival, reinterpretation, syncretism,* and *cultural focus* (Evans 1990), Herskovits set out to unravel the behavioral patterns operating in intercultural contacts. He directed his research especially to African-American cultures as well as those of the Guinea Coast (Herskovits 1938a, 1938b, 1941).

A league of researchers dealing with the history of jazz, blues, and other African-derived musics began to operate from concepts developed by Herskovits, applying refined field interview techniques supplemented by the evaluation of written, pictorial, and other historical sources. Frederick Ramsey, Rudi Blesh, Richard A. Waterman, and others all belong, in a certain sense, to that school. In Cuba, Fernando Ortiz adopted a related approach, although he rejected Herskovits' original concept of acculturation in favor of the two-way concept of *transculturation* (Ortiz 1940). More recently, Dena Epstein (1973, 1977) has been in the forefront among researchers working with historical methods, scrutinizing an enormous number of seventeenth-, eighteenth-, and nineteenth-century sources from the United States and the Caribbean to reconstruct African-American music history. Although the work of these scholars often also incorporates interpretive schemes of the kind I have discussed above, and although the historical-particularist approach has not always been extended to the African continent, it warrants consideration as an independent scientific strategy. Within this school of thought, major musical expressions in the Americas, such as jazz, have been studied as specifically American cultural phenomena arising in the context of particular social situations.

Obviously, there are deficiencies in historical particularism if it is practiced only descriptively, thereby yielding an abundance of detail unrelated by cause and effect. A compensatory reaction to this accusation may be seen, for example, in the zeal of some jazz historians of the 1940s and 1950s to impose an artificial order onto fortuitous[6] style changes in jazz, postulating a ten-year cycle of change from Dixieland and Chicago jazz of the 1920s to swing of the 1930s, bebop of the 1940s, cool jazz of the 1950s, etc. Such simplistic schemes are, of course, easily sold because they are so easily impressed upon the popular mind, but they only vaguely reflect the realities of history.

Cultural Materialism

Karl Marx and Friedrich Engels considered that economic factors determine social structure and ultimately cultural expression, including the arts. From this perspective, the major forces that have determined analogies and differences in African-American cultures, including music, would appear to be economic. Cultural manifestations by African Americans are explained as a social response to particular socio-economic situations characterizing various time periods in New World cultures. Marvin Harris (1968, 22) for example, pointed out that the differences in race relations that could be observed in Brazil and the United States during the 1960s could never adequately be explained by stressing "Portuguese national character and Catholicism" versus "Anglo-Saxon racism and Protestantism." He proposed a cultural-materialist explanation that would start with "the ecological potential of colonial Brazil as compared with colonial North America, differences reflected in sugarcane plantations, as opposed to tobacco and cotton plantations." He also enumerated other factors, such as differences in migratory patterns and the more balanced sex ratio that existed among the English colonists in the U.S., as opposed to "a markedly unbalanced one among the Portuguese." Finally, he pointed to economic factors that dictated a different treatment in Brazil and the U.S. of the offspring of "miscegenation" with African slaves and to the totally different demographic pattern in the two countries during the early nineteenth century.[7]

By analogy, in the cultural-materalistic view, the rise of reggae music in Jamaica would have to be explained solely as resulting from a particular socio-economic situation during the 1970s and the economics of the international record market in that period (see Johnson and Pines 1982; Martin 1982). However, economic factors are better understood as catalytic.

6. My use of "fortuitous" here does not suggest any absence of causality. It simply means that the interface of incalculable factors creates patterns that we cannot predict and that those patterns tend to be chaotic.

7. For demographic development in Brazil from 1835 to 1890, see the figures in Kubik and Pinto (1994, 214).

Their importance and catalytic function in the rise of new musical forms in the United States can be demonstrated. After the invention of the cotton gin in 1793, cotton plantations began to be established profitably to the west of the Appalachian mountains, and with these developments came the transfer of many slave workers from South Carolina, Virginia, and other eastern states. That was the beginning of a development that culminated culturally in the rise of the blues during the last decades of the nineteenth century. To be sure, economics did not create the blues, but without the new social environment created in what was to be called the Deep South, through the establishment of large cotton plantations with relatively scattered settlements, the highly individualistic music called blues would probably not have emerged in the form it did.

Here it must be added that economic interdependence, even between antagonistic population segments, can also turn into a powerful integrative force. A current example is the rise of what is gradually assuming the shape of a "United States of Europe" through economic integration and monetary union, in spite of distinct cultural and language differences. Africa has provided brilliant examples of how interdependence between different population groups based on economic specialization has attenuated the probability of war and genocide. In the seventeenth and eighteenth centuries, the Bantu-speaking peoples who migrated into southeastern Angola eventually reached a state of peaceful coexistence with the autochthonous hunter-gatherer !Kung Bushmen through an economic symbiosis whereby each ethnic group contributes to a common market on the basis of technological skills the other group lacks. Technological exchanges also include music—musical instruments in particular. The !Kung Bushmen have adopted iron-age instruments such as lamellophones from the Bantu; the Bantu learned much from the Bushmen about the techniques of using certain musical bows. A similar example is provided by Bantu-Pygmy economic symbiosis in many parts of Central Africa. Bantu neighbors of the Pygmies have adopted the latter's polyphonic singing style, and the Pygmies adopted several musical instruments from the Bantu. In the New World, whatever ghastly structures of exploitation have been at work, African-American artists have successfully stepped into the limelight through specialized skills in music, dance, and theater that no one else could match. In turn, the development of African-American musical forms drawing on European as well as African traditions heavily determined the shape of mainstream American music.

Cultural Diffusionism

Interpretive schemes based on this model tend to explain analogies and differences in African-American cultures as resulting from different cultural transplantation patterns deriving from the various ethnic backgrounds of Africans deported to the New World during the slave trade. Thus, the presence of a strong Dahomeyan population element in Haiti accounts for the transplantation of Fō religious concepts such as *vodu* (Courlander 1962), while the presence of many Angolans in early nineteenth-century Brazil has been considered responsible for the numerous Angola-related traits in Brazilian music (Kubik 1979). Equally, most of the *candomblé* religious manifestations in Brazil have been identified as Yoruba (Nagô)-based or Ewe (Gêge)-based (Herskovits 1944; Merriam 1956–1957). With the deepening of our knowledge of both contemporary and past African cultures, culture-diffusionist schemes have recently gained in detail. Increasing attention has been given to the cognitive dimension, and concepts such as *vodu* and *òrìsà* in two different West African cultures have been semantically compared (Kubik 1996). From a generalizing, panoramic outlook linking African-American cultures vaguely to the African continent, the culture-diffusionist approach has evolved research models based on the strict use of historical methods, whether working with present-day field materials, the oral tradition, or archival sources (see, for example, Evans 1970, 1972, 1990, 1994; Kubik 1990, 1991b, 1993b; Pinto 1991).

Karl Wernhart (1994, 318) has emphasized that speculations about possible diffusion on the basis of cross-cultural analogies must be separated from factual, historically verified processes of human migration and cultural transplantation. There are two different methodological approaches to the question of diffusion: the first tries to diagnose diffusion through cross-cultural comparison of present-day culture traits; the other attempts to do so by cross-cultural comparison of contemporaneous historical sources from the areas in contact. It can be misleading, therefore, to include these very different approaches under one blanket term.

With regard to the first method, it is never sufficient merely to build the evidence on the criteria of *similarity of form* and *quantity of resemblances*, as systematically described by Fritz Graebner (1911, 108). Graebner's *Formkriterium* stated that similarities between two culture traits found in different places and not arising out of the nature, material, or purpose of the trait should be interpreted as the result of diffusion, regardless of the distances separating the two places. In addition, his *Quantitätskriterium* held that if more such parallels are found between the two cultures compared, the likelihood of contact and diffusion between them is increased.

As sound as these original proposals were, their validity depends on cultural stability. In order to show that a given culture trait is a conclusive *diagnostic marker* of a historical connection between two cultures that are now separate, one has to examine whether the particular trait in question could have been inherently stable over long periods. In social structure, the evidence is very difficult to procure. In music, certain pentatonic scales seem to have been stable in several African cultures for a long time; but transferred elsewhere, they can be easily projected upon and reinterpreted within a heptatonic framework, as the tonality of the blues demonstrates. In the realm of material culture, finally, characteristics such as the shape of drums, the type of resonators in xylophones, and the materials used can change quickly in history, depending on what is available locally for their construction and therefore on environmental factors. Such traits can be stable for a long time, but they can also change overnight in a radically new environment. They are therefore not very useful in building conclusive evidence for culture contact.

Conversely, the mathematics of so-called asymmetric time-line patterns in African music (see Fig. 4) is a realm that is immune to all social, cultural, and environmental influences (see Kubik 1979). Accentuation, mnemonic syllables, and instrumentation of the time-line patterns are all highly variable, but no one can change their intrinsic mathematical structure. Any such attempt simply destroys the pattern. African time-line patterns are therefore either transmitted or not transmitted. Their absence in the blues and virtually all U.S. African-American music (unless affected by Caribbean styles) and their selective presence in Afro-Brazilian, Afro-Cuban, and other cultures further south constitute one of the surest indicators of the historical connections of these African-American cultures to *specific* regions of Africa. Asymmetric time-line patterns are not found everywhere in Africa. They are concentrated on the Guinea Coast and in West-Central Africa and are characteristically absent in most of East Africa, in southernmost Africa (among both Khoisan and Bantu speakers), and in the western and central Sudan among speakers of Nilo-Saharan and Afro-Asiatic languages. The longest asymmetric time-line pattern (24 pulses) in the pyramid stump occurs among the Bangombe pygmies of the southwestern Central African Republic; this surprising discovery was made by ethnologist Maurice Djenda and me in 1966.

In material culture, comparisons based on form and quantity of resemblances have to be expanded by an assessment of technological complexity and uniqueness. The so-called *cord-and-peg tension* (Wieschhoff 1933, 15–16) is found in drums of the candomblé religion of Bahía, Brazil (see Fig. 5), as well as in the drums called *apinti* in Surinam. It is unique to the cultures of the Guinea Coast and can have been carried to these New

Kubik • Analogies and Differences   219

Figure 4. The mathematics of West and Central African asymmetric time-line patterns, shown as a pyramid stump

Cycle number	Pattern structure	Notation	Predominent geographical distribution
8	3+5	[x x • x • x x •]	Universal
12	5+7	[x • x x • x • x • x x •]	Guinea Coast, West-central Africa, Zambezi valley
16	7+9	[x • x • x x • x • x • x • x x •]	Central and West-Central Africa
20	9+11	[x • x • x • x x • x • x • x • x • x x •]	(no data available)
24	11+13	[x • x • x • x • x x • x • x • x • x • x • x x •]	Pygmies of the Upper Sangha (Central African Republic, Congo)

World places only by deportees from those areas in West Africa, especially speakers of Akan languages, Ewe, Fõ, or Yoruba. The name *apinti*, the Yoruba designation of a specific type of drum, hand-played and often used for talking (Laoye 1959, 10–11), is an additional indicator. Equally diagnostic is the presence in Brazil, Colombia, and Panama of drums showing the so-called *wedge-and-ring tension* (see Fig. 6). David Evans observed it also in and near Maracaibo in western Venezuela in 1996, with the ring made of rope (Evans 1997). This tension is native to the west-central region of the African continent, including southeastern Nigeria, southern Cameroon, Gabon, and parts of the Republic of Congo. Its presence in Freetown, Sierra Leone, is just as much a diaspora phe-

Figure 5. Cord-and-peg tension in drums played by Nagô and Gêge religious groups in Bahia

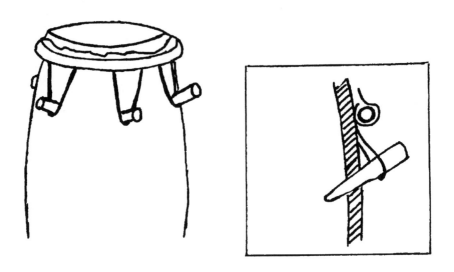

Figure 6. Wedge-and-ring tension in drums played by Congo religious groups in Bahia

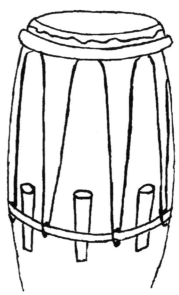

nomenon as is its presence in cultures of the New World, where it was transplanted with the slave trade. The general test for artifacts that can serve as diagnostic markers for historical connections between cultures that are now separated is their degree of technological complexity. The more complex an artifact is, the more unlikely is its multiple, independent invention and the more appropriate is its assessment as a diagnostic marker in a diffusionist explanatory scheme. Until we reach the stage of expressing technological complexity by a general mathematical formula which can then be correlated with the probability scale of unique versus multiple invention of a trait, this criterion can serve at least as a rule of thumb.

One feels tempted to call culture-diffusionist explanatory schemes the "organ transplant" model, which suggests both their merits and their deficiencies: transplanted organs can be beneficially assimilated by their new host, but they can also generate unexpected reactions in the new environment or be rejected entirely. A plain culture-diffusionist approach in African-American studies—unless it is applied comparatively to *several* African-American cultures—tends to emphasize identities and analogies while downplaying the differences. It is thought to give insufficient weight to the forces of adaptation and innovation that have characterized New World developments (wa Mukuna 1994; Martin 1991). Without at least a strong infusion of awareness of the "mechanisms" of culture contact as conceptualized, for example, by Herskovits (1938a) and recently expanded by David Evans' formulation of trends of "revival" on the basis of eclectic borrowings from elsewhere (Evans 1994), culture-diffusionist approaches are sometimes limited to the earliest stages of African-American cultural history.

Some Recommendations

It is obvious that the six theoretical interpretive models that I have summarized above lend themselves to combinations. In practice, very rarely have individual authors followed just one line of thought. Although each scheme can be submitted to decisive criticism, it would be an overreaction to deny any of them the legitimate right to exist. The purpose of my summary is to make my fellow scholars a little more aware of what we and our colleagues are actually doing and from what sorts of silent assumptions we sometimes proceed. One could further analyze the implications of each scheme in terms of competing perspectives: individualistic or collectivistic worldviews, factual-historical or idealized evolutionary assessments of events in time, belief in a purposeful or a fortuitous nature of history, whether or not there is anything like conscious and deliberate human decision (free will), or belief in "born-so" fatalism programmed by genes or, in John Locke's view of the human mind at birth as a "blank slate" on which the sociocultural environment then inscribes its unmistakable hieroglyphs.

Perhaps a reasonable starting position conducive to a realistic assessment of cultural development in the Americas during the past four hundred years is to keep the time dimension constantly in mind, regardless of the interpretive schemes adopted—and not only the American (or African-American) part of the story, but the simultaneous and interconnected African and European parts as well. Whether we realize it or not, from the early sixteenth century on, the whole world was being increasingly linked by a worldwide web of information exchange. Its carriers, in the absence of electronics, may have taken a little more time to reach their destinations, but they did reach them. A new musical fashion coming up in Luanda, Angola, in the 1750s could possibly have been heard in Rio de Janeiro or Lisbon six weeks later. There were probably few simple one-way transplants of cultural ideas without any returns in one form or another. For example, Pierre Verger (1968) has written of the flux and reflux of people and cultural commodities between the Gulf of Benin and Bahía, Brazil, in the sixteenth and seventeenth centuries. Dena Epstein (1973, 65–68) has uncovered some eighteenth- and early nineteenth-century sources that testify to the use of African musical instruments on slave ships for the purpose of "encouraging the captives to dance as a means of preserving their health." It is here that the myth of the Middle Passage as the cutting of an umbilical cord, followed by the victims' cultural amnesia, dissolves. The Americas were permanently connected to Africa and Europe from the sixteenth century onward by a two-way information highway that affected all the communities involved, with notable repercussions even in remote areas of the African interior.

Certainly, such understanding does not make our task easier. Reconstructing at least part of the ever-changing picture across the ages requires the meticulous application of historical methods, preferably working within one delimited period at a time, and with sources from both sides of the Atlantic. We simply cannot afford uncontrolled time-journeys in African-American studies.

Luckily, during the past thirty years historians and archeologists in Africa have uncovered an abundance of intra-African as well as external precolonial sources, so that periodic comparisons across the Atlantic are now often feasible. Where this is still not possible, a second comparative approach can be used, though with precautions concerning the projection of present-day data from either continent into the past. Whenever this path is chosen for the purpose of reconstructing and interpreting past sequences of events, one must be aware of the underlying assumption of *cultural stability*. Anthropological research cannot subscribe *a priori* to that assumption; on the contrary, from the study of factual data we have learned that cultures around the world are naturally unstable and have always been. They drift from one configuration into another. Change is, therefore, an inherent cultural phenomenon. Another stunning observation has been stressed recently (Kubik 1994a, 17), namely, that individuals do not necessarily belong to one and the same culture from cradle to grave. Individual cultural profiles can change considerably during one's lifetime. Processes of enculturation are in principle lifelong, and the learning processes released by any culture contact can be compared to the enculturation experienced by individuals earlier in their lives. Anyone who has done fieldwork in language communities other than the one in which he or she grew up is bound to realize sooner or later that with every acquisition of a foreign language one's overall inner cognitive landscape changes.

The study of culture contact and transculturation in any area of the world, including the Americas, is bound to be deficient if one proceeds from a concept of rigid cultural membership and a monolithic model of culture to analyze "miscegenation," "hybridism," "dialogue" (a surrogate term that became fashionable during the 1970s), or simply "contact." Culture understood from that viewpoint is at best a nonoperational, shadowy concept. It is devalued outright by the simple, observable fact that any culture, whether of the present or the past, is multicultural: at every stage of its history, it is the result of forces of invention, borrowing, reinterpretation, and innovation. The very word "hybrid," borrowed from genetics, loses its qualifying capacity from the moment one realizes that all cultures have never been anything else.

One can, of course, trace where such and such a trait in an actual cultural configuration comes from, and possibly even where it originated, thereby splitting a culture into interactive functional components. An example of a longstanding transculturation process that occurred in Africa is the city of Luanda, founded by Paulo Dias de Novais in 1575, which over a period of four centuries developed a distinctive culture with reinterpreted Portuguese and Kimbundu elements of various periods of history. Luanda is different from any other culture area of Angola or Portugal.

The learnability of culture is also vividly demonstrated by the phenomenon of "cultural drift," i.e., the shifting of distribution areas of cultural goods, technology, and single traits, often by chance. All these can migrate from one population group into another or from one social stratum to another during any given historical period. The versions of

224   BMR Journal

African xylophones in the New World present an instructive example of migration of African cultural goods and technologies into the Amerindian population (Garfias 1983; Kubik and Pinto 1994). Richard Graham (1994) has presented another case of instrumental migration in his analysis of African-derived musical bows and playing techniques (as well as the presence of the banjo) in Euro-American communities of the Appalachian mountains. Graham's observations are not surprising, in view of the relative proximity of this area to South Carolina, where African descendants were concentrated in the eighteenth century (see also Epstein 1973, 62).

When people are transplanted from one cultural environment to another, the new environment always initially tends to challenge and weaken old patterns of behavior, pressing for their modification. The individual transplanted into a different cultural environment is suddenly faced with alternatives to familiar modes of behavior. This may be experienced by some as threatening to deeply entrenched attitudes, traditions, and structures, but by others as liberating them from these forces. Individual reactions can range from enthusiastic acceptance to total rejection. A crucial factor in determining the outcome is how the "receiving" culture reacts to the newcomer. Viewed from the theoretical framework of psychoanalysis, it appears that every cultural encounter is accompanied by projections of one's unconscious onto the other group (Kubik 1991a, 325). The outcome depends on what kind of content is projected. Culture contact, therefore, is always to be understood as an encounter on parallel psychological levels: the conscious and the unconscious. For example, conscious rejection of the "other" is quite often accompanied by secret, unconscious identification with the rejected "other." Many cultural encounters are therefore characterized by an ambivalence that is difficult to dismantle.

The history of African-American cultures in this hemisphere is a history of many different cultural encounters. Phenomenologically, any culture contact, and all that results from it, is just one variant in the panorama of all forms of group interaction. In the absence of a scientifically useful definition of "culture," in fact, we are liberated from the constraints of an all-too-narrow definition of acculturation. We discover that the same psychological patterns of interactive behavior rule all kinds of contact between groups, irrespective of size and content. Whether we are considering group formations based on profession, gender, age, religion, genealogy, or any other organizational criteria appropriate to a stratified society, or large groups such as communities speaking the same language, nationalities, and nations, the observable patterns of interaction are psychologically identical.

Thus, even if "culture" is a misty or fuzzy concept, this does not hurt our research attempt, so long as we know it. We can continue to do cultural research, using the term loosely, as long as we realize that what we are actually studying are oscillating groups of people and their ever-changing interactions. Free of dogmatic concepts, we can then simply define each interacting group empirically, within the changing landscape of time and space, by its momentary state. Instead of proceeding deductively from undefinable sociological jargon, we can look at the language/culture profile of specific groups with accountable memberships, preferably on a small scale, and try to delineate each group's characteristics, the beliefs shared by its adherents, its economic basis, its institutions, its habits and customs, and its value systems determining normative behavior. If the group interacts frequently with a different one, we can repeat the same data-gathering process with the contact group and possibly elicit prevalent patterns of interaction. Ideally, if we have understood the meanings of these interactions in depth, it should then be possible to test our findings by trying to predict what sort of interactions between the two groups will take place in the near future.

Analogies and differences in African-American cultures across the hemisphere can be understood as the result of a complex interplay between social, economic, psychological, and other factors spread out along four dimensions in space and time. This ever-changing picture can be analyzed—on the basis of written, pictorial, artifactual, and aural sources—more effectively if current methods and interpretive schemes are employed within the framework of a new scientific consciousness that includes self-analysis.

REFERENCES

Begley, Sharon. 1997. Infidelity and the science of cheating. *Newsweek* (January 6):33–65.

Boone, Benjamin V. 1994. A new perspective on the origin of the blues and blue notes: A documentation of blues-like speech. Paper presented at the Conference on America's Blues Culture and Heritage, University of North Florida, Jacksonville.

Courlander, Harold. 1962. *The drum and the hoe: Life and lore of the Haitian people.* Berkeley: University of California Press.

Douglas, Mary, ed. 1966. *Thought styles: Critical essays on good taste.* London: Sage.

Eibl-Eibesfeldt, Irenäus. 1972. *Die !Ko-Buschmann-Gesellschaft: Gruppenbindun̦ ·d Aggressionskontrolle bei einem Jäger- und Sammlervolk.* Munich: Piper.

Epstein, Dena. 1973. African music in British and French America. *Musical Quarterly* 59, no. 1:61–91.

———. 1977. *Sinful tunes and spirituals.* Urbana: University of Illinois Press.

Evans, David. 1970. Afro-American one-stringed instruments. *Western Folklore* 29:229–245.

———. 1972. Black fife and drum music in Mississippi. *Mississippi Folklore Register* 6:94–107.

Evans, David. 1990. African contributions to America's musical heritage. *The World and I* 5, no. 1:628–639.

———. 1994. The music of Eli Owens: African music in transition in southern Mississippi. In *For Gerhard Kubik: Festschrift on the occasion of his 60th birthday*, edited by August Schmidhofer and Dietrich Schüller, 329–359. Frankfurt: Peter Lang.

———. 1997. Personal conversation with the author, March 1.

Garfias, Robert. 1983. The marimba of Mexico and Central America. *Latin American Music Review* 4, no. 2 (Fall/Winter):203–228.

Gibbs, W. Wayt. 1997. A matter of language: The popular debate over Ebonics belies decades of linguistic research. *Scientific American* 276, no. 3 (March):18–20.

Graebner, Fritz. 1911. *Methode der Ethnologie*. Heidelberg: Karl Winters Universitätsbuchhandlung.

Graham, Richard. 1994. Ethnicity, kinship, and transculturation: African-derived mouth bows in European-American mountain communities. In *For Gerhard Kubik: Festschrift on the occasion of his 60th birthday*, edited by August Schmidhofer and Dietrich Schüller, 361–380. Frankfurt: Peter Lang.

Haley, Alex. 1976. *Roots: The saga of an American family*. Garden City, N.Y.: Doubleday.

Harris, Marvin. 1968. *The rise of anthropological theory*. London: Routledge and Kegan Paul.

Herskovits, Frances, ed. 1973. *Cultural relativism*. New York: Random House.

Herskovits, Melville J. 1938a. *Acculturation: The study of culture contact*. New York: J. J. Augustin.

———. 1938b. *Dahomey: An ancient kingdom*. 2 vols. New York: J. J. Augustin.

———. 1941. *The myth of the Negro past*. Boston: Harper and Brothers.

———. 1944. Drums and drummers in Afro-Brazilian cult life. *Musical Quarterly* 30, no. 4:477–492.

———. 1948. *Man and his works*. New York: Alfred Knopf.

Horgan, John. 1996. Trends in psychology: Why Freud isn't dead. *Scientific American* 275, no. 6 (December):74–79.

Johnson, Howard, and Jim Pines. 1982. *Reggae: Deep roots music*. London: Proteus.

Kremser, Manfred. 1993. Organizing charity since slavery: The example of the rivaling St. Lucian flower societies "La Rose" and "La Marguerite." In *Slavery in the Americas*, edited by Wolfgang Binder, 305–316. Würzburg: Könighauser and Neumann.

Kubik, Gerhard. 1979. *Angolan traits in black music, games and dances of Brazil: A study of African cultural extensions overseas*. Estudos de Antropologia Cultural, no. 10. Lisbon: Junta de Investigações Científicas do Ultramar.

———. 1989. *Musikgeschichte in Bildern: Westafrika*. Leipzig: Deutscher Verlag für Musik.

———. 1990. Drum patterns in the "Batuque" of Benedito Caxias. *Latin American Music Review* 11, no. 2:115–181.

———. 1991a. Documentation in the field: Scientific strategies and the psychology of culture contact. In *Music in the dialogue of cultures: Traditional music and cultural policy*, edited by Max-Peter Baumann, 318–335. Intercultural Music Studies, no. 2. Wilhelmshaven: Florian Noetzel.

———. 1991b. *Extensionen afrikanischer Kulturen in Brasilien*. Aachen: Alano Verlag.

———. 1993a. U.S. diary notes, January–February. Held at the Oral Literature Research Programme, Chileka, Malawi.

———. 1993b. Transplantation of African musical cultures into the New World. In *Slavery in the Americas*, edited by Wolfgang Binder, 421–452. Würzburg: Könighauser and Neumann.

———. 1994a. Ethnicity, cultural identity and the psychology of culture contact. In *Music and black ethnicity*, edited by Gerard Béhague, 17–46. New Brunswick, N.J.: Transaction Publishers.

———. 1994b. Das "ethnische" Panorama Ostangolas und der Nachbargebiete. *Baessler-Archiv*, n.s., 42:25–59.

Kubik, Gerhard. 1995. Kindheit in außereuropäischen Kulturen: Forschungs-probleme, -methoden und -ergebnisse. In *Kinderwelten: Pädagogische, ethnologische und literaturwissenschaftliche Annäherungen*, edited by Erich Renner, 148–166. Weinheim: Deutscher Studien Verlag.

———. 1996. West African and African-American concepts of *vodu* and *òrìsà*. In *Ay Bobo: African-Caribbean religions*, edited by Manfred Kremser. Vol. 2, *Voodoo*, 17–34. Vienna: WUV.

Kubik, Gerhard, and Tiago de Oliveira Pinto. 1994. Afroamerikanische Musik. In *Die Musik in Geschichte und Gegenwart* 1:194–261. Kassel: Bärenreiter.

Laoye I, Timi of Ede. 1959. Yoruba drums. *Odu: A Journal of Yoruba and Related Studies* (Ibadan) 7:5–14.

Leland, John, and Joseph Nadine. 1997. Education: Hooked on Ebonics. *Newsweek* (January 13):50–51.

Martin, Denis-Constant. 1982. *Aux sources du reggae: Musique, société et politique en Jamaïque*. Marseille: Parentheses.

———. 1991. Filiation or innovation? Some hypotheses to overcome the dilemma of Afro-American music's origins. *Black Music Research Journal* 11, no. 1:19–38.

Mecklenburg, Carl Gregor Herzog zu, and Waldemar Scheck. 1963. *Die Theorie des Blues im modernen Jazz*. Strasbourg: Heitz.

Merriam, Alan P. 1956–1957. Songs of the Ketu cult of Bahía, Brazil. *African Music* 1, no. 3:53–67; 1, no. 4:73–80.

Ortiz, Fernando. 1940. *Contrapunteo cubano del tabaco y el azúcar*. Havana: J. Montero.

Pinto, Tiago de Oliveira. 1991. *Capoeira, Samba, Candomblé: Afro-Brasilianische Musik im Recôncavo, Bahia*. Berlin: Museum für Völkerkunde.

Renner, Erich, ed. 1995. *Kinderwelten: Pädagogische, ethnologische und literaturwissenschaftliche Annäherungen*. Weinheim: Deutscher Studien Verlag.

Richburg, Keith B. 1997. *Out of America: A black man confronts Africa*. New York: Basic Books.

Riesman, Paul. 1993. Stimmt Freud in Afrika? Über das Verhältnis von Erziehung und Person. In *Kinder: Ethnologische Forschungen in fünf Kontinenten*, edited by Marie-José van de Loo and Margarete Reinhart, 157–183. Munich: Trickster Verlag.

Spindler, Paul. 1988. Ethologie. In *Neues Wörterbuch der Völkerkunde*, edited by Walter Hirschberg, 137. Berlin: Reimer.

Trudgill, Peter. 1974. *Sociolinguistics: An introduction to language and society*. Harmondsworth: Penguin.

Verger, Pierre. 1968. *Flux et reflux de la traite des nègres entre le golfe de Bénin et Bahia de Todos os Santos du dix-septième au dix-neuvième siècle*. Paris: Monton.

wa Mukuna, Kazadi. 1994. Resilience and transformation in varieties of African musical elements in Latin America. In *For Gerhard Kubik: Festschrift on the occasion of his 60th birthday*, edited by August Schmidhofer and Dietrich Schüller, 405–412. Frankfurt: Peter Lang.

Wernhart, Karl R. 1994. Zur Bedeutung der Kulturübertragung für die Erforschung Afro-Amerikas. In *For Gerhard Kubik: Festschrift on the occasion of his 60th birthday*, edited by August Schmidhofer and Dietrich Schüller, 317–327. Frankfurt: Peter Lang.

Williams, Juan. 1992. What the author of "Roots" wanted to trace for us all. *International Herald Tribune* February 21:5.

Wieschhoff, Heinz. 1933. *Die afrikanischen Trommeln und ihre außerafrikanischen Beziehungen*. Stuttgart: Strecker and Schröder.

[4]

Love and Theft:
The Racial Unconscious
of Blackface Minstrelsy

ERIC LOTT

I

THE BOUNDARIES SEPARATING black and white American cultures in the nineteenth century were marked most vividly along the lines of property and sexuality. Traffic in slave commodities was as defining a racial practice as the preservation of white racial purity. The blackface minstrel show, we now commonly believe, dedicated itself to staging or constructing these boundaries. Eclectic in origin, primitive in execution, and raucous in effect, a theatrical affair principally of the urban North, minstrelsy has been summed up as, in Alexander Saxton's words, "half a century of inurement to the uses of white supremacy."[1] While it was organized around the quite explicit "borrowing" of black cultural materials for white dissemination (and profit), a borrowing that ultimately depended upon the material relations of slavery, the minstrel show obscured these relations by pretending that slavery was amusing, right, and natural. Though it arose from a white obsession with black (male) bodies that underlies white racial dread to our own day, it ruthlessly disavowed its fleshly investments through ridicule and racist lampoon. Yet I am not so sure that this is the end of the story. In light of recent work on race that proceeds from postmodern accounts of subjectivity, we probably ought to take these facts and processes as merely a starting orientation for inquiry into the great complexities of racism and raced subjects in the United States.[2] In the following pages, I want to put some of this work to use in the area of blackface, the first, formative public or institutional acknowledgment by whites of black culture. In doing so I hope to show that blackface performance arose from and embodied what we might call a mid-nineteenth-century "racial unconscious"—a structured formation, combining thought and feeling, tone and impulse, and at the very edge of semantic availability, whose symptoms and anxieties make it just legible.[3] A reading of these symptoms and anxieties suggests, contrary to current wisdom, that blackface minstrelsy was based on small but significant crimes against settled ideas of racial demarcation, which indeed appear to be inevitable when white Americans enter the haunted realm of racial fantasy. Ultimately I am after some sense of how precariously nineteenth-century white people lived their own whiteness. This will later involve an argument about the uses of ethnography in the historical study of readers and audiences.

Of course there is no doubt that blackface witnessed the efficient expropriation of the cultural commodity "blackness"—a fact well demonstrated in an 1867 *Atlantic Monthly* article rather hypothetically recounting blackface "originator" T. D. Rice's first blackface performance, in Pittsburgh in around 1830.[4] Confronted one day with the dazzling spectacle of black singing, the story goes, Rice saw his "opportunity" and determined to take advantage of his talent for mimicry. Fortunately, intones *Atlantic* writer Robert P. Nevin, "There was a negro in attendance at Griffith's Hotel, on Wood Street, named Cuff,—an exquisite specimen of his sort,—who won a precarious subsistence by letting his open mouth as a mark for boys to pitch pennies into, at three paces, and by carrying the trunks of passengers from the steamboats to the hotels." After some persuasion, "Cuff" agrees to accompany the actor to the theater. There Rice blacks his face, orders Cuff to disrobe, and "invest[s] himself in the cast-off apparel." As Nevin puts it, on stage "the extraordinary apparition produced an instant effect."

At this point something very curious happens, and it bears quoting at length. A steamer appears on the Monongahela Wharf, and Cuff—"who meanwhile was crouching in dishabille under concealment of a projecting *flat* behind the performer"—begins to think of his livelihood:

Between himself and others of his color in the same line of business, and especially as regarded a certain formidable competitor called Ginger, there existed an active rivalry in the baggage-carrying business. For Cuff to allow Ginger the advantage of an undisputed descent upon the luggage of the approaching vessel would be not only to forget all "considerations" from the passengers, but, by proving him a laggard in his calling, to cast a damaging blemish upon his reputation. Liberally as he might lend himself to a friend, it could not be done at that sacrifice. After a minute or two of fidgety waiting for [Rice's] song to end, Cuff's patience could endure no longer, and, cautiously hazarding a glimpse of his profile beyond the edge of the flat, he called in a hurried whisper: "Massa Rice, Massa Rice, must have my clo'se! Massa Griffif wants me,—steamboat's comin'!"

The appeal was fruitless. Massa Rice did not hear it, for a happy hit at an unpopular city functionary had set the audience in a roar in which all other sounds were lost.... [Another appeal went unheeded, when,] driven to desperation, and forgetful in the emergency of every sense of propriety, Cuff, in ludicrous undress as he was, started from his place, rushed upon the stage, and, laying his hand upon the performer's shoulder, called out excitedly: "Massa Rice, Massa Rice, gi' me nigga's hat,—nigga's coat,—nigga's shoes,—gi' me nigga's t'ings! Massa Griffif wants 'im,—STEAMBOAT'S COMIN'!!"

The incident was the touch, in the mirthful experience of that night, that passed endurance. (609–10)

This passage, in all its woozy syntax and headlong rush, is probably the least trustworthy and most accurate account of American minstrelsy's appropriation of black culture. Indeed it reads something like a master text of the racial economy encoded in blackface performance. For one thing, it calls on minstrel devices (ventriloquized dialect, racial burlesque) to narrate the origins of minstrelsy, as if this particular narratable event generated or secreted "naturally" the formal means appropriate to it; its multiple frames (minstrelsy within minstrelsy) amount to so many techniques of black subordination. True to form, a diminished, not to say "blackfaced" Cuff has replaced Rice as this account's center of attention. And its talk of opportunity and investment, lending and ownership, subsistence and competition is more preoccupied with cultural value than we might have expected. Its racial unconscious, we might say, reveals a great deal of anxiety about the "primitive accumulation" it ostensibly celebrates.[5] The fascination with Cuff's nakedness, moreover, highlights this as an affair of male bodies, where racial conflict and cultural exchange are negotiated between men. Cuff's stripping, a theft that silences and embarrasses him on stage but which nevertheless entails both his bodily presence in the show and the titillating threat that he may return to demand his stolen capital, is a neat allegory for the most prominent commercial collision of black and white cultures in the nineteenth century. The cultural expropriation that formed one central drama of the boundary-staging minstrel show was already an unsettled matter of racial intercourse and an injection of "blackness" into the public sphere. But this simultaneous construction and transgression of racial boundaries is something that itself needs explaining, as one performer's enthusiasm for his blackface act suggests: "I shall be rich in black fun."[6]

A strong white fascination with black men and black culture, that is to say, underwrote this popular expropriation. Blackface performers were conspicuously intrigued with the street singers and obscure characters from whom they allegedly took the material that was later fashioned to racist ends. There are several accounts of these men's attraction to their "donors," and it is no wonder that an aura of illicit sexuality—nineteenth-century observers called it "vulgarity"—shadowed the most chaste of minstrel shows.[7] From the start it appeared that a sort of generalized illicitness was indeed one of minstrelsy's main objectives. So much is suggested, at least, by the lengths to which reviews and playbills typically went to downplay (even as they intimated) its licentious atmosphere:

First Night of the novel, grotesque, original, and surpassingly melodious ethiopian band, entitled the VIRGINIA MINSTRELS. Being an exclusively musical entertainment, combining the banjo, violin, bone castanetts, and tambourine; and entirely exempt from the vulgarities and other objectionable features, which have hitherto characterized negro extravaganzas.[8]

One wants to know more about those other objectionable features. Whatever they were, no one took very seriously their alleged absence from the minstrel show, as an 1843 songsheet illustration of the Virginia Minstrels only begins to suggest (fig. 1). Frank Brower the bone player with legs splayed wide; Dick Pelham on the

FIGURE 1. Sheet music cover, *The Celebrated Negro Melodies*, 1843.
Photo: Harvard Theater Collection, Cambridge, Mass.

verge of forced entry of the tambourine; Billy Whitlock in ecstasy behind a phallic banjo: there is no attempt at realism here. The whole scene has rather the air of a collective masturbation fantasy—true enough, we might guess, in capturing the overall spirit of the show. That spirit depended at the very least on the suggestion of black male sexual misdemeanor, and the character of white men's involvement in this institutional Other of genteel culture will bear some scrutiny. While in Rice's act alone one might have seen predominantly black dancing set to music of the British Isles (often Irish jigs) with lyrics of a more or less racist nature, audiences appear to have believed the counterfeit (as we shall see), often so as to border on sexual fervor or, alternately, distaste.[9]

We ought to make some sense of these obfuscations, the hints and denials of vulgarity, the uneasy affirmations of cultural exchange. This language was aimed at a racial structure whose ideological and psychological instability required its boundaries continually to be staged, and which regularly exceeded the dominant culture's capacity to fix such boundaries. Indeed the very notion of secure racial markers, Stuart Hall has argued, is displaced when one acknowledges the constitution of white subjectivity by the constant coupling or complex play of racial fear and desire, "othering" and identification, ambivalence and attraction; at any moment, as in the examples above, the "surreptitious return" of desire or guilt may unsettle the whole business.[10] In blackface minstrelsy this dynamic often tilted toward transgression. Of course I take for granted the casual and undocumentable racial intercourse that creolized black cultural forms as it "blackened" the dominant culture, a process that in one sense makes it difficult to talk about racial transgression at all. Yet in the antebellum years a kind of raw commodification was the economic context out of which blackface display emerged, and this display, in turn, depended upon the dangerous, imaginary proximity of "raced" bodies. My subject here is the affective consequences of that proximity—an affair of dollars and desire, theft and love.

II

The form of the early minstrel show (1843 to the 1860s) underscores the white fascination with commodified "black" bodies. What minstrelsy was not is as important as what it was. Narrative, for instance, seems only to have been a secondary impulse, even though T. D. Rice's blackface burlesque afterpieces were tremendous successes in the 1830s. In their first performances, the Virginia Minstrels gave what they termed "Negro Concerts," containing certain burlesque skits, to be sure, but emphasizing wit and melody; the skits themselves, like Dan Emmett's "Dan Tucker on Horseback," seemed little more than overgrown circus acts.[11] An 1844 playbill publicizing a "Vocal, Local, Joke-all, and Instrumental Concert" conveys both the tenor and the substance of early minstrel shows.[12] In

"sporting saloons" and indeed circuses, among other New York working-class leisure sites, the Virginia Minstrels featured burlesque lectures, conundrums,
equestrian scenes, and comic songs, finally settling into an early version of the
show form that would become standard minstrel procedure. The evening was
divided in two; both parts consisted mainly of ensemble songs interspersed with
solo banjo songs, and were strung together with witticisms, ripostes, shouts, puns,
and other attempts at Negro impersonation. There was as yet no high-minded
"interlocutor" at whom some of the jokes were later directed.[13] Very soon the
program's first part came to center on the "northern dandy negro," while its
second put the "plantation darky" at center stage. In the late 1840s and early
1850s, as the first part began to be devoted to more sentimental music (sometimes
performed without blackface), Emmett's and other companies added a stirring
middle or "olio" section containing a variety of acts (among them a "stump
speech"), the third part then often comprised of a skit situated in the South.
Seated in a semi-circle, the Emmett troupe placed the bone and tambourine
players at either end of the band, and though originally all were comic performers, these two "endmen" began to assume chief importance in most minstrel
companies, particularly after the addition of the interlocutor—genteel in com-
portment and, popular myth notwithstanding, in blackface.[14]

The early emphasis was on what film theorists have called "spectacle" rather
than narrative. The first minstrel shows put narrative to a variety of *uses*, but it
relied first and foremost on the objectification of black characters in comic set
pieces, repartee, physical burlesque. The primary purpose of early blackface performance was to display the "black" male body, to fetishize it in a spectacle that
worked against the forward motion of the show and froze "the flow of action in
moments of erotic contemplation," as Laura Mulvey has written of women in
cinema.[15] With all their riot and commotion, contortion and pungency, performers in these shows exhibited a static, functional unruliness that, in one commentator's words, "seemed animated by a savage energy," nearly wringing
minstrel men off their seats—their "white eyes roll[ing] in a curious frenzy" and
their "hiccupping chuckles" punctuating the proceedings.[16] Here was an art of
performative irruption, of acrobatics and comedy, ostensibly dependable mechanisms of humorous pleasure.[17] "Black" figures were there *to be looked at*, shaped
to the demands of desire; they were screens on which audience fantasy could rest,
securing white spectators' position as superior, controlling, not to say owning,
figures. Behind all of the circumlocution going on in descriptions of blackface
performance, then, we must begin to glimpse the white male traffic in racial degradation whose cardinal principle was yet a supreme disorderly conduct—a
revealingly equivocal means of racial containment.

In this affair, "blackness" provided the inspiration as well as the occasion for
preposterously violent, sexual, or otherwise prohibited theatrical material that
evinced how unsettling was the black power white performers intended to sub-

jugate. Even the ugly vein of hostile wish-fulfillment in blackface songs reads as a sort of racial panic rather than confident racial power (though, to be sure, the result was hegemonic enough). One notes in particular the relentless transformation of black characters into things, as though to clinch the property relations these songs fear are too fluid. The sheer overkill of songs in which black men are roasted, fished for, smoked like tobacco, peeled like potatoes, planted in the soil, or dried and hung up as advertisements is surely suspicious; these murderous fantasies barely conceal the vulnerability they mask, are refined down to perfect examples of protesting far too much. Here is "Gib Us Chaw Tobacco" (early 1850s):

> Natur planted a black baby,
> To grow dis weed divine,
> Dat's de reason why de niggers
> Am made a 'baccy sign.[18]

Although this verse comes on in the mimed accents of a cut-rate Aesop, self-buttressing fairy tales like the above are so baroque that one imagines their concoction requiring a considerable amount of anxious attention. They are not unlike the "atrocious misrepresentations" (as John Quincy Adams called them) in the infamously rigged 1840 U.S. Census, its imagined North populated with frightful hordes of black lunatics and idiots.[19] Indeed, in "My Ole Dad" (early 1850s), the ridiculous titular figure mistakenly throws his washing in the river and hangs himself on the line; he goes in after his clothes but drowns. His son subsequently uses fishing line to catch him, a bloated ghost who returns at song's end, interestingly enough, to haunt his mistress.[20] In the realm of blackface impersonation, one might say, the house was always haunted, the disavowals never enough to halt the enslaved Other's encroachment upon white self-identity; the continual turn to the mask itself, its obvious usefulness, suggests as much.

Some songs came even closer to the heart of the matter. More successfully prophylactic than "My Ole Dad" is "Ole Tater Peelin" (early 1850s):

> Oh, yaller Sam, turn'd a nigger hater,
> Ah, oo! ah, oo!
> An' his skin peeled off like boiled potatoe,
> Ah, oo! ah, oo![21]

The protagonist of this little rhyme is called "tater peelin"; blacks snub him because he becomes colorless, neither "yellow, blue, nor black." Finally hogs eat him, and plant his bones. It is difficult to say whether one's speechlessness before this sort of thing owes more to its merciless brutality or its perverse inventiveness. In any case, the concern with fluid, not to say skinless, ego boundaries, together with the imagined introjection of objectified black people, acknowledges precisely the fragility of the racial boundaries the song attempts to police. Obviously the

The Racial Unconscious of Blackface Minstrelsy   29

dilemma of "race" is a matter of the marking not of white people themselves but only, in particular, of the liminal "yaller" produced by intermixture, signifier of the crossed line, of racial trespass. In such songs it is as though whites were at a loss for language to embody the anxiety that in effect constituted the color line, and this indicates how extreme the consequent defensiveness must have been.

Often this essentially reifying effort in the minstrel show ran up against more intimate dangers. To get the force of those charges of "vulgarity," one must attend to the way certain material—and, we should recall, performers themselves— pressed home a sort of violent corporeal reality, as in the following stump speech (1849):

> Den I 'gin to sweat so ... I sweat half de clothes off my back—tumbled ober a sweat-cloth— took a bite ob dar steaks in de bottom ob my pocket—and absquatulated, just for all de world like a California feverite when he's bound for de gold region![22]

Or consider this white man's bad (if not wet) dream, "Astonishing Nose" (1859):

> Like an elephant's trunk it reached to his toes,
> An wid it he would gib some most astonishing blows
> . . . .
> No one dare come near, so great was his might
> . . . .
> He used to lie in his bed, wid his nose on de floor,
> An when he slept sound his nose it would snore,
> Lik a dog in a fight—'twas a wonderful nose,
> An it follows him about wherever he goes.
>
> De police arrested him one morning in May,
> For obstructing de sidewalk, having his nose in de way.
> Dey took him to de court house, dis member to fine;
> When dey got dere de nose hung on a tavern sign.[23]

The immediacy of the object supervising a loss of the spectatorial subject—the anointing of an unsettled spectator with mud and manure, the blows of disembodied phalluses directed against the Law—seems immanent in the "objectionable features" (to recall the first shows of the Virginia Minstrels) of blackface representation. Why indeed might this have been pleasurable at all? Fredric Jameson has noted that fear, "the aesthetic reception of fear ... the enjoyment of the shock and commotion fear brings to the human organism," is well-nigh central to the experience of pleasure.[24] From eighteenth-century notions of the sublime to Roland Barthes's *jouissance*, Jameson argues, the dissolution of the subject in a paroxysm of threatened menace constitutes one way of transforming "sheer horror" into "libidinal gratification." How much more must this have been the case when, as in minstrelsy, the horror itself was based on a libidinal economy; when precisely the threat of blackface acts was their promised undoing of white male sexual sanctity. If all the hilarity here seems suspicious, it is perhaps because it was both a denial and a pleasurable conversion of a hysterical set of racial fears. Images of the body may be of particular help in this project, offering a symbolic map of psychic, spatial, and social relationships, or a site for the particular concerns of these realms to be secured or dissolved.[25] By way of the protuberant, "grotesque" blackface body, which, in the words of Peter Stallybrass and Allon White, denied "with a laugh the ludicrous pose of autonomy adopted by the subject at the same moment as it re-open[ed]" the normally repressive boundaries of bodily orifices (183–84), the white subject could transform fantasies of racial assault and subversion into riotous pleasure, turn insurrection and intermixture into harmless fun—though the outlines of the fun disclose its troubled sources.[26] Minstrelsy's joking focus on disruptions and infractions of the flesh amounted to a kind of theatrical dream-work, displacing and condensing those fears, imaged in the "black" body, that could neither be forgotten nor fully acknowledged.[27]

The overdetermined nature of these fears comes through in Mark Twain's reminiscences of blackface. For the way in which he chooses to celebrate the "genuine nigger show"—he devotes an entire chapter in his autobiography to it—is through a complicated narrative that involves escorting his mother to a Christy's Minstrels performance in St. Louis. This doubled comic situation, in which Twain pays tribute to the fun of blackface acts by a dose of superadded humor at his mother's expense, not only places Twain himself in the position of son but evokes from him a certain amount of oedipal hostility. His mother is a woman of the church, and while she delights in all sorts of novelties she must also square these with her religious proclivities. She was, writes Twain, "always ready for Fourth of July processions, Sunday-school processions, lectures, conventions, camp meetings, revivals in the church—in fact, for any and every kind of dissipation that could not be proven to have anything irreligious about it."[28] Twain means to immerse his mother in some real dissipation—a desacralizing impulse on the part of the son inspired by the unease minstrelsy has provoked in the writer.

Twain gets his mother and one Aunt Betsey Smith to go to the minstrel show by telling them it is an exhibition of African music by some lately returned missionaries:

When the grotesque negroes [Twain here gets carried away with his own conceit] came filing out on the stage in their extravagant costumes, the old ladies were almost speechless with astonishment. I explained to them that the missionaries always dressed like that in Africa.

But Aunt Betsey said, reproachfully, "But they're niggers." (62)

Of course the novices are soon merrily enjoying themselves, "their consciences . . . quiet now, quiet enough to be dead," Twain writes. They gaze on "that long curved line of artistic mountebanks with devouring eyes" (63), finally reinvigorating with their laughter the whole house's response to a stale joke from the endmen. As is so often the case in accounts of the minstrel show, Twain's actually

The Racial Unconscious of Blackface Minstrelsy   31

reproduces standard elements of blackface joking, here at the expense of blacks
and women both. Indeed the linking of these humorous objects is registered in
the syntactical ambiguity as to who possesses the devouring eyes, and this double
threat, along with the aggression Twain aims at his mother, points toward the
sources of pleasure involved. Twain's enjoyment of blackface fooling and funning
arises from a source of humor Freud calls "degradation to being a child."[29] This,
of course, was neither the first nor the last time an ambivalent white male attraction to blacks, (self-) degradation, and infantile pleasure were conjoined by way
of an imaginary racial Other.

One might speculate with Melanie Klein that Twain's infant sadism owed to
blackface's engendering of a longing for oral bliss whose absence he felt was his
mother's fault and the "devouring" privilege of which was hers alone.[30] The black
and female goads to such extreme ambivalence naturally came together in blackface representations of black women, who generally fared far worse than Twain's
mother. "Lubly Fan" (1844) offers one of the most famous examples. (Twain has
Jim sing "Lubly Fan" in chapter 2 of *Tom Sawyer*—a scene that again conjoins the
naked powers of blackness and femaleness: Jim sings the song as he discovers
Tom painting his aunt's fence in punishment for his truancy.) The reader will
recognize "Lubly Fan" as "Buffalo Gals," though not, perhaps, its original lyrics:

> Den lubly Fan will you cum out to night,
> > Will you cum out to night,
> > Will you cum out to night,
> Den lubly Fan will you cum out to night,
> An dance by de lite ob de moon.
>
> I stopt her an I had some talk,
> > Had some talk,
> > Had some talk,
> But her foot covered up de whole side-walk
> An left no room for me. . . .
>
> Her lips are like de oyster plant,
> > De oyster plant,
> > De oyster plant,
> I try to kiss dem but I cant,
> Dey am so berry large.[31]

The singer on the Smithsonian Institution's collection of popular American music
gets the ambiguous, almost uncontainable edge of that rising last phrase exactly
right.[32] "Dey am so berry large": allusive promise and exaggerated threat; desire
so deep and consequential that it scarcely bears uttering, revulsion so necessary
that utterance is ineludible.

What Mikhail Bakhtin called "grotesque realism," which in *Rabelais and His
World* provides the occasion for so much antibourgeois celebration, here offers up

its less than liberatory effects.[33] This is, to be sure, antibourgeois, but it is black people, black *women*, as the world's body. While minstrel grotesquerie surely had some hand in constructing a raceless popular community-ideal of the "low" and vulgar, it was in this sense more historically useful to some of the people than to all of them. Whether because images of black women abetted the return of rowdy audiences to the pleasures of childhood—to the totalizing, and thus terrorizing, connectedness of pre-oedipal bliss—or because their excess, troubling enough in itself, seemed additionally activated by black male potency, blackface performers tilted their staves at the black female power they simultaneously indulged:

> The other day while riding
>   With two ladies by my side,
> I hardly knew which one to chose [*sic*]
>   To make my happy bride;
> . . . .
> I took them into Taylor's shop
>   To get some ginger beer—
> They flirted up and down the room—
>   The white folks they looked queer.
> One swallow'd six milk punches,
>   Half a dozen eggs as well;
> But fore de bill was brought to pay
>   This darkey thought he'd shell.
> The other ate six mince pies,
>   Twelve juleps quickly sped;
> And when dey axed me for de tin,
>   Now what do you think I said?[34]

The minstrel show's "black" female body clinched the horror of engulfing womanhood, gorging women depleting the bankbook. Here, it seems, the extraordinary energy of antebellum misogyny, perhaps even that contempt for white women intermittently repressed through men's "protection" of them from savage black manhood, was displaced or surcharged onto the "grotesque" black woman. These images indeed make Klein's point that the child's longing for union with the absent mother—a longing both precipitated and symbolized by some blackface images; witness, indeed, the lingering resonance of the black mammy figure—is inextricable from its primitive desire for vengeance against her. In this case it is the black woman as the *world's mother*.[35]

Black women apparently called up related fears of castration, about which there was in blackface minstrelsy an inordinate amount of anxiety and fantasy. Blackface fetish-images substituted in complex ways for the terror of the (b)lack.[36] For example, a great deal of disguise tends to be put in play around this fear (as perhaps when Jim sings "Lubly Fan"). Here is "Gal from the South" (1854), which attempts to meet the threat with the white male prerogative of ownership:

Ole massa bought a colored gal,
   He bought her at the south;
Her hair it curled so very tight
   She could not shut her mouth.
Her eyes they were so bery small,
   They both ran into one,
And when a fly light in her eye,
   Like a June bug in de sun.

Her nose it was so berry long,
   It turned up like a squash,
And when she got her dander up
   She made me laugh, by gosh;
Old massa had no hooks or nails,
   Or nothin' else like that,
So on this darkie's nose he used
   To hang his coat and hat.

One morning massa goin' away,
   He went to git his coat,
But neither hat nor coat was there,
   For she had swallowed both;
He took her to a tailor shop,
   To have her mouth made small,
The lady took in one long breath,
   And swallowed tailor and all.[37]

By now this is pretty familiar stuff. The anxieties here aroused are also familiar: the empowering insistence of the two "boughts" attempts to cancel the threatening open mouth (later to be "made small") while the phallic nose and the engulfing, vaginal throat finally wreak revenge on the master. As we have seen, white men's fear of female power was dramatized with a suspiciously draconian punitiveness in early minstrelsy, usually in the grotesque transmutations of its female figures. It is as if that fear were so fundamental that only a major effort of surveillance—again, like a dream, revealing its anxieties even as it devises its censors—would do. This song's wish to buy women seems an especially suspicious compensatory demand, a commodification that the unruliness of these figures both rationalizes and requires (one doubts that such figures themselves contained the castration threat). Yet the vehemence of this wish, together with the "gal's" hermaphroditic shape, may also point us in the direction of omnipresent nineteenth-century fears of the black penis.[38]

Especially instructive examples in this regard are the many songs in which black women get their eyes put out, as in "Old Blind Josey" (1854), whose violent protagonist is already (perhaps revealingly) blind:

But den one night he [Josey] danced so high,
He run his heel in a black gal's eye—
Oh! Golly me, but didn't she cry!
Unlucky Old Blind Josey.[39]

Repeated ad infinitum such representations signify, if we are to take seriously Freud's connection of Oedipus' blinding and castration. It is perfectly clear, moreover, that this fantasy resonated against the erotic white male looking inherent in "black" theatrical display. So variable are the possibilities of spectator identification in the theater, however, that we might inquire as to just whose castration was being constantly bandied about. On the most immediate level, collective white male violence toward black women in minstrelsy not only tamed an evidently too-powerful object of interest, but contributed (in nineteenth-century white men's terms) to a masculinist enforcement of white male power over the black men to whom the women were supposed to have "belonged." Indeed the recurrence of this primal scene, in which beheeled black men blind black women, certainly attests to the power of the black penis in American psychic life, perhaps pointing up the primary reason for the represented violence in the first place. Yet it is still puzzling that black *women* were so often "castrated"—even if, to follow the metaphor, they were allegorical stand-ins for white men whose erotic looking was undone by the black men they portrayed as objects of their gaze (no doubt this racial undoing, phallic competition and imagined homosexual threat both, was the fear that underlay the minstrel show *tout court*). Or perhaps, extrapolating from Lacan, to castrate the already "castrated" woman was to master the horrifying lack she stood for.

The elastic nature of spectator identifications, I would argue, suggests another possibility, one that does not contradict the general air of male vulnerability being managed or handled here. The blackface image, I have suggested, constituted black people as the focus of the white political Imaginary. Black figures (male and female) became erotic objects both for other characters on stage and for spectators in the theater—with a constant slippage between these two looks. It follows that white men found themselves personified by "black" agents of desire on stage; and this was of course an equivocal ideological effect because, in allowing white men to assume imaginary positions of black male mastery, it threatened an identification between black and white men that the blackface act was supposed to have rendered null. "Old Blind Josey," conversely, uses white men's imaginary "blackness" to *defend them* against black male power. The song calls on tricks of (cross-racial) disguise that Michael Denning has shown to be endemic to working-class cultural production, and it does so in order to make the black male figure of "Old Blind Josey" a representative of white men—already unfortunately castrated, as I have noted—striking out at a black woman who seems not only female but also a cover for black maleness.[40] Her typically jutting protuberances and general phallic suggestiveness (recall the master's hat on the black "woman's" nose) bear all the marks of the white-fantasized black men who loomed so large in racialized phallic scenarios. It makes perfect sense that castration anxieties in blackface would twin the black penis and the woman, as not only in "Old Blind Josey" but "Gal from the South" and other representations. Another referent for whites of Lacan's threatening (m)other, Frantz Fanon argued, is precisely the black male—an overlap too pressing to ignore in songs such as these.[41]

Thus the "castration" scene played out so often in minstrel songs was an iterative, revealingly compulsive rebutting of black men by momentarily empowered white men. Such dream-work disguises are telling proof of minstrelsy's need to figure black sexual power and white male supremacy at one and the same time. In fact their imaginary resolutions speak perfectly to the structure of feeling behind them: the violence against black women vicariously experienced but also summarily performed; the spectacle of black male power hugely portrayed but also ridiculed, and finally appropriated. Just as attacker and victim are expressions of the same psyche in nightmares, so they were expressions of the same spectator in minstrelsy. This dynamic of mastery was both the genesis and the very name of pleasure in the minstrel show.[42]

We might, after Laura Mulvey, call this dynamic the "pale gaze"—a ferocious investment in demystifying and domesticating black power in white fantasy by projecting vulgar black types as spectacular objects of white men's looking. This looking always took place in relation to an objectified and sexualized black body, and it was often conjoined to a sense of terror. This may recall the common charge, leveled most compellingly by Nathan Huggins in *Harlem Renaissance*, that minstrel characters were simply trash-bin projections of white fantasy, vague fleshly signifiers that allowed whites to indulge at a distance all that they found repulsive and fearsome. I would take this line of thinking much further; for, as Stallybrass and White argue, "disgust bears the impress of desire," and, I might add, desire of disgust.[43] In other words, the repellent elements repressed from white consciousness and projected onto black people were far from securely alienated—they are always already "inside," part of "us." Hence the threat of this projected material, and the occasional pleasure of its threat. (I do not assume that black people escape such splits, only that these occur by different means.) It is important to grasp that for white Americans the racial repressed is by definition retained as a (usually eroticized) component of fantasy. Since the racial partitioning so necessary to white self-presence opens up the white Imaginary in the first place, the latter's store of images and fantasies is virtually constituted by the elements it has attempted to throw off. Which is to say that white subjectivity, *founded* on this splitting, was and is (in the words of Stallybrass and White) a "mobile, conflictual fusion of power, fear and desire" (5), absolutely dependent upon the otherness it seeks to exclude and constantly open to transgression—although, in wonderfully adaptive fashion, even the transgression may in certain cases be pleasurable.[44] And if only to guarantee the harmlessness of such transgression, racist "othering" and similar defenses must be under continual manufacture. *This* is the color line W. E. B. Du Bois was to speak of a half century later, more porous and intimate than his graphic metaphor allowed, and it is the roiling jumble of need, guilt, and disgust that powered blackface acts. It should therefore come as no surprise that minstrel comedy went great strides to tame the "black" threat through laughter or ridicule, or that, on the contrary, the threat itself could sometimes escape complete neutralization. Blackface representations were something like compromise formations of white self-policing, opening the lines of property and sexuality to effacement in the very moment of their cultural construction.

III

Is there any way to know whether our surmises about such representations bear a relation to the way they were perceived in the nineteenth century? While the attractiveness of an "ethnographic" reception study has recently grown, few have had the temerity to attempt it in any but the present moment; what Janice Radway has called the "dispersed, anonymous, unpredictable nature of the use of mass-produced, mass-mediated cultural forms" has perhaps seemed an insuperable barrier to the reconstruction of a cultural form's public even in earlier formations of the culture industry.[45] Moreover, a series of questions immediately arises: How construct a public? If one uses blackface reviews, fictionalizations, mentions-in-passing, and other such responses, what is the relation of critical discourse to audience response? How gauge such response? I would like here to attempt one sort of approach to these problems. To begin with, we might observe the practice of Marxist art historian T. J. Clark. Clark has read mid-nineteenth-century French painting through "symptomatic" analyses of its contemporaneous critics, and in this way—by a kind of historical ethnography—produced what are arguably some of the most materialist readings of historical texts in recent criticism. Clark makes an analogy with Freudian theory: if the unconscious is visible only in slips, silences, and (in)admissions in conscious life, so the political unconscious of the public, though usually hidden by official representations that are made of it in the discourse of the critic, can erupt out of gaps in this discourse:

Like the analyst listening to his patient, what interests us, if we want to discover the [public], are the points at which the rational monotone of the critic breaks, fails, falters; we are interested in the phenomena of obsessive repetition, repeated irrelevance, anger suddenly discharged—the points where the criticism is incomprehensible are the keys to its com-

The Racial Unconscious of Blackface Minstrelsy   37

prehension. The public, like the unconscious, is present only where it ceases; yet it determines the structure of private discourse; it is the key to what cannot be said, and no subject is more important.[46]

The nineteenth-century written response to blackface minstrelsy cries out for such analysis. For the relationships of property and sexuality we have seen to be crucial to minstrel representations of black people tended, somewhat surprisingly, to disrupt many accounts of blackface. Most commentators believed minstrelsy to have derived at least in part from slave culture, and found affinities between the two that effectively displaced the differences. Given this perception of origins, anxieties arose about the precise nature of the cultural relationships encoded in minstrelsy, a problem that was fleeting and murky but unmistakably present to most of those who wrote about the minstrel show. It was in the rather obsessive accounts of minstrelsy's origins that these anxieties were most extreme. In what follows, I want to look at how even offhand contemporaneous narratives of the minstrel show's origins attempted to legitimate or resolve pressing ideological questions raised by their subject. For all positions on the origins and make-up of blackface minstrelsy implicitly or explicitly rely on a theory of the racial politics of American culture.[47]

In these tales of minstrelsy's "ancestry," the moment of "racial" exchange between white and black men returns with a vengeance. We should understand this as the desire to fix the object of study in the moment of its emergence, as if to uncover the pure thing (unadulterated by later, superfluous changes or events) were finally to grasp its essence. One notes in this project the development of a discourse on cultural "blackness," narratives of cultural acknowledgment by one race of another, accounts of a relatively trivial cultural form that find themselves worrying the minstrel show's racial economy. They reveal how white performers and audiences conceived of what they were doing in minstrelsy, and the extent to which ventriloquized cultural forms confronted them with a rather more troubling prospect than has been recognized. The moment that interests me in these narratives is the one in which black sounds fill the air and fascinated white men understand for the first time that there are fame and money to be made. We have already seen an account of Rice's first performance; the same *Atlantic Monthly* writer, Robert P. Nevin, fixes this earlier moment as well:

As [Rice] sauntered along one of the main thoroughfares of Cincinnati, as has been written, his attention was suddenly arrested by a voice ringing clear and full above the noises of the street, and giving utterance, in an unmistakable dialect, to the refrain of a song to this effect:—"Turn about an' wheel about an' do jis so, / An' ebery time I turn about I jump Jim Crow." Struck by the peculiarities of the performance, so unique in style, matter, and "character" of delivery, the player listened on. Were not these elements—was the suggestion of the instant—which might admit of higher than mere street or stable-yard development? As a national or "race" illustration, behind the footlights, might not "Jim Crow" and a black face tickle the fancy of pit and circle, as well as the "Sprig of Shillalah" and a red nose? Out of the suggestion leaped the determination; and so it chanced that the casual hearing of a song trolled by a negro stage-driver, lolling lazily on the box of his vehicle, gave origin to a school of music destined to excel in popularity all others. (608–9)

Rice is credited here with the higher development or logical conclusion of the culture of the street and stable yard. Minstrelsy is claimed as the *completion* of black culture, its professional emergence. For all the belief in the minstrel show as authentic "national illustration," then, there is also in this account a submerged melting-pot version of American culture *avant la lettre*—cultural mixing almost unconsciously acknowledged, and hastily forgotten. These narratives, in other words, are riveted by the moment of cultural expropriation, and we should look to them, as Pierre Macherey's work suggests, as much for what they do not say as for what they do—the way they construct, and then sometimes blur, racial boundaries.[48]

The cultural mixing in these narratives, however, usually takes place as it were *en l'air*; there is rarely any actual meeting between racial representatives (unlike the exceptional, harrowing, and probably fanciful account of Rice and "Cuff"). When there is such a meeting, the issues of ownership, cultural capital, and economics arise (as in the Rice and "Cuff" account). These are the two narrative paradigms of minstrelsy's origins: one in which mixing takes place by an elision of expropriation, through absorption (in both senses), the other in which it takes place by a transfer of ownership, through theft (or occasionally payment). In the accounts I have come across it is nearly always one or the other—obvious attempts to master the fears and anxieties I discussed in the last section. Both, it is safe to say, share an anxiety over the fact of cultural "borrowing." And both, I would like to suggest, have as their purpose the resolution of some intractable social contradiction or problem that the issue of expropriation represents. That of the first, I would argue, is miscegenation; that of the second, slavery itself. If, as Joseph Litvak has suggested, "anxiety itself has a narrative (i.e., implicitly history-making) structure," both anticipating and deferring the "deconstructive cancellation of its sustaining techniques," these narratives of love and theft are manipulations of historical anxiety meant to overcome the threatening implications of their primary concerns.[49]

It should hardly seem strange that miscegenation be suggested (if in oblique and displaced form) in accounts of white men's fascination with and attraction to black men and their culture, accounts in which the cultures merge. And the logic of such accounts is that fascination may be permitted so long as actual contact is avoided; that is the way the passage above works. The white man is "arrested" and "struck" by a voice only. At the passage's end, when we do finally see the black man "lolling lazily on the box of his vehicle"—by what means, through whose eyes, where was he before?—this suggestive appearance indicates the reason for his absence throughout: black male sexuality is one component of his arresting voice. In accounts like this there is a relatively transparent white male attraction to and repulsion from the black penis, for which, as in minstrel songs themselves, the preoccupation with miscegenation serves as a kind of shorthand. These two concerns—a jealous guarding of the prized white female body and a fascination with black male sexual potency that either precedes or follows it—amount in any case to the same thing: the twitchy "love" of my title. James Kennard, Jr.'s discussion (in an 1845 *Knickerbocker*) of the racial mixing attendant upon minstrelsy—he is careful to say that it happens "by proxy" (i.e., in blackface performance)—clarifies the nature of the threat. A brief account of the beginnings of T. D. Rice's "imitative powers" is given, and then whimsy turns to distressed irony:

From the nobility and gentry, down to the lowest chimney sweep in Great Britain, and from the member of Congress, down to the youngest apprentice or school-boy in America, it was all: "Turn about and wheel about, and do just so, / And every time I turn about I jump Jim Crow."
    Even the fair sex did not escape the contagion: the tunes were set to music for the piano-forte, and nearly every young lady in the Union, and the United Kingdom, played and sang, if she did not *jump*, "Jim Crow". . . . [Negroes themselves] were not permitted to appear in the theatres, and the houses of the fashionable, but their songs are in the mouths and ears of all. . . . (332–33)

"Contagion" indeed. Later in the article the author tries unsuccessfully to wish away the miscegenating music (personified as "Dan Tucker"):

Depend upon it, he will do no such thing, so long as the young ladies speak to him in such fascinating tones, and accompany their sweet voices with the only less sweet music of the piano. Dan takes it as an invitation to stay; and doubtless many a lover would like to receive a similar rejection from his lady-love; a fashion, by the way, like that in which the country lass reproved her lover for kissing her: "Be done, Nat!" said she, "and (*soto voce* [*sic*]) begin again!" (335)

No wonder, then, that in this first paradigm minstrelsy's "origins" are ordinarily so displaced and disembodied; talk of cultural merging is too dangerously close to a discourse of "amalgamation." A bizarre amalgaphobia infects even the briefest of accounts: "These songs, spawned in the very lowest puddles of society, at length found their way, like the frogs of Egypt, into places of admitted respectability. On so *dark* a subject it can hardly be expected that we should be quite precise in reference to dates."[50] The repetitive, even obsessive insistence on black sexuality in these encounters and in descriptions of their "offspring" has a vaguely unconscious or unmotivated quality; it is less a rhetorical tic or standard reference than something that has slipped by. In an article sympathetic to minstrelsy, one writer imagines "the hum of the plantation":

I listen with attentive ears—for I know by experience the gratification in store for me— and soon catch the distant tones of the human voice—now more faintly heard, and now entirely lost. . . . Now, anew, I hear the sound of those manly negro voices swelling up upon the evening gale. Nearer and nearer comes the boat, higher and higher rises the melody, till it overpowers and subdues the noise of the oars, which in their turn become subservient to the song, and mark its time with harmonious beating.[51]

If black men could do this with their voices, imagine what they could do in the flesh! But they remain voices, without presence, imaginative projections: these accounts seem to require that they remain so, even as the black male is compulsively referred to. The accounts all suggest fears and desires that come in the shape of a social narrative involving overpowering black men. That narrative surfaces in many contexts, but refers us in the end to the unresolved—and to these writers fascinating—threat of intermixture suffusing the minstrel phenomenon. Emblems of a relationship between the races that has been culturally repressed, minstrel songs, like the mulatto child of Thomas Jefferson in William Wells Brown's *Clotel* (1853), returned to haunt the most respectable of places.

But miscegenation/homoerotic desire is not the only kind of relationship whites would rather have forgotten, and the other narrative paradigm that organizes tales of minstrelsy's origins expresses an overriding concern with exchange value, the economics of race—slavery itself. Recall that in the *Atlantic Monthly* account above Rice gets the minstrel idea without meeting the black man; it is only later that "Cuff's" clothes come in handy, and the issue of ownership, and value generally, emerges. (This is the only account containing both paradigms.) The central issue of the second paradigm is so pressing that a later writer, in retelling Nevin's *Atlantic* account nearly word for word, nevertheless amends it in a striking way. Nevin writes that "Cuff was precisely the subject for Rice's purpose. *Slight persuasion* induced him to accompany the actor to the theatre" (609, my italics). Amidst an almost verbatim account, H. P. Phelps writes that "a darkey . . . was induced, *for a slight consideration*, to go with the actor to the theatre" (166, my italics). Given the monotony, the happy plagiarism of the general run of these accounts, such minute shifts are quite revealing, slips of the tongue in a "public" discourse. And what they disclose is white guilt or anxiety around minstrelsy as a figure for the plundering of black culture. Generally the intention of this second paradigm is a denial or forgetting of slavery's unremunerated labor—often difficult to sustain as repressed economic facts return.

In the most benign of these accounts, there can be no meeting between racial representatives without some kind of reparation made by whites to blacks—as in the following:

One spring season of the Louisville Theatre, on a clear, bright morning, during the rehearsal of some play in which Mr. Rice had but little to do, as he was standing on the stage, at a back door that looked out upon the rear of a stable-yard, where a very black, clumsy negro used to clean and rub down horses, he was attracted by the clearness and melody of this negro's voice, and he caught the words, the subject of his song; it was the negro version of "Jump, Jim Crow." He listened with delight to the negro's singing for several days, and finally went to him and paid him to sing the song over to him until he had learned it.[52]

The Racial Unconscious of Blackface Minstrelsy   **41**

This is obviously the legitimating story of cultural "borrowing": all accounts have been paid in full. The mention of a "negro version" of "Jim Crow" is no doubt a nice touch, implying as it does the neutrality and simple difference of versions; but it reveals, even as it attempts to disguise, precisely the *difference* of versions, the implied inaccuracy of blackface minstrelsy's appropriating "delineations." Even in accounts that would deny the notion of imbalance—in the evaluation of cultures or in cultural indebtedness—that imbalance, perhaps inevitably, returns.

It does so most forthrightly in references to the monetary or commodity status of minstrel songs, as well as that of their black "inventors." Most accounts at some point take up the issue of minstrelsy's authenticity, and are therefore littered with defenses against or assertions of its "counterfeit" nature: "Base counterfeits as they are, they pass current with most people as genuine negro songs."[53] Hence the false currency implied in the same writer's quip that "white men have blacked their faces to represent [Negroes], [and] made their fortune by the speculation" (333). The disapproval of this practice suggests an uneasiness with the surplus value thus generated; its falseness seems to stem from the fact that its black "owners" are not equal buyers and sellers on the market but are "represented," bought and sold, by brokers. On the other hand, the disapproval may not have directly to do with slavery; a distrust of the "speculation" of minstrelsy may only be a cautious approach to the main chance—made risky in the aftermath of the Panic of 1837, perhaps. But though the "blackness" minstrelsy peddles may be a commodity like any other, it ultimately derives, as these references continually remind us, from a certain southern commodity: "Those of us who have for so many years been looking anxiously forward to the advent of the coming poet who is to take away from America the sin and the shame of never having produced an epic, or a lyric, commensurate with Niagara and the Rocky Mountains, will do well to get up a subscription and buy the author of [these songs], if his owner can be persuaded to part with him."[54] The claims of Young America notwithstanding, one wants to reply that the sin and shame lie somewhere else. What all this suggests, in any case, is that blackface minstrelsy figured less as a palliative to the economics of slavery than as an uncomfortable reminder of it.

In this context we should recall the most horrific of the accounts organized by this second paradigm. It is Nevin's narrative in which outright theft and public embarrassment are indulged; but here too, as I have suggested, simply narrating the "primal scene" introduces issues of economy, value, and ownership almost behind the author's back. A great deal of space is allotted to Cuff's mode of subsistence, too much in fact for the part he plays as the lender of his "blackness" to Rice. He carries passengers' trunks from steamers to shore; he is, moreover, in active competition with another black man, "Ginger," for business. Revealingly, it is midway through Rice's performance in Cuff's clothes that the "near approach of a steamer"—Cuff's livelihood—intrudes, and requires the song somehow to end. And it must end because, as Nevin writes, "liberally as [Cuff] might lend himself to a friend, it could not be done at that sacrifice" (609). This allegorically suggestive scene—suggestive against the grain of what its author wants to convey—is yet marked by certain complex displacements. The first is the odd overemphasis on Cuff's free labor—here located not in slave-holding Louisville but in Pittsburgh, a swerve away from most other accounts, such as those of Noah Ludlow, T. Allston Brown, and Edmon S. Conner, which make the cultural "donor" a Louisville slave. It is as if, in this first displacement, the fact of slavery will be jettisoned in favor of industrious black men "liberal" enough to "lend themselves" to white friends. But the shape of that last phrase, in which black people offer up their selves like the talking commodities in *Capital* or in Dreiser's *Sister Carrie*, already suggests the slave economy that "lending" is there to cover over.[55] And indeed the scene as a whole, with its successive subordinations of Cuff in Rice's minstrel performance and in Nevin's use of dialect, enacts a second displacement, this time from the free labor by which the passage initially sought to distance itself from slavery. It narratologically reenslaves a black man who has evidently turned out to be more competitive and enterprising than he should be. This rather desperate shifting indicates the ambivalence that minstrelsy's debt to black cultural production called forth—and which this origin-narrative paradigm, I believe, was invented to mediate or "manage."

But we have yet to deal with the most curious detail of this scene, that in which Cuff "let[s] his open mouth as a mark for boys to pitch pennies into"—suspiciously close to white fantasy, but possibly observed. Then again, perhaps Nevin had read Melville's *The Confidence-Man* (1857). In the third chapter, Black Guinea, a "grotesque negro cripple, in tow-cloth attire and an old coal-sifter of a tambourine in his hand," makes his appearance:

Shuffling among the crowd, now and then he would pause, throwing back his head and opening his mouth like an elephant for tossed apples at a menagerie when, making a space before him, people would have a bout at a strange sort of pitch-penny game, the cripple's mouth being at once target and purse, and he hailing each expertly-caught copper with a cracked bravura from his tambourine. To be the subject of alms-giving is trying, and to feel in duty bound to appear cheerfully grateful under the trial, must be still more so; but whatever his secret emotions, he swallowed them, while still retaining each copper this side the oesophagus. And nearly always he grinned, and only once or twice did he wince, which was when certain coins, tossed by more playful almoners, came inconveniently nigh to his teeth, an accident whose unwelcomeness was not unedged by the circumstance that the pennies thus thrown proved buttons.

While this game of charity was yet at its height, a limping, gimlet-eyed, sour-faced person . . . began to croak out something about his deformity being a sham, got up for financial purposes, which immediately threw a damp upon the frolic benignities of the pitch-penny players.[56]

By the end of the scene, we realize with a jolt that this is probably a blackface performance;[57] the attentive reader recognizes another of the confidence man's disguises. This is more than the *Fidele*'s passengers do, hence the dramatic irony here—Melville lifts the mask for the reader only. Indeed, a "purple-faced drover," by implication a slave trader, actually hints at capturing what he takes to be this black man (which casually links minstrelsy with the human traffic of slavery); the accusation of fraud only extends to Black Guinea's lameness. Melville thus exposes the minstrelization of Cuff in Nevin's account: what these passengers and Nevin himself take as "blackness," Melville reveals to be part of a white discourse undergirding the minstrel phenomenon.

However, this turn only takes place when the limping man levels his accusation. Before that the reader sees a pitiable cripple doing his best amid a brutal "game of charity," though Ann Douglas has rightly noted that our sentimentalized pity is itself being savaged here.[58] We soon pay the price in embarrassment, but Melville briefly tries to make us as sympathetic as he possibly can; for all its fakery, the passage above is mightily effective. We have no way of knowing that Black Guinea's "secret emotions" are probably those of a white man pretending to be a black man, and so we are shocked, drawn in. It is an act of blackness as "target and purse," object of derision and repository of market value. Only then does the accusation break up the illusion, "got up for financial purposes." But that, of course, is what Melville has himself been so careful to construct—a sham that works, if only to embarrass—and he has done it by commodifying the blazes out of Black Guinea. The consciousness of black commodification that the writing forces upon us works all the more to make "blackness" into a marketable thing of white interest, this time for the reader. In order for the passage to possess any kick, the racial economy so bitterly exposed here must arouse before it exposes. Commodification is, in a sense, its *attraction*; it is what seems "blackest" about it. It is precisely what is calculated to evoke the foolish pleasure of our pity, and Melville's grim irony only confirms that the attempt to reveal minstrelsy's financial purposes has itself proved to be an act of minstrelization.

Blackface here is one more con game. But Melville's rejection of it accords in striking ways with the thing itself. Far from a happily secured distribution of cultural needs and desires, racial counterfeiting in Jacksonian America appears actually to have defeated the efforts to master it—whether the mastery was attempted by mystification or exposure—no less than it haunted its partisans. The writings I have surveyed were ineffectual, if various, plays for control of the questions minstrelsy apparently raised and tried to resolve. What these narratives seem to have realized is that the minstrel show flaunted as much as hid the fact of expropriation and its subtexts, enslavement and intermixture. Such seemingly coherent and purposive accounts, in short, constituted part of a volatile discourse on "blackness"—examples in themselves of blackface minstrelsy's racial unconscious.

Notes

My deepest thanks to Michael Rogin and Carol Clover for their acute and sympathetic editorial advice.

1. Alexander Saxton, "Blackface Minstrelsy and Jacksonian Ideology," *American Quarterly* 27, no. 1 (1975): 27. For similar emphases see Ralph Ellison, "Change the Joke and Slip the Yoke" (1958), in his *Shadow and Act* (1964; New York, 1972), 45–59; LeRoi Jones, *Blues People: Negro Music in White America* (New York, 1963), 82–86; James H. Dorman, "The Strange Career of Jim Crow Rice," *Journal of Social History* 3, no. 2 (1969–70): 109–22; Alan W. C. Green, "'Jim Crow,' 'Zip Coon': The Northern Origins of Negro Minstrelsy," *Massachusetts Review* 11, no. 2 (1970): 385–97; Nathan Irvin Huggins, *Harlem Renaissance* (New York, 1971), 244–301; Robert C. Toll, *Blacking Up: The Minstrel Show in Nineteenth-Century America* (New York, 1974); Sylvia Wynter, "Sambos and Minstrels," *Social Text* 1 (1979): 149–56; Joseph Boskin, *Sambo: The Rise and Demise of an American Jester* (New York, 1986), 65–94; and Houston A. Baker, Jr., *Modernism and the Harlem Renaissance* (Chicago, 1987), 17–24. This work revises more genial (and often complacent) earlier work such as Carl Wittke, *Tambo and Bones: A History of the American Minstrel Stage* (Durham, N.C., 1930); and Constance Rourke, *American Humor: A Study of the American National Character* (New York, 1931), 77–104.
2. Since this work is still in the process of formation, any listing of it must be eclectic and inexhaustive: John F. Szwed, "Race and the Embodiment of Culture," *Ethnicity* 2, no. 1 (1975): 19–33; Barbara J. Fields, "Ideology and Race in American History," in *Region, Race, and Reconstruction: Essays in Honor of C. Vann Woodward*, eds. J. Morgan Kousser and James M. McPherson (New York, 1982), 143–77; Houston A. Baker, Jr., *Blues, Ideology, and Afro-American Literature: A Vernacular Theory* (Chicago, 1984); Homi K. Bhabha, "The Other Question: The Stereotype and Colonial Discourse," *Screen* 24, no. 6 (1983): 18–36; and Bhabha, "Of Mimicry and Man: The Ambivalence of Colonial Discourse," *October* 28 (Spring 1984): 125–33; Barbara Johnson, "Metaphor, Metonymy, and Voice in *Their Eyes Were Watching God*," in *Black Literature and Literary Theory*, ed. Henry Louis Gates, Jr. (New York, 1984), 205–19; the essays in Gates, ed., *"Race," Writing, and Difference* (Chicago, 1986); Stuart Hall, "Gramsci's Relevance for the Study of Race and Ethnicity," *Journal of Communication Inquiry* 10, no. 2 (1986): 5–27; Hazel Carby, *Reconstructing Womanhood: The Emergence of the Afro-American Woman Novelist* (New York, 1987); Paul Gilroy, *"There Ain't No Black in the Union Jack": The Cultural Politics of Race and Nation* (London, 1987); Henry Louis Gates, Jr., *The Signifying Monkey: A Theory of African-American Literary Criticism* (New York, 1988); Philip Cohen, "Tarzan and the Jungle Bunnies: Race, Class, and Sex in Popular Culture," *New Formations* 5 (Summer 1988): 25–30; the essays in Kobena Mercer, ed., *Black Film/British Cinema* (London, 1988); Richard Dyer, "White," *Screen* 29, no. 4 (1988): 44–64; the essays in Cheryl Wall, ed., *Changing Our Own Words: Essays on Criticism, Theory, and Writing by Black Women* (New Brunswick, N.J., 1989); and Andrew Ross, "Ballots, Bullets, or Batmen: Can Cultural Studies Do the Right Thing?," *Screen* 31, no. 1 (1990): 26–44.
3. Here I am calling on Raymond Williams's definition of "structures of feeling," certainly an apposite conception to that of a racial or political unconscious. See *Marxism and Literature* (New York, 1977), 132–34; as well as Fredric Jameson, *The Political Unconscious: Narrative as a Socially Symbolic Act* (Ithaca, N.Y., 1981).

The Racial Unconscious of Blackface Minstrelsy   45

4. Robert P. Nevin, "Stephen C. Foster and Negro Minstrelsy," *Atlantic Monthly* 20, no. 121 (1867): 608–16.

5. As does the minstrel "conundrum": "Why are minstrel companies like midnight robbers? Because they live by their deeds of darkness"; *White's New Book of Plantation Melodies* (Philadelphia, 1849), 31.

6. See Mrs. Anne Mathews, *A Continuation of the Memoirs of Charles Mathews, Comedian,* 2 vols. (Philadelphia, 1839), 1:239.

7. See, for instance, the "Interview with Ben Cotton" in the *New York Mirror* (1897, clipping in New York Public Library Theatre Collection):

> I used to sit with [blacks on Mississippi riverboats] in front of their cabins, and we would start the banjo twanging, and their voices would ring out in the quiet night air in their weird melodies. They did not quite understand me. I was the first white man they had seen who sang as they did; but we were brothers for the time being and were perfectly happy.

8. *New York Herald,* 6 February 1843.

9. For his part, Mark Twain (like Margaret Fuller and Walt Whitman) was intrigued by what he called the "happy and accurate" representations of the minstrel show. See *The Autobiography of Mark Twain,* ed. Charles Neider (1924; New York, 1959), 60; and Eric Lott, "'The Seeming Counterfeit': Racial Politics and Early Blackface Minstrelsy," *American Quarterly* 43, no. 2 (1991): 223–54.

10. Stuart Hall, "New Ethnicities," in *Black Film/British Cinema,* 28–29. This is suggested also by the historical coexistence in the mid nineteenth century of white supremacy and what George Fredrickson has called "romantic racialism"; see *The Black Image in the White Mind: The Debate on Afro-American Character and Destiny, 1817–1914* (New York, 1971), chap. 4.

11. Hans Nathan, *Dan Emmett and the Rise of Early Negro Minstrelsy* (1962; Norman, Okla., 1977), 118.

12. Quoted in George C. D. Odell, *Annals of the New York Stage,* 12 vols. (New York, 1928–31), 5:33.

13. Hans Nathan is very precise about the make-up of the first minstrel shows; see *Dan Emmett,* 118–34, 143–53.

14. On the basis of late-nineteenth-century performer Lew Dockstader's recollection that the early interlocutor's lack of "darky dialect" contrasted with his black make-up, Robert Toll concludes that interlocutors generally appeared in blackface; see *Blacking Up,* 63, n. 63.

15. Laura Mulvey, "Visual Pleasure and Narrative Cinema" (1975), now in her *Visual and Other Pleasures* (Bloomington, Ind., 1989), 19.

16. See the pamphlet collecting English reviews of the 1846 British tour of the Ethiopian Serenaders, *Ethiopian Serenaders,* 22. The pamphlet is located in the Harvard Theater Collection.

17. In this the minstrel show is not unrelated to television situation comedy. I am indebted here to Patricia Mellencamp, "Situation Comedy, Feminism, and Freud," in *Studies in Entertainment: Critical Approaches to Mass Culture,* ed. Tania Modleski (Bloomington, Ind., 1986), 80–95.

18. *The Negro Forget-Me-Not Songster* (Philadelphia, early 1850s), 90.

19. See Leon F. Litwack, *North of Slavery: The Negro in the Free States, 1790–1860* (Chicago, 1961), 45.

20. *Negro Forget-Me-Not Songster,* 30.   21. Ibid., 102.

22. "Peabody's Lecture, On the Great Soger Camp-Meeting," *White's New Book,* 79.

23. Charles H. Fox, *Charley Fox's Sable Songster* (New York, 1859), 74–75.

24. Fredric Jameson, "Pleasure: A Political Issue," in his *The Ideologies of Theory: Essays 1971–86*, 2 vols. (Minneapolis, 1988), 2:72.

25. Peter Stallybrass and Allon White, *The Politics and Poetics of Transgression* (New York, 1986), 192. This argument refines ideas drawn from symbolic anthropologists such as Mary Douglas, who have written of the body as a symbolic representation of the social forces that produced it—bodily functions and boundaries, points of entry and of exit signifying societal relations and values, in this case racial ones; see Douglas, *Natural Symbols: Explorations in Cosmology* (New York, 1970), esp. 65–81.

26. In the realm of fantasy, blackface degraded also the white men who made use of it—including, I would guess, spectators themselves. The material capacity of burnt cork or greasepaint, mixed with sweat and smearing under the flickering gaslights, to invoke coal, dirt, or their excremental analogues was often acknowledged—Tom's humiliating escape in the "Whelp-hunting" chapter of Dickens's *Hard Times* (1854), for instance, a blacking-up that is a not-quite tarring-and-feathering. Likewise, it was said of T. D. Rice that his reputation depended "upon his blackface; and how he contrives to keep it white, might be matter of grave debate, begrimed as it has been for the last ten years, at least three hours in each of the twenty-four"; F. C. Wemyss, *Theatrical Biography; or, The Life of an Actor and Manager* (Glasgow, 1848), 179.

27. For the notion of popular fiction's plots, types, and disguises as a kind of "dream-work of the social," see Michael Denning, *Mechanic Accents: Dime Novels and Working-Class Culture in America* (London, 1987), 81.

28. Twain, *Autobiography*, 62.

29. Sigmund Freud, *Jokes and Their Relation to the Unconscious*, trans. James Strachey (1905; New York, 1960), 227.

30. Melanie Klein, *Contributions to Psycho-analysis, 1921–1945* (London, 1948), 267–77, 282–338.

31. S. Foster Damon, comp., *Series of Old American Songs* (Providence, R.I., 1936), no. 39.

32. *The Smithsonian Collection of American Popular Music* (CBS).

33. Mikhail Bakhtin, *Rabelais and His World*, trans. Helene Iswolsky (1965; Bloomington, Ind., 1984).

34. "Now Hold Your Horses, Will You!," *Christy and Wood's New Song Book* (Philadelphia, 1854), 9.

35. Another possibility is that audiences experienced a marginally more positive nostalgia for nurture rather than infant rage; this was true of the wave of sentimental black images that also ruled the minstrel stage.

    I have been influenced here by Michael Rogin's psychohistorical interpretation of white attitudes toward Native Americans in the antebellum period; see *Fathers and Children: Andrew Jackson and the Subjugation of the American Indian* (New York, 1975), 3–15, 114–25.

36. See Christian Metz, *The Imaginary Signifier: Psychoanalysis and the Cinema*, trans. Celia Britton et al. (1977; Bloomington, Ind., 1982), for an account of how the castration threat is managed by replacing it with a fetish-substitute: "The fixation on [the fetish's] 'just before' [castration] is thus another form of disavowal. . . . The fetish signifies the penis as absent, it is its negative signifier; supplementing it, it puts a 'fullness' in place of a lack, but in doing so it also affirms that lack" (70–71).

37. *Christy and Wood's New Song Book*, 85–86.

38. In a talk entitled "Mirror Stages: Jacques Lacan and Frantz Fanon" (University of Virginia, 30 October 1991), Barbara Johnson remarks that if the phallus is almost by

definition white, the penis must be black—which accounts here for its unruly and threatening potential. Thanks to Michael Rogin for a similar point in regard to my essay.

39. *Christy and Wood's New Song Book*, 30.

40. Denning, *Mechanic Accents*, 146–48.

41. Frantz Fanon, *Black Skin, White Masks*, trans. Charles Lam Markmann (1952; New York, 1967), 161.

42. In thinking about racial and gender disguise, and about theater-spectators' varying identifications with blackface characters, I am indebted to Mark Nash, "*Vampyr* and the Fantastic," *Screen* 17, no. 3 (1976): 29–67; and to Carol J. Clover's brilliant "Her Body, Himself: Gender in the Slasher Film," *Representations* 20 (1987): 187–228.

43. Stallybrass and White, *Transgression*, 77.

44. Stallybrass and White have an excellent statement of how this formation comes about in ibid., 193–94.

45. Janice Radway, "Reception Study: Ethnography and the Problems of Dispersed Audiences and Nomadic Subjects," *Cultural Studies* 2, no. 3 (1988): 361; in the same issue see Lawrence Grossberg's "Wandering Audiences, Nomadic Critics." More generally see, for example, Carlo Ginzburg, *The Cheese and the Worms: The Cosmos of a Sixteenth-Century Miller*, trans. John and Anne Tedeschi (1976; Baltimore, 1980); Stuart Hall, "Encoding/Decoding," in *Culture, Media, Language: Working Papers in Cultural Studies, 1972–79*, eds. Stuart Hall et al. (London, 1980), 128–38; Janice Radway, *Reading the Romance: Women, Patriarchy, and Popular Literature* (Chapel Hill, N.C., 1984); Ien Ang, *Watching Dallas: Soap Opera and the Melodramatic Imagination*, trans. Della Cooling (New York, 1985); the essays in James Clifford and George Marcus, eds., *Writing Culture: The Poetics and Politics of Ethnography* (Berkeley, 1986); David Morley, *The Nationwide Audience* (London, 1980); and Morley, *Family Television: Cultural Power and Domestic Leisure* (London, 1986); the essays in Robert C. Allen, ed., *Channels of Discourse: Television and Contemporary Criticism* (Chapel Hill, N.C., 1987); especially Allen's own essay, "Reader-Oriented Criticism and Television"; James Clifford, "On Ethnographic Authority," in his *The Predicament of Culture: Twentieth-Century Ethnography, Literature, and Art* (Cambridge, Mass., 1988), 21–54; Tania Modleski, "Some Functions of Feminist Criticism; or, The Scandal of the Mute Body," *October* 49 (1989): 3–24; and Guenter H. Lenz, "'Ethnographies': American Culture Studies and Postmodern Anthropology," *Prospects* 16 (1991): 1–40.

46. T. J. Clark, *Image of the People: Gustave Courbet and the 1848 Revolution* (1973; Princeton, N.J., 1982), 12. Clark's remarks are evidently (although not explicitly) based on Pierre Macherey's *A Theory of Literary Production*, trans. Geoffrey Wall (1966; London, 1978). One ought to note that Clark makes a distinction between the actual audience of art and a generalized or postulated "public," which, because they are more continuous in the case of popular culture, I conflate in my account of audience response. See also Richard Dyer, *Heavenly Bodies: Film Stars and Society* (New York, 1986) for a related practice of reconstructing the racial and sexual discourses in which, for example, movie stars become intelligible.

47. This section owes much to Edward W. Said, *Beginnings: Intention and Method* (New York, 1975), chap. 2; and to J. F. Lyotard's reflections on the function of "legitimating narratives" in *The Postmodern Condition: A Report on Knowledge*, trans. Geoff Bennington and Brian Massumi (Minneapolis, 1984), 18–20.

The many accounts of the rise of minstrelsy, some briefer than others, include "Origins of Jim Crow," *Boston Transcript* 27 May 1841; James Kennard, "Who Are Our

Negro Poets?," *Knickerbocker* 26, no. 4 (1845): 332; F. C. Wemyss, *Theatrical Biography*, 178–79; and Wemyss, *Theatrical Biography of Eminent Actors and Authors* (New York, 1852), 122; G. W. Curtis, "Editorial Notes—Music," *Putnam's Monthly* 2, no. 11 (1853): 572; "Letter from a Teacher at the South," *Journal of Music* 2, no. 21 (1853): 164; Sol Smith, *The Theatrical Journey* (Philadelphia, 1854), 53; "Obituary, Not Eulogistic: Negro Minstrelsy Is Dead," *Journal of Music* 13, no. 18 (1858): 118; Nevin, "Stephen C. Foster," 608–9; T. A. Brown, *History of the American Stage* (1870; New York, 1969), 310; and "The Origin of Negro Minstrelsy," in *Fun in Black; or, Sketches of Minstrel Life*, ed. Charles H. Day (New York, 1874), 5–10; H. D. Stone, *Personal Recollections of the Drama* (1873; New York, 1969), 240–41; Olive Logan, "The Ancestry of Brudder Bones," *Harper's New Monthly Magazine* 58, no. 347 (1879): 687–98; H. P. Phelps, *Players of a Century: A Record of the Albany Stage* (1880; New York, 1972), 166–67; Noah M. Ludlow, *Dramatic Life As I Found It* (1880; New York, 1966), 392–93; E. S. Conner, "An Old Actor's Memories" (1881), in Marshall Stearns, *The Story of Jazz* (New York, 1956), 111–12; J. J. Jennings, *Theatrical and Circus Life* (St. Louis, 1882), 368; Walter Leman, *Memories of an Old Actor* (San Francisco, 1886), 92; Laurence Hutton, "The Negro on the Stage," *Harper's New Monthly Magazine* 79, no. 469 (1889): 131–45; E. L. Rice, *Monarchs of Minstrelsy from "Daddy" Rice to Date* (New York, 1911), 7–10; M. B. Leavitt, *Fifty Years in Theatrical Management* (New York, 1912), 23–24; and Brander Matthews, "The Rise and Fall of Negro Minstrelsy," *Scribner's Magazine* 57, no. 6 (1915): 755.

48. Macherey, *Theory of Literary Production*.

49. Joseph Litvak, "Back to the Future: A Review-Article on the New Historicism, Deconstruction, and Nineteenth-Century Fiction," *Texas Studies in Language and Literature* 30, no. 1 (1988): 127. On cultural texts as symbolic or "magical" resolutions to lived social contradictions, see, for instance, Stuart Hall et al., eds., *Resistance Through Rituals: Youth Subcultures in Post-War Britain* (London, 1976), 9–74; and Fredric Jameson, "Reification and Utopia in Mass Culture," *Social Text* 1 (1979): 130–48; and *Political Unconscious*, 77–80.

50. "Obituary, Not Eulogistic," 118.

51. "Negro Minstrelsy—Ancient and Modern," *Putnam's Monthly* 5, no. 25 (1855): 76–77.

52. Ludlow, *Dramatic Life*, 392.

53. Kennard, "Who Are Our National Poets?," 336.

54. "Negro Minstrelsy—Ancient and Modern," 73–74.

55. Here is Marx:

> Could commodities themselves speak, they would say: "Our use-value may be a thing that interests men. It is no part of us as objects. What, however, does belong to us as objects, is our value. Our natural intercourse as commodities proves it. In the eyes of each other we are nothing but exchange-values."

Capital, Vol. I, trans. Samuel Moore and Edward Aveling, ed. Frederick Engels (1867; New York, 1967), 83. Here is Dreiser:

> Fine clothes to her were a vast persuasion; they spoke tenderly and Jesuitically for themselves. When she came within earshot of their pleading, desire in her bent a willing ear. The voice of the so-called inanimate! Who shall translate for us the language of the stones?
>
> "My dear," said the lace collar she secured from Partridge's, "I fit you beautifully; don't give me up."
>
> "Ah, such little feet," said the leather of the soft new shoes; "how effectively I cover them. What a pity they should ever want my aid."

Theodore Dreiser, *Sister Carrie*, ed. Donald Pizer (1900; New York, 1970), 75. What allows commodities to talk is precisely their exchange-value; it is this that masks their social character as labor and gives them a life of their own. Under slavery the opposite happens; self-owning human beings become voiceless things, pure socio-economic values. "Lending oneself" occupies a strange middle ground between the two, suggesting both self-ownership and an invitation to self-enslavement, particularly given the uses to which Cuff's loan is put. It is in any case *Nevin's ambivalence* toward black labor that is represented here, comfortable with neither slavery nor free labor; this ambivalence accounts for the shifting displacements going on in his narrative.

56. Herman Melville, *The Confidence-Man: His Masquerade* (1857; New York, 1954), 17–18.
57. Carolyn Karcher has argued forcefully that the confidence man's race is finally a riddle, that Melville's manipulations leave us no way of knowing whether he is "really" white (here in blackface) or black. While this is generally persuasive, and while I agree with Karcher's important argument that the issue of slavery is at the heart of *The Confidence-Man*, the specific implications of blackface are central to Black Guinea's first appearance; in the sixth chapter, Melville himself invokes the minstrel show, and it is only later that race is successively destabilized. This hardly calls Karcher's point into question—indeed it is probably central to it. See Karcher, *Shadow Over the Promised Land: Slavery, Race, and Violence in Melville's America* (Baton Rouge, La., 1980), 186–257.
58. Ann Douglas, *The Feminization of American Culture* (1977; New York, 1978), 361.

[5]

"That Wild Mercury Sound": Bob Dylan and the Illusion of American Culture

Barry Shank

The goal of man and society should be human independence: a concern not with image or popularity but with finding a meaning in life
that is personally authentic: a quality of mind not compulsively driven
by a sense of powerlessness, nor one which unthinkingly adopts
status values, nor one which represses all threats to its habits, but
one which has full spontaneous access to present and past experiences, one which easily unites the fragmented parts of personal history, one which openly faces problems which are troubling and unresolved; one with an intuitive awareness of possibilities, an active
sense of curiosity, an ability and willingness to learn.
— "The Port Huron Statement," June 1962

I always hear other instruments, how they should sound. The closest
I ever got to the sound I hear in my mind was on individual bands in

I would like to thank Charlie McGovern, Joane Nagel, Jonathan Arac, Graeme Boone, and
the audiences at the Mid-America American Studies Association conference in April 2000
and the Musicology group of the Department of Music at the Ohio State University for their
helpful readings and comments on this essay.

98   boundary 2 / Spring 2002

the *Blonde on Blonde* album. It's that thin, that wild mercury sound. It's metallic and bright gold, with whatever that conjures up. That's my particular sound. I haven't been able to succeed in getting it all the time. Mostly, I've been driving at a combination of guitar, harmonica, and organ.

—Bob Dylan, interview in *Rolling Stone*

Even as it articulated the political agenda for the New Left in the United States, "The Port Huron Statement" situated its vision of modern life within a paradoxical longing for both authentic connection and autonomous freedom. In laying out the cultural underpinnings of progressive politics, it seemed to state that any truly effective collective must consist of healthy, personally authentic individuals. These individuals should feel connected to their past and their present, but they must not concern themselves with the good opinions of others. Their interactions with each other should be as fully independent, as free of the constraining ties of status competition or the struggle for distinction, as particles of silicate suspended in salt water. Linking a monadic autonomy to the concept of authenticity, the philosophy of "The Port Huron Statement" reflected the contradictions of life in consumer culture, where socially necessary dependence on the managed productivity of others can seem like so much empty acceptance of the detritus of mass production. The personal authenticity that is capable of supporting individual autonomy seeks dignity and grace outside of the superficial everydayness of modern life. As folklore theorist Regina Bendix puts it, "The quest for authenticity is a peculiar longing, at once modern and anti-modern. It is oriented toward the recovery of an essence whose loss has been realized only through modernity and whose recovery is feasible only through methods and sentiments created in modernity."[1] The historiography of the New Left and its legacy remain haunted by this contradictory search for both autonomy and authenticity.

Much of the story of American music is also caught up in the search for authenticity. But the curious history of American music is such that the search for authenticity has so often proceeded through artifice. For the history of American popular music is, in large part, a history of illusions and masks, of whites pretending to be black, of women pretending to be men, of sophisticated stage performers pretending to be rubes (and, of course, vice versa). Another way to put it would be to say that American popular music

1. Regina Bendix, *In Search of Authenticity: The Formation of Folklore Studies* (Madison: University of Wisconsin Press, 1997), 7–8.

gives us a history of more or less successful attempts at self-recreation—a reconstruction created out of songs and dreams shared by strangers. The most curious aspect of all of this pretense is that so many times the illusion works. And it works authentically. It does not work as a trick that fools its audience but as an artfully constructed connection to a past and a tradition that can only be accessed through, because it is wholly constructed out of, commercially structured experiences (music produced for profit and distributed as commodities). Throughout the twentieth century, the artificial authenticity of American popular music has successfully linked performers and audiences in the remaking of traditions, in the creation of changing sames, in the collective construction of identities and histories. Perhaps even more curiously, it has worked not in spite of but in alliance with the creative powers of the commercial culture industry—those perpetrators and arbiters of image, opinion, and popularity—not in spite of but as a result of its ability to play with surfaces and hide behind masks.

In this essay, I want to use the early part of Bob Dylan's career to explore the artificial authenticity that lies at the core of American popular music—the legacy of blackface minstrelsy. By historicizing his work in the context of the Civil Rights movement and the New Left, I hope to show that the debates about the Left in the 1960s have been haunted by a search for a transparent authenticity that denies its artificial status. By disavowing any engagement with the complexities and masks of minstrelsy, historians of the New Left have been able to construct a tragic narrative of the sixties. They have argued that the latter years of the decade traced a political decline characterized by a failure of moral purpose: While the first half of the decade was focused on serious social issues, most centrally the Civil Rights movement, the second half of the decade saw a fall away from seriousness and a descent into issues of personal fulfillment. This argument suggests that the move from collective political engagement to the search for individual meaning was a collapse of authentic purpose—marked, among other things, by the dissolution of the dream that the original promise of the United States could be saved through a transparently authentic cross-racial alliance. I want to argue here that the music Dylan made during the first half of the 1960s helps us to come to a more useful understanding of the cultural politics of the period. Just as his fabled transition from being a folksinger to being a rock star was not so much an abrupt change as an outgrowth of the very skills that had been the source of his early effectiveness, so the apparent shift from the moral seriousness associated with the Civil Rights movement to what has been termed the self-indulgence of the late years

100   boundary 2 / Spring 2002

of the decade represented a working through of the philosophical contradictions that enabled the cross-racial alliances of the earlier period.[2] American culture, to the extent that one can define and characterize such a unity, is itself a culture of illusions—of artificial authenticities such as those produced in blackface minstrelsy. Dylan's rock music helps us to understand the power and the effectiveness of artificial authenticities even as it refuses the old illusions of a transparent authentic American identity.

Dylan was certainly not the first major American artist to advance a dialectic between autonomy and authenticity, identity and illusion. Working in a tradition that includes Herman Melville, Billie Holiday, Orson Welles, and Ralph Ellison, his obsession mines a rich vein that has yielded much ore. Yet Dylan's particular struggle details an intense engagement with two central illusions of American culture that characterize the philosophical contradictions of "The Port Huron Statement." The trajectory of his music and career questions the powerful dream that, through consciously planned and managed effort, progressive change toward social justice can be directly achieved. His best songs illustrate the inevitable disruptions of contradiction, pleasure, and desire that frustrate such plans. The second illusion challenged by Dylan's music is simply the American promise of freedom, where freedom is understood as autonomy—the power of individual self-determination, self-creation, self-transformation. Dylan's career cycles between two poles of immersing oneself in an authentic social group, with its own history and its dreams of solidarity and progress—that is, of being a folksinger—and of autonomy, of standing completely apart from any group —of being a rock star. Yet his desire to be a rock star both preceded and enabled his effectiveness as a folksinger—both of these personae were equally effects of his engagement with minstrelsy. Dylan's most powerful musical statements, even those among his early acoustic songs, illuminate the power of this contradictory legacy throughout the struggles of the 1960s. Listened to carefully, they demonstrate the powerful hold that minstrelsy exerted on the white New Left during the Civil Rights movement.[3]

2. For left historians who subscribe to the fall thesis, see especially Todd Gitlin, *The Sixties: Years of Hope, Days of Rage* (New York: Bantam Books, 1987); and Jim Miller, *Democracy Is in the Streets: From Port Huron to the Siege of Chicago* (New York: Touchstone Books, 1987). For some views of those who challenge it, see Alice Echols, *Daring to Be Bad: Radical Feminism in America, 1967–1975* (Minneapolis: University of Minnesota Press, 1989); Van Gosse, *Where the Boys Are: Cuba, Cold War America, and the Making of a New Left* (New York: Verso Press, 1993); and David Farber, ed., *The Sixties: From Memory to History* (Chapel Hill: University of North Carolina Press, 1994).
3. As a curiously American practice, American studies often shares in these illusions.

The New Left claimed an affinity with the music of Dylan from the moment it became widely (commercially) available. Several of the leaders of Students for a Democratic Society (SDS), the important New Left organization of the early sixties, claimed immediate historical significance for his songs. Richard Flacks, one of the early leaders of SDS, claimed, "To understand 'The Port Huron Statement,' you have to understand Bob Dylan." In the summer of 1963, Dylan's song "Blowin' in the Wind" went to number two in the national pop charts (of course, it was not Dylan's but Peter, Paul and Mary's recording of the song that achieved this commercial success). Flacks and Tom Hayden, two of the most prominent members of SDS at the time, got the sense that this commercial popular success meant that they "were really on to something." The chart success of "Blowin' in the Wind" seemed to confirm and legitimate the value of progressive white students organizing for the establishment of civil rights. Testifying to the immediacy of Dylan's work, Carl Oglesby, a former president of SDS, remarked, "Dylan's early songs appeared so promptly as to seem absolutely contemporary with the civil rights movement. There was no time lag. He wasn't a song writer who came into an established political mood, he seemed to be a part of it and his songs seemed informative to the Movement as the Movement seemed informative to the song writer. . . . [Dylan] gave character to the sensibilities of the Movement." Even when he rejected the role of political spokesperson, Dylan's songs suggested an orientation toward life that was shared by many of his contemporaries. Todd Gitlin remembered listening to "Mr. Tambourine Man" and thinking, "This was the transcendentalist fantasy of the wholly, abstractly free individual, finally released from the pains and distortions of society's traps, liberated to the embrace of nature and the wonder of essential things, in an America capable of starting the world again." In these two

---

Many of us want to believe that our study of American culture will result in progressive effects that are due to our individual agency. Without aiming to produce anger, I hope to expand on Dylan's work to suggest that, to the extent that our work might have progressive effects, it will not be because of our intentions but rather because of complex social interactions that we not only cannot plan but often cannot see. William T. Lhamon has described Bob Dylan as "the contemporary heir to blackface history who perhaps most consciously registers [its] unseen weight." Lhamon refers to two recordings that Dylan made in the mid-90s that feature minstrel songs. I am working with a less literal understanding of Dylan's engagement with blackface. I find Lhamon's book to be quite suggestive in the way it sees an irreducible contradiction and "compaction" at the core of blackface and in the way that it traces the continuance of this set of contradictions in the very recent past. See Lhamon, *Raising Cain: Blackface Performance from Jim Crow to Hip Hop* (Cambridge: Harvard University Press, 1998), 160.

quotes, each taken from a leader of SDS, both of Dylan's apparently contradictory positions—authentic connection to a group and transcendent individual autonomy—are recognized and applauded.[4]

For a group of relatively affluent, well-educated, and, to a large extent, white young people, torn between the contradictory pulls of autonomy
and authenticity, Dylan managed for a short while to articulate the artificial
union of both. And he did it by writing pop songs that became commercial
hits. While many cultural historians and popular music scholars have discussed the uncanny synchronicity between Dylan's lyrics and the ideologies
of the Civil Rights and antiwar movements of the sixties, I am much more
interested in his music. I want to explore the musical representations of the
habitus, or orientation toward life, that Dylan shared with the members of
SDS and other young people of the time, an orientation that remained consistent across his career.[5] Shaped by the currency of the struggle for racial
equality, this habitus, I will argue, was based on the structuring effects of
minstrelsy. The white branch of the New Left believed in the possibility of
uniting autonomy and authenticity—individual freedom and social connection. They achieved the linkage of these two opposed values by displacing
their union onto black culture and then reabsorbing the possibility of the

4. Flacks, Oglesby, and Hayden are quoted in Miller, *Democracy Is in the Streets*, 160–61;
Gitlin, *Years of Hope, Days of Rage*, 200–201.
5. Here, see Miller, *Democracy Is in the Streets*; Gitlin, *Years of Hope, Days of Rage*; Greil
Marcus, *Invisible Republic: Bob Dylan's Basement Tapes* (New York: Henry Holt and Com-
pany, 1997); Wilfrid Mellers, *Darker Shade of Pale: A Backdrop to Bob Dylan* (New York:
Oxford University Press, 1985); Anthony Scaduto, *Bob Dylan: An Intimate Biography* (New
York: Grosset and Dunlap, 1971); Robert Shelton, *No Direction Home: The Life and Music
of Bob Dylan* (New York: Beech Tree Books, 1986); and George Lipsitz, "Who'll Stop the
Rain? Youth Culture, Rock'n'Roll and Social Crises," in Farber, ed., *The Sixties*, 206–34.
By my use of the term *habitus*, I am drawing on the work of Pierre Bourdieu. Akin to Raymond Williams's concept of "structure of feeling," the concept of habitus emphasizes that
those aspects of life that we call feeling, taste, or intuition are indeed structured by material, social, and historical conditions. The term also suggests that these structures exist
at a social level, subsuming the experiences of individuals. For Bourdieu, *habitus* conveys
the early encoding of socially specific assumptions about value and the ways of living in
an individual's most basic approaches to everyday life. The habitus explains a similarity
of taste and attitude across fields or domains and within a social group. In this essay, I
am using the term to describe an orientation toward life that can be discerned in musical
structures and that saw some of its effects in the history of the Civil Rights movement.
See Raymond Williams, *Marxism and Literature* (Oxford and New York: Oxford University
Press, 1980); and Pierre Bourdieu and Loic Wacquant, *Invitation to a Reflexive Sociology*
(Chicago: University of Chicago Press, 1992).

union through an imaginary identification with that culture—through black-face. The artificial authenticities constructed in and through blackface constituted an antifoundationalist cultural practice that enabled the individualist yet political voluntarism of the period. This cultural practice determined no political effects, guaranteed no progressive outcome. But for a brief moment, the antifoundational artificial authenticities of blackface were misrecognized as a set of cross-racial alliances that were believed to be the foundation for the progressive work of the New Left. Hayden first encountered a group of African American activists working for the Student Non-Violent Coordinating Committee in 1960. His romantic idealization of those activists both enabled and constrained the effectiveness of the work he would go on to do for SDS. "They lived on a fuller level of feeling than any people I'd ever seen," Hayden said, "partly because they were making history in a very personal way, and partly because by risking death they came to know the value of living each moment to the fullest. . . . I wanted to live like them." Supported by the belief that identity was individual, not social, dedicated young white individuals could cut themselves free (if only for a moment) from their social origins, could identify with those different from themselves, and could locate the possibility of achieving the goal of autonomous authenticity in that identification. This move evoked the strategies of blackface minstrelsy; it enabled the cross-racial alliances that characterized this movement but also, in the end, marked its limitations.[6]

Dylan was born Robert Zimmerman. He spent most of his early life in Hibbing, Minnesota, a small mining community of about 17,000. Hibbing was

6. Michael Rogin has described the effects of blackface as akin to those of Freud's phallus or Marx's commodity: the irreducible fetish at the core of an antifoundationalist logic. "The fetish condenses the unanalyzed magical significance assigned to blacks." Rogin's analysis is more concerned with uncovering the historical crimes that have been carried out in the name of blackface, the reaffirmation of white over black that the strategy has consistently reproduced. If I am correct, however, that blackface is an antifoundationalist cultural practice, then no politics—either progressive or cruelly regressive—follows from it necessarily. See Rogin's *Blackface, White Noise: Jewish Immigrants in the Hollywood Melting Pot* (Berkeley: University of California Press, 1996), 182. Hayden's description of African American activists is heavily influenced by existentialism. The impact of existentialism on the social movements of the sixties has yet to receive its full accounting. Such an accounting would demonstrate the threads of this brand of individualism through the writings of C. Wright Mills, Saul Alinsky, Paul Goodman, and other influential figures. For a theoretical critique of existentialism, see Theodor Adorno, *The Jargon of Authenticity* (Evanston, Ill.: Northwestern University Press, 1973). Tom Hayden is quoted in David Farber, *The Age of Great Dreams: America in the 1960s* (New York: Hill and Wang, 1994), 78.

not all that different from mining towns in the South or the West. There was a strong local memory of the mine owners' violent strike-breaking strategies, which were an enduring source of bitterness. Bobby's father was part owner of an electronics firm that sold and serviced modern appliances on credit. And when Bobby Zimmerman was young, he used to have to work for his father, going to the homes of laid-off miners either to collect their overdue payments or to repossess the appliances. The Zimmermans were not particularly wealthy, but they were doing fine. Theirs was not an atypical life for successful assimilated Jewish merchants in the midwestern United States.[7]

While growing up in Hibbing, Zimmerman was immersed in a small community, a face-to-face world of aging miners, small shopkeepers, and high school cliques. He was intimately familiar with what remained of the small community romanticized by folklorists, Southern Agrarians, and anti-modernists of all stripes, and he hated it. According to Echo Helstrom, Zimmerman's high school girlfriend, living in Hibbing was like living in a gold-fish bowl, where "the plain gold fish would kill the fancy gold fish just for being fancy" (Scaduto, 5). It should not be surprising that, when out of his radio came the music of Hank Williams, Fats Domino, Elvis Presley, and, most importantly, Little Richard, the young Zimmerman absorbed not only these sounds but the promises of independence, individuality, and freedom that this music seemed to carry. His first high school band gave Bobby the chance to be "pretty much a personality. He was Little Richard, with rhythm in the background" (Scaduto, quoting Larry Fabro, 11). Borrowing musical materials from southern African American traditions, the skinny high school kid who did not want the confinement of a face-to-face community, who did not want to be the son of a small shopkeeper, who did not want his weekend job of collecting past-due payments on appliances, transformed himself into a jumping piano-slapper, who played "Little Richard style" (Scaduto, 11). In an archetypal move of American popular musical culture, Zimmerman began to remake himself into "Little Richard, with rhythm in the background."

This effort at personal transformation, whereby a young white male attempts to remake himself through performing black music, is the classic trope of the great American tradition of blackface minstrelsy. From at least as early as the 1830s, when T. D. Rice observed a dancing slave and created the international sensation "Jump Jim Crow," American popular music

---

7. The details of Dylan's early life can be found in Scaduto, *Bob Dylan: An Intimate Biography*; and Shelton, *No Direction Home: The Life and Music of Bob Dylan*. I draw most heavily from Scaduto, and subsequent references will be cited parenthetically in the text.

has formed a crucial cultural ground, where the meanings of blackness and whiteness have been reproduced, renegotiated, and renewed.[8] Certainly, Elvis Presley must be considered among the most significant participants in this tradition in the post–World War II period, and when Zimmerman was not trying to sound like Little Richard, he was telling everyone he knew that he was going to be bigger than Elvis. Dylan's earliest musical tastes, desires, and ambitions were profoundly intertwined with the history of race relations in the United States; he learned about race through his study of popular music.[9]

While still in high school, Zimmerman traveled through northern Minnesota, tracking down black men who were or had been musicians or disc jockeys. He would look them up and drop in unannounced, trying to discover, or create, a more direct relation to the experiences he believed were encoded in the records he had studied, experiences that he believed were the source of the recordings' power (Scaduto, 24). Yet even as he was searching for mentors, for teachers who could help him learn how to be Little Richard, young Zimmerman believed that he knew how to play that music better. According to Dylan, Little Richard's records could have been even greater. His "mistake was that he played down too low" (Scaduto, 11).

Zimmerman's high school band performed Little Richard's song "Jenny Jenny." Recorded in the key of F major, the song begins with the piano hitting a C-major chord. The highest note in the chord is middle C. The song's intro bangs through the standard changes of the dominant and subdominant to the tonic (C – B-flat – F), with each note of each chord played firmly with the left hand, which stays beneath middle C. Indeed, through-

8. See Eric Lott, *Love and Theft: Blackface Minstrelsy and the American Working Class* (New York: Oxford University Press, 1993); Dale Cockrell, *Demons of Disorder: Early Blackface Minstrels and Their World* (New York: Cambridge University Press, 1997); and Lhamon, *Raising Cain.*

9. Jeffrey Melnick has articulated the complex power dynamics that structured the encounter between Jewish men and African American musical forms in the period before World War II. Melnick sees the musical field as a particularly fertile arena for the continuing development of "Black-Jewish relations"—his real topic. I take his point that Jewish men were able to work their way into and through the music industry for particular historical reasons. Yet I agree with Rogin that the Jewish appropriation of blackface (whether through films or music) is a particular example of a larger strategy of whiteness. To the extent that the racial classification of Jews was less problematic in the 1950s, I read Zimmerman's attraction to blackface as less specifically Jewish and more directly engaged in the black-white encounter. See Melnick, *A Right to Sing the Blues: African Americans, Jews, and American Popular Song* (Cambridge: Harvard University Press, 1999).

106   boundary 2 / Spring 2002

out the recording, Little Richard's piano part never leaves the left side of the keyboard. Not only Richard's piano playing but the entire arrangement of the song emphasizes the lower to middle ranges of each instrument. The saxophones and voice stay low, with the exception of Richard's trademark falsetto "whooo," which stands out all the more by its distance from the musical background. When Dylan said that Little Richard played too low, he was referring to this emphasis on the lower frequencies.

In the fall of 1959, Zimmerman moved to Minneapolis to attend the University of Minnesota, where he began introducing himself as Bob Dylan. He also began inventing new identities for himself, telling wondrous stories about hoboing around the West, of touring with circuses and carnivals, of playing the piano for Bobby Vee, a successful but relatively unimportant pop singer. Perhaps most significantly, he had ceased to imitate the rock and roll star Little Richard and had begun to transform himself into a folksinger. A folksinger is an odd sort of performer. Perhaps best exemplified by Pete Seeger, the folksinger is supposed to be an insulated conduit between a tradition and an audience. Even while singing and playing the connection to the folk, the folksinger has to erase his or her individuality in the performance of that connection. When Seeger insists that his audience sing along, and when he simply stops singing himself in the enjoyment of the performance of the collective, he has immersed himself in the anonymous passing on of tradition that is the romantic view of the folklore process. As Benjamin Filene has recently put it, "The sing-along is the musical technique for which Seeger is most famous, and it is the ultimate testament to his passion for the folk song process."[10] The performance by a folksinger is an opportunity for the performance of community and the performed reconnection to an otherwise lost past. Pop singers and rock stars focus on the reconstruction of self through image and craft, that is, artifice. Folksingers erase self in the authentic performance of community. Bobby Zimmerman could never be a folksinger. But for a while, Bob Dylan tried to be.

Dylan worked at this new persona as carefully as he had worked at trying to be Little Richard, using the same tools—a powerful belief in self-determination, a willingness to create new identities for himself, and the musical lessons found on commercially distributed recordings. But this time,

10. Filene emphasizes Seeger's actual social position as an outsider to the folk, even as he remained committed to the integrity of the folk process. See Benjamin Filene, *Romancing the Folk: Public Memory and American Roots Music* (Chapel Hill: University of North Carolina Press, 2000), 197. For another discussion of these issues, see Robert Cantwell, *When We Were Good: The Folk Revival* (Cambridge: Harvard University Press, 1996).

the relevant recordings were a little more difficult to find. These records were not played on the radio; you could not step into any neighborhood store and find them. They were produced and released by obscure labels such as Folkways, and to find out about them, you had to know someone who already knew about them. In the Dinkytown area of Minneapolis, near the University of Minnesota, there were many initiates into the mysteries of folk music. According to Tony Glover, a young white folk and blues musician who arrived in the Dinkytown bars at almost the same time as Dylan, "the music around the U was . . . made by people who were enamored of mountain banjo melodies and old string bands with names like Gid Tanner's Skillet Lickers. These people had big record and tape collections. Some even sent off to the Library of Congress to buy tape dubs from the field recording collections at $17 an hour. A Folk Society was formed—people met to discuss and play these songs and it was all pretty academic."[11] Folksingers in Minneapolis had created a restricted field of cultural production (just as had other folksingers in Cambridge and Greenwich Village). These folksingers were mostly interested in singing for other folksingers and in developing a cultural history that was focused directly on their imagined connection to folk songs of the past.[12] The obscurity of the knowledge they were producing made it seem that much more powerful and important; not everyone knew about the Skillet Lickers, only those who had already invested considerable time and effort in developing that knowledge. While many of the folksingers reached for the most authentic, by which they meant the most difficult to find and, therefore, most valuable, music, Dylan was entranced by the songs found on a six-LP collection on Folkways called *The Anthology of American Folk Music* and by the songs of and stories about Woody Guthrie.

Woody Guthrie was an author, a songwriter, an illustrator, an instigator, whose life and songs appeared so deeply intertwined that he gave off the aura of being an authentic creator of folk song. But that was the paradox. Folk songs are not supposed to have been created but are supposed

11. Tony Glover, booklet essay accompanying Bob Dylan, *Live, 1966: The "Royal Albert Hall Concert,"* Columbia Legacy Records/Sony Records, 1998.

12. Pierre Bourdieu explains his concept of the restricted field of cultural production in several places. The most clear introduction to this concept is probably in his essay "The Field of Cultural Production, or the Economic Field Reversed," in *The Field of Cultural Production* (New York: Columbia University Press, 1993), 29–73. The restricted field is his term for that group of cultural producers who are most interested in the prestige and honor they earn from the opinions of other cultural producers who are engaged in the same field: that is, folksingers who were most interested in singing for other folksingers.

always already to have been. By insistently and yet apparently effortlessly writing (that is, authoring) hundreds of songs, Guthrie asserted that not only was he a folksinger, he was an artist. Quite probably, the Guthrie work that had the greatest impact on Dylan was his autobiography, *Bound for Glory*. Dylan already knew several of Guthrie's songs and was aware of the fact that he was lying in a hospital room somewhere back East. But it wasn't until a friend loaned him a copy of Guthrie's autobiography, which he read straight through in one afternoon while sitting in a coffee shop, that Dylan's fantastic identification with Guthrie commenced. Dylan was strongly taken by a scene early in the book in which Guthrie's guitar was saved from a downpour by fellow hoboes who offered up their shirts to keep it dry. Throughout the narrative, Guthrie tells stories like this that demonstrate the significance of his music to the dispossessed. Later in the book, Guthrie describes walking through "the crowded side of your big city," wondering where all the poor people came from, what they did, where they were going. Guthrie's narration makes it possible for his readers to identify with those who had lost everything in the Great Depression, those who "had a house and a home just about like your own," who "had a job of work just about like you. And then something hit them and they lost all of that." Passages such as this must have resonated with the young man who had repossessed appliances from laid-off miners. But Guthrie follows that scene with the pledge that, "if you think of something new to say . . . [y]ou'll hear people singing your words around over the country . . . and these are the only kind of songs my head or my memory or my guitar has got any room for." That was the promise that solidified Dylan's identification with Guthrie. Dylan's connection to the dispossessed was indirect and conflicted, but his yearning to have his own songs sung all over the country was immediate.[13] With Guthrie as a necessary imaginary link, Dylan then studied the music on the "Harry Smith Anthology," as the Folkways collection came to be known. It is important to point out that Dylan was a follower here. *Everyone* in Dinkytown was listening to the "Harry Smith Anthology." But not everyone heard the same things. What Dylan heard was an indirect and imaginary connection to a people and a tradition of music making that was shaped by his ability to disconnect, his own insistent, if illusory, autonomy. When he listened to the folk music on the "Harry Smith Anthology," he did not hear the folk, he heard singers.

13. Woody Guthrie, *Bound for Glory* (1943; reprint, New York: E. P. Dutton and Co., 1968), 330–31, 338. David Whittaker's story of borrowing *Bound for Glory* from a professor at the University of Minnesota and loaning it to Dylan is in Scaduto, *Bob Dylan: An Intimate Biography*, 39–40.

Dylan's self-titled first album for Columbia contains his version of one song from the Folkways collection, "See that My Grave Is Kept Clean." The version that Smith had collected and anthologized was originally recorded in 1928 for Paramount Records by Texas blues singer Blind Lemon Jefferson. He sings it in E-flat (probably performed on a guitar tuned one-half step down from standard). If you have a copy of this recording, I encourage you to listen to it. When you do, listen carefully to the timbre of Jefferson's voice. Dylan's version was recorded for Columbia in 1961. He sings the song in the slightly lower key of D major. Despite being performed in this lower key, Dylan sings "Grave" an octave higher, and so his version of the melody is sung at a higher pitch than Jefferson's. But I want to point out something more important than this choice of basic pitch. When you listen to Dylan's version, notice that the entire timbral feel of Dylan's voice is higher. This is not simply an effect of the higher basic pitch. There is more power, greater amplitude, in the lower overtones or harmonics of the basic note in Jefferson's voice than there is in Dylan's voice; the overtones sounded by Dylan's voice are higher relative to his basic pitch. Dylan tries to make up for this difference in sound by growling as much of the song as he can. But he can't change the way his voice sounds. His chest cavity and vocal tract simply resonate a higher set of overtones than do Jefferson's. A culturally produced and differentially distributed disciplining of the body results in these musical differences.

Remember that Dylan thought that Little Richard played the piano too low during "Jenny Jenny." And now we know that his body resonated "Grave" higher than the source from which he learned it. If we take Dylan at his word, that he really believed that Little Richard was playing the piano too low, then we must accept that his ears preferred a higher range, as well. What is the significance of this shift to a higher set of tones? I want to suggest that this upward tonal shift characterizes the historical performance practice of blackface minstrelsy. It is important for me to emphasize that this is not just a matter of individual differences. This shift to an upper range of either basic notes or overtones is common in white appropriations of black musical forms and styles. I trust that it is clear that I am not making an essentialist or biological argument. Rather, this argument is about broadly based cultural differences that have been reinforced over a long history. The tonal difference, particularly the difference in overtones or harmonics, is an audible trace of the earliest white investigations into a specific black difference in African American musical practice.

These investigations were both an effect of and a reinforcement of a romantic white urge to supplement the losses believed to have been induced by civilization with "the missing link of American identity," what was believed to be the "the purity and wholeness" of black music. As Ronald Radano has shown, "from the 1830s onward," white listeners to black music described "a peculiarly audible sensation whose special properties tested the outer limits of the Western imagination." The dominant means of recording music in the nineteenth century was notation, and transcribers regularly commented on the "difficulty of capturing in Western notation the nuances of slave singing." Radano argues persuasively that "black singing assumed the form of a discernible *difference*," and this "racialized, sound-filled difference became the key reference point for white writers," who invented new ways to suggest in writing this apparently essential difference between black and white vocalizing.[14] The entire tradition of blackface minstrelsy, indeed perhaps the central racial problematic within American popular music, is based on this imaginary yet perceptible difference. By calling this difference in harmonics imaginary, I want to characterize it as the result of fantasy. That is, the awareness of an unnotatable difference between black and white singing styles was made possible by a fantastic racialized approach to the study of song, shared by academic scholars and popular minstrel hall performers— blacks were different from whites, therefore black singing was different from white singing. I also want to emphasize the social and historical processes by which cultural differences are produced. Over time, through the efforts of scholars and promoters, as well as performers white and black, this perceptible difference became the overdetermined evidence of racial difference— the artificial authenticity of black singing.

    To bring this abstract argument back to the ground, remember that of all the songs on the "Harry Smith Anthology," Dylan first chose to record Blind Lemon Jefferson's "Grave." Jefferson was born in 1897 in Texas and apparently made his first recordings in "the rug department of a Dallas store" in 1924. His most important recordings were made in Chicago during 1927–28 for Okeh and Paramount as part of the effort of white-owned recording companies to find music that would appeal to the significant African American demand for phonograph records. Jefferson was chosen by several different white representatives of the recording industry to make recordings designed for sale to blacks. They hoped to use the relatively new technology of recording to capture the imaginary perceptible difference in

14. Ronald Radano, "Denoting Difference: The Writing of the Slave Spirituals," *Critical Inquiry* 22 (spring 1996): 522, 511, 508.

Jefferson's powerful deep voice. Indeed, he became one of the most influential of early recorded country-blues singers. His imaginary perceptible difference became a key marker of the blackness of authentic blues performance
for contemporary singers and for scholars and collectors in the generations
that followed. Over time, such imaginary perceptible differences came to be
treated as the artificial signs of authenticity. In Dylan's gruff yet constrained
recording of "Grave," you can hear both a tribute to Jefferson's influence and
Dylan's unmistakable acknowledgment of difference. Both of these aspects,
the tribute and the difference, the recognition of the contradictory artificial
conventions that constructed this difference and the insistence that this difference mattered—that it was authentic—are central elements signified and
masked through the long American tradition of minstrelsy.[15]

    Okay, so Dylan's appropriations of black music partake of minstrelsy.
So What? To a certain extent, that could be equivalent simply to saying that
Dylan was making American music. I want to suggest that his participation
in the long tradition of blackface minstrelsy—his simultaneous identification
with and recognition of his difference from African Americans—shaped his
cultural participation in the social movements of the sixties. His ability to
imaginatively identify through black music even as he marked his difference
from its origins reflected an orientation to life that was based on the quick-
silver fluidities of artificial authenticity. Just as importantly, two significant
musical consequences followed from this appropriation of black music in
Dylan's mature style. The first is that in blues culture—however firmly rooted
in folk practices—the singer does not disappear into either the audience
or an anonymous tradition. Blues singers individuate commonly known and
widely performed songs. In effect, the singer matters more than the song,
a fact that helps Dylan deal with his contradictory desires to be both authentic and autonomous.[16] Secondly, by raising the timbral and tonal focus
of his music, Dylan was able to add a crucial instrument into his mix, the harmonica. His harmonica style, awkward and idiosyncratic, is the key to "the

15. For information on Blind Lemon Jefferson, see Sam Charters, *The Country Blues* (New
York: Da Capo Press, 1959). For discussions of his influence, see Pete Welding's essay accompanying the CD *Great Blues Guitarists: String Dazzlers*, Sony Roots n' Blues series,
1991. For a particularly influential discussion of the emphasis on the simultaneous tribute
and difference encoded in blackface minstrelsy, see Lott, *Love and Theft*.
16. On this point, see Samuel Floyd, *The Power of Black Music: Interpreting Its History
from Africa to the United States* (New York: Oxford University Press, 1995). See also
Angela Davis, *Blues Legacies and Black Feminism* (New York: Vintage Books, 1998); and
Cantwell, *When We Were Good*.

wild mercury sound . . . metallic and bright gold," that, later in his career, he claimed to have always been striving for. Like an alchemist taking basic, commonly found materials and creating something of inestimable worth, Dylan took this "primitive country instrument, invented in about 1820," and, by simply breathing into it, created a high tonal center, a core sound around which his musical representation of the continuity and coherence of American popular music and the illusory possibility of self-constructed, authentic yet autonomous, identity could be projected.[17]

Dylan's use of the harmonica began in Dinkytown, while he was studying the "Harry Smith Anthology" and "trad[ing] a few harp riffs" with Tony Glover.[18] In 1965, Glover published "an instruction method for playing the blues harmonica" that provides some insight into the styles and traditions of music making that had been influential in the folk scene in Minneapolis. Glover starts his book by cautioning against overvaluing technical mastery. "The flashiest, fanciest, fatastic-est [sic] mouth harp technique is wasted unless it's used to help tell the story or paint the mood. Mechanics are only a tool. Don't make the mistake of letting them become an end in themsel[ves]." Against technique, Glover emphasizes the significance of "the hard-core center of the blues" that "has to come from the inside out." He seems to assume that his readers are white and rushes to reassure them that "the blues is no longer the exclusive property of the Negro." Yet his brief history of harp styles focuses on Sonny Boy Williamson, Little Walter, and Sonny Terry—classic African American masters of the harmonica. While Glover encourages his readers to study the recordings of these musicians, he warns his readers that they will never be Sonny Terry (for instance); they should, therefore, avoid trying to sound just like him. Rather, they should "play [their] own sound." Here, Glover echoes the widely shared belief in an autonomous authenticity that had been displaced by white listeners and performers onto the blues tradition yet that could be reappropriated through the study of black styles. By studying the recordings of Sonny Terry and Little Walter, white harmonica players will learn how to sound like themselves.[19]

Glover's instruction manual does not restrict itself solely to classic blues harp sounds. He discusses other black southern styles, in particu-

17. Wilfrid Mellers, *A Darker Shade of Pale: A Backdrop to Bob Dylan* (New York: Oxford University Press, 1985), 138.
18. Glover, essay in the booklet accompanying Bob Dylan, *Live, 1966*. Glover went on to record with Dylan in the 1970s.
19. Tony Glover, *Blues Harp: An Instruction Method for Playing the Blues Harmonica* (New York: Oak Publications, 1965), 7, 8, 11–13.

lar, mentioning the harmonica sound commonly found on the recordings of jug bands from the 1920s and 1930s. He makes the point that in these musical contexts, "much of the playing [was] done in the upper register so that the sound would carry over the booming jugs and thumping backing rhythm." Dylan's harmonica style never approximates the sound of the great blues harpists. In line with his musical preferences for the upper ranges of instruments, Dylan's harmonica style takes up this higher register associated with jug bands. No doubt both Dylan and Glover were familiar with the jug band music that Harry Smith had collected for his anthology, which featured two songs by Gus Cannon's Jug Stompers. Gus Cannon's parents had been slaves. Cannon first performed professionally in a "colored minstrel troupe," one of many such groups of black performers who reappropriated the sounds and jokes of blackface minstrelsy, claiming to be more authentic in their renditions of the form than the white musicians who blacked up before they performed.[20] In the 1920s, the Jug Stompers were one of the more successful jug bands playing on the streets of Memphis. Both songs that appear on the "Harry Smith Anthology" feature the harmonica work of Noah Lewis, who does not bend the instrument's reeds into the howls common to the style of classic blues harpists but who also does not restrict his tones to the upper range of the instrument. During "Minglewood Blues," first recorded in January 1928, Lewis keeps his harp playing high and well out of the range of the jug. But on "Feather Bed," recorded half a year later, Lewis focuses on the middle range of his instrument, significantly lower than that recommended by Glover.[21]

A page from the original booklet that accompanied the anthology includes Smith's original notes for "Feather Bed." At the bottom of the page is an ad for a harmonica holder, an "entire frame of strong, nickel-plated wire to fit shape of neck and is adjustable to any position." Ernest Stoneman, a white folk and bluegrass performer, had to have used one of those harmonica holders when The Stoneman Family recorded their version of "The Spanish Merchant's Daughter" (which is discussed by Smith on the preceding page of the booklet). Stoneman recorded with a number of bands from

20. A discussion of colored minstrel troupes can be found in Robert Toll, *Blacking Up: Minstrel Shows in Nineteenth-Century America* (New York: Oxford University Press, 1974). Ma Rainey first achieved fame as a singer with the Rabbit Foot Minstrels. See Davis, *Blues Legacies and Black Feminism*.
21. For information on Gus Cannon and his Jug Stompers, see Jeff Place, "Supplemental Notes on the Selections," essay accompanying *The Anthology of American Folk Music*, ed. Harry Smith, reissued by Smithsonian Folkways Recordings, 1997, 57.

the twenties through the fifties, recording topical ballads that achieved some popularity as the bluegrass scene developed in Virginia. On this recording from 1928, he plays both guitar and harmonica while his wife sings. His harmonica playing is pitched higher and features even fewer bent notes than Lewis achieved. When held by a wire holder, the harmonica is an instrument that is wholly dependent on and therefore completely reflective of the respiring body, echoing the effort of the body to breathe in and out. Stoneman's harmonica struggles to convey the regularity of breathing; with its strained lungs and wheezing tone, it seems to suggest that breathing is an accomplishment, not something to be taken for granted.

Although nearly everyone in the folk music scenes in Minneapolis and in New York was studying these recordings, only Dylan's harmonica style began to conjure up the space between Lewis and Stoneman. Perhaps sounding most directly like the harmonica style of Frank Hutchison, Dylan's style is distinguished by his ability to make a particular breathing body audibly present.[22] Like Hutchison, Stoneman, and Lewis, Dylan does not struggle to bend the reeds of the harmonica into a full and deep sound but exploits its squeaky treble. He does not shy away from the upper range of this cheap instrument but seems most comfortable exploring the top end of its sound. This harmonica sound is ugly. It is rough, raw, crude. It sounds like the black lung of dying miners. It conveys the opposite of sophistication, and it is far from the expressive modal wails of expert blues harmonica performers such as Little Walter, Sonny Boy Williamson, or Sonny Terry. It is an audible image of lives crushed by commerce, industry, and modernity. In its refusal of mastery, Dylan's harmonica sound is the skeleton key that unlocks his blackface imaginary. This purposefully awkward timbre performs the impossible union of black and white cultures, an illusory union made possible by the creative use of the masks and reflective surfaces that characterized the commercial exploitation of the imaginary perceptible difference in the tradition of minstrelsy.

Which is not to say that Dylan was incapable of great lyricism on the harmonica. "The Lonesome Death of Hattie Carroll," a song from his third album, the last recording to feature what Dylan called "finger-pointing

22. Somewhere in between the styles of Stoneman and Lewis lies the harmonica sound of Frank Hutchison. Hutchison's version of "Stackolee" graces the first volume of "The Harry Smith Anthology." Hutchison grew up in the coal mining districts of West Virginia, where he worked "mostly as a musician, occasionally doubling as a blackface comedian." In the early 1990s, Dylan recorded his own version of Hutchison's version of this black ballad. For more on Hutchison, see Marcus, *Invisible Republic*, 52–55, 60–62.

songs," contains one of his most melodic harmonica solos. The song is important to my argument for other reasons, as well. Lyrically, it details the murder of Hattie Carroll, a middle-aged black cook who worked in a hotel in Baltimore, by William Zanzinger, a young white member of the Maryland elite. It is a finger-pointing song in the tradition of "Masters of War," "Only a Pawn in Their Game," and "The Times They Are A-Changin'." It eloquently describes the justice system's blatant devaluing of the lives of poor black women. While the words of this song seem to maintain Dylan's commitment to folk songs of protest, it is important to note that the music suggests a feeling of exhaustion with this style. Recorded in 1963, after Dylan participated in the Civil Rights March on Washington, "Hattie Carroll" marks the momentary end of this line of his work. (He would take it up again a decade later in "George Jackson" and "Hurricane.") Through a musical trope that suggests the inadequacy of civil rights marches and the inherent limits of romantic images of cross-racial solidarity (images that Dylan had both internalized and disavowed in his intricate dance through the tradition of minstrelsy), and that foregrounds the apparent inevitability of privilege, hatred, and evil, "Hattie Carroll" is one of Dylan's most haunting articulations of the contradictions internal to the white New Left. As he sings the verse, the guitar strums a simple three-chord descending pattern, and the melody stair-steps upward, straining against the harmony. The first verse is six lines long; the second is seven lines long; the third and fourth verses are each eleven lines long. At the end of each verse, the tension between the harmony and the melody inverts; the melody descends as the chords rise up, and Dylan sings, as if to his devoted white, college-educated listeners, "You who philosophize disgrace and criticize all fear"—those of you who believe in your own righteousness and your own ability to change the world—"take the rag away from your face, this ain't the time for your tears." The murder of Hattie Carroll might bring tears of sympathy, tears of rage, to those listening to this song, but those tears—sympathetic identification—are inadequate to the task at hand. As each verse of this song grows, the tension between the melodic line and the guitar chords repeats, growing more intense, stretching out the description of injustice, giving Dylan more room for his understated disgust, leading up to an apparently inevitable yet immensely sad harmonica solo. This solo, played near the top of the harmonica's range, where its reedy harmonies sound almost hollow, echoes not rage but an exquisite anguish, breathing in time with Dylan's body as it marks the distance between that body and the murdered body of Hattie Carroll. And only then, after the solo and after the final verse that ends with the pronouncement of

116   boundary 2 / Spring 2002

Zanzinger's six-month sentence for the murder of Hattie Carroll, only after this ludicrously inadequate sentence is announced, does Dylan announce that it is time for the philosophers' tears. The song, with its musical depiction of human callousness, might be said to represent the stubborn inertial recalcitrance of hatred and injustice. It seems to say that songs, folk songs, songs of protest, finger-pointing songs, cannot prevent such things; they can only cry out afterwards. The song's power comes from its precise objectification of the habitus common to many of Dylan's listeners. The musical structure of "Hattie Carroll" is a prescient representation of the strong yet limited commitment most young affluent whites could feel toward the long-term project of the Civil Rights movement. It prefigures the exhausted abandonment to come.

Anyone who had listened carefully to "Hattie Carroll" should not have been surprised at the transformation in Dylan's music that his fourth album, *Another Side of Bob Dylan*, signaled. With this record, he began to distance himself explicitly from any politics that was not personal. Fighting with Phil Ochs at about this time, Dylan declared, "Politics is bullshit. It's all unreal. The only thing that's real is inside you. Your feelings. . . . The world is, well . . . it's just absurd" (Scaduto, 182). The exhaustion that hummed beneath "Hattie Carroll," that musically pointed its finger not so much at the Zanzingers of the world but at those who believed the Dylans of the world could lead them in righteous battle against the Zanzingers of the world, found lyrical expression in "It Ain't Me Babe" and in the awkward ranting in "Ballad in Plain D." The liner notes, "Some Other Kinds of Songs," decry "the mob. each member knowin that they all know an see the same thing they have the same thing in common. can stare at each other in total blankness they do not have t speak an not feel guilty about havin nothin t say. everyday boredom soaked by the temporary happiness of that their search is finally over for findin a way t communicate a leech cookout giant cop out. all mobs I would think. an I was in it an caught up by the excitement of it."[23] This album made clear Dylan's position that "involvement in causes was lifelessness" (Scaduto, 176).

Yet the most common stories told about Dylan's career skip over this record as they emphasize the apparently abrupt disruption of his 1965 transformation from a "folksinger" to a "rock star." Released in the spring of that year, Dylan's fifth album, *Bringing It All Back Home*, publicly introduced arrangements for a full rock band—drums and electric instruments—even as

23. "Some Other Kinds of Songs," liner notes to *Another Side of Bob Dylan*, Columbia Records, 1964.

it figured "the transcendentalist fantasy of the wholly abstractly free individual."[24] The turning point most frequently described by critics and music historians is his performance at the Newport Folk Festival that summer. The Newport performance seems so significant because of the coincidence of opposing gestures on the same stage. Dylan's status within the folk scene had been confirmed during the same festival two summers before, where he had achieved the full flowering of folk song success, where his claim to being the most significant songwriter of the scene had been verified, where his own song, "Blowin' in the Wind," had indeed been sung by Joan Baez, Seeger, Peter, Paul, and Mary, and the Freedom Singers, and by thousands of others as a sign of solidarity with the dispossessed. Yet only two years after his coronation, Dylan seemingly abdicated the throne.

In the summer of 1965, Dylan wanted to perform in the style of the electric half of his new album. He played with a pick-up group taken from the racially integrated Paul Butterfield Blues Band and, according to legend, provoked nothing but hostility from the crowd, who had expected pure commercial-free guidance from their troubador.[25] At the time, some fans accused Dylan of selling out. Which did not mean that they had not wanted his songs to be on the radio or that they did not want him to sell records. The appearance of his songs on the radio, after all, had signified to many the cultural success of the New Left. Instead, loud electric instruments and drums made it impossible for them to hear the musical references to premodern life that had promised to purify Dylan's listeners from the stains of modern commercial interdependence. Acoustic instruments had enabled a connection to an imaginary noncommercial youth of the nation, where the wounds of racism, slavery, Jim Crow, and lynching could be imagined never to have taken place. When Dylan turned to electric instruments, his music no longer resounded this particular artificial authenticity for his folk listeners. Instead, he seemed to be aligning himself with the teenagers of America, with the Beatles and the pop music industry. While his move was not free of commercial motives, he was not aligning himself strictly with the Beatles. He was, rather, reattaching himself with the music that had first promised him his own artificial freedom, the music that had first enabled his construction of autonomous authenticity—the rock and roll of Little Richard, Elvis

24. Gitlin, *The Sixties*.
25. Benjamin Filene lists a variety of interpretations and responses to Dylan's performance at Newport, providing a calmer-than-most description of this event, in *Romancing the Folk*, 215–17.

118   boundary 2 / Spring 2002

Presley, Fats Domino, and the rest. The fans who booed Dylan's electric rock and roll at Newport were booing his refusal to imagine a more pure past and his overt embrace of the complexities of the commercial minstrelsy tradition.

With the hindsight of thirty years and the benefit of the official release of previously obscure and bootlegged recordings, it has become difficult to hear much of a radical break in Dylan's music. For his first single for Columbia, Dylan chose a song called "Mixed Up Confusion." It was recorded in 1961 after the first album was completed, but it was not released until 1985. Throughout the song, Dylan plays the piano higher than Little Richard does in "Jenny Jenny." In the middle of an already tightly condensed musical range, squeezed between a very high-end electric bass and the piano and guitar, are Dylan's voice and his harmonica. The song is an insufficiently developed amalgamation of rock and roll with the intensity of Dylan's Guthrie-like ambitions, and it failed for that reason. Nevertheless, the song is important because it shows how even this early in his career, before he became a spokesperson for the New Left, Dylan wanted a rock and roll hit single, a song that, like Presley's best performances, would seem to represent racial difference even as it masked it in an illusory union of American music. And he wanted the value of this recording to be recognized in the marketplace. It would be another four years before he achieved this.

Dylan's first hit single was "Subterranean Homesick Blues," released in the spring of 1965, just as he was about to begin his final all-acoustic tour of England. This tour was filmed by Don Pennebaker for the documentary "Don't Look Back." Throughout the film, Dylan performs the role of the rock star, despite the fact that he is still working as a folksinger. No longer dressed in jeans and work shirts but in the sharp black that has defined understated hip for decades, surrounded by apparently idiotic interviewers, followed by screaming teenage fans, protected by his entourage from any substantive engagement with either intrusive group, Dylan dominates every interaction—as though the point of each interaction selected for the film is to demonstrate precisely that dominance. In "Don't Look Back," you see Dylan thoroughly removed from the face-to-face community, with all the autonomy that his artificially constructed persona could allow him. In the documentary, a young fan chastises Dylan for the change of style indicated by "Subterranean Homesick Blues." The rock star replies that the song is "early authentic folk music." While this is certainly one of Dylan's throwaway lines, meant to keep his fan at a distance while only seeming to engage, this comment also points us toward the contradictory positions that grew out of the shared simultaneous desires for authenticity and autonomy, the positions that linked even Dylan's rock songs to the New Left. This linkage was reproduced and mediated through the commercial culture industries and the tradition of blackface minstrelsy. Even as the leaders of SDS waited for the next Dylan record to be released, finding their most powerful images of themselves immediately sung back to them, Dylan's most important musical connections reached back through the recordings of Presley and Little Richard, back through the recordings of Blind Lemon Jefferson, the Stoneman Family, Gus Cannon's Jug Stompers, and others, back to the artificial authenticity of the imaginary perceptible difference and the artificial blackface promise of wholeness. Rather than dream of a past that never was in an acoustic construction of soft folk harmonies, Dylan's embrace of the minstrelsy tradition refused to deny the horrors of racism and the continuing legacy of slavery, while it drew from and helped to reconstitute the boundaries of "black" music.

Even in jest, Dylan always seemed uncomfortable with the term *folk music*. In 1966, in another attempt to keep his interlocutor at bay, he tried to separate clearly his own work from that form. "Folk music is a bunch of fat people," he insisted. Dylan wanted to connect his work instead to something he called "traditional music."

> Traditional music is based on hexagrams. It comes from legends, Bibles, plagues, and it revolves around vegetables and death. There's nobody that's going to kill traditional music. All these songs about roses growing out of people's brains and lovers who are really geese and swans that turn into angels—they're not going to die. . . . *[T]raditional music is too unreal to die*. It doesn't need to be protected. Nobody's going to hurt it. In that music is the only true, valid death you can feel today off a record player. But like anything else in great demand, people try to own it. It has to do with a purity thing. I think its meaninglessness is holy. Everybody knows that I'm not a folk singer.[26]

"Subterranean Homesick Blues" reworks that tradition, not with hexagrams or vegetables but with a lyrical and musical structure that revels in the traditional power of blackface by emphasizing through its musical form the meaning of above ground and underground, by pointing out in its lyrics

---

26. Dylan is quoted in Tim Riley, *Hard Rain: A Dylan Commentary* (New York: Alfred A. Knopf, 1995), 144–45.

that Maggie's black face was colored by soot and that even antiheroes in trench coats and coonskin caps are trickster figures who simply want your money. This song can be called old and authentic when we recognize that the tensions it describes and enacts are the tensions between autonomy and authenticity, between blackness and whiteness in American culture, between the longing for an impossible-to-recover past and the speeding toward an ever more nervous future. There are two bass lines in the song, one played standard, the second played on fuzz bass. The effect of playing a bass through a fuzz box is that it strips out the bottom frequencies. Thus, those sounds that Ralph Ellison cautions us might speak for all Americans are both present and masked in Dylan's blues, which does not use a blues lyric at all but seems more like a series of placards, of cue sheets reminding us all of the roles we must play. And like the cue sheets that Dylan famously throws away during the beginning of "Don't Look Back," this song gets it all just a little bit wrong. "Subterranean Homesick Blues" is not really a blues; in its immediate popular success, it was never subterranean; and it evinces nothing of the nostalgia of homesickness. Yet, in the field conjured by that name lies a certain fury, an anger at the apparently inevitable webs of contradiction, greed, ambition, and desire that frustrate and disrupt the illusions—the broken dreams and false promises—of American culture. "Subterranean Homesick Blues" renders explicit the continuing traditional power of blackface minstrelsy. As the two bass lines stomp up and down and up and down, as the harmonica wails at the end of each chorus, marking the ground line between pavement and basement, and while Maggie's face is only full of black soot, Dylan exhorts us all to jump down the manhole and light ourselves a candle, reminding us of Ellison's invisible man and that character's doppelgänger, Rinehart.[27]

It is while the invisible man lies beneath the sidewalk that he dreams a nightmare of castration and is asked how it feels to be stripped of illusions. "Like a Rolling Stone," Bob Dylan's first number one hit record, takes a little more than six minutes to ask with a sneer how it feels to be free of

27. In the prologue to *Invisible Man*, the narrator refers to himself as "Jack the Bear." "Jack the Bear" is the title of a famous recording by the Duke Ellington Orchestra, in which Jimmy Blanton is featured as a soloist on the bass. When Ellison speaks at the end of the book about the "lower frequencies," he is including such sounds as those made by Blanton's bass. Of course, the invisible man begins and ends the book in a hole beneath the sidewalk, while Rinehart, the numbers man, pimp, and preacher, walks above. Ralph Ellison, *Invisible Man* (New York: Vintage, 1952).

such illusions. The song begins with the snap-crack-flame of snare, kick-drum and organ that announces the deadly seriousness of the question. Dylan is not joking as he addresses a privileged young woman who went to the finest schools but who now has to live on the streets and make deals with tramps. She is a figure for Dylan's core audience, precisely that group of well-educated, relatively affluent, mostly white young people who had been the fans of "Blowin' in the Wind" and "The Times They Are A-Changin'." What is curious about this song is that the anger and the vengeance that motivate the attack on his audience, that powerfully drive Dylan's voice over the rolling unending waves of organ, piano, guitar, and jug-band-style harmonica do not seem overwrought. Rather, the emotions conveyed in the strain and rhythm of Dylan's voice feel right—precisely focused, acutely tuned. At the end of the first verse, he hesitates just half a beat between the "Now you don't" and the "talk so loud," and in the following line, between the "Now you don't" and the "seem so proud." These hesitations force him to rush the end of each line to fit the music, a rushing phrasing that almost takes over the last line of the verse as he squeezes in "About having to be scrounging" in only a bit more than half the beats it should take. Often, when he rushes to fit words to a melody line, it can sound awkward, but here the combination of hesitation and rush produces a tension that is hardly released with the extended "Ahhhh" that begins the first chorus line, "How does it feel." As the chorus and the song continue, with the rise in the mix of the minstrel echoes of a tambourine, it becomes evident that Dylan is not simply singing to his audience but that this set of questions and admonishments is directed just as much at the rock star himself. His voice steadily screams out the painful contradictions of late-modern America, the simultaneous incorporation and denial of blackness that is the minstrelsy of rock, and the impossibility of autonomous authenticity. "Like a Rolling Stone" is Dylan's most successful objectification of the orientation toward life that he shared with so many of his listeners. It expresses anger, disgust, and betrayal. Yet it remains passionate in its refusal to stop caring. Which is why the last verse ends with the couplet, "You're invisible now, you've got no secrets to conceal." To be stripped of illusions is to be left pained and empty, with no secrets to conceal and no romantic images left to blur the history of violence and conflict that is the legacy of slavery.

When historian Jim Miller describes the meaning of that record within the New Left, he emphasizes the loss of "the spirit of open-minded tolerance that had once characterized SDS."

> The new spirit rising within SDS—and within the avant-garde of the youth culture—was impatient, raw, hard with anticipation. The song of the moment was "Like a Rolling Stone," not "Blowin' in the Wind." Bob Dylan wasn't strumming an acoustic guitar and singing broadsides in the artless manner of Woody Guthrie any longer; now, he was shouting over a welter of amplified instruments, plunging headlong into dreamlike poems of betrayed love and apocalypse with the fevered, deranged conviction of a rock-and-roll Rimbaud.[28]

From a spirit of openminded tolerance to fevered deranged conviction, from "Blowin' in the Wind" to "Like a Rolling Stone," this is the journey of the New Left in the 1960s as some have narrated it. This position on the sixties might not be accurately described as "left conservatism," but it does conjure a sort of left fundamentalism. To narrate the sixties as a fall from grace is to imagine such social struggles as the Civil Rights movement stripped of the complexities and confusions of blackface pleasure. It is to claim that the early years of the decade, the years of white northerners traveling south to work with the blacks that had inspired them to live more fully in the history of the moment, were free of blackface desire. It is to argue that they were motivated instead by a belief in an authentic cross-racial alliance based on a mutually shared foundational understanding of the meaning of this alliance that was equally available to all participants. It yearns for a transparent meaning to history and the ability of well-intentioned individuals to escape the legacy of that history.[29]

But perhaps there is another set of meanings that can be drawn from the shift in the middle of the decade. What would happen if we saw the white engagement with the Civil Rights movement not as a break from the previous history of cross-racial identifications and alliances but as wholly within that tradition? What if the inspiration motivating these white struggles was derived from the artificial authenticities and antifoundational logics of blackface? If we put Dylan's music at the center of the culture, if we believe the claims made for the significance of his music for understanding the politics of

---

28. Miller, *Democracy Is in the Streets*, 254.

29. I do mean to conjure up the explosive debates about "left conservatism" that were generated initially by a conference at the University of California at Santa Cruz in January 1998. I am trying to align this project of rethinking the sixties with an antifoundationalist approach to historical and cultural analysis that was one of the objects of debate at that conference. For the proceedings of this conference, see *Theory and Event* 2, nos. 2 and 3 (1998). For a continuation of the debates, see *boundary 2* 26, no. 3 (fall 1999).

the period, and if we take his musical development seriously as an object of cultural analysis, then we are forced to consider the crucial factor of his participation in this fantastic tradition. We are forced to think through the possibility that the tradition of masks and surfaces, of borrowing and stealing, of violence and passion, that is the history of minstrelsy might have provided a more honest framework within which to address the difficulties of cross-racial identification and alliance building in the Civil Rights movement than did the folk-revivalist illusions of a return to a precommercial, preslavery, and preracism past that wanted to dream away the horrors of American history. Rather than conceptualizing the trajectory of the New Left as a downward fall from moral purpose, then, we might come to see that shift as a movement toward a full engagement with the complexities and contradictions of our history.

Dylan's career helps us to rethink the meaning of the sixties by forcing us to take seriously the legacy of blackface minstrelsy as a factor in the strategies of the Civil Rights movement. The struggles of the sixties can be better understood when they are recognized as having been built upon a set of illusions—the belief that individuals can disavow their socially overdetermined identities and engage in voluntaristic struggles for social change; the belief that there is a unified American culture that is shared equally by the diverse groups that produce it; that conscious struggle produces social progress. By reading the movement for racial equality through the analytical framework of minstrelsy, we can see the disruptive yet historically necessary element of blackface pleasure that underlay white participation in the Civil Rights movement. This recognition does not undermine the significance of these struggles but better enables us to evaluate the responsibility of those who participated in them and the strategies they promoted. Blackface remains a central cultural practice in the production of whiteness; its pleasures remain with us. The temporary donning of the black mask enables the projection and reabsorption of an imagined essence, an artificial authenticity, a mercurial longing for solidity that dissolves into liquid complexity. The confusions and asymmetries engendered through cross-racial alliances are inescapable. But the responsible approach is not to abandon all efforts at creating these alliances because authentic unity cannot take place. Rather, true responsibility comes only after the recognition that these confusions will occur, that the masks of blackface are not easily removed but neither are they totally enervating if left on. If we recognize that we are all wearing masks, then we can begin to be responsible for how those masks function and what they mean.

Part II
Roots, Experienced

[6]

Zydeco/Zarico: Beans, Blues and Beyond

Barry Jean Ancelet

Like the blues and jazz, rock and reggae, the music of the Louisiana black Creoles usually called zydeco is the result of a typically American experience which blended European (primarily French, but also Spanish, German and English), native American and Afro-Caribbean musical traditions. Lawrence W. Levine describes a similar blending process in Afro-Caribbean music that produced "a hybrid with a strong African base" (Levine 1977: 24). The American colonial context was basic to the development of these hybrid music forms. Nothing quite like them developed in Europe where direct contact with African culture is rare and exotic. In Africa, the closest parallel is the high-life tradition, born of the influence of the colonial French on native African culture. In America, both European and African cultures were far from home, on new ground. Settlers and slaves learned some old ways from each other and made up lots of new ways for themselves as they carved out a new world on the frontier.

Among the most important influences in this new blend was percussion. This new music was hard-driving polyrhythmic dance music. Early planters tried with more or less success to prohibit drumming on the plantation (Epstein 1977: 52). For one thing, planters supposedly feared that slaves would use a secret language of drums to communicate among themselves. For another, drumming was the heartbeat of African cultural expression. Eliminating the practice would help to assimilate any reluctant subjects. Yet, it is impossible to prevent people from drumming in real life. There are too many opportunities to improvise. A log, box, table or chair can easily become a drum with the simple addition of two sticks. Even without any additional objects, the body can be used to produce rhythmic sounds: hands on thighs, clapped hands, stomping feet, etc. Put several people doing complementary rhythms together with such improvised "drums" and the result is remarkably close to the polyrhythmic beat of an African musical event. This critical African tradition may also have been reinforced by an overlap with native American drumming. In any case, it survived to provide a beat for zydeco and Cajun music, as well as rock, rhythm and blues, jazz, soul, hip hop and other black-influenced American music styles.

Zydeco, zarico, zodico, zordico, and even *zologo* represent a few of the spellings used by folklorists, ethnomusicologists, record producers, and filmmakers, as well as dance hall owners and fans, to transcribe the word performers use to describe Louisiana's black Creole French music. The word *creole*, which originally meant simply "native or homegrown, not imported," served, among other things, to distinguish "esclaves africains" [African slaves] from the more valuable "esclaves créoles" [Creole slaves]. In South Louisiana, where the French language is an important cultural identity marker, French-speaking blacks often call themselves "Créoles noirs" [black Creoles] or "Créoles de couleur" [Creoles of color] to distinguish themselves from French-speaking whites, who might be either "Créoles français" [French Creoles] or "Cadiens" [Cajuns], as well as from English-speaking blacks who were called "nègres américains" [American Negroes]. Historically black Creoles spoke a French-influenced Creole dialect. Many who live in the old plantation belt along the Mississippi River and on the western edge of the Atchafalaya Basin still speak a version of that Creole dialect. Eventually most of those living on the southwest prairies came to speak a French dialect resembling that of their Cajun neighbours. Today many members of the older generations still speak French or Creole or both, as well as the English they learned in school, while members of the younger generations tend to speak little or no French or Creole.

Because its first language was French or Creole, the zydeco tradition remained a mystery to most outsiders. Native Louisiana Creoles explain that the word comes from *les haricots* because of the expression, "*Les haricots sont pas salés*" [The beans aren't salty], often heard in traditional songs. The spelling *zydeco* was the first one to appear in print. It was first used by record producer Mack MacCormack to transcribe the sound he heard from musicians in the Houston area in the early 1960s and is the most widespread. Most record companies favor it, including Chris Strachwitz's California-based Arhoolie Records which released most of "Zydeco King" Clifton Chenier's major recordings. This spelling comes from an Anglo-American's attempt to render the flapped [r] in *les haricots*. The [z] sound would then come from the liasion with the "s" of "les" as in *les hommes* or *les hôtels*. Although contemporary French grammar frowns on this liaison because the "h" in *haricot* is now considered aspirate, Cajun and Creole French dialects preserve the former pronunciation of *les haricots* without the aspirate "h."

So then, what's in a name? Sometimes that depends on how you spell it, and who's doing the spelling. Québecois filmmaker André Gladu drew criticism from Strachwitz for entitling his 1984 film on Louisiana black Creole music *Zarico*. Strachwitz maintained that the standard spelling of the term was *zydeco*, and that derivations unnecessarily cloud the issue and dilute the potential for interest. Gladu claimed this was a colonialistic foul and countered with the explanation that *zydeco* is based on superimposed English phonetics, while *zarico* respects the tradition's own French language connection by using French phonetics to render the term. Ironically, this French connection is the result of an earlier colonial influence. Thus the politics, not to mention the economics, of culture spilled over into the realm of linguistics. The debate over whether to spell the term according to precedent or to perceived culturel appropriateness continues. This question is complicated further by the recent discovery of apparent African influences that may need to be taken into account.

Folk spellings and folk etymologies often develop to explain or rationalize words and expressions whose origins or exact meaning have become unclear, especially among people who had no way of knowing what a word looked like until relatively recently when they learned to read. The attempts of folks to make sense of a term which has strayed, for one reason or another, from its original usage often yield related, though indirectly connected meanings, much like "for all intents and purposes" can become "for all intensive purposes," and "taking something for granted" can become "taking something for granite." Similarly, in South Louisiana, the name given to the nocturnal witch-rider, the widely perceived cause of what is medically described as sleep apnea, is *couche-mal*, literally "sleep poorly," an adaptation of *cauchemar*, French for "nightmare."

In the same way, words sometimes survived the efforts of ante bellum planters to eliminate African languages among their slaves, but shifted slightly in the process. In Louisiana French Creole animal tales, for example, the dupe of Lapin [rabbit] is named Bouki. The word *bouki* is Wolof for "hyena," traditionally the hare's dupe in West African animal tales. No traditional storytellers report knowing the original meaning of *bouki*, yet the term has survived and been extended to cover generally any foolish character or person. Another African survival, *gumbo*, is still used in its original sense to refer to okra, but also has come to mean the soupy dish it is used to make. Similarly, *congo* came to mean "dark" or "black," and by extension, "water moccasin," a snake which is dark grayish brown or black in color, by association with the color of the slaves who came from that area of Africa. The popular Cajun song "Allons danser, Colinda," in which a singer exhorts a young lady named Colinda to dance with him while her mother is not around, is a borrowing from Creole tradition (Bernard and Girouard 1992). The calinda or Kalinda was an African dance slaves performed despite the interdictions of their masters (Epstein: 30-33), and the expression "*Allons danser calinda*" probably meant "Let's dance the calinda."

The explanation that zydeco comes from the expression "Les haricots sont pas salés" has generally been "taken for granite" by musicians, record producers and scholars. A collection of traditional Creole music recorded by French Ethnomusocologist Jean-Pierre LaSelve (1980) on Rodrigue, a remote island in the Indian Ocean, includes an intriguing song entitled "Car zarico," a group song accompanied by clapping hands, stamping feet, drums and a triangle, with the following verse:

Idée moi, idée toi, Azéline.	I'm thinking the same thing you're thinking, Azéline.
Cari zarico.	Hot bean soup
Quand la lune fé séga mouliné.	When the moon dances the séga we'll harvest.
Cari zarico.	Hot bean soup

(LaSelve 1980)

Despite the literal translation, it seems safe to assume that bean soup was not uppermost on the singer's mind; courtship was. Yet the singers used the expression "cari zarico" as a repetitive, seemingly unrelated chorus throughout the song. When asked about this, LaSelve explained that singing about beans is part of a musical tradition called "séga zarico" which exists on Rodrigue and several other Creole-speaking islands in the Indian Ocean. The traditional dance associated with this music re-enacts the planting of beans, the woman walking backwards pretending to make a hole with her heel by stamping on the floor, and the man walking toward her placing an imaginary seed in the hole and covering it with his foot. The obvious connection between beans and dance, harvest and fertility rituals among Indian Ocean Creoles suggests that a look beyond the surface of the Louisiana Creole zydeco tradition might prove interesting.

Louisiana Creole and Rodrigue Creole cultures share similar origins and development patterns. They were both colonized by French planters in the 18th Century. The first slaves brought to the Indian Ocean islands were not from the nearby East African coast, but from the west coast, the same area exploited for the American slave trade. Both cultures speak closely related varieties of French-based Creole. Both share preoccupations derived from a common heritage, such as the setting sun and the rising moon, stemming from both harvest rituals and ordinances which forbade slaves to be away from the plantation after dark. From Rodrigue, we hear:

Soleil couché, maman, la lune levé, no allé.	The sun is setting, mother, the moon is rising, we go.
O hé, la saison là.	O hey, the season (the time) has arrived.
La saison, la saison, la saison là, no allé.	The season, the season, the season (the time) has arrived, we go.
O hé, la saison là.	O hey, the season (the time) has arrived.

(LaSelve 1980)

and from Louisiana:

O soleil après coucher,	Oh the sun is setting,
O la lune après lever.	Oh, the moon is rising.
Mmm, mon nègre est pas arrivé	Mmm, my man has not arrived.
Mmm, malheureux, nègre,	Mmm, unhappy one, man
O c'est malheureux...	Oh it's sad...
O mais quinze jours passés,	Oh fifteen days ago
O les promesses tu m'as fait,	Oh the promises you made to me,
O chère amie, mon nègre.	Oh dear friend, my man.
O soleil après coucher	Oh the sun is setting
To connais la promesse tu me fais moi	You know the promise you made to me
Sur un jeudi soir qui passé.	On a Thursday night past.
O la lune après lever,	Oh the moon is rising,
O soleil après coucher,	Oh the sun is setting,
Mmm, là-bas chez Moreau.	Mmm, over at Moreau's place.
O cherche ton candi, nègre...	Oh seek your candy, man...

(Lomax 1934)

In Louisiana, instrumental dance bands play waltzes and two-steps. In Rodrigue, they play waltzes and ségas. In both cultures, they are built around an accordion, a fiddle and a triangle. Since they share so many elements, it is at least plausible that their preoccupation with beans is more than coincidental. English blues scholar Samuel Charters alluded to a similar realization in his book *The Roots of the Blues: An African Search;* when, faced with a ceremonial procession in Banjul which looks for all the world like the black Mardi Gras Indians of New Orleans, it occurs to him that "To Weh Bakaweh" (a traditional Mardi Gras chant) "must be African, a phrase from one of the languages along the coast, though I was never able to locate it" (Charters 1982: 69).

The languages of West African tribes affected by the slave trade may provide some clues as to the origins of zydeco, though they are admittedly still vague. In at least a dozen languages from this culture area of Africa, the phonemes [za], [ré], and [go] are frequently associated with dancing and/or playing music, most notably among the Yula where "a zaré" means "I dance" (Sigismund 1963). With the cultural and circumstantial evidence enhancing the case, it is tempting to pursue the link between these tribal languages and the proverbial expression concerning unsalted beans. The recurring refrain supposedly about unsalted beans may be built upon older sounds, no longer understood, and now distorted into more familiar, intelligible words, changing the denotation while preserving the connotation.

Levine maintains that "in America as in Africa Negro music, both vocal and instrumental, was intimately tied to body movement" (1977: 16). In South Louisiana, zydeco refers to dance styles as well as the music associated with them. The meaning of the term has expanded (or survived) to refer also to the music, the musicians, the dance, and the entire social event. Creoles go to a zydeco to dance the zydeco to zydeco music played by zydeco musicians. The term is used to exhort dancers, as in the opening dialogue between zydeco king Clifton Chenier and his brother Cleveland on their classic recording of the tradition's title song, "Zydeco est pas salé:"

Clifton: Hé, toi. Tout quelque est correct?	Hey, you. Is everything all right?
Cleveland: C'est bon, *boy.*	It's good, boy.
Clifton: Tout quelque chose est magnifique, hein?	Everything's wonderful, eh?
Cleveland: O oui. Qui tu veux dire avec ça?	Oh yes. What do you mean by that?
Clifton: Allons les haricots/zydeco, nègre!	Let's --------, man!
Cleveland: Allons couri à la yé.	Let's run after them.

(Arhoolie 1082)

If zydeco meant only beans, then Clifton's last sentence would not be grammatically sound: "Let's go the beans, man!" Yet neither the late Clifton Chenier nor his Creole compatriots were in the habit of speaking nonsense in their own language. If, however, zydeco is taken to be a verb, with "les" being a direct object pronoun, instead of an article, Clifton makes much better sense: "Let's zydeco them, man!" or "Let's go zydeco, man!" One connotation seems to be associated generally with Creole music and dancing. There are many other examples of this usage, such as "Nous autres va zydeco," "Zydeco tout la nuit," or in English, "Zydeco, baby!" "Zydeco down!" and "We're going to zydeco all night long." Community dance events, which provide the primary opportunity for courtship, are announced as zydecos. Dance events are also referred to as "la-las" or simple French dances, to distinguish black Creole events from disco, soul or rhythm and blues gatherings.

Clifton Chenier's classic song, recorded in the 1950s, is thought by some to have given a name to this musical style. It is based on "Hip et Taïau," a French Acadian folksong about two thieving dogs:

C'est Hip et Taïau, [cher],	It's Hip and Taïau, dear,
Qu'a volé mon traineau, [cher].	That stole my skid, dear.
Quand [ils ont] vu j'étais chaud, [cher],	When they saw that I was mad, dear,
Ils ont ramené mon traineau, [cher].	They returned my skid, dear.

(cf. Whitfield 1939 [1969]: 106)

Clifton's version continues to tell basically the same story in fractured form, but adds seemingly unrelated bridges ostensibly about unsalted beans:

O Mama!	Oh Mama!
Quoi elle va faire avec le nègre	What's she going to do with the man?
Les zydeco est pas salé.	The beans/zydeco aren't salted.
Les zydeco est pas salé.	The beans/zydeco aren't salted.
T'as volé mon traineau	You stole my sled.

T'as volé mon traineau	You stole my sled.
Regarde les Hip et Taïau...	Look at Hip and Taïau...

(Arhoolie 1082)

The occurrence of the expression, 'Les zydeco sont pas salés,' in the seemingly unrelated bridges of several Louisiana Creole songs from the 1934 collection of Alan Lomax as well as in modern zydeco music suggests origins even beyond its functional folk etymology. In one Lomax recording, Wilbur Charles, a Creole migrant farm worker, concludes an unusual song, again borrowed from French Acadian tradition, about Italians lying in ditches apparently ill from having eaten rotten bananas with the following verses:

Quoi il n-a? Quoi il n-a avec ma femme?	What's the matter? What's the matter with my wife
Ma femme, elle est malade, couchée côté de les vieux Dégos	My wife is sick, lying next to the old Italians
Dégos.	Italians.
Les haricots sont pas salés.	The beans/zydeco aren't salted.
Quoi il n-a, mon cher ami?	What's the matter, my dear friend?
Quoi il n-a?	What's the matter?
Les haricots sont pas salés.	The beans/zydeco aren't salted.
O yaie! O mon nègre!	Oh yaie! Oh my man!
Les haricots sont pas salés.	The beans/zydeco aren't salted.
Pas mis de la viande, pas mis à rien,	Didn't put meat, didn't put anything else,
Juste des haricots dans la chaudière.	Only beans in the pot.
Les haricots sont pas salés.	The beans/zydeco aren't salted.

(Lomax 1934)

The beans are unsalty because the cook has no meat to add to the pot. Before the days of refrigeration, a common way of preserving meat was to salt it away. Adding this salt meat to sauces, soups and beans provided seasoning as well as protein. 'Les haricots sont pas salés,' then, may refer to hard times and, by association, to the music that helped to endure them. One is left to wonder what the singer's wife is doing laying in the ditch with the old Italians in the first place, sick or not. Thus 'Les haricots/zydeco sont pas salés' seems also to appear in situations that feature frustrated courtship, or unhappy relationships. In English-speaking African American tradition, this music is called the blues, whether it be a "low-down" blues lament which relieves by purging or a jumping, juking blues which relieves by distracting.

The laments and field hollers that were in English in the rest of the plantation south were in French in South Louisiana. Consequently, zydeco's bluesy side is sometimes based on melodies and rhythms which resemble those of the Southern blues tradition. Other times, the confluence of European and Afro-Caribbean rhythms and sources produced haunting songs in 3/4 time which function equally well as blues laments and as waltzes. Creole fiddler Canray Fontenot explained that as late as his own youth and young adulthood, in the 1930s and '40s, the blues were considered barroom music, and respectable families did not allow the blues to be played at their house dances (Fontenot 1977). Musicians circumvented this proscription by converting their blues into acceptable dance forms such as the waltz. Fontenot's recording of "Les barres de la prison" is an excellent example of this style (Arhoolie 1070).

An important step in the development of what is now called zydeco was juré tradition, recorded in Louisiana by Alan Lomax during 1934. The Louisiana Creole counterpart of French Acadian "danses rondes" and Anglo-American play party songs, these unaccompanied group songs were performed for dancers during times when instrumental music was either proscribed (Lent or periods of mourning) or simply unavailable. They resemble the Rodriguais séga zydecos in style and beat as well as in the frequent, seemingly unrelated reference to beans in the chorus or bridge. *Juré* is apparently derived from the French word for "sworn" or "testified," though Epstein notes that a similar word, Juddy, was reported by seventeenth-century trader Ben Jobson as used to refer to "professional" musicians in Guinea and Benin (Epstein: 4). In Louisiana, jurés are the Louisiana French parallel for shouts and spirituals resulting from the blending of Afro-Caribbean, French-Acadian and southern Protestants traditions. Some texts were religious, as in the case of "Feel Like Dying in [Joining] His Army," a bilingual recording made by Lomax in 1934:

O Lord, Lord, Lord, my God.
   Feel like dying in [joining] His army.
O oui, mon cher amie, o quoi tu vas faire?   Oh yes, my dear friend, oh what will you do?
   Feel like dying in [joining] His Army.
O quoi tu vas faire, comment, hein, petit monde?   Oh what will you do, how, eh, dear one.
   Feel like dying in [joining] His Army.
O oui, ma petite, si to pries pas...   Oh yes, my little one, if you don't pray...
   Feel like dying in [joining] His Army
O si to pries pas, tu vas brûler dans l'enfer.   Oh if you don't pray, you'll burn in hell.
   Feel like dying in [joining] His Army.

                                                     (Lomax 1934)

Others were secular, often adapting the story line of French-Acadian folk songs to a highly syncopated Afro-Creole style. In similar vein, Gilbert Chase reported that "The English musician Henry Russell, who lived in the U.S. in the 1830s, was forcibly struck by the ease with which a slave congregation in Vicksburg, Mississippi, to a 'fine old Psalm tune' and by suddenly and spontaneously accelerating the tempo, transformed it 'into a kind of negro melody'" (1966: 235–36; quoted in Levine: 26). This is the case with Clifton Chenier's signature song "Les zydeco est pas salé," and with several of the Lomax recordings, such as "Je veux me marier, je peux pas trouver," based on the French Acadian song, "Je veux me marier, mais les poules pendent pas." Compare the two:

French Acadian:

Je veux me marier	I want to marry
Je veux me marier	I want to marry
Je veux me marier	I want to marry
Mais la belle veut pas	But my sweetheart does not.
La belle veut,	My sweetheart accepts,
La belle veut,	My sweetheart accepts,
La belle veut,	My sweetheart accepts,
Mais les vieux vut pas.	But her parents do not.
Les vieux veut,	Her parents accept,
Les vieux veut,	Her parents accept,
Les vieux veut,	Her parents accept,
Mais j'ai pas d'argent.	But I have no money.
J'ai pas d'argent,	I have no money,
J'ai pas d'argent,	I have no money,
J'ai pas d'argent,	I have no money,
Et les poles pend pas.	And the chickens aren't laying.

(traditional: e.g. Gilmore 1970)

Juré:

Je veux me marier,	I want to marry,
Je peux pas trouver,	I can't find,
O, c'est malheureux.	Oh it's sad.
Je veux me marier,	I want to marry,
Je peux pas trouver,	I can't find,
Mais comment done je vas faire?	What am I going to do?
Je veux me marier,	I want to marry,
Je peux pas trouver,	I can't find,
Mais Mam et Pap veut pas.	And Mother and Father don't want.
Je veux me marier,	I want to marry,
Je peux pas trouver,	I can't find,
Mais o, c'est malheureux.	Well oh, its sad.
Je veux me marier	I want to marry,
J'ai pas d'argent,	I have no money,

J'ai pas de souliers,	I have no shoes,
Mais o, c'est malheureux	Well oh, its sad.
Comment donc	What then
Tu veux moi, je fais,	Do you expect me to do,
Mais comme un pauvre misérable...	Well, like a miserable wretch...

(Lomax 1934)

The French Acadian version is lyrically and rhythmically structured in typically European-influenced fashion. The juré is lyrically reformulated and impressionistic, with a fragmented storyline, uneven lines, and a completely retooled melody, all of which comes from the African influences of its singers' past. The juré version preserves the basic theme of the young suitor whose courtship is frustrated because he has no money, but develops the story in a completely different way.

Juré singers provided dance music during times of Lent or official mourning periods when instrumental music was forbidden, or whenever musicians simply could not be found or afforded. The French Acadian counterpart to this tradition was called *danses rondes,* or round dancing. In Anglo-American tradition, this was sometimes called play-party singing. ("London Bridge" and "Ring around the Roses" are two well-known examples of play-party singing.) Lomax called juré style "the most African sound I found in America." The singers are accompanied only by improvised percussion (stamping feet, clapping hands, spoons rubbed on corrugated washboards...) and a vocal counterpoint.

Sexuality is a common feature in African tradition and survives in Afro-American cultural expression. "Jazz" and "rock" which describe other related African-American musical styles originally were euphemisms for making love in the black oral tradition. The connection between music and dance and sexuality and courtship may give additional clues to the origins and meaning of zydeco. In "J'ai fait tout le tour du pays," based on the French Acadian "J'ai fait tout le tour du grand bois," the story line concerns another frustrated young lover who cannot visit his sweetheart again because he is poor (his clothes are tattered, his horse is sickly...), but the bridge is a complaint ostensibly about unsalted beans. If one considers that zydeco has possible roots in courtship and fertility ritual music and dancing, however, a possible relationship appears between the bridge and the verses which describe frustration in courtship.

J'ai fait tout le tour du pays	I went all round the land
Avec ma jogue au plombeau	With my bottle on the pommel
Et j'ai demandé à ton père pour dix-huit piastres, chérie	And I asked your father for eighteen dollars, dear.
Il m'a donné que cinq piastres.	He gave me only five dollars.
O Mam, mais donnez-moi les haricots.	Oh Mama, give me the beans.
Mais o chérie, les haricots sont pas salés.	Well, o dear, the beans ain't salted.
O Mam, mais donnez-moi les haricots.	Oh Mama, give me the beans.
Mais o yé yaïe, les haricots sont pas salés.	Well, o yé yaïe, the beans ain't salted.
Toi, comment tu veux je te vas voir	You, how do you expect me to visit you.
Mais quand mon chapeau rouge est fini.	When my red hat is worn.

Toi, comment tu veux je te vas voir	You, how do you expect me to visit you.
Mais quand mon suit est tout déchiré?	When my suit is all torn.
O Mam, mais donnez-moi les haricots.	O Mama, give me the beans.
Mais o yé yaïe, les haricots sont pas salés...	Well, o yé yaïe, the beans ain't salty...

(Lomax 1934)

Again, compare the French Acadian source with its even lines and lyrical narrative style:

J'ai fait [tout le] tour du grand bois	I went all around the land
Avec ma [jogue] au pombeau,	With my bottle on the pommel,
Mon [pe]tit [cheval] blanc tout blessé	My little white horse lame
Et mes culottes rapiécetées.	And my clothes in tatters.
Comment tu [veux] que [je vas te] voir?	How do you expect me to visit you?
Tu [restes l'autre] bord du grand bois.	You live on the other side of the woods.
Comment tu [veus je te] marie?	How do you expect me to marry you?
J'ai [rien qu'] une paire de souliers.	I have only one pair of shoes.

(Whitefield 1939 [1969]: 96–97)

Juré and zydeco may be even more directly linked to courtship and its results. The Rodrigue Island dance tradition described earlier is obviously associated with courtship rituals. In ante bellum Louisiana, part of the planters' systematic efforts to eradicate their slaves' African heritage included outlawing slave dances like the calinda. The pretext that they were lewd and lascivious was not entirely unfounded, however, especially from a European point of view. Descriptions of these dances suggest that they may have been associated with African courtship and fertility rituals (Levine 16; Epstein 30). Contemporary black Creole dance styles associated with zydeco are often considered suggestive, to say the least, by Cajun and Anglo-American observers. Zydeco lyrics are often more than suggestive. It doesn't take blues scholars long to figure out the sexual metaphors in such songs as Clifton Chenier's version of the Blind Lemon Jefferson classic, "Black Snake Blues." Nor is there much doubt about the meaning of Canray Fontenot's "Joe Pitre a deux femmes" [Joe Pitre has Two Women], Buckwheat Zydeco's "Give Me a Good Time Woman," Boozoo Chavis's "I'm Going to Dog Hill" ("...where the pretty women're at..."), and Clifton Chenier's version of "I'm a Hog for You, Baby" ("...rooting, rooting, rooting around your door..."). Much of African American expressive culture features double-entendre and sexual imagery, often using foods as euphemisms for female sexual organs (e.g., cabbage, cookie, cake, candy, jelly roll, shortening bread) (Levine 242–243). More recently zydeco hits are even more obvious: "I Want a Big Butt Woman" and "Take Off Your Clothes, Throw'em in the Corner."

There is an unmistakable tendency toward soul and rhythm-and-blues among contemporary Louisiana Creole musicians. Yet the same band leaders who insist on singing English lyrics and adding saxophones, trumpets and electric guitars in their groups demonstrate their deep understanding of the essential tradition when they play what they sometimes call "du vrai zydeco" [real zydeco]. After receiving a Grammy Award in 1984 for his album "I'm Here," Clifton Chenier commented, "Soul didn't get me that Grammy. Rock-and-roll didn't get me that

Grammy. Zydeco got me that Grammy" (1984). Ironically, producer Chris Strachwitz had a hard time convincing Chenier to record zydeco for his first Arhoolie Records releases in the 1960s and '70s (Strachwitz 1980). Chenier wanted to record rock and blues. He was quick to notice, however, that zydeco was what distinguished him from the rest of the crowd of musicians. Whether he was in a local dance hall or on the main stage of a major festival, he never failed to include some of the "real stuff" which featured his brother Cleveland on frottoir and Robert St. Judy on drums. The rest of the Red Hot Louisiana Band dropped out while Clifton and the percussionists beat out a jumping rhythm. Clifton transformed his piano accordion into a melodic drum, using it almost like a complicated version of an African thumb piano. The "real stuff" was also marked by exclusively French vocals and a percussive frenzy that clearly reveal the style originated in the cultural creolization of Afro-Caribbean and Franco-American traditions.

Whatever its linguistic origins, zydeco is, like the blues and rock and roll, a product of the American blending process with a strong African base. But like its fellow Louisiana product, jazz, zydeco has an important French element. A few years ago, anthropologist Alan Lomax predicted that zydeco could become as big as reggae, another result of the creolization process. At the time, that was hard to believe because of the language barrier of hard-core zydeco. Yet, what had begun as a gradual drift towards English lyrics accelerated during the 1980s, as young Creoles were less and less capable of performing in French. Beyond South Louisiana, Queen Ida's 1982 Grammy, Clifton Chenier's 1984 Grammy for "I'm Here!" (one of the most English-orientated of his career) and Rockin' Sidney's 1986 Grammy for "Don't Mess With My Toot Toot" have lots of folks, from Patti LaBelle and Fats Domino to John Fogarty and Paul Simon, interested in zydeco.

Of course, what pop zydeco for national consumption gains in understandability, it loses in some other important areas, including contact with its French elements and intangibles that might be attributed to the social warmth (and even heat) of South Louisiana Creole dance halls. But the form is undeniably enjoying national attention. In South Louisiana, a veritable army of young Creole bands have become interested in the music of their heritage, and it is clear that zydeco has taken its place as part of the national music scene.

If there is a problem with today's zydeco, it is ironically, rooted in the success of its major figure. To understand zydeco today, one must understand Clifton Chenier. Born in the country near Opelousas in 1925, Clifton and his brother Cleveland left Lousiana in 1946 to work in the post-war boom in east Texas. Later, they moved back to Louisiana, though Clifton never completely gave up his foothold in the Houston area.

The Chenier brothers were among the first to popularize their adaptation of the older juré tradition. They turned what had been an unaccompanied group singing tradition into instrumental dance music, performed on an accordion and frottoir. They may not have invented zydeco, but they certainly defined it with every performance. At first, they played for neighbourhood house dances while holding down regular jobs. They decided to devote themselves to music full-time when Clifton was fired from his job in an east Texas oil refinery because he could not and would not climb a tower. When he went back the next day to ask for his job, he played his accordion around the sandwich wagon while waiting for the foreman, and picked up more money during the lunch hour than he had made working hard all week. Clifton and Cleveland quickly became very popular on the weekend dance circuit. Former owners of abandoned dance halls throughout southwest Louisiana speak proudly of the times that he had played at their place.

Clifton's zydeco was culturally between Houston and New Orleans, between the blues and jazz, between the delta and the gulf. It was an ideal illustration of anthropologist C. Paige

Gutierrez's notion that French Louisiana is actually south of the South (Gutierriez 1992: 4). In the 1950s, the influence of rock-and-roll and rhythm-and-blues imposed changes and Clifton succeeded in translating his percussive zydeco sound into modern terms. The group grew to include electric guitars, a bass, drums, a saxophone, and even a trumpet, as Clifton carefully built what he perceptively named the Red Hot Louisiana Band. Together, they strained the floor joists under most of the area's dance halls during the four-hour sets which are still common (even necessary) among performers who play real music for real people in South Louisiana. There is little time for stargazing when folks want to dance.

The principles of the local zydeco music scene will tell you the recipe for success was (and still is) to make a record and get it played on local radio and jukeboxes. It's not clear whether Clifton had a plan for getting ahead, but he had the goods and, whether you're making better mousetraps or playing hotter accordion, people will beat a path to your door. After recording a couple of tunes for Specialty Records in 1955, he drifted from one regional company to another. He finally returned to the national scene in 1964 with Chris Strachwitz's Arhoolie label for whom he made his most memorable recordings. The Arhoolie releases also attracted the attention of young, hip whites in South Louisiana's urban, college-town center, Lafayette. Some overcame their nervousness at being the only whites for blocks to hear the master in his own element, in black clubs such as the Blue Angel and the old Bon Ton Rouley. Clifton's growing popularity soon raced past racial barriers and he became a mainstay of un-air-conditioned student hangouts such as Willie Purple's and the legendary Jay's Lounge and Cockpit.

Clifton believed that his hot zydeco sound could also transcend regional and cultural barriers and he made annual forays to the edges of America. He recorded for numerous labels, including Tomato, Blue Star, Jinn, and Free Bird, and was the subject of several films, including Les Blank's *Hot Pepper*. The fears of those who expected Lawrence Welk-style music from his piano accordion was invariably and immediately laid to rest. The list of musicians Clifton played with during those years reads like a who's who of American blues men and women, old and new, from Big Joe Turner to Big Mama Thornton, B. B. King to Johhny Winter, Ray Charles to Elvin Bishop, Lightnin' Hopkins to Gatemouth Brown. Aware of Europe's long fascination with American jazz and blues, Clifton arranged tours of France, England, Germany, Scandanavia, and Switzerland.

Throughout all of this, Clifton managed to blend success with real life, playing concerts for concert audiences and dances for dance hall audiences. He was keenly aware of his status as a culture hero. In 1971, the King of Zydeco first delighted audiences by appearing with a very conspicuous rhinestone-studded crown (e.g. Gould 1992: xix). By the 1975 Tribute to Cajun Music festival in Lafayette, all the members of his Red Hot Louisiana Band had smaller, prince-sized crowns as well. Yet, the King of Zydeco maintained a warm closeness with his bread-and-butter constituency on the local zydeco circuit, regularly holding court over the bandstand rail in little dance halls throughout South Louisiana.

Clifton Chenier dominated the world of zydeco, as his title "King of Zydeco" implies. He was such a creative genius that he transformed anything he played into his own, including pure blues, country, rock, western swing and big band tunes. He was so important to the tradition he helped define that after his death in 1987, the zydeco community fell into disarray. There was a power vacuum at the top. A well-intentioned attempt to stabilize the situation made by one of Clifton's heirs, Alton "Rockin' Dopsie" Rubin, only made things worse because of the volatile cultural politics of the times. Eventually, several musicians emerged to provide some much-needed leadership. Musicians such as Delton Broussard, John Delafose and Preston Frank brought forward a renewed rural style, featuring the simpler, single-row diatonic accordion. Wilson

"Boozoo" Chavis, one of Clifton's colleagues from the 1950s, came out of retirement to assume the position of elder statesman with a few new hard-driving old-style zydeco recordings. A new generation of musicians such as Stanley "Buckwheat" Dural and his protégé Nathan Williams, as well as the Sam Brothers and Clifton's own son C. J. Chenier, have distinguished themselves with excellent musicianship in the urban tradition developed by Chenier, characterized by the use of a chromatic piano-key accordion. An even younger generation led by the creative forces of musicians such as Terrance Simien, Zydeco Force, and Beau Jocque are exploring new trends, using a variety of instruments, including a chromatic three-row button accordion.

Yet it is sometimes difficult to tell the differences between what passes for contemporary zydeco and the rock, soul and blues it imitates. Clifton was such a huge presence that it was difficult to see past him to explore the sources he used and the styles that had influenced him. Unlike the young Cajun musicians who were reviving Cajun music with a strong sense of history and language, exploring the unaccompanied ballads and instrumental dance tunes of centuries past, it seems that most young Creole musicians only see as far back as the Zydeco King. And when these young musicians look back for inspiration from his recordings, they assume everything he did was zydeco, though he knew the difference. So their own music goes off in as many directions as his experiments, but often without a clear sense of what is the "real stuff". Furthermore, the tradition's poetic quality suffered in the shift from French to English lyrics. The state of contemporary zydeco is a good barometer for the contemporary black Creole society that has only recently begun to explore the complex and specific nature of its history, culture and language. During the decades following World War II, when the Cajuns became interested in preserving their culture and language, the black Creoles were in the throes of the Civil Rights struggle, and rightly so. Though there is still work to be done in this area, today no one really notices who's drinking out of the water fountain and where people are sitting on the bus. The black Creole community has begun to explore its special nature, apparently feeling that it can afford such "luxuries" as culture and language. As organisations such as Creole, Inc., have emerged to lead this effort, so there are musicians who reflect its early results. Lynn August, who grew with zydeco, turned to rock and popular music and recently returned to the music of his heritage, has released several recordings which include jurés he learned while exploring the historical recordings of Alan Lomax (e.g. *Creole Cruiser*, Black Top 1074).

Zydeco may be tempted by its brush with national appeal and move into the fast lane, developing in new directions which distance it from the traditions which gave it birth. Old-time French zydeco might then be relegated to a few South Louisiana versions of jazz's Preservation Hall where only a handful of nostalgia groups play the old stuff, while contemporary groups produce wave after wave of experimental new sounds. Or the tradition may preserve itself and develop in its own terms enough will to continue stirring its pot of "unsalted beans." The current generation will, as it always does, determine the future.

References:

August, Lynn. *Creole Cruiser*. Black Top 1074
Bernard, Shane, and Julia Girouard. 1992. "'Colinda:' Mysterious Origins of a Cajun Folksong." *Journal of Folklore Research* 29:37–52.
Broussard, Delton and the Lawtell Playboys. *Zodico*. Swallow 6009.
Charters, Samuel. 1982. *The Roots of the Blues: An African Search*. New York: Perigree/Putnam.
Chase, Gilbert. 1966. *America's Music, from the Pilgrims to the Present*. New York: McGraw-Hill.

Chenier, Clifton. 1984. Field recording, Barry Jean Ancelet collection, Center for Acadian and Creole Folklore Archive, University of Southwestern Louisiana.

Chenier, Clifton. 1984. *Classic Clifton.* Arhoolie 1082.

Epstein, Dena J. 1977. *Sinful Tunes and Spirituals: Black Folk Music to the Civil War.* Urbana: Univeristy of Illinois Press.

Fontenot, Canray. 1977. Field recording, Barry Jean Ancelet collection, Center for Acadian and Creole Folklore Archive, University of Southwestern Louisiana.

Fontenot, Canray, and Alphonse "Bois-sec" Ardoin. *Boisec: La musique créole.* Arhoolie 1070.

Gould, Philip. 1992. *Cajun Music and Zydeco.* Baton Rouge: Louisiana State University Press.

Gutierrez, C. Paige. 1992. *Cajun Foodways.* Jackson: Univeristy Press of Mississippi.

Levine, Lawrence. 1977. *Black Culture and Black Consciousness: Afro-American Folk Thought from Slavery to Freedom.* Oxford: Oxford University Press.

Lomax, Alan. 1934. Field recordings released as *Louisiana Cajun and Creole Music, 1934: The Lomax Recordings.* Swallow 8003-2.

Sigismund, Wilhelm Koelle. 1963. *Polyglotta Africana.* Graz, Austria: Academische Druck

Strachwitz, Chris. 1980. Personal communication.

[7]

Sounding out the city: music and the sensuous production of place

Sara Cohen

The relationship between music and place is explored through biographical information on one particular individual and his social activities and networks in the city of Liverpool. Music plays a role in producing place as a material setting comprising the physical and built environment; as a setting for everyday social relations, practices and interactions; and as a concept or symbol that is represented or interpreted. This production of place through music is shown to be a contested and ideological process, whilst the dynamic interrelationship between music and place suggests that music plays a very particular and sensual role.

key words Liverpool place ethnicity music local identity

Institute of Popular Music, University of Liverpool, PO Box 147, Liverpool L69 3BX

revised manuscript received 10 May 1995

Introduction

Within the social sciences, studies of the social production of place usually allude to visual representation;[1] this paper, however, explores the role of music and sound. It does so through biographical information on 88-year-old Jack Levy, drawn from a case study in which he participated on popular music and Liverpool's Jewish 'community'. The paper points to connections between some of the musical styles and places, varying in scale from neighbourhoods and cities to the national and multinational or global, that have been particularly important to Jack.

The first part of the paper discusses music and place in terms of everyday social relations, practices and interactions, looking in particular at the ways in which place is 'produced' (defined, represented, transformed) through musical practice. The second part emphasizes the fact that this 'production' is always a contested and ideological process, whilst the third part considers the dynamic interrelationship between music and place. It suggests that music plays a very particular and sensual role in the production of place partly through its peculiar embodiment of movement and collectivity.

I first met Jack in 1992. His wife had died two years previously, after which he had become bored, depressed and unwell. He found walking difficult and his trips outside were less frequent than he would wish. He occasionally visited a nearby home for the Jewish elderly and, when he could manage it, he walked to the synagogue round the corner. Each week he attended social activities held at the Jewish community centre a couple of miles away or at the complex of flats where he lived which was built and serviced for the Jewish elderly by Liverpool Jewish Housing Trust. Through such activities, Jack keeps in contact with people he has grown up with but frequently tires of. A friend of his, Les, used to visit him everyday and a volunteer sometimes came to help with the shopping but last year Les moved abroad and the volunteer can no longer spare the time. Jack regularly telephones his sister who lives in a home for the elderly in Southport but he has no children, his only daughter having died in the early 1970s.

Since our initial meeting, I have visited Jack at his home on a regular basis. His front room is dingy and cramped. The walls are a dark yellow and the patterned carpet has faded. There is a table, a television which is rarely turned on, an armchair and a pale brown sofa. A dark patch at one end of the sofa marks the spot worn by the familiar pressure of Jack's head. Beside the sofa is a wooden chair upon which sits a small radio and a telephone. The sideboard is crammed with old photographs. To help pass the time alone in that room, Jack listens to music on the radio, particularly dance band music. In 1992, he also began to write what he refers to as 'stories'. He would choose a particular subject familiar to him – a Liverpool Jewish family, street, event or activity – and write a paragraph or several pages on what he remembered about it. With his life savings he published some of his reminiscences in two small booklets (Levy 1993, 1994).

Talking to Jack has often proved a frustrating experience. He frequently contradicts himself, he can appear surprisingly naive and he could not be described as particularly articulate or perceptive. His memory, however, is phenomenal. He can take a particular Liverpool street of the 1920s and list by number all the houses or businesses along it, describing the Jewish people who lived or worked in them and tracing their family histories. In addition, Jack has a tremendous sense of humour and he adores music. Like others, he finds it hard to describe music, often relying upon commonplace statements and clichés to explain the way it can make him feel, but he talks of music and dance with a passion and intensity that colours and animates his face and gestures. Recalling some of the people and events he has known, he has introduced me to a world of music through which places are produced and reproduced.

Living and defining place

Relations of kinship and community
Jack was born in London's East End in 1906. His parents were part of a wave of Jewish immigrants who came to Britain from eastern Europe in the late nineteenth century, many of them fleeing the Crimean War. The port of Liverpool acted as a staging post for hundreds of thousands of Jews who passed through it on their way westwards. Some, however, remained in Liverpool and, when Jack moved there with his family at the age of eight, the city's Jewish population had increased to around 11 000, creating what is generally referred to as a Jewish 'quarter' around a street called Brownlow Hill, a name that retains symbolic significance for many Liverpool Jews. Jack's family finally settled in that street after occupying a series of dilapidated

flats in neighbouring streets. His sisters ran a milliner's shop on the street.

Jack left school at fourteen, after which he had 37 different jobs including, for a long time, that of door-to-door salesman selling trinkets and other items largely to Jewish people within the city, collecting money for Jewish charities, selling advertisements for the local Jewish newspaper and working on commission for other Jewish organizations. Over the years, Jack was also hired by various Jewish tailors whenever work was available. Jack's employment experiences have been typical of many Jewish immigrants. Throughout the nineteenth century, Liverpool suffered chronic unemployment; it had relatively little manufacturing industry and, as a port, it attracted large numbers of unskilled labourers. Fluctuations in trade made for an unstable labour market, a situation exacerbated by the flow of Irish, Jewish and other immigrants to the city during the latter half of the nineteenth century. Most of the Jewish immigrants thus lived in poverty. About 40 per cent were unskilled and took to some form of peddling (selling drapery, crockery, furniture, tobacco, stationery, pirated sheet music, etc.). At the same time, there existed within Brownlow Hill a small-scale industrial economy of Jewish tailoring and cabinet-making workshops, many of which were cramped and situated in people's homes. (Jack's mother worked as a button-holer, his father was a tailor, his father-in-law a cabinet-maker.) There were also quite a few Jewish shops in Brownlow Hill – bakers, butchers, booksellers, etc. In contrast to Manchester and Leeds, commerce predominated amongst Liverpool's new immigrant Jews, perhaps largely because of the city's lack of manufacturing industry.

The first generation of immigrants, including Jack's parents, aunts and uncles, tended to work, socialize and worship only with fellow Jews and they spoke Yiddish. They established tightly knit social networks based on relations of kinship and fellowship with those from the same country of origin. Together these groups constituted quite an isolated population. As a young boy, Jack also associated only with fellow Jews. Later, he and his Jewish peers had Gentile friends but never visited their houses or entertained the idea of marrying a Gentile. In 1939, Jack eventually had, like his sister, an arranged marriage.

The impoverished situation of the new immigrants, and that of Liverpool's labouring classes generally, contrasted greatly with the wealth of the

436

city's élite which included a small established Jewish population. By the beginning of the nineteenth century there were already about 1000 Jews in Liverpool, including a middle class of merchants, bankers and shopkeepers (largely of German and Dutch origin) which was well integrated into the upper echelons of Liverpool society but, as a minority, was concerned to be seen to be well-behaved and to fit in with wider society. This highly anglicized Jewish élite lived a few miles outside the 'Jewish quarter' in the large mansions situated around two of Liverpool's finest parks. They had little in common culturally or economically with the new immigrants. In 1906, a lawyer and renowned member of this élite, Bertram L Benas, gave a presidential address to the Liverpool Jewish Literary Society in which he said

> a self-imposed ghetto is for the first time in process of formation in our city. Entire streets are being wholly occupied by Russo-Polish immigrants in the Brownlow Hill district . . . The non-Jewish residents are removing to the more distant outskirts . . . To see them at prayer is quite a revelation to modern Liverpool Jewry. Their services are full of emphatic, vivid, even uncouth devotion. To listen to their ready and soulful responses, to see the weird swinging of their bodies during their orisons, to hear the loud and earnest sounds of their great Amen, their hearty unison in songs of praise, wanting perhaps in musical culture, yet giving food for inspiration.

Class and other distinctions amongst Liverpool Jews were reinforced in the popular press. A series of articles entitled 'The Liverpool Jew' appeared in the *Liverpool Review* of 1899. The articles were full of anti-Semitic references to Jewish character and culture. Four classes of Liverpool Jew ('specimens') were portrayed, from the uppermost 'English Jew', down to the 'newly-imported Foreign Jew' based in the 'little colony' as the Brownlow Hill neighbourhood was referred to, a term which, like 'ghetto' or 'quarter', implies a position of powerlessness and incarceration. Second-generation immigrants, comprising the second class, were typified as frequenters of music and dance halls: 'exhibiting his "light fantastic toe" at cheap cinderellas and dances' (*ibid.*, 25 February 1899), whilst the English Jew was portrayed as much more 'cultured', artistic, literary and '[m]usical – to an acute degree'; 'found at almost every concert devoted to the classical productions of the world's great composers' (*ibid.*, 4 March 1899). Such stereotypes illustrate the way in which

music (in this case through writing and verbal discourse) is used to distinguish people and places according to class and ethnicity, thereby underlining the emphasis of Stokes (1994b, 6) on the importance of turning from

> defining the essential and 'authentic' traces of identity 'in' music . . . to the question of how music is used by social actors in specific local situations to erect boundaries, to maintain distinctions between us and them.

Musical performance, exchange and interaction

Yet social practices involving the consumption and production of music also draw people together and symbolize their sense of collectivity and place. For the immigrant Jews of Brownlow Hill, music (religious, folk, popular and classical) played an important role in everyday life and the rituals, routines and discourses that comprised it. Music was the focus of many social gatherings, helping to establish and strengthen the immigrants' relations with each other or their relationship with God. Such relations were also established and defined through other musical practices, such as the exchange of musical recordings. In addition, music framed particular events such as wedding ceremonies and religious festivals, setting them apart from other daily activities, heightening their symbolic significance (Finnegan 1989).

Most of the immigrant Jews were indeed very religious, and religious music and practice undoubtedly helped maintain individual and collective identity in a context of considerable uncertainty and unfamiliarity. The immigrants set up *Chevra*, societies through which those who had originated from a particular eastern European town or district met together to worship and socialize, often in someone's house. Gradually, they set up their own synagogues which contrasted greatly with the austere opulence and grandeur of those frequented by the Jewish élite. (They also set up their own welfare organizations, assisted by the Jewish élite for whom charitable activity played an important role, as it has done in many Euro-American Jewish circles, acting as a source of collective cohesion and prestige.)

Within Judaism, particularly its eastern European traditions, vocal music is believed to provide the closest communication with God, with the Hasidic song or wordless chant possessing 'more power than any other prayer; representing pure religious ecstasy' (Werner 1980, 629) and embodying the notion that, while the life of a text is limited, the melody lives on forever. The chanting is traditionally done by and for men. The Hasidic song has left a strong imprint on eastern European Jewish music as a whole. Today, synagogue attendance has declined among Liverpool Jews but the symbolic meanings and ritual imagery of the synagogue are deeply internalized. Jack's stories often incorporate religious references and synagogue music has great emotional significance for him. It 'shows you your place', he explains, and it is

> traditional. They daren't alter it. That music goes on and on and on. Fathers play to sons, and sons play to sons. Always the same. It never alters . . . that music is there forever.

He thus depicts the music as a timeless (and gendered) tradition, representing security and stability.

When Jack was young, his parents used to listen on the gramophone at home to recordings of the great *chazans* imported by a nearby record retailer from a Jewish wholesalers in London. They also listened to recordings of Yiddish folk music. One of Jack's memories of music as a young child is of his mother and aunts sitting together to sing Yiddish songs and weeping to their mournful sounds as they reminded them of Poland, their homeland (*der heim*). Such songs typically depict aspects of daily life – songs about separation and parting, work, children's songs, women's songs, etc. Jack said of the women, 'They loved to weep, that was their pleasure'. Many people maintain a link with their past through attachment to specific places and music is often used to remember such places. The Yiddish music provoked and structured particular emotions in Jack's female relatives, through which they expressed their feelings about their country of origin and the relations and practices they had left behind. The music brought them together and symbolized their collective identity. Listening to that music today, Jack is reminded of those women and the female domestic space or home that they represented.

Referring to the recordings that his relatives listened to, Jack said

> And somehow those records came around. And one person got hold of one, and it was passed all round . . . And bit by bit we used to have records.

This description conforms with Jack's depiction of Liverpool Jews as living 'in one circle', a spatial

metaphor for neighbourhood that incorporates Jewish records and songs as part of the circle and part of the process of defining it. Likewise, there existed for a short period a Liverpool Yiddish book publisher, Ghetto Press, and a regional Yiddish newspaper that Jack also described as being passed around the neighbourhood from house to house.

But what Jack talks about most in relation to the past is popular culture, particularly music and dance which he describes as 'the whole life and soul of (his) generation'. As a young man, he attended the cinema on a weekly basis and the films and music he saw and heard there greatly inspired him. He has sung, for example, the songs of Al Jolson for me, demonstrating through his voice and the movement of his arms the emotional intensity that they evoke. Jolson was also the son of Jewish immigrants struggling to find their place in a new country and Gabler (1989, 145) wrote that he was 'Caught between the old life and the new . . . of both and of neither'. Jolson's on-screen performances often articulated this experience, which is perhaps partly why his music appealed so strongly to Jack.[2]

Since he left school in 1920, Jack's major obsession has been the music and dance of the dance halls. 'Dancing', he said, 'was my life'. At one time he was dancing six nights a week at Jewish functions, at the tailor's club and at various dance halls in the city. During his early twenties, he started running dances himself and acted as MC in various local dance halls. Jack's reminiscences indicate the attraction that dance-hall culture had for him, the sense of excitement and occasion, as well as the anticipation and preparation that a dance provoked, and the escape it offered from the worries and routines of everyday life. He describes in vivid detail the women he danced with, their beauty and glamour, and the fashionable dress of both them and the men.[3] Sitting on his sofa, he sways his torso and arms, closing his eyes in an expression of blissful engrossment, attempting to convey to me the physical attraction of the dance and the heightened sensuality and pleasure it evoked, displaying a sense of pride in the talents he had as a dancer and the proficiency and skill with which he mastered the steps.

For Jack's bar mitzvah, his parents bought him a piano and, although none of his family could play it, there was always someone in the neighbourhood who could. Jack remembers social gatherings in his house when people would stand around the piano and sing popular songs of the day (*Rambling rose*,

438

for example). Others in the neighbourhood played instruments on a semi-professional basis and during the 1920s and 1930s there were quite a few Jewish dance bands based in the Brownlow Hill neighbourhood. Jack was close friends with these musicians and he refers to them with affection and pride as 'local musicians', local here meaning not just musicians from the Brownlow Hill neighbourhood but that neighbourhood's Jewish musicians (i.e. claiming them as the community's own). Similarly, Jack sometimes talks of 'Liverpool' or 'this town' when he is referring only to its Jewish community. Hence 'local' is a discursive shifter or variable determined by factors such as ethnicity and class.

Jack yearned to perform in a dance band himself and later, during the 1940s, he took the plunge and spent all his savings on a saxophone. He joined a band but eventually decided that he wasn't good enough. Like many of his peers, he also dreamed of being a professional dancer but again decided that he wasn't good enough:

> And the only place to be a professional was London, and all my family was in Liverpool. I wouldn't leave them for the world to go to London.

However, the beginnings of the modern British entertainment industry coincided with Jewish immigration from eastern Europe and attracted many enterprising immigrants. Access was relatively easy compared with other industries due to lower financial barriers and less discrimination. It was an area not yet dominated by Gentile talent and capital, partly because it was considered risky and disreputable. Consequently, Jews entered the industry at every level. Close inspection of reports and publications on Liverpool's theatres and cinemas, for example, and of local Jewish archives, reveals passing references to Jewish performers, entertainment agents and owners, managers and promoters of clubs and cinemas. (This situation was mirrored in other British cities, particularly London, Manchester and Birmingham. It was magnified in America.) On the music retail side, there have been several Jewish-owned music instrument and record shops in Liverpool.[4]

Music and the social, cultural and economic production of place

The above account of the social and cultural life of the immigrant Jews of Brownlow Hill has been brief, fragmented and rather superficial. It has promoted a view of music and place not as fixed and bounded texts or entities but as social practice involving relations between people, sounds, images, artifacts and the material environment. It has also highlighted the importance of place in defining Jewish ethnicity[5] and indicated some of the ways in which music is involved in the social, cultural and economic production of place.

Jack is very proud of Liverpool and its history. Explaining why he feels so strongly about the city, he said

> I live here. My home's here. My mother and father, my daughter, they're buried here. So where they're buried is my home.

Places thus reify or symbolize social relationships and kinship relations are obviously of particular emotional significance.[6] Although Jack has few living relatives in Liverpool, he is bound to the city through relations with dead kin and relations of affinity with fellow Jews. Music is one means through which such relations are established, maintained and transformed. For Jack, it is sound as well as sight and smell that conjures up images, emotions, memories of Brownlow Hill. His attempts to demonstrate the physical pleasures of music and the way in which it is experienced within the body, stimulating movement and emotion, emphasize the intensity of experience evoked by music and its effectiveness in producing a sense of identity and belonging. The musical practices and interactions of the immigrant Jews helped to define the particular geographical and material space within the city that they inhabited and, at the same time, they invested that space with meaning and a sense of identity and place, thus distinguishing it from other places within the city.

Hence, places are socially produced as practical settings or contexts for social activity but, through such activity, places are also produced in a conceptual and symbolic sense. Appadurai (1993) has thus described locality as both figure and ground, representing a combination of the material and the conceptual, and Stokes (1994a, 4) underlines the importance of turning from the notion of music *in* a place to look at the ways in which place is evoked through music:

> Music does not then simply provide a marker in a prestructured social space, but the means by which this space can be transformed.

Comparative material on Liverpool's Irish and black populations emphasizes the role of music in the practical and symbolic organization of space, in the spatial politics of everyday life and in the expression of ethnic identity. One musician, for example, describes how, in the 1930s, a black neighbour of his would play his records loudly and open all the windows so that the sound would travel and publically proclaim his status as the owner of a gramophone player. Meanwhile, a colour bar operated in many of the city's clubs and dance halls which led to a situation where black musicians performed in 'white' spaces and the leisure activities of black people were restricted to one particular area of the city. Elsewhere in the city, marching concertina bands acted as a focus and trigger for Irish sectarian conflict, representing an appropriation or invasion of public space and a marker of territory (McManus 1994).

Whilst music defines a sense of 'this place', it also marks relations of kinship, alliance and affinity with places elsewhere. Yiddish music, for example, was commonly used by the immigrant Jews to maintain relations with eastern Europe and, from the 1920s onwards, various Hebrew songs were used to forge relations with another home or promised land and to express Jewish nationalism.[7] Zionism and other political movements have used music to reify particular places in the pursuit of common goals so that those places come to embody the future and alternative ways of living. Many songs of *Eretz* Israel represent a synthesis of elements from east European and middle eastern folk song. They are usually about the land and those who work on it and many have an assertive, patriotic ring, thus contrasting with the Yiddish songs that conjure up images of everyday life in homelands like Poland. Jack finds it hard to relate to songs of *Eretz* Israel, partly perhaps because – unlike his contemporaries who have established connections with other places (especially London and Israel) through their middle-class children and grandchildren – Jack has few such connections. The songs are in a language he cannot understand and he sees them as belonging to another generation.

> I don't want to know. They're not in my era. Once we became a land of our own, a State, the whole thing changed. The youngsters took over ... and it was different then.

Thus Jack sometimes expresses a sense of alienation from his contemporaries and from the younger

middle-class Jewish establishment in Liverpool, yet says at the same time, 'I knew their parents', again expressing a sense of community and belonging through kinship ties.

Relations between Liverpool Jews and Jews in Israel, America or elsewhere are reinforced through visiting musicians and other musical exchanges. Jack's reminiscences frequently allude to Liverpool Jews now, in his words, 'scattered all over the world'. Like other Jews of his generation, he discussed the music of Jewish immigrants from eastern Europe, such as Irving Berlin and Sophie Tucker based in America, in a manner that suggests a sense of affinity with those sharing similar heritages and experiences. In addition, however, Jack frequently cites Irish songs and songs of black slaves in America, acknowledging through them a sense of unity with other immigrant or oppressed peoples. He said of the latter

> They all had their songs ... they've got their roots here, their roots there ... Nobody wants them. They're a misfit. They get out, but where can you go? They've got no home.

The images and information that Jack has acquired about such people have been obtained largely through popular song and film. He talks with affection about the 'black mammy women' from the American South, describing the little spectacles they wore and their warm-heartedness. He also quotes at length from the song *Danny boy*, linking the lyrics to Irish experiences of oppression and linking that to Jewish experience and history, thus suggesting the marking of 'families of resemblance' through music (Lipsitz 1989, 136).

This highlights the way in which music enables Jack to travel in an imaginary sense to different times and places. Illustrating how music inspires his fantasy, transporting him from one place and immersing him somewhere else, Jack described his Monday afternoons at a Liverpool ballroom during the 1920s. Monday, he explained, was traditionally washing day. The women used to take off their aprons after a hard morning's work, do their hair, put on their finery and take the bus to the city centre, arriving at the ballroom for the 2.30pm start. Jack once danced there to a tune entitled *In a garden in Italy* and he enthused about how the music made him picture that garden and

440

how wonderful that experience was. Jack said of music

> It doesn't matter if it's dance music or what, it's there in my radio, and you're in another world. It takes you to a new world.

He cited songs with American places in their titles, such as *Back home in Tennessee, Chicago, Memphis blues, California here I come*. He depicted the scene at the Swanny River:

> all the women with their wide dresses. The men with their bowler hats. So there you are, that's the Swanny. I don't even know where it is. I don't even know if there is a Swanny River ... I used to lie awake at night going through all the districts of the tunes ... Marvellous ... You'd go off to sleep thinking of them.

In a completely different sense, music, as a profession, also offered some Liverpool Jews a 'way out' of the place they were in and the possibility of creating a new place. In his portrayal of the eastern European Jewish immigrants who founded and built Hollywood, Gabler (1989, 4) argued that the desire of these immigrants to assimilate and achieve status and power led them to a 'ferocious, even pathological embrace of America'. Through film, these Jews created an idealized image of the America to which they aspired.

> Prevented from entering the real corridors of power, they created a new country, 'an empire of their own', and colonised the American imagination to such an extent that the country came largely to be defined by the movies.

The same was achieved through song by George Gershwin, Irving Berlin, Jerome Kern and other Jewish composers. The experience of migration may not only exaggerate attachments to romanticized homelands but also lead migrants stridently to assert an adoptive belonging (Lowenthal 1985).

In the biography of Vesta Tilley, well-known music-hall performer and wife of Walter de Frece – a Liverpool Jew and theatrical entrepreneur involved with the music-hall business – Maitland (1986) suggests certain parallels with the experience of the Hollywood Jews. De Frece spearheaded the move to make music hall more respectable and enhance its appeal to the middle classes. He had political and social aspirations which eventually led him and Vesta Tilley to drop their associations with music hall. Later on he was awarded a knighthood

and in 1924 he became a Member of Parliament and a Deputy Lieutenant. This suggests that music hall both helped and hindered De Frece's efforts to achieve upward mobility and represent respectable Englishness and it points to the ideological significance of music in the production of place.

Representing and transforming place

Music, ideology and social mobility

Jews like Jack gradually assimilated with wider Liverpool culture not just through interaction with Gentiles at dance halls and elsewhere but through pressures brought to bear upon them by the Jewish establishment. Whilst Jack's mother and aunts wept to Yiddish music at home, Jack and his peers were singing *Land of hope and glory* at school, undergoing a social and educational programme instigated by the Jewish élite. The programme was designed to anglicize the immigrants, ridding them of their Yiddish language and culture; to control their leisure, directing it away from disreputable activities (e.g. gambling and dance halls); and to depoliticize them, exorcizing the socialist, anarchist and trade-union activity that some of them promoted. The élite were motivated by a variety of impulses. They perhaps feared, for example, that the foreign ways of the newcomers would threaten their acquired respectability and standing and attract hostility to the Jewish population as a whole. Alternatively, popular culture has commonly acted as a focus for moral panic and social control, particularly in connection with working-class or immigrant youth. The concern of the Jewish Liverpool élite with anglicization and with adapting Jewish tradition to wider culture can be detected early on in the rapid changes they introduced to their synagogues. A choir was introduced in one Liverpool synagogue at the beginning of the 1840s, for example, and an organ in another during the 1870s. These and other changes have continually reflected and provoked divisions among British Jews regarding processes of assimilation and distinctiveness.

The social and educational programme aimed at the new immigrants was instigated through a framework of Jewish societies and clubs, many of which were based upon models in the wider English society. They included a working men's club which ran classes in English and a branch of the Jewish Lads' Brigade – a national Jewish cadet force based on the Church Lads' Brigade – whose letterheaded paper states that its object

> is to train its members in loyalty, humour, discipline and self respect that they shall become worthy and useful citizens and be a credit to their country and their community.

The Brigade was backed by a number of social clubs, including the Jewish Lads' Club, the Jewish Boy Scouts, and the Jewish Girls' Clubs. The process of anglicization continued in the Hebrew school founded in 1840. Pupils were encouraged to change their names, mark British celebrations and enter choral competitions and similar events.

These societies and clubs represented leisure and entertainment but they were also highly politicized, combining both power and pleasure. Music was used to mould particular identities and allegiances, whether it be the military brass band music of the Jewish Lads' Brigade, the choral and orchestral societies of the Jewish working men's club, or songs and anthems which acted as symbols of Englishness and expressions of national loyalty and unity. The programme indicates pressures of assimilation but also the simultaneous concern with maintaining distinctiveness as Jews. Jewish societies, clubs and dances were regarded as safe contexts in which Jewish people could meet and form suitable friendships with people of their own kind. The programme was extremely successful. Within a single generation, Yiddish had practically disappeared from the cultural scene.

Yet the production of national or other place-bound identities is always a contested process and not all the immigrants were totally influenced by the social and educational programme instigated by the élite. Many kept to their own more informal leisure activities based around their homes. Some, like Jack, attended rambles, played football and participated in other activities organized by Jewish societies but also attended 'outside' functions such as local dance halls frequented by Gentiles and forbidden to many Jewish young people. Meanwhile, the Jewish élite patronized different clubs and venues, and Jack never mixed with them. They also had their own social and cultural institutions – literary societies, for example, which gradually began to encourage the more up-and-coming of the new immigrants to join their activities, until members of this *nouveau riche* started setting up their own similar organizations. Most such societies

organized regular dances, concerts and gramophone recitals in addition to dramatic, sporting and fundraising activities, and debates and lectures. According to their minute books, many talks focused on politics and high culture.[8] Debates addressed issues such as the division between established and immigrant Jews, and the generation gap between immigrants and their 'English children'. These societies gradually died out in the face of growing competition from the newly flourishing entertainment industries.

Music, stability, security

Like many other immigrant Jewish populations, Liverpool's immigrant Jews experienced rapid social and economic advancement, and within two generations a significant transformation of the class position of the immigrants had occurred. This was due to a mixture of social, cultural and economic factors, including the fact that the city's high rate of unemployment discouraged further Jewish immigration. Most of the pedlars progressed as entrepreneurs. They came into contact with Gentiles because they moved around a lot and did better economically than the masses of skilled cabinet-makers and tailors who worked long hours in small outfits for a fixed wage. However, the latter's occupational structure also eventually shifted, towards clothing, drapery and furniture businesses, and towards the professions into which many were encouraged as a means of improving themselves and their families.

Biographical information on some of the Jewish individuals and families involved with the Liverpool entertainment industries illustrates the way in which they were able quickly to establish themselves in those industries but also indicates the cultural transformation that enhanced status and respectability might demand. Mal Levy, for example, had a recording contract in the 1960s and toured the country as a performer until he succumbed to parental pressure and returned to Liverpool to join the family tailoring business:

> I think it was 'don't put your son on the stage'. You know the old fashioned Jewish outlook – it's not a good job, it's not a decent job . . . They looked down on music in those days.

Such attitudes help explain why Liverpool Jews have tended to work in music business and management rather than performance, although there are far

442

fewer now than there used to be, and why rock and pop music have received such little attention from the city's Jewish institutions.

Brian Epstein came from a respected Liverpool family that ran a lucrative furniture business. He opened a record retail branch within this business before taking up management of the Beatles and setting up his own music-management company. According to Coleman (1989, 83), Epstein's father, along with other relatives, wasn't too thrilled about Brian's association with the Beatles ('those yobbos'), and persuaded him to take on his brother, Clive, as joint director. Although Epstein's success eventually earned him respect from Liverpool's Jewish community, his obituary in the *Jewish Chronicle* stated

> The sad thing is that Brian was never completely *au courant* with the music that he was so much involved in . . . His strength of character came from the solidarity of his upbringing and the integrity of his background. It was this strength that he relied on when his artistic judgement failed. (*ibid.*, 415)

During Epstein's funeral in Liverpool, the officiating rabbi ignored his achievements and fame and described him as 'a symbol of the malaise of the 60s generation' (*ibid.*, 410). News of Brian's death in the *Liverpool Jewish Gazette* was limited to a few short lines in the obituary notices at the back. It began, 'Brian Epstein, manager of the Beatles' and went straight on to mention his donations to Jewish charities.

Whilst the first part of the paper pointed to music as a fundamental part of everyday life and to its role in the production of identity, belonging and place, the second part has emphasized the ideological dimension to this process. Particular musical styles and activities come to symbolize particular values and they can be used as a tool to transform notions of place and identity in order to maintain or challenge a particular hierarchical social order. Music is thus bound up with the struggle for power, prestige, place. It reflects but also influences the social relations, practices and material environments through which it is made.

Place, image, status

As the immigrants made their way up the economic and social scale, they gradually moved out of the Brownlow Hill neighbourhood. During the 1930s the area underwent massive slum clearance which hastened the Jewish exodus. By the late 1930s only a small minority remained in Brownlow Hill. The Jews moved along Smithdown Road to settle in the more affluent neighbouring suburbs of Allerton, Woolton and Childwall where the overwhelming majority of Liverpool Jews are now based. As one informant put it, 'it is easier to be Jewish when you live with other Jews'. During Jack's lifetime a great transformation in Liverpool's Jewish population has thus taken place. It has involved a shift from notions of Russian or Polish Jews to Anglo Jews; from notions of a Jewish 'quarter' or 'ghetto' to a Jewish 'area' or 'district'; from a split between the élite, more established Jews and the immigrant Jews to a single middle-class Jewish community based in that area or district. Notions of being inside, outside or 'on the fringes' of the community have strengthened as socio-economic homogeneity amongst the Jewish population intensified, increasing pressures for conformity.

Many young Liverpool Jews describe the community as 'incestuous' and 'traditional'. The head of music at the Jewish school told me that Jewish religious 'rules' make it impossible for many of the Jewish children to join in some musical events and activities and that, even if they aren't religious, they have to be seen to be. 'That's why it's such a close knit community', she said, 'because they make their fun together'. When Liverpool's economic situation worsened after the 1960s, young Jews, along with those from other social groups, began to leave the city in search of economic and social opportunities elsewhere. This, along with emigration to Israel, a drop in the birth rate and the high rate of inter-marriage, led to a significant decline in the Jewish population. At present there are around 4000 Jews in Liverpool and the Jewish authorities recently launched a 'Come back to Liverpool' campaign and video to encourage younger people to stay in, or return to, the city. The video emphasizes the uniqueness of the Jewish community and the area in which it is located. The smallness and safeness of the community is also emphasized, pointing out that it is easier to be someone in such a context rather than be a small fish in a big pool somewhere else. The video features leisure amenities that project an image linked to classical music, emphasizing, for example, long-standing Jewish associations with the Royal Liverpool Philharmonic Orchestra. Notions of 'community' and 'Jewishness' have thus become more commonly defined through so-called 'high' culture.

The place of music

Embodying place

Travel and migration

The story of Jewish migration is a familiar one that features strongly in Jewish collective memory. Judaism has been likened by one Liverpool Jew to a 'mental map by which we find each other as Jews in every part of the globe' (Kokosolakis 1982, 199). Jack's mental maps of the world, of Britain, of Liverpool, are partly based upon collective knowledge and experience of the geographical global movements of Jewish people, especially the movement of Jews from eastern Europe to particular British and American cities, and the movement of Liverpool Jews from the city centre to the suburbs.

In contexts of change and mobility, the production of place is often intensified. Writing about Turkish and Irish migrants, Stokes (1994b, 114) points out that

> place, for many migrant communities, is something constructed through music with an intensity not found elsewhere in their social lives.[9]

Of today's global mobility, Stokes wrote that 'the discourses in which place is constructed and celebrated in relation to music have never before had to permit such flexibility and ingenuity' (*ibid.*, 114). Musical sounds and structures reflect but also provoke and shape such movement. Hebrew songs, for example, helped inspire the Zionist movement, whilst Irish traditional music has developed through continual movement between Ireland (the 'home country') and the more distant countries adopted by Irish emigrants. Irish music influenced and blended with different musical styles in America, for example, and some of the resulting hybrid styles and sounds were then reimported to Ireland and treated as authentic, traditional expressions of Irishness.

Many musical compositions address the experience of migration or travel more directly through lyrics or through the culturally specific semiotic coding of musical sounds and structures. American country and blues musicians, for example, have written about the experience of being on the road[10] and Jack sings songs about leaving and returning written by Irish and other migrants. Such songs are prevalent in ports like Liverpool with their mobile and displaced populations, for whom concepts of 'home' and 'homeland' can evoke strong emotions, although relations with, and notions of, homeland depend on the particular circumstances of those involved, e.g. whether they emigrated individually or, like the Jews, in family groups. Today in Liverpool, songs from *Fiddler on the roof* are often played at social gatherings of elderly Jews like Jack, songs that remind them of their collective origins and experiences of homelessness and emigration.

Place is also produced through the shorter journeys, routes and activities of everyday life. All Jack's stories are about the city and the people and places within it. Sitting in his front room, he has taken me on a tour of parts of the city, house by house, dance hall by dance hall, street by street,[11] pointing out relevant events, individuals, family and other relationships as we pass by and transforming my own view of the city. Jack's phenomenal memory of, and emotional investment in, these buildings, locations and social networks may be due in part to the daily door-to-door journeys he conducted around the city by foot as a travelling salesman.[12] His leisure activities as a dancer, which took him on a nightly basis to various parts of the city, have added to his perspective on the city and its spatial geography.

> I've been round this town for the last 70 years and I know it backwards. I know everybody, and almost everybody knows me, except the growing generation.

In this sense, places can be seen to be literally embodied. Through their bodies and bodily movements (whether through long-distance travel, walking or conversation), people experience their environment physically. Depending upon the circumstances surrounding them, some movements, such as long-distance travel, can be quite stressful. Other more repetitive movements, such as the day-to-day journeys involved with work or the sensual and expressive movements of dance, can be particularly memorable or intense. All can have a deep impact upon individual and collective memory and experiences of place, and upon emotions and identities associated with place.

Bodies, sounds, sentiments

Music can evoke or represent this physical production of place quite well. There is no space here to explore evidence for this in detail but personal observations supported by the work of several critical musicologists indicate, without essentializing music, the particular way in which music produces place.

444

First, music is in a sense embodied. Musical performances represent repetitive physical movements, whether through the fingering of instrumentalists or the gestures of dancers. Music moves bodies in a way that distinguishes it from everyday speech and action and from the visual arts and, although it is part of everyday life, it is also perceived as something special, different from everyday experience (Finnegan 1989). Hence, many people in Liverpool and elsewhere have prioritized music, making enormous financial sacrifices so that their children might learn and create it.

In addition, we listen to music and hear the presence and movements of the performing musicians. Hence, Tagg (1981, 1) describes music as an 'extremely particular form of interhuman communication', involving

> a concerted simultaneity of non-verbal sound events or movements . . . [which makes music] particularly suited to expressing collective messages of affective and corporeal identity of individuals in relation to themselves, each other, and their social, as well as physical, surroundings. (*ibid.*, 18)

Music also creates its own time, space and motion, taking people out of 'ordinary time'.[13] Blacking (1976, 51) points out that

> We often experience greater intensity of living when our normal time values are upset . . . music may help to generate such experiences.

Furthermore, as sound, music fills and structures space within us and around us, inside and outside. Hence, much like our concept of place, music can appear to envelop us.

The images and experiences engendered by music are, of course, dependent upon the particular circumstances in which the music is performed and heard, and upon the type of musical style and activity involved. But, through its embodiment of movement and collectivity, and through the peculiar ambiguity of its symbolic forms,[14] music can appear to act upon and convey emotion in a unique way and it represents an alternative discourse to everyday speech and language, although both are ideologically informed and culturally constructed. Hence, male working-class rock musicians in Liverpool use music to express sentiment in a manner that is discouraged in other public settings (see Cohen 1991). Their music is very personal, although, at the same time, it is created for public

performance. For the general listener, just one simple musical phrase can simultaneously represent a private world of memory and desire and a collective mood or a soundtrack to particular public events (hence, the contrasting use of music in BBC Radio 4's *Desert island discs* and BBC1's *The golden years*).

For Jack, sitting and listening to music alone on the radio, or simply talking about music, can evoke some of his most intense feelings and experiences. His musical tastes and experiences are individual, reflecting his personal biography. At the same time, however, his reminiscences have been shown to be shaped by the social relations, networks, collectivities that he has been a part of. All this indicates the effectiveness of music in stimulating a sense of identity, in preserving and transmitting cultural memory and in the sensuous production of place. Individuals can use music as a cultural 'map of meaning', drawing upon it to locate 'themselves in different imaginary geographies at one and the same time' (as Hall 1995, 207, has written of 'diaspora') and to articulate both individual and collective identities.

Conclusion

This paper has explored the relationship between music and place through a specific biography bound up with specific social relations and situations rather than through more abstract discussion. Place has been presented as both concept and material reality, representing social and symbolic interrelations between people and their physical environment.

Music reflects social, economic, political and material aspects of the particular place in which it is created. Changes in place thus influence changes in musical sounds and styles (hence the gradual anglicization of eastern European synagogue music brought to Liverpool). The discussion has highlighted, however, ways in which music not just reflects but also produces place. First, music is bound up with the social production of place. The discussion has illustrated ways, for example, in which music acts as a focus or frame for social gatherings, special occasions and celebrations; provokes physical movement or dance; and involves everyday social interactions such as the exchange of records and other musical artefacts, as well as business and industrial activity. Such musical practices have been shown to establish, maintain, transform social relations and to define and shape material and geographical settings for social action.

At the same time, music has been discussed as conceptual and symbolic practice. Music can, for example, be intentionally used to represent place. Lyrics might refer directly to specific places but musical sounds and structures might also represent place, either through culturally familiar symbols (accordions, for example, to represent France, or the augmented fourth to represent the Orient (Stokes 1994a)), or in more particular ways, as illustrated by the musical stereotyping of Brownlow Hill (the 'little colony') in the Liverpool press. Such collective musical symbols associate places with particular images, emotions, meanings and they provoke or shape social action. Hence, anthems and Zionist songs inspire nationalist sentiments and movements whilst other musical styles might be linked in similar ways with issues of class and hierarchy.

Music is not only bound up with the production of place through collective interpretation, it is also interpreted in idiosyncratic ways by individual listeners, with songs, sounds and musical phrases evoking personal memories and feelings associated with particular places, as revealed by Jack's interpretations of Yiddish music and the songs of Al Jolsen. Places like Liverpool, Poland and parts of America have been shown to have emotional and symbolic significance for Jack because of the relations of kinship, affinity and alliance that they embody. Such relations are maintained, strengthened and transformed through social practice and cultural interaction. This includes listening to and producing music, the verbal discourse and physical movements surrounding such practices and the ideology informing them.

Music thus plays a unique and often hidden role in the social and cultural production of place and, through its peculiar nature, it foregrounds the dynamic, sensual aspects of this process emphasizing, for example, the creation and performance of place through human bodies in action and motion. Stokes (1994a, 3) suggests that

> The musical event, from collective dances to the act of putting a cassette or CD into a machine, evokes and organises collective memories and present experiences of place with an intensity, power and simplicity unmatched by any other social activity.

The production of place through music is always a political and contested process and music has been shown to be implicated in the politics of place, the struggle for identity and belonging, power and prestige.

Acknowledgement

I would like to thank the Leverhulme Trust for funding the research project that enabled the study to be carried out.

Notes

1. See also Jackson (1989); Stoller (1989) and others on the visualist bias in 'western' culture.
2. This common experience of being caught between different places, or of 'bifocality', has, of course, been widely studied. Much has been written, for example, on the dual allegiance experienced by Anglo-American Jews, with a Jewish nationality existing alongside a British or American one (e.g. see Goldstein and Goldscheider 1985).
3. Fashion played an important role in the lives of Jews like Jack, largely perhaps because of their domination of the local tailoring industry. An emphasis upon being fashionably dressed might also have given them a sense of status and prestige. Gabler (1989), writing on the immigrant Jews of Hollywood, frequently refers to their smart and fashionable attire, as do the satirical articles on 'The Liverpool Jews' published in the *Liverpool Review* (1899).
4. Hence the Jewishness of the entertainment infrastructure surrounding the Beatles, including clubs, agents, managers, retailers and solicitors.
5. See Hall (1995) for a reconception of ethnicity as a politics of location.
6. See Werlen (1993) writing on Pareto (1980).
7. Zionism was brought to Liverpool by immigrant Jews early in the century when anti-Semitism was rife throughout Europe. The movement was opposed by the Jewish élite who saw it as a threat to their acquired respectability, status and Englishness.
8. One, for instance, was on Mendelssohn as an example of a fine Jewish composer.
9. See also Clifford (1992) on 'Travelling cultures'.
10. Metaphors of roads, trains, etc. have infused much of Euro-American popular culture, which may also be attributed to fantasies of escape and celebrations of distance or modernity.
11. He is particularly proud of the fact that he can list every dance hall that ever existed in the city.
12. Lynch (1960) and other human geographers have studied people's mental maps of their immediate locality in relation to their habitual movements through the locality.
13. See Tagg (1979) on musical time.
14. See Tagg (1981) on the non-referentiality of music.

446

References

Appadurai A 1993 The production of locality Unpubl. paper delivered at the decennial conference of the Association of Social Anthropologists, Oxford University, July

Blacking J 1976 *How musical is man* Faber, London

Clifford J 1992 Travelling cultures in **Grossberg L, Nelson C and Treichler P A** eds *Cultural studies* Routledge, London 96–112

Cohen S 1991 *Rock culture in Liverpool* Oxford University Press, Oxford

Coleman R 1989 *Brian Epstein: the man who made the Beatles* Viking, Harmondsworth

Finnegan R 1989 *The hidden musicians: music-making in an English town* Cambridge University Press, Cambridge

Gabler N 1989 *An empire of their own: how the Jews invented Hollywood* W H Allen, London

Goldstein S and Goldscheider C 1985 *Jewish Americans: three generations in a Jewish community* University Press of America, Lanham

Hall S 1995 New cultures for old in **Massey D and Jess P** eds *A place in the world? Places, cultures and globalization* vol. 4 *The shape of the world: explorations in human geography* Oxford University Press, Oxford

Jackson M 1989 *Paths toward a clearing* Indiana University Press, Bloomington

Kokosolakis N 1982 *Ethnic identity and religion: tradition and change in Liverpool Jewry* University Press of America, Washington

Levy J 1993 *Yiddisher Scousers* Liverpool

Levy J 1994 Memories are made of these: more stories by Jack Levy *Yiddisher Scousers No. II* Liverpool

Lipsitz G 1989 *Time passages: collective memory and American popular culture* University of Minnesota Press, Minnesota

Lowenthal D 1985 *The past is a foreign country* Cambridge University Press, New York

Lynch K 1960 *The image of the city* Massachusetts Institute of Technology Press, Massachusetts

Maitland S 1986 *Vesta Tilley* Virago, London

McManus K 1994 *Ceilies, jigs, and ballads: Irish music in Liverpool* Institute of Popular Music, Liverpool

Stokes M ed. 1994a Introduction in *Ethnicity, identity: the musical construction of place* Berg, Oxford

Stokes M ed. 1994b. Place, exchange and meaning: Black Sea musicians in the west of Ireland in *Ethnicity, identity: the musical construction of place* Berg, Oxford

Stoller P 1989 *The taste of ethnographic things: the senses in anthropology* University of Pennsylvania Press, Philadelphia

Tagg P 1979 Kojak – 50 seconds of television music: toward an analysis of affect in popular music *Studies from Gothenburg University, Department of Musicology, II* Gothenburg University Press, Gothenburg

Tagg P 1981 On the specificity of musical communication: guidelines for non-musicologists *Stencilled papers from Gothenburg University Musicology Department* 8115 Gothenburg University Press, Gothenburg

Tagg P 1994 Introductory notes to music semiotics Unpubl. paper University of Gothenburg, Sweden

Werlen B 1993 *Society, action and space: an alternative human geography* Routledge, London

Werner E 1980 Jewish music: liturgical, Ashkenazic tradition in **Sadie S** ed. *The new Grove dictionary of music and musicians* vol. 9 Macmillan, London

Williams B 1987 Liverpool Jewry: a pictorial history Exhibition guide. Liverpool Jewish Youth and Community Centre, Liverpool

[8]

Techniques of Blues Composition among Black Folksingers*

DAVID EVANS

ANYONE FAMILIAR WITH AMERICAN FOLKSONG knows there are a number of basic differences between the Anglo-American and Afro-American traditions, despite more than three centuries of contact and musical interaction between blacks and whites in this country. These differences are due in part to the separate cultural and musical heritages from Great Britain and from Africa, as well as to the American pattern of social segregation, which has forced separate cultural development (though not without many mutual influences) upon the two groups. Newman I. White noted in 1928 that the black tradition displayed three important attributes absent in the white folksong tradition: the black tradition emphasized improvisation ("highly characteristic; . . . a racial trait"), variation, and the accumulative tendency.[1]

Today, in accordance with more modern terminology, we would probably change White's characterization of improvisation as a "racial trait" to a "cultural trait." He later states that it is "the continuation of a habit brought from Africa."[2] The statement that the cumulative tendency is characterized by "fishing stanzas out of a spacious but none too accurate or discriminating folk memory"[3] must not go unchallenged, however. Although a cumulative tendency is found in many black folksongs, White has committed the error of judging black folksongs by the standards of the white tradition, which emphasizes memorization of songs by their singers. The inevitable result of such judgment is a negative assessment of the black tradition.

In the light of White's statement, I will examine blues, currently the most popular and prevalent genre of black nonreligious folksong, and will show how these songs are learned and composed by black folksingers. These findings will be contrasted with the ways in which white folksingers learn and compose their songs. It will be shown that the differences in approach to learning and composi-

* This paper was read at the annual meeting of the Southern California Academy of Sciences, May 4, 1974, at Fullerton, California. I am indebted to Jeff Titon and my wife for their comments on an earlier version.
[1] *American Negro Folk-Songs* (Cambridge, Mass., 1928), 26.
[2] Ibid., 29.
[3] Ibid., 26.

TECHNIQUES OF BLUES COMPOSITION AMONG BLACK FOLKSINGERS   241

tion are not only due to separate musical heritages but are also reinforced by attitudinal differences held by singers and audiences within the two groups.

Almost all white secular folksongs tell a story or develop a theme. If the message is told from the first-person point of view and its emotional dimension is stressed, then the song is called a *lyric*. If action is stressed, then the song is called a *ballad*. A third type is the *dialog song*, in which there is a verbal confrontation of characters. All three types, though, are essentially story-songs,[4] that is, where the story is not overt it is easily reconstructable. Furthermore, white folksongs display comparatively little variation in oral tradition. This partly results from the fact that, as story-songs, they have a theme or plot as a built-in constant structural feature. But more importantly, the minimal variation is due to certain values and attitudes held by white folksingers toward their songs.

Normally the white folksinger will attempt to learn his text and tune exactly as the piece has been performed by his source. Then, once he has learned the piece, he will attempt to perform it the same way each time he sings it. The greatest variation in the process of learning and subsequent performance is likely to be in the instrumental accompaniment, but we may ignore this because, with the exception of instrumentally-based musical genres such as bluegrass and banjo and fiddle dance-tunes, instrumental accompaniment is not essential to the performance of white folksongs. Instead, accompaniment, if used, remains in the background of the vocal performance and serves simply to enhance the singing harmonically and rhythmically. In general, then, in white folksong tradition "the singer views himself as a voice for whatever piece he is performing; he places himself in the background, letting the piece speak for itself. He attempts to reproduce the song exactly as he has heard it and learned it."[5]

The preceding statements, of course, represent an ideal situation. In reality, change does take place in the white folksong tradition, and some changes are even made consciously by the folksingers.[6] These changes may occur because the singer forgets a portion of the song while performing or mishears a portion in the process of learning it. More rarely, a singer may actually delete those parts of a song inconsistent with his worldview (such as references to the supernatural) or offensive to his moral outlook (such as sexual and scatological references). On the other hand, the singer may feel that a song as he has learned it is incomplete and therefore will attempt to "patch it up." Variation may also result from the singer either combining two or more different versions of a song he has heard or borrowing elements from another song and incorporating them into his version. In virtually all cases the singer ultimately establishes his own stable version of the song. Subsequent patching up, combining, and borrowing simply serve to produce what one might call a "revised standard version." Thus, the singer's performance at any one time represents the result of his attempts to develop a definitive version of the song. The white tradition, then, on the whole

[4] Roger D. Abrahams and George Foss, *Anglo-American Folksong Style* (Englewood Cliffs, N.J., 1968), 37–38.
[5] Ibid., 12. See also G. Malcolm Laws, Jr., *Native American Balladry* (Philadelphia, 1964), 82.
[6] The ways changes are made are discussed in Abrahams and Foss, 12–36, and Laws, 68–82. For an excellent discussion of eleven white folksingers' attitudes toward changes in their songs see John Quincy Wolf, "Folksingers and the Re-creation of Folksong," *Western Folklore* 26 (1967), 101–111.

is resistant to change. The attitude typical in this tradition has been expressed by Mrs. Almeda Riddle, a folksinger from Cleburne County, Arkansas: "I never change anything just to be changing, but I know that songs are supposed to make good sense."[7]

Rather little attention has been paid to the manner in which black blues singers learn and create their songs, despite the fact that over thirty books have been published on various aspects of the blues in the last decade alone.[8] Instead, research has tended to focus on the lives and life styles of blues singers, on the content of the songs and its relationship to Black American Society, and on the history of the blues genre, with particular emphasis on the commercially issued blues designed for the black record-buying public.[9] Earlier writers, like Newman White, tended to view blues and other Afro-American folksongs in terms of the standards of white folksong. Blues were frequently considered to be random composites of lines and stanzas with no very clear or consistent meaning as whole songs.[10] This attitude failed to consider that such a manner of composition might be an advantage for the blues singer and the audience and that it might in many cases be preferred by them.

Because of the scarcity of published information on how blues are learned and composed, I am basing the following description on my own fieldwork with black folk musicians. Since 1965, I have recorded close to a thousand blues from about one hundred performers and have questioned many of them about how they learn and compose their songs. In many cases I have revisited my informants and recorded their blues on different occasions in order to note variations in performance.

With the decline of minstrelsy and balladry in the last few decades, blues have become today the most important genre of black nonreligious folksong. All blues are lyrics in the sense that they are told from the first-person point of view and their emotional dimension is stressed. Unlike most white folksongs, however, blues are frequently the original compositions or combinations of the persons who sing them. Furthermore, blues normally require an instrumental accompaniment, which serves as an integral part of the song itself. It is not simply a background sound which enhances the vocal: throughout the performance it responds to and interacts with the vocal lines.[11]

In spite of these two major differences, many blues still display the same kind of stability in tradition that is characteristic of white folksong. For the most

---

[7] Wolf, 108. For another statement of the same view see Roger Abrahams, "Creativity, Individuality, and the Traditional Singer," *Studies in the Literary Imagination* 3 (1970), 11.

[8] Exceptions to this statement are Harry Oster, *Living Country Blues* (Detroit, 1969), 76–95; William Ferris, Jr., *Blues from the Delta* (London, 1970), 34–60; John Fahey, *Charley Patton* (London, 1970), 52–70; David Evans, *Tommy Johnson* (London, 1971), 45–68, 91–107.

[9] An excellent summary of much of the recent blues scholarship is Paul Oliver's *The Story of the Blues* (London, 1969).

[10] See, for example, Howard W. Odum and Guy B. Johnson, *Negro Workaday Songs* (Chapel Hill, N.C., 1926), 27.

[11] Some writers, as well as some blues singers themselves, have called certain unaccompanied Negro lyric folksongs "blues." These songs may indeed use many of the same textual and melodic conventions as instrumentally accompanied blues, but for analytical purposes I prefer to call them by the separate term "hollers" because their character and functions when unaccompanied by an instrument are quite different from those of real blues.

part, however, such songs can be traced to origins in the popular commercial recordings of blues that have been appearing by the thousands since 1920. Other
blues singers hear these records and try to reproduce them for local audiences.
Most of the variation from the original phonograph record is in the accompaniment, where the performer may use a different instrument from that on the record or may play a different set of figures on the same instrument, either by
preference or from inability to play the part on the record. As for changes in the
words of such blues, they generally occur as a result of the same factors that
cause change in the white folksong tradition, although Mrs. Riddle's position
against change for its own sake applies to a lesser extent for blues such as these.
Black singers in general tend to personalize their songs and are less likely to see
themselves as simply carriers or vehicles for the performance of traditional
pieces. For example, "Boogie" Bill Webb, a blues singer from New Orleans
whom I have recorded extensively, sang a version of "Red Cross Store," a song
about the government relief program for the poor during the Depression and
World War II and derived ultimately from a commercial blues recorded by
Walter Roland in 1933. Webb's version is close to his recorded source in words
and melody, but he has personalized the lyrics somewhat by inserting his wife's
name in several appropriate places and by adding a spoken introduction which
connects the events in the song to a particular period in his life. His two performances for me of this blues were virtually identical.

Commercially issued blues are usually thematic and therefore could be called
story-songs. Their performers are frequently also the composers. Other singers
learn to perform these blues from the records and may even compose a few blues
of their own, usually story-songs with thematic texts on the model of other commercial blues. Some of these singers later get an opportunity to make commercial
recordings themselves. "Boogie" Bill Webb is such a blues singer with an orientation toward commercial records. He recorded four blues for Imperial Records
in 1953, two of which were issued on a record. It sold poorly, and Webb was
not recorded again until my sessions with him beginning in 1966. The majority
of songs he performs were learned from popular blues records, and on them his
singing is close to the originals, with very little variation from one performance
to another of the same blues. Most of the rest of his blues were learned in person from other singers, primarily from John Henry "Bubba" Brown and Tommy
Johnson. Brown, whom I have recorded in Los Angeles where he now resides,
was a prolific composer of blues, who almost always worked out stable versions
of his songs, which he would then perform the same way every time.[12] Webb's
versions of these songs are in most cases very close to Brown's, even to the guitar
playing, which Webb learned note for note. Webb also has developed stable
versions of Tommy Johnson's blues, despite the fact that Johnson himself apparently varied his lyrics considerably from one performance to another.[13]

Webb has composed only a handful of blues himself. All of them are thematic and almost unvarying from one performance to the next, like his other

[12] See David Evans, "Bubba Brown, Folk Poet," *Mississippi Folklore Register*, 7 (1973), 15–
31; "The Bubba Brown Story," *Blues World*, 21 (October, 1968), 7–9; *Tommy Johnson*,
71–72.
[13] Evans, *Tommy Johnson*, 91–94.

blues. Typical of his original compositions is "Drinking and Stinking," a blues which tells in lyric style the story of a specific event in Webb's life. He even has a story about how he came to compose this song.

I made some songs. One I made was "Drinking and Stinking." It may sound funny, but that's what it is. A friend of mine is the cause of that. He's in California today. I don't want none of the ladies who hear this to get mad with me, but this actually happened. We knowed three ladies that had been playing hookey for around three days then. I want you to know they wouldn't go home. We knowed it was time for a bath or something, you know. And so, he's the one that said, "Man, you ought to put a song out about 'Drinking and Stinking.'" They had been drinking three days and nights and stinking. So me and him right then started the "Drinking and Stinking."

The words of this song are as follows:[14]

1. You've been drinking and stinking all night long.
   You've been drinking and stinking all night long.
   Well, I'm gonna say, babe, I'm gonna say to you,
   Girl, you smell like a garbage can, and I don't know what I'm gonna do.

2. You smell like a garbage can late at night.
   If I tell you what you been doing, it make you want to fight,
   When you've been drinking and stinking all night long.
   You've been drinking.
   Girl, you've been drinking, pretty babe, and stinking all night long.

3. *Repeat stanza 2.*

4. You don't never want to brush your teeth, but you always want to be up
      in my face.
   You smell like something I never smelled before.
   Well, you've been drinking and stinking all night long.
   Well, you've been drinking.
   You've been drinking, pretty babe, and stinking all night long.

5. *Repeat stanza 2.*

6. *Repeat stanza 4.*
   Spoken: Kiss me, baby!

A few blues singers are adept at improvising thematic blues on the spot at the time of performance. These spontaneous creations are usually quite original in their texts, and frequently, because of lack of time for more careful composition, they contain a good number of unrhymed lines; often the singing is interspersed with spoken passages. Such songs appear to issue forth from the singer in a "stream of consciousness," and they are seldom performed a second time. Napoleon Strickland of Como, Mississippi, is a singer who frequently improvises such spontaneous blues. His songs combine startling, sometimes almost surrealistic, images related to his current thoughts or events in his life, such as the following blues about an uncooperative mule, "Black Sam."[15]

[14] Recorded in New Orleans, Louisiana, August 27, 1970, and issued on Arhoolie 1057, *Roosevelt Holts and His Friends*, 12″ LP. Stanzas 3 and 4 were deleted on the record.
[15] Recorded in Como, Mississippi, June 27, 1971.

TECHNIQUES OF BLUES COMPOSITION AMONG BLACK FOLKSINGERS 245

1. Come over here, Black Sam. You know I want to plow your hams down.
   Come over here, Black Sam. Believe I'm gonna plow your black hams down.
   You know, your legs so long, Lord, you gonna run my short legs down.

2. You ain't gonna hold your line in the wagon, and your plow's all down on the ground.
   Lord, I plowed Black Sam so long, 'til the old coot, he done got straightened wrong.

3. Lord, when Black Sam got hungry, Lord, I had to take him out and carry him to the barn.
   Lord, I carried him to the trough. Lord, he sure didn't want no water.

4. Lord, his bell ringing all day long. Lord, Black Sam would holler up and hoot.
   Lord, I'm leaving here. Black Sam, good day!
   What Black Sam will do—he wouldn't eat, he wouldn't eat, he wouldn't eat when he got hungry.

Many other blues singers, however, have little interest in putting their momentary thoughts or episodes in their life's story into song form. Instead, they rely on a vast body of traditional formulaic lines and stanzas for composing their blues. A few dozen to a few hundred of these formulas comprise the repertoires of many blues singers. To form a blues they will combine about five or six of these stanzas, usually only loosely related in theme and sometimes even inconsistent and contradictory. Most of these formulaic stanzas and lines treat some aspect of the man-woman relationship and express thoughts relevant to almost anyone's life experience. Consequently they are known by many blues singers and are quickly recognized by their audiences, in contrast to the verses of a blues like "Drinking and Stinking," which will probably always be associated with their composer.

A singer who frequently avails himself of formulaic lines and stanzas in improvising blues is Roosevelt Holts of Bogalusa, Louisiana. He uses all of the stanzas of the following blues, "Let's Talk It All Over Again,"[16] in other blues, and I have also heard most of the lines used by other singers in various combinations. No specific central theme unites the various thoughts expressed in these verses, nor do any of them refer to specific dateable events in Holts's life. They are, however, experiences which he or anyone else could easily have undergone.

1. Well, come on, baby. Let's talk it all over again.
   Well, come on, baby. Let's talk it all over again.
   'Cause you know we love each other. Let's try to hold out to the end.

2. Well, wake up in the morning feeling sad and blue.
   Well, wake up in the morning feeling sad and blue.
   Well, I woke up this morning, didn't hardly know what to do.

3. Well, I got a red rooster, crow every morning 'fore day.
   Well, little red rooster, he crow every morning 'fore day.
   Well, I can always tell when my baby gone away to stay.

---

[16] Recorded in New Orleans, Louisiana, February 3, 1966, and issued on Blue Horizon 7-63201, *Presenting the Country Blues: Roosevelt Holts*, 12" LP.

246   DAVID EVANS

4. Well, the lead in my pencil done gone dead on me.
   Lord, the lead in my pencil done gone dead on me.
   Well, that's the worst old feeling that a poor man ever had.

Holts had never sung this particular combination of verses before and to my knowledge has never sung it since. Instead, each stanza as well as the melody and guitar part are separable elements in his repertoire, which he recombines with other stanzas, melodies, and guitar parts to form new blues.

Some times a blues that combines traditional formulaic stanzas and musical elements becomes fixed in a singer's repertoire and is repeated in the same way on different occasions. When this happens, the singer usually associates the blues with another performer he has known. This association with a particular singer gives the piece a certain sanctity so that others become unwilling to alter what they conceive to be the song's "original" version. A similar attitude has been seen to prevail toward blues learned from phonograph records. One might expect, then, that such fixed combinations would enter the repertoires of several singers if the "original" singer enjoyed wide popularity. Such stability of tradition, however, does not usually occur. Even when a blues singer claims to be performing a song in exactly the same way as another singer, a check usually reveals considerable difference. Such was the case with the few fixed combinations in Roosevelt Holts's repertoire in all instances where it was possible to compare his version with that of his source, and such is the case in most other comparable instances I have encountered among blues singers. The reason for this is that often the original singer does not perform the blues in the same way every time. Only a part of it is fixed in his repertoire. This part, which we shall call the blues "core," usually consists of the melody, instrumental accompaniment, and a single stanza of the text. The remaining stanzas are drawn from the repertoire of traditional formulaic stanzas and vary with each performance by the singer.

A singer who uses the core technique for composing most of his blues is Mager Johnson of Crystal Springs, Mississippi. The following version of "Big Road Blues"[17] is typical of this technique. The core of the song for him consists of the melody, guitar accompaniment, refrain, and first stanza. The remaining stanzas vary considerably in his other performances of this blues.

1. Lord, ain't going down that big road by myself.
   Now don't you hear me talking, pretty mama?   (*refrain*)
   Lord, ain't going down that big road by myself.
   If I don't carry you, gon' carry somebody else.

2. Mmmm, Lord, have mercy, mama now, on my wicked soul.
   Now don't you hear me talking, pretty mama?
   Crying, Lord, have mercy on my wicked soul.
   If the good Lord don't help me, the devil will damn my soul.

3. Mmmm, take me back to my same old used-to-be.
   Now don't you hear me talking, pretty mama?
   Lord, take me back to my same old used-to-be.

[17] Recorded in Crystal Springs, Mississippi, March 30, 1969.

Crying, Lord, I ain't got no special rider here.

4. Says my special rider, mama now, done been here and gone.
   Now don't you hear me talking, pretty mama?
   Mmmm, done been here and gone.
   Crying, Lord, I ain't gon' be here long.

I have recorded versions of "Big Road Blues" from many singers, all of whom combine the same core with various other stanzas. Isaac Youngblood of Tylertown, Mississippi, recorded the following version of this blues.[18]

1. Well, I ain't going down the big road by myself.
   Don't you hear me talking to you, mama?   *(refrain)*
   Oh, going down that big road by myself.
   If I don't carry you, I'm gonna carry me someone else.

2. Well, I got a riding horse. She's already trained.
   Don't you hear me talking to you, mama?
   Oh, got a riding horse. She's already trained.
   If you want to ride easy, tighten up on your reins.

3. Hey, what good is your bulldog, he won't bark or bite?
   Don't you hear me talking to you, mama?
   Oh, good is your bulldog, he won't bark or bite?
   Well, what service is your woman, she won't let you in at night?

4. Hey now, see, see, rider, see what you done done.
   Don't you hear me talking to you, mama?
   Oh, see, see, rider, see what you done done.
   You done made me love you. Now your man done come.

Unlike Mager Johnson, Isaac Youngblood has established the text as a stable item in his repertoire and performs it in the same way every time, except for omissions. Youngblood does not consider the song to be completely his own because he learned it many years ago from Tommy Johnson, Mager's brother. Mager Johnson, however, considers it to be very much his own song and feels free to add verses to the core as he sees fit at the time of the performance.[19]

In use among black folksingers, then, are five main types of blues, which vary according to the degree of stability of the song in the performers' repertoire and whether or not the text is thematic. The five types are:

1. Thematic/Stable. Examples: "Drinking and Stinking" and most commercially recorded blues.

2. Thematic/Improvised. Example: "Black Sam."

3. Nonthematic/Stable. Example: Isaac Youngblood's "Big Road Blues."

[18] Recorded in Tylertown, Mississippi, August 25, 1966, and issued on Matchbox SDM 224, *The Legacy of Tommy Johnson*, 12" LP.

[19] Tommy Johnson apparently shared his brother's attitude. I have recorded this song from many blues singers who learned it from Tommy Johnson at various times. Each has a standard version he performs in the same way every time, yet each singer has a different version from every other singer. All versions, however, contain the core of this blues. For the text of Tommy Johnson's own 1928 recording of "Big Road Blues" see Evans, *Tommy Johnson*, 49–50. It has been reissued on RBF 14, *Blues Roots/Mississippi*, 12" LP.

4. Nonthematic/Improvised. Example: "Let's Talk It All Over Again."

5. Nonthematic/Partly Stable ("core" blues). Example: Mager Johnson's "Big Road Blues."

There may well be a sixth type, Thematic/Partly Stable (a thematic blues using the core technique). I have not encountered it in my fieldwork, however.

Each blues performer usually exhibits a preference for one of the above types, but most can and do compose in more than one way. For instance, most of Roosevelt Holts's blues are Nonthematic/Improvised, but he also performs some which are Thematic/Stable, Nonthematic/Stable, and Nonthematic/Partly Stable. Napoleon Strickland prefers to compose Thematic/Improvised blues, but he also performs many that are Nonthematic/Stable, Nonthematic/Improvised, and Nonthematic/Partly Stable.

This range of approaches to blues composition stands in marked contrast to the situation for white secular folksong. In the white tradition the vast majority of folksongs are Thematic/Stable (and basically are not the performers' original compositions), almost all the rest being Nonthematic/Stable. The other three approaches are virtually nonexistent in white tradition. The differences, then, lie in the common use of improvisation and original composition in much blues singing and the less common occurrence of these processes in white folksong.

The reasons for these differences are related to both the history and the social context of the blues. In terms of their history, blues are, of course, only a recent branch of the great stream of Afro-American music, which is itself an offshoot of African music, adapted to the New World social environment and containing various borrowings from European musical traditions. Many other types of African and Afro-American music allow improvisation within the limits of their traditions, so that blues are by no means unusual in this respect.

Furthermore, the particular context in which blues were first sung encouraged improvisation. The blues genre arose from the field hollers sung by black farmers working alone behind a mule and plow or chopping weeds with a hoe. Hollers were sung mainly to pass the time and to take the singer's mind off his rather tedious and uninteresting work. There was seldom any audience. Thus the singer could holler whatever thoughts might come across his mind as well as sing traditional lines and stanzas or set pieces that he had memorized. These hollers became blues when the singer later set them to an instrumental accompaniment.

Blues today, however, are not normally sung in fields but are instead performed for audiences at parties and dances. They express in their words and music moods the singer feels or would like to create. They must also express moods and thoughts to which the audience can relate, or else they will be unsuccessful. Since the audience is varied and the moods are constantly shifting, a blues singer must have considerable variety to his repertoire. His ability to improvise offers a simple but effective means of achieving this variety. It enables the singer to meet the needs of the moment, to try out new ideas to see if they will be successful, and to abandon unsuccessful ideas. The blues audience is a demanding one, and it needs excitement as well as rhythm for dancing. Improvisation assures that a blues singer's repertoire will not become too familiar to the audience and thus will continue to provide excitement.

Most white folksingers rarely compose original songs but instead learn their pieces from other singers and try to perform them exactly as heard or with a few revisions. In contrast, most blues singers claim the majority of their songs as original compositions, even when they have simply recombined traditional musical and textual elements. The ability to improvise and the fact that such recombinations have never before been performed in exactly the same way give the singer a feeling of originality highly valued among blues singers and their audiences. Among white folksingers and audiences originality is valued less than correct and accurate performance of the song. To whites the song and its message are more important than the person who happens to be singing it, but the opposite is true for blues singers and their audiences. Improvisation in blues allows the singer to be an individualist while at the same time expressing sentiments familiar and important to himself and the audience.

California State University
Fullerton, California

[9]

Changing Contexts for Traditional Dance Music in Ireland: The Rise of Group Performance Practice*

HAZEL FAIRBAIRN

IRISH INSTRUMENTAL MUSIC is most often heard today played by groups. Bands like The Chieftains are known all over the world and many more people are familiar with the *céilí* band sound than with solo instrumental performances. Visitors to Ireland could be forgiven for assuming that the large groups of musicians they see playing in west coast pubs are representative of an ancient tradition of music-making; the assumption is hardly discouraged by the Irish Tourist Board.

Yet, most traditional musicians insist that Irish music is essentially a solo art, its skill lying in the subtle variation of the melodic line, and that it is best heard played by one instrumentalist. Until forty years ago, there was very little ensemble playing and the group sound was virtually unheard outside the (then newfangled!) *céilí* band. The pub session, an informal musical gathering which fascinates many thousands of tourists every year, was an entirely unknown phenomenon and no one had considered playing tunes in any kind of formal group arrangement. Despite the solo genesis of the tradition, group playing forms the main musical outlet for most of today's traditional Irish musicians.

The Traditional Irish Music Session

Like most non-native players, my first experience of traditional Irish music was in the context of the session. The session is an informal

* This article is based on the author's unpublished Ph.D. thesis, 'Group Playing in Traditional Irish Music: Interaction and Heterophony in the Session' (University of Cambridge, 1992). The field recordings from which Examples 2, 3, 4 and 8 are taken are on deposit at the University Library, Cambridge, together with the thesis. All the musical examples reproduced here are transcribed by Hazel Fairbairn unless stated otherwise.

social and musical event which takes place either in a private house or, more often, in a public bar. In neither case is the session a performance as such; the musicians sit in a closed circle around a table and attention is focused into this musical circle rather than at an audience.

A shared repertory of traditional dance tunes, usually played in sets (medleys), forms the shared musical basis of the event. The characteristic sound of the session is of a rapid and high melodic line played in an amorphous unison, very often accompanied by chordal, stringed instruments (such as guitar and bouzouki) and sometimes by percussion (for example, *bodhrán* or bones). The audible backdrop from other activities occurring in the same room (conversation, bar noise), as well as responses to the music (shouts, claps or intermittent 'whoops'), are part of this characteristic session sound.

Sessions follow no precisely preconceived or rehearsed plan, they involve flexible numbers of musicians, and in principle they usually welcome both strangers and beginners. In my experience, a newcomer demonstrating respect through initially passive participation is generally readily accepted. In musical terms, continued acceptance depends on a sensitive level of contribution — not joining in on unfamiliar tunes, for example, and not trying to dominate in terms of volume. Usually, at some point, a more established member of the session group will acknowledge a newcomer, asking them to start a tune. Beyond this point, integration depends on the way that relationships evolve through social and musical interaction. A musician who is 'good crack' is often valued just as highly as an extremely accomplished player. The expression, 'he's a good musician but he's an awful bollocks', refers to a musician whose behaviour is considered antisocial and often particularly refers to arrogance or unfriendliness. The inseparability of the musical and social aspects of the session is always emphasised by the musicians themselves, as demonstrated by the following remarks:

There's more to it than sitting down and playing a tune; there's the talk and the drink and the humour.[1]

It's not just the music it's the meeting of musicians.[2]

I think we do certainly react globally with the person with whom we are playing . . . to the person's self, to the style of playing and also to the instrument they are playing.[3]

The learning and performing processes are also inseparable in the session. O Súilleabhain expresses their integration when he describes 'the pure play of the child which is at once a learning experience and an affirmation of life — a definition in itself of a good traditional session'.[4] Sessions often involve beginners, and this is accepted by the more accomplished players who remember their own early efforts and know that participation is the best way to internalize the rhythmic style and melodic patterns of traditional tunes. However, learning is not restricted to beginners; even very active players know only a fraction of the traditional repertory. Most musicians regard the session as the best place to hear new tunes, as well as new versions of an already familiar tune, and also for consolidating tunes learnt from another source, such as disc or tape recordings. Frequent playing with a variety of people also helps to maintain a wide repertory, prompting recollections of half-forgotten tunes learnt in the past.

Sessions reflect the balance of individuality and communality in the tradition as a whole. The tunes and the style are shared, and the activity of group playing expands this shared basis. For the individual musician, the activity of playing is very personal, 'an extension of some deep inner life rather than simply an entertainment'.[5] In a good session, this deeply personal relationship between each player and his or her musical tradition is retained, creating both intimacy and intense excitement. Sessions of this kind are often described as 'flying'. Another expression associated with group playing is that of 'lift', referring to rhythmic vitality. Although a solo performance can also be praised for having 'great lift', the notion of other musicians adding lift to one's own playing is widespread. When a session 'flies', the tempo will often increase, a strong melodic accentuation emerges, and the sets of tunes become longer, with fewer breaks for conversation in between. There is a magic about these 'flying' sessions. Everyone's individual playing is at once celebrated and transcended. As a traditional Irish flute player living in Cambridge has described, 'a really good session has an indefinable element of unrestrained energy and sensitivity, something which is only occasionally present, even with the same people.'[6]

My initial interest in traditional Irish music was as a player, catalysed by the excitement of participating in sessions. The fact that communication in sessions is not a matter of musicians directing their efforts toward an audience, but is contained within the musical circle, means that the session can only really be experienced and observed from a playing seat. The musical process is integrated into a social and drinking environment, and interactive detail is often obscured to all but the participants themselves.

In many ways the session is a very personal experience and the insights presented in this paper are necessarily limited by my own social and musical experiences. No doubt some of my observations will conflict with the experiences of other players. Participation may limit one's perception of the whole and creates a fieldwork problem in that one's own playing features on many of the audio recordings of the events. However, the session presents a musical situation which can only really be studied subjectively.[7]

I had been playing in sessions in Ireland and England for a couple of years before I realized that the situation was a relatively new context for traditional Irish music. This was quite a startling revelation; sessions seemed such a natural, spontaneous and suitable environment for traditional music. Many deeply committed musicians are passionate about playing in sessions and it is hard to imagine Irish music thriving without them. This article considers the transition from solo to group performance practice. How and why did Irish dance music move into the group context? Have the style and repertory adapted to group playing? What implications do contemporary developments hold for the future of the tradition? The article traces the way in which the public session has evolved from its solo roots, and compares it to more formalized traditional music groups. It also suggests ways in which the session provides a contemporary context for musicians denied their traditional role by the technological and social changes of the twentieth century.

The Heritage of the Solo Tradition: Regional Styles and the Art of Variation

The word 'style' can be used to refer to three distinct but interacting aspects of traditional music performance. As a generic term it refers to a national idiom, within which there are regional distinctions. Individual style refers to a musician's unique relationship with one or both of these. According to McCullough, style is intrinsically linked to the creative process of varying a melody, connecting the idea of style with individual interpretation rather than shared idiom:

The term 'style', as used by traditional Irish musicians, denotes the composite form of the distinctive features that identify an individual's musical performance. The elements of style can be divided into four main variables: ornamentation, variation in melodic and rhythmic patterns, phrasing, and articulation.[8]

Players sharing regional styles have a common approach to rhythmic emphasis and accent as well as pursuing closely related melodic versions. Although the placing of ornamental devices is generally considered to be an entirely individual decision, the kind of ornamentation used is an element in the distinction between different regional styles. For example, the Donegal fiddle style uses no rolls and favours the use of single bow strokes, creating a characteristically strident and energetic regional sound.[9] By contrast, Sligo fiddling uses more varied and slurred bowing, and employs a greater variety and quantity of gracing devices. The Kerry fiddle style has strong and regular rhythmic accents and uses drones and chords to create emphasis.[10]

Example 1 shows the simultaneous performance of a reel by brother and sister players, Julia Clifford and Denis Murphy, and their teacher, Padraig O'Keefe. All three players represent the *Sliabh Luachra* style of fiddle playing associated with the East Kerry region.[11] The three players each treat the tune individually within a detailed, shared melodic-rhythmic skeleton which synchronizes on most of the main beats. The doubling of the tune in the lower octave by one of the three players is characteristic of rural dance music partnerships in many regions. In this example it combines with droning on the open string to create a full-bodied sound. All three players emphasise the second and fourth beats of each bar, creating a strong accent system, and the upper melodic lines reinforce this, catching two strings on the second and fourth beats of the first, third and fifth bars of the phrase.*

This example is representative of the small ensembles and gatherings which have long existed on the periphery of rural music traditions in Ireland. Informal gatherings of musicians meeting to play and exchange tunes moved into the public bar during the 1950s and 1960s, and raised the profile of the musical group as a context for traditional dance tunes. In the last three decades, group playing has assumed a central role in

---

* Transcriber's Note: The arrows above the notes on the top stave indicate subtle pushes and pulls in timing shared by all three players.
→ = pull (the onset of the note occurs slightly later than the beat).
← = push (the onset of the note slightly anticipates the beat).

Changing Contexts for Traditional Dance Music in Ireland   571

Example 1
'McLeod's Reel', played by Julia Clifford, Denis Murphy and Padraig O'Keefe
on *Kerry Fiddles: Music from Sliabh Luachra Vol. 1* (12-inch L.P., 12T309,
Topic, 1977).
By permission of Topic Records

traditional music-making and large groups have become much more common.

The House Dance and its Decline

Since the 1930s, instrumental music has become increasingly dis-associated from its primary function — to accompany dancing — although in the last few years a set dance revival has reversed the process to some extent. The traditional setting for the music is the country house dance, remembered vividly by today's oldest generation of musicians:

I miss the grand get-together. The country house dance had something anything else hadn't. Then you were a closely knit crowd around a small country kitchen and they were all locals and you were altogether.[12]

Micho Russell, the famed whistle player and storyteller from Doolin, County Clare, and one of the main informants for my research, remembers house dances in the years 1920–50, and mentions the 'American wakes' (send-off parties for emigrating local people) which were common before that time. When asked why they declined he was vague, but mentioned that the priests objected to people 'collecting in small houses'.[13]

Another account describes the American wake and the importance of the house dance in the depleted rural community:

Emigration was very high and every emigrant was given a send off in the form of an American wake . . . In one way they were a great boon to the local musicians who remained at home, providing a meeting place for them and an outlet for their talents. In fact most occasions of any importance in the country-side would be celebrated with a dance. The people had to make their own entertainment since there was nothing else available. Many of them lived out their lives within a short radius of where they were born, so that they all knew each other and knew what was going on.[14]

Most accounts describe house dances going on well into the small hours, singing and storytelling taking over from the music and dance as dawn approached. The dances themselves were usually sets, danced by groups of four couples, but individual contributions characterized the other events of the evening. Step dancing was performed by a single man, and singing and storytelling were solo efforts, delivered by one

unaccompanied voice. According to Micho Russell, the musicians playing for the dance took turns, rarely more than two playing together
and more often a single player providing the music.[15]

From the mid-1930s a number of factors contributed to the disappearance of the house dance. As in so many other parts of the world,
traditional music suffered the effects of technological revolution and the
subsequent domination of media and market forces. Radio and gramo-
phones opened up a new world of entertainment and created a much
greater consciousness of town culture among young country people.
The media installed new aspirations, and suggested alternative lifestyles
and value systems. The cultural life of the community fell into dissolution as it was rejected for urban and cosmopolitan models. Combined
with the 1936 Dance Hall Act, which effectively made the house dance
illegal, this change in consciousness saw the end of the custom. The
house dance took with it the role of traditional music in rural social life.

Having lost their primary social function, many musicians stopped
playing.[16] Emigration slowed down, but rural depopulation continued,
young people tending to leave for the cities where independence had
created new job opportunities. There were fewer young people to inherit
indigenous rural musical skills and all these factors combined to reduce
significantly the number of active musicians.[17]

Traditional music became associated with tinkers, a class of travelling craftsmen who epitomized all that the aspiring rural landowner
wished to forget. Consequently, traditional music became unacceptable
in many circles. Feldman and O'Doherty point out that those few
who continued to play did so from a sense of individualism which
distinguishes the artistic and creative musician:

> There were many factors inherent in the tradition to foster an individual
> musician's resistance to the de-culturalisation process . . . The orientation in
> Irish music has always been on the soloist; ensemble playing was not a strong
> practice in Ireland. Thus, the emphasis on the music is on the master musician
> who can engrave his own distinct identity on the repertoire through superior
> technique and inventiveness. The tradition of the virtuoso, possibly an inherit-
> ance from the ancient harpers, coexisted with the communitarian functions of
> the music. It was this ethic of musical individualism that provided many players
> with a self-perpetuating impetus to continue playing in the face of social
> indifference.[18]

The low esteem in which music was held in the 1940s and 1950s
sorted those with an intense personal relationship with the music from

more pedestrian and socially-oriented players. Only those who related to the music as a purely personalized and solitary art form had any real reason to keep playing. The emphasis upon variation in contemporary performance is partly the heritage of these gifted and creative musicians.

The subsequent evolution of the music in the hands of the solo player moved away from the basic requirements of the dance which, as Michael Tubridy has pointed out, had exerted a conservative influence on the music:

> The fact that a lot of musicians do not play for dances any more releases them from a lot of constraints. They do not have to pay the same attention to phrasing, and they can put in notes and decorations wherever they will fit.[19]

The separation of music from social dance activity catalysed change in musical style as well as in performance contexts. This was demonstrated to me by Micho Russell. Now aged nearly eighty, Micho has witnessed firsthand the divorce of music from its rural cultural context and its subsequent development. One distinction he draws very clearly is that between dance music and listening music:

> Playing for listeners and playing for dancers are two different things. I think myself that people should more or less choose their company wherever they go. They have different ways of thinking.[20]

The three reels reproduced in Examples 2–4 were all played on the whistle and they illustrate three contrasting styles of playing. Micho described the first tune as an accompaniment to 'dancers wearing strong boots, hobnailed boots' and he called it (perhaps off the top of his head) 'The Days that Are Gone' (Example 2). The tune is played slowly with clear phrasing created through silences and minimal ornamentation. Micho followed his demonstration with the remark: 'It wouldn't be played as slowly as that in 1950, that would be going back to 1930 maybe, the old days.' His next example demonstrated the style and tempo in the 1950s (Example 3). Micho played this tune faster and used more ornamentation to articulate the line. It retains a clarity of phrasing achieved through breaking the quaver flow of the tune with silence. The tune itself is built around the transposition of one simple motivic figure, the figure itself built around a grace note. The tempo of the final example (Example 4), demonstrating 'the speed of the reel today', is the same as that of the tune in Example 3. The phrasing of

Changing Contexts for Traditional Dance Music in Ireland 575

Example 2
'The Days that Are Gone', played by Micho Russell, February 1992, recorded
by Hazel Fairbairn.

Example 3
Unnamed reel, played by Micho Russell, February 1992, recorded by
Hazel Fairbairn.

Example 4
Unnamed reel, played by Micho Russell as an example of 'a modern reel',
February 1992, recorded by Hazel Fairbairn.

the final tune propels the melody across the natural phrase breaks
creating an impression of greater speed and energy. To some extent the
performance sacrifices the shape and sense of proportion which was
created in the earlier examples through the balance of silence and sound.
The ornamentation is more florid and this combines with the phrasing
to give the performance a more impulsive character.

In all three examples, melodic variation is created by octave transposition of isolated notes. On the whistle this is an element of breath
control, the fingering remaining the same. There is more variation in
the final example, occurring in both the rhythmic and melodic dimensions. Clear phrasing is an element of Micho's personal style and is

Changing Contexts for Traditional Dance Music in Ireland   577

evident in all three examples, transcending the distinction he was demonstrating.

The combining forces of rural depopulation and the mass media led to another significant influence on traditional music-making in Ireland. Recordings of émigré Irish musicians made in New York in the 1920s caused a sensation in rural communities back in Ireland. Marty O'Malley describes how people gathered to hear recordings of Michael Coleman, James Morrison and Paddy Killoran, three Sligo musicians living in New York:

> The gramophone, needles and records were usually brought in from the States by visiting relatives and were somewhat of a sensation at the time as people flocked in to hear the mechanical music. 'Twas the era of Coleman, Killoran and Morrison, and when you got the tip, 'We have a new record . . . it came from America' . . . you all met and went to the house.[21]

These recordings popularized the intricate and highly ornamented Sligo style, and the tunes from the region represented on these early records form the backbone of what has emerged as a mainstream national style and repertory in Ireland.[22]

The decline of regional styles has been recognized just in time for musicians and scholars to collect much of the rapidly disappearing material from musicians of Micho's generation. Some of today's young urban players are turning to these recordings and basing their styles on them. The accumulation of archive recordings and their subsequent use as an oral source is an ironic contemporary backlash. It demonstrates a displaced learning process which uses the very medium (recording technology) which all but destroyed traditional music and the mechanisms of rural lifestyle and community which generated it.

Although the phenomenon of players learning tunes and styles from old recordings may preserve and even regenerate the surface technical features of regional styles, by definition these styles cannot be reproduced. The intimate relationship between music, dance and social gathering, and their high profile in rural lifestyle, is the source of regional styles. There is an integrity about the practitioners of these styles, who employ a form of musical expression inherited from and evolved among local musicians and players in the family. It is the exclusivity of this relationship between an individual and the music of his or her area which imparts the great value of the resulting musical styles, and the respect and regard they command today.

Regional styles are in danger of extinction, eroded along with the traditional lifestyle with which they are integrated. There is no musical commodity which can replace a musician's life. The spirit of traditional music is that of the personal utterance, a musical expression of life experience. As lifestyles change, so does the music they generate.

Revival and Group Playing

As with many indigenous music forms threatened by social change, the Irish tradition has been subject to revival through institutional support and interest. The activities of revival groups provided new outlets which brought isolated musicians together and Irish music demonstrated its resilience by adapting to social change in this century, regenerating its social function through changes in performance practice.

The first wave of revival goes back to the end of the last century. Whilst the depleted rural population was losing interest in its linguistic, cultural and musical heritage, the urban intelligentsia was attempting to fight a wave of Anglicization. They promoted a sense of national pride using cultural symbols, aiming to restore Irish as a spoken language and encouraging tradition-based social activities. *Conradh na Gaeilge* (The Irish League) was established before the 1916 uprising and McCartney suggests that it was the activities of this movement that gave the uprising conviction and power, imparted by cultural meaning.[23]

The birth of the *céilí* band, the first identifiable group arrangement in Irish music, can be traced to the activities of *Conradh na Gaeilge* in London. The *céilí* as promoted by the new Gaels was a public dance organized more along the lines of Scottish communal dancing than the Irish sets of the house dance. The *céilí* band was a directly functional development, existing in the form required to provide a volume of music suitable for large public dances. The classic *céilí* band line-up comprised the traditional fiddle, flute and accordion backed by vamp piano and military-style snare drum. In American cities *céilí* bands became big business, sharing the vaudeville and music hall circuit. Taylor describes how the influence of these musical styles was reflected in the addition of instruments such as string bass, saxophone and trombone to the basic line-up of bands, like the Chicago-based O'Leary's Irish Minstrels.[24]

Changing Contexts for Traditional Dance Music in Ireland   579

Returning emigrants and exported American recordings took the *céilí* band sound back to Ireland and it started to become popular in the 1950s. The *céilí* band arrangement introduced the concept of group playing to an essentially solo tradition, the tunes being played in unison over a rhythmic backing of piano and snare drum:

First they added piano and drums, then double bass, then the final insult, saxophones, guitars and banjos. The most important principles of traditional music, the whole idea of variation, the whole idea of the personal utterance, are abandoned. Instead, everybody gets hold of a tune and belts away at it without stopping. The result is a rhythmic and meaningless noise with as much relationship to music as the buzzing of a bluebottle in a jam jar . . . The ideal *céilí* band/orchestra must not flog away at the tunes all the time, with all the instruments going at once like present day *céilí* bands. Ideally it would begin with stating the basic skeleton of the tune to be played; this would then be ornamented and varied by solo instruments or by small groups of solo instruments. The more variation the better, so long as it has its roots in the tradition and serves to extend that tradition rather than destroy it by running counter to it.[25]

Despite criticism such as this, the *céilí* bands remained popular and provoked this commentator, Seán Ó Riada, into an attempt to redefine the direction that group playing in Ireland was to take. Ó Riada, who was a composer and professor at University College Cork, formed his own group, *Ceoltóirí Chualann*, in the early 1960s, as described by Éamon de Buitléar:

O Riada had this idea of forming a group. He discussed it with me and wondered what kind of musicians we should have. I suggested he should very definitely have Sonnie Brogan and John Kelly because they were old traditional musicians and they would certainly have all the old tunes, and they would soon tell us if we were doing something radically wrong as far as traditional music was concerned.[26]

In *Ceoltóirí Chualann*, Ó Riada tried to incorporate the learning processes and performance skills of respected traditional players into arrangements inspired by his own background in western art music composition. His idea was to incorporate the variation of the monodic line, which he perceived as central to traditional music-making, into a structure which maximized the textural variety offered by the group context. His first aim was to counteract the 'musical abomination' of the *céilí* band sound.

Ó Riada's ideas met with a lot of resistance from traditional players. As argued by Taylor, the *céilí* band has its roots in the fundamental aspect of the instrumental tradition in that the music is tailored to the needs of dancers. As far as the dancer is concerned, lift and good rhythm is more important than variation.[27] Contrary to Ó Riada's view, some individual ornamentation and nuances of melodic interpretation can be heard in regional-based bands like The Tulla and The Kilfenora. These bands have also produced many fine traditional solo players. Ó Riada finally won the support of the musicians with whom he worked because of his willingness to integrate his compositional creativity (on the level of arrangement) with the restraints of traditional style (on the level of melodic variation and ornamentation):

They [traditional musicians] didn't welcome at all some of the things Seán was doing. At the time they thought he was gone completely crazy, playing this kind of musical arrangement to some of the traditional tunes they had been playing for years and years. They were very much against it, but later they were very much in agreement with what Seán did. Although Sonnie and John would say to Seán on occasion: 'Look, you just can't do that, that's wrong.' Sonnie and John would very soon tell Seán if the playing or the construction of a particular tune was so way out that it wasn't acceptable to them.[28]

Example 5 shows part of one of Ó Riada's arrangements of a reel. The use of an ostinato on the _uilleann_ pipes and the counter-melodic activity between the fiddles depart from the essentially unison sound of the _céilí_ band. Sections like the one reproduced, where a heterophonic texture is created between the melodic lines, contrast with solo sections, varying groups of instruments and percussive riff-based breaks, in a large-scale orchestrated arrangement of eight cycles of the thirty-two bar tune.

In Ó Riada's own view _Ceoltóirí Chualann_ was a failure. Ultimately, it was the integrity of the solo musician, the very thing he had set out to protect, that frustrated his efforts. Ó Riada's excitement about the textural possibilities of group playing faded as he realized how much expressive power remained locked into the relationship between the player, instrument and tradition. He recognized the richness of a creative dimension which was inaccessible through the channels of extended group arrangement and compositional manipulation.

Despite his own disappointment, Ó Riada's position as Assistant Music Director for Radio Éireann had allowed him access to media channels to promote his band and he unwittingly catalysed a popular revival of interest in traditional material. The new band concept took on a life of its own, generating new treatments of traditional material.

Changing Contexts for Traditional Dance Music in Ireland   581

Example 5
'Toss the Feathers', played by *Ceoltóirí Chualann*, on *Reacaireacht an Riadaigh*
(12-inch L.P., CEF 010, Gael-Linn, 1962). This section was accompanied
by *bodhrán* and bones which are omitted from the transcription.
By permission of Gael-Linn Available on oriadacd08 *Pléaráca an Riadaigh* (2008).

The Chieftains, formed by Paddy Moloney, piper with *Ceoltóirí
Chualann*, continued to work with Ó Riada's ideas about arrangement.
Group interpretations of traditional dance tunes became popular, and
traditional sounds started to fuse with popular music styles. Donal
Lunny, a traditional musician and record producer, introduced driving
Afro-American rhythms in his early projects, The Bothy Band and The
Moving Hearts, creating a powerful sound which won new audiences
for Irish music, both at home and abroad. These groups forged a way
for traditional music by generating public awareness and interest.
However, the vitality of the popular revival of tradition came not from
these media-based experiments but from a grass roots regeneration of
musical activity in the form of the pub music session.

Comhaltas Ceoltóirí Éireann and the Emergence of the Session

The pub session emerged at about the same time in Ireland and in Irish
communities in London. In both countries, it seemed to be a response

to alienation and a reaction catalysed by the meeting of urban and rural culture. During the 1940s, commercial dance halls became more and more oriented towards popular music. This left *céilí* bands, the main traditional music pursuit, to find new environments. In London, the music found its place in the public house where musicians from different parts of Ireland, representing different regional styles, met and played together. The session became intrinsic to social life and a general sense of identity amongst the emigrant community:

> For many an Irish country man, London proved an inhospitable place except for the joyous occasions of Irish music sessions and the camaraderie of an 'Irish' pub. In the fifties it was not uncommon to find fifty musicians at the Eagle in Camden Town on a Monday lunch time. In the pub the musician was in a different element: the music was a trigger in a mechanism which allowed people who had to work and live in a strained environment to regain their composure in a neutral way.[29]

In Ireland in the 1940s, traditional music was at a particularly low ebb and, as in London, show bands and discos were fulfilling the social function once provided by traditional activities. It was a Dublin-based organization, *Comhaltas Ceoltóirí Éireann*, who revived interest in traditional music. Their music festivals, the *Fleadhanna Cheoil*, instigated a similar phenomenon to the London sessions described above, bringing together musicians from all parts of the country.[30]

Established in 1951, *Comhaltas Ceoltóirí Éireann* is a government-funded educational body responsible for the promotion of the traditional performance arts. It has taken the urban revival of cultural awareness back into the countryside by organizing competitions there. Although the concept of competition is in many ways alien or opposed to traditional music, the festivals which sprang up around these *Fleadhanna Cheoil* have become important meeting places for musicians.

Isolated from their own communities after the demise of the house dance, players formed their own musical community and, with it, the session. Although discouraged by the official organizers of the events, musicians met in the pubs and on the streets for 'a few tunes' and the session was born. Today's *Fleadhanna* are mainly popular for their sessions, and the vast majority of musicians who attend are not there to compete.

The *Fleadhanna*, based on regional heats and national champion-ships, instigated a new nationwide network of musicians which gave performers the opportunity to play with a much wider and more diverse selection of people than they would normally encounter. Musicians, isolated for decades, were keen to extend their circle of musical acquaintance, to encounter new styles, melodies and versions.

Public music sessions were born into this festival environment and as a result they have evolved in such a way as to include a flexible number of musicians. The session is, almost by definition, an open event. Players join and leave the session at their leisure and, as already described, previously unfamiliar musicians can be accommodated as well as familiar ones. Thus, the session provides the maximum opportunity for players to make new musical acquaintances.

Sessions dissolve boundaries, bringing together large numbers of musicians, with or without previous experience of one anothers' playing, and representing diverse musical backgrounds, styles and experience. The large and eclectic sessions associated with the *Fleadhanna* both accelerate and reflect the demise of regional styles. One aspect of this is the reinforcement of the national repertory of tunes, based on widespread familiarity with the tunes recorded by Coleman and his contemporaries.

The *Fleadh* and the pub music session reinstated a sense of community and music, but by drawing together such diverse musical sources they inverted the role of the music in the social group. The house dance brought together local people. These people shared a rural and relatively consistent lifestyle and their music expressed individual responses to the shared routines of local daily life. Instead of music expressing *different* approaches and reactions to shared life experience, musicians in the *Fleadh* session, coming from all walks of life, express their *communality* through the activity of playing music together.

It also seems to be the *Fleadhanna* sessions that established an inseparability between music and drink. The holiday atmosphere, the pub venue and the strong social element, with musicians meeting for the first time or for the first time in a number of years, all combined to call for celebration. Scenes of excessive drunkenness provoked disapproval, as demonstrated by the view of one of the longstanding adjudicators:

The Fleadh in certain areas was no longer, in the bourgeois term, acceptable. The fools! Centuries of oppression could not kill our culture and surely to God, a few beer swilling thullatans were not going to succeed where the might of the ruling class failed. The delicate flower that is our music drooped, but it did not die. Maybe the folk book of the sixties sent people, unconsciously perhaps, in search of musical roots.[31]

Towns that had hosted a *Fleadh* in the early years often continued to be meeting places for musicians. Members of the urban intelligentsia recognized the importance of traditional culture; their interest combined with musical activity to establish these towns as rural centres for traditional activity. Micho Russell remembers a transition in Doolin, where pub sessions and the beginning of the village's snowballing success as a popular resort went hand in hand:

I suppose it started to get popular in 1950 and 1960. Maybe in 1956, the *Fleadh Cheoil* in Lisdoonvarna was the first. Writers and professors used to come after that. My brother he was a good cause for all those people to come, because he was very smart and he used to talk to them and entertain them and tell them about the old things and the Irish language . . . Different people would come that wouldn't be interested in the music at all, [but the] culture you know, and scenery, folklore and so on.[32]

The *Fleadhanna* in Clare in the early years were instrumental in putting the county on the 'musical map'. The Miltown Malbay *Fleadh* in 1957 re-established it as a musical stronghold, as explained by Marty O'Malley:

Come '57 then it was to change Miltown totally, tourist-wise, every-wise. It was the start of the boom for Miltown. That Fleadh brought in a new crowd. They started comin' back and back. They came weekends and played in pubs.[33]

Many of the musicians who continued to visit '*Fleadh* towns' were young city players. The session was the main musical environment for these players. The majority of them would have learnt their tunes via the mass media and may have had some previous experience in another musical field. Many of the musicians now living in rural musical centres such as Miltown and Doolin are from this eclectic background; amongst musicians resident in Doolin, Dubliners far outnumber local players.

The new community between musicians, and their divorce from social life in general, is reflected in the invariable spatial arrangement of the session-type event. Musicians sit in a closed circle with their backs to the audience and attention is focused into the musical group. Although inclusive, the session is essentially introverted, drawing newcomers into the group but not projecting into the environment.

Informality and Heterophony in the Session

The flexibility and informality of the session group is partly the heritage
of the solo tradition. The following observations apply to melodic
instrumentalists rather than percussive and harmonic 'backers'. The
fact that each musician retains the autonomy of his or her own melodic
line, contributing a line which is a complete musical performance in its
own right, means that there is no interdependence of musical roles.
There are a number of other musical traditions where group activity is
essential to the basic structure of the music. The hocket techniques used
in the Bolivian Andes,[34] the antiphony and polymeter which characterize
African ensembles,[35] the stratification of the western orchestra — in
each case the individual contributes a specific musical role and skill to
the group, and mutual responsibility for the overall sound may be a
catalyst for or a source of social interaction.

In the Irish session group this is somewhat reversed. The structure
of the group is created through interaction within each event and
depends on social and environmental factors rather than musical necessi-
ties. The shape of the room, the personnel and size of the group, the
relationships between the musicians present, the mix of instruments
being played, the inclinations of the individual participants, all of these
and countless other factors combine as the session groups, regroups
and shapes itself during the course of the event, and this in turn governs
the overall sound. The very unpredictability of many of these factors
is essential to the session and this aspect of group performance practice
seems to recreate a level of spontaneity associated with individual
variation-making.

The informality of the group generates a subtle and complex session
protocol. The idea of the session as an egalitarian musical gathering is
an attractive one, but inaccurate. In fact, the musical structures characteristic of the African or Bolivian ensemble are much better examples
of musical democracy. The status of individual musicians is an
important organizing principle, contributing to the creation of a
hierarchy expressed through spatial organization and the proportional
distribution of the melodic lead. Colin Hamilton lists technical skill,
background, instrument played, repertoire and reputation (social as
well as musical) as factors which contribute to the evaluation of a
musician.[36] The combination of these factors, together with the personality, whether the musician is forceful or passive, the volume of the

instrument played, and the existing relationships between the players, tends to create roles of leader, filler and beginner. In regular events, these roles become relatively static. Visiting players who are already known to the stable nucleus of musicians play an important part in transforming such events and recreating the group.

The spatial organization limits the interactive involvement of unfamiliar or beginner musicians but does not restrict their personal playing. Again, this contrasts with the apprentice role in many other musical ensemble traditions where a beginner is fully involved but plays a relatively simple part. Providing a rhythmic, droned accompaniment to the tune in a Transylvanian string ensemble is a step in the learning process and can be a step toward leading one's own ensemble. A more closely related example exists in the way that American old-time fiddle music is often taught in group workshops. The basic 'shuffle' rhythm (one long and two short bow strokes) is often introduced as a foundation, and then stripped-down versions of tunes are introduced in short phrases, at first repeated individually and then combined in sequence, gradually building up the tune. Players of different aptitudes may contribute anything from the shuffle rhythm on single notes to a varied and more complex version of the tune.[37] In the Irish session, the hierarchical roles described above form the initial basis for a session and will often dissolve as the session starts to take off. In my experience, sessions involving musicians of the same level of experience and accomplishment are more likely to 'fly'.

Sessions themselves vary enormously, from large sessions involving a wide cross section of different styles to small and intimate affairs where the players can all hear one another. The instrumentation also varies considerably, no instrument is specifically excluded, and I have heard sounds as diverse as saxophone, didgeridoo and electronic keyboard contributing to sessions alongside the more traditional fiddles, accordions and flutes. In general, musicians favour a balanced cross section of different instruments, but will play alongside whatever turns up.

Whatever the size and instrumentation of the session, musicians have a strong tendency to maintain individual autonomy. The structure of individual melodic contributions to a session is often indistinguishable from solo performances, tunes tending to remain intact, and variation pursued within traditional limits. The way in which a musician goes about learning a tune in the session demonstrates a principle of melodic autonomy at work. Following the movement of another player's lead, the new material is worked into familiar melodic structures to create an integrated line which follows the shape of the simultaneous perform-ance. The resulting overall sound is the heterophonic, simultaneous variation of a single melody.

The creative element in the session group lies with the individual musicians' interpretations of the melodic line. Even when all those playing know the same version of a tune, there is still a heterophonic dimension, created by the spontaneous variation-making of individuals. Variation may be catalysed by the simultaneous hearing of someone else's version of the same basic monody. Individual differences in the treatment of the melodic line can be obscured in large groups and the interaction between soloistic and subtle variations of the melodic line is best heard in small sessions.

Example 6 reproduces one phrase of the three melodic contributions to a session version of the reel, 'The Liffey Banks'. The extract is taken from the third cycle of the tune. The example demonstrates individual

Example 6
'The Liffey Banks', played by Connie O'Connell and Matt Cranitch (fiddles),
Colin Hamilton (flute) and Tom Stevens (guitar) in a session at the Old
Triangle, Macroom, County Cork, February 1992, recorded by
Hazel Fairbairn.

approaches to the rhythmic configurations of the melodic line which are contained within a closely related framework of main beat pitches. Although the musicians are treating the tune individually, there is detailed melodic coordination between their versions. All three players have a relationship with the *Sliabh Luachra* regional style and this gives a natural affiliation. They are also meeting in a quiet situation where they are able to hear each others' versions and variations of the tune.

The very nature of spontaneous improvisation — new ideas conceived in the process of playing a tune — defies attempts to link it with any specific catalyst. This kind of improvisation constellates events in a new way and in a sense it relates to the integrating capacity of the 'in performance' learning process described above. Spontaneous improvisation may be a response to almost any stimulus, not necessarily a musical one, and it is the preserve of neither group playing nor the session. However, there is an extent to which the informality of the session-type event and the contribution from other musicians combine to provide an element of uncertainty that can be the source of inspiration. On one level this exists in the form of the possibility of unexpected musicians joining the session, but it also exists within the playing itself.

Although session-type events follow certain tendencies — the inclusive and open group, the introverted nature of the performance practice, the informality which allows musicians to leave or join the group at their leisure — there are as many kinds of session as there are different gatherings of musicians. Example 6 demonstrates a small and intimate affair where musical interaction can be pursued within the constraints of shared regional style. Criticisms of the session are particularly levelled at the large, diverse and noisy festival session. The most commonly expressed criticisms are eloquently summarized by Tony MacMahon's view:

Over the past number of years, in my travels in Ireland at traditional music festivals or other traditional music events, I have been, if you like, horrified by the way playing in pubs has degenerated. By that I mean big numbers of people playing very fast in a charged atmosphere. I mean it's very good for having a good time and other pleasant social functions, the emphasis on the word social. But if you want to listen to the music, or take any interest whatsoever in the tunes being played, or in the ornamentation, you will get nothing. And for that reason, I feel, if you have a number of people, be it three, four, five, six or ten people playing together in a pub . . . traditional Irish music . . . reels, jigs and hornpipes, the detail is killed. So what you get is the skeletal form of the music only. And even that is twisted and pushed out of shape, because the atmosphere of the pub charges the whole thing up, pushes the speed up, accelerates it. These tunes start faster than they should be, and as drink and excitement gets hold of people, you have an increase in tempo and what you end up with is what I call a 'musical brawl'.[38]

Yet, even in these large sessions, often accused of ironing out individual style, the individual is emphasised in the informality of the performance practice which allows each player to pursue their own musical preferences. Players may pursue their own variation-making within the framework of the traditional monodies which form the basis of the event and any player may start their own choice of tune, so that the event is structured around the desires and moods of the individual participants expressed through social and musical interaction.

Change to the actual musical structure and monodic-based style occurs when the interactive dimension is obscured and displaced. In small and intimate events, the heterophony created between individual versions of the same tune can be heard. The musicians are able to react to one anothers' individual gestures and respond to variations introduced during the performance. In large, noisy and diverse events, musical communication may be transferred to a structural level which accommodates prolonged departure from the tune skeleton and a resulting enlargement of musical texture and focus.

One example of this occurs in the evolution of a reel, '*An Pinsín Snaosín*' ('The Pinch of Snuff'), from a rather eccentrically structured five-part tune, transcribed in Example 7 from the playing of Johnny Doherty, a Donegal fiddler who represents the old regional style of the area. This tune consists of three basic strains, the first two of which are transposed into the upper octave to create a further two parts. The overall structure of the parts is therefore A:B:C:A'(↑8ve):B'(↑8ve).

Example 8 shows the contemporary popular session version of 'A Pinch of Snuff' which rises through three keys. Advances in instrument technology have developed chromatic counterparts for most diatonic traditional instruments and this has combined with the incorporation of accompanying chordal instruments to raise the awareness of key and modulation amongst traditional players. The version now becoming popular in sessions adds no new motivic material but extends the melody to nine parts through transposition. Figure 1 compares the part structures of the two versions. Parts A″, B″, A‴ and B‴ are simply

Example 7
'*An Pinsín Snaosín*' ('The Pinch of Snuff'), played by Johnny Doherty, edited by
Breandán Breathnach, in *Ceol Rince na hÉireann*, 2 vols (Baile Átha Cliath:
Oifig an tSoláthair, 1982), II, 95.
By permission of An Gúm, Dublin (copyright Government of Ireland)

Changing Contexts for Traditional Dance Music in Ireland

592

HAZEL FAIRBAIRN

Changing Contexts for Traditional Dance Music in Ireland   593

Example 8
'The Pinch of Snuff', played in a session at Fahey's bar, Miltown Malbay,
County Clare, July 1990, recorded by Hazel Fairbairn.

Johnny Doherty	Session
A: On D	A: On D
B: On D	B: On D
	A″: On G
	B″: On G
	A‴: On A
	B‴: On A
	A′: On D (↑8ve)
	B′: On D (↑8ve)
C: Descending	C: Descending
A′: On D (↑8ve)	
B′: On D (↑8ve)	
C: Descending	

Figure 1

Variation in the Part Structure between the Doherty and the Session Versions of
'The Pinch of Snuff'.

transpositions of the A and B parts shared by both Johnny Doherty's version and the session version.

Thus, the session version of the tune simplifies motivic construction within the parts. Simple repetition replaces intricate motivic variation generated through inversion and transposition in Doherty's version. Instead, transformational processes of transposition, modulation and extension into new key areas are used to generate new and distinct parts.

In addition, the session treatment of the descending phrase (C) gives an unusual example of the transformation of the melodic structure to suit the needs of group rather than solo playing: the answering phrase in bars 3–4 of Johnny Doherty's version is treated in the session as a short break, allowing a single musician to extemporize.

The session participants treat this kind of group activity very light-heartedly, but nonetheless this setting of the tune has evolved independently in a number of different session performances of the tune. In Fahey's bar in Miltown Malbay, 'The Pinch of Snuff' became a performance ritual evolved by a relatively stable group of musicians over a period of four years of the Willie Clancy week.[39] The tune was played at midnight on each night of the festival week. As the tune rose from the B part into the A″ part, changing to the key of G, the musicians would all stand up for the duration of the key change. As the tune rose again, to the key of A, they would stand on their seats. The high A′ section would find them all standing on the table and, as the tune descended, they returned to their seats, repeating the entire sequence with each round. All this happened at the expense of a fair number of the notes of the tune. By the time I experienced 'The Pinch', then in its fourth year of development, the whole ritual became so predictable as to be incorporated into the bar schedule: the bartender's children were sent running underneath the mounted musicians to collect the empty glasses on the table.

The evolution of this tune demonstrates the development of certain musical parameters at the expense of others as a consequence of group playing. Changes transfer the interactive dimension to a more purely social level in the large group, the music sometimes becoming an excuse for 'the crack' rather than an equal partner with it. This often results in impoverishment on the level of motivic detail and subtle melodic variation.

The festival session context does not preclude detail in the individual versions, but it does inhibit it in two important ways. The general increase in tempo in the large session is a consequence of the excitement generated between large numbers of players meeting informally, combined with the skeletal treatment of the melodies. The faster pace does not accommodate detail for musicians who have an older and gentler style of playing, and can also preclude the use of phrasing as an expressive device, as demonstrated by Micho Russell (see Example 2). Secondly, even for a player who is used to today's faster versions of traditional tunes, the musical subtlety of an accomplished and experienced traditional musician has less impact on the group than a steady backing or the structural clarification of a basic version played on a loud instrument. Hence, the contribution of the quality solo player and of traditional performance aesthetics is devalued.

The kind of enlargement of texture illustrated in 'The Pinch of Snuff' is ultimately not sustainable. The rhythmic and tonal structure of Irish traditional dance tunes is so similar that to approach the large-scale building blocks at the expense of melodic detail leads to uniformity between pieces in the traditional repertory. In the case of 'The Pinch of Snuff', it is the eccentricity of the old setting which has allowed the development of structural variety. The session and the performance tradition as a whole continue to rely on the detailed knowledge of individual tunes. Amongst musicians I have met and played with, even those who pursue the session as their only musical outlet still attach importance to complementing learning in the session situation with individual application to tunes using commercial recordings or personal tapes as source material. As such, the musical blind alley of diversity at the expense of detail does not threaten the mainstay of the tradition.

In general, sessions are based on fundamentally individualistic concerns. The actual group product is secondary to the effect that the interactive process and performance context has on each solo participant. Through interaction, musicians stimulate one anothers' creative capacities, but the resulting variation is usually conceived in the linear context of the individual version of the melody. Melodic variations create heterophony with simultaneous versions of the same tune.

The traditional emphasis on creative individual effort has survived in the session group. It has also survived the introduction of the kind of group arrangements proposed by Ó Riada. Since the late 1970s commercial folk groups have returned to the integrity of the eight-bar phrase. Formal experiments — such as Ó Riada's ostinatos, or extemporization such as that on the album, 'The Storm', by The Moving Hearts, which extends the melody beyond its dance-based, eight-bar construction — have given way to the concentration of the creative element in the solo dimension and the interaction between solo elements.[40]

Interdependent group arrangements restrict the scope of the spontaneous element. They require organization, either in the form of musical direction or by rigorous rehearsal that predetermines musical behaviour. In the session, and in most contemporary groups, arrangements have reverted to the traditional eight-bar phrase structure, within which the players retain the reins of their own creativity whilst interacting with simultaneous versions of the tune. The invariability of the eight-bar phrase structure of the dance tunes and a detailed shared repertory allow the spontaneous musical behaviour and interaction which is particularly associated with the unpredictable musical environment of the session.

Conclusions

The *Fleadhanna Cheoil* thus instigated a revival of traditional music performance and their efforts combined with the emergence of group playing to repopularize Irish music. In many ways, Irish music is thriving and has found itself an unlikely niche in an increasingly commercial world. As well as the very many young Irish people, living at home and abroad, who play traditional music to a very high standard, the Irish tradition has attracted a large number of foreigners. There are particularly large numbers of German, Dutch, Scandinavian and American musicians who have become inspired to commit themselves to learning the craft of traditional Irish music. Traditional music is also a significant tourist attraction in Ireland and is directly responsible for new prosperity in some areas along the western seaboard.

There is a strong association between these achievements and the rise of ensemble playing in both its informal and formal settings. The group context has become the most widespread mode of performance of traditional dance tunes providing a sustainable modern context for traditional music. The session recreates the intimate involvement between local people at a house dance. Musicians play for and with other musicians, the session is a participatory event and experience, providing its own community and making audiences redundant. Bypassing the formalized modes of group interaction explored by contemporary ensembles, the performance practice of the session reflects the social function of the house dance and the individual monodic expression of the solo tradition.

Notes

[1] Matt Molloy quoted on the sleeve notes to *Music at Matt Molloy's* (C.D., RW 26, Real World, 1992).

[2] Peter O'Grady quoted on the sleeve notes to *Music at Matt Molloy's*.

[3] Matt Cranitch, interview, February 1992, Cork, Ireland.

[4] Mícheál Ó Súilleabhain, from a set of draft programme notes written for a performance of his orchestral work, *Homo Ludens*.

[5] Mícheál Ó Súilleabhain comparing Irish and Cape Breton musical traditions on the sleeve notes to *Traditional Music from Cape Breton Island* (12-inch L.P., N15 383, Nimbus, 1993).

[6] Niall Kenny, questionnaire response, 1992.

[7] Cf. K. A. Gourlay, 'Towards a Reassessment of the Ethnomusicologist's Role in Research', *Ethnomusicology*, 22 (1978), 1–35.

[8] Lawrence E. McCullough, 'Style in Traditional Irish Music', *Ethnomusicology*, 21 (1977), 85–97 (p. 85).

[9] The roll is a device which decorates a main note with a sequence of rapidly executed upper and lower auxiliary notes. The group of notes is played so quickly as to create an impression of rhythmic emphasis rather than melodic embellishment.

[10] These are general observations based on listening, and supplemented by what little documentation there is of regional styles in traditional Irish music. Two such sources are: David Lyth, *Bowing Styles in Irish Fiddle Playing: Vol. 1* (Monkstown: Comhaltas Ceoltóirí Éireann, 1981), which describes elements of the Sligo fiddle style, and Caoimh Mac Aoidh, 'Aspects of Donegal and Kerry Fiddle Music', *Ceol*, 7.1–2 (December 1984), 20–28.

[11] *Sliabh Luachra* is a mountainous area on the East Kerry/West Cork border which has a strong regional style associated with the set dance.

[12] Tom Munnelly and Harry Hughes, 'Marty O'Malley', *Dal gCais*, 9 (1988), 85–91 (p. 87).

[13] Micho Russell, interview, January 1992, Doolin, County Clare.

[14] Michael Tubridy, 'The Musical Heritage of Mrs Crotty', *Dal gCais*, 10 (1991), 82–92 (p. 83).

[15] Micho Russell, interview, January 1992.

[16] Allen Feldman and Eamonn O'Doherty, *The Northern Fiddler* (Belfast: Blackstaff Press, 1979; repr. London: Oak Publications, 1985), pp. 25–26.

[17] Colin Hamilton, 'The Session, A Socio-Musical Phenomenon in Irish Music' (unpublished master's thesis, Queen's University of Belfast, 1978).

[18] Feldman and O'Doherty, p. 26.

[19] Tubridy, p. 89.

[20] Micho Russell, interview, February 1992, Doolin.

[21] Munnelly and Hughes, p. 87.

[22] Some of these 78 r.p.m. recordings have been reissued on 12-inch L.P.s by Shanachie Records as follows: *The Legacy of Michael Coleman* (33002, 1976), *Paddy Killoran's Back in Town* (33003, 1977), *The Pure Genius of James Morrison* (33004, 1978), *The Classic Recordings of Michael Coleman* (33006, 1979).

[23] Donal McCartney, 'The Founding of the Gaelic League', in *Milestones in Irish History*, ed. by Liam de Paor (Cork: Mercier Press in collaboration with Radio Telefís Éireann, 1986), pp. 117–27.

[24] Barry Taylor, 'The Irish Ceili Band: A Break with Tradition?' *Dal gCais*, 7 (1984), 67–74 (p. 70).

[25] Seán Ó Riada speaking on 'Our Musical Heritage', a series of programmes first broadcast on Radio Éireann, 7 July 1962–13 October 1962.

[26] Interview with Éamon de Buitléar, in Grattan Freyer, 'From "Ceoltoiri Chualann" to "The Chieftains": Two Interviews', in *Integrating Tradition: The Achievement of Séan Ó Riada*, ed. by Bernard Harris and Grattan Freyer (Terrybaun, Bofeenaun, Ballina, Ireland: Irish Humanities Centre; Ballina and Sligo: Keohanes; Chester Springs, Pa.: Dufour Editions, 1981), pp. 120–30 (p. 120).

[27] Taylor, p. 74.

[28] Éamon de Buitléar, quoted in Freyer, p. 123.

[29] Brendan Mulkere, 'A Heritage Abroad', *Dal gCais*, 9 (1988), 87–93 (p. 91).

Changing Contexts for Traditional Dance Music in Ireland   599

[30] *Fleadhanna* is the plural of *fleadh*, meaning 'feast', and *cheoil* means 'music'.

[31] Cormac MacGiolla, 'The Changing Fleadh Scene', *Treoir*, 15.4 (1982), 17.

[32] Micho Russell, interview, January 1992.

[33] Munnelly and Hughes, p. 91.

[34] Henry Stobart, public lecture, 10 February 1994, Anglia Polytechnic University, Cambridge.

[35] John Miller Chernoff, *African Rhythm and African Sensibility: Aesthetics and Social Action in African Musical Idioms* (Chicago: University of Chicago Press, 1979).

[36] Hamilton, pp. 42–43.

[37] These are general observations based on my own experience of workshops. See also Michael Frisch, 'Notes on the Teaching and Learning of Old Time Fiddle', *Ethnomusicology*, 31 (1987), 87–102.

[38] Tony MacMahon, interview, February 1992, Dublin.

[39] The Willie Clancy Summer School is a week-long event consisting of traditional music classes and concerts. In addition to the organized events, a festival of informal sessions has sprung up in the twenty-two pubs of Miltown Malbay.

[40] The Moving Hearts, *The Storm* (12-inch L.P., 3014, Tara, 1985).

[10]

"A Special Kind of Courtesy"

Action at a Bluegrass Festival Jam Session

Michelle Kisliuk

Live musical communication is action, and it can be as truly dramatic as any other mode of performance. The bond of music, musicians, and on-lookers to each other and to the immediate environment distinguishes live music from mechanically reproduced sound. And when it comes to blue-grass, many connoisseurs assert that recorded bluegrass is hardly blue-grass. Only when the music is acoustic—meaning not even miked—can you get the pure bluegrass experience. Only then can you "feel that fiddle goin' right into your ear," as one onlooker once put it.

Bluegrass jam sessions provide an opportunity to look at that area of performance which falls between stage performance, where audience and performers are clearly separated, and private rehearsal. Unlike a rehearsal, the jam session is an end in itself, and unlike stage performers, jammers focus on performing with and for each other. While much learning goes on in the jam session setting, the emphasis is on enjoying the music sociably.

Though many people come to bluegrass festivals primarily to see the amplified stage show, others use the show as a good excuse to have infor-mal jam sessions in the campground or parking lot. Many from this seg-ment of the festival-going public, both players *and* listeners, agree, as I was told in Lexington, Kentucky in 1984, that jam sessions are "about the only reason I come to these." Why do some connoisseurs say that the music is more real at a jam session? Partly because there is a special energy that comes from the anticipation of the unexpected and the unrepeatable within the temporary jam session alliance. Jammers implicitly follow an interac-tional etiquette which helps to channel this energy into the music. This etiquette is manifested in the conventions that help strangers come together to make music, and it is expressed microcosmically in the choices made while playing. In the jam session context, ethics and musical aesthetics are fused as jammers learn to negotiate guidelines for interaction in order to reach a heightened musical and social communion.

142   *Michelle Kisliuk*

1. A picnic table serves as a centerpiece for this campground jam session, where performers and spectators are barely distinguishable. (Photo by Michelle Kisliuk)

Bluegrass originated with the stringband music of Bill Monroe and his Blue Grass Boys on the radio and at Nashville's Grand Ole Opry in the late 1930s and early '40s. Other bands imitated the style and by the early '50s fans were beginning to call any music with that special sound "bluegrass."[1] Though bluegrass evolved in a professional radio and stage setting, its roots (and Bill Monroe's) are in white Appalachian (Scots-Irish) music, black blues and gospel, and other American folk traditions. The living body of the genre is held largely in the hands of people who either cannot or choose not to make a living at it, but who have assimilated the music of the professionals into a less-formal jam session tradition.

Since the late 1950s, bluegrass has attracted more and more people from outside its cultural roots in the upland South. A main factor contributing to this growth has been the bluegrass festival. In 1965 Carleton Haney, a country music promoter, organized the first weekend-long bluegrass festival, held at Roanoke, Virginia (Rosenberg 1985a:205). The format was comprised of an outdoor stage show, day and evening, with several bluegrass bands playing short sets. There was rough camping for those who were staying for the weekend, instrumental workshops for enthusiasts, band and instrument contests, and informal jam sessions in the parking lot. Though the idea of the bluegrass festival was influenced by the folk revival festivals of the '60s, it was also based on several interrelated types of events including fiddle conventions, old-time music contests, religious camp meetings, and country music concert parks.

There are now hundreds of independently organized festivals every summer all over the United States, in Canada, and even in Europe and Japan. A significant number of the people who go to bluegrass festivals are bluegrass musicians themselves and may travel hundreds of miles to spend

2. The stage at Bill Mon-
roe's festival at Bean Blossom, Indiana. Monroe is on
stage with Ralph Stanley
and other bands for the Sunday morning gospel sing.
(Photo by Michelle Kisliuk)

3. Jammers such as these at
Bean Blossom often ignore
the stage show completely.
(Photo by Michelle Kisliuk)

long weekends picking and singing with their friends, family, fellow band
members, and strangers—all of whom might blend into one category
during a good campsite jam. Neil V. Rosenberg reports that at the first
festival in Roanoke "one of the things mentioned by almost everyone who
attended was the high quality of the informal music sessions" (1985a:208).

Musicians of every category, from novice to professional, come to jam,
and certain annual festivals, such as Bill Monroe's festival in Bean Blos-

som, Indiana, are known for their high concentration of jam session enthusiasts. The jam session network forms a social and musical core at these
festivals, and for some people the stage show is only a benign presence on
the jam session scene.[2] People of various ages and backgrounds come
together in the campground sessions, and Rosenberg notes that even at the
first festival in Roanoke, "while there was some polarization between the
citybillies and the hillbillies in the small crowd, many of those present
shared an enthusiasm for the music which transcended cultural differences"
(1985a:207). They also shared a repertoire of songs and tunes—traditional
old-time material, and a growing body of recorded bluegrass that was
newly written or appropriated into the style from other sources such as
country western, swing, and rock and roll. This emerging bluegrass repertoire and its special form of ensemble playing, modeled after Monroe's
band, provided the basis for a distinct stringband jam session culture.

Bluegrass instruments form a combined picture of antiquity and modernity. The streamlined shape of the bluegrass classic Gibson F-5 mandolin
reminds some people of a mini–electric guitar, while the bluegrass banjo is
designed to augment its ringing and punching sound with more bronze,
chrome, and just plain flash than the old-time banjo. But the stand-up bass,
the fiddle, and the guitar are of standard design, and all bluegrass instruments, strictly speaking, are acoustic. This acoustic property lets the music
resonate elementally with its surroundings, and also underlines both socially and sonically what bluegrass is not—not rock and not commercial
country western music.

Since the 1950s bluegrass has expanded in many musical directions,
including "newgrass" and "jazzgrass." But what is called the "traditional"
sound almost always includes the rhythmic and tonal elements of Monroe's mandolin style and Earl Scruggs' three-finger banjo, along with a
solid beat and off-beat laid down by the guitar and bass, and accented by

*4. Monroe rides through the
campground at Bean Blos-
som, hobnobbing regally
with an admiring jammer.
(Photo by Michelle Kisliuk)*

the whole band. Fiddle and dobro guitar are also common bluegrass instruments. Characteristic bluegrass singing favors a "high lonesome" sound with tense, spine-tingling harmonies, and the voices often interlock or "line-out" the verse. These types are inspired by Afro-American and white Appalachian church singing.[3]

While "session" is used by Irish musicians to describe impromptu musical gatherings, the term "jam" comes from jazz.[4] The linguistic fusion in "jam session" echoes the musical and cultural fusion that is bluegrass. Bluegrass is sometimes presumed to be a hyper-white or even racist music, while those who understand the form rarely deny the extensive debt bluegrass owes to Afro-American culture.[5] Many aspects of bluegrass have been borrowed from jazz, and bluegrass jamming overlaps in form and meaning with the classic jazz jam session. The jazz jam has been described as a musical and spiritual escape from the aesthetic binds of commercialism, and as a setting for aspiring musicians to learn the social and musical intricacies of the form (see Cameron 1954). But perhaps more importantly, both in jazz and in bluegrass the collective jam session gives the musician access to a level of experience and self-expression unlike any other. Often going unnoticed by the casual listener, jamming is a central part of the artistic lives of many musicians, both professional and nonprofessional.

The endurance of the physical ordeal is an active ingredient in the transcendent experience that some bluegrass festival-goers look for. The challenge for jammers to stay up all night and "pick till you puke," as one fellow jammer put it at Bean Blossom in 1984, is part of the ethos of a bluegrass festival jam session—and its ultimate drama. This is consistent with the theory that at festivals in general people look for a "bombardment of the senses" that leads to a feeling of dizziness (Abrahams in Rosenberg 1985a:277). At a bluegrass festival jam the special combination of the outdoors, good bluegrass music, alcohol, and the excitement of cooperation and competition with strangers and friends makes for an atmosphere charged with potentiality. Jammers who pursue this potential to its limit by picking all night may overcome fatigue and reach a penetrating musical, social, and spiritual harmonic.

But not all jam sessions live up to the ideal. There are as many different kinds of jam sessions as there are combinations of people who play in them. As with any type of ensemble performance based on structured improvisation, the subtle social interactions of participants are inseparable from their artistic (in this case musical) interactions. It is in this unity of art and social life that the meaning of the event lies. Cueing between musicians is one focal point for such interaction.

Especially when strangers are just starting to play together, someone must be the leader to give cues about who is to take a break (instrumental lead),[6] when the tune will end, and other eventualities. The leader's role can be traded around within a song, depending on who is in the musical focus at a given time. For example, if I am playing and I finish my break, I can glance at the guitar player who, when she is done, might nod to the mandolinist. But sometimes this cueing system is superfluous, or it breaks down completely. If at one moment there is no leader, or if the jam session is very large, two people may be cued at once or may just start playing of their own accord. Then, if both stop playing, there will be a moment of hesitation before one of them makes a decided move. Also, if someone is taking a longer break than is appropriate, or has already had a turn when someone else has not, somebody may just butt in by beginning his or her own break. But cueing problems are sociomusical problems, and they

146   *Michelle Kisliuk*

5. Far from bluegrass's cultural roots in the upland South, these yankees jam at a festival in Boxboro, Massachusetts. (Photo by Michelle Kisliuk)

indicate the level at which the jammers are communicating interpersonally. In a happening jam session cueing is tight and exciting—not that cueing is emphasized, but rather it is taken for granted as part of the alertness necessary for playing good bluegrass. Unlike tunes rehearsed for stage performance, a measure or two lag of chording between breaks or singing is not usually seen as a problem in a jam session. But the cueing system, as part of an overall structure for extemporaneous interaction, can be employed as strictly or as loosely as fits the occasion.

During the summer of 1984 I attended and participated in jam sessions at Bill Monroe's festival in Bean Blossom, Indiana, and at the Festival of the Bluegrass in Lexington, Kentucky. Though I have attended festivals and played in jams since 1979, this time I was interested in taking a detailed look at what makes jam sessions work—or not work. I compared sessions at both festivals; each jam shed light on the code of behavior that permeates both the musical and the social interaction. For example, in a discussion after one unsuccessful jam session at Lexington, a jammer named Jim complained that "people kept comin' over and interrupting us. And it just bothers me, you know, 'cause along with picking I like to think goes a special kind of courtesy." This "special kind of courtesy" must be set in motion for a jam session even to get under way. It is the tacit basis of bluegrass jamming culture, the aesthetic that merges social and musical interaction.

Bill Monroe's Bean Blossom festival, June 1984.[7] Friday night, after the show. It's 11:30 and the jamming in the campground fields is already going full blast. As I walk through the campground one session just off of the dirt path sounds particularly good. I listen in the dark a few feet away and notice a man standing between two camper-trailers, confidently fretting the neck of a guitar. His right hand picks a bass string and then strums down, his wrist repeating the percussive, circular movement of bluegrass rhythm guitar. He sounds the strings with resonance and interlocks rhythmically with the banjo player who now switches from playing to backup. But before I can listen to the guitar break a man seated on a beer cooler next to the players motions for me to come over.

"I think my ears are outta whack," laughs the guitar player as I approach, tuning up after his skillful playing. The man who had called me over offers me a beer and plays host: "That's Greg, that's Ronnie, that's Verna, I'm Jimmy, and who are you?" After I make sure that they don't mind having another banjo in the session I go to my tent and get my instrument. When I come back I see that Jimmy, the one who had called me over, has gotten up to sing. Greg is standing too, and the jammers form a small circle inside a larger one marked by their seats. They're doing "I Know You're Married But I Love You Still," a slow Reno and Smiley song. Greg starts a guitar break, smoothly splitting it with Ron on the banjo, and after the next verse Ron starts the break and splits it with Greg. I think to myself that these guys are very tuned-in to each other—they must be used to playing together.

"I couldn't figure out where to pick it," says Greg when they're done.

"I thought you done a pretty good job there, myself," protests Jimmy.

"I couldn't figure out whether to go high or low," Greg insists good-naturedly, "or sideways or crooked or what."

I tune up. Their patience as they give me their pitches makes me feel welcome. This kind of incidental musical message is a mode of nonverbal communication in jam sessions.

They like the looks of my banjo so I can sense that they expect something impressive from me. "If we get some hot pickin' goin' here I'm bailin' loose," says Greg, picking a run on his guitar. "Go ahead and pick something," he says to me—a modified version of the classic jam session challenge, "kick one off." I hesitate.

"Ummm. . ."

"She's got the same problem we got!" exclaims Greg, "sit at home and play thousands of songs, and then get out here like this and you can't think o' nothing'." I decide on "Mountain Girls," one that everybody will know. Our playing is fueled by the creative tension between strangers all intent on making good music and having fun, and the simultaneous risk of missed social and musical cues.

I play an opening break and then start to sing the verse. By the time we get to the chorus any tentativeness is gone and we're in the swing of it. Ron, a chemical plant worker from southern Ohio, is playing a sensitive banjo backup. A fiddle player emerges from the dark to join our circle just in time for Greg to nod to him, a signal that he should take a lead. He splits a break with Ron who takes it up on the chorus. Then we realize we have run out of verses.

"That's it," I say as we keep up the beat, "let's do the chorus again." Laughing, we all sing it.

Get down, boys, go back home,
Back to the girls you love.
Treat her right, never wrong.
How mountain girls can love.

Some of us know an ending in which the final "How mountain girls can love" is repeated, so half of us sing that while the others play a more abrupt ending. But a final "shave-and-a-haircut, two-bits" brings us together for a resounding finish.

"That's a good one," says Greg with a drawl. "I couldn't remember the cotton-pickin' words—I knew what you wanted to do but I couldn't get on the beat there." While Greg had actually been right on in his playing, he often finds something to criticize himself about after a tune, courteously making it known that he thinks his playing leaves room for improvement. His playing as well as his social skills help the jam along by making people feel comfortable. A tension exists in bluegrass jamming between egalitarian ideals on the one hand, and a hierarchy created by differing levels of technical skill on the other. Good jammers often resolve this tension by casting their skill in egalitarian terms. For example, Greg, in answer to an onlooker who lamented that he himself could never get the knack of playing the *gui*tar, told him cheerfully, "If I can do her you can do her."

A little later in the jam, beers are being passed around. "Boy, that's embarrassing," says Greg, "somebody gives you a can of beer and you try to open the wrong end." He feigns confusion, then laughs, but suddenly he snaps back to business: "Now what was the one I said . . . 'Pearlie Blue'?"

" 'Down the Road,' " Ron and Joe (the fiddle player) correct him on the title. Greg starts out with a lively guitar intro. Ron looks over at me inquiringly but I say I don't know it. He is surprised I don't know it because Flatt and Scruggs recorded the tune. Joe marks the off-beats on the fiddle and Ron joins with a backup as Greg starts the verse:

6. Some enthusiasts spend the entire summer in a camper, going cross-country from festival to festival. (Photo by Michelle Kisliuk)

Down the road 'bout a mile or two,
Lives a little girl named Pearlie Blue.
'Bout so high, hair is brown,
Prettiest thing, boys, in this town.

"Wait a second," says Greg, stopping everybody just before the chorus.
"Do you guys know the chorus of it the way they used to do it?[8] Do you
know the chorus the way it goes [he sings], 'Down the road / down the
road / I got a sugar baby down the road' or 'pretty girl down the road,' one
of the two."

Ron sings it, "Down the road / down the road / I got a pretty baby
down the road."

"That's it," says Greg. "It's 'pretty baby,' split the difference," he
laughs. "Want to do it that way?" We all make noises of approval. "I think
that'd be . . . Kick it off," he tells Ron. I am wishing that I knew this song,
not just because it's a good song, but because this is one of those moments
in a jam session when the music and the awareness of ensemble feeling are
beginning to come together. Something begins to dawn on me as I listen to
them play. These guys are more than just good players and friendly people. Both Ron and Greg have idiosyncratic though traditional styles (musically and socially) which have obviously been steeped in lots of casual
interaction with other players. It's not so much an ability to improvise that
is important. Although they have great ability to vary what they do, they
do not focus on variation at the expense of action and interaction. "Extemporaneous improvisation" conveys more accurately than "improvisation"
the process of making music with presence. As Robert Cantwell observes:

*7. Greg, Ron, and others
sing gospel tunes on Sunday
morning after a long night of
jamming. (Photo by
Michelle Kisliuk)*

Extemporaneity implies spontaneity, and spontaneity implies originality; yet extemporaneous improvisation is rarely as original as that
which has been labored over. [. . .] What the musician plays may
show his mind; but the way he plays shows his sensibility. [. . .] It is
far more the fruit of intelligence in action, a kind of readiness, than
intelligence in contemplation, the reflective inquiry that belongs to
the composer. [. . .] The musician most interested in his capacity to
perform will favor it [extemporaneity] at the expense, perhaps, of
the originality, the magnitude, and the permanence of his art. For it
is the "tradition"—the availability of the formulae and the embrace
of performing conventions—that promotes extemporaneity
(1984:157–8).

In the extemporaneous aspect of jamming, in the play of formulae in
response to the moment, the sociomusical aesthetic comes together. Good
jammers have learned by jamming, and in so doing have learned how to
respond musically to a social situation. The "special kind of courtesy" is as
much a musical awareness that reveals social concerns as it is a social
awareness that supports musical concerns. There are many jammers, however, who are less aware than are Greg or Ron of the delicate balances of
sociomusical interaction. Bluegrass hobby magazines such as *Bluegrass Unlimited* regularly publish anecdotes about infringements of jam session etiquette. Examples of such enter our own jam session as it continues.

An hour after "Pearlie Blue," the fiddle player has left and a bass player
has joined us. About 15 spectators have gathered around us and they join in
eagerly on the singing. After a version of "Dark Hollow" which has been
overpowered by too many singers, a young guy with a mandolin moves
into the inner circle, and an onlooker shifts to give him room.

"You got a guy here who wants to tune with you," says the onlooker.

"OK," says Greg. "Shoot, I thought he was already tuned up, sorry
about that."

"No," says the guy with the mandolin. "You're all a little higher than
standard."

"Oh, are we?" says Greg, not impressed. "Just tell me what you need
there." Greg plays him his pitches and the guy tunes his mandolin. His
opening comment foreshadows his behavior for the rest of the evening.
This mandolin player, whom I'll call Hal, proceeds uninvited to take over
the jam session, suggesting a string of songs that are over-played in jams
and that most jammers are sick of.

Later: It's almost 2:30 in the morning. Many onlookers have left. The
bass player, a friendly teenager, lifts up his bass: "It was good picking with
y'all, I'll see you tomorrow," he says.

"Yeah, nice meetin' ya," Greg calls out after him. Then there is a pause.

"Cop off somethin' of the Stanley Brothers,"[9] says one neighborly
sounding onlooker.

"Ohhhhhh," says somebody else.

"Wanna do some Stanley Brothers' stuff?" asks Hal.

It seems to have been decided. Then Ron, the banjo player, says blandly:
"Uh, I don't care for Stanley Brothers." A pause. Then quickly, "Don't
hit me, don't hit me, I'm lyin', I'm lyin'," he confesses.

"I was gonna come over there and beat ya," jokes Greg.

"No, he's my—he's one of my idols," Ron says quietly, referring to
Ralph Stanley, a banjo player. "Him and Bill" (Bill Monroe). Everything
is quiet. "What do you want to do by them?" he asks.

"Uh, let's see," says Greg, strumming in anticipation, trying to think of which Stanley tune would be just right. We have reached a precious moment in a late-night jam session when everyone's energy and attention are tuning in together. To make the feeling gel it's important to choose a tune that most of the central players know. This is the negotiation of jamming etiquette at its most delicate.

"You know 'Handsome Molly'?" Hal bursts in loudly, interrupting an onlooker who had started to suggest something. "Handsome Molly" is not even particular to the Stanley Brothers, it's an Anglo-Celtic ballad. Hal starts to sing it. Greg tries to join him, and then Ron starts to come in, but they are unsure of it. Ron starts to improvise a break but loses steam in the middle.

Jimmy, who has been with us all evening, suddenly gets up. "See you tomorrow," he says. "I'm gonna go to bed."

"You're turning in?" Greg asks, keeping the beat. "That's un-American!" he jokes, in the spirit of all-night jam sessions. Hal starts to sing again, and then takes a feeble mandolin break. Ron is ready to try one after that but Hal has already ended it. Two of the older, neighborly spectators are getting ready to leave, and through the din of plucked strings one of them says to Greg, "I really liked your pickin', it was real good."

Everyone plucks strings absent-mindedly, perhaps wondering if we can regain that precious tuned-in feeling. I start to fool with the beginning of a Ralph Stanley banjo tune in an attempt to keep up the Stanley idea. Everybody suddenly goes silent and Greg starts to back me up, stopping momentarily to be sure of the chords, but picking it up right away, putting in parallel runs and fill-in echoes. I stop short; Greg's backup is so nice that it takes me by surprise. I wasn't expecting such sudden attention. "It's just a Ralph Stanley banjo thing that I just . . ."

"Oh," says Ron sympathetically in his quiet voice, "it's hard to do Stanley. I don't know why but nobody can do it just like him." Ron starts to noodle around.[10] Greg follows him and soon they're playing a lively Stanley tune. They glance at me but I indicate with a head shake that I don't know the tune. Ron starts to sing it. I play some soft backup while Greg joins Ron for a high harmony on the chorus:

> Love me darlin' just tonight,
> Take these arms and hold me tight.
> Tomorrow you may hold another;
> Love me, darlin', just tonight.

Greg lets his voice trail off on the high part in classic "high lonesome" style. Ron plays a simple, clear banjo break, and then sings the next verse in a soft, raspy voice:

> Tomorrow you say that you'll be leavin',
> I hope you know the way that's right.
> I pray to God that you won't leave me;
> So love me, darlin', just tonight.

This is one of the finest moments we've had all evening, and since it's so late the silence around us presses in, magnifying each sweet sound and heightening every feeling. This is the kind of moment jammers strive for. The song is about ephemeral love, but it has some unspoken correspondence to our more immediate situation: The delicate feeling with us now could pass or be disrupted at any moment, and even if we could sustain it, our jam session alliance is necessarily temporary. Like all powerful music, bluegrass can be a manifestation of pure love of life, and of course life itself is ephemeral too—ephemeral love, ephemeral jam session, ephemeral moment, ephemeral life. Although these metaphors may not be consciously apparent to us as we play, the *feeling* of them is apparent, as is the fact that Ron and Greg, both of them master jamming artists, are finally in control of the musical and social atmosphere. Even Hal, the mandolin player, has been subdued, just "chunking" nicely on the off-beats. For a moment Ron can't remember the last verse. Greg chuckles; it doesn't matter anyway. But then Ron remembers it:

> Try to find true love in your heart,
> Tomorrow we may not have to part.
> But if you feel you must leave me,
> Love me, darlin', just tonight.

Ron plays an elegant final break and then an ending lick, going straight into an instrumental and not letting Hal interrupt the flow. Ron and Greg trade breaks and Ron is about to end the tune when Greg verbally alerts him that Hal looks like he wants to have a go at it. It seems unusual for Ron to have to be told such a thing, since he's such an aware musician, and I wonder if he was trying to get away with ignoring Hal. This would have been a breach of jamming etiquette, so Greg made sure to avert the transgression. Unfortunately, the mandolin, which has never been quite in tune, sounds pretty bad—and Hal still takes it twice through the verse. Ron can only try to salvage the moment with a final break at the end.

Participation in bluegrass has boomed over the past 15 years, and many people have joined the bluegrass ranks from outside its cultural and contextual roots in the rural upland South. As a result, many people who have learned to play through mediated sources such as tablature books, records, and formal instruction come to the festival jam session scene with only a partial understanding of what jamming is about. Some have developed virtuosic technique, while others have minimal technique but much aggressive, competitive spirit. Most, like Hal, have only a partial grasp of the underlying sociomusical aesthetic of jam sessions—or are totally oblivious to it. They therefore fill in randomly with whatever interactional style they are used to—in Hal's case the inept smoothness of a college fraternity-type entertainer. Tension arises when these relative newcomers meet with the minority of jammers who have grown up with jamming or who have learned to balance their technical knowledge with social skills.

Learning the tacit rules of jam session etiquette is not necessarily easy if you have not grown up in an environment infused with similar social values. Brian, a banjo player from Minnesota and a Bean Blossom regular, told me that when he first began to play the banjo he came to a bluegrass festival with his parents who pushed him into joining a jam session before he was ready: "I was annoyed that people were playing in my break . . . I didn't know that you were supposed to stop and let somebody else have a chance." The people he had imposed upon took radical action: " 'Looks like rain,' they said. . . . The sky was blue. One poor guy was left with me. He didn't want to insult me."

When someone ruins the picking, others may want to "lock him in a hot box out in the field somewhere," as Brian said during a daytime discussion at Bean Blossom. But to be overtly rude would be much worse than letting

8. " 'Looks like rain,' they
said. . . . The sky was
blue." Brian (right) has
since matured into an accomplished jammer. (Photo by
Michelle Kisliuk)

the spoiler ruin the jam session. If those who know the etiquette are rude, the basic values which allow jams to form in the first place are thrown into question. The ideas of equality and hospitality must be maintained, even if it means leaving a jam session open to ruin. An individual session can be sacrificed in order to preserve the values of the system as a whole. This explains why Greg so patiently smoothed over Hal's obnoxious behavior.

   Jam session performance is neither a rehearsal nor a formal performance, and it is because of this fairly open frame that jamming discourse can take place. When bluegrassers perform on stage they can avoid the risky openness of the jam session by doing their rehearsed act with musicians whose actions they can pretty well predict. But jammers, particularly those who come to festivals in order to play with new people and to learn, set themselves up for a potentially heightened experience. By balancing the tensions inherent in the jam session situation, jammers create a temporary alliance, a vital focal point for artistic energy that is imbedded in sociability.
   Like the front- and backstage of stage performances, front and back regions exist in jam sessions, but not as literally. A stage performance encourages a conscious sifting and monitoring of social and musical behavior for the sake of the audience, while backstage performers presumably do not sift their behavior, or at least not in the same way. In contrast, jammers play for their own enjoyment and there are no clear lines between performers and onlookers. Someone may join or quit playing at any moment, and the energy and commentary of everyone present contributes to the ambiance of the particular jam session. In jam session performance the back regions are determined by the implicit interaction between participants

154   *Michelle Kisliuk*

*9. & 10. These jammers
started their session seated,
trading licks on a hillside.
As others began to join them
the energy was heightened.
(Photo by Michelle Kisliuk)*

*11. The country values of
low tech and high human energy are often touted by
bluegrassers. This old trailer
is "Bluegrass Powered."
(Photo by Michelle Kisliuk)*

who communicate according to the immediate musical and social situation. Front and back regions exist simultaneously, the back regions accessible at any moment only to those with a certain level of awareness, such as
Greg, who interact with the front region people like Hal. But since awareness and sensitivity can shift from moment to moment even within the
same person, part of the challenge of jam sessions is to manage the ever-
changing borders between "front" and "back" awareness.

The jam session situation, unlike the stage, allows for more risk-taking
and unknown potential. Whereas on stage the limits are bounded and
highly framed, in jams there is the license to be as solemn or rowdy, as
experimental or as faithful to tradition as the moment dictates. But just as a
jam can sometimes reach the heights of experience, it can also disintegrate
into the depths of bad music and lack of communication. As jammers
balance the tensions of their circumstances, they rely on each other and on
the group as a whole to create a temporary, transcendent community.

Understanding how jammers manage the subtle flow of interaction may open up an area of research, helping us to understand the social bases of ensemble performances more generally and consequently gain insight into the many modes of cooperation-based social life.

Notes

1. For more on the development of professional bluegrass see Rosenberg (1985a).
2. There is often, however, a reciprocal relationship between the jamming atmosphere in the campground and the stage show; an inspired show often precedes a hot night of jamming and vice versa. Many jammers enjoy the show and many stage performers join the campground jam sessions.
3. For more on the roots of bluegrass see Cantwell (1984).
4. "Jam" was an Afro-American term meaning sex, but it has lost this meaning. In black West Indian English "jamming" does include a sexual reference.
5. Other forms of American music, such as rock, are also fusions of black and white traditions and use the term "jam session."
6. "Break" is bluegrass jargon for a melodic lead, or a foregrounded instrumental interpretation of a song.
7. The following descriptions are based on comprehensive tape recordings of the jams, field notes, and my memory.
8. By "they," Greg means the groups Greenbriar Boys and Country Gazette, both of whom recorded a chorus like this (Rosenberg 1985b).
9. The Stanley Brothers recorded many classic bluegrass and bluegrass gospel songs, and are loved by many of the most devoted bluegrassers.
10. A "noodle" is the musical counterpart of a doodle, and can be a means of nonverbal communication.

References

Cameron, William Bruce
1954   "Sociological Notes on the Jam Session." *Social Forces* 33:177–81.

Cantwell, Robert
1984   *Bluegrass Breakdown: The Making of the Old Southern Sound.* Urbana: University of Illinois Press.

Rosenberg, Neil V.
1985a   *Bluegrass: A History.* Urbana: University of Illinois Press.
1985b   Personal communication, 7 July.

Michelle Kisliuk *studies ensemble music, both as a musician and as a scholar. A PhD candidate in NYU's Department of Performance Studies, she is currently in Central Africa researching the group singing of the Biaka pygmies.*

[11]

Composition, Authorship, and Ownership in Flamenco, Past and Present

PETER MANUEL / John Jay College and the CUNY Graduate Center

Among the most fundamental musical developments accompanying the advent of modernity has been the emergence of new conceptions of authorship, ownership, and the roles of composition. A growing body of literature has emerged which addresses various aspects of these processes in relation to diverse music cultures (e.g., Talbot 2000, Vaidhyanathan 2001, Frith 1993). In the realm of Western art music, scholarly attention has focused in particular on the celebration, especially from the Romantic period on, of the composer as an individual genius, and on the special importance of "the work," as an original, reproducible, structurally unified, aesthetically unique, and privately owned entity (Goehr 1992). Concepts of authorship can be particularly problematic in the case of oral traditions that evolve into or become absorbed into commercial popular musics, entailing new conceptions of and a new prominence of the "song" and its individual composers, and new notions of ownership as embodied in copyright. Meanwhile, however, instead of promoting pre-composed "songs" and "works," modernity can also reinforce and rearticulate approaches which in fact de-emphasize composition, via, for example, the legitimization and elaboration of existing oral traditions, the elevation of individual, soloistic virtuoso expression and interpretation (as in jazz)—as opposed to composition per se—and the promotion of trends toward the standardization and codification of an existing repertoire, which thenceforth becomes in its own way resistant to accretion and new composition.

In this article I explore how some of these processes have operated in the modernization of flamenco, in the various forms in which it has flourished over the last century. Paralleling developments in certain other genres, in commercial pop flamenco, collective oral-tradition recycling of stock musical materials can be seen to give way to mass mediated, pre-composed songs, as new dimensions of finance and copyright precipitate polemics and legal actions. At the same time, however, the new importance of compositions and composing in the realm of this mass-mediated "*nuevo flamenco*" (new flamenco) has been counterbalanced in mainstream, neo-traditional flamenco by a certain codification of the existing repertoire, which has become less accommodating to new creations. The contradictions and complexities of these processes acquire various sorts of importance—as revealed by polemics and disputes—involving issues of aesthetics, ownership, and even ethnicity (as concerning Gypsies and non-Gypsies). Their complexity derives in part from the heterogeneity of forms of flamenco—from traditional to pop—and from the way that even traditional flamenco (in some respects like jazz) defies categorization as folk, classical, or pop.

Traditional Flamenco: *Cantes* and *Estilos*

If flamenco is understood as comprising *cante* (singing), *toque* (guitar), and *baile* (dance), it is cante which is traditionally regarded as structurally and aesthetically the most important and representative aspect of the art, and which accordingly is the primary focus of this essay. Traditional flamenco is based on a body of basic song-types which are called *palos* or *cantes* (aside from the general meaning of cante as "singing"). The mainstream repertoire comprises around a dozen basic and familiar cantes/palos, and some two dozen subsidiary or less common variants of these. The palos are distinguished variously in terms of poetic form, characteristic vocal melodies, in some cases metrical scheme, called *compás* (with distinctive internal accents), and guitar tonalities and conventional accompaniment patterns.[1]

The basic cantes/palos themselves may be regarded as general categories, and as frames or molds which accommodate a variety of more specific stock tunes, which could be called "sub-cantes" but are traditionally referred to by some vocalists as *estilos*—literally, "styles." Generally, an estilo—to those who use this term—comprises a distinctive melody, which accommodates a *copla,* which is a verse of from three to five lines. Thus, a typical rendition of a *soleá* (one of the palos) might consist of a string or "set" of four or five coplas or verses, which would probably be in different estilos, punctuated by guitar interludes (*falsetas*), all conforming to the characteristic twelve-beat compás and familiar chordal progressions of that cante. In practice, most soleá sub-cantes follow fairly similar melodic patterns.[2]

While a vocalist might sing a familiar copla in the estilo traditionally associated with it, the estilos function as stock tunes in the sense that a singer is free to set a new (or old) lyric to a suitable estilo. Writers on flamenco—notably Soler Guevara and Soler Díaz (1992) and Norman Kliman,[3] elaborating the work of Antonio Mairena (with Molina, 1979)—have identified almost one hundred distinct estilos of soleares and of *siguiriyas*, which are associated variously with places or with the names of singers who created or popularized them. While many singers might be unaware of such associations, a knowledgeable vocalist might announce, "Now I'll sing a soleá of Alcalá," which would imply any suitable copla or verse set to one of the loose stock soleá melodies supposedly deriving from the Gypsy singers from Alcalá; or it might be announced as "la soleá de cierre de El Mellizo," meaning a standard closing estilo attributed to Enrique Mellizo (1848–1906). Only literati familiar with the erudite taxonomies of Kliman and the Solers would be able or inclined to further identify the estilo as, for example, "La Andonda 2." Estilos in other palos could be similarly catalogued.

If the cantes constitute traditional song-types providing the basic mold or structure, the estilos or sub-cantes, in combination with the words to which they are set, are somewhat more "song-like" in their greater melodic specificity. Some of the lighter, metered sub-cantes—especially *fandangos de Huelva, tangos,* and familiar tunes like "Tanguillo Castillo de Arena"—are fairly "hummable" in the sense that their melodies are relatively fixed and tuneful, and are largely syllabic rather than melismatic in style. Such items can even be sung in unison by two or more singers, especially as lighter fare accompanying a commercial dance show (a *tablao*) at a club. However, estilos in the more serious flamenco cantes like *soleares, siguiriyas,* and *tientos* are better understood as flexible schematic outlines, which place greater demands on the singer's creativity of rendition. Accordingly, as *cante jondo* ("deep song"), they are more highly regarded by connoisseurs, and could never be sung in unison. Free-rhythmic fandango styles, including *malagueña* and *granaína*, although not seen as *cante jondo* or *cante gitano*, can also be quite melismatic, loose, demanding, and soloistic in their own way. Certain singers, to be sure, developed fairly fixed ways of rendering even melismatic estilos, such that they acquired some of the character of pre-composed entities, although they would be treated as stock tunes to be used strophically with different verses.

Despite the known authorship of many estilos, a typical traditional flamenco item, whether in concert or on a commercial recording, has few of the essential attributes of a "song" or composition, being instead a "set" of two to five coplas, which each constitute thematically unrelated and wholly independent and complete lyric statements. Insofar as the coplas are sung in similar or identical estilos, the rendering is thus loosely strophic and additive rather than organically structured like, for example, a 32-bar AABA song. Although in the case of cantes like soleares, there are certain conventions as to sequence of estilos (including a gradual increase in intensity), there is no particular overall structure, symmetry, or design, nor is there any particular form of closure, aside from the occasional use of short, closing cadential patterns (*remates*). The "title" of a piece that appears on the label of commercial recording is typically the first line of the first copla, or perhaps a distinctive line from another copla, rather than constituting a phrase relevant to the set as a whole. Further, in traditional singing, a vocalist need not make any particular attempt to reproduce any particular sequence of coplas and estilos that (s)he has sung previously, in concert or recordings (unless the artist is specifically attempting to promote a recent recording). For its part, an individual estilo—whether of a "hummable" tango or a flexible soleá—differs from a "song" in being short and constituting a manner of singing a single strophe or verse, rather than a blueprint for an entire piece of four or five minutes.[4] The distinctions between a "song" and a rendering of a cante are reflected, albeit idiomatically and imperfectly, in flamenco terminology and discourse. Outsiders might be tempted, if only for sheer convenience, to refer to a four-minute rendering of, say, a soleá, as a "song," especially when it appears on a CD with a "title." As we have seen, though, the term "song" is misleading in suggesting a "work" that is original, reproducible, through-composed, and subject to proprietary concerns. Hence it might be more appropriate, in English, to refer to a typical flamenco rendering of a cante as a "set." In Spanish discourse there is, unfortunately, no vernacular term for this, but the cognates for "song"—such as *"canción"*—are generally and deliberately avoided, as they specifically suggest pre-composed entities (which are hence generally lighter and less demanding). Thus, a singer, rather than announcing "Voy a cantar una canción por bulerías"—"I'll sing a song in bulerías"—will say "Voy a cantar por bulerías," which means, "I'll sing in bulerías," and implicitly means, "I'll sing a few coplas, in a few different estilos, in bulerías." By contrast, "To sing a song in bulerías"—("cantar una canción por bulerías")—would imply precisely that, i.e., to take an existing commercial popular song, like "María de la O," and sing it in the compás of bulerías—a practice that has been common in some contexts but is somewhat distinct from flamenco per se. Similarly, instead of saying, "She sang two tangos" ("Ella cantó dos tangos"), one might more properly say, "Ella cantó por tangos dos veces" or "ella cantó dos letras por tangos"—"She sang twice in tangos." (The use of the plural "tangos" is idiomatic in references to palos.)

Composition, Ownership, and Individuality in Traditional Flamenco

Although flamenco became a professional and commercially performed art by the 1860s-70s, it continued to be an overwhelmingly oral tradition in character, whether performed on stage, for partying *señoritos* (playboys), or in private Gypsy fiestas. As in many other oral-tradition music genres (such as, for example, Indian classical music), singers of traditional flamenco have been valued primarily for their expressive delivery of existing repertoire—in this case, a body of core palos and estilos that was largely in place by the mid-twentieth century. Compositional talent, and the originality and size of a vocalist's repertoire (lyrics and melodies) constitute features that might be appreciated in certain contexts, but are largely secondary to the flair with which the vocalist renders a largely inherited body of song-types. A singer lacking in such expressive delivery, however abundant in other talents, would not achieve renown.

Nevertheless, notions of composition and ownership are complex and have in some respects been contested, as reflected in attempts to compose palos and estilos, or, to codify them as a fixed repertoire, or to claim ownership of them, whether as a general ethnic patrimony or as legally protected entities. The distinctions between cantes and estilos as precomposed entities are analytically important and merit further individual treatment.

Cantes/Palos

For the purposes of understanding the role of composition, it is noteworthy that most of the basic repertoire of cantes, including their conventional guitar accompaniment patterns, was standardized by the early twentieth century. The innovation that abounds today in neo-traditional flamenco—even as played by innovative guitarists—consists primarily of various sorts of elaboration and expansion within these inherited cantes rather than invention of new ones. Accordingly, creation of the basic palos is not attributed to any individuals; rather, they are assumed to have evolved in a collective and anonymous fashion (especially in the mid- and latter nineteenth century). However, certain individuals are regarded as having played key roles in developing, refining, codifying, and popularizing them (e.g., Juan Breva with malagueñas and Antonio Chacón with *granaínas*). Meanwhile, scholars like Lefranc (2000) have reconstructed plausible, if speculative, evolutions of basic cantes like soleares and siguiriyas out of precedents like *romances* and the Muslim call to prayer (*azan*), but it is not possible to attribute these processes of creation to known individuals, except in the most speculative fashion. Even the now-popular and basic bulerías, despite evolving in the relative historical daylight of the early twentieth century, appears to have developed in a collective manner, rather than being the creation of any particular known artists.

The actual attempts of certain individuals to create cantes in the twentieth century stand out as exceptions to the rule. Virtually the only cante to have been successfully created and popularized by an individual after the beginning of the century is *colombianas*, which was invented around 1930 by *cante bonito* ("pretty flamenco") singer Pepe Marchena. After fashioning the colombianas as a light, Caribbean-flavored palo, Marchena was able to popularize it as a cante per se by performing and recording it repeatedly, with different verses. Given his prodigious stardom, Marchena's imitators also began singing colombianas, and the idiom effectively entered the canonic repertoire of established cantes. However, like the rococo cante bonito in general, the colombianas fell out of vogue in the 1970s and is seldom sung nowadays.

Subsequent attempts to invent cantes enjoyed less success. In the 1970s, vocalist Camarón de la Isla and guitarist Paco de Lucía created and attempted to popularize a palo which they called "*canastera*" (literally, "basket carrier" or "basket weaver," connoting a nomadic Gypsy woman). Camarón and Paco recorded two canasteras, with different lyrics, which were labeled on LP liner notes as cantes per se (e.g., in parentheses after the track titles, like the other indications of palos).[5] The two songs—as we may retrospectively characterize them—attained some popular appeal, being used, for example, by various dance ensembles. But unlike the colombianas of an earlier generation, the canastera did not come to be used by other singers as a palo—that is, as a vehicle for new song texts and interpretive elaboration (Gamboa and Nuñez 2003:349). Conservative critics were also dismissive of it as a palo per se, characterizing it as a pastiche of elements of tango and fandango de Huelva, and opining, explicitly or implicitly, that the repertoire of palos and estilos was quite adequate and allowed ample scope for creativity and innovation, and as such had no need of being expanded. Such, indeed, seems to be the general verdict regarding mainstream flamenco, which, since the 1970s, has consisted overwhelmingly of elaboration of the existing palos—alongside performance of pop and "nuevo flamenco" newly-composed songs.

In 1976, a similar attempt by vocalist Juan el Lebrijano to create two new palos, which he called *galera* and *caravana*, met a similar fate.[6] Both creations could, in retrospect, be regarded essentially as original "songs" in that they did not adhere to any known cantes. However, El Lebrijano specifically presented them, with some fanfare, as new palos per se, in the hopes that, like colombianas, they would become accepted in the canon. Like the canastera, their names appeared in the LP liner notes as palo indications, following the titles of the tracks. Also like the canastera, the galera and caravana were essentially failures in that while the specific songs enjoyed some ephemeral popularity, neither palo came to performed as a palo per se—that is, a framework used by other singers for new estilos with new lyrics.

Estilos and *Mairenismo*

Creating and popularizing an estilo is in some respects a less formidable undertaking than adding a palo to the canon, although, as with cantes, the core repertoire of estilos in basic palos like soleares and siguiriyas was largely in place by the mid-twentieth century. Most of the estilos catalogued by Kliman and the Solers (1992) appear to have been standardized by the 1930s, and many presumably or even demonstrably took shape well before then. It is partly for this reason that early-twentieth-century flamenco recordings by singers like Manuel Torre do not necessarily sound archaic to modern ears, except in the poor recording fidelity; both in terms of style and repertoire, they are essentially cognate with the mainstream flamenco of today.

Successful creation or "composition" of estilos continued until around the 1950s. The standard flamenco repertoire contains many sub-cantes that are attributed to singers who flourished in the 1930s-40s, such as El Niño de Gloria and Pastora Pavón, along with Manolo Caracol's 1950–60s versions (which he called *caracoleras*) of palos like tientos, siguiriyas, and fandangos. Lefranc insists that creation of estilos in cante jondo continued through the '60s and '70s, but it is not at all clear whether many, if any, of these new estilos have actually entered the repertoire as stock tunes used by others (especially insofar as his informants were reluctant to disseminate their art). As such, the basic flamenco repertoire of cante jondo sub-cantes, like that of cantes, was largely fixed by the 1950s.

The codification of the flamenco repertoire in the mid-century was both embodied in and promoted by the career of Gypsy vocalist and scholar Antonio Mairena (1909–83). Mairena came of age in the most culturally stultifying period of the Franco era, when cante jondo—while still cultivated in Gypsy circles and señorito parties—was being largely neglected in favor of lighter styles—especially fandangos, Latin American-inspired cantes like *guajiras*, and quasi-pop *cuplé* (discussed below), which were quintessentially presented in the context of theatrical variety shows called "*ópera flamenca.*" Mairena took it as his mission to rescue cante jondo in a project which Lefranc (2000:197) characterizes as the "Great Salvage." Mairena energetically collected estilos from all possible informants and singers, whether known or obscure, and endeavored to popularize and codify them through his own performances and commercial recordings, and through his written collaborations with flamenco scholars. Subsequently, Luis Guevara and Ramón Soler Díaz classified, organized, and related the supposed origins of Mairena's entire recorded repertoire of soleares and siguiriyas in their book, *Antonio Mairena en el mundo de la siguiriya y la soleá* (1992).[7] Mairena also authored two books: *Mundo y formas del cante flamenco* (with Ricardo Molina, 1963), a general and widely read study of the history and current forms of flamenco; and *Las confesiones de Antonio Mairena* (1976), an engaging musical autobiography.

Mairena has been criticized for allegedly exaggerating the role of Gypsies in creating flamenco and, especially, cante jondo. Also controversial was his attempt to establish the flamenco repertoire as a fixed body of forms which was complete and should not be added to. One of Mairena's goals, clearly, was to salvage and revitalize cante jondo not only by performing and promoting it per se, but, more importantly, by giving it a new legitimacy as a codified, documented, standardized, and almost "classical" repertoire. In these endeavors he must be regarded as achieving prodigious success and having made a remarkable contribution to the art. At the same time, his purist insistence that the repertoire was thenceforth fixed and inviolate promoted a kind of ossification, which predominated in the 1960s and had its own sorts of affinities to the climate of the Franco era (Mitchell 1994:217). During that decade, both innovative young performers like Paco de Lucía and even some conservative "flamencologists" like Don Pohren (1962:57) were coming to regard *mairenismo* as a stultifying orthodoxy (in Pohren's words, a "mummification") that had to be overcome. An occasionally noted irony is that Mairena himself, in his neo-classicist zeal to present a complete and codified repertoire, appears to have effectively composed several estilos, which, however, he generally attributed to other obscure past singers. Thus, for example, he recorded and catalogued more than twice as many forms of siguiriyas as had previously been recorded. Similarly, he "improved" several other forms by rationalizing and standardizing their forms. For instance, flamenco authority Estela Zatania notes, regarding the *tangos de Málaga* associated with the singer Piyayo,

> The original Piyayo styles [estilos] were long rambling verses, almost *romances*, that Piyayo often made up on the spot recalling his adventures in Cuba. However Antonio Mairena felt the need to clean them up and put order, so he devised the neat and manageable four-line verse and melody most of us know today.[8]

Similarly, Lefranc (2000:197) cites the comments of renowned vocalist Pastora Pavon, interviewed by Georges Hilaire: "As for the resurrections of *estilos* by the likes of Mairena and Pepe Torres, she opined that they were 'for intellectuals' and wouldn't fool any legitimate enthusiast."[9]

The codification of repertoire prevails in much mainstream traditional flamenco singing today. New lyrics continue to be composed and performed, but the melodic repertoire of cantes and estilos largely remains that inherited from before 1950. In the somewhat lighter palos of tangos and bulerías, it is possible to discern several melodies that have arisen in recent decades and have acquired the status of estilos, although no flamenco scholar has undertaken an enumeration of these in the manner of Kliman's study of soleá and siguiriyas. Nevertheless, in these latter core cantes, and even in others—whether fandango variants or the flexible tangos and bulerías—most of the singing one hears today comprises either, in mainstream flamenco, established estilos or else, in the realm of nuevo flamenco (and, to some extent, dance performances), new compositions which are not treated by others as estilos or stock tunes, as discussed below.

The process of codification and standardization clearly owes much to the exertions of Mairena, the general cultural stagnancy of the 1960s in Francoist Spain, and a sentiment—voiced by singers like Rafael Romero (in Sevilla

1995:60)—that the repertoire of cantes and estilos was forged by the great past masters out of the depth of Gypsy suffering, and should not be supplemented with the inevitably lesser creations of the prosaic and petty-bourgeois modern era. However, the codification must also be seen as relating to broader trends, including a desire to legitimize flamenco performances by grounding them in a past, inherited repertoire, the aesthetic emphasis on interpretation rather than composition, and a shift of compositional creativity to the realm of pre-composed songs rather than cantes or estilos.

Songs and Flamenco

As we have seen, neither palos nor estilos—the basic structural constituents of mainstream flamenco—share the key aspects of a "work," or of what has come to be a standard modern conception of a "song," in the sense of being an original, reproducible, structurally unified, or privately owned entity. At the same time, ever since the latter nineteenth century when flamenco was performed in public in the *cafés cantantes* ("singing cafés"), it has coexisted and to some extent overlapped with parallel traditions of commercial, pre-composed forms of music which tend to fall unambiguously into the category of "songs." Many flamenco musicians have earned much of their living performing or even composing such songs, which in some contexts—such as the "ópera flamenca" shows—were performed alongside mainstream flamenco (see Washabaugh 1996:43–45). In the first half of the twentieth century the most important genre in this category was the cuplé, a term deriving from French *couplet*, which in Spain denoted a variety of light, romantic, and often "naughty" song, marketed in cabarets and on recordings (see Salaün 1995), especially by songstresses like Conchita Piquer. The cuplé overlapped to some extent with another genre called copla, here connoting not verse or couplet but a variety of popular song—especially Andalusian—often aspiring to greater expressive and lyric depth than the cuplé, and flourishing particularly in the mid-century decades. The Andalusian copla, particularly as performed by singers like Lola Flores (1923–95), Juanito Valderrama (1916-2004), and Rocío Jurado (1945-2006), was typically rendered in an "*aflamencado*" manner, with flamenco-style melismas, chord progressions, and the like. Nevertheless, both copla and cuplé differed structurally from flamenco in constituting pre-composed songs with original chord progressions, whose verses are thematically interrelated rather than being a random suite of independent, detachable strophes sung in various estilos.

Starting around 1970, a virtual revolution occurred in the flamenco world, with the advent of what has come to be called nuevo flamenco. Although "new flamenco" is a heterogeneous phenomenon, its most prominent aspect has been the vogue of original pre-composed songs (or passages thereof), rendered by flamenco artists in more or less flamenco style, generally set to the compás of *tangos*, *rumba*, or *bulerías*. Collectively, in a genre where composition had been effectively marginalized, they represent an unprecedented explosion of compositional creativity.

Nuevo flamenco songs typically alternate verses with a catchy, singable refrain (sometimes sung in parallel thirds by two vocalists) and pre-arranged instrumental interludes. The latter generally foreground guitar, but the accompaniment as a whole often includes bass, percussion, and perhaps other instruments. In such songs—which might be called *canciones aflamencadas* ("flamenco-style songs")—the verses are thematically interrelated and are not detachable entities which would be recycled independently in, for example, a live bulerías set. A tendency toward such compositions was evident in early 1970s recordings by Camarón and Paco de Lucía, such as "Son tus ojos dos estrellas" and "Al padre santo de Roma" (1971), in which the verses are more or less related (see Sevilla 1995:34). More quintessentially representative of the new flamenco are songs (and here the word "song" may be used unproblematically) like "Rosa María" (1976) and "Como el Agua" (1981), recorded by Camarón and de Lucía.[10]

Nuevo flamenco has a somewhat ambiguous and uneasy relationship with traditional flamenco. Much nuevo flamenco, both in its musical structure and the slick promotion of its performers, lies clearly in the realm of commercial popular music, and is disparaged accordingly by flamenco purists (who are more likely to be middle-class zealots rather than Gypsies). Even composer and vocalist Pepe de Lucía, although clearly a gifted songwriter, has stated that he would prefer to make his living singing cante (in Calvo and Gamboa 1994:143). Many singers and audiences shun nuevo flamenco entirely, and it is largely kept out of several important performance contexts (such as flamenco *peñas* or clubs, and many festivals and concerts in Andalusia and elsewhere). However, most modern commercial recordings contain mixtures of both traditional and modern styles, and a performer like José Mercé, in a full-fledged concert, might perform the first half in traditional style, accompanied only by guitar, and devote the second half to his semi-pop hits (like "Aire"), accompanied by five or six instrumentalists and background singers.

Not surprisingly, endless polemics rage over the pros and cons of nuevo flamenco, upon which we need not dwell here, except to point out the importance of the role of compositions in this debate. For many of those who value traditional flamenco and especially cante jondo primarily for their interpretive spontaneity, the more pop-style nuevo flamenco "ditties," with their jingle-like refrains and pre-arranged instrumental passages, are anathema. On the other hand, it might be pointed out that the nuevo flamenco vogue has unleashed a virtual explosion of dynamic compositional creativity in the flamenco world, which had been effectively denied another outlet in main-stream flamenco, with its codified, fixed repertoire of palos and estilos.

The vogue of compositional activity emerging in flamenco from the 1970s did not occur in a vacuum, nor is it simply the result of a few creative individuals' efforts, but rather must be seen as part of a larger socio-musical context. On the surface level, as suggested above, the trend can be viewed as a reaction against the stultifying mairenista orthodoxy of the 1960s, which impeded any composition of new palos or estilos. Paco de Lucía said of this period,

> When I was growing up there was no freedom to compose. You had to repeat the old. The *flamencólogos* ["flamencologists"] and flamenco people regarded as sacrilegious any note outside of what was already established. Camarón and I disrupted somewhat this purist sentiment, which I regard as false. This wasn't purity, it was putting the music in a box and archiving it in a museum. I've always believed that one should respect traditions but not obey them with a blind faith—trying to express your epoch, to be in the moment in which you live, with all the musics you hear, all the evolution, and always, always, without losing flamenco's essence, force, and personality. (In Gamboa and Nuñez 2003:93)

The "epoch" that de Lucía refers to would have been quite distinct from that of the previous generation. New musical styles—especially rock, with its emphasis on instrumental "hooks" and tuneful refrains—were becoming familiar in Spain. Although the xenophobic regime of Franco continued until his death in 1975, the last decade had nevertheless been one of prodigious and belated cultural opening in Spain, in which all manner of artistic creativity, from cinema and literature to flamenco, came to flourish anew. The expansion of the record industry further conditioned the trajectory of nuevo flamenco, as commercial flamenco passed from an early, almost pre-industrial stage of cabarets to a modern capitalist mode more oriented toward mass-mediated production. As Paco Sevilla (1995:42) wrote of the new era, "It is an age of composers and songwriters. The recording industry ate up most of the traditional material and the public demanded something new" (see also Washabaugh 1993:42–43). In a broader sense, the nuevo flamenco era was quintessentially modern in that it was characterized by the coexistence of a neo-classical, relatively fixed traditional repertoire and a flourishing quasi-pop genre based to a large extent on new, commercially-oriented compositions. The advent of new norms of composition also introduced new conceptions of ownership and new challenges for legal copyright.

Authorship and Copyright

As we have seen, neither palos, estilos, nor a typical rendering of them as a "set" exhibits the sort of originality, reproducibility, uniqueness, and integrated structure that constitute the key features of a "work" or composition in the modern sense. At the same time, notions of authorship and ownership are not entirely absent or irrelevant to them. One "song"-like feature of the estilos is that, as mentioned, many of them—unlike cantes—are attributed to specific singers, who either transmitted, popularized, or "composed" them in the sense of elaborating, altering, or refining existing melodies. While such attributions were and to some extent remain transmitted primarily through oral tradition, they have also been catalogued—albeit in a manner heavily deriving from oral tradition—by various writers, especially Antonio Mairena. However, Mairena, like others, explicitly acknowledged the difficulty and even arbitrariness of distinguishing between actual "creators" of estilos and those who merely alter existing ones (Mairena and Molina 1979:179–84).[11]

Accordingly, the extent to which such attributions of estilo authorship are known or accepted in the flamenco world varies considerably. As mentioned, aside from intellectuals who have perused the studies of Kliman or the Solers, no one, whether a singer or enthusiast, would refer to a given estilo as "Frijones 3" or "Juaniquí 4." Further, there might be several who would share the opinion of renowned singer Pastora Pavón that the attribution of estilos to individuals is a misleading enterprise. In a 1955 conversation on the subject,

> She said that for her part she refused to go along with the publishing houses in referring to "tangos of la Grabiela" [*sic*] or "soleá of la Sarneta" etc; that neither la Sarneta, nor her own brothers Tomás and Arturo [Pavón], nor "El Nitri," nor Agustino [*sic*] Talega ever sang the same thing; . . . [she insisted that] every respectable singer improvises within the given formulas, making his or her own creation, and that is how it has always been. (Georges Hilaire, quoted in Lefranc 2000:197)

Pavón is clearly correct to stress the importance of personal interpretation and the danger of regarding the estilos as fixed tunes which the interpreter merely mechanically reproduces. At the same time, many in the flamenco milieu might agree that with all due respect to the great singer, the lady doth protest too much. Although writers on flamenco acknowledge, for example, that Manuel Torre (d. 1933) probably only transmitted rather than created the siguiriya which bears his name, it remains quite standard, and probably accurate, in flamenco discourse to identify other estilos with specific singers, as, for example, with the "fandango of El Gloria," the "soleá of La Sarneta," or the "malagueña of Enrique Mellizo." Further, more extensive and detailed attributions are common in such contexts as liner notes, concert reviews, and flamencological books like those of Gamboa and Nuñez (2003). Moreover, many performers—including people such as Camarón who are not known as bookish "intellectuals"—have taken great interest in acquiring (primarily via oral tradition) a wide repertoire of estilos (whether or not they use that term) and learning the supposed pedigrees of these melodies.

On the whole, by mid-century most cantes and sub-cantes had come to be seen—both in vernacular and legal senses—as being in the public domain. Thus, if a modern vocalist announces that he is going to sing a "malagueña of Enrique Mellizo," his intent is not to provide a legally required attribution of authorship, but to render homage to the venerable creator, and to invoke and perpetuate a sense of tradition and historicity (especially of Gypsy creators).

Gypsies and Non-Gypsies

Despite the sense of impersonality of cante jondo singing, the authorship of estilos has acquired some importance not only in the sense of invoking legendary stalwarts of the past, but also in ongoing polemics about the role of Gypsies, as opposed to non-Gypsies, as creators and composers. This controversy constitutes a vast and sensitive topic, which need only be outlined here insofar as it relates to more general questions of authorship and ownership. At stake here is the role of Gypsies in the creation—whether collective or individual—of cantes and estilos. It has often been asserted—whether in reference to the Balkans or Spain—that however skilled Gypsies have been as interpreters and performers, they have never been significant as actual creators of repertoire. In reference to flamenco, this point of view has been argued by such flamencologists as Blas Infante (1980) and Manuel Barrios (1989), and recurs in various other contexts.[12] Similarly, historian Timothy Mitchell, in his engaging and polemical book *Flamenco Deep Song* (1994), argues at length that the flamenco repertoire must be seen as a product of Andalusian music culture rather than Gypsy subculture—which itself, as he points out, developed as a mixture of not only ethnic *gitanos* but also Jews, Moors, and other assorted lumpen bohemians. As Mitchell and others have noted, all the fandango forms derive ultimately from Andalusian rather than Gypsy music, and even the supposedly Gypsy cantes of soleá and siguiriyas can be seen to derive ultimately from hoary Spanish traditions of *romance* and *seguidilla*, respectively, and took their modern form in the professional contexts of public café cantante stages and the fiestas of rich señoritos.

Attempts to highlight Gypsy compositional creativity commenced in the late 1950s, when, for example, when vocalist Manolo Caracol included printed attributions of items in the liner notes to a double-LP of his (see Lefranc 2000:35). Shortly thereafter Mairena commenced his "Great Salvage." Mairena, while acknowledging the non-Gypsy origins of lighter genres like the fandango, insisted on the exclusively Gypsy origin of all significant estilos of cante jondo, especially soleá and siguiriyas. Mairena's discussion of the origins of these estilos (with Molina 1979:179-98) was thus intended not only to codify them and establish a sense of historical legitimacy to them, but also to foreground the role of Gypsies in creating them. Lefranc (2000) corroborates this approach, at once attempting the trace the roots of these cantes to (non-Gypsy) sources like the *romance*, but also stressing how the transformation to soleá and siguiriyas, and the composition of standard estilos, were undertaken overwhelmingly by Gypsies, especially in private festivities.

Traditional Proprietary Concerns

Aside from such features as originality, reproducibility, uniqueness, and integrated structure, one of the key features of a "work" or composition in the modern sense is its status as property. Traditional attitudes towards and treatment of the flamenco repertoire are contradictory and irregular—as are other aspects of how that repertoire relates to the notion of a composition. On the one hand, palos and estilos have never enjoyed formal senses of protection and exclusivity. Flamenco cantes or estilos have never been extensively marketed as sheet music, nor has there been a particularly common or significant practice of singing "cover versions" of recorded items—i.e., reiterating identical series of verses and estilos in the manner of a pre-composed "song."

On the other hand, flamenco has certainly involved commercial practices, to some extent, for well over a century, as it was performed in public from the latter 1800s café cantante period on, and from around 1900 it came to be marketed on commercial recordings. For flamenco professional singers, as with singers in other orally-transmitted traditional music genres, public dissemination—via live performance or recordings—constituted at once a necessary means of livelihood and a potentially damaging avenue for the spread of otherwise exclusively retained repertoire. Commercial recordings were particularly double-edged, in that they provided prestige and publicity but made it easy for rivals to copy repertoire. A complicating factor was the sense, among Gypsy artists, that flamenco was their distinctive and unique creation, and that discretion had to be exercised in sharing it with the non-Gypsy public, not to mention rival non-Gypsy musicians.

Accordingly, many Gypsy performers did have a strong sense of ownership of their repertoire and would impart it only under certain conditions. Lefranc, writing of his informants in the late 1950s to the '70s, notes:

> In the relation of the Gypsies of lower Andalusia to the cante, we noted a ferocious sense of propriety—it is "what's ours [*lo nuestro*], we don't have anything else"—and in effect, they have little sense of collective memory, nor knowledge of the past, even the recent past. This sense of ownership is so strong that, in the early '60s, the initiative of [Antonio] Mairena, who went in search of old cantes, was regarded critically in the villages; they called him a *robacantes* [cante-thief]. The basis of this reticent sense of ownership is the fear of being dispossessed—which to a large extent is what has happened. In effect, the phonograph record

has not only rendered the inheritance accessible to everyone but has also disassociated it from the livelihood that had been its basis. (2000:28)

The reluctance of some Gypsy musicians to disseminate their repertoire in the cafés cantantes was particularly strong. Lefranc continues:

> We can surmise the existence in Triana, in the last third of the nineteenth century, of a veritable taboo against selling such cantes: according to a formula attributed to Juan el Pelao, a blacksmith Gypsy of Triana, to sell cante is like selling a woman, that is to say, it is prostitution. In a general sense this taboo persists: if at times it seems to be bypassed, it is with ingenuity. The real cante is *given*, behind closed doors. That which is sold, in most cases, is a bit less real, and its quality will depend on the level of competence of the listener and his manner of hearing: "one sings according to the face"—of the listener . . . In a public performance, Gypsies, probably since centuries ago, perform what they are asked to, but typically limit themselves to offering something harmless ["anodyne"]; later, they get together amongst themselves and delight in singing the real thing; I've seen this many times. (2000:34; emphasis in the original)

Thus, he notes, the commercial recording of bits of traditional cante by early-twentieth-century Gypsy singers like Manuel Torre would constitute only an occasional and somewhat exceptional occurrence in relation to the ongoing, more mainstream transmission in private Gypsy fiestas and song sessions. A few singers refused to record, or, like Pepe el de la Matrona, did so only late in their lives, and famed vocalist Tomás El Nitri reportedly refused to perform in front of Silverio Franconetti (1831–89), who popularized, standardized, and professionalized much flamenco via his famed café cantante. Franconetti's presentation of private Gypsy repertoire to the general paying public is variously lauded as the effective creation of an art form,[13] or, as Lefranc suggests, it could be regarded as a "*Gran Indiscreción*" (2000:29). Similarly, while one of Mairena's motives in publicizing and recording cante jondo repertoire was to illustrate the breadth of Gypsy contribution to the flamenco repertoire, in doing so he undermined in some respects the privileged status of Gypsy performers by making that repertoire available to any interested singer, Gypsy or *payo* (non-Gypsy). Hence the harshness of Lefranc's critique of the mairenistas: "In the mid-1950s . . . certain ill-tempered Gypsies became angered to the point that they conceived the demented idea of making available to everyone the authentic repertoire of Gypsy origin, with the aim of putting an end to adulterations and to the myth that Gypsies hadn't contributed to the cante" (Lefranc 2000:191).

Such protective attitudes toward traditional family repertoire have been common in other professional oral music traditions, as in North Indian classical music culture, where some early-twentieth-century singers refused to record and some still refrain from performing certain family-jewel songs in public.[14] In the long run, of course, such singers, with their secret repertoire, can end up being largely forgotten, except as vaguely revered names. Moreover, in flamenco and in India, the hoarding of repertoire has largely come to be seen as an archaic practice, especially as so much repertoire becomes available via commercial recordings. Certainly since the mid-twentieth century, most flamenco singers would welcome the prestige that a commercial recording offers, and the knowledgeable listening public would not throng to hear a vocalist who was known to present only "anodyne" on stage.

Copyright in Mainstream Flamenco

Some of the ambiguities, contradictions, and tensions involved in traditional proprietary conceptions of ownership in flamenco have carried over into the realm of copyright, which also introduced its own norms and, in some cases, abuses. In many respects, the challenges flamenco has posed to copyright law and practice have been typical of other oral-tradition musics that enter the world of commercial marketing, especially when such traditional genres evolve into commercial popular idioms. At the same time, the conceptions of authorship and ownership in flamenco, as we have seen, are in some respects unique, and have posed their own idiosyncratic difficulties to copyright observance.

In theory, and to a considerable extent in practice, modern copyright law and its representative institutions have been able to handle much flamenco, whether traditional or modern, without difficulty or conflict. Artists' incomes from recordings could come from a combination of three sources (all of which might be referred to as *derechos de autor*, a term which could variously translate as "copyright," "royalties," or other phrases, depending on context). First, performers are paid by the recording company, at a rate and in a form that is subject to negotiation; thus, a singer might accept a flat fee, or negotiate a royalty rate linked to record sales, or some combination of those two formats. Second, performers are also paid royalties by AIE (La Sociedad de Artistas Intérpretes o Ejecutantes de España), which collects appropriate percentages from record companies to be distributed to its members. Third, composers, lyricists, and/or arrangers (if any) are paid royalties by SGAE (Sociedad General de Autores y Editores), which in this context functions like the American institutions ASCAP and BMI, collecting appropriate payments from record companies.[15] If the music and/or lyrics are assumed to be *"popular"* (i.e., in the public domain), then SGAE retains the amounts that would otherwise be distributed to authors.

As can be imagined, different sorts of flamenco records would involve distinct sorts of payments. At one end of the spectrum would be newly-composed nuevo flamenco songs, which could be treated like any commercial popular songs, with their clearly delineated and properly recompensed composers, interpreters, producers, session accompanists, and the like. At the other end of the gamut are renditions of traditional flamenco, which can also be accommodated into copyright norms. Thus, for example, if a songstress records a traditional siguiriya, using an estilo of Manuel Torre (d. 1933), with traditional lyrics, such as "De Santiago a Santa Ana," no royalties need be paid to the estate of Torre for the melody, nor to anyone for the lyrics, as they are both in the public domain. There would be no composer's or publisher's rights involved in the recording. The singer would thus be paid an artist's fee by the AIE and, as negotiated, by the record company. If she tried to falsely register a lyric as her own (in order to receive royalties from SGAE as a lyricist), she might be able to do so, unless the lyric title appeared in SGAE's database as "*popular*," in which case SGAE would refuse payment to her, on the basis that it could not verify the lyrics as being her original creation.[16]

In the first half of the twentieth century, it is safe to say that relatively little attention was paid to copyright in the realm of traditional flamenco. Most material was regarded as coming from oral tradition. Most singers who recorded did so primarily for the publicity, and were generally happy to accept a flat fee rather than royalties, which might never materialize. Further, sales of most flamenco records were small. Moreover, although mechanical rights might conceivably be involved if, for example, the particular recording were relicensed or reused, composition or publisher's rights appear to have been effectively non-existent. Such compositional copyright would not have been remunerative or operative in any case, since there is little tradition of singing "cover versions" of recorded items—i.e., reiterating identical series of verses and estilos in the manner of a pre-composed song. Oddly enough, some of the most profitable recordings were those made at the very dawn of the industry, especially in the case of vocalist Antonio Chacón, who earned considerable sums (as flat fees) from his recording contracts, including those for eleven thousand phonograph cylinders produced in 1899.[17]

As in other world musics during this early period of the recording industry, some abuses certainly occurred. Even in the supposedly more regulated realm of the commercial cuplé, as Salaün relates (1995:91), "One has to remember that the idea of copyright was not yet firmly established and singers poached material from each other freely." Further, given flamenco's frequent mixture of traditional material and other material—whether music or lyrics—of known and recent authorship, some irregularities were bound to occur. A recording of soleares, for example, might well include one verse handed down from oral tradition, one written by the singer's uncle and allegedly provided by verbal agreement, and another written by a professional poet and taken from another commercial recording. The vocalist might go to great lengths to ensure scrupulously proper compensation of all parties involved; alternately, he might claim the lyrics as his own, or, more likely, he might simply register the lyrics as "*popular*," i.e., understood to be in the public domain. The main factor limiting the scope for disputes would be the likelihood that the recording would not in any case generate much income for anyone. In flamenco discourse one hears occasional reports of singers listing protected lyrics as "*popular*" in order to avoid paying royalties, but these sorts of indiscretions are common to many genres and, further, would generally not involve large sums of money.

Complications began to emerge when, especially from the 1970s, it became more common for authorship, whether of music or lyrics, to be registered by persons other than the singer, whose status would thus be explicitly relegated to that of an interpreter of material legally owned by someone else. Such complications are not necessarily injustices, but often embody the distinctive, and in some cases competing, kinds of authorship involved. A significant grey area has involved whether or the extent to which anyone could legitimately claim compositional authorship—and subsequent royalties—from SGAE. Such a claimant might be the guitarist, whose guitar introduction and interludes (falsetas) might be to some extent original creations of his. Alternately, the guitarist, the singer, or perhaps even a "producer" might claim credit for "arranging" the music. Disagreements over such claims are not unheard of.[18]

While I discuss the case of Camarón de la Isla in greater detail below, here we may look at a few typical recordings by that vocalist, in collaboration with guitarist Paco de Lucía as well as Paco's father, Antonio Sánchez, and brother, Pepe de Lucía (b. 1945), both of whom were active as composers and lyricists. A typical breakdown for such a recording might be as follows: from the ten dollars, for example, collected from the sale of a cassette (after the vendor's profit is accounted for), seven might go to the record company, two (via the record company and AIE) to the artists as interpreters (primarily, Camarón and Paco de Lucía), and one (via SGAE) to the composer(s) and lyricist(s).

We may take as a typical track the fandango "Donde una ermita poner," on a 1970 album.[19] The liner notes on the cassette version of this attribute the authorship (in an unspecified capacity) to "Francisco Sánchez" (the birth name of Paco de Lucía). By contrast, Gamboa and Nuñez—presumably citing the original LP release—indicate that while the music is credited to Francisco Sánchez, the lyrics are credited to Antonio Sánchez, his father, who wrote many of the lyrics for Camarón's recordings. As is often the case, attributions on liner notes are imprecise, if not simply false, and they do not constitute legal documents of ownership in any case. Accordingly, they are in this case at variance with the current SGAE database, which attributes fifty percent of the authorship to Antonio Sánchez and twenty-five percent to Pepe de Lucía. In fact, while Paco de Lucía's guitar interludes are to some extent original, the vocal estilo of this fandango is "traditional," being that fashioned by Rafael el Tuerto and popularized by Antonio el Rubio (see Gamboa and Nuñez 2003:330–31). Similarly, for example, Camarón's "No naqueres más de mí"[20] is registered to Antonio, although in musical form, as listed on the liner notes, it is a "Tangos del Titi," that is, a tango estilo attributed to vocalist El Titi. The same album also contains a fandango "Ni que me manden a mí," whose melody was composed by Enrique Morente but first recorded by Camarón (Gamboa and Nuñez 2003:129, 396) with Morente's amicable permission; the SGAE database attributes the authorship (of the lyrics?) to Antonio Sánchez, such that Morente's estilo has effectively become public domain, in legal terms. Neither he nor Camarón nor Paco de Lucía receive any credit as composers.

The practice of claiming compositional rights to essentially traditional music appears to have begun around 1970; Paco de Lucía stated that he was one of the first to do so (in Grimaldos 1993:83). For a figure like de Lucía, it could be argued that not only were his guitar interludes (falsetas) original, but that he was the effective arranger of the music. Potentially problematic and misleading is the occasional practice of registering authorship of traditional lyrics, whether deriving from oral tradition or from anthologies like that of Antonio Machado in 1881. In a typical flamenco record, such attributions might garner some negligible royalties for a supposed author. They also might occur if, for example, someone registered as his own the lyrics to a song consisting of an original verse of his along with some traditional ones (just as liner notes might say "Tangos of Pastora," when in fact only the first verse is of Pastora). Although a few sources have cited the practice of claiming authorship to traditional public-domain lyrics (see, e.g., Calvo and Gamboa 1994:208), it is not clear how widespread this practice is. In any case, such an attribution would not be illegal if the documented original source—such as Machado's book—were more than sixty years old and the material had entered the public domain (see, e.g., Peregil 1993:192); nor would any such pseudo-author be likely to attempt to collect royalties on someone else's use of those lyrics if they could be easily found in such a source. Nor would such a claim, involving lyricist's royalties paid by SGAE, decrease the money earned by the performers (as paid by the record company and AIE). A converse practice is that of singers registering lyrics by known authors as "*popular*," i.e., public domain, in order to avoid paying royalties to the real author. Both practices—claiming ownership of public-domain material, and registering as "*popular*" material in fact owned by someone else—are not unique to the flamenco world but occur in various genres worldwide. While in flamenco they may occasionally generate expressions of alarm or indignation, there is no evidence that they have constituted serious and widespread problems. On the whole, individual authorship and ownership of compositions are not important concerns in mainstream (traditional) flamenco, even as it flourishes today.

A Polemic Erupts: Camarón and Paco de Lucía

As we have seen, the sorts of irregularities and ambiguities pertaining to authorship and ownership of flamenco generally mattered little as long as the profits involved were inconsiderable. It was not really until the early 1990s that sales of flamenco recordings began to reach levels that could generate genuine concern over compositional rights. It was at that point that an ugly controversy erupted that rocked the flamenco world as a whole and raised, for the first time, serious questions about the nature of ownership, authorship, and copyright in flamenco.

The central figure in this in this controversy was José Monje, or Camarón de la Isla (1950-92), who is generally regarded as the most brilliant flamenco vocalist of the latter twentieth century. Camarón's career took off when he started performing and recording with Paco de Lucía (b. 1947), who was in the process of revolutionizing flamenco guitar. Starting in 1969, Camarón and de Lucía produced a series of outstanding LPs, in which de Lucía's father (Antonio Sánchez) and brothers (Pepe de Lucía and, to a lesser extent, Ramón de Algeciras) were also involved. Antonio Sánchez, a professional guitarist (and with Camarón, a lyricist) had successfully trained his sons as a putative dynasty; Ramón (b. 1938) was a fine guitarist, who frequently accompanied Camarón and others; Pepe, although trained in guitar and, of Antonio Sanchez's sons, the most devoted to singing, has made his living primarily through composing modern flamenco songs and lyrics. Paco turned out to be the family genius, achieving an international renown (and income) unprecedented in flamenco, via his various performances and recordings, whether done solo, with his sextet, with Camarón, with other flamenco singers, or with artists like John McLaughlin and Al DiMeola.

Camarón's recorded repertoire with Paco and family ranged from cantes rendered in more or less traditional style to innovative, catchy, pre-composed songs like "Como el Agua." Camarón became like an additional member of the family, whom they professionally groomed and personally loved, despite the mistrust that sometimes exists between Gypsies, like Camarón, and non-Gypsies, such as the Sánchez family. In the 1980s the links between the two parties became loosened, as Camarón more often worked with other producers, and Paco devoted more time to touring internationally on his own. Camarón's own career became increasingly limited by his lack of enthusiasm for touring (especially abroad) and by his heroin addiction, which started around 1980. Nevertheless, in 1991 Paco and Camarón—who was by then dying of lung cancer—rejoined for a final LP (*Potro de rabia y miel*).

While some Gypsies in Spain have a reputation for being crafty, street-wise hustlers, Camarón conformed to a different stereotype, that of the impulsive artist who paid little attention to financial matters. In his early years of collaboration with the Lucía/Sánchez family, Camarón entrusted his finances largely to Antonio Sánchez. With the Lucías and, later, on his own, he earned well, mostly through performing concerts, as records were not very remunerative for any flamenco performers. He bought a few properties for his family, and refrained from squandering his earnings on luxuries, with the exception of his heroin habit. In other respects he was alternately heedless and grabby, lavishly tipping waiters at a party one day, and trying to sell de Lucía some overpriced socks the next (earning only raucous laughter [Peregil 1993:165–66]). In the final months of his life, with his health and perhaps mental stability fraying, he became especially concerned about the future welfare of his wife and children, and about his prior inattention to his finances and past reliance on the Lucías. In particular, his ears appear to have been poisoned against his collaborators—especially the Lucías—by his personal "handler" and advisor, one José Candado.

His confused head filled with unrealistic figures, recriminatory bad advice, and belated mistrust of the people whom he had allowed to handle or mishandle his past finances, Camarón gave a television interview a month before he died (on July 2, 1992) in which he said of his recordings, "I've discovered, after the great shock that it's given my family, that the work isn't mine … So if it's true that I've contributed something to flamenco, then I'd like for some of it—at least half—to remain for my family." Camarón was referring specifically to the compositional rights to his recorded oeuvre, of whose 164 songs he was a registered author of only six songs, and shared credits for a few others, the remainder of the recorded repertoire being either assumed to be "traditional," i.e., in the public domain, or else signed by various lyricists and composers, such as Ricardo Pachón, Antonio Humanes, Paco de Lucía, Antonio Sánchez, and especially Pepe de Lucía. Candado and Camarón's wife (later widow) Chispa subsequently made various inconsistent statements, some of which specifically exonerated the Lucías from any accusations, but others of which clearly implied that they and the other non-Gypsy collaborators and producers had cheated Camarón by not registering him as co-author of his recorded songs.[21]

Many in the Gypsy community, who had idolized Camarón, were inflamed by the notion that their guileless hero had been exploited by the wily Lucía clan. At Camarón's funeral, some of them shouted "Thief!" at Paco de Lucía, who also received telephonic death threats, uttered in strong Gypsy accents. Camarón's family, with Candado's evident guidance, hired a team of five lawyers to pursue the issue. The lawyers' report insisted that the authorship of Camarón's recorded work was "collective," such that he merited composer's royalties. While they did not pursue litigation, they called upon his various collaborators, who held the authorial rights, to cede parts of those rights to Camarón's heirs in a spirit of good faith.[22] Chispa also made specific requests via intermediaries to those registered authors.

Paco de Lucía was traumatized by the affair, succumbing to a prolonged depression and hardly touching his guitar for the next year. He had had great affection for Camarón, had helped him financially on several occasions, and, with his family, had always had close and amicable relations with other Gypsies. From all published accounts, Paco behaved in this affair, as in all other aspects of his life, as a perfect gentleman. Whether judiciously or not, he refrained from speaking in public about the matter until a year later, when he gave an interview with a magazine (Grimaldos 1993). On that occasion he related that, among other things, he had requested from SGAE a precise accounting of all the sales of his records with Camarón and the composer's royalties Paco had received from them. These data were supplemented by other journalistic investigations (especially Saenz 1992), which collectively illuminated much about the nature of flamenco commercial recordings.

SGAE's statistics revealed how surprisingly, even pathetically, low the sales of the records were. Camarón's nineteen records, as of the time of his death, had only sold a total of 361,172 copies (aside from pirate sales). Thus, for example, although the 1981 album *Como el Agua*, with its catchy title tune, was a classic in the flamenco world, it had sold only a piddling 7,541 copies. Only in Camarón's final years did sales pick up, with, for example, *Potro de rabia y miel* going gold after selling fifty thousand and later surpassing seventy thousand. Paco de Lucía, in his capacity as a registered author or co-author of several songs on the first three albums, had received well under $8000 in royalties.[23] Although Camarón's records were expected to enjoy ongoing steady sales, the revenues generated by their sales to date were only around a tenth of the giddy sum publicized by Candado.

In most cases, as mentioned, flamenco recordings have not been significantly remunerative for performers. Artists made recordings primarily for publicity, as documents for posterity, and as creative endeavors in themselves, rather than for expected royalties. Paco de Lucía related that every record made with Camarón involved spending three or four months in the studio and forfeiting three or four hundred thousand dollars of profits that his group could have earned touring; in his later years Camarón himself could earn as much as $30,000 for a single concert (though he turned down most requests and on occasion failed to show up for concerts). On the other hand, someone like Pepe de Lucía, whose performing career has been only moderately successful, might well depend for his livelihood on author's royalties from the many songs he had composed for other singers.

Most relevant for the purposes of this article are the general issues that the polemic raised about ownership of flamenco repertoire. Camarón's recorded oeuvre could be grouped into a few different categories. One of these would comprise renditions of traditional cante in which neither lyrics nor music were claimed by anyone; neither Camarón nor anyone would properly have any legitimate claim to authorship of such items, which abounded in the early recordings.[24] At the other end of the gamut would lie recordings of catchy songs like "Como el Agua," whose lyrics and melodies were composed by individuals like Pepe and taught to Camarón. In between would lie the many songs which mixed old and new elements, or contained strikingly innovative and original renditions of familiar cantes. Camarón was allegedly especially upset when he discovered that he had no royalties from the composition of the cante "Canastera" (Fernández Zaurín and Candado 2002:62–63). For all these recordings Camarón would have received some royalties as a performer—especially after the renegotiation of his contract with Polygram in the 1980s, when he was granted the relatively high interpreter fee of twelve percent (see Peregil 1993:193). At issue, however, were the potentially larger royalties that could conceivably in the future accrue from compositional rights.

One question is whether Camarón, or anyone, would have a right to claim compositional rights to renditions of traditional cante. As we have seen, Paco de Lucía, Pepe, and their father appear to have claimed authorial rights on several such items. Aside from the fact that royalties earned from these claims were inconsiderable, Paco could legitimately claim some credit for the originality of his guitar interludes (falsetas), and as he asserted, "They've accused me of claiming as mine things that weren't mine, but the truth is the opposite. In Camarón's discography there is much material I composed but didn't register as mine" (in Grimaldos 1993:83). The issue arises as to whether Camarón should have claimed partial compositional rights for his innovative renderings. Singing a flamenco cante is not like singing a pop song; as we have seen, the palos and estilos are less fixed melodies than skeletal, flexible frameworks, whose successful rendering depends on the singer's interpretive nuances and flourishes—precisely the elements that distinguish an ordinary singer from a brilliant one like Camarón. Was he merely an interpreter of material that was either traditional or composed by others, or were his renderings of that material so structurally distinctive and original as to render him an effectual "co-composer"? Indeed, given the flexibility inherent in almost any rendition of cante, should flamenco singers as a whole not be justified in claiming partial authorial rights? The report prepared by Antonio Agesta, who headed the team of lawyers contracted by Camarón's family, claimed that the authorship of his work was at least "collective," arguing, "At least he should be seen as a co-author in all [the songs not registered to him] ... based on our study of the musical structure of the themes" (in Soto

Viñolo 1992). However, it is hard to imagine what sort of study of the music could reveal such an assessment; rather, in order to judge Camarón's role as composer one would need to know something about the actual processes of composition and recording.

To some extent, these processes have been described by Camarón's collaborators, especially Paco de Lucía and family, although ambiguities clearly remain.[25] It is clear that except in a very few cases, Camarón would arrive at a recording session without any particular material except his considerable knowledge of traditional cante. In recording, he would to a large extent rely on his collaborators for original repertoire, including many details of rendition. In a typical session, Pepe de Lucía would bring a demo tape in which he sang the items (with lyrics written by himself, his father, or family friend and vocalist Fosforito), which Camarón would copy. Often, as they related, Pepe would have to repeat a phrase twenty times, while Camarón struggled to get the hang of it; then, just as the de Lucías were ready to give up from exasperation, Camarón would finally get it, rendering it with an original flourish that astounded and delighted everyone (see, e.g., Gamboa and Nuñez 2003:247). Paco Sevilla sums up the argument as follows:

> Camarón had no right to [composer's] compensation for songs he didn't compose. But in his case there was a catch. Camarón de la Isla sang no song as it was written. His genius lay in his ability to totally recreate a song, to convert a trite ditty into a work of art, to create from a simple song that might pass unnoticed if sung by another, a flamenco experience guaranteed to survive in flamenco history and become a part of tradition. (Sevilla 1995:172–75)

Such considerations have led some to fault Spanish copyright law for not granting greater rights to flamenco interpreters (see, e.g., Telléz 2003:194). As it is, however, both the law and extant published opinions tend to favor the legitimacy of the distinction between composer and interpreter, both in the abstract and in reference to the specific case of Camarón. Camarón's brilliance as an interpreter gained him his high concert fees and his artist fees as a performer on recordings, but not retrospective rights as a composer (except, of course, in so far as he had negotiated such rights in his original recording contracts).

Given these considerations, despite the personal sympathy felt for Camarón and his bereaved family, both Camarón's collaborators as well as journalists and flamencologists writing on the subject were largely unimpressed by the claims that he merited half the compositional rights to his recordings. Accordingly, most authors of songs recorded by Camarón rejected Chispa's petitions to cede composition royalties, especially since such an action would suggest prior wrongdoing on their part (see Peregil 1993:193).[26] Pepe de Lucía, while saying he would sing innumerable benefit concerts for Camarón's family, told Camarón before his death that he wouldn't give up a penny of what was rightfully his: "Camarón got the rights that he earned, via the AIE . . . but not the rights to my songs, because if I gave him those then I would have four hundred Gypsies demanding the same" (in Peregil 1993:190). Similarly, Ricardo Pachón, who composed songs like "La leyenda del tiempo," spoke of the hard work he put into such compositions, and asserted, "There is nothing to discuss regarding those rights. [Camarón] never demanded any percent of those royalties and was not an interpreter who changed the songs . . . The author must be respected" (in Telléz 2003:198, Peregil 1993:189, Saenz 1992).

One subtext in the controversy was the old argument about whether Gypsies (such as Camarón) should be recognized as composers, or were merely gifted and flamboyant interpreters of music composed by non-Gypsies, such as the Lucía family, and Antonio Humanes. Another underlying theme was the way the conflict embodied the tensions inherent in the collision of an oral tradition with modern notions and practices of composition and copyright.

Conclusions

In the introduction to this essay I suggested that the changing conceptions of composition and ownership in flamenco are related to broader processes of modernity. Apprehending flamenco in relation to these themes can highlight both parallels with other genres of world music, and also distinctive features of flamenco culture—all of which, however, can be seen as representing encounters with modernity in some fashion.

In a general sense, the processes outlined in this paper represent the encounter of, on the one hand, an oral tradition, and its attendant "folk" or "urban folk" modes of composition, with, on the other hand, modern compositional norms as conditioned by copyright, a music industry, and other phenomena. What is particularly characteristic about flamenco is the transformation of a traditional form of composition into a modern one, and the way that the products of each now coexist side-by-side. Until sometime before the mid-twentieth century, traditional-style composition of estilos was to some extent common and successful, in the sense that a sub-cante developed by an artist—no doubt by altering an existing one—would come to be used by other singers as a stock melody, perhaps bearing the name of its creator. By the 1950s, this sort of successful composition declined dramatically, in that a canonic repertoire of estilos (not to mention palos) in the core cantes became codified, and newly created melodies were unlikely to be used as stock tunes by other singers. Singers copy Camarón's *style* without singing his estilos. Despite, or perhaps even partly because of such ossification, the period since 1970 has seen an explosion of compositional activity, in the form of "canciones aflamencadas" which may be more or less "pop" in orientation, and which are not used—and are not designed to be used—as estilos or stock melodies for the settings of new lyrics.

These two modes of composition can be seen in some respects as pre-modern and modern, respectively, although the process of codification of the traditional repertoire is in its own way a modern phenomenon. The neo-classicist standardization of repertoire promoted by Mairena and his collaborators invites obvious comparison with similar projects in other music cultures. One thinks in particular of the early-twentieth-century efforts of musicologist V.N. Bhatkhande to codify the repertoire of North Indian *râgas*, and the similar endeavors of Mirza Abdollah and later Nur Ali Boroumand to compile and document the *radif* (traditional repertoire) of Persian classical music (see, e.g., Nettl 1992:4, Bakhle 2005). All these projects can be seen as essentially modernist attempts to strengthen and rescue for posterity a threatened and otherwise disorganized traditional repertoire by documenting and classifying it via learned publications and, in Mairena's case, commercial recordings. A more general sort of analogy could even be made to the trajectory of composition in Western music culture, whose concert repertoire now consists overwhelmingly of an inherited body of music from the eighteenth and nineteenth centuries, with more modern compositions either managing only marginally to penetrate the concert halls, or else being oriented toward commercial popular music. Western art music culture can be said to resemble traditional flamenco in that its locus of creativity and aesthetic interest has shifted from composition to interpretation of a fixed body of material.

With the advent of modernity, however, come new dimensions of financial considerations, as embodied in contracts, royalties, and formal ownership of repertoire.[27] Flamenco, as we have seen, poses special challenges to copyright, especially insofar as neither cantes, estilos, nor their renderings cohere with established conceptions of "works." Ambiguities are inherent to the genre. At what point, or to what extent, can a guitar falseta adapted from earlier prototypes be considered an original "composition," meriting author's royalties from SGAE? To what extent, if any, should a flamenco singer, whose interpretive nuances are the very essence of the art form, be credited as a co-composer, as opposed to a mere interpreter of traditional or pre-composed repertoire?

As long as the sums of money, and especially those accruing from authors' royalties, are inconsiderable, then such legal grey areas may not be of great concern to the parties involved. However, the case of Camarón de la Isla illustrates that in flamenco, as in other genres, there operates a certain basic rule of copyright: ambiguity plus money equals litigation—that is, where there is ambiguity of ownership, and where real money is involved, legal action will follow. Such conflicts may continue to erupt in flamenco, whose international record sales now generate something like thirty-five million dollars annually.[28] Nor are these issues confined to music: in 2001 flamenco choreographer Javier Latorre issued a manifesto in which he bitterly denounced the plagiarism of choreographies in the professional flamenco dance world—activities that involve formidable sums of money.[29] While such conflicts may generate much bitterness, they also oblige the parties involved to confront and articulate issues of authorship, composition, and ownership.

It has often been noted that new genres like hip-hop, Jamaican dancehall, and remixes present new challenges to copyright and to the notion of a "work."[30] Flamenco, unlike these genres, involves no use of new technologies, but in its own way it poses similar challenges, in ways which are at once distinctive, and distinctively modern.

Acknowledgments

While taking full responsibility for the contents of this article, I wish to acknowledge the particular insights I have gained from Norman Kliman, Estela Zatania, and especially John Moore and Brook Zern, who provided detailed comments on an earlier version of this article.

Notes

1. See, e.g., Skierra 1990.

2. The features of and distinctions between cante and estilo are further elucidated in Manuel 2006, which notates and analyzes a representative recording of soleares.

3. Kliman's website is *http://www.ctv.es/USERS/norman/*.

4. Malagueña might constitute one sort of exception, in that "a malagueña" typically implies the singing of a single copla (rather than a series of three or four), whose elaborate, melismatic, drawn-out rendering might easily last two or three minutes.

5. The canasteras appear on the albums *Canastera* (1972) and *Rosa María* (1976). Paco also recorded an instrumental version of canastera on *El duende flamenco de Paco de Lucía* (1972: Philips 824417-2), reissued on *Entre dos aguas* (1976: Smash 7166071).

6. Both can be heard on El Lebrijano's LP *Persecución* (Philips 7166037).

7. Norman Kliman's erudite website (see note 3), while lacking staff notation, extends the catalogue of the Solers, and provides short MP3 excerpts of all known estilos in soleares and siguiriyas. Pierre Lefranc's impressive book *El cante jondo* (2000) constitutes a parallel and largely corroborating documentation (again, however, without staff notation) of the soleá and siguiriyas repertoire.

8. Zatania, in a post in 2004 on the flamencodisc/yahoogroups email list.

9. Lefranc specifies some of these "resurrections" (2000:198).

10. Most of the leading composers of such songs have been flamenco guitarists, including Paco Cepero, Diego Carrasco, Manzanita, Vicente Amigo, Paco de Lucía, his father Antonio Sánchez, and his brother, Pepe de Lucía. Some have made quite good money composing and producing, as has Cepero with singers El Turronero, La Marelu, Juanito Villar, and Chiquitete (whom he groomed as pop stars), and Pepe de Lucía with Remedios Amaya, La Susi, and La Venta (Sevilla 1995:107–08). A few singers, such as El Torta, José de la Tomasa, and El Capullo, have enjoyed success at writing their own material. Space does not permit discussion of authorship and compositional practices in flamenco guitar music.

11. See Gamboa (2005 142–43) for further discussion of the mairenista attributions of estilos.

12. For example, the liner notes to the influential and ground-breaking 1954 *Anthologie du Cante Flamenco* (Ducretet-Thomson, reissued on Hispavox) assert that Gypsies have not made any significant contribution to the flamenco repertoire aside from their talent at expression. See also Lefranc 2000:35. Note that I use the term "Gypsies" (rather than Roma or Romani) in accordance with standard English-language writing on flamenco.

13. For example, in 1881 Antonio Machado y Alvarez wrote: "The Gypsy genre, in leaving the tavern for the café, became 'Andalusianized' and was converted into what everyone calls flamenco. Silverio created the genre of flamenco, a mixture of Gypsy and Andalusian elements" (1975 [1881]:180–81).

14. For example, at a recording session of vocalist Girja Devi I once suggested to her that she sing the rare râg Gandhâri-Bahâr, which I had heard her sing many years before; she smiled and replied that it was a special treasure of her *gharâna* (family tradition) that was not to be recorded.

15. SGAE, although technically a private institution, operates in many respects like a state monopoly and extends its activities to such realms as mechanical rights, broadcast mechanical rights, grand rights, film, theater, choreography, and mimes. As with ASCAP and BMI, those parties from whom SGAE collects fees—whether a restaurant playing recorded music, or an individual hiring a band for a party—may regard SGAE as onerous, while on the other hand, artists represented by SGAE may appreciate its efforts in collecting dues on their behalf.

16. Thus, for example, in a meeting with New York SGAE employee Alex Garcia, I verified that the familiar guajiras lyric "Contigo me caso indiana," which has been recorded several times, is correctly listed as *"popular"* and thus could not be claimed by any party.

17. See his 1922 interview, reproduced in *http://www.flamenco-world.com/artists/chacon/entrevista.htm.*

18. For example, such disagreements emerged over the compositional rights involved in the album *La leyenda del tiempo* of Camarón, in which were also involved producer Ricardo Pachón and innovative singer-composer Kiko Veneno. See, for example, the discussion in "20 years later: Twenty takes on 'La leyenda del tiempo'," by Luis Clemente, in *http://www.flamenco-world.com/magazine/about/leyenda/leyenda.htm.*

19. On *Mi cante: El Camarón de la Isla con la colaboración especial de Paco de Lucía.*

20. On *Arte y Majestad*: Philips 848527-2.

21. For more expansive discussion of the entire affair, see also Gamboa and Nuñez 2003; Peregil 1993; Sevilla 1995; and Téllez 2003. Candado also co-authored a book (Fernández Zaurín and Candado 2002) which addressed the subject. Although the book's tenor is moderate rather than polemical, it insists that Camarón was denied his share, and reiterates the wildly inflated figure of six million dollars of royalties allegedly generated by Camarón's record sales (2002:133–35).

22. Lawyer Antonio Agesta wrote: "Camarón didn't sing anything the same way twice, and I repeat that his work is of collective creation, and his heirs should receive royalties accordingly …I think that what would be humane and just would be for those people who have made so much money with him, reach an agreement. But it should be done willingly, not through lawsuits" (in Saenz 1992).

23. Peregil gives a figure of $7000 (1993:190); de Lucía himself stated he only earned half that much (in Grimaldos 1993).

24. However, as mentioned above, some critics, such as Antonio Humanes, have asserted that several of the lyrics claimed by Antonio Sánchez were in fact derived from public domain sources like Machado's 1881 anthology (in Téllez 2003:198). No examples of such false claims are given (also alleged by Candado), except for some public domain lyrics that are in fact acknowledged on liner notes as "traditional" (Peregil 1993:191).

25. Some of these ambiguities may derive from Paco de Lucía's generosity in granting compositional royalties to others—especially Pepe and Antonio, who depended on them for their livelihood. Thus, while Pepe is registered as the author of songs like "Como el agua," Ramón de

Algeciras claims that Paco was the composer, and Pepe merely the lyricist (in Peregil 163, 191). There is no doubt, however, that Pepe composed successful songs for many artists.

26. Paco de Lucía originally indicated that he intended to turn over all his royalties to Camarón's heirs, but subsequently decided not to do so (see Telléz 201). Antonio Humanes, who had much of the credits for the album *Te lo dice Camarón*, gave most of his shares to Camarón's family (Telléz 1997:66).

27. Here as in other respects, parallels can be found in other traditional music cultures, such as that of North India (see, e.g., Manuel 1993:132).

28. See "The flamenco industry, under scrutiny," in *http://www.flamenco-world.com/ noticias/negocios26032004.htm* (accessed 12/2005).

29. "Latorre denounces the present state of 'flamenco dance'," in *http://www.flamenco-world .com/artists/latorre/latorre.htm* (accessed 10/2005).

30. Regarding dancehall, see Manuel and Marshall (2006).

References

Bakhle, Janaki. 2005. *Two Men and Music: Nationalism in the Making of an Indian Classical Tradition*. New York: Oxford University Press.

Barrios, Manuel. 1989. *Gitanos, moriscos y cante flamenco*. Sevilla: Rodríguez Castillejo.

Calvo, P., and José Manuel Gamboa. 1994. *Historia-Guía del Nuevo Flamenco: El Duende de Ahora*. Madrid: Ediciones Guía de Música.

Cenizo, José. 1997. "San Camarón de la Isla (genio mito, y mártir)," in *Camaron: Cinco años despues* (*Olivo* 45/46). Jaen: Excmo. Ayuntamiento de Vva de la Reina

Fernández Zaurín, Luis, and José Candado Calleja. 2002. *Camarón: biografía de un mito*. Barcelona: RBA Libros.

Frith, Simon. 1993. *Music and Copyright*. Edinburgh: Edinburgh University Press.

Gamboa, José Manuel. 2005. *Una historia del flamenco*. Madrid: Editorial Espasa Calpe.

———, and Faustino Nuñez. 2003. *Camarón: Vida y Obra*. Madrid: Sociedad General de Autores y Editores.

Goehr, Lydia. 1992. *The Imaginary Museum of Musical Works: An Essay in the Philosophy of Music*. Oxford: Clarendon Press.

Grimaldos, Alfredo. 1993. "Si Camarón estuviera vivo, le arrancaría la cabeza a más de uno." *Interviú*, no 898, July 19-25 [interview with Paco de Lucía].

Infante, Blas. 1980. *Orígenes de lo flamenco y secreto del cante jondo*. Sevilla: Junta de Andalucía, 1980

Kliman, Norman. Website: *http://perso.wanadoo.es/siguiriya/soleares.htm*

Lefranc, Pierre. *El cante jondo: del territorio a los repertorios: tonás, siguiriyas, soleares*. Sevilla: Universidad de Sevilla, 2000.

Machado y Alvarez, Antonio. [1881] 1975. *Colección de cantes flamencos*. Madrid: Ediciones Demófilo.

Mairena, Antonio. 1976. Sevilla: *Las confesiones de Antonio Mairena*. Universidad de Sevilla.

———, and Ricardo Molina. [1963] 1979. *Mundo y formas del cante flamenco*. Sevilla: Librería Al-Andalus.

Manuel, Peter. 1993. *Cassette Culture: Popular Music and Technology in North India*. Chicago: University of Chicago Press.

———. 2006. "Flamenco in Focus: An Analysis of a Performance of Soleares." In *Analytical Studies in World Music*, edited by Michael Tenzer, 92-119. New York: Oxford University Press.

———, and Wayne Marshall. 2006. "The Riddim Method: Aesthetics, Practice, and Ownership in Jamaican Dancehall." *Popular Music* 25(3): 447-70.

Mitchell, Timothy. 1994. *Flamenco Deep Song*. New Haven: Yale University Press.

Nettl, Bruno. 1992. *The Radif of Persian Music: Studies of Structure and Cultural Context*. Champaign, IL: Elephant and Cat.

Peregil, Francisco. 1993. *Camarón de la Isla: El dolor de un principe*. Madrid: El País.

Pohren, Don. 1962. *The Art of Flamenco*. Bimport, UK: Musical New Services Limited.

Saenz de Tejada, Nacho. 1992. *El País*, "La herencia de un principe" 2 August.

Salaün, Serge. 1995. "The *Cuplé*: Modernity and Mass Culture," In *Spanish Cultural Studies: An Introduction: The Struggle for Modernity*, edited by Helen Graham and Jo Labanyi, 90–93. New York: Oxford University Press.

Sevilla, Paco. 1995. *Paco de Lucia: A New Tradition for the Flamenco Guitar*. San Diego: Sevilla Press.

Skierra, Ehrenhard. 1990. "Musical Forms and Techniques for the Flamenco Guitar." In *Flamenco*, edited by Claus Schreiner, 136–46. Portland: Amadeus Press.

Soler Guevara, Luís, and Ramón Soler Díaz. 1922. *Antonio Mairena en el mundo de la siguiriya y la soleá*. Málaga: Fundación Antonio Mairena and Junta de Andalucía.

Soto Viñolo, Juan. 1992. "Una polémica de 1000 millones." *El Periódico,* 13 October.

Talbot, Michael, ed. 2000. *The Musical Work: Reality or Invention?* Liverpool: Liverpool University Press.

Téllez, Juan José. 1997. "Palabra y letra de José Monje." in *Camaron: Cinco años despues* (*Olivo* 45/46) 1997. Jaen: Excmo. Ayuntamiento de Vva de la Reina, 63–66.

———. 2003. *Paco de Lucía en Vivo*. Madrid: Plaza Abierta.

Vaidhyanathan, Siva. 2001. *Copyrights and Copywrongs: The Rise of Intellectual Property and How it Thwarts Creativity*. New York: New York University Press.

Washabaugh, William. 1993. *Flamenco: Passion, Politics, and Popular Culture*. Oxford and Washington D.C.: Berg.

[12]

'Funky Drummer': New Orleans, James Brown and the rhythmic transformation of American popular music

ALEX STEWART

The singular style of rhythm & blues (R&B) that emerged from New Orleans in the years after World War II played an important role in the development of funk. In a related development, the underlying rhythms of American popular music underwent a basic, yet generally unacknowledged transition from triplet or shuffle feel (12/8) to even or straight eighth notes (8/8). Many jazz historians have shown interest in the process whereby jazz musicians learned to swing (for example, the Fletcher Henderson Orchestra through Louis Armstrong's 1924 arrival in New York), but there has been little analysis of the reverse development – the change back to 'straighter' rhythms. The earliest forms of rock 'n' roll, such as the R&B songs that first acquired this label and styles like rockabilly that soon followed, continued to be predominantly in shuffle rhythms. By the 1960s, division of the beat into equal halves had become common practice in the new driving style of rock, and the occurrence of 12/8 metre relatively scarce. Although the move from triplets to even eighths might be seen as a simplification of metre, this shift supported further subdivision to sixteenth-note rhythms that were exploited in New Orleans R&B and funk.

From the 1950s on, songwriters working in the new styles of R&B and rock 'n' roll based on even eighths often collaborated with drummers in inventing distinctive patterns to drive their tunes. New Orleans drummers excelled in the creation of catchy beats (usually one- or two-bar repetitive patterns) that were innovative while being rooted in their city's percussive traditions. Americans may have become acquainted with the 'New Orleans sound' through the warm Creole voice of Fats Domino, but the unique rhythms brewed in this city profoundly influenced American popular music and played a vital role in the development of funk.

After briefly examining the emergence of straight rhythms in the larger context of American music history in general, this essay develops three interrelated themes in connection with this metric transformation and the New Orleans roots of funk: (i) mixed metre or 'open shuffle', (ii) highly syncopated 'second-line' or street processional drumming patterns, and (iii) Caribbean influence. The careers of some popular artists span the entire period of this shift in metre. The next section briefly describes some of the elements that one of the most important of these performers,

James Brown, put together in his music of the 1960s, specifically examining his aesthetic of 'the one' and its relationship to New Orleans rhythms.[1] The final part takes a look at the funk style around the time it began to be perceived as a distinct genre in the early 1970s.

'Boogie Down'

By the 1950s certain musicians in the popular realm, such as Little Richard, Chuck Berry, Bo Diddley and Jerry Lee Lewis, began to break away from shuffles or 12/8 metre. The voluminous literature on American popular music has seldom discussed this phenomenon except in terms like 'boogie', 'shuffle', 'rocking', 'driving', 'rolling', 'dotted', etc., that are often used imprecisely and unclearly to imply metric qualities (for a few examples, see Palmer 1979; Gillett 1996 [1971], pp. 95, 133). Traditional musicological approaches (such as Hamm 1979), which prioritise melody and harmony, tend to neglect rhythmic analysis – an avenue with great pertinence to the study of popular music of the United States (for discussion of this issue, see Middleton 1990, pp. 101–26).

The study of this rhythmic transformation offers an illuminating glimpse into the productive and complicated interactions between classes, ethnic groups and rural and urban populations in the United States. Swing feel had begun to infect America's musicians in the 1920s and gradually came to pervade almost every corner of popular music, from jazz, blues and boogie-woogie, to Western swing and Hawaiian.[2] Straight rhythms, of course, never entirely disappeared and remained present, however much in the background. Before turning to the role of New Orleans, other areas that need to be discussed with respect to the shift to even beat subdivision are gospel, boogie-woogie piano and downhome blues, country music, Caribbean-flavoured songs, and dance styles.

Scholars have long noticed the high degree of exchange between African-American sacred and secular genres (see, for example, Work 1949; Courlander 1963; Szwed 1969; etc.). Black gospel had absorbed large doses of jazz and jump blues rhythms by the 1930s and 40s (for example, Sister Rosetta Tharpe's 'Strange Things Happening Every Day'). More traditional gospel, however, as represented in the records of southern quartets, remained relatively free of swing rhythms (two examples are the Norfolk Jubilee Singers' 'Jonah in the Belly of the Whale' (1938) and the Dixie Hummingbirds' 'Book of the Seven Seals' (1944)). In addition to these 'rhythmic spirituals', hard-driving rhythms were also found in a style of gospel singing and clapping known as 'rocking and reeling'. An example recorded by Courlander in rural Mississippi in 1950, 'Move, Members, Move', illustrates the kinds of rhythms that fed funkier styles of R&B.[3] Many performers (Little Richard, Ray Charles, James Brown and Aretha Franklin, to name but a few) have acknowledged their debt to the sanctified churches. Black gospel is an obvious source for not only the soulful singing style of R&B, soul and funk, but also the syncopated rhythms and subdivision of the beat by two or four rather than by three.

Boogie-woogie piano blues may also have been a source of these rhythms. From its obscure origins in the southern barrelhouses and juke joints, this idiom went on to exert an enormous impact on American popular music. Its popularity surged in the 1930s, surfacing in the Kansas City swing of Count Basie and Mary Lou Williams, and making its way into the repertory of many Swing Era big bands. This trend was central to the development of the rhythm and blues styles of Louis

Jordan, Lionel Hampton and Amos Milburn. Most of these early artists (as well as the arrangers) came to R&B from a swing or jazz background and played boogie-woogie style with a shuffle feel. Although the boogie-woogie fad had diminished by the early 1950s, boogie bass patterns and piano styles continued to exert a powerful influence on American popular music. Rock 'n' roll's early practitioners, who had grown up during boogie-woogie's heyday, drew heavily from this genre.

Boogie-woogie pianists, as the earliest recordings make clear, performed not only in shuffle time, but also frequently in even eighths. For example, Romeo Nelson's 'Head Rag Hop' (1929), Speckled Red's 'Wilkins Street Stomp' (1929), and Cow Cow Davenport's 'Cow Cow Blues' (1928) are mostly in 8/8. Though shuffle rhythms may have become predominant in boogie-woogie, the even-eighth variety did not disappear (for example, Champion Jack Dupree's 1940 records on Okeh, 'Cabbage Greens No. 1' and 'No. 2'). Little Richard Penniman's string of rock 'n' roll hits, from 'Tutti Frutti' (1955), 'Long Tall Sally' (1956), 'Lucille' and 'Keep A Knockin' (1957) to 'Good Golly Miss Molly' (1958), mostly featured straight eighths. He and other early rock 'n' roll pianists such as Jerry Lee Lewis did not have jazz or swing backgrounds – their blues-based rock 'n' roll has more in common with non-swinging styles of boogie-woogie.

Straight rhythms were also common in country blues as, for example, in Charlie Patton's 'Green River Blues' (1929). In 1920s blues recordings, both duple and triple rhythms are found, often in the same song (see Titon 1994 [1977], pp. 144–52). These rhythms remained evident in later blues recordings (such as those of Robert Johnson from 1936–7). In the 1940s, a huge influx of southern black migrants poured into northern cities to supply the wartime demand for labour. In clubs such as those on Chicago's South Side, 'itinerant Mississippi Delta blues musicians, playing their downhome style of blues for fellow migrants, found a receptive audience'. After World War II, amplification was introduced yielding a 'louder, more intense, and percussive style' (Barlow 1989, p. 328). Although more often than not these electric blues were shuffles (perhaps reflecting the influence of jump blues), southern bluesmen brought to northern cities a harder driving variety of blues (often containing duple subdivision) that had an enduring influence on rock 'n' roll.

Even eighths (and sixteenth-note rhythms) were prominent in bluegrass style, which emerged in the 1940s and was based on the classic string bands. Chuck Berry drew upon his familiarity with these country styles in creating his distinctive style of rock 'n' roll. His debut hit song 'Maybellene' (1955) was inspired by the string band tune, 'Ida Red', which he had first appreciated as a teenager for its 'rhythmic' and 'amusing' qualities (Berry 1987, p. 143).

The metric shift in the 1950s could also have been influenced by the influx of Caribbean-flavoured songs. Pérez Prado reached a 'crossover' audience with songs like 'Que Rico el Mambo' (1950), 'Mambo No. 5' (1950) and 'Mambo No. 8' (1951). In 1953, calypso swept the nation, led by Perry Como's 'Pa-paya Mama' and Harry Belafonte's 'Matilda'. Over the next several years, songs such as 'Cindy, Oh Cindy', 'The Banana Boat Song', 'Mangos' and 'Yellow Bird' made the hit parade (Shaw 1974, pp. 171–2). John Storm Roberts cites many examples of Latin-tinged 1950s rhythm and blues, from artists such as Professor Longhair, Ruth Brown, Clyde McPhatter and Ray Charles. Roberts believes that R&B became a 'vehicle for the return of the Latin tinge to mass popular music' (Roberts 1985, p. 136).

Another aspect to the shift must have involved changes in dance styles. Wendell Logan has discussed the link between certain dances 'such as the chicken, the

funky chicken, the popcorn, the twist, the yoke – all of which had unique steps'
and the change to 'even two and four-part subdivisions of the quarter-note' (Logan
1984, p. 200).[4] These dances, which feature physically separated partners instead of
a joined couple, also have intriguing similarities with secular Afro-Latin dances
such as the rumba. However, in the absence of corroborating testimony from individuals involved, it is difficult to establish more than a tenuous connection between
Latin and Caribbean music, new dances, boogie-woogie piano styles, downhome
blues, and the sweeping metric shift in popular music that began in the 1950s. What
seems clear is that, though early rock 'n' roll often maintained the 12/8 metre along
with other things it borrowed from R&B, by the early 1960s an even-ing of the
basic subdivision of the beat linked to new styles of dance movement had become
emblematic of modern youth, while jazz, swing and shuffles were largely relegated
to the previous generation.

The Crescent City

Having glanced at some of the many musical strands that came together in producing rock 'n' roll, we now turn to the role of a particular city. Though the importance
of New Orleans is sometimes exaggerated, the musical traditions cultivated here
contributed not only to the creation of jazz and rock 'n' roll, but also to the development of a funkier style of R&B.

New Orleans' mélange of Caribbean, European and African cultures and its
distinctiveness from other North American cities are familiar tropes. The city was
never governed by the English and, until the Louisiana Purchase of 1803, it was
ruled by either the French or Spanish. Its early history saw large influxes of Caribbean populations, culminating in the migration of thousands of Creole landowners
and their slaves around the time of the Haitian revolution of 1804. The site of the
first permanent opera company in the United States, New Orleans was also
unusually tolerant (at least until 1845) of open manifestations of African culture
such as the Sunday gatherings in Congo Square. In keeping with its Caribbean and
Catholic heritage, the Crescent City has also been home to North America's most
important Carnival tradition.

In an issue of *Black Music Research* devoted to New Orleans (Spring 1988),
Samuel A. Floyd, Jr describes the city as 'the wellspring of black music in the United
States'. It is not surprising that many musicians, journalists and fans have claimed
an important role for New Orleans in funk's development (Berry, Foose and Jones
1986, pp. xiii, 20; Rose 1990, p. 47; Rebennack 1994, pp. 186–7; Broven 1995 [1974],
pp. xxi–iii; Vincent 1996, pp. 68-70). A distinctive style of rhythm and blues was
fostered in the city's clannish and somewhat ingrown atmosphere. Crescent City
musicians, savouring the musical traditions, culinary delights and unique cultural
mix, were understandably reluctant to leave. Even when they did depart, to escape
endemic racism or to seek opportunity in Los Angeles, Chicago or New York, they
tended to form close-knit communities and mutual-aid networks. Earl King, a local
singer and songwriter, attributes this bond to a common 'rhythm attitude' involving
'a concentrated rhythm and stiffness', which enables musicians from the Big Easy
to feel comfortable playing with each other even without rehearsals (Broven 1995
[1974], p. xxi).

In the early 1950s, unable to reproduce convincingly the New Orleans sound
without indigenous musicians and singers (Gillett 1996 [1971], p. 69), record com-

pany executives and producers flocked to the city. The engineering skills and primitive recording facility of Cosimo Matassa were central in the creation of this distinctive music. Nearly every R&B song recorded in New Orleans from the 1940s until the late 1960s was taped in his legendary studio (Broven 1995 [1974], p. 13). Earl Palmer was part of the studio's in-house rhythm section and drummer on most of Little Richard's hits and many songs of Fats Domino, Professor Longhair and Lloyd Price. Palmer encouraged the other musicians to bring out this 'rhythm attitude'.

I had tried to make them understand that people were comin' down here just to record with this band and they were just goin' through the motions. ... I said, 'Well you got to do something with the music, make it a little funkier!' (Thress 1993)

In producing this intense or 'funkier' effect, at least some of the musicians played straighter eighth notes. The result was recordings that exhibit subtle shadings of time and mixtures of triplets and even eighths, which are analysed below.

'Nervous Boogie'

By the late 1950s and early 1960s, when the general trend in popular music was back to straighter rhythms, much R&B seemed to be caught between two worlds – that of shuffle or 12/8 metre and that of even eighths or straight time. Some tunes seem to be in both metres simultaneously; others have passages that momentarily shift from one to the other. Occasionally, soloists (such as saxophonists) appear to have difficulty negotiating the new style. Only in New Orleans, however, did the mixture of shuffle and straight eighths become a trademark of sorts. Sometimes it is found *between* members of the group, for example with the bass player in 8/8 and the pianist in 12/8, or the drummer in 12/8 and the pianist in 8/8; and at times it is found *within* one member such as the drummer (a straight feel on the hi-hat and a swing feel on the snare) or the pianist (between the two hands).

The New Orleans drummer Johnny Vidacovich demonstrates this hybrid groove, which he calls 'open shuffle', on a CD included with his recent instructional book *New Orleans Jazz and Second Line Drumming*. This 'in-between-ness' is achieved, he states, by that emphasising the upbeat so 'it lags into the downbeat' (Thress 1995, p. 98). Straight eighth notes are played on the bell cymbal while offbeat snare and tom-tom figures are behind the beat or swung.

Piano players were central to the distinctive style of black music that evolved in New Orleans after World War II. In their formidable capacities as singer/performers, bandleaders, songwriters and arrangers, they drew inspiration from a wide range of sources such as boogie-woogie, jump blues, jazz, street music and Latin-flavoured popular songs. Jeff Hannusch begins his invaluable guide to this city's R&B with a chapter on pianists Isidore 'Tuts' Washington, Professor Longhair (Henry Roeland Byrd), Huey 'Piano' Smith, James Booker and Allen Toussaint (Hannusch 1985, pp. 3–68). To this list could be added Fats Domino, Mac Rebennack (Dr. John) and Art Neville, as well as pianists who spent significant time performing or recording in New Orleans, such as Ray Charles and Little Richard.

Professor Longhair (or 'Fess') was a key figure bridging the worlds of boogie-woogie and the new style of rhythm and blues. From the perspective of Mac Rebennack:

... Fess put funk into music. I don't think ... a Allen Toussaint or a Huey Smith or a lot of other piano players here would have the basics of style without Fess. ... Longhair's thing

298   *Alex Stewart*

had a direct bearing I'd say on a large portion of the funk music that evolved in New Orleans. (Berry *et al.* 1986, p. 20)

Born in Bogalusa, Louisiana in 1918, Byrd moved with his mother to New Orleans when he was only a couple of months old. The Crescent City, in addition to being the home of more 'high-class' pianists who worked in the brothels (such as Jelly Roll Morton), was a centre for the itinerant barrelhouse and honky tonk 'professors' who provided entertainment for the black labourers in the surrounding lumber industries and levee-building camps. Adopting the region's hard-driving style, Byrd developed a percussive style of performance that included kicking the sound-board of his upright pianos (and resulted in the destruction of more than one). His distinctive style of piano playing became known locally as 'rumba-boogie'. Tad Jones described his playing as 'a marvel of blues keyboardists all over the world, superimposing very fast triplets on a syncopated 8/8 rumba beat' (Jones 1976, p. 17). In Example 1 (taken from a remake of his most famous tune, 'Tipitina'), Byrd has placed a common boogie-woogie triplet gesture over a left hand habanera-like figure in even eighths and an underlying current of sixteenth notes played on the snare. This passage exhibits a remarkable layering of beat subdivisions: two, three and four.

Example 1. 'Misery' (1957), 4th chorus, mm. 2–5 (1:10). H.R. Byrd (Professor Longhair).

The next two examples illustrate rhythms more frequently found in boogie-woogie piano (especially by the late 1930s). In Example 2, both hands play in 12/8 without contrasts in subdivision of the beat. Cross-metric accents (through odd-numbered groupings of notes, in this case, five triplets), can lend interest to this more rhythmically homogeneous style.

Example 2. 'Boogie Woogie Blues' (1939), beginning of 8th chorus (2:32). Albert Ammons.

One of the most common forms of polyrhythm in boogie-woogie is the playing of quarter-note triplets against a shuffle or 12/8 ostinato in the bass. Example 3 is taken from Meade Lux Lewis's March 1937 version of 'Honky Tonk Train Blues'. Though this could be considered polymetric (6 against 4), it is not 'New Orleans mixed metre' or 'open shuffle', in which eighth-note triplets are superimposed over duple eighth notes.[5]

Example 3. 'Honky Tonk Train Blues' (1937), beginning of 2nd chorus. Meade Lux Lewis.

Open shuffle or this peculiar 'in-between-ness' can be found on many New Orleans R&B recordings. Paul Gayton's aptly named 'Nervous Boogie' (1957) illustrates an interesting psycho-acoustical aspect of this phenomenon.[6] As in the visual paradoxes of M.C. Escher, the perspective of the listener/viewer can shift – the metre is perceived as shuffle or straight, according to which instrument the listener focuses on. This mixture of shuffle and straight or 'vestigial swing', for which musicians from New Orleans became renowned, contributed to a funkier style of rhythm and blues.

A similarly mixed groove, described as 'schizophrenic' in one text (Slutsky and Silverman 1996, p. 13), was used by drummer Nat Kendrick on James Brown's 1960 tune, 'Think'. A slight swing feel flavours later James Brown tunes, like 'Funky Drummer' (1970), and is an important element of 'nastay' grooves (especially in medium tempos, around 100 beats per minute, such as comprise the majority in Parliament/Funkadelic's repertoire). It is still heard on many hip hop and contemporary R&B drum tracks ('New Jack Swing').

Many aficionados describe funk as an attitude 'impossible to completely describe in words' and the experience as something that makes you want to *'get off your ass and jam* [italics original]' (Vincent 1996, p. 3). Adjectives such as 'dirty', 'filthy', 'raw', 'stanky', and 'nastay' underscore funk's associations with bodily functions and sexual odours. Subtle accentual and timbral variations also contribute to groove. These somewhat intangible elements, along with the 'little discrepancies' in time (Keil and Feld 1994, p. 98), are interpreted as physical involvement in the performance and invite listeners' active participation. As James Brown puts it, 'in funk you dig into a groove, you don't stay on the surface' (Brown 1986, pp. 242–3). Because these musical traits have been prominent in the dense, churning grooves of New Orleans R&B from the beginning, it is understandable why funk is so often linked to New Orleans.

Second line

The influence of marches on American song, recognised in ragtime and other forms, did not end at the turn of the century but continued to have an impact through the training of drummers in marching styles and, more specifically, through New Orleans street processional music. Drummers in the Crescent City absorbed these street rhythms and passed them along to players from other cities. Eventually, non-New Orleans drummers such as Clayton Fillyau and Clyde Stubblefield incorpor-ated these patterns in the music of James Brown.

Among the black working class of New Orleans, carnival activities are organ-ised around the social networks of the Mardi Gras Indians. In each neighbourhood, members of the various rival tribes (e.g. the Wild Tchoupitoulas and the Wild Magnolias) spend considerable time and energy throughout the year preparing elaborate 'Indian' costumes for Mardi Gras. At Carnival time, as they wend their way through the city streets to a syncopated march beat, they are joined by dancers or 'second liners' who may add their own rhythms on sticks, bottles, shakers and body percussion. Field recordings in New Orleans by Samuel Charters in 1956 illus-trate two typical 'Indian' marching patterns (Examples 4(a) and (b)).

The attitude expressed in the lyrics of 'Red, White, and Blue' demonstrates what Michael Smith has described as the Indians' refusal 'to subject themselves to the humiliation of being monitored and controlled by hostile authorities, . . . which they consider to be largely racist'. Through their taking over of the streets and their flamboyant public display, the Indians are able to reaffirm 'a broad range of African cultural concepts, celebrations and folkways' (Smith 1994, pp. 45, 48).

In the instructional video, *New Orleans Drumming: From R&B to Funk*, Herman Ernest, drummer with the Neville Brothers, demonstrates a basic Indian marching cadence that he says was usually played on a tom-tom (Example 5). This pattern and those in Example 4 illustrate an important element of New Orleans drumming – the accent on the 'and' of beat four. (Drummers often conceive these figures in cut time and call this accent beat four of every other measure; the difference is purely a notational matter.)

This percussion style has not been confined to street processions and has been a marker of New Orleans music at least since early jazz. 'Second line' has flavoured the playing of Crescent City drummers from Warren 'Baby' Dodds (Armstrong's drummer and featured on Frederic Ramsey's 1940 recording, *Footnotes to Jazz; Talk-ing and Drum Solos*) to Vernel Fournier (Ahmad Jamal's 1958 recording of 'Poinciana') and Herlin Riley (currently with Wynton Marsalis).

One of the earliest examples of this drumming style on an R&B recording is Professor Longhair's 1953 record 'Tipitina' (Example 6). Underpinning this song's descending melodic phrases, eight-bar blues structure and Indian street jive lyrics, is a second line drum groove laid down by Earl Palmer. Palmer describes how he arrived at this kind of beat:

The funk thing came about because it was a street thing that we all just inherently got. . . . It was a mixture of the bass drum beat that one guy was playing and the snare drum beat that another guy was playing. And not just the basic beat on the bass drum. They were playing syncopated things that were meshing with the snare drum. I tried to do that on a set of drums. And that's where that came from . . . I combined what the snare drum players were playing and what the bass drum players were playing with a little more up-to-date funky thing. (Payne 1996, p. 5)

New Orleans street beats, especially the bass drum parts, were often simplified when transferred to the drum kit and used on commercial recordings. Palmer plays the bass drum on the downbeats and the hi-hat on the upbeats. This became a common way of rendering the New Orleans march feel in the early years of R&B (as in Example 9). The snare part's flurry of notes leading to beat four and a strong accent on the 'and' of four are important elements of Indian marching patterns.[7]

(a)

(b)

($\downarrow$ = lowered pitch)

Example 4. (a) 'To-Wa-Bac-A-Way'; (b) 'Red, White, and Blue Got the Golden Band' (from The Music of New Orleans, recorded by Samuel Charters, 25 October 1956).

Example 5. Street beat (N.B. the note in parentheses is not often played).

302   *Alex Stewart*

Example 6. 'Tipitina' (1953), basic drum groove.

Herlin Riley has likened these grooves to 'hitting a speed bump'. As the synco-pated energy builds up, it 'reaches a hump' on beat four (or the 'and' of four) before its release on beat one. Riley also describes grooves as sometimes having longer cycles, hitting 'bumps' every two or even four measures (personal communication).

On his recordings with New Orleans pianist and singer Fats Domino, Palmer incorporated some of these techniques. Most tunes are basic shuffles, but on some, such as 'I'm Walkin'' and 'I'm Gonna Be a Wheel', he plays straight eighths on the snare (executed with a two-handed single stroke roll) with accents on the 'afterbeat'. Because they are played on the snare rather than the hi-hat or ride cymbal, these figures are evocative of parade music. 'I'm Walkin'' starts out with a drum introduc-tion that is pure 'street beat' and continues with a groove that could be considered second line with a strong backbeat (Example 7). This Example also illustrates a characteristic that Mac Rebennack has noted in New Orleans drumming. Instead of the typical one-bar patterns used in much rock and early R&B, drummers from this city often use two- and even four-measure patterns (Rebennack 1994, p. 186). Palmer also plays a basic (and again somewhat simplified) street bass drum pattern in which the fourth hit is anticipated.

Example 7. 'I'm Walkin'' (1957), basic drum groove.

Implied sixteenth-note triplets, made explicit in 'fills' at important junctures in the tune (e.g. the transition to the tenor sax solo), subdivide the eighth notes. Thus, though fundamentally straight, these tunes combine a straight eighth and shuffle feel in a metre that could almost be considered 24/16 or four beats subdiv-

Example 8. 'I'm Walkin'', drum fill (0:39).

ided by six (Example 8). This Example illustrates how tunes with even eighth notes can acquire a swinging lilt through the use of slightly uneven sixteenth notes or sixteenth-note triplets.

Eventually, musicians from outside of New Orleans began to learn some of the rhythmic practices discussed above. Most important of these were James Brown and the drummers and arrangers he employed. Brown's early repertoire had used mostly shuffle rhythms, and some of his most successful songs were 12/8 ballads (e.g. 'Please, Please, Please' (1956), 'Bewildered' (1961), 'I Don't Mind' (1961)). Brown's change to a funkier brand of soul required 4/4 metre and a different style of drumming. Alfred 'Pee Wee' Ellis, Brown's bandleader and arranger after 1965, credited Clyde Stubblefield's adoption of New Orleans drumming techniques:

If, in a studio, you said 'play it funky' that could imply almost anything. But 'give me a New Orleans beat' – you got exactly what you wanted. And Clyde Stubblefield was just the epitome of this funky drumming. There was a way his beat was broken up; a combination of where the bass and snare drums hit which was topsy-turvy from what had been goin' on'.

But *James* . . . did a tune early in the '60s called 'I Got Money' [sic]. And *it's* funky. For him the thing was always there. (Rose 1990, p. 47)

'I've Got Money' (1962) is the first recorded example of Brown's shift to a funk style based on sixteenth-note rhythms. In composing this tune, Brown relied heavily on the contribution of a new drummer from St Petersburg, Florida: Clayton Fillyau. Thanks to the research of Jim Payne, much more information is now available on this musician 'who invented the James Brown beat' and who has been called 'one of the most influential "unknown" drummers of our time' (Payne 1996, p. 20). Fillyau was taught the second-line rhythms by a New Orleans drummer (whose name he doesn't remember) with Huey 'Piano' Smith and the Clowns when they passed through his hometown.[8]

Smith recorded numerous sides for Johnny Vincent's Ace Records beginning in 1955 (his most famous song, 'Sea Cruise', became a best seller in 1959 after it was released with a vocal by a white singer, Frankie Ford, which Vincent had surreptitiously overdubbed). A 1961 recording by Huey Smith and the Clowns features the kind of beat Fillyau could have learned (Example 9). This Example illustrates what drummers refer to as 'linear' playing, in which virtually every sixteenth note is played on one or more pieces of the drum set.[9]

Example 9. 'Susie Q' (1961), introduction, mm. 1–2, drum solo (brushes).

Fillyau acknowledges: 'Now this [New Orleans] is where funk was really created! That's where funk originated.' Smith's drummer also told him, "Use your imagination. Only thing you got to remember is *where is 'one'*? I don't care where you put it on those drums, remember where 'one' is, and you'll never lose the time.'

Fillyau began experimenting but found the shuffles limiting:

Everything back then was shuffles, but I didn't like those shuffles, I like syncopation. I like to play rhythms against rhythms. So I started practicing, getting into my style of playing. When I started, nobody liked the way I played. It was too fast. It wasn't *definite*. It wasn't straight, you know, *dup-da, dup-da*, like the shuffle thing. (Payne 1996, pp. 21–2)

Shuffles favoured the kinds of triplet rhythms illustrated in Examples 2 and 3. These grooves typically did not employ two or four-bar drum patterns. By making the basic unit of time sixteenth notes, musicians were liberated from the 'rolling' uneven eighth notes of the shuffle (often erroneously referred to as 'dotted').[10] Players were still free to use triplets (as Professor Longhair does in Example 1), but also had a rich palette of sixteenth-note rhythms at their disposal. Almost anything was possible. The strong conception of beat one allowed musicians to employ disorienting syncopations and hemiolas that are attributes of some of the funkiest music.

When he was asked to join Brown's band in 1961, Fillyau told the bass player 'your days of leanin' on the drummer are over with. You're gonna have to *play*. I'm not carryin' no straight time.' (Payne 1996, p. 24) Ever vigilant for a distinctive

304   *Alex Stewart*

sound, Brown supported Fillyau and eventually hired a bass player more adept at handling the syncopation. He also became so possessive of Fillyau's rhythms that he put him under contract and told him not to share his ideas with other drummers (in contrast to customary New Orleans practice). Fillyau's first recording with Brown was the now legendary 1962 *Live at the Apollo*, and one of his first studio dates included 'I've Got Money' (Example 10). This Example exhibits a high degree of linearity, as do Examples 4, 5, 6 and 9. Fillyau has incorporated more syncopation in the bass drum part, landing on the beat only on 'one' of each measure. Vernel Fournier has attributed an important difference between New Orleans drummers and most others to the use of dynamics and syncopation in the bass drum.[11] 'It comes from the street bands, the bass drum.' (Thress 1995, p. 46) The independence required for such syncopations is, of course, much easier in parades where each part is played by a different drummer. Apparently, Brown did not force Fillyau to simplify his playing in order to be more 'commercial' as Earl Palmer suggests often happened in studio sessions (Thress 1993).

Example 10. 'I've Got Money' (1962), introduction, mm. 1–2, drum solo.

Brown's high level of artistic control (unique among soul artists of that time) enabled him to bring a virtuosic style of drumming to the forefront of his music. Musicians and listeners perceived African qualities and, especially during an era of rising black nationalism, the intricate, more 'in-your-face' style of drumming easily became identified as a funky celebratory march of ethnic difference (Hirshey 1984, pp. 284–5; Guralnick 1986, pp. 239–43; Brackett 1992).[12] During the mid-1960s, Brown often carried five or even six drummers on the road. His four-hour extravaganzas and unamplified drums demanded frequent changes of drummers. Although typically only one drummer played at a time, Brown seems to have liked the visual impact of several drum sets on stage. Certain drummers were entrusted with specific grooves: Clyde Stubblefield for hard and driving, for example, and 'Jab'o' Starks for more subtle and finessed (Slutsky and Silverman 1996, p. 58). Fillyau remained in Brown's retinue, lending a hand by driving the bus or equipment truck and by teaching the show and passing along his 'secrets' to newcomers like Stubblefield (who joined the band in 1965).

    In Stubblefield's playing on 'Mother Popcorn', note the similarity to Earl Palmer's 'Tipitina' beat in the first measure of the two-bar cell: the accents fall on two and on the 'and' of four. The main difference is that Stubblefield has transferred part of the pattern to the hi-hat (Example 11).

Example 11. 'Mother Popcorn' (1969), basic drum groove.

    On 'Funky Drummer' (1970), Stubblefield has incorporated running sixteenth notes on the hi-hat, accented snare backbeats and a syncopated bass drum part. In the drum break, the snare figure is once again similar to Palmer's 'second-line'

pattern (Example 12). This complex and difficult break has resurfaced in the 1990s
in numerous hip-hop tracks. As Tricia Rose has pointed out, the whole of the James
Brown discography is 'the foundation of the break beat. . . . Drum samples, which
are particularly difficult to claim (in copyright terms), are the most widely used
samples in rap music.' (Rose 1994, pp. 70, 92)

Example 12. 'Funky Drummer' (1970), drum break (5:34).

The Table shows that most of the percussion patterns in Examples 4–12 can
be seen to contain 5 or 6-note cells extracted from the accented and syncopated
notes. Their most striking characteristic is the playing of beats one and two (and
often the 'and' of one). Beat two is always accented and 'the one' is stressed even
if it is sometimes not played.[13] This on-the-beat playing at the beginning of the
measure sets up a sort of springboard for the profusion of sixteenth notes around
beats three and four. The connection with parade drumming is clear: drum cadences
used in marches share this structure. In second line and funk, however, these sixteenths are syncopated. These rhythmic cells provide songs with a repeating 'open'
and 'closed' foundation that oscillates between downbeats and syncopation. This
kind of asymmetrical time cycle is also suggestive of West African drumming.

Stubblefield and his co-drummer and eventual successor, John 'Jab'o' Starks,
created figures similar to the second line/Palmer/Fillyau pattern in tunes that are
too numerous to illustrate with transcriptions.[14] Related figures, though often found
on the guitar (for example 'Soul Man' (1967)) or bass rather than the drums, or
played in unison by all three rhythm section instruments ('Expressway to Your
Heart' (1967) and the chorus of 'I Want You Back' (1969)), are common in the soul
music and proto-funk of the late 1960s. Such unison would be unthinkable in the

	1			2			3			4		
Red, White & Blue	X	X		X			X			X		X	
Tipitina	X	X	X				X					X	
Susie Q	X	X		X					X		X		
I've Got Money	X		X			X	X			X			
Popcorn	X	X	X			X	X					X	
Funky Drummer	X	X	X			X	X			X			

	1			2			3			4		
	X	X		X			X			X		X	
	X	X	X				X					X	
	X		X			X			X		X		
	X		X				X			X			
		X	X		X	X			X				
	X	X	X			X	X			X			

music of James Brown, in which a striking characteristic is the *independence* of the drum and, indeed, all the instrumental parts.

This section has followed the use of a particular march-derived rhythmic model from post-World War II New Orleans through James Brown's music to the popular music of the 1970s. This model, it should be noted, is different from a time line (such as clave and tresillo) in that it is not an exact pattern, but more of a loose organising principle. As such it has served musicians well, offering flexibility and variability. Carnival drumming styles of Cuba, Trinidad, Haiti and Brazil have also influenced popular musics within those countries and beyond and offer opportunities for future research and cross-cultural comparison.

'Mardi Gras Mambo'

New Orleans is often depicted as a 'melting pot' through its importance as North America's premier Caribbean port and as a former colony of the Spanish and French. Discussing the 'Creole origins of jazz', Thomas Fiehrer describes New Orleans music of the late nineteenth century as reflecting 'a social context at great variance from mainstream America. . . . [I]ts musical expression reflected its physical proximity to the Caribbean, its spiritual affinity for Europe, and its distance from the "gauchesquerie" of gilded age America' (Fiehrer 1991, p. 29). Gradually, the rest of the country absorbed some of this city's unique cultural blend. In one of the best-known examples, Jelly Roll Morton, to whom the 'Spanish tinge' was an essential ingredient in the recipe for jazz, brought his habanera-influenced pieces to many other musicians, such as the Chicago pianist Jimmy Yancey.[15]

Numerous writers have heard Afro-Cuban rhythms in boogie-woogie (Russell 1962; Harrison 1959; Giddins 1981; Silvester 1989; Narvaez 1994; etc.). Peter Narvaez argues that in New Orleans, 'Cuban rhythms particularly affected a school of blues pianists who developed the New Orleans "sound" of rhythm and blues.' (Narvaez 1994, p. 203) 'The Latin inflections that Professor Longhair melded with blues were the remarkable rhythmic syncretisms of Spanish and African music cultures that evolved in Cuba; such Afro-Cuban rhythms have been evident in New Orleans since the nineteenth century.' (Ibid., p. 216)

Like Morton, Longhair also acknowledged his interest in Latin rhythms, which he said was stimulated by hearing some Latin groups during a short stint in one of Roosevelt's public works projects in 1937 (Hannusch 1985, p. 18). In an oft-quoted interview he described his playing as a mixture of rumba, mambo and calypso (Leadbitter 1989). Longhair's 'Hey Little Girl' (1949) and 'Go To the Mardi Gras' (1959) exhibit a left-hand figure strongly suggestive of a 'tresillo' bass figure (Example 13). Both Morton and Yancey used similar figures, though in the latter's case they were played with a swing feel more often than not (as in Example 2, with both hands playing triplet subdivisions).[16]

Example 13. 'Go To the Mardi Gras' (1959), bass line.

The Mardi Gras Indian chants recorded by Charters (Examples 4(a) and (b)) offer intriguing similarities with Afro-Cuban musical practices. Besides the basic alternating solo and response structure, both pieces contain the ubiquitons 'cinquil-lo' rhythm (e.g. 'To-Wa-Bac-A-Way').

New Orleans musicians also drew upon commercial mass-mediated Latin music. Robert Palmer reports that, in the 1940s, Professor Longhair listened to and played with musicians from the islands and 'fell under the spell of Pérez Prado's mambo records' (Palmer 1979, p. 14).[17] The Hawketts, in 'Mardi Gras Mambo' (1955) (featuring the vocals of a young Art Neville), make a clear reference to Prado in their use of his trademark 'Unhh!' in the break after the introduction.

As R&B musicians began to turn away from the blues progression, Latin music may have presented some alternatives. For example, Sugar Boy Crawford's 'Jock-A-Mo', recorded for Chess in 1953, adopts a familiar Caribbean tonic/dominant chord progression. This tune, based on a Mardi Gras Indian chant, eventually became famous as the New Orleans anthem 'Iko Iko'. It was recorded by the Dixie Cups in 1964, and by Dr. John in 1972, and is frequently performed in concert by groups such as the Neville Brothers.

Many drummers, such as Johnny Vidacovich and Bobby Sanabria, claim to hear clave in second line drumming and funk drumming styles. A good example of such compatibility is 'I'm Walkin'' (Example 7) which can be seen to suggest a 2–3 clave (Example 14).

Example 14. 2–3 clave.

A tune clearly 'in clave' is Huey 'Piano' Smith's 'We Like Birdland'. Originally entitled 'We Like Mambo', this song was first recorded when Ace Records owner Johnny Vincent placed it on the B-side of a record by Eddie Bo (without proper credit). Smith was finally able to record the tune under his own name in 1958 (the same year the Champs' more watered-down mambo, 'Tequila', reached number one on the pop charts). This version is an interesting amalgam of Latin and R&B influences. At mid-point in this rocking mambo (in 2–3 clave), Smith abandons its mixolydian vamp for the more familiar harmonic territory of the blues.

For several years in the early 1950s, Ray Charles lived and worked in New Orleans. Drawing from his experience here and with the encouragement of producers like Ahmet Ertegun, Ray Charles 'incorporated gutsy New Orleans R&B techniques' in his music (Ellison 1985, p. 230). As Charles' recordings reveal, he moved away from shuffle beats to tunes based on straight-eighth rhythms. On his 1959 hit, 'What'd I Say', he incorporates figures reminiscent of the conga 'tumbao'

Example 15. 'What'd I Say' (1959), basic drum groove.

patterns basic to much Latin music (Example 15). The basic groove in another Charles tune, 'Tell the Truth' (1960), uses a bell cymbal pattern that bears some similarity to Melvin Parker's drum break on James Brown's 1965 hit 'I Got You (I Feel Good)' (Examples 16(a) and (b)). These two tunes also share the now-famous

308   *Alex Stewart*

Example 16. (a) 'Tell the Truth' (1959), basic drum groove; (b) 'I Got You (I Feel Good)' (1965), drum break (0:41).

Example 17. (a) 'Tell the Truth' (1959); (b) 'I Got You (I Feel Good)' (1965).

ascending pattern notated in Examples 17(a) and (b). In Brown's tune the chord is arpeggiated up to the ninth instead of the upper root.

The demands of tourists as well as local audiences, and the economic rewards bestowed by the recording industry for their singular sound, led New Orleans musicians to cultivate and seek out distinctive ways of playing. Sometimes they chose to accentuate their 'Caribbean' identity by borrowing from commercially popular Latin music (such as Pérez Prado) that would have been available to any musician in the United States, not just in New Orleans. By the 1950s, the Haitian migrations and colonial eras were in the distant past. We should not exaggerate the importance of the 'Caribbean connection' as a survival of 'authentic' (i.e. Afro-Haitian) musical traditions. New Orleans R&B became increasingly 'Caribbeanised' in the 1960s and 1970s by incorporating more Latin percussion instruments, clave patterns and reggae rhythms that were part of the emerging transnational popular music scene. This process can easily be heard by comparing different versions of the same tune over a couple of decades (such as 'Jock-A-Mo' and its later incarnations as 'Iko Iko'). In any case, wherever obtained, there *are* Latin borrowings in early New Orleans R&B. Caribbean-flavoured popular songs of the 1950s, as well as the Latin currents that indirectly entered rock 'n' roll and funky R&B through their presence in jazz and boogie-woogie, clearly influenced Crescent City musicians.

Certain elements in funk bear a strong resemblance to Latin music (and the related African idioms). For example, the textures typically consist of independent interlocking parts that combine to make complex rhythms and resultant patterns. Latin and funk often use binary 'open' and 'closed' rhythmic cells, though in Latin idioms less emphasis is placed on the first beat (salsa, particularly in the bass parts, avoids 'one'). Both share a predominance of quadruple subdivision of the beat and a tendency towards static harmonies. There was also a profusion of percussion instruments in soul and funk: congas, bongos, maracas, claves, cowbells, etc. These affinities with Latin music suggest a connection but do not prove that funk was the product of Latin influence on R&B.[18] By the 1970s, groups such as Santana and War fused manifestly Latin and Caribbean rhythms with funk and rock. Borrowings were also in the other direction, as evidenced in Latin bugalú of the 1960s.

'Make It Funky'

James Brown's recordings of the mid-1960s brought funk to a national audience and melded it into a cohesive, rhythmically locked musical structure. In the summer of 1965, Brown released 'Papa's Got a Brand New Bag'. In his autobiography he comments, 'I had discovered my strength was not in the horns, it was in the rhythm. . . . Later on they said it was the beginning of funk . . . I just thought of it as where my music was going.' (Brown 1986, p. 158) In saxophonist Maceo Parker's words, 'It was just a way to play: funky as opposed to straight. Just a form, a style of music. *James* made it a craze.' (Rose 1990, p. 47)

In creating this new style, Brown not only drew upon his drummers' knowledge of New Orleans rhythms but also assimilated elements of jazz. Brown explains that 'when people talk about soul music they talk only about gospel and R&B coming together'. Jazz, he says, is what made his music 'so different and allowed it to change and grow after soul was finished' (Brown 1986, p. 120). Many of his band members, especially his music directors, came to R&B with a jazz background. His use of ninth chords, chromaticism, extended improvisation and 'modal' harmonies (as discussed below) confirm his interest in jazz. Because of these affinities with jazz, his music was appreciated by many jazz musicians and in turn influenced the development of jazz/funk fusions by Miles Davis, Herbie Hancock and others.

Brown apparently guards the funk recipe closely. In an interview with Lenny Henry for London Weekend Television, he refused to divulge his 'trade secrets'. At the beginning of 'Make It Funky' (1971), Brown's sidekick Bobby Byrd asks what he's going to play. Brown playfully replies, 'I don't know, Bobby, but whats ever I play, it's *got* to be funky.' As if to affirm a link between food and funk, Brown proceeds to call out the names of various soul foods (neckbones, ham and yam, turnips, grits and gravy, etc.).

Though Brown won't reveal his cooking methods, some of the raw musical ingredients of the incipient funk style he put together could be enumerated as follows:

(1) Sixteenth note as the basic rhythmic unit – one of the characteristics that distinguishes funk from soul which, though also highly rhythmic and syncopated, was built fundamentally on eighth-note rhythms. Even if it is not played, in funk the sixteenth note is always felt or implied.

(2) 'Linear' drumming which was often highly syncopated and stressed the first beat of the measure, permitting deviations from the accented second and fourth beats (backbeats) and offbeat eighth notes found in jazz and R&B shuffles. As James Brown puts it, 'I changed from the upbeat to the downbeat. Simple as that.' (Rose 1990, p. 59)

(3) A style of singing derived from gospel and shared with soul. Shouting, screaming, melismatic vocalisations often featuring call and response with a backup 'chorus' inspired by sanctified churches. (Brown, like Wilson Pickett, Sam Cooke, Aretha Franklin and so many other soul singers, began his career in the church.) Sly Stone and P-Funk later introduced vocals that were repetitive unison chants ('We want the funk').

(4) Importance of improvisation, both collective and solo (a distinguishing characteristic from

soul, in which 'jamming' and spontaneous instrumental expression figure less prominently). Use of short phrases set in relief by silent spaces.

(5) Influence of Southwestern (i.e. Kansas City, Texas, Oklahoma, etc.) horn players, especially rhythmic and, at times, screaming saxophone solos. Economical horn riffs and orchestrations à la Count Basie, often consisting of one or two-note punctuations in an almost percussive use of horns.

(6) A more percussive style also from the string instruments, especially 'scratch' guitar (three strings squeezed quickly against the frets with little or no sustain), bass performance techniques eventually leading to the thumb-slapping innovations of Larry Graham (bassist with Sly and the Family Stone and leader of Graham Central Station).

(7) A prominent role for the bass player. More emphasis on heavy repetitive lines, often containing no thirds (unlike blues and boogie-woogie lines) and consisting mostly of roots, sevenths and fifths (similar in this respect to Latin music). In the 1970s, the bass increasingly liberated from harmonic and time-keeping duties – more improvised and complex.

(8) Large bands and revues often with collective 'family' or 'tribal' image: e.g. P-Funk, Ohio Players, Sly and the Family Stone, Tower of Power, etc. Collaborative compositional process (also common in rock).

(9) Static harmonies often modulating to a bridge. Abandonment of the blues progression. Extended jamming on one chord as in modal jazz of the 1960s. Preference for chords including upper partials such as ninths.

How these ingredients are combined is, of course, central to Brown's artistry. A basic rhythmic organising principle often used in his tunes, similar to the bass drum parts of 'I'm Walkin'' (Example 7) and underlying the rhythms in the Table, is the accenting of 'one' and anticipation of beats three and/or four. Proving that he can't help but be funky, even his count-offs reflect this pattern. For example, to bring in the drum break on 'Funky Drummer' and repeatedly behind Maceo Parker's sax solo in 'Mother Popcorn', Brown shouts in the rhythm shown in Example 18.

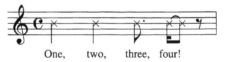

One,   two,   three,   four!

Example 18. James Brown's count-off.

Many of his sidemen (Parker, Fred Wesley, Bootsy Collins, etc.) mastered Brown's lessons. For example, Maceo Parker's sax solos not only follow the guiding philosophy of 'the one', but exhibit his internalisation of the rhythmic patterns of each tune. In 'Mother Popcorn' he carefully builds a percussive solo (also demonstrating his mastery of modal improvisation) by playing sparsely around the accents on beats one and two, saving most of his activity for the second half of each measure. In his memoirs, Brown relates how 'the one' aesthetic helped bassist Bootsy Collins to control his ample, yet at times undisciplined chops. 'I got him to key in on the dynamic parts of the one instead of playing all around it. Then he could do all his other stuff in the right places – *after* the one.' (Brown 1986, pp. 218–19)

'Everybody on the One'

In 1967 the term 'funk' entered general parlance through Dyke and the Blazers' hit song, 'Funky Broadway'. Initially many disc jockeys had been reticent even to say the word on the air. Though not yet perceived as a distinct genre of music separate from 'soul', a funky style of playing R&B had become widely recognised.

Various regions of the country had distinctive styles of this funky brand of soul; for example, the boogaloo in Chicago, the 'tighten up' of Archie Bell and the Drells out of Houston, the more jazz-influenced sound of Kool and the Gang (originally called the Jazziacs) in the Northeast, the laid-back grooves of Charles Wright's Watts 103rd Street Rhythm Band on the West Coast, and the slick soul of Isaac Hayes in Memphis. The New Orleans tradition was carried forward in the percolating grooves of the Meters and their dynamic drummer, Joseph 'Zigaboo' Modeliste.

As the bass parts became progressively more syncopated in the 1970s, the drums resumed more of their time-keeping function. Perhaps too much syncopation from the rhythm section infringed on 'danceability'. Sly Stone's rock- influenced funk featured a simpler style of drumming with a heavier emphasis on all four beats (see Example 19). Complicated linear drumming could still be found in the jazz/funk of Herbie Hancock and in the music of Tower of Power, but the drum parts in funk's most popular styles became noticeably less complex and syncopated than those played by Brown's drummers.

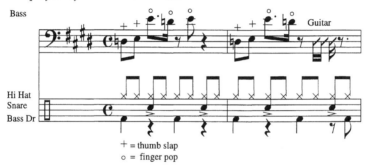

Example 19. Thank You (Falettinme Be Mice Elf Agin) (1970).

The accentuation of beat one and its importance as a point of arrival or depar-ture in one- or two-bar cycles was at times carried to a minimalist extreme by Clinton and Parliament/Funkadelic. This style (as in Example 19) is epitomised by bass drum hits on beats one and three and snare hits on beats two and four. The optional eighth note pick-up in the bass drum, which is sometimes swung, could be a vestige of New Orleans marching patterns (in which the accent on the 'and' of four is an important element). Instead of eighth notes, sixteenth notes (which also may be given a slight swing) are sometimes played on the hi-hat. These running sixteenths have precursors in New Orleans drumming (where they were played on the snare, as in Example 1) and in the tambourine playing of gospel and of some 1960s R&B songs. Cymbal crashes on beat one and occasional silences on beat four further accentuate the one. George Clinton has elevated this emphasis on the first beat, or the 'funk bomb', to an overriding funk spiritualism ('the One'). As the high priest, Dr. Funkenstein (Clinton) leads the faithful in chants of 'Everybody on the one'.

The foregrounding of the bass, which Atlantic Records engineer Tom Dowd helped pioneer,[19] was also attempted, with somewhat less audio fidelity, on

Motown recordings, most of which featured in-house bassist James Jamerson. Larry Graham, bassist with Sly and the Family Stone, further innovated with his finger-popping, thumb-slapping technique which he had developed while playing without a drummer. Further special effects (such as distortion, wah-wah and mutron) were introduced in funk bass playing by Bootsy Collins. When he joined the JB's in 1970, Brown, recognising his charisma, inventiveness and flashy style, immediately gave him a prominent role in the band. Bass lines, which had been fairly set until this point, became freer and more improvised. Collins, of course, later became a driving force in George Clinton's Funkadelic and its spin-off, Bootsy's Rubber Band. The central role of the bass player continued under stars like Rick James and Louis Johnson.[20] In a move that anticipated the techno-pop and rap of the 1980s, Clinton's keyboard player Bernie Worell exploited the synthesizer bass with its greater range, timbral possibilties and sonic force. Tunes like 'Flashlight' (1978) feature endlessly varying bass improvisations against vocal, horn and drum ostinatos. Hit tunes such as 'Fire' (1974) by the Ohio Players, 'Do It ('Til You're Satisfied)' (1974) by B.T. Express, and 'Give the People What They Want' (1975) by the O'Jays were built around bass 'hooks'. The funky drumming rhythms made popular by James Brown were increasingly usurped by bass players.

The mature funk style of the 1970s, with its emphasis on glamour and spectacle, is not as far removed from the streets of New Orleans as it might seem. The zany costumes of George Clinton's Afronauts and the colourful splendour of the Mardi Gras Indians share a spirit of 'strategic anti-essentialism'. Lipsitz has described how, by adopting personas such as the Indians, performers use resonances of an 'unfamiliar' culture to 'defamiliarise' their own culture with the ultimate goal of 'refamiliarising' it from a new perspective (Lipsitz 1994, p. 161). In a similar vein, John Corbett sees Clinton's outer space imagery as 'subtly signify[ing] on the marginalisation of black culture' (Corbett 1994, p. 7). In Clinton's own words, his ultimate goal was 'putting black people in situations they have never been in . . . – I knew I had to find another place for black people to be. And space was that place.' (Mills, Alexander, Stanley and Wilson 1998, p. 97)[21]

Conclusions

It has been claimed that 'all genres of black music [have] at least some of their roots in the city [of New Orleans]' (Floyd 1988). While I hope to avoid giving the impression of a unilinear development, this essay has made a case for the important role of New Orleans in the transition to even eighths and in the evolution of a specific genre: funk.

As the rhythmic underpinnings of American popular music at mid-century began to move away from swing and 12/8 metres, more assertive rhythms and dances emerged in R&B and soul music. Rising black consciousness in the 1950s and 1960s stimulated interest in southern black roots on the part of those African Americans who had earlier turned away from such 'backwoods' practices brought by recent migrants to the north. 'My generation rebelled against that simplistic music [blues and gospel]', explained New York City jazz pianist, Walter Bishop, Jr. 'I had to reach a certain level of confidence, of being secure in my power to know that it wasn't a drag to play the blues.' (Rosenthal 1992, p. 72) The desire of many jazz musicians (and their audiences) to reconnect with these traditions, which resulted in hard bop or soul jazz, coincided with their dues paying on R&B gigs and session work as players and arrangers in studios such as Atlantic Records in New York and later, Motown in Detroit. The eventual emergence of soul music directly from the south (eloquently portrayed by Peter Guralnick in *Sweet Soul Music*) was brought about by performers who had experience of and admiration for these unabashedly black cultural practices (as did the white studio players who brought their own versions of southern culture).

A complicated picture of cross-fertilisation among genres and styles comes more clearly into focus as we look at how musicians drew on their personal experiences, learned from other players, or were exposed to regional styles through the mass media. A primary fount of the new style, vocally and rhythmically, was the music of the sanctified churches. Hard-driving straight (and mixed) rhythms had also remained present in barrelhouse piano and rural blues, even though these genres had absorbed a heavy influx of swing rhythms. Musicians in New Orleans actively pursued their interest in Caribbean music. In addition, with the encouragement of bandleaders and songwriters, Crescent City drummers introduced second-line march cadences. Musicians such as Earl Palmer, who came to R&B with a love of modern jazz, had realised that it was nearly impossible to make a living playing bebop. Still, he and many others attempted to incorporate elements of this demanding music when possible. 'The music of the 1960s blurred the lines between jazz, soul, and funk', says Dan Thress, 'and created a new type of player proficient in various musical styles.' (Thress 1995, p. 8)

The emergence of straight rhythms in American popular song was a decisive break with the softer, more relaxed (but not necessarily less energetic or intense) shuffle and swing rhythms of the past. To some African Americans, the shuffle (originally an African–American dance in which the feet were rhythmically slid along the floor without lifting them) may have been tainted by associations with the shuffling steps seen in the subservient roles and the stereotypical images of blacks depicted in the media.[22] Dance styles became less patterned and more free-styled with less physical contact.

The metric shift took several (not entirely separate) paths: simpler, equal-eighth varieties (rock and soul) and a strain based more on sixteenth notes (funk). Guralnick sees the 'explosive' style of rock as expressing 'the vague proletarian yearnings' of a new generation of white suburban youth (Guralnick 1971, p. 15). The rhythms of soul articulated the sense of urgency felt by many African Americans during an era of aspirations toward upward mobility. Funk combined the emphasis on improvisation and the technical accomplishment of jazz with the inflections and rhythmic spirit of soul. As in New Orleans street processional music, the prominence of complex percussive patterns asserted cultural pride and functioned to reconnect with African traditions. Black music, particularly funk, represents a core of musical values and practices that has contributed to, in Paul Gilroy's words, the 'lived sense of a racial self' for people of the African diaspora (Gilroy 1993, p. 109) and has spread throughout the 'black Atlantic' and beyond. Largely through funk's influence, sixteenth-note subdivision now permeates American and European popular music.

At the close of the twentieth century, there is some evidence of a revived interest in music and dance forms based on triplet rhythms. A swing dance craze is sweeping North American college campuses and has even reached suburban high schools. The re-emergence of these rhythms in popular music encompasses not only this (largely white) revival of swing era, jump blues and rockabilly classics, but also includes contemporary styles of funk, hip hop and jazz fusions. Whether this trend is merely a quickly passing fad or is the beginning of a widespread shift back to triplet subdivision remains to be seen. Perhaps with the profusion and coexistence of multiple styles (both old and new, local and global) and their easier availability through cable and the internet, neither swing nor straight rhythms will become as predominant as in the past.[23]

Copyright acknowledgements

'Misery' words and music by Henry Roeland Byrd © Copyright 1957 Professor Longhair Music. Reproduced by kind permission of Don Williams Music, Inc.

'Honky Tonk Train Blues' by Meade (Lux) Lewis © Copyright 1939 Shapiro, Bernstein & Co. Inc., New York. Copyright renewed. International copyright secured. All rights reserved. Used by permission.

'Boogie Woogie Blues' by Albert Ammons © Copyright 1941 MCA Music (a division of MCA Incorporated, USA). MCA Music Limited, 77 Fulham Palace Road, London W6. Used by permission of Music Sales Ltd. All rights reserved. International copyright secured.

'Tell The Truth' words and music by Lowman Pauling © Copyright 1962 Fort Knox Music Co. Inc. and Trio Music Co. Inc. Reproduced by kind permission of Lark Music Ltd (Carlin).

'I've Got Money' words and music by James Brown © Copyright 1962 Fort Knox Music Co. Inc. and Trio Music Co. Inc. Reproduced by kind permission of Lark Music Ltd (Carlin).

"I Got You (I Feel Good)' words and music by James Brown © Copyright 1966 Fort Knox Music Co. Inc. and Trio Music Co. Inc. Reproduced by kind permission of Lark Music Ltd (Carlin).

Endnotes

1. 'The one' refers to the first beat of the measure. Brown's grooves are based on one- or two-measure cycles that accentuate beat one. The section below entitled 'Make It Funky' will explain this principle further.
2. 'Swing feel' is used here in its most rudimentary sense, that is, to convey the idea of unequal eighth notes consisting of approximately two-thirds and one-third of a beat or a quarter and eighth in 12/8.
3. A partial transcription of this performance (from *Negro Folk Music of Alabama, Volume 2.* Ethnic Folkways Library FE 4418) can be found in Courlander's *Negro Folk Music, U.S.A.* (New York, 1963), pp. 230–2.
4. See 'Chicago Black Dance', pp. 187–210, in
6. A few other representative examples are: 'Baby, Let Me Hold Your Hand' (1957) by Pro-

Chicago Soul by Robert Pruter (Urbana and Chicago, 1992) for vivid descriptions of various dances and an illuminating critique of writing on rock 'n' roll dance.
5. In his discussion of contrasts in beat subdivision in downhome blues, Titon notes that, although triple rhythms are occasionally used against duple in the guitar accompaniment, 'once singing in triplets, [a downhome blues singer] tends to switch his bass accompaniment from the duple to the triple' (Titon 1994 [1977], p. 146). Ensemble playing, as opposed to solo performance, would seem to demand more rhythmic consistency from the performers, but New Orleans R&B styles seem intentionally looser.
James Brown as a common feature of US African–American music.

fessor Longhair, 'Rockin' Pneumonia and the Boogie-Woogie Flu' (1957) and 'Second Line' (1965) by Huey 'Piano' Smith.

7. Some of the many other songs driven by a kind of New Orleans street beat are: Longhair's 'Misery' (1957, with Charles 'Hungry' Williams on drums), his 'Go to the Mardi Gras' (1959, with John Boudreaux on drums), the Hawketts' 'Mardi Gras Mambo' (1955, also with Boudreaux), Little Richard's 'Slippin' and Slidin'' (1956) (with Earl Palmer), 'Genevieve' (1958) by Huey Smith, and Aaron Neville's 'Over You' (1960).

8. Earl Palmer believes it was Charles 'Hungry' Williams or Joseph 'Smokey' Johnson (Jim Payne, personal communication). According to Herlin Riley, it was probably Williams, 'but it could have been anyone. All the New Orleans drummers shared information and often switched bands' (Herlin Riley, personal communication). Williams became the leading drummer at Matassa's studio after Earl Palmer left for Los Angeles in 1957. Williams, described as the 'funkiest thing out' by songwriter Al Reed, was, according to singer Earl King, especially well schooled in Latin rhythms (Broven 1995 [1974], p. 95). Whether or not Williams was the Clowns' drummer on that particular tour is not crucial – as the drummer on the recordings he would have had a hand in creating the grooves that would be more or less duplicated on the road.

9. The offbeat hi-hat in this example, as in Palmer's drumming on 'Tipitina' (Example 6) and Fournier's on 'Poinciana', is a common element in New Orleans street beats.

10. Around this same time John Coltrane was making double-time figures or sixteenth notes the basic units of his improvisation. His style has proved particularly adaptable to funk as can be heard in the playing of Michael Brecker.

11. Unfortunately, lower frequencies presented great problems for the recording technology of the period (even when state of the art) and bass drum parts are often difficult to hear in early rock 'n' roll and R&B recordings. In today's recordings, bass drums leave a much greater sonic 'footprint' by being recorded with individual microphones and with much more treble.

12. This could be seen in the context of an 'appropriation–revitalisation' cycle in African–American music (see Keil 1966; Wilson 1974; Palmer 1992 [1976]; Garofalo 1997, p. 217; and others) or 'a perhaps unconscious reference to West African music' (Rose 1990, pp. 117–; Brackett 1992, p. 320).

13. In his article, 'Robert Johnson's rhythms', Ford mentions the 'heavily weighted second-beat riffs' of Howling Wolf and horn dyads of

14. A partial list is: 'Think' (1967), 'Licking Stick', 'Pass the Peas', 'Papa Don't Take No Mess', 'Jabo', 'I Can't Stand Myself', 'Get Up (I Feel Like Being A) Sex Machine', 'Soul Power', 'I Know You Got Soul', 'Get On the Good Foot' and 'I Got Ants In My Pans' (slightly modified with a triplet feel).

15. It has been a subject of speculation whether Yancey encountered Morton during the latter's sojourn in Chicago in 1914–17 and later in 1923. Harrison thinks the relationship with the 'Spanish tinge' 'should not be overstressed' (Harrison 1959, p. 125). Silvester believes that 'the most plausible explanation for Yancey's use of Latin American rhythms is that he absorbed them from his days in Vaudeville' (Silvester 1988, pp. 15, 75).

16. Christopher Washburne, in a recent article, analyses early jazz with respect to underlying 'time lines'. He believes that, in New Orleans, Caribbean rhythms based on clave, tresillo and cinquillo 'became part of the rhythmic foundation of jazz' (Washburne 1997, p. 75).

17. In a 1975 interview with Tad Jones, Professor Longhair credits a 'Hungarian kid' who 'wasn't white or black' with helping him 'develop the calypso and the Spanish beat because he played a lot of off-beat Spanish beats'. This mysterious figure, whose name he didn't remember, was responsible for Longhair naming his band the 'Shuffling Hungarians' (Jones 1976, pp. 19, 24).

18. The Latin drummer and lecturer Bobby Sanabria has helped gain recognition for the Latin influence on music of the United States. In the process, however, he has perhaps too extreme in hearing clave as *the* essential element in African–American music. Johnson and Chernoff are more cautious, inserting the following disclaimer in their comparative study of African–American rhythms: 'In the American context, we cannot always assume that things that sound alike are the same. . . . Thus, for example, the rhythmic similarity of some forms of Brazilian samba to an American funk beat cannot be taken as indicating a cross influence.' (Johnson and Chernoff 1991, p. 62)

19. Dowd was among the first to take advantage of new studio technologies such as eight-track recorders (Wexler and Ritz 1993, p. 189). Record companies also eventually began to record less time on each side of a disc, the increased groove width permitting lower frequencies to be recorded louder.

20. On a 1990 tour, Miles Davis dispensed with guitar altogether and carried two bassists – one fulfilling the normal role of timekeeping and providing a 'bottom' and the other functioning as a 'lead' bass by chording, using harmonics and soloing.

316   *Alex Stewart*

21. Clinton's statement echoes that of another 'Afronaut', bandleader Sun Ra (Herman 'Sonny' Blount), whose words form the title of John Szwed's recent biography, *Space is the Place: The Lives and Times of Sun Ra* (New York: 1997).

22. 'Shuffling' is often associated with less assertive movement. In *Black Dance: From 1619 to Today*, Emery equates Step 'n' Fetchit's role as a 'shuffling, acquiescent, funny servant' with 'the minstrel stereotype of the contented slave' (Emery 1988 [1972], p. 231). By the early 1950s, the clowning antics and shuffle beats of such jump blues performers as Louis Jordan and Lionel Hampton experienced a precipitous decline in popularity with black audiences.

Vincent points out in his book on funk that a popular civil rights marching song contained the words, 'Ain't gonna shuffle no more' (Vincent 1996, p. 62). Interestingly, descriptions of the original shuffle dance suggest similarities to the gliding movements of Michael Jackson's moonwalk.

23. I am grateful to David García, Peter Manuel and Stephen Blum for their comments on earlier versions of this essay, and to Rob Bowman for his Huey 'Piano' Smith recordings. The insights of Lee Finkelstein, drummer with the Funk Filharmonik, and bassists Peter Dowdall and Peter Mathews were also extremely helpful.

References

Barlow, W. 1989. *Looking Up at Down: The Emergence of Blues Culture* (Philadelphia)

Berry, C. 1987. *Chuck Berry: The Autobiography* (New York)

Berry, J., Foose, J., and Jones, T. 1986. *Up From the Cradle of Jazz: New Orleans Music Since World War II* (Athens, GA)

Brackett, D. 1992. 'James Brown's "Superbad" and the double-voiced utterance', *Popular Music*, 11(3), pp. 309–24

Broven, J. 1995 [1974]. *Rhythm & Blues in New Orleans* (Gretna, LA)

Brown, J., with Tucker, B. 1986. *James Brown: The Godfather of Soul* (New York)

Corbett, J. 1994. *Extended Play: Sounding Off from John Cage to Dr. Funkenstein* (Durham/London)

Courlander, H. 1963. *Negro Folk Music, U.S.A.* (New York)

DeCurtis, A., Henke, J., with George-Warren, H. 1992 [1976]. *The Rolling Stone Illustrated History of Rock and Roll*, 3rd edn, original editor, J. Miller (New York)

Ellison, M. 1985. 'Real Gone Gal, by Lavern Baker; etc. . .' (essay review of 10 records), in *Popular Music 5: Continuity and Change*, ed. R. Middleton and D. Horn (Cambridge), pp. 225–34

Emery, L.F. 1988 [1972]. *Black Dance: From 1619 to Today* (Princeton, NJ)

Fiehrer, T. 1991. 'From quadrille to stomp: the Creole origins of jazz', *Popular Music*, 10(1), pp. 21–38

Floyd, S. 1988. Introduction to papers of the 1987 National Conference on Black Music Research (in New Orleans), *Black Music Research Journal*, 8(1)

Garofalo, R. 1997. *Rockin' Out: Popular Music in the USA* (Boston)

Giddins, G. 1981. 'Professor Longhair Woogies', in *Riding on a Blue Note* (New York), pp. 103–10

Gillett, C. 1996 [1971]. *The Sound of the City* (London)

Gilroy, P. 1993. *The Black Atlantic: Modernity and Double Consciousness* (Cambridge, MA)

Guralnick, P. 1971. *Feel Like Going Home* (Cambridge, MA)
    1986. *Sweet Soul Music* (New York)

Hamm, C. 1979, *Yesterdays: Popular Song in America* (New York)

Hannusch, J. 1985. *I Hear You Knockin'; The Sound of New Orleans Rhythm and Blues* (Ville Platte, LA)

Harrison, M. 1959. 'Boogie-Woogie', in *Jazz*, ed. N. Hentoff and A.J. McCarthy (New York)

Henry, L., and Bragg, M. 1992. *A History of Funk*, South Bank Show, London Weekend Television. 12 January 1992 (London)

Hirshey, G. 1984. *Nowhere to Run* (New York)

Johnson, H.S.F., and Chernoff, J. 1991. 'Basic conga drum rhythms in African–American musical styles', *Black Music Research Journal*, 11(1), pp. 55–73

Jones, T. 1976. '*Living Blues* interview: Professor Longhair', *Living Blues*, 26, pp. 16–21, 24–9

Keil, C. 1966. *Urban Blues* (Chicago)

Keil, C., and Feld, S. 1994. *Music Grooves* (Chicago)

Leadbitter, M. 1989. Liner notes to *New Orleans Piano* by Professor Longhair. Atlantic SD 7225, 1972. Reissued on CD, Atlantic 7225-2

Lipsitz, G. 1994. *Dangerous Crossroads: Popular Music, Postmodernism and the Poetics of Place* (London and New York)

Logan, W. 1984. 'The ostinato idea in black improvised music: a preliminary investigation', *The Black Perspective in Music*, 12, pp. 193–215

Middleton, R. 1990. *Studying Popular Music* (Milton Keynes)

Mills, D., Alexander, L., Stanley, T., and Wilson, A. 1998. *George Clinton and P-Funk: An Oral History* (New York)

Narvaez, P. 1994. 'The influences of Hispanic music cultures on African–American blues musicians', *Black Music Research Journal*, 4, pp. 203–24

Palmer, R. 1979. *A Tale of Two Cities: Memphis Rock and New Orleans Roll* (Brooklyn)

1992 [1976]. 'James Brown', in DeCurtis et al. (1992), pp. 163–70

1995. *Rock & Roll: An Unruly History* (New York)

Payne, J. 1996. *Give the Drummers Some: The Great Drummers of R&B, Funk and Soul* (Katonah, NY)

Rebennack, M. (Dr. John), with Rummel, J. 1994. *Dr. John: Under a Hoodoo Moon* (New York)

Roberts, J.S. 1985. *The Latin Tinge* (Tivoli, NY)

Rose, C. 1990. *Living in America: The Soul Saga of James Brown* (London)

Rose, T. 1994. *Black Noise: Rap Music and Black Culture in Contemporary America* (Hanover, NH)

Rosenthal, D.H. 1992. *Hard Bop: Jazz and Black Music, 1955–1965* (New York)

Russell, W. 1962 [1940]. 'Three boogie woogie blues pianists', in *The Art of Jazz* (London)

Shaw, A. 1974. *The Rockin' '50s* (New York)

Silvester, P. 1989. *A Left Hand Like God* (New York)

Slutsky, A.. and Silverman, C. 1996. *The Funkmasters: The Great James Brown Rhythm Sections, 1960–1973* (Miami)

Smith, M. 1994. 'Behind the lines: the Black Mardi Gras Indians and the New Orleans second line', *Black Music Research Journal*, 14(1), pp. 43-73

Szwed, J. 1969. 'Musical adaption among Afro-Americans', *Journal of American Folklore*, 82, pp. 112–21

1997. *Space is the Place: The Lives and Times of Sun Ra* (New York)

Thress, D. 1993. *New Orleans Drumming: From R&B to Funk*, DCI Music Video (Miami)

Thress, D. (ed.), with Riley, H., and Vidacovich, J. 1995. *New Orleans Jazz and Second Line Drumming* (Miami)

Titon, J.T. 1994 [1977]. *Early Downhome Blues: A Musical and Cultural Analysis* (Chapel Hill)

Vincent, R. 1996. *Funk: The Music, the People, and the Rhythm of the One* (New York)

Washburne, C. 1997. 'The clave of jazz: a Caribbean contribution to the rhythmic foundation of an African-American music', *Black Music Research Journal*, 17, pp. 59–80

Wexler, J., and Ritz, D. 1993. *Rhythm & Blues, A Life in American Music* (New York)

Wilson, O. 1974. 'The significance of the relationship between Afro-American music and West African music', *The Black Perspective in Music*, 2, pp. 3–22

Work, J.W. 1949. 'Changing patterns in Negro folk songs', *Journal of American Folklore*, 62, pp. 136–44

Discography

Albert Ammons, *Albert Ammons – Boogie Woogie Man*. Pavilion Records TPZ 1067. 1997

Boogie Woogie Rarities 1927–1932. Milestone MLP 2009. 1969

James Brown, *Star Time*. CD boxed set. Polydor 849 108-2. 1991

Henry Roeland Byrd, *'Fess: The Professor Longhair Anthology*. CD boxed set. Rhino Records R2 71502. 1993

Ray Charles, *The Best of Ray Charles: The Atlantic Years*. Rhino Records R2 71722. 1994

Chess New Orleans. MCA CHD2-9355. 1995

Cuttin' the Boogie: Piano Blues and Boogie Woogie 1926–1941. Recorded Anthology of American Music. New World Records NW259. 1977

Fats Domino, *My Blue Heaven: The Best of Fats Domino*. EMI CDP-7-92808-2. 1990

Champion Jack Dupree, *New Orleans Barrelhouse Piano*. Columbia Legacy CK52834. 1993

La Grande Époque du Gospel 1902–1944. Best of Gospel Records 21. 1995

The History of Funk: In Yo' Face! Volume 1/2. Rhino R2 71615

The History of Funk: In Yo' Face! Volumes 1–5. Rhino R2 71431-5

A History of New Orleans Rhythm & Blues. Volumes 1–3. Rhino RNC 70076-8

The Music of New Orleans. Volume 1. The Music of the Streets, The Music of Mardi Gras. Recorded by Samuel Charters. Folkways Records FA 2461. 1958.

Negro Folk Music of Alabama. Volume 2. Recorded by Harold Courlander. Ethnic Folkways Library FE 4418. 1956 (rec. 1950)

Piano Jazz Vol. I: Barrel House and Boogie Woogie. Brunswick Records BL 54014. 1957

318   *Alex Stewart*

Huey 'Piano' Smith & the Clowns, *Good Ole Rock 'n Roll*. Ace Records ACE 2038. 1990
Huey 'Piano' Smith & the Clowns, *Somewhere There's Honey for the Grizzly Bear, Somewhere There's a Flower for the Bee*. Ace Records CH 100-A
Jimmy Yancey, RCA LX-3000. rec. 1939
Jimmy Yancey, *Eternal Blues*. Blues Encore CD 52031. 1994

[13]

AFRO-AMERICAN GOSPEL MUSIC:
A CRYSTALLIZATION OF THE BLACK AESTHETIC

Pearl Williams-Jones

INTRODUCTION

If a basic theoretical concept of a black aesthetic can be drawn from the history of the black experience in America, the crystallization of this concept is embodied in Afro-American gospel music. The cultural traditions and ideals of West Africa are the ultimate source from which the basic concept of a black aesthetic definition is derived. There are many aspects of black American culture, such as folktales, speech patterns, religious beliefs and musical practices, which reveal connecting links to African roots in subtle and sometimes obvious ways. Black gospel music, however, retains the most noticeable African-derived aesthetic features of all (Washington 1973:19-35, 78-79). In concept and practice there has been some, but little significant deviation in gospel from many of the basic traits found in the traditional music of West Africa and the various phases of evolvement in the Afro-American cultural continuum. Deviation from or conformity to ancestral traditional practices is influenced by environmental factors. According to John Szwed, "Song forms and performances are themselves models of social behavior that reflect strategies of adaptation to human and natural environments." Black gospel music, then, reflects changes and retentions of West African musical style and context that can only be "understood within a synthesis of social and cultural change" (Szwed 1970:220).

The consistent and persistent retention in gospel music performance and practice of a clearly defined black identity growing out of the black experience in America is indicative of the indomitability of the African ethos. The process of acculturation and syncretism has done much to alter the social fabric of black life in America. In spite of this fact, cultural ties of the ancestral lineage have been preserved in various forms within the enclave of the black gospel church and its music—black gospel. Black gospel music is one of the new seminal genres of contemporary black culture which continually maintains its self-identity while it nourishes and enrichens the mainstream of the world's cultural sources.

THE FOUNDATION FOR A BLACK AESTHETIC DEFINITION

The concept of a black aesthetic definition has been increasingly debated in recent years among black intellectuals. Poets, writers, critics, and philosophers appear aware of the importance and desirability of formulating a comprehensive statement concerning the essential elements of the black aesthetic in black arts.

One essential purpose of the definition is the establishment in American cultural thought of the existence and profound significance of distinct and unique African-American art forms. The proper assessment of the black art forms, gospel music included, must emerge from aesthetic criteria which have been evolved through black thought and tradition. It must be realized, according to McPherson, *et al.* that,

> ... white aesthetic terminology, for all its avowed lack of social involve-
> ment, is rooted in racism of white society and therefore inappropriate for
> judging black expression (1971:264).

Stephen Henderson continues,

> ... the recognition of Blackness in poetry is a value judgment which on
> certain levels and in certain instances, notably in matters of meaning that go
> beyond questions of structure and theme, must rest upon one's immersion
> in the totality of the Black experience (1973:65).

In order to establish a black aesthetic definition as applied to black art forms, the implications of the black gospel church and the music associated with it should be brought into focus.

THE BLACK GOSPEL CHURCH

If it is true, as it has been commonly claimed, that the church is a conservative institution, then we can assume that it is likely that many of those cultural characteristics which are typical of blacks would be preserved in their truest form in the black church and hence, in black religious music. This assumption appears valid if consideration is given to the ethnic-styled mode of worship and the style and function of music in this setting. Many of the black churches in urban as well as rural communities maintain worship services which are essentially unchanged from those of the slave's praise houses and and the early black churches of the freed men. There are several accounts of these which have been historically documented. *Readings in Black American Music* (Southern, ed. 1971:62, 68, 70, 112, 113, 146, 147) give an indication of the close relationship of early black church worship with some contemporary carry-over. Hale Smith, eminent black composer and an articulate spokesman on black music has stated:

WILLIAMS-JONES: AFRO-AMERICAN GOSPEL MUSIC   375

> On the North American continent the Black musical definition is most clear
> in that music of the Black man who is closest to the soil or in the lower
> cultural or economic levels ... you will find blues singers out of Mississippi
> or singers in the various store-front churches which come as close as
> anything can to the essence of the black experience through music (de
> Lerma 1970:69).

The singers "in the various store-front churches" referred to by Smith are performers of gospel, as well as other forms of black religious music.

Many of the practices which we commonly associate with the gospel church, such as dance, the emotional and musical delivery style of sermons, and the spontaneous verbal and non-verbal responses by preachers and congregations, have been appropriated and often emasculated by secular performers who seek to recreate what is essentially a genuine spiritual element in an authentic gospel performance. Ben Sidran states:

> Both the association of music with magic in African cultures and the
> importance of music to the development of black Christianity in America
> have been cited as proof of connection between black music and black
> spirituality (1971:xvii).

While this spirituality may be one of the most emotionally potent forces in the arsenal of the black aesthetic, it has not necessarily remained the exclusive property of the black church. In the "world" it is known colloquially as "soul."

Significantly, black religious music more than secular music was one of the most potent moral weapons in the human rights struggle of the 1960s. A whole generation of young blacks were introduced to the power of gospel songs and spirituals to "... galvanize a group of individuals on an emotional, non-verbal level of experience" (Sidran 1971:xiv), which provided a bond of cohesiveness and strength to the movement. At the same time, generations of older blacks were reminded of the similar role which the spirituals had played in the course of black history from the period of slavery.

Because black gospel music is inadequately recorded and has had limited access to radio, television and the publication media (source and books), some blacks and many white Americans are totally unaware of the existence of this music. The black spirituals of slavery were similarly unknown outside of the southern slave community until the Fisk Jubilee Singers introduced the songs during their tours of the 1870s. Among musicologists and ethnologists there is a beginning awareness of black gospel music, and as a result, increasing numbers of articles and scholarly studies on the subject have begun to appear. Much of the difficulty in developing a body of materials about gospel music is the paucity of researched primary data on an idiom which exists principally and most authentically in an oral tradition. Since gospel music is transmitted primarily through oral tradition it is necessary to define this genre in the context of the black gospel church.

BLACK GOSPEL MUSIC

Black gospel music, a synthesis of West African and Afro-American music, dance, poetry and drama, is a body of urban contemporary black religious music of rural folk origins which is a celebration of the Christian experience of salvation and hope. It is at the same time a declaration of black selfhood which is expressed through the very personal medium of music. Having been for most of its fifty years of existence an underground or counterculture body of music, gospel is among the least known or understood of the many black cultural expressions today.

While the influences of Western religious concepts and music upon black religious music are indisputable and have been factually documented through musicological and historical analysis, the overriding dominance of the African-ization of these Western influences is equally indisputable (Washington, 1973). "The very importance of song in black worship is an Africanism hard to overestimate" (Roberts:1972:174). Without negation of the presence of European-derived harmonies, forms, and instances of actual usage of white hymn tunes in gospel music, the principle emphasis is upon the utilization of these elements in an unusual way to create new forms. Unlike the art song arrangements of black spirituals, or the movement in "third stream" jazz techniques, which actively and deliberately incorporated European classical musical concepts and practices, black gospel music has not consciously sought the assimilation of European religious music practices or materials into its genre. If this has occurred, the materials have been improvisationally re-created to conform to black aesthetic requirements of performance. Donald Byrd, jazz artist, lecturer and music educator was quoted in the Washington Post as having stated:

> Gospel music is one of the few black art forms that hasn't evolved into something else. There hasn't been any evolution in it like there has been in jazz, or folk, with the changing of the beat, the basic construction, and even harmonic techniques. It's one of the pure strains in the black heritage that hasn't changed from its birth in Africa, except for the first adaptation to the white man's church (Smith 1969: magazine section).

Gospel has distilled the aesthetic essence of the black arts into a unified whole. It is a colorful kaleidoscope of black oratory, poetry, drama and dance. One has only to experience a gospel "happening" in its cultural setting to hear black poetry in the colorful oratory of the black gospel preacher, or to see the drama of an emotion-packed performance of a black gospel choir interacting with its gospel audience, and the resulting shout of the holy dance. It is indeed a culmination of the black aesthetic experience.

As a relatively new manifestation of a long historical tradition of religious music, black gospel music has drawn upon such source music as spirituals, ring shouts, jubilees, chants, and camp meeting songs which themselves had numerous retentions of Africanisms. Bruno Nettl (1965:180) takes the position that African features are retained and in evidence in the music most closely associated with religion or ritual. He and other scholars (Bastide 1971) maintain that while music of the U.S. blacks exhibits the least Africanisms of those areas in the Americas and the islands where there were African slaves,

> U.S. Negroes retained much of the structure of the African heritage, and while their folk music does not sound African in the sense that the music of Haiti and Bahia does, it contains some African stylistic features (Nettl 1965:180).

Nettl's basic concept is one which adheres to the philosophy that, "only in the style of performance can we detect definitely African roots" (1965:180). Evidence of this concept is recognized in a comparative analysis of the stylistic performances of two well-known gospel singers: James Cleveland, Afro-American gospel singer and George Beverly Shea, Anglo-American gospel singer.

The vocal timbre, phrasing, rhythmic emphasis, and dramatic projection of the text in such a time-honored white gospel hymn as, "Peace Be Still" reflects the contrasting conceptual aesthetic form which each performance emanates. James Standifer (1972:100) notes that "the black performer makes a rendition strikingly 'black' by bringing himself and the black experience to that rendition." In "quasi-sermon" fashion, Cleveland utilizes the vast arsenal of vocal devices which are at his disposal through cultural tradition: moans, grunts, wails, shouts, gliding pitches, and song speech. Shea, on the other hand, has a style of delivery which stresses clear enunciation of words, clean, clear phrasing, and incorporates few glides or slides to and from pitches. In general, his delivery is a typical "straight" or literal representation of the song text and music. Stylistic comparisons of performance practices can also ". . . reveal much about the acculturation and assimilation process constantly working in reciprocity with blacks and whites in America" (Standifer 1972:100). The African and Afro-American concept of the "beautiful" singing voice does not entirely concur with Western concepts. Harold Courlander has noted,

> In most traditional singing there is no apparent striving for the "smooth" and "sweet" qualities that are so highly regarded in Western tradition. Some outstanding blues, gospel, and jazz singers have voices that may be described as foggy, hoarse, rough, or sandy. Not only is this kind of voice not derogated, it often seems to be valued. Sermons preached in this type of voice appear to create a special emotional tension. Examination of African singing tradition indicates that there, too, "sweetness" of voice is not a primary objective, and that other considerations are regarded as more relevant to good singing (1963:23).

Some facets of West African musical practice are seemingly more dominant in the gospel idiom than in the primary black religious forms such as the spirituals. The role and significance of accompaniment in gospel music is a case in point. Traditional spirituals were unaccompanied and limited in rhythmic accompaniment to swaying, footpatting, and handclapping. Instruments were generally unavailable or forbidden. This tradition of non-instrumental accompaniment (whether by choice, custom or circumstance singularly or combined) of the spirituals was continued long after slavery and well into the period during which blacks established their own churches. John W. Work stated that:

> The folk church has forbidden instruments to be used in the service in the past apparently because the instruments available in the community, the piano, the guitar, harmonica, and the banjo were too closely identified with secular life or "the world," as opposed to the sacred church (1949:137).

Instrumental as well as rhythmic accompaniment in gospel is an integral part of the performance just as in African music.

What are some of the specific aesthetic requirements of black music which have necessitated the retention of certain Africanisms in the black religious musical continuum? The following list of distinctly African related traits are present to a large extent in Afro-American gospel performances, techniques, and form:

1. The use of antiphonal response.
2. Varying vocal tone.
3. Endless variation on the part of the lead singer.
4. Use of falsetto.
5. Religious dancing or "shouting."
6. Percussive-style playing techniques.
7. Handclapping and footpatting.
8. Emphasis on dynamic rhythms.
9. A dramatic concept of the music.
10. Repetition.
11. Improvisation.
12. Communal participation.
13. Immediacy of communication.
14. Oral transmission of the idiom.
15. Functionalism of the music.

It might appear that the retention of so many Africanisms would make gospel music more African than Afro-American. However, it is in the process of syncretism or synthesis that aspects of some or all of the clearly discernible Africanisms have become assimilated into the Afro-American style. An example in point is the alteration of the rhythmic element in Afro-American music.

The relationship of the rhythmic element in African and Afro-American music is somewhat obvious; however, the special quality known as "swing" in

WILLIAMS-JONES: AFRO-AMERICAN GOSPEL MUSIC   379

black music in general as well as gospel, is peculiarly an adaptation of the African rhythmic fundamental. "Swing" is a term that has never been satisfactorily defined, but it is a tangible quality in rhythmic emphasis which distinguishes the complex metronomic polyrhythms of African drumming from the swinging rhythms of black American music. In his book, *Where's the Melody?*, Martin Williams says of "swing":

> It is a quality empirically present or not present in a performance, and the
> particular rhythmic momentum of "swing" can be felt and heard (1961:10).

In black gospel, the special use of rhythms which are distinctly gospel, and which swing, were derived out of the holiness shout music of the early 1900s revival movements. Courlander in commenting upon the rhythms of the black church noted that:

> It is commonplace that Negro church music and secular music not only
> "swing" but also have much more sophisticated elements of off-beats,
> retarded beats, and anticipated beats than does Euro-American folk music in
> general. . . . As remote as U.S. Negro rhythm is from the African today, it is
> certainly closer to it in rhythmic concepts than to either English or French
> folk tradition (1963:29).

Euro-American traits in Afro-American gospel music are evidenced primarily in form, employment of certain characteristic scales, European harmony, and the surge singing technique which had origins in the New England psalmody practice of "lining-out." The concept of individual authorship of a composer is also primarily European, and the creation of gospel songs by individual composers was begun by Thomas A. Dorsey and continued by an early generation of gospel composers who followed his example, notably: Lillian Bowles, Lucie Campbell, Theodore Frye, Roberta Martin, Kenneth Morris and others. The form which these early writers used most often was the traditional protestant hymn type of verse and chorus. Some of the well-known examples are: "Precious Lord, Take My Hand" by Dorsey, "Just to Behold His Face" by Lucie Campbell, "Just a Closer Walk With Thee" by Kenneth Morris. Form, however, was merely the framework around which improvisation could take place. Gospel songs are composed songs but within the clearly discernible gospel performance tradition which is often more reflective of general folk stylistic traits than distinct compositional techniques of the individual composer. In this regard, gospel music may be considered "composed folk song" which is transmitted primarily through oral performance traditions in much the same fashion as folklore. The musical score of any gospel song gives faint clue to the vocal or instrumental improvisation which is assumed by the composer. There existed a similar tradition of improvisation in European music in the seventeenth century when the figured bass and the da capo aria styles were in vogue.

Gospel music utilizes the diatonic and pentatonic scales for the most part which, according to Chase, is not incompatible with some African tonal systems. "The diatonic scale is common to both systems and forms, indeed, the strongest link between them as well as the mark that distinguishes them from all other systems" (1955:75). The rock/blues musician, Al Wilson, has suggested, according to Roberts that

> ... both the blues and soul music use basically five-note scales, but different ones ... C, D, E, G, A, C, to gospel music and soul, and C, E-flat, G, A, B-flat, C, to the blues. ... If Wilson were right, it would certainly help to explain why the blues element in much soul music, though there, is far less obvious than gospel music (1972: 190).

Harmony in gospel music is based upon the European tradition coupled with blues tonality which results from the use of certain blue notes with primary and secondary chord changes. This combination, as we have seen in other forms of black music, gives the music its distinct harmonic sound.

There is strong evidence to support the belief that black gospel singing style has been influenced by the practices of "lining out" which occurred in New England psalm singing during the seventeenth century. It is a practice which was carried on in early black churches and is still practiced in a large number of Baptist and Methodist churches today. Chase states that this practice

> ... opened the door of the introduction of the florid style ... Negro singing in America developed as the result of the blending of several cultural traditions is certain; and it seems equally certain that one of these traditions was the folk style of early New England psalmody and hymnody, carried southward in the late eighteenth and early nineteenth centuries (Chase 1955:239).

This performance style when combined with the special vocal timbres and sonorities of the black sound aesthetic produces the unique black gospel singing style which has been so widely copied or carried over by the black soul singers, many of whom were former gospel singers. This leads us into a discussion of the art of gospel singing and performance practices.

Gospel singing style is in a large measure the essence of gospel. It is a performers art and a method of delivering lyrics which is as demanding in vocal skills and technique as any feat in Western performance practice. Learning or acquiring the art takes time, practice, and dedication. The performing process is so intuitive as to be almost unteachable. The greatest gospel artists are usually those who were born nearest the source of the tradition. There are high aesthetic standards which are evident in the performances of many of the best known gospel singers, but these standards can also be observed in many obscure and unknown gospel churches throughout the U.S. where gospel talent often flourishes in abundance unrecognized by all except the knowledgeable few. Emerging from some such beginnings to achieve honor and recognition among their peers and the gospel cognoscenti has been the late Mahalia Jackson, the late Clara Ward, James Cleveland, Alex Bradford and others. In addition there are the innumerable known and unknown choirs, congregations, quartets, and groups which proliferate throughout the country. What is the model for achieving the gospel singing ideal?

There are two basic sources from which gospel singing has derived its aesthetic ideals: the free-style collective improvisations of the black church congregation and the rhetorical solo style of the black gospel preacher. In seeking to communicate the gospel message, there is little difference between the gospel singer and the gospel preacher in the approach to his subject. The same techniques are used by the preacher and the singer—the singer perhaps being considered the lyrical extension of the rhythmically rhetorical style of the preacher. Inherent in this also is the concept of black rhetoric, folk expressions, bodily movement, charismatic energy, cadence, tonal range and timbre. Aretha Franklin, a consummate vocal artist in the gospel tradition, has credited her father, a noted black gospel preacher, with having had the greatest influence on her in his singing style and fusion of rhythm with words and preaching. She said: "I learned vocally from him. He gave me a sense of timing in music" (Garland 1969:198). The gospel preacher does not act alone. The total gospel experience is one in which congregation and preacher interact in an African related call and response pattern. For example,

(Call) What's the matter with Jesus?
(Response) He's alright!
(Call) I say, what's the matter with Jesus?
(Response) He's alright!
(Call) He's bread when I'm hungry,
(Response) He's alright!
(Call) Water when I'm thirsty!
(Response) He's alright!

This typical up-tempo gospel shout song leads inevitably into a series of chants and the holy dance.

Chant I. "Well, Well, Well"

Chant II. "Ho-ly Gho- -st"

This gospel experience is almost ritualistic in its sustained drama and spiritual intensity. People are possessed and overcome in this state of high religious ecstasy.

These dual influences reflect the general aesthetic preference for an intensity which use of the chest voice or open tones can produce. It enables gospel singers to create innumerable variations of vocal color from the strident quality of traditional hollers and laments to tonal utterances and nuances in vocal contour which may be meaningful only to those who are sensitive enough to cultural practices to understand such subtleties. Singing styles are highly prized for the individuality which the gospel singer can bring to the music. Originality is greatly esteemed. Some of the important gospel stylists, such as Shirley Ceasar, and James Cleveland, are noted for the quasi-preaching approach to a gospel song. There is the country gospel flavor of the Staple Singers; the rock-gospel of Andrae Crouch and Edwin Hawkins; the surge singers such as Robert Anderson and J. Robert Bradley. There are the balladeers such as the Reverend Charles Watkins and Archie Dennis; and the holiness shouters such as Isaac Douglass, Myrna Summers, Madame Ernestine Washington, Mattie Moss Clark and the many quartet leaders. The soloist in the gospel idiom has been as important in the historical development of the gospel music style as the solo blues artist in the development of blues concept and form. In both the blues and gospel, the projection of the individuality of the performer, his feelings, beliefs, and desires become known. The solo medium is very personal. LeRoi Jones thoroughly explores the socio-cultural implications of solo forms through his analysis of blues and blues structure. He said:

> The whole concept of the solo, of a man singing and playing by himself, was relatively unknown in West African music (Jones 1963:66).

The solo concept is more an acculturated pattern which the black artist adapted to his own needs. As stated earlier, the gospel singer may be considered the lyrical extension of the gospel preacher. In the early days individual street singers carried on a gospel singing tradition that originated in rural churches. The soloist was usually the preacher himself or one whose voice was exceptionally suited to song leading and skillful improvisation. The gospel soloist is virtually a stylized representation of the preacher or congregational song leader.

An essential element in gospel singing technique is a breathiness in tone production which adds a certain emotional intensity to the performance. Breathing between words and short phrases is not considered improper to the idiom. The audible breath intake and expulsion of air acts as a rhythmic factor and is an essential part of black timing and rhythmic pacing. This is heard to particular advantage in black gospel sermons and has a seeming direct connection to the practice of rhythmic timing in work songs. It is a distinctive ethnic phenomenon firmly rooted in tradition. The melismatic embellishments of gospel singing can achieve dizzying heights of virtuosity among the most skilled gospel singers. Two of the most noted exponents of this style are Marion Williams, former lead singer with the all female Clara Ward Singers, and Dolores Barrett Campbell, formerly of the Roberta Martin Singers. Each of these artists has a vocal instrument of beauty (by conventional Western criteria) with exceptional range and considerable vocal agility comparable to the coloratura. And like the coloraturas, Miss Williams and Miss Barrett

WILLIAMS-JONES: AFRO-AMERICAN GOSPEL MUSIC 383

incorporate a barrage of pyrotechnics into a gospel song which lifts the simplest one to aria status in mere moments.

Black speech is a significant aspect of the gospel performance idiom, and as such it is often equated with black poetry. In the introduction to *Understanding the New Black Poetry* by Stephen Henderson, the author defines black speech as follows:

> By Black speech I mean the speech of the majority of Black people in this country, and I do not exclude the speech of so-called educated people. By Black speech, I also imply a sensitivity to an understanding of the entire range of Black spoken language in America. This includes the techniques and timbres of the sermon and other forms of oratory (1973:31).

There are several forms of black speech which Henderson refers to as "Black linguistic elegance." One such category is called, "worrying the line,"

> ... the folk expression for the device of altering pitch of a note in a given passage or for other kinds of ornamentation often associated with melismatic singing in the Black tradition (Henderson 1973:41).

As a solo technique, worrying the line is most often encountered in the gospel selections which are in slow tempo. This allows the maximum opportunity for the inventiveness of the soloist in improvisation and building an emotional climax. Aretha Franklin's early gospel recording of the hymn, "We'll Never Grow Old" is a classic example of worrying the line with the added device of word repetition to build dramatic impact:

> There is a land where we'll never, never,
> n - e - v - e - r grow old. . . .

Interaction between the congregation and the gospel performer is a tradition which has been observed in a similar pattern among Africans by Herskovits (1958:152). Audience involvement and participation is vitally important in the total gospel experience. Interjections and responses to singers such as, "go 'head," "that's alright," "yes, suh," and "sho' nuf" are common practices which act as an emotional catalyst to spur the singers on. Among the Africans, Roberts (1972:176) noted that during the narration of traditional tales by the griots it was considered impolite to listen "dumbly" without response in some appropriate comment. This response trait is clearly traceable in the accounts of black sacred and secular situations. One is as likely to encounter interaction between performer and audience at Harlem's Apollo theatre as in the gospel church. Passive audience attitudes are Western European aesthetic norms.

The charismatic appeal of the gospel singer's performance style has been effective in dramatizing the song lyrics as well as serving as a gauge of his intense emotional involvement, often called "gettin' happy" or "feeling' the spirit." The greatest gospel performers utilize movement, tonal contours, and verbal expressiveness in a manner of total consummation. Ben Sidran makes the following description:

> The ability to perform music at the peak of emotional involvement, to be able to maintain the pitch of this involvement, and continue the process of spontaneous composition separates black entertainment from almost all of Western tradition. This stage presence, which accounts for the impact of the black personality on the entertainment industry in general and the music industry specifically, is reinforced in black churches today (1971:47).

The dance which is an essential part of African religious ritual was carried over into the religious worship practices of the slaves where it was known as "ring shouts." Several accounts of these were published in magazines around the 1860s, the most famous of these being found in the *Nation* of May 30, 1867. There are descriptive parallels which also occurred in the camp meetings of the white revivalists of the 1890s. However, the shout, or the holy dance may be an instance in the mutual accommodation of similar cultural patterns of African and American origins.

Finally, in the broad spectrum of Afro-American arts which retain roots of the African heritage, black gospel music has the unique position of close proximity to purely African related origins. It is that which is instantly heard and felt in the presence of the gospel sight-and-sound experience. Furthermore, it is to be desired and anticipated that gospel music will not abandon its significant and singular role as the dominant force in the preservation of black cultural identity. Because it is a profound statement of black culture, it is hoped that the acceptability, respectability and universal receptivity to gospel music will not eventually bring a "kiss of death" and route to the dilution of this art form. It is imperative that black gospel maintain its strong self-identity and continue as the positively crystallizing element in the emerging black aesthetic.

REFERENCES CITED

Bastide, Roger
    1971   African Civilizations in the New World. London: C. Hurst & Co. First published in 1967 as Les Amériques noires.

Chase, Gilbert
    1955   America's music. New York: McGraw-Hill Book Co., Inc.

Courlander, Harold
    1963   Negro folk music, U.S.A. New York: Columbia University Press.

de Lerma, Dominique-Rene, et al.
    1970   Black music in our culture. Kent Ohio: Kent State University Press.

Garland, Phyl
    1969   The sound of soul. Chicago: Henry Regnery.

Gayle, Addison Jr., et al.
    1971   The Black Aesthetic. New York: Doubleday and Co., Inc.

Heilbut, Tony
    1971   The gospel sound. New York: Simon and Schuster.

Henderson, Stephen, et al.
1973   Understanding the new black poetry. New York: William Morrow and Co.,
       Inc.

Herskovits, Melville
1958   The myth of the Negro past. Boston: Beacon Press.

Jones, LeRoi
1963   Blues People. New York: William Morrow and Co., Inc.

McPherson, Holland, Banner, Weiss, Bell
1971   Blacks in America. Garden City, N.Y. Anchor Books/Doubleday & Co., Inc.

Nettl, Bruno
1965   Folk and traditional music of the western continents. Englewood Cliffs, N.J.:
       Prentice-Hall, Inc.

Roach, Hildred
1973   Black American music past and present. Boston: Crescendo Publishing Co.

Roberts, John Storm
1972   Black music of two worlds. New York: Praeger Publishers.

Sidran, Ben
1971   Black talk. New York: Holt, Rinehart and Winston.

Smith, Donald
1969   "The Gospel Way" Sunday magazine. The Washington Star Newspaper. Jan.
       26.

Southern, Eileen, ed.
1971   Readings in Black American Music. New York: W. W. Norton and Co.

Standifer, James, Barbara Reeder
1972   Source Book of African and Afro-American Materials for Music Educators.
       Washington, D.C. Music Educator's National Conference.

Szwed, John F.
1970   "Afro-American Musical Adaptation," in Afro-American Anthropology. New
       York: The Free Press.

Washington, Joseph R.
1973   Black Sects and Cults. New York: Anchor Press. First published in 1972.

Williams, Martin
1961   Where's the melody? New York: Minerva Press.

Work, John W.
1949   "Changing patterns in Negro folk song," Journal of American Folklore
       (April-June).

DISCOGRAPHIC REFERENCES

Aretha Franklin: Amazing Grace (1972). 33 1/3 rpm. Two 12″ disc. Atlantic Records
2-906.

Clara Ward: Packin' Up. 33 1/3 rpm. Savoy 14020.

Edwin Hawkins: More Happy Days. 33 1/3 rpm. Buddah M 85064.

James Cleveland: Peace Be Still. 33 1/3 rpm. Savoy Records MG 14076.

Mahalia Jackson: At Newport (1958). 33 1/3 rpm. Columbia CL 1244.

Negro Church Music: 33 1/3 rpm. Atlantic 1351.

Sam Cooke and the Soul Stirrers: 33 1/3 rpm. Specialty S 2116.

Staple Singers: The Best of the Staple Singers. 33 1/3 rpm. Buddah 2009.

The Gospel Sound: Twenties to the Sixties. 33 1/3 rpm. Columbia G 31086.

[14]

The Significance of the Relationship Between
AFRO-AMERICAN MUSIC AND
WEST AFRICAN MUSIC

By Olly Wilson

Any musically sensitive person who has experienced both West African and Afro-American music is aware of the similarities of these musics simply on the basis of the empirical musical evidence. In addition, common sense informs us that the shared history of these peoples would probably be reflected in some cultural similarities. It was only the ethnocentrism of some Euro-American writers that prompted the notion of a tenuous relationship between African and black-American music.[1]

This attitude toward the relationship of African to Afro-American culture was not limited to music. It was part of a larger view of the interrelationship of these peoples which held that there was little remaining of Africa in Afro-American cultures. Herskovits, in his monumental study *The Myth of the Negro Past*, describes this attitude as the "cultural *tabulala rasa*" theory; that is, the theory that Afro-American culture is essentially devoid of any important vestiges of African culture, that the ravages of slavery and contact with a powerful Euro-American culture have destroyed all remnants of Africa and created a cultural *clean state*. Herskovits launched a devastating attack on this position and demonstrated, through the marshalling of a wealth of data, that black cultural practices in America, particularly in religion and the arts, have shown an amazing ability to retain or adapt African practice to conform to the demands of the new environment.[2] With the recent growth of scholarship informed by a black perspective, on both sides of the Atlantic, Herskovits's studies have been amplified.[3] The purpose of this paper is to attempt to show some of the retentions and adaptations of West African musical practices in Afro-American music and to explore the nature of this relationship.

The question of the relationship of the Afro-American music to African music must be seen in the context of the meaning of the general term "African Music." The people of a continent as vast as Africa, with their cultural and historical differences, necessarily reveal this diversity in their music. It is because of these differences that some musicologists refer to "African musics"[4] and not African music. As a matter of fact, it appears that the more conversant one is with a specific musical style, the more he resists generalizations about African and Afro-American music. Nevertheless, as long as one recognizes the limitations of such generalizations they may be useful in tracing relationships which might otherwise be ignored. It is for this reason that, although the individuality of specific musical cultures must be recognized as the basic source of the richness of African music, the commonality of larger stylistic areas must not be overlooked. As Kwabena Nketia has stated:

4   THE BLACK PERSPECTIVE IN MUSIC

> A plural concept of African music based on the "ethnic" group as a homogeneous musical unit can be misleading, for divergencies merely represent areas of musical bias. They are the result of specializations or differences in emphasis on the selection and use of common musical resources, common devices, and procedures, specializations which have over the years tended to group African peoples into different communities of taste.[5]

The recognition of the importance of an overview of the entire continent has led to comparative studies of African cultures as a whole, as well as specific aspects of these cultures. Among these, the pioneering work of Herskovits in comparative studies of African cultures and a study of Joseph Greenberg in African languages may be cited.[6] The implicit assumption behind both of these studies is the existence of an interrelationship of large areas of Africa in terms of culture or certain aspects of culture.

In music there have been several comparative studies. Perhaps the best known is that of Alan Merriam, published in *Continuity and Change in African Cultures*.[7] Though his study was preceded by studies of Waterman [8] and others, Merriam's work had the advantage of drawing upon more recent research from specific areas. The basic criteria for the establishment of music cultural areas has been "a matter of specialization within a common practice." Hence, Merriam suggests that there are seven distinguishable musical areas in Africa, each having special areas of concentration:

> (1) Bushman; Hottentot; (2) East Africa; (3) East Horn; (4) Central Africa; (5) West Coast; (6) Sudan; Desert, divided into [a] Sudan and [b] Desert; and (7) North Coast. [These coincide in the main with the culture areas delimited by Herskovits.] [9]

To these must be added an eighth area which does not have geographic unity, the Pygmy area, found in rather widespread locations in central Africa. As Waterman had suggested, Merriam accepts (in a qualified way) the idea of a common sub-Saharan African musical practice. He differs from Waterman, however, in the delineation of common characteristics. Waterman has listed the following five characteristics as common throughout sub-Saharan Africa:

> (1) Metronomic sense (2) Dominance of percussion (3) Polymeter (4) Off-beat phrasing of melodic accents (5) Overlapping call-and-response.[10]

Merriam contests this list as not being applicable to the entire area. He holds that these characteristics are salient features of West Africa but not of East Africa. He is less explicit in specifying common characteristics for the entire sub-Saharan continent, though he points to "the importance of rhythm and percussive-rhythmic techniques" as indicators of a "reasonably cohesive musical system in Africa." [11] It should be pointed out that Merriam is not suggesting a monistic approach to African music but is simply underlining elements of commonality that he finds running through independent musical practices. The most important contribution of Merriam's study is the clear statement of specific characteristics of each of the musical areas. Others have also made comparative studies of African music. Of particular note is A. M. Jones's use of the practice of singing in fixed intervals of thirds (or fourths), fifths, and octaves as a criterion for the establishment of musical areas.[12]

With a few notable exceptions, the scope of most of the comparative studies of African music culture has been limited to peoples living within the continent. This is surprising in view of the fact that the cultural influences of people outside of the continent on the music of the continent has received much notice, if not systematic analysis. Nevertheless, comparatively few studies have been published that give attention to the influence of African music on music outside of the continent.

Among the exceptions to this, however, have been the work of Waterman; [13] Merriam, Whinery and Fred; [14] Courlander; [15] and A. M. Jones.[16] The first two studies deal with the relationship of African music to the music of African descendants in the New World. The most detailed of these is that of Merriam, Whinery and Fred. In this study, there is a comparative analysis of Gege (Dahomean derived music of Brazil), Rada (Dahomean derived music of Trinidad), Ketu (Yoruban derived music of Bahia), and Cheyenne Indian music. Specific variables of the musical structures (incidence of melodic intervals, etc.,) are subjected to a statistical analysis. This study has shown that stylistic studies, though limited, may be a valuable tool in indicating continuity of musical styles.

Jones's work, *Indonesia and Africa,* is the most novel and problematical of the comparative studies because it is not based upon a known historical connection. It suggests that cultural similarity might be used to suggest a historical relationship. Jones's study compares the Chopi, Malinke, and Bakuba peoples of Africa with peoples of Cambodia and Java. He notes the similarity of the beginning absolute pitches of xylophones used by both groups in addition to similarities in scalar arrangements, techniques of singing in thirds, decorative patterns, game forms, and other characteristics. Jones concludes with the statement:

> The thesis we have propounded alters our perspective of Africa; it calls for a map with the Indian Ocean in the center; a basin whose rim is Indonesia on the east, Madagascar in the south, and Africa on the west, all to a greater or less extent, sharers in a common sphere of influence.[17]

Though his theory has been questioned,[18] it is of interest to us here because it suggests that a large cultural area might involve a sphere of influence outside of its geographical focal point.

6   THE BLACK PERSPECTIVE IN MUSIC

It is the position of this paper to offer another hypothesis which has more credibility, at least, in terms of known historical connection.[19] I propose that a black-music cultural sphere exists which includes the music of the African and African-descendant peoples of the following geographical areas: the Atlantic Ocean in the center, bounded by West Africa on the east with the northern part of South America and the Carribean Islands on the south-west and the United States on the north-west. The resultant sphere of influence, which is divided geographically and culturally into three large sub-groups (West Africa, South America, North America), represents an extension of the West-African music area cited by Merriam. The common factors used to identify West-African music are all present in the same or adapted form in music of the two areas in the Americas. The earlier cited study of Merriam, Whinery and Fred, as well as others, has already established this relationship between West African music and that of selected areas of the Carribean and Northern Brazil. The fact that similarities exist in regard to the kind of slavery practiced, the probable origin of the slaves, the ratio of blacks to whites, and the geography between other areas in the Carribean and the northern part of South America implies that the same kind of close relationships also may exist between these areas and West Africa.

The inclusion of North America is admittedly more problematic since culturally the overall relationship of African descendants in the United States to West Africa is considerably less demonstrable than that of their brothers in the Carribean and South America.[20] A careful investigation, however, may add validity to my position. If one considers the five criteria given by Waterman as cluster characteristics for West African music, one finds that three have been well documented as being characteristic of Afro-American music. Call-and-response organizational procedures, dominance of a percussive approach to music, and off-beat phrasing of melodic accents have been cited as typical of Afro-American music in virtually every study of any kind of Afro-American music from work songs, field or street calls, shouts, and spirituals to blues and jazz. The degree to which systematic comparative analysis of these characteristics is dealt with in extant studies varies from being virtually nil in the descriptive works of early chroniclers of Afro-American music to tentative attempts by writers like Sargeant [21] and Schuller.[22]

Another of Waterman's characteristics, "metronomic sense," is really not a musical characteristic at all but a psychological one which proports to explain a cultural psycho-physical reaction to music. Such claims are conceivable, but given the embryonic state of psycho-cultural analysis they remain dubious and, under any circumstance, outside the range of competence of most musicologists, especially musicologists who are not native to the group whose collective psychology they attempt to explain.

Waterman's final characteristic, "polymeter" or "multi-meter" deserves special attention. Defined as the "simultaneous use of two or more meters," [23] its exact nature has remained a matter of controversy.[24] Most observers have found it usually results from the metrical interaction of the various drums of the common multi-voice drum family to each other, and from the interaction of the drums with the gongs, rattles, and hand clapping which normally accompany them in West Africa. The exact manner in which these strata interact has been the subject of much musicological debate,[25] but the following statement of Jones is generally accepted as being representative of the fact:

> Whatever be the devices used to produce them, in African music there is practically always a clash of rhythms; this is a cardinal principle.[26]

If one assumes that the essence of the multi-meter practice is the clashing of rhythmic accents or the creation of cross-rhythms (and not the manner in which this is produced), then the incidence of multi-meter in Afro-American music is large. Unlike in black musical cultures of South America and the Carribean, the typical multi-drum ensemble is virtually non-existent within North America. Nevertheless, the usage of cross rhythms is a persistent characteristic feature of Afro-American music. The frequency with which this occurs, in contrast to its more limited usage in musics of the Euroamerican tradition, also points to an African derivation. Early descriptions of Afro-American music consistently refer to the special rhythmic qualities of the music. Observers, such as Dr. James Eights in the eighteenth century and Francis Kemble in the early nineteenth century, all make reference to these unusual rhythmic qualities. Henry Krehbiel and the black composer-musicologist Nicholas J. G. Ballanta-Taylor, writing at the turn of this century, also comment upon this characteristic in the black spirituals they describe. None of the above, however, gives a detailed analysis of the rhythm.

Don Knowlton, writing in 1926,[27] pointed out that a black guitar player told him that there was a distinction between "primary rag" and "secondary rag"—terms used to refer to typical rhythms commonly employed in the then popular instrumental form called ragtime. By "primary rag" he meant simple syncopation (or the momentary displacement of the regular accent implied by the metrical framework of the piece); by "secondary rag" he meant "the superimposition of one, two, three upon the basic one, two, three, four." (See Example 1.)

Aaron Copland, in his article "Jazz Structure and Influence on Modern Music," [28] points out that secondary rag is really an example of the polyrhythm, or the interplay of two or more contrasting meters. He feels that the notation commonly used to indicate rag rhythm is misleading, that another kind of notation would be more explicit. (See Example 2.)

The difference in these rhythmic notations reveals the distinction between one metrical system in which all rhythms are subsumed under a single all-encompassing metrical background and another one in which contrasting metrical backgrounds coincide.

8   THE BLACK PERSPECTIVE IN MUSIC

Example 1

Example 2

Example 3

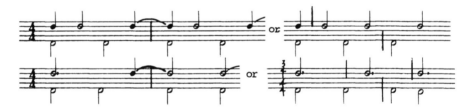

Example 4

Example 5

AFRO-AMERICAN AND WEST AFRICAN MUSIC   9

Winthrop Sargeant, in reviewing Knowlton's and Copland's work, suggests that the distinction between syncopation and polyrhythm has to do with the relative length of the patterns superimposed on one another since certain kinds of syncopations may also be polyrhythmic. He states his position as follows:

> In extended simple syncopation the accents of the superimposed rhythm are spaced similarly to those of the basic rhythm [i.e., a half note apart; see Example 3a]. In the secondary rag type of syncopation, on the other hand, the accents of the superimposed rhythm are spaced differently from the basic rhythm [i.e., three quarter notes apart; see Example 3b]. This would appear to be the fundamental difference between extended simple syncopation and polyrhythmic syncopation.[29]

The application of newer analytical procedures to this question suggests that the distinction between syncopation and polyrhythm is a function of the rhythmic hierarchic level upon which the displacement occurs. Hence, if the foreground rhythm (i.e., basic metrical pulse) is not displaced or is displaced only momentarily, the result will be syncopation (see Example 4), but if the foreground rhythm is displaced (see Example 3b or 5) or a lesser rhythmic level is displaced over a long time span, the effect of polyrhythm will occur.

It should be pointed out that Knowlton, Copland, and Sargeant, while recognzing polyrhythm as a non-European element of black rhythmic practices, tended to isolate it as the principle which governed black music. They therefore confused much music written in the twenties and thirties with black music because it superficially contained one of the characteristic elements of Afro-American music, although it lacked most of the others.

The polyrhythm described above is an Afro-American adaptation of the West African practice of multimeter. The adaptation became necessary because it was common practice in the slave states of North America to outlaw drums for fear of slave rebellions. Hence, although the multi-drum choir was impossible, the cultural propensity for cross rhythms was fulfilled by new practices.

Example 6 is a transcription of an excerpt from an Agbadza, an Ewe social dance. As is customary in West African music, the ensemble is divided into two rhythmically-functional sections: a fixed rhythmic section consisting of instruments whose basic rhythmic patterns are maintained essentially unchanged throughout the duration of the piece and a variable rhythmic section consisting of instruments whose rhythmic patterns change in the course of the piece. The Gankoqui (metal gong) and the Axatse (calabash rattle with external beads) form the fixed rhythmic group. The Kagan (small membrane keg drum), Kidi (medium-sized keg drum), and the Sogo (medium-large keg drum) comprise the variable rhythmic group.

Example 6

AGBADZA

Transcribed by Olly Wilson

In the course of most pieces, the master drummer will play a series of rhythmic patterns which will be answered by a corresponding series of counter-rhythms performed on the smaller drums. The polymeter results from the dynamic interaction of the drum rhythms with one another, the interaction of the master-drum rhythms with the counter-rhythms of its paired associates (i.e., Kidi and Kagan), and the interaction of the entire variable rhythmic group with the fixed rhythmic group.

Specifically, in Example 6 the polymeter results from a clash of the implied 2/4 meter in the fixed group with the implied 12/8 meter being performed simultaneously in the variable group (see Example 7).

Example 7

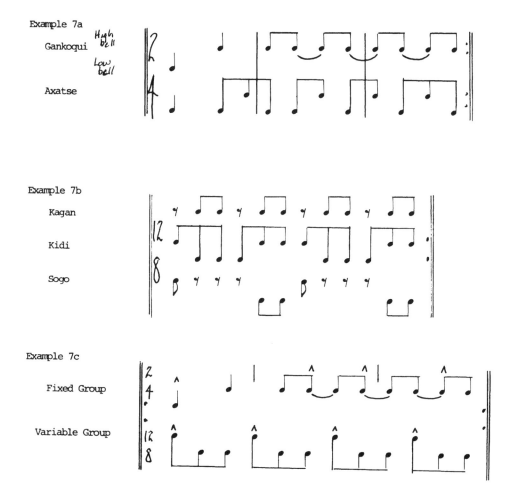

A composite polymetric rhythm is set up because the basic accents of the fixed rhythmic group and the variable rhythmic group are not coincident except at the terminal point of the bell pattern, which is precisely what makes the end of the pattern a perceptible focal point. The polymeter is thus the result of the simultaneous occurrence of several rhythmic strata, each with an independent meter.

In the James Brown transcription, (see Example 8), we find a refinement of the Afro-American adaptation of West African polymetric rhythmic practice described earlier in the ragtime examples. Although the wind instruments (along with the snare drum) may be written in 4/4 meter for ease of reading, the pattern that they play is really one of alternating meters (i.e.,   ). The second chord in the first measure is equal in stress to the first and therefore must be properly conceived as a downbeat, not an upbeat. The following notation—   —implies the second eighth note is weaker than the first. In addition to this alternating metrical pattern, a contrasting meter is created by the strong accents that occur every four quarter notes, thus suggesting a regular 4/4 meter. This 4/4 meter is reinforced by the entry of the voice (in measure four) anticipating the downbeat, but still accenting the first beat of the next five measures. The first entry of guitar as well as the low E-flat, the melodic goal of the bass, also occurs on the first beat.

A third metrical pattern is produced by the bass instrument, which begins on the second beat of the first measure. This repetitive eight-beat pattern is subdivided into two groups of four beats each: (1) by the occurrence of heavy stress and agogic accents on the high E-flat every four beats and (2) by the repetition of the pitch pattern from high E-flat to low E-flat. The fact that this four-measure pattern begins on the second beat of the implied 4/4 meter creates a counter-rhythmic effect.

In Example 9 is a graphic representation of the resulting polymetrical composite rhythm.

Example 9

AFRO-AMERICAN AND WEST AFRICAN MUSIC   13

Example 8

SUPER BAD, sung by James Brown

Transcribed by
Olly Wilson

Example 8 (Continued)

SUPER BAD

It is vital to understand the concept of adaptation of African practices if there is to be an understanding of Afro-American music. It provides a conceptual framework that can explain the diversity of practices within the sphere of West African music culture. Another area in which adaptation is operative is in the Afro-American approach to instruments. Eileen Southern cites many examples from colonial accounts of blacks in the United States which show that as early as the seventeenth century many slaves and former slaves had mastered European instruments.[30] In most accounts, blacks were sought out for their peculiar ways of performing, especially for performing music for the dance. What this suggests is that the slave dance-musicians performed differently than their white counterparts, that they approached the instruments with a certain stylistic bias. I would suggest that this stylistic bias was a percussive polyrhythmic manner of playing which was part of their West African tradition, that they adapted the European instruments and the English jigs that they probably played to an essentially African way of doing things. The adaptation of European instruments, from the violin to the electronic organ, has been a continuing process in the history of Afro-American music. It is well known that the performance technique a black jazz musician uses is not the same as that of his white symphonic counterpart and that this distinct manner of playing an instrument as if it were an extension of the voice has been a unique Afro-American feature throughout the history of black-American music.

In addition to the above characteristics cited as distinct features of both West African and Afro-American music, the following features common to both may be briefly noted. There tends to be an intensification of the stratification of the musical lines by means of emphasizing the independence of timbre (color) for each voice. Just as the different tonal colors of various size drums are clearly differentiated from each other and from the gongs, rattles, hand clapping, and voices in West African music so we find that the typical violin, banjo, bones, and tambourine of the eighteenth century or the clarinet, trumpet, trombone, guitar, bass, and drum set of early twentieth century Afro-American music maintain this independence of voices by means of timbral differentiation. The sound-ideal typical of the West African sphere of influence is a heterogeneous one.

Another common characteristic is the high density of musical events within a relatively short musical space. There tends to be a profusion of musical activities going on simultaneously, as if an attempt is being made to fill up every available area of musical space. This is partially a result of the stratification commonly found in the instrumental music of the entire area we are considering, but it is also present in solo songs—where the singer seems to furnish his own countervoice. This also partially explains the abundance of tonal and other vocal nuances as well as the overlappings and anticipations of phrase beginnings and endings that frequently occur.

Finally, another common characteristic is the inclusion of environmental factors as integral parts of the musical event. The thumping of the feet, for

16   THE BLACK PERSPECTIVE IN MUSIC

example, or the patting of parts of the body and the sympathetic vibrations of anything on the dancers, the instruments, or in the physical surroundings are all considered an integral part of the musical experience. As someone has said, there are no observers in the traditional West African multi-media experience; everyone is a participant. The same thing could be said of most Afro-American musical experiences.

The above survey of the common musical characteristics shared by West African and Afro-American musical cultures is given in support of my contention that the West African musical sphere should include Afro-American music as an important sub-group. This does not mean that diversity between the musical practices of these groups is non-existent or unimportant. Nketia warns us:

> One need not over-simplify the musical situation by ignoring differences or variations in which, in fact, the richness of the African heritage lies. It is by taking into account what each African society has done, what each has been able to achieve musically that we can see the African musical heritage in its entirety. This aggregate must include also those forms integrated into African tradition and regarded as part of their musical culture by those who use them, but which, nevertheless, can be traced to some outside influence. Rigid immutable cultures, we are told, are barely to be found, and we must expect the same kind of situation in the African field.[31]

Among the obvious instances of divergencies of Afro-American music from West African music has been the adaptation of West African practices to incorporate functional harmony. The fact that most Afro-American music is functionally harmonic has led some observers to describe this music as representing a combination of European and African influences—African in its rhythmic principles and European in its melodic and harmonic principles. Indeed, African-American music, and particularly jazz, has been proclaimed as the only true American art form, with the emphasis on the American, the implication being that jazz consists of approximately equal elements of European and African cultures. Though this view appears plausible at first glance, careful examination reveals that it represents a gross over-simplification. Like the studies of Knowlton, this position ignores the fact that it is the combination of many interrelated parameters that defines the Africanness of a musical practice, not the presence or absence of a single one. The approach to metrical organization with cross rhythms as the norm, the percussive technique of playing any instrument resulting in an abundance of qualitative accents, the density of musical activity, the inclusion of the environmental factors as part of the musical event, the propensity for certain "buzzy-like" musical timbres—all these are African features which have been consistently maintained in Afro-American music.

The confusion has arisen because most musicologists, trained in Western music, unconsciously approach the musical event as one in which the most important elements are melody, harmony, and rhythm. All other aspects are seen as secondary. The traditional Western notation system reflects this bias. That is why transcribed African or Afro-American music seems a pale distillation of the musical reality—in which factors other than melody and harmony are of as equal, or more, importance.

Herskovits, in considering the dynamics of acculturation between two cultures, has stated that only those elements of a foreign culture which are compatible with the original culture will be adapted.[32] It has been pointed out by several reviewers that scalar types and methods of voice production found in West African and Euro-American music have a high degree of compatibility. In addition, although research has shown that most traditional West African music is modal and that structural organization is governed by rhythmic and melodic principles, some studies have suggested that a functional modality might be operative as a means of organizing melodic phrases. For example, in a study of melodic organization of music in Ghana (especially Asante music), Nketia found that the determination of the final tone of a melody was often indicated by the placement of the final tone of the penultimate phrase.[33] If this common practice in Asante music is typical of other West African modal usage, then one could postulate that the concept of functional relationships between tones exploited as a larger structural principle is present in African music. The same principle applied to harmonic aggregates can be regarded as compatible with West African practices.

This is not to say that the adoption of functional tonality in Afro-American music, with its regulatory principles, was not a significant departure from the West African tradition. What is suggested, however, is that functional tonality was not completely alien to West African practices. An investigation of the usage of functional harmony in Afro-American music remains to be undertaken, but a few of its common features suggest that its usage in this context is unique. First, the standardized harmonic patterns which evolved in Afro-American music (coincident with the development of the spiritual and later classic blues) tended to be strophic, short, and not dependent upon large-scale harmonic relationships for their continuation. Second, the usage of much melodic dissonance has been a characteristic feature of the music. This is because the harmonic rhythm tends to be slow, thus allowing for a large degree of melodic independence.

Another divergence of Afro-American music from the main West African tradition is represented by the lack of specificity of musical types for particular functions. This is a reflection of the difference in the social institutions of the two ethnically-related but geographically-separated peoples. Music in West African societies is usually associated with a specific social function. The specificity of musical type is shown by special music performed by specific groups on special occasions [34] (i.e., Fontomfrom, Kete, Adowa). This specificity of musical type is not present in Afro-American music. The closest thing to the complicated West African system of musical types is the use of general designations for various kinds of music—such as "church music" or "dance hall music," or as the old folks used to say "God's music" or the "devil's music." This general distinction between sacred and profane music has always been more of a verbal one than a musical one, since musical styles, instruments, specific songs, and even the musicians themselves have been commonly shared by both the church and the dance hall. Performers from the early blues players to such contemporaries as Ray Charles and Aretha Franklin have played both sides of this street, frequently at the same time. Indeed, a study of Afro-American musicians would reveal that typically they serve an apprenticeship in the church prior to their professional performances on the stage. This is not surprising if one recalls that the black church in the United States was the strongest black-controlled social institution in the community for decades and hence the major reservoir of cultural practices. Although there are other divergencies of Afro-American music from West African music, the two cited above, along with the language differences, are the most important.

Two books written independently which explore the complicated psycho-sociological relationship of the black minority in the United States to the white majority appear to add support to my hypothesis about the relationship of Afro-American to African music. The two books are Leroi Jones's *Blues People* and Charles Keil's *Urban Blues*. The uniqueness of Jones's work derives partially from the fact that he approaches the problem of the black man's attitude toward himself and the white majority through a study of changes in black music and partially from the fact that Jones writes from a consciously black perspective—that of a man on the inside looking out. He states in the book's introduction:

> I am saying that if the music of the Negro in America in all its permutations is subjected to a socio-anthropological as well as musical scrutiny, something about the essential nature of the Negro's existence in this country ought to be revealed, as well as something about the essential nature of the country.[35]

and later:

> The one peculiar referent to the drastic change in the Negro from slavery to citizenship is his music.[36]

In his survey of change in Afro-American music, he concludes that important changes in the music were derived from reinterpretations of an older, basically African tradition, partially in reaction to dilutions of this music by whites who imitated it. Speaking of the development of the so-called Bebop movement of the 1940s he says:

> What seems to me most important about the music of the forties was its reassertion of many "non-western" concepts of music.[37]

Charles Keil accepts Jones's thesis, applies it to recent developments in contemporary American society, and codifies it into what he calls the "appropriation-revitalization process." He writes:

> Negro music, since the days of the first recordings but especially during the last two decades has become progressively more "reactionary"—that is more African in its essentials—primarily because the various blues and jazz styles are, at least in their initial phases, symbolic referents of in-group solidarity for the black masses and the more intellectual segments of the black bourgeoisie. It is for this reason that each successive appropriation and commercialization of a Negro style by white America through its record industry and mass media has stimulated the Negro community and its musical spokesmen to generate a "new" music that it can call its own. In every instance the new music has been an amalgamation of increased musical knowledge (technically speaking) [sic] and a re-emphasis on the most basic Afro-American resources.[38]

The appropriation—revitalization theory tends to support my basic premise that African-American music is a unique branch of West-African music in that it suggests that there is a basic store of African ways of creating music buried deep in the collective psyche of black Americans which historical and sociological forces make necessary for them to tap in order to retain some semblance of a unique identity. The tenaciousness of this fundamental base of West African characteristics, in spite of enormous sociological and environmental changes, suggests that Herskovits's assertions about the durability of subliminal aspects of culture might have credibility.[39] Thus, although the history of black music in the United States shows movement from hollers, chants, and worksongs to spirituals, ragtime, blues, jazz, gospel, soul, and avant-garde black music—all of which differ from one another—the characteristic West African core, clearly demonstrable in each practice, is the essential element which unites and defines these musical expressions.

Although Jones and Keil both seemingly recognized this, neither formulated the relationship in this manner, partially because the exact nature of the relationship of African-American to African music was peripheral to their major concerns. Keil, as a matter of fact, betrays a lack of understanding of the nature of this "West African Core," the source of revitalization, when he states:

> In the light of recent and current events in American music it looks as if this process (appropriation-revitalization syndrome) may now be entering its final cycles. Once gospel music has been brought to white night clubs and tambourines have been passed out to patrons at the door, it would seem that there isn't much left to be appropriated. Jazz musicians—sensing that

> Afro-American resources have now been thoroughly explored,
> re-integrated, and appropriated—are turning with increased fre-
> quency to Africa itself and to other ethnic traditions as well
> for revitalizing force.[40]

This statement implies, first, that there is a major difference between African and Afro-American elements, and second, that these elements are quantitative. Keil apparently did not grasp that the relationship between African and Afro-American music consists not only of shared characteristics but, more importantly, of shared conceptual approaches to music making, and hence is not basically quantitative but qualitative. Therefore, the particular forms of black music which evolved in America are specific realizations of this shared conceptual framework which reflect the peculiarities of the American black experience. As such, the essence of their Africanness is not a static body of something which can be depleted but rather a conceptual approach, the manifestations of which are infinite. The common core of this Africanness consists of the way of doing something, not simply something that is done.

The work of anthropologists studying continuity and change in African culture supports this view of conceptual framework. Herskovits and Bascom, for example, frequently refer to the tenacity of various aspects of African culture—sometimes reinterpreted, but always essentially African. In speaking of the religion they say:

> Despite the intensity of Christian missionary effort and the
> thousand years of Moslem proselytizing which have marked
> the history of various parts of Africa, African religions continue
> to manifest vitality everywhere. This is to be seen in the wor-
> ship of African deities, the homage to the ancestors, and the
> recourse to divination, magic, and other rituals.[41]

They could have added to this list the rapid contemporary development of African spiritualist churches which exhibit an adaptation of Christianity to traditional African modes of worship.

If my view of the relationship of African and Afro-American music has validity, then fears of the imminent demise of black musical culture on both sides of the Atlantic seem unfounded. Contemporary developments in Afro-American music certainly seem to belie such claims, even in the face of the mass commercialization it is currently undergoing. The simultaneous development of this music in so many areas is astonishing. In addition, recent reinterpretations of this tradition have occurred on the mother continent, partially as a reflection of significant social changes and partially as a reaction to the impact that western music in general, and Afro-American music in particular, has had on the continent. Witness the development of highlife and more recently the so-called Afro beat of Fela Kunti. In each case the basic Africanness of the new development is undeniable.

The widespread popularity of James Brown throughout West Africa is a vivid testimony of the close relationship of Afro-American to African music. Brown's style is based upon an intensification of the most salient aspects of West African music, modified by the divergencies referred to earlier as characteristic of Afro-American music and the peculiarities of Brown's individual musical personality. The result is a style which is consonant with traditional West African approaches and yet different enough to benefit from the advantages of novelty. It is for the same reason that Louis Armstrong on his tours was immensely popular in Africa or that the young performer Fela Kunti, given proper exposure, would be popular in black America. To be sure, every Afro-American style could not find great popularity in Africa or, conversely, every African style in the United States. Some are too inextricably tied into a peculiar social experience to be understood by an audience unfamiliar with those circumstances. Billy Holiday speaks a musical dialect that people in Koforidua, Ghana, would have difficulty comprehending, and the essence of songs by the Ewe composer Akpalu would probably be lost in the streets of Harlem. Yet, in styles where the basic elements common to both cultures are emphasized the reaction is similar. For musical meaning, as studies have shown, is a complex phenomenon which exists on many levels, all of which have a cultural context. And in some instances the levels are so refined as to have relevance only to a select group. Yet, the communicability of certain aspects of music (especially those that are common to different groups although in distinct forms) appears to transcend these parochial distinctions.

In this paper I have limited myself to a general overview of the nature of the relationship of Afro-American to West African music. In order for my hypothesis to have meaning, it is necessary that there be more detailed study of music throughout the entire area. The basic point of this paper has been to develop a viable hypothesis which would give direction to the consideration of the relationship of African and Afro-American music. While the notion of a West African musical culture sphere united by a commonality of shared conceptual approaches to music making seems plausible, I recognize that because of the limited knowledge presently available in the field of comparative musicology such formulations must be primarily speculative. Nevertheless, it is hoped that such an overall view will bring together ideas from current independent studies to support or refute the hypothesis and hence serve to clarify a very complicated relationship.

University of California at Berkeley

NOTES

[1] There are many such studies, most of them written before 1950. One of the best known is George Pullen Jackson, *White and Negro Spirituals* (New York, 1943).

[2] Melville J. Herskovits, *The Myth of the Negro Past* (New York, 1941). Herskovits has been criticized for overstating the case by applying his concept of retention and

adaptation too freely to sociological patterns. Nevertheless, his position on religion and art has been incontrovertible.

³ See particularly Joseph Washington, *Black Religion* (Boston, 1964) and Paul Oliver, *Savannah Syncopators; African Retentions in the Blues* (New York, 1970).

⁴ See, for example, Hugh Tracey, "A Short Survey of Southern African Folk Music" in African Music Society Newsletter 1, no. 6 (1953).

⁵ J. H. Kwabena Nketia, *Unity and Diversity in African Music: A Problem of Synthesis* (Accra, 1962), p. 11.

⁶ Herskovits, "A Preliminary Consideration of Culture Areas of Africa" in *American Anthropologist* 26 (1924), pp. 50-63; Joseph Greenberg, *African Linguistic Classification* (New Haven, 1955).

⁷ Alan P. Merriam, "African Music" in *Continuity and Change in African Cultures*, edited by William Bascom and Melville Herskovits (Chicago, 1958), pp. 49-86.

⁸ Richard Waterman, "African Influence on the Music of the Americas" in *Acculturation in the Americas*, ed. by Sol Tax (Chicago, 1952), p. 212.

⁹ Merriam, "African Music," p. 80.

¹⁰ Waterman, "African Influence," p. 212.

¹¹ Merriam, "African Music," p. 80.

¹² A. M. Jones, *Studies in African Music* (London, 1959).

¹³ Waterman, "African Influences," pp. 139.40.

¹⁴ Alan Merriam, Whinery and Fred, "Songs of a Rada Community in Trinidad" in *Anthropos* 51 (1956), pp. 157-74.

¹⁵ Harold Courlander, *Negro Folk Music: U. S. A.* (New York, 1963).

¹⁶ Jones, "Indonesia and Africa" in *African Music* 6 (1960), pp. 36-47.

¹⁷ *Ibid.*, p. 46.

¹⁸ M. D. W. Jeffreys, "Negro Influence on Indonesia" in *African Music* 7 (1961), pp. 10-16.

¹⁹ The historical derivation of the majority of African-descendent peoples from West Africa is so well known it need not be belabored here.

²⁰ Herskovits, *Myth*, pp. 146-47.

²¹ Winthrop Sargeant, *Jazz: Hot and Hybrid* (New York, 1938).

²² Gunther Schuller, *Early Jazz* (New York, 1968).

²³ Merriam, "African Music," p. 61.

²⁴ Jones, *Studies*, p. 53.

²⁵ Merriam, "African Music," pp. 57-65.

²⁶ Jones, "African Rhythm" in *Africa* 24 (1954), pp. 26-27.

²⁷ Don Knowlton, "The Anatomy of Jazz" in *Harper's Magazine* 152 (1926), pp. 578-85.

²⁸ Aaron Copland, "Jazz Structure and Influence on Modern Music" in *Modern Music* 4 (1927), pp. 9-14.

²⁹ Sargeant, *Jazz*, pp. 63-63.

³⁰ Eileen Southern, *The Music of Black Americans* (New York, 1971).

³¹ Nketia, *Unity and Diversity*, p. 11.

³² Herskovits, *Myth*, p. 85.

³³ Nketia, *African Music in Ghana* (Evanston, 1963), p. 20.

³⁴ *Ibid.*, p. 107.

³⁵ Leroi Jones, *Blues People* (New York, 1965), p. x.

³⁶ *Ibid.*

³⁷ *Ibid.*, p. 194.

³⁸ Charles Keil, *Urban Blues* (Chicago, 1966), p. 46.

³⁹ Herskovits, "Patterns of Negro Music" in *Transactions* 34 (1941), p. 19.

⁴⁰ Keil, *Urban Blues*, p. 46.

⁴¹ Herskovits, *Continuity and Change*, p. 4.

Part III
Offshoots

[15]

Metaphors of Power, Metaphors of Truth: The Politics of Music Professionalism in Bulgarian Folk Orchestras

DONNA A. BUCHANAN   NEW YORK UNIVERSITY

> For every belief, practice, ideal, or institution that is condemned as backward, one, often the same one and by the same people, is celebrated as the very essence of contemporaneity; for every one attacked as alien, one, again often the same one, is hailed as a sacred expression of the national soul (Geertz 1973:319).

The evolution of neotraditional musical styles in Bulgaria from the *Vŭzrazhdane* (the late nineteenth-century national renaissance) to the present illustrates the complex interface of cultural heritage, aesthetics, political ideology, nationalism, and socio-economic change embodied in the history of music professionalism in twentieth-century culture.[1] As in many other parts of the world, the professionalization of Bulgaria's diverse musical traditions during this period manifests an aspiration toward the West European standards and structures of art music performance practice. In socialist Bulgaria, this aspiration was accompanied by a concomitant institutionalization of musical styles through the establishment of a hegemonic cultural administrative network comprising political organizations, such as the Committee for Culture of the Bulgarian Communist Party, and academic bodies like the Institutes for Musicology and Folklore of the Bulgarian Academy of Sciences. These organizations set the national standards whereby cultural forms were judged as aesthetically and socially valuable for Bulgarian society, frequently requiring that previous musical practices— those which are often perceived by culture members and outsiders alike as "traditional"—be reshaped as official, modern, symbolic, neotraditional expressions of the Bulgarian socialist state.

Professional and amateur state-sponsored folk song and dance ensembles developed and maintained by Bulgaria's cultural administration

382   Ethnomusicology, Fall 1995

during the socialist period (1944–1989) demonstrate the melding of West European socio-aesthetic ideals with aspects of rural Bulgarian musical life. When I arrived in Sofia in 1988 to begin the bulk of my dissertation research, my goal was to investigate Bulgarian folk orchestras, which may be defined as musical ensembles of traditional Bulgarian instruments modeled on the Western classical philharmonic, as symbolic of the socialist construction of Bulgarian national identity between 1944 and 1990. My hypothesis was that the state's creation of the professional folk orchestras, choirs, and dance troupes comprising folk ensembles exemplified the anthropological notion of cultural performance, in which a culture plays out aspects of its world view through vibrant symbolic displays such as parades or festivals on the national and international stage.

While this supposition proved valid as a cursory model of Bulgarian cultural development, it did not account for the dynamic, entangled collection of stylistic nuances, musical concepts, attitudes, and experiences that I encountered in conjunction with the daily implementation of musical practices among musicians at the State Ensemble for Folk Songs and Dances (SEFSD)-Filip Kutev, the Ensemble for Folk Songs of the Bulgarian Radio (hereafter EFSBR), and similar groups.[2] What I discovered was a much more complex situation that located folk orchestras within a web of symbolic discourses which (1) elucidated the distribution of political power at every level of Bulgarian society, (2) highlighted the contradiction between Bulgarian premier Todor Zhivkov's ideological typification of his country as a monoethnic nation-state and the reality of its multi-ethnic composition, (3) revealed the superimposition of pre- and post-1944 world views shaping Bulgarian culture, and (4) linked microcosmic questions of musical style and aesthetics to macrocosmic formulations of Bulgarian national identity in an international context.

The forced retirement of Todor Zhivkov on 10 November 1989 added an unexpected dimension to my research. His fall from power prompted a heated struggle for democracy and political pluralism shadowed by the Romanian civil war, a horrifying event which many of my friends and colleagues in Sofia feared would also befall Bulgaria. The intensive jockeying for power among emergent political factions, especially between the Union of Democratic Forces, the Bulgarian Socialist Party (formerly the Bulgarian Communist Party), and the Turkish minority's Movement for Rights and Freedoms Party, accompanied a sharp rise in tensions between Bulgarians and the country's ethnic minority populations, a resurgence in public religious activity, and widespread demonstrations of popular solidarity and dissent in response to each of these issues (cf. Silverman 1989; Karpat 1990; Poulton 1991; and Tomova and Bogoev 1992 on the Bulgarian government's discriminatory policies toward minorities). The people's demand for accurate information about the Bulgarian government and its actions during the course of the political transition revealed the corrupt and decrepit nature of the state administration and disclosed the carefully woven official vision of Bulgarian life as, in the words of Václav Havel, "a world of appearances trying to pass for reality" (1991b:135; see Fuhrman 1989 on corruption in the Bulgarian government).

Truth, Identity, and Hegemony

Havel's writings, like those of Michel Foucault, address the important question of how truth, as a fluid and relativistic concept, is culturally structured and socially validated. Both envision truth as a network of discourses emerging from the dissemination of knowledge and implementation of socio-political power. This sense of a "régime" or "general politics" of truth constitutes those culture-specific views of the world, redundantly legitimized and justified through socio-cultural structures, symbols, and other expressive forms, which enable us to discriminate right from wrong, good from bad, and the real from the illusory (Foucault 1980:93, 131–32). As such, truth is deeply connected to cultural ideology and interactively experienced as one's sense of morality and identity within the confines of a particular group. During Bulgaria's socialist period, monolithic state projections of social reality often conflicted sharply with the fragmented, labyrinthine machinations of "lived socialism" (Creed 1992:3). In 1989, as the gap between appearances and reality in Bulgarian society widened, it was precisely the inability of the socialist system to establish cultural truth on both ideological and experiential levels that led to its breakdown.

This article examines how the post-1944 professionalization of pre-1944 Bulgarian musical culture incorporated indigenous music production into the dominant order of socialist reality. However, the transformation of music in this manner cannot be viewed merely as forced political domination by the socialist regime. Rather, like Bulgarian political hegemony itself, this transformation results from a dialectical and dynamic process that implicates the lives of individuals within "a realized complex of experiences, relationships, and activities, with specific and changing pressures and limits" (Williams 1977:112). The music of Bulgarian folk orchestras sonically embodies the life experience of its performers; its shape and content are defined through the interaction of individual musicians with the "complex interlocking of political, social, and cultural forces" (ibid.:108, 110) that comprise hegemony, and which continually shift in accordance with particular political and economic realities at specific historical junctures (Hall 1979:333; Williams 1977:115.)

The conceptualization of music, identity, and hegemony proposed above stems from the works of Antonio Gramsci and his followers, especially Stuart Hall and Raymond Williams. Gramsci maintains that for a socio-

384   Ethnomusicology, Fall 1995

politically dominant group to sustain power, it must forge alliances that establish comprehensive social authority by winning the consent of subordinate groups, thus making this authority seem a natural and legitimate construction of social reality—a reality taken for granted by culture members as the truth of common sense (Hebdige 1979:15–16 after Hall 1979:332; Hall 1986:14). The consensual aspect of Gramscian hegemony implies an active reciprocity between dominant and subordinate, state and individual, which constantly reshapes the nature of power relations. Here specific actors, in this case musicians, continually negotiate between their own, internalized senses of self—their individual and localized world views—and the multilayered interpretations of reality constructed by their government. Viewing hegemony in this manner focuses upon the human contribution to state and identity construction, on hegemony as multifariously encountered and lived experience, rather than on hegemony as a monolithic, faceless force. As the writings of Havel demonstrate, the distinction between the two poles of this discourse—between the normative reality diversely experienced by individuals and the philosophical reality presented through political ideology— is especially strident in a socialist society of the Soviet model, where what he calls a "peculiar dialectical dance of truth and lies" characterizes many aspects of life (1991a:5). To succeed in such societies people are forced to live out a schizophrenic existence that often prostitutes the essence of their morality, individuality, and identity (1991b:143–45). For Bulgarian musicians under the socialist regime, this meant sometimes performing certain types of music because it was politically or economically expedient, even though they disliked or questioned the worth of this music because of its association with the government's control of musical expression, or sadly, because of its connection with ethnic groups denigrated within Bulgarian society.

Whether we speak of localized senses of identity, national identity, social affiliations, ethnicity, or gender, a major theoretical reorientation, traceable to the Gramscian conception of the human personality as "strangely composite" (Forgacs 1988:326; Turino 1990:401), is evident in recent ethnomusicological and anthropological literature.[3] That both human identity and the forces resulting from the alliances creating hegemony at any given moment are heterogeneous, fluid, and dynamic, and that these two social phenomena are often variously shaped and experienced in a dialectical relationship to each other is one of the seminal contributions of Gramscian scholarship to our understanding of how individuals, power, and expressive culture intersect in the construction of social identity at any level. Gramsci acknowledges that consciousness and identity are multidimensional, and that this "plurality" results from "the relationship between 'the self' and the ideological discourses which compose the cultural terrain of a society" (Hall 1986:22).

I found the dialectical tension between the individual and the "terrain" of Bulgarian society captured in metaphors musicians used to describe the music they performed. These expressions revealed the role of music professionalism in establishing the socialist interpretation of reality as the only official cultural truth, and alluded to the international influences framing the configuration of power relations within Bulgaria's borders. As my research progressed, it became clear that the nature of Bulgarian political hegemony must be viewed not just within the context of the Bulgarian nation-state, but within the international hierarchy of economic and political power. The orientation of the Bulgarian Communist Party's political agenda at the national level was predicated upon the government's image of Bulgaria's position within a global environment structured by the country's membership in the Warsaw Pact and role as a Soviet political satellite, its rejection of Ottoman cultural and historical influences, and more recently, its aspiration to membership in the European economic community. Each of these parameters impacted the shape and conceptualization of musical styles performed by folk orchestra members, both within and outside the folk ensemble network, illustrating the extent to which political ideology is often "lived" through poetic or symbolic discourse (cf. Hall 1985:103–4, 111; Hebdige 1979:13–14; Geertz 1973; and Herzfeld 1985:100).

In considering the significance of specific styles of expressive culture within a transnational forum I am following a precedent set by many recent anthropological (Rosaldo 1989; Appadurai 1991) and ethnomusicological studies (Keil 1985; Meintjes 1990; Feld 1992; Noll 1991; and Slobin 1992). The methodological focus of these studies is suggestively intertwined with the current attention devoted to reflexivity and to textual representation and authority in ethnomusicological (Gourlay 1978, 1982; Keil 1982; Feld 1987; Turino 1990; Becker 1991) and anthropological ethnography (Clifford and Marcus 1986; Wolf 1992; Silverman Forthcoming). Both types of investigations adopt a dialogical—and even multilogical—approach that is sensitive to the simultaneous and myriad truths, voices, perspectives, and poetics that characterize any aspect of socio-cultural life. Such studies recognize process— temporality and the multitude of shifting variations it engenders—as a critical factor in ethnographic analysis (Rosaldo 1989:103, 105). Further, they make us aware that life-time does not operate simply as a linear construct; rather, it is experienced holographically. This is leading us to view culture as a multiplicity of life processes, multifigured and multivocal, rather than as an object conducive to formal or structural analysis (cf. Clifford 1986:12).

Economics of Village Musical Life

In traditional Bulgarian musical culture the West European-derived notion of music professionalism, which largely signifies the performance of

386   *Ethnomusicology, Fall 1995*

music for economic gain in the context of a career, did not emerge until the late nineteenth century and even at that time was more frequently associated with the performance of symphonic style *akademichna* [academic] music by Czech- and Russian-directed school choirs, community chorales, and military or wind bands than with the performance of Bulgarian *narodna muzika* [indigenous or folk music]. According to Bulgarian musicologists such as Venelin Krŭstev (1978:175), such groups were in fact responsible for introducing the repertoire of West European classical music and its attendant performance practice, aesthetics and values into Bulgarian society. By contrast, indigenous instrumental and vocal music remained, with some exceptions, mutually exclusive and gender-specific solo traditions performed in conjunction with calendrical customs, life cycle events, or as entertainment by male instrumentalists and female singers who earned their living through non-musical means.[4] Payment of village instrumentalists was minimal, spontaneous, and often absent altogether. Women rarely received payment for their singing, and if this occurred, such remuneration took place secretly (Iordanova 1987:10).

To pursue a career as a performer of narodna muzika was in fact regarded negatively in pre–twentieth-century Bulgarian culture (Buchanan 1991:314–18). Within the Bulgarian village this type of lifestyle symbolized moral and financial impoverishment and was associated directly with Gypsy, Turkish, or Vlach musicians hired to perform narodna muzika at community weddings and festivals. Although Bulgarian villagers appreciated the musical talents of these performers—and hired them because of this—the fact that the musicians belonged to ethnic groups living on the fringes of Bulgarian society, and indeed, at least in regard to ethnic Turks, often were located physically along Bulgaria's borders (see Poulton 1991:106) stigmatized the pursuit of music as a profession, associating it with foreign ways. This was "*tsiganska rabota*" [Gypsy work, the Gypsy way]—a phrase used even today to describe a task or event accomplished improperly or with insufficient effort—despite the fact that a villager's ability to employ several musicians for a wedding celebration in some cases signified status within the community.

The contradiction between the discriminatory perception of minority musicians as lazy, shiftless and irresponsible, and the value attributed to their music-making is demonstrated by a variety of expressions like "a violinist cannot feed a household" or its more telling variant, "a violinist cannot feed a household, but gloomy is the house that lacks one" (Buchanan 1991:334). Such idioms, found throughout the country in everyday discourse, illustrate that from the standpoint of a traditional Bulgarian villager, the music profession was no way to support a family, and that only a foreigner anxious to escape the daily drudgery of agricultural work would try such a thing.

The association of the violin with non-Bulgarian professional musicians in the above metaphor is both socially and historically important, as it was the *lautari* (professional Vlach or Banat Gypsy musicians living in northern Bulgaria), *chalgi* (Gypsy wedding musicians), and *svirdzhi* (a Turkish-derived term referring to Gypsy wedding musicians) who introduced this instrument to Bulgarian culture, utilizing it in the performance of narodna muzika. The affiliation of this instrument with foreign professional musical culture is thus doubly significant, symbolizing both the performance practice of Bulgarian minority musicians, and the symphonic tradition of Western Europe as personified in the presence of Czech and Russian music directors during the late nineteenth century.

The Road to Professionalism

> There is . . . no simple progression from "traditional" to "modern," but a twisting, spasmodic, unmethodical movement which turns as often toward repossessing the emotions of the past as disowning them (Geertz 1973:319).

The concept of European musical professionalism therefore entered Bulgarian society comparatively late and contrasted sharply with traditional social codes. However, the establishment of radio in Bulgaria during the early twentieth century and the subsequent development of musical "ensembles for songs and dances" provided social legitimacy and govern-ment sanction for the pursuit of professional music careers. The continued popularity of school choirs and of wind bands connected with the country's fifty military garrisons, and the concomitant passion for sentimental *gradski pesni* (urban songs, often of Turkish derivation and especially prominent in Pirin-Macedonia, marked by triadic harmony, melody lines in parallel thirds, and an accompaniment of Western or mixed Western and indigenous instruments) all helped spread the aesthetic of classical music during the early twentieth century. In these contexts a *svirach*, or nonprofessional player of a traditional instrument, could become a *muzikant*, or professional musician in the symphonic sense.

The idea of combining traditional Bulgarian instruments together in groups did not exist before the late 1800s. Village instrumentalists instead performed *horos* alone on the village square or at local fairs. This was demanding work, because instrumentalists found it difficult to project the volume of their instruments in the open air and any mistakes were clearly audible. In fact, some ensemble musicians with whom I worked, such as my *kaval* [rim-blown wooden flute] teacher, Stoyan Velichkov, recounted that they believed village instrumentalists began playing together to ease the strain brought on by the lengthy periods of solo playing required at village events, and to provide some aural contrast (cf. Buchanan 1991:156). With

388   Ethnomusicology, Fall 1995

time, village performers on *gaida* [bagpipe], *tŭpan* [frame drum], *gŭdulka*
[three-stringed short-necked bowed lute], *kaval*, and *tambura* [long-necked
strummed lute] began to play together in groups of two to five, but in the
beginning, they did not necessarily play the same song or in the same key
(Rice 1994:151; see Atanasov 1976; Buchanan 1991; and Kachulev 1978 for
more complete descriptions of Bulgarian instruments). Rarely were two
instruments of the same type used together. Eventually instrumentalists
devised a structure in which they performed a melody in unison or as a series
of successive solos, each musician improvising the melody in turn.

After the establishment of radio in Bulgaria in 1929, small instrumental
ensembles for the performance of narodna muzika, such as the Bistrishka
Chetvorka [The Bistritsa Quartet], founded in 1936, the Trakiiska Troika
[Thracian Trio], established around 1935, the Ugŭrchinska Grupa (1939–
1946), and the Strandzhanska Grupa (1956) emerged to meet the demands
of radio programming. These groups were recruited by Radio Sofia's chief
editors to perform traditional, unarranged melodies in unison settings, often
with an added drone or rudimentary bass line, during live radio broadcasts.
The groups' repertoires were defined according to the country's major
ethnographic regions; the Trakiiska Troika, for example, specialized in the
music of Thrace, while the Bistrishka Chetvorka performed music from the
Shop region that encompasses Sofia and the town of Bistritsa, for which the
group was named. All songs and melodies stemmed from the repertoires of
individual group members, who had learned these pieces from other
musicians in the course of oral tradition. The new instrumental groups grew
quickly in popularity and communities soon hired them to entertain at
weddings, christenings, and other social events. Such groups became the
prototype for the larger folk orchestras that developed in conjunction with
the creation of professional folk ensembles in the 1950s. The members of the
Ugŭrchinska Grupa, for example, later became the core around which the
EFSBR's folk orchestra was established.

In 1951 Filip Kutev, inspired by the Soviet folk ensemble "Pyatnitski,"
created the first professional, state-supported Bulgarian folk ensemble.
Eventually the leading exponent in a larger system of fourteen such
organizations established in urban centers throughout Bulgaria, Kutev's
ensemble performed arrangements of traditional music and song characterized by harmonies, contrapuntal techniques, and formal structures associated with Western classical music on many of the world's concert stages. The
goal of such ensembles was to popularize the musical traditions of Bulgaria's
six primary ethnographic regions (the Shop area, the Rhodopes, Thrace,
Pirin-Macedonia, Northern Bulgaria, and Dobrudzha) in a new, sophisticated theatrical venue. Cultural policy directors considered the formalized
concert performance context and symphonic style of the arrangements

representative of and appropriate for the new socialist Bulgarian nation, because the administration upheld Western classical music as a cultural ideal of the highest value, and strove to carve a niche for Bulgaria within the European fine arts world by devising a uniquely Bulgarian symphonic practice manifested in the performances of folk orchestras and choirs. The resulting sound was both distinctively Bulgarian and one to which foreigners, including tourists, could relate.

Each folk ensemble featured a women's choir, a dance troupe comprised of equal numbers of male and female dancers, and a predominantly male orchestra. The professional folk orchestras, which featured twelve to twenty-five musicians, expanded the prior instrumental group of diverse instruments into a neotraditional philharmonia of orchestral families. Not only were the five principal instruments found in traditional Bulgarian culture (kaval, gŭdulka, tambura, gaida, and tŭpan) represented by multi-part orchestral sections, but new instruments like the viola, cello, and bass gŭdulka, and piccolo kaval (*kavalche*) were commissioned by Kutev from Ivan Katsarov, a master instrument craftsman, who manufactured them on the basis of symphonic models to extend the range of the instrumental spectrum. For a time, some of the new instruments were equipped with fingerboards derived from the western violin. The forms and sizes of all of the instruments were reshaped and standardized. Tunings, also, were modified and regularized.

The construction of these new instruments was accomplished to create orchestral consorts capable of performing melodies in four-part harmony. However, once built, the fledgling ensembles also had to train instrumentalists to play them. This posed a problem, as most of the new folk orchestras lacked personnel experienced in performing on the Western instruments from which the new instruments were designed. Folk orchestras therefore opted to audition instrumentalists trained at the State Conservatory on classical viola, violoncello, and double bass. Sometimes the performer hired was female, a break with tradition justified by the fact that gender specificity was not an issue for instrumental art music performance.

The alterations made to musical instruments facilitated the composition and collective performance of symphonically-styled arrangements of traditional melodies and songs called *obrabotki* (singular, *obrabotka*), for which the ability to read Western musical notation became requisite. In fact, musical literacy emerged as one of the most important components of a musician's professional identity, a factor which set apart a muzikant, *orkestrant,* or *instrumentalist*—terms clearly derived from the discourse of Western classical music that folk orchestra members used to refer to themselves—from a svirach. As the network of *narodni ansambli* [folk ensembles] grew, the Bulgarian government developed an elaborate system

390 Ethnomusicology, Fall 1995

of cultural administration to oversee the training, repertoire, and employment of musicians seeking careers in the performance of neotraditional orchestral music. Future folk orchestra personnel were trained at secondary schools located in Shiroka Lŭka and Kotel, and following this, at the *Vissh Muzikalno Pedagogicheski Institut* [Higher Musical Pedagogical Institute, hereafter VMPI] in Plovdiv, all establishments whose curricula emphasized traditional instrumental music, singing, dance, and ethnography from the late nineteenth century to the present. The goal of these schools was to generate enough artists to fill the employment vacancies within the folk ensemble network.

Within the schools students learned how to perform instrumental narodna muzika according to an approach christened by Bulgarian music educators as the *sluhovo-notno-podrazhatelen-metod*, or aural notational mimetic method, which emphasized both listening skills and notereading ability. Many of the teachers at these schools were older folk orchestra instrumentalists who had themselves learned to read musical notation only after becoming professionally employed by an orchestra. Therefore, the very conceptualization of performance practice by an orkestrant—regardless of his age and training—constantly manifested a tension between these two parameters of musical ability. Students gained specific knowledge of the repertoires and styles of their native regions, especially in terms of ornamentation, within a broader understanding of the country's other musical idioms. They learned the essence of musical style in a modified form of oral tradition, by listening extensively to the performances of older musicians in a variety of contexts—including recordings, radio broadcasts, concerts, lessons, and daily interaction—absorbing idiomatic features of regional performance practice, and making them a fundamental source of their own expressive vocabularies. Students developed virtuosic instrumental techniques and strong notereading skills through the study of conservatory-inspired scalar and technical etudes, through chamber compositions resembling American high school solo and ensemble contest pieces, and by mandatory participation in school folk orchestras and chamber groups, which both familiarized students with the written repertoires of the professional folk orchestras, and heightened their sense of ensemble musicianship.

The institutionalization of traditional music produced a contemporary national musical style grounded in centuries of custom but aspiring to the values promoted by Western classical music, resulting in a confrontation between older musical values and Western ideals of music professionalism. Central to this confrontation were the changes in Bulgarian musical practice wrought by musical notation. The notation of traditional instrumental music in arrangements for folk orchestra introduced the concepts of fixed and authored composition to traditional Bulgarian musicians. It also accompanied the implementation of the value-laden hierarchy of power associated with the Western symphony, personified in the figures of the orchestral maestro, assistant conductor, and concert master, into traditional music-making. These factors highlighted the non-traditional emphasis on precision playing that the creation of the folk orchestra engendered, and as trademarks of West European music professionalism, were iconic of the socialist philosophy for cultural progress. Indeed, the term obrabotka used to describe folk orchestra arrangements derives from the verb *obrabotvam,* meaning to rework or cultivate in a manner that improves the original.

The creation of compositions for folk orchestras was dominated not by musicians schooled in Bulgaria's musical instruments, performance practice, ethnography and folklore, but by members of the Bulgarian Composers Union, primarily conservatory-trained composers, musicologists, and administrators educated in Western classical music and music theory. While folk orchestra musicians trained at special folk music schools, composers certified to create the professional repertoires of these musicians were educated at the State Conservatory. Instrumentalists with compositional talent were almost never allowed to publish their own obrabotki, to record them, or to have them performed publicly. On the rare occasions when this occurred, the instrumentalists were required to submit their compositions for approval before a commission of Union members who advocated common practice harmonies and symphonic forms that ignored the improvisatory and frequently modal implications of most Bulgarian melodies.

Several folk orchestra members at the Ensemble of the Bulgarian Radio who wished to try their hand at composing recounted, for example, how humiliated and frustrated they felt at being required to furnish the Radio Commission with a sketch of the melody line that they wished to arrange together with a reduced harmonic analysis (using Roman numerals) of the potential obrabotka, only to have the commission return their efforts covered with corrections in red ink—as if their creative work were a collegiate music theory assignment. Once the commission approved the harmonization, the musician was permitted to orchestrate the piece. Upon completion, the commission again evaluated the obrabotka according to the part-writing rules of the Western common practice period before allowing it to be performed or recorded (Buchanan 1991:404–13).

The Radio Commission consisted of a production and programming committee whose members were selected from the department of Narodna Muzika at Bulgarian Radio (ibid.:407). Instrumentalists were quite close-mouthed about the specific constituency and activities of the Radio Commission, which they considered an ugly and unpleasant aspect of creative musical life. Often they referred to this administrative board simply

392   Ethnomusicology, Fall 1995

as "the commission." Musicians frequently became physically agitated and emotionally upset when I asked about the commission's role in the production of obrabotki, and much of the information I received was given on conditions of anonymity and in a hushed tone of voice. Commission members clearly carried great political clout that could affect musicians' careers adversely.

The aspiring composer's creative instincts were constrained further by the fact that the commission would only consider arrangements of melodies from his native ethnographic region, because cultural administrators believed that a musician could only portray this style accurately.[5] As one musician pointed out, this policy contradicted the fact that most instrumentalists who wished to compose today had been trained in the network of state folk music schools—two of which were located in the Thracian ethnographic region and all of which emphasized the Thracian musical style as predominant (cf. Buchanan 1991:221–28; Silverman 1983:59). Having spent his formative years in Thrace, the same musician explained that it was ridiculous that the cultural administration now confined him to arranging or publicly performing (as a soloist) only melodies from northern Bulgaria, simply because he was born there. In addition, all professional folk orchestra instrumentalists were trained and in fact required to be able to perform all of the country's regional styles, for cultural administrators charged state folk ensembles with popularizing the musical traditions of the entire country. While instrumentalists freely admitted to me that ensemble repertoires accentuated the Thracian style, they were also proud of their ability to accurately portray the country's other musical idioms, and could articulate, both musically and verbally, the differences between them. Many musicians angrily blamed cultural administrators and conservatory-trained arrangers of obrabotki directly for the homogenization of the country's musical diversity manifested by folk ensemble repertoire, which they believed stemmed from the composers' lack of attention to regional musical characteristics, and superimposition of art music structures on narodna muzika.

In order to provide a steady supply of new obrabotki for radio airplay and releases produced by the state recording firm Balkanton, it was common for members of the folk orchestra at Bulgarian Radio to supply Union-certified composers with traditional melodies for use in ensemble arrangements. Composers reworked the horos as instrumental solos with folk orchestra accompaniment that featured the contributing instrumentalist. Indeed, this was the only way that these musicians could solo with their orchestra, and again, they could only supply and perform melodies from the ethnographic area of their birth. Once the arrangements were approved by the Composer's Union and Radio management, the folk orchestra of the EFSBR recorded them for radio broadcasts. This process was fraught with difficulties; musicians sometimes had to bribe composers to persuade them to use their horos. Many also complained about the length of time (sometimes years) it took for a composer to produce such obrabotki.

The power invested in the Union of Composers by the Bulgarian government was such that it was economically advantageous for the Union's members to discourage and even forbid musicians versed in tradition from producing folk orchestra obrabotki. During 1988 and 1989, for a single recorded obrabotka three minutes in length, the arranger received 200–400 *leva* (depending on the renown of the composer and the strength of his social and political connections) and official credit as the author of the composition, while the instrumentalist who supplied the melody and recorded the solo part of the arrangement received eighteen leva. Accompanying instrumentalists received as little as six leva.[6] Neither soloists nor orchestra members earned much money in terms of royalties for these recordings. In fact, in 1988 the amount was so small that in protest the musicians refused to collect the royalties at all.

The rules and regulations developed by the Union of Composers made it nearly impossible for the talented graduates of VMPI to reap the creative and economic rewards associated with writing obrabotki. These musicians, with their profound knowledge of ethnography and village tradition, posed a tremendous artistic and financial threat to Union members. Union commissions therefore returned many obrabotki to orkestranti with claims that the music was, in the experience of one instrumentalist, "unworkable" because "the harmony was not correct." In this way the Union of Composers kept a stranglehold on the composition of folk ensemble repertoire, functioning like a mafia whose primary concerns were money, prestige, and power (Buchanan 1991:410).

Truth and Power in Metaphors of Musical Experience

Václav Havel, Michel Foucault, and Pierre Bourdieu assert that the maintenance of hegemony depends upon the continual reproduction of dominant interpretations of social reality as cultural truth. Intellectuals are the guardians of the production of cultural truth; the academy and university are important sites in which power and truth intersect (cf. Foucault 1990:127, 131–32; Bourdieu 1990:146). The production of truth is the basis of power (Foucault 1980:93), or as Havel succinctly declares, "the center of power is identical with the center of truth" (1991b:130). In this regard, organizations representing the cultural bureaucracy of the Bulgarian central government, such as the State Conservatory, the Union of Composers, and the Institutes of Folklore and Musicology, were the hubs of truth, power, and authority within the domain of professional folk ensembles during the socialist period.

394   Ethnomusicology, Fall 1995

The tension that emerged between muzikanti and composers because of the government's institutionalization of cultural truth via the power of cultural policy—between the instrumentalists' knowledge of pre-socialist tradition and the European ideals of music professionalism espoused by the Union of Composers—was encoded by musicians in two metaphors of musical experience that they used to discuss the relative worth of a folk orchestra composition: "playing from the heart" and playing "*notno*," or in a style bound to the musical notation of an obrabotka.

To understand the implications of these metaphors and the processual nature of their significance it is important to consider briefly the stylistic evolution of obrabotki during the fifty-year history of Bulgarian folk orchestras. As stated earlier, the performance of traditional music by small instrumental trios and quartets at Bulgarian Radio during the first part of the twentieth century was largely improvisatory and modeled closely on village custom. The music was neither arranged nor performed from notation, and integral aspects of Western symphonic compositions, like the use of harmony, sequences, counterpoint, and countermelody, were absent entirely. Tuning was largely untempered. The musicians performed melodies learned in their own villages in unison or as a series of improvisatory individual solos underneath which the other instrumentalists provided a tonic drone. The musicians did not execute these melodies with symphonic precision; each instrumentalist wove ornamentation into the melodic line as he felt it, resulting in a multitude of variations on the underlying melodic contour.

As time went on, it became standard practice to accompany each melody with rudimentary bass lines and harmonic progressions in the form of strummed tambura chords. In addition, the form of the horos performed by these small groups became more rigidly structured to facilitate live broadcasts. While a horo performed for a village dance could continue for an extended period, Radio Sofia limited the length of each selection to about three minutes. The performers accommodated Radio policy by devising a cohesive structure called the *kolyano* form through which they could present the essence of a horo in a narrow time frame.

A kolyano is a musical phrase or statement that comprises one section of a horo. Most are repeated, giving every kolyano a binary structure. Musicians say that they build horos "*kolyano sled kolyano*" [kolyano after kolyano]. Each kolyano represents an organic development of the previous musical idea. This development is accomplished often through motivic manipulation. While village musicians always "thought" horos in *kolyana*, the phrase lengths they employed were generally uneven. Because in village contexts musicians performed primarily as soloists, they were able to extemporize freely upon a melodic motive for as long as they liked. Their ability to improvise upon kolyana in fact helped them to play for long periods of time. With the advent of ensemble radio performance, the kolyano structure became symmetrical. The use of even phrase lengths helped groups determine approximately how many kolyana were required to fill a particular time slot. Each instrumentalist still improvised upon the motives of previous kolyana when taking a solo, but he now improvised this material within phrases of equal length. This practice helped indicate to the other members of the group when the solo would end, especially as the duration of a solo could be determined prior to performance. Horos now possessed definitive introductions and conclusions, and manifested a "good, natural development" throughout (Buchanan 1991:365–74; Stoyan Velichkov: interview, 1988).

The orchestral style described above also characterizes the earliest obrabotki for professional folk orchestras. As early recordings of the Kutev Ensemble or Sider Voyvoda Ensemble illustrate (*Koutev Bulgarian National Ensemble* Monitor MFS 402 and *Bulgarian Songs & Dances: The Sider Voyvoda Ensemble* MFS 712), these arrangements featured unison melodies performed predominantly by the *gaidi, kavali,* and *gŭdulki,* bass lines typified by drone, stepwise motion, or leaps of fourths and fifths, and limited supporting harmony. Individual sections of the orchestra often alternated kolyana in a manner not unlike earlier horo performance. The expanded instrumental format and added harmonies rarely interfered with the linear development and exposition of the original horo melody; their goal was rather to enhance it. The ensemble still did not place great emphasis on precision playing, and tuning, by western symphonic standards, remained tenuous. The orchestral timbre was reedy, buzzy, and thick, a result of the preponderance of overtones created by the presence of untempered intervals.

Despite the standardization of narodna muzika performance practice that the creation of folk ensembles eventually engendered, during the initial period of folk orchestra development ensemble directors depended upon the musicians themselves for repertoire and strove to maintain an atmosphere of collective composition that reflected the philosophy of working together to produce a new socialist society. All of the musicians had some say in the shape of the final product. For example, whenever the instrumentalists encountered a problematic section in one of his obrabotki, Filip Kutev would ask each orkestrant how it should be played. Once a consensus was reached among the musicians as to the most idiomatic solution, Kutev instructed the orchestra to "throw away the notes" and play the melody as they felt it (Buchanan 1991:245).

Between 1988 and 1990 members of the Kutev Ensemble's folk orchestra regaled me with anecdotes like this one time and again to illustrate Kutev's understanding and love of Bulgarian custom, which respected the individual

396   Ethnomusicology, Fall 1995

music maker as a knowledgeable contributor to tradition. Such stories became metaphors of empowerment for current orkestranti—references to a time when instrumentalists, individually and collectively, could help determine the style of their ensemble's repertoire.

The impact of folk ensemble performances on the Bulgarian public was enormous. Tsenka Iordanova, a Bulgarian musicologist who was a small child at the time that the Kutev Ensemble was established, reminisced that audiences were completely entranced by the visual and aural beauty of ensemble spectacles, which contrasted strongly with the drab reality of everyday life, the dearth of material goods, and arduous labor necessitated by the industrialization of the country.

By 1970 obrabotki for folk orchestra became much more complex and *avtorsko*—authored by composers and directors less interested in the traditional wisdom of orchestra members. The kolyano form was eliminated or became embedded in lengthy dance suites that accompanied large-scale *postanovki*—dramatic presentations of village custom acted out through dance, pantomime, and song by the choral and dance components of the folk ensemble. From 1970 to 1990 obrabotki increasingly featured countermelodies and internal harmonic lines, chromatic harmonies, altered chords, arpeggiated passages, and internal modulations. The earlier emphasis on the linear evolution of a horo melody kolyano by kolyano now contended with the vertical or synchronic orientation of harmony. Melody lines consisted of fragmented motives exchanged (often awkwardly) between individuals, orchestral sections, or mixed instrumental groups, always with harmonic accompaniment. Pieces became steadily more symphonic and technically difficult. Tempos increased greatly. Intonation became standardized and playing style polished and precise. (Compare Monitor MFS 402 and MFS 712 with *35 years: Philip Koutev-State Ensemble for Folks Songs and Dances* Balkanton BHA 11871/72.) Additionally, by 1990 obrabotki began to incorporate musical practices more characteristic of *gradski folklor* [urban folklore], including the utilization of jazz harmonies or idioms. Pieces such as Dimitŭr Trifonov's duo for clarinet and accordion recorded by the folk orchestra of the EFSBR featured Western instruments associated with gradski folklor in a solo capacity. Despite the length, difficulty, or relative unconventionality of such compositions, orkestranti performing publicly (as opposed to in a recording studio) were required to play them from memory to create the visual impression of the oral improvisation germane to village musical culture.[7]

The best of these arrangements were, in the opinion of orchestra members, fresh, innovative, and creative—a welcome challenge to the technical skills of those instrumentalists trained in folk music schools. More often, however, orchestral obrabotki of the 1980s arrived on the stands of musicians featuring a plethora of inconsistencies, including inaccurate metric designations, copy errors, incorrect ornamentation, unidiomatic passages, and pitches outside the range of the designated instruments, in stereotypical forms boasting common practice harmonic progressions that showed limited sensitivity to Bulgaria's regionally distinct musical styles or traditional modes of music-making. For musicians these compositions symbolized the ugly political and economic realities of their position within the music world's hierarchy of power. They supported the musicians' belief that composers wrote arrangements as quickly as possible and "only for money" [*samo za pari*], rather than "from the heart" [*ot sŭrtseto*]—that is, out of love for and understanding of musical tradition. In 1988 such sentiments were echoed by my non-musician acquaintances, one of whom described the style of obrabotki as "false," "mechanically done," and as a government strategy to promote national pride (Buchanan 1991:534–35).

At this point it is important to note that in 1988 the average monthly salary for a member of the Kutev Ensemble's folk orchestra was about 230 leva. The most highly paid member of the group, the concertmaster, earned 400 leva per month. These were considered good salaries. A composer gifted in harmonizing melody lines, however, could earn 1000 leva per month or more by producing several obrabotki—a much easier task than composing a symphony, which would bring the composer the same amount of money. Thus it was to a composer's advantage to write obrabotki rapidly, resulting in haphazard workmanship and predictable western musical formulae that musicians found trite, boring, and detached from tradition. Additionally, many composers received salaries as directors of orchestras or ensembles, or as scholars in academic institutes, further increasing the financial and political disparity between their social positions and those of musicians.

Musicians labelled such pieces "notno" because the music existed only in the notes, as an academic exercise in part writing, lacking feeling, expression, and style. A horo became "notno" when the performer was unable to realize the music as he felt it, according to his own internalized sense of tradition, gained from years of listening to and absorbing the *izvor* [spring, source], characterized by musicians as the fount of all cultural truth and traditional creativity. One instrumentalist defined the izvor in musical terms as the "music of the old masters," the playing of older generations of musicians, which contemporary musicians rearticulated in varied forms through individual improvisation, ornamentation, and style. This is the essence of "playing from the heart," the personalized transformation and manifestation of interiorized musical style and experience (ibid.:423–30). The emphasis on executing melodic lines with unified precision, including ornamentation, within the folk orchestra idiom, the inviolability of the score, and the authority of the composer and conductor clashed directly with this fundamental attribute of traditional music-making. In terms of the instrumentalists' knowledge of tradition, it was the skills learned aurally that signified good musicianship; but in the workplace it was their notereading ability that implied musical competence.

A brief vignette from my field experience may help illustrate how the conflict between performing a notno horo and playing from the heart was articulated in the everyday experience of Bulgarian musicians belonging to the folk orchestra of the prestigious Kutev Ensemble.

One morning, as an exercise in ensemble musicianship and musical memory, the director of the Kutev Ensemble's folk orchestra selected an instrumentalist at random and asked him to play the first two phrases of a slow, unmetered, and intricately ornamented melody (a genre called *bavna melodiya* [slow melody]) from his own repertoire, and then requested that each of the other instrumentalists imitate this melody precisely in terms of pitch, timbre, rhythm, ornamentation, and overall character—one by one. None of the musicians could perform the phrases in exactly the same manner, and they quickly became incensed with the director's criticism and insistence that they achieve this seemingly impossible goal. Two instrumentalists grew so furious that they left the rehearsal altogether in protest—a highly uncharacteristic reaction that strained interpersonal relations within the orchestra for several days (ibid.:420).

While this event may not seem important on the surface, orchestra members talked about it for months afterward. One of them explained to me that the director hoped to achieve the standardized ensemble sound associated with symphony orchestras, but his directive essentially negated the role of the musician in traditional performance practice, which demands that the performance of every melody be filtered through the idiosyncracies of instrumental technique, the regionally-associated stylistic vocabulary of the performer, and his personalized sense of ornamentation—factors that one instrumentalist described as "having a *verno chuvstvo* [true feeling] for the style" (ibid.:421, 425). No two musicians could perform any melody, but especially one of this type, in precisely the same way, because the aesthetic pertaining to these pieces mandated that they be performed as external manifestations of each musician's internalized, localized experience (ibid.:422). The instrumentalists resisted playing in such a standardized format because in the words of one orchestra member, "*muzikata stava akademichna—stava notna—i ne narodna*" [the music becomes academic—it becomes *notno*—and not *narodno*] (ibid.).

By contrasting an arrangement liked by musicians in the EFSBR's folk orchestra because of its traditional properties with one that they disliked intensely, the following discussion highlights other ramifications of the notno metaphor. Musicians often praised the arrangements of Kosta Kolev because of the composer's intimate knowledge of folklore and ability to enhance a traditional melody without disrupting its customary stylistic and structural implications. For example, in his "Lyavata," a horo for solo kaval with folk orchestra accompaniment recorded by the folk orchestra of the EFSBR, Kolev allows the kaval melody, which he was given by Stoyan Velichkov, to stand on its own without alteration (*Narodni Pesni i Hora - Obrabotil Kosta Kolev* [Folk songs and horos arranged by Kosta Kolev], Balkanton BHA 10822). The orchestral parts are simple, light, and at times derive from the melodic material of the kaval tune. They serve to reinforce the rhythmic elements of the horo and make little use of homophonic chords, relying on the bass line instead to imply harmonic movement. In order to write an obrabotka like this a composer must, in the words of one orkestrant, "feel narodna muzika, be acquainted with it from childhood, listen to it, feel it in [his] heart." Such composers "write the truth," claimed this same musician, because they understand the nuances of tradition.

In comparison, musicians in the Radio Ensemble's folk orchestra derisively christened Stefan Kŭnev's "Veleshko Horo" (Figure 1) and "Kavadarsko Horo" (Figure 2) the "Oriental Horos" and the "Turkish Horos" because in their opinion these arrangements were "full of *turtsism*-s"—atypical musical features characteristic of Turkish music. The arrangements became the subject of jokes and slurs in rehearsal as the musicians vented their anger about being forced to perform material they considered untraditional. One orkestrant angrily remarked that the obrabotki were "absolutely Turkish," to which another added "pure Istanbul" (Buchanan 1991:129–30). And while one gŭdulka player attempted to correct some problem spots in a Turkish-sounding passage, another instrumentalist shouted, "You play that line and you can call a taxi to take you south!"

To be sure, both horos are rooted in *makam Hičaz* [Bulgarian *Hidzhaz*]. The melodic lines of both pieces emphasize the important "chromatic" or lower tetrachord of this makam (see Dzhudzhev 1970:308). Both subsequently feature prominent augmented seconds and chromatic, scalewise ascending and descending passages that not only signify makam Hičaz, but which instrumentalists associated with "*orientalna muzika*" [oriental music] and the "*iztok*" [East]. They employed these terms in a homogenizing "us against them" manner similar to that described by Edward Said (1979:7), underscoring their perception of their nation and their work as affiliated with Christian Europe rather than the Islamic Near East. Central to their perception was "the idea of European identity as a superior one in comparison with all the non-European peoples and cultures," and that the Orient represented backwardness (ibid.:7). Further, "oriental" called to mind Bulgaria's lengthy struggle against the Ottoman Empire, a conflict of intense hatred chronicled in history books, movies, song texts, tales, jokes, and metaphors.

Figure 1: "Veleshko Horo," transcription of melody line, m. 49–92

Figure 2: "Kavadarsko Horo," transcription of melody line, m. 1–24 and 65–87

402   Ethnomusicology, Fall 1995

Beyond these elements, there are other musical and contextual considerations against which the musicians were reacting. First, it is important to note that there are many, many Bulgarian melodies and songs that utilize makam Hičaz, and which Bulgarian musicians and scholars alike (see Dzhudzhev 1970:307–11) identify as traditional and authentic. Thus the use of makam Hičaz by itself is not enough to characterize an arrangement as "*orientalno.*" On a musical level the persistent play of the melodic line around the makam's lower tetrachord is coupled with other problematic elements.

It is probable that the two horos are named for the towns of Titov Veles and Kavadarci, both located in Vardar Macedonia. The music of urban Macedonia manifests a great deal of Turkish influence and has been widely popularized by Muslim Gypsies (cf. Rasmussen 1991). Thus the musicians opposed the pieces both because of their probable Macedonian origin, and subsequent Turkish/Gypsy flavor. Beyond this, both obrabotki include several internal modulations that increase the chromaticity of the material. Musicians found these technically awkward and stylistically academic. One orkestrant went so far as to describe "Kavadarsko Horo" as *grubo* [crude, uncultivated] and "without finesse." The technical obstacles were exacerbated by the fact that the arrangements came to the orchestra without most of the necessary accidentals written in the parts, creating total chaos in rehearsal. In "Kavadarsko Horo," the melody is fragmented further by orchestrated registral contrasts, as small sections of the horo are traded between each instrumental faction. Although not shown in the transcriptions, both arrangements make use of countermelodies, occasional doubling in thirds or sixths, and three-part chords performed by the kavali in their uppermost register to accompany the horo tune. Finally, the melodic content of "Veleshko Horo" is untraditional in that it amalgamates three distinctive musical styles together in one piece: a heavy, Turkish line that strongly emphasizes Hičaz (Figure 1: "A"), a lighter section whose musical content is more typical of Pirin-Macedonia and which is performed by the tambura (Figure 1: "B"), an instrument also emblematic of that area, and a brief section which is reminiscent of Thrace (Figure 1: "C") in playing style (full, legato gŭdulka sound, slides into pitches) if not in musical content.[8]

For musicians, each of these problematic factors demonstrated the composer's inability or unwillingness to artistically and appropriately set traditional Bulgarian melodies for a national orchestra whose primary goal was to promulgate a representative, mass-mediated Bulgarian musical style throughout the country. In fact, these arrangements were so detested by the musicians that when I recorded them, they told me that I should not waste such good cassette tapes on such "*gluposti*" [stupidities, inanities]. Their reaction resonated with the cultural administration's racist insistence that

Bulgarian music bore no Turkish influence, a policy that prompted ensembles to cleanse foreign words from obrabotka song texts and, during the 1980s, which led to proscriptions against the production of Turkish and Gypsy music recordings and the playing of the *zurla* [zurna], an instrument connected by the administration to Turkish and Gypsy culture (Silverman 1986:56, 1989:151, 154–55). Yet the musicians' attitude also contradicted other aspects of their behavior and the historical reality of musical style.

Many of the orkestranti who objected to the "oriental" style of the horos performed a type of Turkish- and Gypsy-influenced instrumental music heavily restricted by the Bulgarian government until the late 1980s, termed *svatbarska muzika* [wedding music], on the weekends to earn extra money (see Buchanan 1991:495–602; Rice 1994:231–50; Silverman 1989). At the same time, some of these same orkestranti claimed that the popularity of wedding music threatened the future of folk orchestras, and that *svatbarski orkestri* [wedding orchestras] were taking work away from state-sponsored folk orchestras. Thus the style of Kŭnev's obrabotki called to mind both the fact that orkestranti had to moonlight on the side to make enough money to survive in the rapidly disintegrating economic climate, and the threat posed by wedding orchestras to the musicians' primary source of employment. Like the Trifonov arrangement mentioned above, these pieces also symbolized composers' attempts to gain access to the lucrative wedding music scene (Buchanan 1991:399–400; Rice 1994:250). Further, the label "oriental" seemed to be related as much to the fact that Kŭnev's obrabotki were written poorly for the instruments as to the actual Turkish musical characteristics heard within them. The political debate over civil rights for Bulgarian minorities that rocked Bulgaria at the time that these obrabotki appeared added another dimension to their interpretation. In this context, "oriental" was a logical term of denigration for such unidiomatic writing.

Another way of analyzing this situation is to emphasize that *notno/akademichno* and *orientalno/tursko/tsigansko* map onto each other as vilifying adjectives in a way that highlights a perpetuation of the self versus other dichotomization of personal identity that characterized Bulgarian society during the socialist period (Verdery 1993:194). While under socialism individuals frequently blamed the state for the country's social problems, during the transition away from socialism the scapegoat for social ills became ethnicized—in the actions of ethnic Turks and Gypsies, who many held responsible not just for threatening the jobs of orkestranti, but for problems such as the severe food shortages that followed the mass exodus of ethnic Turks (many of them agricultural workers) to Turkey in the summer of 1989—and then nationally politicized in the platform of the Movement for Rights and Freedoms Party (cf. Verdery 1993:197; Buchanan 1991:127). In 1989–1990 several Bulgarian friends expressed their fear that if ethnic Turks

were granted civil rights they would push their way into elevated government positions that would allow them to work together with Turkey to
overthrow the Bulgarian leadership. This hysteria was fueled by the
Bulgarian news media (Buchanan 1991:127–28). Unable or afraid to cope
with the prospect of the freer society heralded by glasnost, my friends could
envision only another era of domination that would extend the previous
historical pattern of subordination to the Byzantine Empire, the Ottoman
Empire, and Soviet-directed socialism.

In this context, the musical situation described above symbolizes the
large-scale conceptual conflation of the socialist hegemony (of which
akademichno and notno are markers) with both the historical Ottoman
hegemony (again, ethnicized as Turkish and responsible, in Bulgarian eyes,
for the country's historical isolation from Europe), and the potentiality of a
second Turkish takeover. The historical basis for the entanglement of these
concepts stems, at least in the domain of neotraditional expressive culture,
from their role in socialist bureaucratic nationalism. While all of these terms
pertain to musical styles outside the idealized notion of village tradition that
urban professional performers of neotraditional orchestral music understand
as "playing from the heart," their use as denigrative markers derives directly
from and was strongly reinforced by nationalistic political policies utilized to
construct the socialist state—namely, the whitewashing of ethnic diversity and
the contradictory reconceptualization of rural folklife as both a homogeneous
source of Bulgarian pride and identity, and a regressive peasant lifestyle
requiring reformulation in the image of West European models.

Music, Identity, and Political Change

> It is in a country unfamiliar emotionally or topographically that one needs poems and road
> maps (Geertz 1973:218).

> The wound is still open which the revolutionary shrapnel of modern society, guided by
> symbols of future and progress, inflicted on the rural, indigenous past. Through this
> wound the political culture wheezes; in the name of pain for the shattered past it devises
> a profile of contemporary man that corresponds, point by point, with the myth of paradise
> subverted (Bartra 1992:19).

I lived in Bulgaria during a period of extreme social, political, and
cultural stress in which the daily disintegration of the dominant order of
reality produced a sense of cultural vertigo; the deterioration of the
extensively institutionalized premises of former life created a present mired
in quicksand and an elusive, illusory future (cf. Geertz 1973:218–21; Havel
1991a:8–9; Appadurai 1991:202–3). My study of the relationships between
musical style and national identity prompted some difficult questions.

What happens, for example, to people's perceptions of life, self, and
nation when the prevailing construction of cultural truth shatters? Although

it was common for my Bulgarian friends—most of whom had travelled extensively outside Bulgaria—to comment privately upon the discrepancy between the reality constructed through political ideology and the nature of their actual existence, many of them profoundly believed in the ideals of communism. They were stunned by the extent of bureaucratic corruption and disinformation that the political transition disclosed, and bewildered by the rapid breakdown of the economic system, as food, gasoline, and material goods began to disappear from the already meagerly stocked marketplace. How then did the process of hegemony function in such a transitional moment, or was the concept of hegemony not applicable during such a period? What were the implications of the political transition for professional folk orchestra performers given that this transition revealed the state-supported neotraditional Bulgarian musical style as a representative expression of a socialist reality swamped in fabrication, thus signalling the potential disbanding of the folk ensemble network which was the musicians' livelihood? Finally, if in experiencing hegemony we always encounter "'traces' of previous ideological systems and sedimentations" that, again through ideology, register in the present (Hall 1979:333; 1985:111), how did musicians at this crucial political juncture mediate between the many different ideological layers informing their musical experience—these being their newfound aspirations to free creative expression associated with the shift to political pluralism, their grounding in pre-socialist tradition, and official career experience as musical ambassadors of the socialist version of culture and tradition? I can offer only preliminary answers to these questions as the extraordinary events shaping Bulgaria's future continue to unfold.

It seems to me that since 1989 Bulgaria has experienced the reassertion of localized senses of identity as implicated within the global network of power relations. In other words, as the forces of perestroika, glasnost, and popular dissent dismantled the hegemonic allegiances condensed in the apparatus of the Bulgarian state (Hall 1986:18), the country's underdeveloped structure of civil institutions and subsequent dearth of civic experience were laid bare (cf. Hall 1986:17; see Verdery and Kligman 1992:140–47 for a Romanian comparison). During the chaotic, tense period that followed, regional, local, personal, and ethnic interests and alliances were asserted publicly through a variety of symbolic cultural displays such as demonstrations, chants, banners, and television exposés that pertained to the reconceptualization of ideology and the repossession of public life (cf. Kligman 1990; Geertz 1973:221). For the urban Bulgarians with whom I had contact, international considerations became paramount in regard to the reconfiguration of the Bulgarian economy, political system, lifestyle, and position of music within these realms. In the domain of expressive culture, marketing opportunities facilitated by glasnost made the professional performance of narodna muzika both a striking symbol of and dynamic agent responsible for reformulating the image of the Bulgarian state in response to how culture members viewed their position within an economically and politically consolidated Europe unbounded by designations of East and West. The throwing off of the socialist system steadily emphasized Bulgaria's aspiration towards a West European way of life nuanced by local traditions. Bulgarians envisioned themselves as Westerners in a Gramscian sense of both economic and political orientation that extends beyond geographic location (Hall 1986:18). They perceived their country as part of the "common European home," a euphemism for the open market structure that European countries have been trying to implement since 1992. Likewise, on rehearsal breaks over coffee at least one group of Bulgarian musicians jokingly referred to themselves as citizens of the "fifty-first state of the American Union," a reference to their admiration for the United States, their desire to emulate the American economic and political system, and their hope that America, and the West in general, would help transform Bulgaria into a prosperous, democratic nation.

In the realm of Bulgarian instrumental music, the philosophy of freedom of expression engendered by glasnost prompted the appearance of musical genres combining aspects of traditional music with elements of urban folklore, popular music, jazz, and the wildly celebrated music of Bulgarian wedding orchestras, either in symphonic contexts, or in original settings for smaller combinations of instruments not necessarily restricted to the indigenous instrumental arsenal. (Hear *Vissh Muzikalno-Pedagogicheski Institut Plovdiv: izpŭlneniya na solisti, hor i orkestŭr* [VMPI Plovdiv: Performances of soloists, choir and orchestra], Balkanton BHA 12234.) A clear example of this trend was the genre of disco folk music [*disko folk*], which appeared in 1988 at the hands of musicians in the EFSBR in conjunction with composer Dimitŭr Penev, both to turn the attention of Bulgarian youths to their cultural roots in a contemporary form with popular appeal, and to transform Bulgarian music into a style that the musicians thought would be popular and marketable in the West. Their efforts resulted in the Balkanton release "*Folklorna Diskoteka 1: Krŭstopŭt*"[Folk Disco Volume 1: Crossroad] (BHA 12366), whose title, jacket (which depicts a pair of legs straddling the middle of a highway, one clad in the leather shoes and woven socks of the traditional past, the other in contemporary tennis shoes, synthetic hose, and blue jeans), and musical content reflected the turning point faced by narodna muzika and its proponents in late twentieth-century Bulgarian society.

Unhappy with the form of their art and its growing detachment from everyday life, these musicians sought to merge narodna muzika with an already well-liked genre of popular music. All of the record's instrumental pieces featured horo melodies performed on indigenous instruments set by Penev to a disco accompaniment provided by electronic drums and a synthesizer. In doing so, they followed the precedent established by wedding orchestras, which also combine elements of popular music— primarily rock and jazz—with indigenous Bulgarian, Greek, Serbian, Turkish, and Gypsy musics.

In creating disco folk music, musicians counterbalanced their knowledge of tradition and their training with their economic aspirations and visions of Bulgaria's future. For Bulgarian teenagers and young adults, discotheques were one of most popular venues for socializing. Assuming the same was true in the West, Bulgarian musicians anxious to earn hard currency and snare concert tour invitations asked me several times about marketing disco folk in the US as top-40 pop music (cf. Buchanan 1991:560– 64). Although disco folk never really gained popularity among Bulgaria's youth, the musicians pursued this venture with pleasure because it allowed them to be creative and innovative. In a July 1988 interview with Radio Sofia and in informal conversations with me, Stoyan Velichkov described, for example, how surprised and elated he was by the "*kristalen*" [crystalline] and "*veren*" [true] sound that he achieved in these recordings. He characterized the music as wonderful, "pure" [*chista*] narodna muzika because in spite of the accompaniment, he was able to perform the kaval melodies "*bitovo verno*" [true to their traditional form] and "*ot izvora*" [from the source] (Buchanan 1991:563–64).

The word *bitov* describes events, objects, and customs germane to daily life in the villages of late nineteenth- and early twentieth-century Bulgaria. The phrase *bitovi instrumentalni grupi*, for instance, describes "the old masters"—those small instrumental groups that emerged in the first decades of the twentieth century, leading to group performance at Radio Sofia. *Verno* translates as true or correct. Thus to perform music "*bitovo verno*" means to play it in a manner truly representative of music-making in post-Liberation and pre-socialist rural Bulgaria, an historical era romanticized by folk ensembles and their cultural administrators as the source of late twentieth-century Bulgarian national identity. Further, the use of the phrase *bitovo verno* resonates with understanding "playing from the heart" as a musical expression of cultural truth, because "playing from the heart" engenders a musical externalization of the izvor (the mythical and idealized source of all creativity labeled as narodno, traditional, or authentic), which in the minds of folk orchestra instrumentalists like Velichkov was rooted in the regionally-defined *bit* [bitov lifestyle] of that same historical period.

For Velichkov, the disco folk arrangements were in some ways more narodni than many of the obrabotki he performed with EFSBR's folk orchestra. His performance of and attitude toward disco folk represented his attempt to juggle his personal identification with the izvor, his role as a folk orchestra participant charged with popularizing an officially-sanctioned

408   Ethnomusicology, Fall 1995

style of neotraditional music as national, and his desire to create a form of Bulgarian music adaptable to the world music market. Performing this melody bitovo verno, in a manner faithful to his knowledge of village tradition and unencumbered by a score, demonstrated that it is free and personalized musical expression informed by the accumulated wisdom of the izvor which constitutes "playing from the heart." Velichkov could enjoy the disco setting, inspired by Bulgarian perceptions of and economic aspirations to transnational music fame, as long as it embodied the *verno chuvstvo*—the sincerity and truth—of *narodna traditsiya*.

Raymond Williams states that the shape of tradition in daily life exemplifies the nature of a society's hegemonic relations, because as a social force tradition has great power to incorporate the various facets of culture into the dominant order of reality (1977:115). The case presented above illustrates that hegemony is relational as well as oppositional, for while the current concepts of izvor and bitov can differ from narodno, and while these three terms contrast with notno, they are all linked intrinsically to the aims and policies of bureaucratic nationalism. Here tradition serves the creation of hegemony, because as a conceptual marker it is remarkably fluid and totally relative. In the context of folk orchestra performance practice, all of these concepts are twentieth-century constructions which offer "an intentionally selective version of a shaping past and a pre-shaped present, which is then powerfully operative in the process of social and cultural definition and identification" (ibid.:115). Such descriptives mark the performances of folk ensembles as "pastoral modes of ethnographic domination" because they claim to promote "a documentary rather than fictional [presentation of] the lives of actual shepherds" in which "a neutral [and hence manipulable] ethnographic truth can collect itself" (Rosaldo 1986:96–97). By symbolically cultivating rural life in the interests of constructing nationalism, this "neutral ethnographic truth"—this izvor—is established as a "myth of paradise subverted" (Bartra 1992:19).

Postlude

The breakdown of Bulgaria's political system prompted by glasnost and perestroika propelled narodna muzika onto the world music scene with the help of West European, American, and Japanese concert impresarios and recording companies. Suddenly Bulgarian music, in forms ranging from the local (such as the US performances of the Bistritsa Babi) to the national (as in the 1991 American tour of the SEFSD-Pirin) was popularized outside Eastern Europe in the wake of the world's thirst for global and New Age music exotica, and excitement over the end of the Cold War (see Buchanan 1991:571–91).

The most renowned result of this trend was the international tours of the women's folk choir associated with the EFSBR (marketed as the Bulgarian State Radio and Television Female Vocal Choir, hereafter BSRTFVC) and their associated Nonesuch recordings, entitled *Le mystère des voix bulgares* (Nonesuch 79165-1 and 79201-4; a third volume, which includes other choirs, was released by Fontana/Polygram in conjunction with Disques Celliers in 1990). In a brilliant example of media manipulation, the BSRTFVC and its proponents performed an avant-garde style of Bulgarian choral music that exaggerated specific features germane to the Bulgarian musical aesthetic, packaged the resulting sound as "mysterious," and marketed it as traditional. Beginning in about 1968, choral *obrabotki* by Kutev, Stefan Mutafchiev, Georgi Minchev, and others transformed traditional, often regionally associated, diaphonic musical structures into complex eight- to ten-part chromatic sonorities that highlighted the Bulgarian preference for employing seconds, fourths, sevenths, and octaves as consonances. The international commercialization of this dense, ultra-chromatic style in the late 1980s produced a mass-mediated, imagined "ethnoscape" of Bulgarian life that played upon exactly those associations with the Near East that many Bulgarians rebelled against (see Appadurai 1991). The "mysterious voices" phenomenon both catered to and reinforced West European and North American perceptions of the Orient as ancient, mystical, magical, and metaphysical (cf. Said 1979; Buchanan 1991:575–91).

In contrast to the choir's modern arrangements, on the same tours a small instrumental group derived from EFSBR's folk orchestra performed synchronized, unison improvisations of dance melodies in a style reminiscent of the early twentieth century, but at the blistering tempos associated with contemporary musicianship. The nature of these performances exemplified another dimension of Bulgarians' perceptions of the West's expectations of Bulgarian music. Their style was predicated upon the assumption that—as one instrumentalist put it—"in Europe and America they only want to hear authentic instrumental music," but modern arrangements of Bulgarian song.

A host of international tours by Bulgarian musical groups launched, accompanied, and followed those of the BSRTFVC. Because most of these groups were subfactions of state folk song and dance ensembles, the tours turned the ensemble network on its head. Tours heralded new opportunities for professional Bulgarian musicians to earn hard currency, to gain recognition for their skills, to purchase material goods not available in their own country, and to see the world. They promoted intense rivalries between the leading state ensembles as all vied for permission to travel abroad. This competition caused the leading ensembles to restructure their programs in formats they surmised would be more accessible to Western audiences unfamiliar with Bulgarian folklore. Both the Kutev Ensemble and the SEFSD-Trakiya, for instance, created new productions fashioned around a single theatrical theme, such as a display of Bulgarian folklife during the four seasons, which called for ensemble members to utilize their acting skills and mix on the stage as dramatic personae to a much greater degree than before.

Both the administrative heads of state ensembles and individual musicians resorted to *vrŭzki*—personalized networks of political connections utilized by all Bulgarians under socialism as a means of daily survival—in their efforts to go abroad. Everyone from Bulgarian Radio executives to obrabotki composers wanted a piece of the "mysterious voices" gold mine. Suddenly the question of copyright, royalties, *avtorski prava* [author's rights], and the methods by which musicians or groups gained access to tours became crucially important and hotly debated conversation topics. Ugly quarrels and outright hostility developed between musicians selected or invited to travel and those left behind. Conflicts also emerged between instrumentalists and vocalists, for orkestranti were often envious of the greater exposure, and hence, financial rewards, given to the members of touring folk choirs.[9]

Following my departure from Bulgaria in March 1990 state funding for national folk song and dance ensembles plummeted and the rate of inflation skyrocketed. While as of summer 1993 ensemble salaries had risen to approximately 800 leva per month, a good salary was now 1200–1500 leva per month. No longer was ensemble employment one of very few avenues to personal fame, privilege, travel, and fortune. In response, some musicians quit the ensemble circuit for more lucrative employment or to pursue private entrepreneurship. Several ensemble directors, composers, and orkestranti emigrated to other countries or lived abroad for extended periods. In several cases folk ensemble administrators compelled musicians to give up their orchestral positions if they chose to undertake employment abroad, even if this employment was temporary. Many such musicians traveled to the US to present concerts and master classes, to play at festivals, or to teach at Balkan folk music and dance camps. Most looked for ways to stay. Because their knowledge of American immigration policy was predicated upon the ideology of the Statue of Liberty, rather than the red tape of work visas and green cards, and because their visions of America were derived from foreign films and television, they did not understand why once in the US, they could not remain, and why they could not work legally. Because the Bulgarian media presented successful touring artists like the Trio Bŭlgarka as heroes of western popular culture, my Bulgarian friends had little comprehension of the fact that despite the West's love affair with Bulgarian music, the number of Americans actually supporting Balkan folk music and dance was quite small.

I strongly applaud the continuing efforts of Bulgarian musicians to attain recognition on the international music scene. However, I am saddened by the practice of dissimulation that performers have chosen or been forced to adopt in order to achieve economic success, for this extends the earlier patterns of social and moral "bipolarity" that fostered duplicity, complicity, and vrŭzki as coping strategies under socialism (Verdery 1993:193).

For instance, many of the vocalists performing with the BSRTFVC exclaimed to me while on tour in the US in 1990 that they did not even like the chromatic vocal obrabotki so loved by the West, preferring more traditional settings of village songs instead. The "*le mystère*" arrangements were exhausting to sing, difficult to keep in tune, and distant from the women's conceptualization of tradition. Nor was America all that they had envisioned. The weariness and fatigue of constant long-distance travel and performances were stultifying, and the performers' desire for material goods conflicted with the reality of seeing America by bus on a twenty dollar *per diem*. One woman confided that, but for the money she was earning for her children, she would not have continued touring.

As a footnote to this discussion I offer some observations made to me in 1990 by Stoyan Velichkov about the evolution of his own career. By this point a veteran of many tours to Western Europe and North America, Stoyan possessed a keen sense of the socio-economic and socio-political complications posed by the transnational popularization of Bulgarian narodna muzika. After much thinking about the disco folk music venture, his dismay at being obliged to perform dismal folk orchestra obrabotki at home, and requests that he and his colleagues perform musical entertainment as outrageous as the *lambada*—on indigenous instruments—for a New Year's celebration, he seemed to feel compromised. In a tone of voice that mirrored his frustration, he said that from that point on, if someone wanted to hire him, he would play either authentic narodna muzika or nothing at all.

It is important to note that at the time Stoyan made these comments he was operating from a position of relative economic and political strength due to his successful trips with Balkana and his proximity to retirement. Nevertheless, his remarks and the situations above highlight the extent to which the performance of neotraditional narodna muzika, whether in the form of obrabotki for folk orchestra, disco folk music, or mysterious choral music, constituted a kind of "style for sale," in which musicians were not only alienated from the product of their labor, but subsequently were forced—by economic need or political decree—to participate in the alienation of self (Camille Brochu 1992:pers. comm.). Here their attempts to incorporate Bulgarian musical life into Western society entailed a transnational cultural displacement that was both "the root of their problems" and "the engine of their dreams, of wealth, of respectability, of autonomy" (Appadurai 1991:207).

412   *Ethnomusicology, Fall 1995*

Summary

In a critical sense, "playing from the heart" represents an affective, Bulgarian expression of Havel's "living in truth," for both concepts entail rejecting the "world of appearances" in favor of the free expression of life experience (cf. Havel 1991b:135, 148–50, 178). Metaphors like "playing from the heart" or playing a "notno horo" are thus more than descriptive commentary on musical style or aesthetics. They are powerful evaluations of the politics of music professionalism as embedded in the hegemonic relations of the Bulgarian political economy, which in turn resonate dialectically with Bulgarian stereotypes, expectations, perceptions and visions of the Orient and the Occident. The snug correspondence between these metaphors and the social reality of folk orchestra performance practice imbues them with a sense of truth (see Lakoff and Johnson 1980:180). And by highlighting, sanctioning, or rebelling against certain aspects of Bulgarian experience during the period of political transition—especially against the ideology of Soviet-directed socialism—these metaphors not only have carried the burden of truth, they have served as "a license for policy change" within the domain of Bulgarian folk ensembles by encouraging the improvisation of meaningful, neotraditional musical styles that have wrought changes in performers' lifestyles in association with shifts in political and economic doctrine (ibid.:156).

The circumstances that produced the creation of folk orchestras in the 1950s and the Mystery of the Bulgarian Voices of the late 1980s were similar in that both resulted from radical social, political, and cultural changes that fractured pre-existing world views. In both instances Bulgarians renegotiated local, regional, and national identities in accordance with a network of conjectured and reciprocal inter- and intranational relations. At both of these junctures Bulgarian music was modified to meet Western standards of musical beauty, showing the significance of classical and other types of Western music as measuring sticks of professionalism and value, and Bulgaria's desire to gain a foothold in the Western music market. In each case professional Bulgarian musicians mediated between their personal, regionally-defined identification with tradition and the expectations of Western audiences to formulate new images of the Bulgarian nation, demonstrating that, in the Bulgarian context an understanding of the relationship between music and political hegemony must be married to an understanding of the construction of identity. In Bulgaria musicians continue to play a vital role in this process of identity reconfiguration, because they hold the keys to the heart of tradition, while serving simultaneously as their nation's emissaries to the outside world.

Notes

1. This article is based on twenty-one months of dissertation field research undertaken in Sofia, Bulgaria during three separate visits during the years 1986–1990. Research was supported by an International Research and Exchanges Board Specialized Language Training Grant (1986) and East European Long Term Exchange Grant (1988), with funds provided by the National Endowment for the Humanities and the United States Information Agency, and by a Fulbright-Hays Grant for Graduate Study Abroad (1989–1990) administered by the Institute for International Education. Additional support was supplied by the University of Texas at Austin Graduate School in the form of a Graduate Fellowship (1990–1991) during the writing of my dissertation, from which this article is derived. I am deeply grateful to each of these institutions. I am also profoundly indebted to my Bulgarian sponsors at the Institute for Musicology (now the Musical Sector of the Institute for Problems in Art Studies), the Bulgarian Academy of Sciences, and the Bulgarian Ministry of Education for aiding the logistics of my research, and in particular to the members and directors of the State Ensemble for Folk Songs and Dances-Filip Kutev and the Ensemble for Folk Songs of the Bulgarian Radio for their friendship, understanding, patience, and collegial support. None of these organizations or individuals is responsible for the views expressed.

Earlier versions of this paper were presented in 1991 at the Thirty-Sixth Annual Meeting of the Society for Ethnomusicology in Chicago, Illinois, and at the Department of Music, New York University, in February 1992. My heartfelt thanks to Gerard Béhague, Tim Brace, Camille Brochu, David Burrows, Steve Feld, Sandra Graham, Gabriela Ilnitchi, Charles Keil, Paul Klemperer, Kathleen Oien, Tim Rice, Jane Sugarman, and Tom Turino for their comments on previous drafts of this paper.

2. Other groups with which I worked included the children's folk ensemble "Izvorche" of the Palace of Pioneers, Sofia; the SEFSD-Trakiya, located in Plovdiv; the SEFSD-Rodopa, Smolyan; and smaller folk music groups derived from larger ensembles, such as Balkana and the Trakiiska Troika.

3. It is the constant negotiation of the self that underlies Christopher Waterman's definition of Yoruban identity as "mixed, relational, and conjunctural" (1990:367) rather than "self-constituting and essential" (ibid.:377) from an historical perspective. Thomas Turino similarly demonstrates the value of this thesis in his discussion of the fluid aspects of Conimeño community identity as manifested in musical performance and social aesthetics (1990). Likewise, Arjun Appadurai's term "ethnoscape," which constitutes a response to the fact that "groups are no longer tightly territorialized, spatially bounded, historically unselfconscious, or culturally homogenous" (1991:191); Renato Rosaldo's emphasis on "multiplex personal identity" and investigating "culture as multiple border zones" (1989:166, 217), Michael Fischer's exploration of ethnicity as "a process of inter-reference between two or more cultural traditions" (1986:201), and Roger Bartra's utilization of the "cannon of the axolotl" (1992), all mark identity as a dynamic complex of supple personae which interact with each other and the world at large (see also Hall 1985:110).

4. The most striking exception to the preponderance of solo or unison music-making is the use of drone to accompany vocal and instrumental melodies. Many indigenous instruments, such as the *gaida* and *dvoyanka*, are constructed to automatically produce such a sound. See Rice 1977, 1980, 1988; and Buchanan 1991 for in-depth treatments of the diaphonic tradition and its accompanying aesthetic, and Rice 1994 for a more detailed discussion of musical life in rural Bulgaria.

5. The composition of obrabotki is a male dominated activity. The female folk ensemble vocalists with whom I am acquainted gave their songs directly to composers for arrangement. I am unaware of any vocalists who wrote folk orchestral arrangements for their own songs.

6. In 1986 one dollar was roughly equivalent to 1.2 leva at the official exchange rate, although the black market demanded seven leva to the dollar. When I left Bulgaria in March,

1990 the black market rate had skyrocketed to as much as twenty leva to one dollar. By January 1994 the official exchange rate had risen to 31.5 leva to one dollar.

7. This was also a practical consideration. Playing from memory eliminated the need for music stands and allowed the instrumentalists to roam the stage freely when necessitated by the drama of a given *postanovka*. However, visually portraying a connection with tradition was so important that it sometimes superseded sound quality in significance. The use of cello and bass gŭdulki is a case in point, as performers on these instruments told me that they could never extract a satisfactory tone from them. In the folk orchestra of the EFSBR the classical violoncello and bass were utilized almost exclusively, for this orchestra performed mainly in recording studios where visual presentation was less important than aural effect. Nevertheless, the bassist and cellist maintained that for concert performances they sometimes were required to play the neotraditional instruments.

8. I am indebted to Jane Sugarman for helping me come to grips with some of the Turkish elements in these pieces. The historical interweaving of Ottoman Turkish culture with regional folklife in the Balkans is a tremendously tangled area that requires much more attention.

9. These quarrels began to erupt in December 1988 in conjunction with musicians' complaints about disparities between vocalist and instrumentalist salary scales. The extent to which financial considerations were affecting interpersonal relations was not lost on orkestranti, one of whom turned to me and sadly said, "A long time ago we had a saying: 'He who sings or plays an instrument thinks no evil.' But this is no longer true. We are always thinking about money and how much the other person gets."

References

Appadurai, Arjun. 1991. "Global Ethnoscapes: Notes and Queries for a Transnational Anthropology." In *Recapturing Anthropology: Working in the Present,* edited by Richard G. Fox, 191–210. Santa Fe: School of American Research Press.

Atanasov, Vergilii. 1976. "Bulgarian Folk Musical Instruments." In *The Folk Arts of Bulgaria: Papers Presented at a Symposium, October 28–30, 1976,* 188–213. Pittsburgh: Duquesne University Tamburitzans Institute for Folk Arts.

Bartra, Roger. 1992. *The Cage of Melancholy: Identity and Metamorphosis in the Mexican Character.* New Brunswick, NJ: Rutgers University Press.

Becker, Judith. 1991. "A Brief Note on Turtles, Claptrap, and Ethnomusicology." *Ethnomusicology* 35(3):393–96.

Bourdieu, Pierre. 1990. *In Other Words: Essays Towards a Reflexive Sociology,* translated by Matthew Adamson. Stanford: Stanford University Press.

Buchanan, Donna A. 1991. "The Bulgarian Folk Orchestra: Cultural Performance, Symbol, and the Construction of National Identity in Socialist Bulgaria." Ph.D. dissertation, University of Texas at Austin.

Clifford, James. 1986. "Introduction: Partial Truths." In *Writing Culture: The Poetics and Politics of Ethnography,* edited by James Clifford and George E. Marcus, 1–26. Berkeley: University of California Press.

Clifford, James, and George E. Marcus, editors. 1986. *Writing Culture: The Poetics and Politics of Ethnography.* Berkeley: University of California Press.

Creed, Gerald. 1992. "Economic Development under Socialism: A Bulgarian Village on the Eve of Transition." Ph.D. dissertation, City University of New York.

Dzhudzhev, Stoyan. 1970. *Bŭlgarska narodna muzika. Tom I.* Sofia: Nauka i Izkustvo.

Feld, Steven. 1987. "Dialogic Editing: Interpreting How Kaluli Read *Sound and Sentiment.*" *Cultural Anthropology* 2(2):190–210.

———. 1992. "From Schizophonia to Schismogenesis: Notes on the Discourses of World Music and World Beat." Working Papers and Proceedings of the Center for Psychosocial Studies No. 53, edited by Greg Urban and Benjamin Lee. Chicago: Center for Psychosocial Studies.

Fischer, Michael M. J. 1986. "Ethnicity and the Post-Modern Arts of Memory." In *Writing Culture: The Poetics and Politics of Ethnography,* edited by James Clifford and George E. Marcus, 194–233. Berkeley: University of California Press.

Forgacs, David, editor. 1988. *An Antonio Gramsci Reader: Selected Writings 1916–1935.* New York: Schocken Books.

Foucault, Michel. 1980. *Power/Knowledge: Selected Interviews and Other Writings, 1972–1977,* edited by Colin Gordon; Colin Gordon, et al., translators. New York: Pantheon Books.

Fuhrman, Peter. 1989. "The Bulgarian Connection." *Forbes* 143(8)[17 April]:40–44.

Geertz, Clifford. 1973. *The Interpretation of Cultures.* New York: Basic Books.

Gourlay, Kenneth A. 1978. "Towards a Reassessment of the Ethnomusicologist's Role in Research." *Ethnomusicology* 22(1):1–36.

———. 1982. "Towards a Humanizing Ethnomusicology." *Ethnomusicology* 26(3):411–20.

Hall, Stuart. 1979. "Culture, the Media and the 'Ideological Effect'." In *Mass Communication and Society,* edited by James Curran, Michael Gurevitch, and Janet Woollacot, 315–48. Beverly Hills and London: Sage Publications.

———. 1985. "Signification, Representation, Ideology: Althusser and the Post-Structuralist Debates." *Critical Studies in Mass Communication* 2(2):91–114.

———. 1986. "Gramsci's Relevance for the Study of Race and Ethnicity." *Journal of Communication Inquiry* 10(2):5–27.

Havel, Václav. 1991a. "Second Wind." In his *Open Letters: Selected Writings, 1965–1990,* selected and edited by Paul Wilson, 3–9. New York: Alfred A. Knopf.

———. 1991b."The Power of the Powerless." In his *Open Letters: Selected Writings.*

Hebdige, Dick. 1979. *Subculture: The Meaning of Style.* London and New York: Methuen.

Herzfeld, Michael. 1985. *The Poetics of Manhood: Contest and Identity in a Cretan Mountain Village.* Princeton: Princeton University Press.

Iordanova, Tsenka. 1987. Untitled and unpublished paper delivered at the symposium, "Profesionalizmŭt v narodnata muzikalna i srednovekovna pevcheska praktika," held in Razlog, Bulgaria, 26–28 October 1987.

Kachulev, Ivan. 1978. *Bulgarian Folk Musical Instruments,* edited by Walter W. Kolar, translated by Thomas Roncevic. Pittsburgh: Tamburitza Press.

Karpat, Kemal H., editor. 1990. *The Turks of Bulgaria: The History, Culture and Political Fate of a Minority.* Istanbul: Isis Press.

Keil, Charles. 1982. "Applied Ethnomusicology and the Rebirth of Music from the Spirit of Tragedy." *Ethnomusicology* 34(3):399–412.

———. 1985. "People's Music Comparatively: Style and Stereotype, Class and Hegemony." *Dialectical Anthropology* 10:119–30.

Kligman, Gail. 1990. "Reclaiming the Public: A Reflection on Creating Civil Society in Romania." *East European Politics and Societies* 4(3):393–437.

Krŭstev, Venelin. 1978. *Bulgarian Music.* Sofia: Sofia Press.

Lakoff, George, and Mark Johnson. 1980. *Metaphors We Live By.* Chicago and London: University of Chicago Press.

Meintjes, Louise. 1990. "Paul Simon's *Graceland,* South Africa, and the Mediation of Musical Meaning." *Ethnomusicology* 34(1):37–73.

Noll, William. 1991. "Economics of Music Patronage Among Polish and Ukrainian Peasants to 1939." *Ethnomusicology* 35(3):349–79.

Poulton, Hugh. 1991. *The Balkans: Minorities and States in Conflict.* London: Minority Rights Publications.

Rasmussen, Ljerka Vidić. 1991. "Gypsy Music in Yugoslavia: Inside the Popular Culture Tradition." *Journal of the Gypsy Lore Society* 5 1(2):127–39.

Rice, Timothy. 1977. "Polyphony in Bulgarian Folk Music." Ph.D. dissertation, University of Washington at Seattle.

———. 1980. "Aspects of Bulgarian Musical Thought." *Yearbook of the International Folk Music Council* 12:43–66.

————. 1988. "Understanding Three-Part Singing in Bulgaria: The Interplay of Theory and Experience." *Selected Reports in Ethnomusicology* 7:43–57.

————. 1994. *"May It Fill Your Soul": Experiencing Bulgarian Music*. Chicago: University of Chicago Press.

Rosaldo, Renato. 1986. "From the Door of His Tent: The Fieldworker and the Inquisitor." In *Writing Culture: The Poetics and Politics of Ethnography*, edited by James Clifford and George E. Marcus, 77–97. Berkeley: University of California Press.

————. 1989. *Culture & Truth: The Remaking of Social Analysis*. Boston: Beacon Press.

Said, Edward W. 1979. *Orientalism*. New York: Vintage Books.

Silverman, Carol. 1983. "The Politics of Folklore in Bulgaria." *Anthropological Quarterly* 56:55–61.

————. 1986. "Bulgarian Gypsies: Adaptation in a Socialist Context." *Nomadic Peoples* 21/22:51–62.

————. 1989. "Reconstructing Folklore: Media and Cultural Policy in Eastern Europe." *Communication* 11:141–60.

————. Forthcoming. "Who's Gypsy Here?: Reflections at a *Rom* Burial." In *The World Observed: Reflections on the Fieldwork Process*, edited by Bruce Jackson and Edward Ives. Urbana: University of Illinois Press.

Slobin, Mark. 1992. "Micromusics of the West: A Comparative Approach." *Ethnomusicology* 36(1):1–87.

Tomova, Ilona, and Plamen Bogoev. 1992. "Minorities in Bulgaria. Report to the December 1991 International Conference on the Minorities Organized in Rome by the Lelio Basso International Foundation for the Rights and Liberation of Peoples." *The Insider* [February]:15-page insert.

Turino, Thomas. 1990. "Structure, Context, and Strategy in Musical Ethnography." *Ethnomusicology* 34(3):399–412.

Verdery, Katherine. 1993. "Nationalism and National Sentiment in Post-socialist Romania." *Slavic Review* 52(2):179–203.

Verdery, Katherine, and Gail Kligman. 1992. "Romania after Ceausescu: Post-Communist Communism?" In *Eastern Europe in Revolution*, edited by Ivo Banac, 117–47. Ithaca: Cornell University Press.

Waterman, Christopher. 1990. "'Our Tradition is a Very Modern Tradition': Popular Music and the Construction of Pan-Yoruba Identity." *Ethnomusicology* 34(3):367–79.

Williams, Raymond. 1977. *Marxism and Literature*. Oxford and New York: Oxford University Press.

Wolf, Margery. 1992. *A Thrice-Told Tale: Feminism, Postmodernism, and Ethnographic Responsibility*. Stanford: Stanford University Press.

[16]

Native American Contemporary Music: The Women

Beverley Diamond

Abstract

This article explores issues raised in interviews with traditional and contemporary Native American musicians and recording artists of the 1990s. It exemplifies how they view their roles vis à vis *traditional gender structures and community obligations, how they draw upon different media to communicate their messages, and how they use their work as a form of social action. Their narratives reveal a wide variety of strategies by which they negotiate the double consciousness and multiple relationships of their lives, balancing historically rooted values and traditions with modern ones. I attempt to develop a feminist interpretation that is respectful of the cultural values these women expressed in their conversations with me.*

Boston, USA, April 9, 1999: Everything came together in a powerful way. The setting, Trinity Church in the affluent Copley Place was acoustically and visually spectacular, if a little ironic, as a setting for skilful arrangements of stomp dance songs, a song of lost loves as a "string of broken pearls", or a powerful indictment of the cultural loss represented in "museum pieces". The church was jammed with upwards of 1000 people, many of them Harvard University students, fans of the Sisters of Kuumba, an opening African American student ensemble. The Sisters' message was sincere though a bit timid on this occasion, knowing, perhaps the immensity of the vocal spirit which would follow. Four powwow dancers performed next, moving as best they could in the confined space of the church aisles. In my mind, they ironically embodied their peoples' historic confinement by Western institutions.

And then the concert headliners: Ulali, a trio consisting of co-founder Pura Fe (Tuscarora), co-founder Soni Moreno (Yaqui, Apache, and Mayan), and long-time partner Jennifer Kreisberg (Tuscarora).The crowd exploded in applause. At that moment, no one could doubt that Native American women in popular music now had a large, diverse, and enthusiastic audience. The hundreds of fan letters on their web site - many citing the trio's work with Robbie Robertson or the Indigo Girls or that final moving song in the hit film *Smoke Signals*, document the ways the US public has come to know and love them. On this spring evening in Boston, the strength of emerging alliances between African American and Native American artists was one strong theme. Ulali's innovative style itself draws on diverse musical roots. The perfect synchronicity of their close harmony, sliding chord changes, virtuosic phrasing, and polyrhythms

12 •   *the world of music 44 (1) - 2002*

played sometimes on frame drums, sometimes on small can rattles or cowhorn shakers
shifted from delicacy to fierce strength, from sweetness to rough-edged energy.

But there would be more before the evening ended. It just happened that the Six
Nations Women Singers, good friends of the trio, were in the audience and, at the urging of Pura Fe, Soni, and Jennifer, they came on stage. These six Haudenosaunee (Iroquois) women, led by Seneca singer Sadie Buck, matched the vocal strength of the trio
and, together, they nearly raised the roof with the *Unity Stomp* (undoubtedly familiar
to some audience members via the Six Nations Women Singers performance of it with
Robbie Robertson on his album *Contact from the Underworld of Redboy*). They continued the lively and very funny banter that characterizes Ulali's performances. The
audience was on its feet after virtually every song. Finally, they ended with *The Travelling Song*, a statement of aboriginal women's spirit of collaboration. The song had
been jointly composed in 1995 by women who attended the first Aboriginal Women's
Voices Project's workshops at the Banff Centre for the Performing Arts in Alberta,
Canada, one of several new institutionalized structures that have contributed to the
strength of indigenous women's voices on the current scene. This concert was a powerful stop on their travels.

This fragmentary ethnographic description of one event (paralleled by many others
in Canadian and US cities throughout North America) invites a number of questions.
Wherein lies the power of contemporary Native American women musicians: in their
old or new alliances, in the knowledge of travel and new encounters (the knowledge
of *The Travelling Song*) or in the knowledge of home and community? What factors
have enabled their innovativeness, entrepreneurship and collaborations to thrive in
the 1990s? How have new performance contexts changed their roles, their music, or
their sense of who they are? Whose work should be recognized here: the dozen or so
performers of 'star' stature, artists with large CD sales and growing numbers of film/
theatre credits, or the host of other women who are serving as important role models
in hundreds of communities; the new artists or the pioneers whose work of the 1970s
and 1980s faced different challenges, including an industry not yet attuned to "world
music?"

The questions are obviously posed after a decade in which a richer array of recordings and public performances by Native American women is available beyond
the boundaries of their communities than at any time in the past.[1] Their ages vary
enormously from child virtuosi such as the pre-teen Cree duo, Moodie x Two, to elders like Flora Wallace and Alanis Obomsawin. Some of these women (e.g. Joy Trejo, Sissy Goodhouse, Olivia Tailfeathers, or the Six Nations Women Singers) compose and perform repertoires of traditional music they have shared in their
communities throughout their lives. Some women such as Joanne Shanendoah make
contemporary arrangements of traditional songs. Many including Pura Fe, Fara or
Buffy Ste. Marie, are well respected as mainstream performers and singer-songwriters, regardless of the 'aboriginal' modifier. Contemporary First Nations, Inuit, and
Métis women may choose to be primarily classical or folk musicians, reggae or blues
artists, or rappers. But many—in fact most in some part of their work—draw upon a
combination of culturally specific elements and mainstream styles, creating synthe-

Roots Music 351

Beverley Diamond. Native American Contemporary: The Women • **13**

ses or stark juxtapositions in some cases that are unique in feel and in message, while contributing to a redefinition of the genres in which they work.

To catalogue the ways in which their indigenous consciousness is manifested in the work of Native American women musicians of the 1990s would require a monograph rather than this brief description and analysis. Consider a few examples. Barbara Croall, composer-in-residence with the Toronto Symphony Orchestra in 1999-2000, works with the sounds of the Ojibwe language. Mary Youngblood borrows stylistic elements from Plains flute music but also uses classical flute techniques in her entirely original works. Ulali uses call and response patterns and polyrhythmns reminiscent of the leg rattle rhythms characteristic of traditional Southeastern stomp dances. Their close harmony defies generic categorization. Sharon Burch uses a folk style, accompanied often by acoustic guitar but her songs are shaped rhythmically and structurally by the Navajo language and vocables. She uses a slow delivery as well as layers of voice-over, melodic passages, and 'extra' sounds that bridge human, animal and machine worlds. Wayquay creates a new style of rap, one that seems aware of the tradition of spoken poetry with musical accompaniment of an older generation of women including Jeanette Armstrong, Alanis Obomsawin, and Joy Harjo. Joy, herself, developed a unique stylistic synthesis of poetry, jazzy saxophone lines and reggae-inspired rhythms.

A distinctive aspect of the work of many of these enterprising women, exemplified in the ethnographic sketch at the beginning, is a record of extensive collaboration with one another as well as with others. Sometimes their work has engaged their brothers: Syren and Buffy Ste. Marie have worked with powwow drums (Eagle Heart and Red Bull respectively) using new technologies to rework traditional material or juxtaposing powwow music with contemporary popular music. The Six Nations Women Singers remain true to the traditional social dance music of the Haudenosaunee people but they have permitted their performance of this music to be recontextualized in a popular song by Robbie Robertson (who has worked with Ulali, Tudjaat, Walela, Fara and others). Joy Harjo, Joanne Shenandoah, and Mary Youngblood toured together in 1999.

The quotations woven through this chapter are taken from interviews I conducted with only a small proportion of the indigenous women currently active in the public music domain.[2] They are Sadie Buck, Joy Harjo, Pura Fe, Soni Moreno, Jennifer Kreisberg, Alanis Obomsawin, Jani Lauzon, Mishi Donovan, Lucie Idlout, and Mary Youngblood. Joanne Shenandoah and Buffy Ste. Marie both responded generously to emails concerning my project. In addition I relied on workshops and informal conversations with members of the Six Nations Women Singers.

I attempt to put their voices in dialogue about such issues as how they see their roles as musicians, *vis à vis* the cultural communities in which they were raised or those in which they now move. We discussed their choices of media and subject matter, their experiences on stage and in the recording studio, as well as their artistic aims. We also discussed the interplay of tradition and innovation, and issues surrounding appropriation and ownership as they have been affected by the process of

14   •   *the world of music 44 (1) - 2002*

commodification. In some places the narratives resonate strongly, while in others
they diverge. The sub-headings I use are expressions that emerged repeatedly in the
interview process. While the first three sub-headings are perhaps more concerned
with each woman's relationship to her community and her birth Nation, and while
the last three are perhaps more related to the ways they define their work in cross-cultural contexts, I resist the dichotomy. Rather, I urge readers to think about all kinds of
relationships (to environment, to community, to all the Others of individual experience) as fundamentally engaged in relation to each theme.

The framework for considering the work of Native American women in popular
music is crucial. Should we consider First Nations, Inuit, and Métis women as an extension of the enormous impact of women in 'mainstream' popular music in the late
1990s?[3] Visual artists and art historians have addressed this issue more extensively
than musicians and musicologists, to date. In attempting to construct an aboriginal
art history, for example, Gerald McMaster (1999:81) references artist Carl Beam's
view that mainstream is "not a roaring torrent ... it's more like mud puddle, or tiny
creek at best" and challenges the concept of a mainstream as a "duplicitous narrative" of universality. He argues that the very concept of a 'mainstream' wrongly suggests that the music and the discourse about it are not culture specific.

Music differs from visual art, about which McMaster writes, in several regards.
For one thing, both the technological sophistication and 'liveness' of performance
asserts the undeniable vitality and modernity of Native American expressive cultures. The immediacy of performance affords opportunities for new kinds of agency
and alliance. On the other hand, assertions of a 'mainstream' — particularly in popular music — are arguably more aggressive than in the visual arts. Various 'measures'
of 'mainstreamness' (airplay statistics, numerous legitimizing awards) reinforce the
duplicitous narrative McMaster acknowledges. In my view, although Native American women work in relation to these measures of success, Top 40 achievement
would be an inappropriate framework for presenting the artists you will meet in the
pages that follow. Their career paths, their histories and the values they carry forward, their positioning as Native American women are factors that frame their stories
differently. Similarly, however, to consider their work in relation only to Native
American traditional culture might perpetuate the colonial errors of freezing them in
the past or assessing their work in relation to some presumed index of 'authenticity.'
The extent to which 'tradition' resonates in their work is highly variable. Rather,
their stories are complex products of the discursive interaction of colonial history,
community (re)invigoration, corporate manoeuvring, and individual agency.

Roots Music   *353*

Beverley Diamond. Native American Contemporary: The Women • **15**

1. **"Women Who Keep on Singing Because They Must"**
    (Sadie Buck commenting on the Aboriginal Women's Voices Project at Banff
    Centre for the Arts, Alberta, Canada)

It is well established that women's pre-colonial roles in many First Nations cultures
were stronger than in the ensuing centuries.[4] With reference to this, several of the
women artists with whom I spoke described the current surge of aboriginal women's
music as part of a recovery of that power, of "thunderbirds returning" or a "regaining
of balance."

On the other hand, others, particularly Haudenosaunee clan mother Sadie Buck,
emphasized continuity:

> Mostly in our cultures, it's the male that has public roles and that's why the public only
> sees that. But it's been a reality that women do sing, and have sung, and will always
> sing because that's part of their role.

She observed that the change and revitalisation that has occurred in the 1990s is
in attitudes of mainstream audiences rather than in the social position of First Nations, Inuit, and Métis performers. It is easy to verify the important traditional musical roles women have played in many First Nations, as Navajo medicine people, in
Plains Sun Dance ceremonies, or in performance of the Crown Dances of the Mes-
calero Apache, as Inuit 'throat singers' or Pueblo basket dance singers, and so on.[5]
Sadie may have had some of these important roles in mind as well as her own lifelong
work as a Haudenosaunee singer.

The differences among this small group of interviewees reminds us that the history of the traditional roles of women in different nations is a diverse and complicated
one. Practices were locally variable and historically subject to change.[6] Some of the
women I spoke with were well aware of these and other contingencies of gender construction. Joy Harjo, for instance, challenged the naturalization of gender categories:

> I'm always aware of a place where there's no such thing as male and female. You
> know … there are interesting boundaries, so to speak, and real interesting and disturb-
> ing roles. I watched different roles play out for people, both males and females. I've
> certainly been a female in this life, you know. You're going to have a different experi-
> ence if you're a male.

Some shared principles, however, govern the gender systems in different nations
and varying sociopolitical contexts. One is the concept that men and women generally have different but mutually dependent and complementary roles. In some cases,
for instance, ceremonies were given to women who then passed them on to men.[7]
Musical and dance repertories might be distinctive or public performance might be
relegated to men while women play other non-musical roles, as in the case of the
Plains-origin powwow. In some First Nations, particularly Plains cultures, proscriptions against the use of the drum by women is related to the 'power' they already
have through menstruation; men are said to need to sing and drum in order to acquire
power that women already have. An important role for women in many Nations is as

16 • *the world of music 44 (1) - 2002*

"keeper of the fire" or "keeper of the next generation." Another emphasis, which takes different forms in different nations but seems to apply rather generally, is that special or unusual gender styles and the skills or strengths associated with them are held in high esteem. Many of the musicians celebrated here have such skills, ones that may not correspond to traditional public roles for women in their societies but that were encouraged nevertheless. They are, as Sadie Buck describes participants in the Aboriginal Women's Voices Project at Banff, "women who sing because they must."

While these themes of gender complementarity and respect for individuality resonated in the narratives of different artists, the divergences in their individual histories, motivations, and experiences, are equally significant. Some, such as the Six Nations Women Singers, were raised in a strong way by traditional people and their public performance continues the musical work they have always done by raising money for the mutual aid society of which they are an active part. Others were victims of a system that placed aboriginal children in adoptive homes. Mary Youngblood, Jani Lauzon, and Mishi Donovan all engaged in a search for their roots as adults and music was part of that search. Several women, including Alanis Obomsawin and Lucie Idlout (the oldest and youngest of the women interviewed), were raised in urban contexts but spent extensive periods, often during summer vacations, in the small Native communities of their grandparents. Jennifer Kreisburg visits and maintains a relationship with her community. Pura Fe now resides on some of her ancestral homelands while her colleague Soni Moreno has found a supportive community within New York City. Joy Harjo and Buffy Ste. Marie similarly reside far away from their people's land, both choosing Hawaii in the 1990s. Mishi Donovan enjoys rural residence in Onoway, Alberta, not far from the land her grandparents walked near Turtle Mountain, North Dakota.

The language that singers used to describe their roles as musicians often echoed these shared themes even when referencing divergent experience. Traditional Maliseet singer Margaret Paul, and Abenaki musician and film-maker Alanis Obomsawin, related the compulsion to sing to their roles as "keepers of the nation" or "keepers of the next generation." Margaret explained that she "had to [sing] cause there was nothing Indian, nothing of who we are or what we are."[8] Alanis stated that she was "always singing when [she] was a young girl." But because she was very "shy about getting up on stage," she refused many offers to perform, "[but] saying yes when it had to do with children, because that was always my main interest."

Closely related are statements by Oneida recording artist Joanne Shenandoah and Métis songwriter Jani Lauzon, who saw their talent as a special gift and a responsibility to use that gift for the good of the people. Reiterating a story that appears on her album, *Life Blood*, Shenendoah explained that her natural native name is "She Sings," a name given to her as a small girl. She continued:

> The elders seem to know what they are doing when they name you. I began in the computer industry and after 14 years, saw a huge tree being cut down. At that moment I realized, I needed to be doing more with my life and my natural talents.

Roots Music 355

Beverley Diamond. Native American Contemporary: The Women • **17**

For Jani, her success in music related:

> [to] a shift in the sense of responsibility, and it came with the realization of just how incredible being gifted creatively is. And I guess the sense of responsibility comes from a passion or a longing that I feel within myself to see the world working in a better way and a better respect for our own survival and so ultimately for ourselves. And it wasn't until I realized that each of us and every one of us [has] that responsibility.

At that point she found a way "to take the gifts [she has]" and marry them to "a yearning to help make change in the world." She explained that she specifically targeted young women for her first solo album *(Blue Voice, New Voice)*, employing women to perform with her, both in the blues and the powwow influenced song *Wabakii Bezhig*. The structure of this song, furthermore, subtly reflects female roles: at a powwow women generally encircle the ring of male drummers and they may enter the song part way through, an octave above the men's voices. In Wabakii Bezhig, the solo incipit of the lead singer occurs only once and the song's contours circle back to the highest pitch level rather than ending on the lowest, while the drum enters only in the second phrase and is not an essential underpinning of the women's voices, a musical gesture consistent with the belief that they already have the 'power'.

Jani spoke of "honouring [her] gifts in a much more spiritually based way so that [her] music then becomes a vehicle ... for the words and the love that the Creator brings upon the earth." Jani described herself as an intermediary: "I use my body as a vehicle to allow the voices from a larger place to come through me."

Mary Youngblood used a similar metaphor, describing herself as a vessel, an image adopted by musicians from many different cultural backgrounds:

> I don't want it [my career] to get so big that I lose myself in it. And one of the ways I do that is to remember that I'm just a vessel. I really truly believe that. I'm just a vessel between the Creator and this instrument. A long time ago I asked the Creator to use me and to use my art to touch people or for whatever my purpose is. I really believe that, that I'm just a vessel.

Mishi Donovan echoed Jani's vision, also using the metaphor of gifts that must be honoured:

> There are many gifts that are given to help the human race in general, not only First Nations people. And all of us have those gifts. But whether we choose to use them and use them in a good way is the question. You know, same as anything else, there's the good and bad and some choose not to walk a good path. But [there are] those that do honour those gifts that are given and start to use them in their personal life to help others, you know.

Joy Harjo similarly spoke about the responsibility that art entails but she saw this responsibility as directed toward her art itself because she believed "the poem is wiser than me:"

> You've got to have a respect for it, the music and the poetry. You realize that it's something larger than you, and that you're serving it. You're serving the music.

You're serving the poetry. And you have to give time to it, and you have to honour it, and it's not always easy.

Whether expressed as a responsibility or a need to honour one's gift, one's art, or life itself, these descriptions imply that music is fundamentally integrated with other realms of expression and experience. This theme also emerged in relation to the media of their work.

2. Multi-Media Before the Word was Invented (Buffy Ste. Marie)

When I contacted Buffy Ste. Marie about referencing her work, she responded:

> The most important thing you can take home about me is as a longtime multimedia artist before there was an internet or a name for "multimedia artist." The whole do-everything concept has always seemed natural to indigenous people but alien to academics, European traditions, and showbiz in general. (Actually it's easy.) [email 8/9/99].

Indeed, Buffy Ste. Marie has done cyber art, produced an interactive multimedia CD-ROM called *Science: Through Native American Eyes*, and engineered the sound mix on her own albums, *Coincidence and Likely Stories* and *Up Where We Belong*. In the former, she overdubbed the powwow voices (short excerpts of the Ironwood singers and Ben Blackbear are heard but the other voices are all Buffy's) and instrumental lines. In the mixing of *Darling Don't Cry* recorded in conjunction with the popular [powwow] drum, the Red Bull Singers, on her most recent CD *Up Where We Belong*, the drum sounds are digitally manipulated. She has been a strong advocate for technological development in First Nations communities. In an interview for *Runner* magazine (1994:36), for example, she explained:

> I think the new technology is very important for Native people and for artists because as Native people and artists, we usually have reasons for enjoying being at home. Home is where we really live ... As Native people and as artists, we live in our natural environment, in our studios, close to nature, close to our art and our work and our families. The new technology is making it better for Native people to work better at home and to still make our contributions to the world community without ever leaving the reserve. This is important, especially for women who are responsible for family, for artists who don't necessarily want to join the corporate ladder and for elders, who because of health reasons, or for personal reasons, would prefer to stay in the community and still make their contribution on-line through computer networking.

Her belief in community-based uses of technologies extends to a number of education initiatives, including the aforementioned CD-ROM and other projects described below.

The "do-everything" concept seems easy as well for many other aboriginal women in music. Music has, for several, been a natural extension of their literary work. Poet and author of the first novel[9] by a First Nations woman in Canada, Jeannette C. Armstrong (Okanagan), for instance collaborated with musicians to create the powerful album, *Til the Bars Break* (1991), as a message of resistance created during and

Roots Music 357

Beverley Diamond. Native American Contemporary: The Women • **19**

after the Oka crisis in Quebec.[10] This CD puts forward a message of solidarity both in the themes of songs and in the collaboration between Native and Caribbean musicians. Armstrong's recitations challenge stereotypes (e.g. in *Indian Woman* accompanied by a reiterated musical phrase vocalized by her sister Delphine [Derrickson] Armstrong), and offer a strong indictment of the forces which have historically oppressed Native Americans in *Blood of My People* and *Threads of Old Memory*. On the same album, the issue of stereotyping is also addressed in the parodic *High Tech Teepee Trauma Mama* by Ojibway performance artists Rebecca and Florene Bellmore (vocalists in the band 7th Fire).

Another widely acclaimed writer-musician is Joy Harjo (Muskogee) whose unique blend of saxophone interludes, performed poetry, and blues, jazz, or reggae influenced arrangements is a distinctive and powerful voice on the Native American scene. She described the hard work over 12 years to learn the saxophone and face the "utter terror" she had about getting on stage. She explained that her writing was always "aural" and indeed, in addition to her many published collections of prose/poetry,[11] she has produced a number of recorded anthologies.

> I think my voice was always there, somehow, whether it was the horn blowing through the voice, the singing voice ... I think it's a natural evolution, you know. I always loved music. I think music influenced me, even jazz, as a kid ... I wanted to be a painter. My aunt, Lois Harjo is a painter. And that's what I used to do all the time was paint. And then I used to sing all the time too. I always liked singing. And so the poetry came late ... I liked the singing part of it; I liked the musical part of language. And I realize now, that when I started writing poetry, the music was always there in it.

Many other Native American musicians are closely linked to theatre or film.[12] Alanis Obomsawin, acclaimed for her award winning documentary *Kanehsetake: 270 Years of Resistance* (Ottawa: National Film Board, 1993) among many others, described her early career: she fought for changes in the education system, sang, did fashion shows, and made recipes on television. She was recruited to be a film consultant, gaining access to film-making in that way. Her own ability to use whatever tools, media and resources she had access to in order to do the community work that motivated her, no doubt influences her message to other artists:

> Anyone that's a Native person and can express him or herself through words and singing, paintings, whatever, it's very important. And they should be free to do it the way they want.

Mishi Donovan is a documentary film maker and an actor in addition to being a musician. All her work is marked by her courage in addressing difficult social issues, including domestic violence (in songs such as *Letting Go* and *Does It Take Death*) or prescription drug abuse in the film *One Too Many*. She is particular excited by the revisionist history projects in which she has participated. With reference to a recent miniseries on Big Bear, she exclaimed "that's stuff going down in history, you know and it's awesome being a part of it." The Big Bear film shoot:

was conducted in Saskatchewan. It was a miniseries, directed by Gil Cardinal, and it was the historical account of Big Bear and the signing of the treaty with Poundmaker, and how Big Bear tried to spare his people the signing. He was the last one that did that. And finally, he signed because he was forced to for his people, because they were being starved to death ... It was an awesome experience because it was done with a First Nations focus and enacted by First Nations people and filmed right on the land where it happened, the Fort Qu'Appelle Valley.

Jani Lauzon is a similarly multifaceted artist, an actor, singer, song-writer and puppeteer. The latter skill has earned her a number of TV credits, including the *Mr. Dress-Up Show, Little Star* on the Learning Channel (Montreal), and an educational series, *Prairie Berry Pie*, produced in 1999 on the Global television network:

That's actually a skill that I have that really came from my mother because she was a doll-maker and brought her dolls to life. So it was just a natural skill I had. And it's actually the skill that I use ... so that I can support my music and my acting careers.

Aboriginal women are, of course, hardly the only artists who successfully cross among many media, but the emphasis they place on this aspect of their work and the reasons they feel they need to use image, movement, sound, and word in such a rich array of combinations is culturally significant. With all of these artists, there is a certain pragmatism to their choices of media. But, more than that, there are hints that, whatever the professional commitment and training needed in whatever medium, these artists will do what is required to communicate the stories that need to be told as historical correctives or social commentary.

3. Walking the Talk

In most of the interviews, I asked if particular musicians had influenced the artist to whom I was speaking. Perhaps my Euro-Canadian perspective led me to anticipate that people would identify artists whose sound or songs they appreciated. At any rate, I was struck by the fact that many comments related, not to the music *per se*, but to the humanity of the individual, to their capacity to give back to their communities. Mishi Donovan, for instance, has admired Buffy Ste. Marie because "she walks the talk" as Mishi commented:

She truly is one that I've watched and come to learn a little bit about and somebody that I respect for what she's done. And she's one of those front liners that I talked about.

Mishi may have had in mind such projects as Ste. Marie's "Cradleboard Project,"[13] an initiative which puts Native American and non-Native American children in contact via the internet, as well as making information available to students from a Native American perspective, "instead of studying dead text, handed down by generations of non-Indian educators" as Ste. Marie explains (1999:87). The approach to curricular design emphasizes fun, observing that "I think that it's just not

Roots Music   *359*

Beverley Diamond. Native American Contemporary: The Women • **21**

said often enough that self-empowerment comes from *enjoying* what you do" (Cald-well 1999:138). The Cradleboard web site incorporates a Cradleboard Jukebox.[14]

Direct assistance to their community is central to the work of the Six Nations Women Singers who are widely respected for their community service. The performance fees they are given for staged workshops or concerts are handed back to the community. As Charlene Bomberry explained in a recent workshop: "We belong to a larger organization called a Singing Society. So what a Singing Society does is raise money to help out people in our community. Maybe someone lost a relative, or they are sick or something. We give them money or give them groceries or just go help them do something. So that's the purpose of our whole organization" [Workshop at Harvard University, April 1999].

Emphasis on social action is embedded in language itself as their leader, Sadie Buck, explained. Even when speaking English, "around here, [we say] 'he makes up songs' ... Because it's an action oriented phrase, that makes more sense to people than 'composer' does ... when people would call me a composer, I [would] say 'no, I don't think so'. But then I realized the difference because [in English the word] composer is a noun; it means that is what I am and making up songs is only what I do." (interview in Cronk 1990:13)

A means of "walking the talk" employed by every songwriter in the Six Nations Women Singers is the use of music itself as a means of social action. Sadie Buck's very definition of music stresses the "essence of commitment and dedication" and asserts repeatedly that "it's all about caring and sharing." In her workshops, she emphasizes that social music has one objective: to make people want to dance. It plays a fundamental social role in that regard. Maliseet singer Margaret Paul has spoken in a similar way:

> I want to chant so I can send chills up and down somebody else's spine. That is what I want to do. To make somebody feel good, to make somebody feel like dancing. To make somebody feel PROUD, you know, that they are who they are.

The engendering of pride has been achieved by other artists in different ways.[15] Joanne Shenandoah has honoured the women of her community in the production of her CD *Matriarch*. A compilation of women's shuffle dance songs, or *eskanye*, each individual arrangement conveys something of the dedicatee. Hence, for example, track 3 dedicated to her mother, a clan mother and traditional person, has water drum accompaniment (although no cowhorn rattle) like traditional performance. It is also delicately embellished by xylophone-like sounds and the sounds of birds (those creators mentioned in the Haudenosaunee Thanksgiving Address as the sources of song) in the middle verses. On the other hand, a powwow-like drum beat (in tempo and pitch) is adopted on track 11 for a dedicatee who likes the powwow trail, while on track 7, an individual who enjoys travel and appreciates diverse cultural experiences is honoured with layered tuned percussion parts reminiscent of Indonesian gamelan textures.

Other women artists use their music as part of a process of community healing. Mishi Donovan, Lucie Idlout, and her fellow Inuk Susan Aglukark, are among the many who have addressed difficult social issues, for instance.[16] Lucie recounted:

> One song that I perform regularly is a song called *Suicide*. It speaks in the first person, as if it's my experience, about the various things that are going on in the mind leading up to and almost committing the act. And the reason why I wrote that song is because, in my family, as far back as my great-grandfather, there has been one male in each generation who has committed suicide ... It's an issue that affects all people no matter where you come from. But in the North we have the highest suicide rate in the world. And for me, it's not about having the rest of the world acknowledging that we have the highest suicide rate but it's about being honest enough and open enough and safe enough to talk about it. That's always the first step in dealing with any issue.

Several songwriters have been part of the important work of revisionist history, relating the stories of neglected Native American heroes (e.g. *Anna Mae Pictou Aquash* by Joy Harjo; *Tattered Tipi of Chief Seattle or About Geronimo* by Arigon Starr, or *Tears for Kientepoos* by Mary Youngblood); or telling historical events from an aboriginal perspective (e.g. *Louisiana Purchase* by Laura Vinson; *1492* by Wayquay; *Blood of My People* by Jeanette Armstrong; *Bury My Heart at Wounded Knee* or *My Country 'Tis of Thy People They're Dying* by Buffy Ste. Marie).

Joy Harjo expressed the importance of recognizing the 'front liners' of every society:

> I think the issues that draw me are issues about people who stand up and have integrity, no matter the cost, or no matter what they have to suffer. You know, people like Anna Mae [Pictou-Aquash]. People like Nelson Mandela, I think I really admire, who did not turn against the people ... and it put them in prison. Who didn't turn and try to destroy them. Who became the larger person and turned and embraced [their people]. And to me, that's what really moves me, like *A Letter from the End of the 20th Century*, those kinds of stories.

She refers to the title song on her 1997 CD, a story narrated to her by a Nigerian Igbo taxi driver in Chicago concerning a man who found the strength to befriend and redeem the murderer of his closest friend. This courage to resist violence with love is central to Harjo's vision of front liners.

Prior to her better known work in film, Alanis Obomsawin's early musical compositions were also related to her activism. A series of songs with the title *Bush Lady*—two of which are recorded on her CBC-produced LP of the same name—emerged from the need to articulate real life problems as she describes.[17] One musical setting for this song, starkly contrasts a taunting male voice accompanied by dry drum beats with an atonal chamber ensemble, defying generic or stylistic categorization:

> [The recording came together] for the same reasons that I was fighting for stuff in the schools. In my singing, my own experience in travelling across the country and seeing the situation of the women—the men too—the terrible situation, having to do with losing their status and all the hardship to do with that. It came from that and the misery

Roots Music 361

Beverley Diamond. Native American Contemporary: The Women • **23**

[of] leaving your community, losing your status, getting married, or perhaps living with somebody, having children and then being left on your own. And it's still happening but at that time it was like an epidemic or something. And talking with a lot of women and really knowing the situation very well, it's through that. I made several *Bush Lady* songs and it came from those feelings.

The emphasis on music as a form of social action is not presented here in order to romanticize this group of women as somehow more virtuous than other groups, but rather to emphasize that, for many of them, the very definition of music itself is tied to this vision of "sharing and caring." Judgments about the achievement of individuals was repeatedly tied to this capacity and this commitment. In fact, my questions about their 'achievements' made little sense within their frame of reference. Such questions were sometimes dismissed humourously. Mary Youngblood kidded that she wanted a Grammy Award, while Mishi Donovan laughed at the fact that she was home making bannock bread when she was awarded her Canadian equivalent, the Juno Award. Jani Lauzon told a funny story about driving with four friends in a decidedly unglamorous Honda Civic into the limousine line at the Juno Awards ceremony at which she was a nominee. Several argued that such honours spur more artists to get their work out but that winning is not the important thing.

If one thinks again of the metaphors for their own roles as singers—as vehicles, vessels, or individuals entrusted with the responsibility of gifts—it is perfectly logical that my questions about career development and 'achievements'[18] were so often deflected. Pura Fe seemed perplexed, perhaps even annoyed, when I asked the members of Ulali about their achievements. "Achievements? What we've achieved?" she asked with incredulity in her voice. "We've learned so much." She proceeded to describe herself as the lucky recipient of so many gifts: "More knowledge. That's for sure ... We owe, we owe everything that we've learned to so many people. They've given us so much. They've given us so much encouragement. They've given us, everything. You name it." "Food," added Soni. "Support. Place to stay. Laughter, everything," Jennifer chipped in. "Sticking up for us. There's so many," said Pura Fe.

4. "We Feel Those Sharp Edges All the Time" (Jani Lauzon)

Several artists find music an appropriate medium to convey the 'double consciousness' of their lives, at once facing two or more cultures, past and present. Jani Lauzon was the one who coined the sub-heading, for instance, with reference to the lead role she played in Tina Mason's play *Diva Ojibway*.

[My character] is in a place inside herself where she is constantly in that contradiction. She loves opera but she came from and grew up and dealt with that conflict within herself in a Native community where opera was not accepted and was ridiculed, and if you didn't like country music you weren't hip. So it was a contradiction in the play that came out of something she had experienced in her life.

She composed a song entitled *Symphony in E Minor* to articulate this conflict in the Diva Ojibway character she played, a conflict between the music she loved and the music she was raised with. Recorded on *Hearts of the Nation* (1997), the song layers a chorus of vocables (a cry to get the world to look up at her as she perches — ominously — on the edge of an "ancient building"), with acoustic guitar and flute accompaniment.

Jani continued to relate "what she had access to" with the often difficult doubleness of being a Métis woman in the late 20th century:

> For my music, I only respond intuitively to what I have access to. And with my first album, I used the blues as a base, with some jazz influence vocally, from all the years of listening to Frank Sinatra and Billie Holiday. And the horn sections mixed in with the mixture of chanting, which is something that I've really started to incorporate in my own understanding of the songs that come from my culture. So I used only what came from what I had access to ...
>
> We feel those sharp edges all of the time. We find ourselves trying to go back constantly now to the elders to find the old stories, to reconnect with the old ways, and yet we have to bring those old ways and we have to apply them to a modern way of living because this is what we are faced with now. So we're constantly, in our daily lives, dealing with that, and it doesn't surprise [me] that it reflects its way into our music.

Joy Harjo expressed a similar struggle with the complex mix of experiences on which she draws as a writer and musician:

> We're doing music that's about who we are, as Native people in the late 20th century into the next. I listen to jazz and blues, you know; it's all been part of our musical education. Our different tribal music. You know, I've been around a lot of Navajo musics, a lot of Pueblo music; of course powwow music has influenced everyone. A lot of [Rhythm and Blues].

It's not surprising that, at another point in our conversation, she said:

> I don't want to do just pure stuff. I did my first jazz Hawaiian music gig the other day. I try to mix things up a little. I don't want to do just pure jazz; that's not my place in life, just like it's not my place in life to write in European verse forms. It's not really who I am ... I feel my place is to open things up and make something else with them. It's not the easiest place to be.

Do these comments simply reflect the multiplicity of experience shared widely by virtually all postmodern artists? One critic, Gerald Vizenor (1999), suggests Native Americans face a unique challenge as "post-indians;" that is, individuals dealing with centuries of colonial inventions of what it means to be "Indian." As he says, "postindian warriors are wounded by the real" (Vizenor 1999:23). The opportunity and need to defy stereotypes was a topic addressed by virtually every participant in this research.

Jennifer Kreisberg of Ulali regarded the breaking down of stereotypes as perhaps the biggest success of Ulali:

Roots Music 363

Beverley Diamond. Native American Contemporary: The Women • **25**

All kinds [of stereotypes]. Stereotypes of Indians, types of Indian women, of what the music is supposed to sound like. Things like that. I think that's really big ... Sometimes people come to our shows expecting feathers and [expecting] us to talk about our spirituality which is just too personal, not 'for sale'. That's left at home. And I think some people get disappointed, even though they don't realize that, as we educate, blues and all those other kinds of music have roots in traditional Indian music. And I think they get disappointed that we're not stoic and, on the East coast, we're loud. A lot of the tribes are loud. Women are outspoken people. Sometimes they don't welcome the breakdown of the stereotypes. Sometimes they do.

Lucie Idlout, a young Inuit woman from Iqaluit (the capital city of the newly established northern territory Nunavut, Canada) also rejected easy markers of her identity,[19] going so far as to say that she "really hate[s] to be coined as an Inuk singersongwriter":

I don't like to be promoted that way. Because all I'm doing is I'm writing about life, and life as I experience it and life as I understand and feel ... I think definitely there are very strong stereotypes about, not just northern music, but what First Nations and Inuit music are supposed to be. I think people expect throat singing or drum dancing or 'eyo hiyo' music, and I don't understand why we should have to be pigeon-holed. It's beautiful for people who are doing traditional music. I love that. I love traditional music. I love listening to it. I don't personally appropriate any elements of that into my music and I don't see why I should have to, for that matter.

She laughed at a label recently applied to her: the "anti-Aglukark." She hastened to comment that she has nothing against the gentle, Arctic super-star Susan Aglukark but that her own music is harder-edged and 'heavy'.

A number of First Nations musicians, similarly, play on the divergences between their image and message. One of the most radical examples of the latter is Arigon Starr, self-labelled as "The Diva" (http://www.arigonstarr.com). Adept at using computer technology, her web pages present a glamourous socialite, encountering the stars of the First Nations and non-First Nations arts scenes. Her press reads like many 'Around Town' columns in the media. Her songs, on the other hand, for which all song texts and explanations of the issues that inspired them may also be found on the web, are hard hitting critiques and historical commentaries.

The strategies of defying stereotypes related closely in my mind to other instances of resisting cultural oppression. My own feminist orientation led me to see these as small-'p' 'political choices and actions'. On at least one occasion, however, I was stopped short when I tried to proceed with my 'political' frame in place. For instance, when speaking with the women of Ulali, I tried to frame a question about songs of social critique, songs such as *Museum Pieces*. I was interested in the political choices that artists make, the selection of one issue or another as musical material. My question was awkwardly framed. Jennifer kindly tried to help me out by saying:

I don't think we look at it as politics. It's just our experiences ... It's just that we get hassled at the stupid Canadian/US border every single time, and we've had it.

She references a song about border-crossing (and I'm reminded that Joy Harjo has written a song on the same theme, no doubt prompted by similar experiences). Then Pura Fe described the journey, and it was quite a pathway, which gave rise to *Museum Pieces*.

> Well, actually it started out 'cause I used to stay in Arizona a lot with a good friend of mine. He does a lot of work for the treaty council. So I travelled with him on a couple of trips and saw things. And one journey started at Wounded Knee during the memorial. You know, you take that in. And after that, we drove to Minneapolis and we went into the women's prison, the Indian program, and you take that in. And we ended up in Boston at the Peabody ... [My friend] was checking up on some remains and things that were taken ... So, we met with the director of the Peabody Museum. He wouldn't even meet us in his office; he met us in the hallway. So I took that in. So, it wasn't till I got home that it all registered. The way we exist and the everyday struggles ... So ya, it's important that we talk about our [experiences]. The fact that we're able to have a microphone, the fact that we're able to travel, the fact that we have a voice, it's very important we say everything we can say about our people, our communities, our home and everything, to preserve ourselves.

"You take that in" echoed as I listened to Mishi Donovan reflecting on aboriginal 'spirituality'.

> A lot of people misinterpret that fact that it's not a religion, so to speak. It's a way of life. It's a spiritual journey ... That [music] combines with the healing journey because the only way that I found I could express myself was in song. If you track the various albums that I've done, like *Spirit in Flight* was the first one, and that really reflected some of the confusion, some of the surface issues I was dealing with, you know, like family violence and not knowing my mom and identity and suicide and what not, painful relationships. That was the first one. But the second one, *Spirit Within*, goes deeper into the reaches of the soul, where it talks about the connection with the land and how I used the water, mountains, the earth, and the wind, and the animals to help me on my journey. So it's been a progression. It's been a change of writing.

Clearly she must speak with an awareness of the frequent romanticization of Indian women as 'spiritual'. She counters such fictions with pragmatic stories of real life, and with the idea of a journey, in which her creative work plays a role, as it did in relation to several of her songs, including the popular *Vision Quest*. For example:

> I had gone through our 4-day fast ... That was a big step for me, challenging all that I was and all that I hoped to be. To go in there wasn't something that was taken lightly but it was something I knew I had to do. So *Vision Quest* was written before that and actually [it] was a dream. So having that dream and then following that, I think it was a year later, I actually went in and did my fast, my vision quest.

Mary Youngblood also recounted how she is guided by close attention to things she has access to, and messages which intersect in her life in powerful way. She dedicated her second album, *Heart of the World*, and some of its revenue to the U'wa people of Colombia and to three US activists, two of whom were indigenous people. They were killed during a trip to work out an educational exchange and to support the

Roots Music 365

Beverley Diamond. Native American Contemporary: The Women • **27**

U'wa in their struggle to resist oil exploration on tribal land. Youngblood chanced upon a press release about the incident and then experienced an almost 'accidental' encounter with advocates of the U'wa cause on a trip to Washington.

The sharp edges of experience, then, relate to several things in the narratives cited here. They may be disjunctures between value systems within one's own family or community, difficulties of being treated as 'real' in the wake of centuries of stereotypical cultural violence, continuing acts of disrespect and oppression that constitute everyday experience for Native Americans, or indeed twists and unexpected encounters. Music plays a role in reporting, reflecting, and reconstituting those experiences.

5. "The Saxophone Complicates Things" (Joy Harjo)—Tradition and Innovation, Respect and Appropriation

In her poem/song entitled *The Musician Who Became a Bear: A Tribute to Pepper*, Joy Harjo uses the image and sound of her saxophone to symbolize the complexities of Native American, African American and European American interaction. The Native American singer and the saxophone initially share a melody, cadencing the first phrase in unison in "the lush stillness of the end of a world," but they slowly diverge, moving to different musical universes as the poem moves to be "about rearranging the song to include the subway hiss under your feet in Brooklyn." "The saxophone complicates things" in several different ways. Played by a Muscogee woman, the saxophone represents a history of cultural interaction among Native American, African American, European American and others, complicating pictures which isolate or compartmentalize Native Americans. Sounding the falseness of the dichotomy between purity and cultural loss, Joy's saxophone asserts an interactive history.

In such a history, however, issues of cross-cultural appropriation and respect must be engaged. Three aspects of appropriation[20] were addressed in the interviews: the adoption of Native American cultural symbols by non-Native wannabees and others who find uses (often commercial uses) for such symbols; the use of cultural property by Native American musicians from another Nation or social collectivity that is not theirs; the matter of agency in controlling the representation and distribution of Native American artistic work in a globalized economy.

The second issue is the one discussed most frequently in the interviews. Sadie Buck was particularly thoughtful and articulate on the issue since she organized the Aboriginal Women's Voices Project at the Banff Centre, in part, as a solution to the complex problems of interaction and innovation which emerge across First Nations, Inuit, and Métis as well as between aboriginal/non-aboriginal people. She emphasized that the context of the song must be taught with the song: "if it's sung in a certain way or if it's sung at a particular time, or if only certain people sing that, or if it's only sung with certain instruments, then you maintain that." She explained that the women gathered at Banff in "a traditional context of learning and being involved and sharing." They taught one another songs of their particular nation as well as the context for those songs. She described how:

> we learned those songs and got each other used to knowing those sounds, their sound that they have from their region. And then, what we did was, out of that context and those particular songs, we created together as a group.

One particular song, *The Travelling Song* (referenced in the vignette at the beginning of the article) became particularly iconic, referencing the respectful process by which it was created. Sadie recounted the experience:

> Basically we would sit in a circle and we would just sing. We would start with a vocable, any vocable, or whatever, and we would just sing. Then what happened was, if you're in a room, everybody is impacted in some way by the vocable and people start. Usually I start and I'll sing something for a short length of time. Then the next person sings something and the next person sings something and the next person sings something, and what happens is they start to blend together. Not only the lyrics but also the melodies, they blend together. And because all of these individuals come with their own sense of music and their own sense of sound from their land, then all of those things become intertwined and very intrinsic to the actual song that does come out. So, we just go around until we start hearing, and then usually I pull it, but there are other individuals who pull melodies. And all you have to do is really listen to what's being sung and then what you start to hear is a melody that keeps coming out, or else a melody overall that is maintained in the music and as people go around, you just pull that melody out, the lyric that goes with it. And once you've got it, then you cement it. You fix it ... You can embellish it, or structure it in the way that you want.

Her verb choice is interesting here. She "pulls" the collective song from the offerings of each individual. This is not conceptualized as co-creation but respectful attentiveness.

Knowing the 'context' is more difficult, however, for artists who were separated from family and community or those who choose to work outside the traditions of their birth community. Nevertheless, even those who emphasize innovation urged respect for the tradition of each community. It was not surprising to hear repeated emphasis that ceremonial music is not to be used in the commercial domain. However, even social music is often employed only after community permission has been obtained. Joanne Shenandoah in an interview with Andrew McConnell, for instance, described this process in relation to the Iroquois social dance songs she sometimes renames and inevitably rearranges. McConnell quotes her as saying "Admittedly some people were shocked by the combination" but explains that "the majority of elders she spoke to encouraged her to do it" (*Aboriginal Voices* 1996 5/2:12).

Instruments are an issue relating to appropriation as well. Joy Harjo addressed the issue:

> I've had people give me musical instruments or things, rattles and things, as gifts from their cultures and say, 'this is for you,' you know. They want to give it to me, but you, you can't use it in the music. It's used for particular ceremonies.

This respect, however, does not preclude musical inclusivity:

Roots Music   *367*

Beverley Diamond. Native American Contemporary: The Women • **29**

I know some of the band members want to be very strict, where we only want Indian musicians doing Indian things. I don't know that I'm yet quite that rigid. I think that a good musician with the right attitude and a good heart ... can cross over.

Mishi Donovan emphasized that the particular rattle she uses in public performance is what she described as a "people's" rattle, one intended to encourage participation:

These are things passed on to me, that have come my way, I guess. The rattle is a people's rattle. It's the four colours of the races and it's used by whoever wants to try it out and wants to accompany some of the songs.

Like Joy, however, she is not exclusive or "rigid" in terms of social proscriptions. She acknowledged that the drum as well as the sweat lodge were for the males of her Plains Chippewa culture but saw the advent of women at the drum as "a new thing that's come along," a part of the effort "to achieve balance between the male and the female again. That was so terribly, terribly lost."

Mary Youngblood has struggled with gender proscriptions as well particularly since the Plains flute (one type among the over 80 flutes she plays) has traditionally been a male instrument. The flute also was not part of either her Seminole or Aleut heritage. By playing only her own compositions, she avoids appropriating traditional music. Similarly, Ulali commented that they initially discussed the fact that, for some Nations, the drum was not played by women, although this proscription was never operative in their own nations. But they saw this as an issue of the past. Both Ulali and Youngblood now value the fact that their roles as women help to break down stereotypes, as mentioned earlier.

Ultimately, the issue of appropriation raises the larger matter of agency and control, matters that are urgent in the increasingly international circuits of these musicians, their CDs and videos. This issue has often been described as a struggle between the polarities of the local and the global. Stuart Hall (in Boswell and Evans 1999:37), for instance, articulates the issue as follows:

Paradoxically, globalization seems also to have led to a strengthening of 'local' allegiances and identities *within* nation-states; less the revival of the stable identities of 'locally settled communities' of the past, and more that tricky version of 'the local' which operates within, and has been thoroughly reshaped by, 'the global' and operates largely within its logic.

Jani was already cognizant of this when I first interviewed her in 1995. Her excitement about the burgeoning interest in Native American popular music was tinged with vigilance:

What's happening in the marketing world with Native music, on a positive side, is that it is more accessible to the masses and so people are gaining an understanding that was never there before, and gaining an appreciation that was never there before. So there's a tremendous amount of growth potential in that respect, but with that there is also the fact that the market is run by an industry that is controlled by these set of rules and

there is potential for this to become, for the Contemporary Native music scene to become another form of control and genocide in a sense.

In the rapid development in aboriginal music that has occurred in recent years, we
see evidence of strategies, however, that Hall does not seem to consider. Jani's astute
observation is closer to the combination of doubt and wonder that Vizenor has articulated as a marker of "trickster hermeneutics":

> The sources of natural reason and tribal consciousness are doubt and wonder, not nos-
> talgia or liberal melancholy for the lost wilderness; comic not tragic, because melan-
> choly is cultural boredom, and the tragic is causal, the closure of natural reason. The
> shimmers of imagination are reason and the simulations are survivance, not domi-
> nance; an aesthetic restoration of trickster hermeneutics, the stories of liberation and
> survivance without the dominance of closure. (1994:14)

6.   "We'd Pretty Much Have the Place Connected" (Soni Moreno of Ulali)

The theme of full and interactive participation in the world emerged in virtually every narrative, often articulated in terms of the important relationships which musicians forge both within and beyond the community. Often the topic of participation,
relationship, and 'connections' was introduced in conversation when I least expected
it, in relation to career achievements and turning points, for instance, or with regard
to CD production values. Perhaps the strongest statement was Soni Moreno's when
she described the privilege that Ulali had to travel and reach new audiences, changing the image of aboriginal women and growing in knowledge and friendships: "I
think if we could have a string or a length of chain to leave with every community
and place we have travelled, we pretty much would have the place connected."

Part of the tricksterism identified by Vizenor is the fact that many of these artists
opt out of the competitive, hirerarchical values enacted in many parts of the music industry. They generously thanked people like Robbie Robertson and Buffy Ste. Marie
who had inspired them and facilitated their entrée to a wider audience through collaborative CDs such as *Music for the Native Americans, Contact from the Underworld of Redboy*, or *Up Where We Belong*. They valued opportunities to work together. The event described at the beginning of this chapter was one such occasion.
Another was the autumn 1999 tour by Joy Harjo, Joanne Shenandoah, and Mary
Youngblood.

The project most often referenced as an important place of connection, however,
was the *Aboriginal Women's Voices project*, the brainchild of Sadie Buck, facilitated
by the Banff Centre for the Performing Arts. Jennifer Kreisberg of Ulali stated:

> Sadie Buck really made a comfortable space for us to get together and create together
> and share. And we got paid a little bit so it wasn't like our households, our homes, fell
> apart while we were gone. That really helped. We were fed. What they did was they
> took all the worry, the details, and just gave us a space to do it. That was really good.
> It's important.

Her colleagues Soni Moreno and Pura Fe both echoed Jennifer's praise, describing it as "an incredible place" and a project that is really important for aboriginal women's music. Jennifer illustrated both the camaraderie and the respect among the women at Banff with a story about one song for which comical but irreverent words were made late one night. An older participant had as much fun as the rest of the women, although she had not understood two profane and bawdy, English-language references. When she came back the next day, upset because she had found out the meaning of the words, the women agreed to drop the song from their performances and from the recording, *Hearts of the Nations*.

In many narratives the importance of connectedness, trust, and close relationship was emphasized as a key element in producing CDs. When describing the criteria for a successful band, Joy Harjo quickly replied:

> I know in my band, nobody showboats ... And maybe that's a woman doing so [insisting on this cooperativeness] but that's [also] John and Sue [Williams], particularly. They were raised in tribal communities. That's kind of a different attitude. You want everybody to do their best. And it's about not competing with each other. It's about competing with yourself, to really serve the music and serve the place it comes from well.

Mishi Donovan commented that she insists that, during production, "the atmosphere in which we're creating our work has to be a good environment or I won't sing ... that's just the way I am, the way I work, and it has to be something honoured. If it's not, then that feeling won't be represented in the music."

One further discourse of 'connectedness' is noteworthy. Joy Harjo recollected that she thinks of 'home' as a symbolic place of connection in a contemporary world where travel and uprootedness are so much the norm:

> There's a place that's somewhere in your heart that connects all of those things, a place that we all go back to. I was born in Oklahoma, but that's always felt, to me, well we are not here by choice. And so it's made me restless ... I love going back, I go back for ceremonies. And I love the people. And I love being there in that place, but it's not where I can be. It's not my place, to stay there in this life.

As Joy articulated the distinctiveness of music making in Native American contexts, in response to my observation that I hadn't yet found a Native American language that's got a word for 'music', one senses that music is perhaps 'home' for her:

> It's probably because [music is] so integrated into life, you know; it's like breathing. It's a whole different relationship. You don't have artist/audience. You have participant. It's more like participation, not set up [as] artist/admirers ... Everyone is a participant and it's a whole different way to think of your place in the world as a human, and as someone who sings.

32   •   *the world of music 44 (1) - 2002*

7.   Agendas in Dialogue

I have attempted here to counterpoint the perspectives of twelve Native American women musicians (with passing references to several others). My perspective was shaped, in part, by various 'third world' critiques concerning the representation of women's cultures.[21] They observe that much feminist literature written by white women ignores women's situation in the postcolonial world, and considers all women's movements as products of (Western-defined) modernization or development, assuming the same patterns across vastly different cultures and nations. These pitfalls are easy to imagine in my own work. For instance, as I mentioned at the outset, it is tempting to read the 1990s success of aboriginal women performers as inextricably connected with the industry success of women generally in popular music of this decade,[22] but an overemphasis on this connection would repeat the second and third of the errors identified above. The 1990s music of Native American women makes strategic use of the increasing popularity of 'world music' but is certainly not determined by it. Furthermore, the motivations and relationships, musical style choices and performance modes of the performers introduced here vary markedly both from one another and mainstream production.

The interviews with these artists suggest a number of means of rethinking one of the most vexing of issues central to contemporary cultural studies and to feminism: subjectivity. While feminists have sometimes observed the polarization of individuality and community-mindedness, these musicians seem to root their esteem for each individual's pathway, in their community-mindedness. Not surprisingly, then, the star system of the Western music industry has little valence here as a framework for constituting oneself as an artist, although it may be a useful strategy or even a vehicle for masquerade. The many substantial honours and awards garnered by aboriginal women in music are often valued, not as individual achievements, but as means of recognizing First Nations, Inuit, and Métis music generally.

Experience and its relationship to what is often called 'identity' (a word that has its own share of mystery in the academic world in which I spend most of my time) is affirmed over and over in the work of Native American women musicians. But what exactly is 'experience'? And how is its social construction to be understood in its own context? Joan Scott has written about the 'historicity' of concepts of experience: until the early 18th century, its connection to experiment, observation, and the visual; the incorporation of 'reflection' as an element of experience in the writings of the 19thcentury, and the acceptance of "feeling as well as thought" in the 20th; the extension of the concept to "influences external to individuals - social conditions, institutions, forms of belief or perception" in the 20th century (1992:27), but her examples are all Eurocentric.

What does Native American discourse assume and create when 'experience' is referenced in relation to music? Several distinctive emphases fill the stories of the Native American women interviewed for this research. One is their insistence that experience is not divisible into European categories such as politics or religion for in-

Roots Music 371

Beverley Diamond. Native American Contemporary: The Women • **33**

stance. And secondly, that experience is not autonomous but a place of relationship, a place where divergences are reconciled very often, where the sharp edges of simultaneously different worlds are brought together. A third is that experience is an unfolding, a journey or pathway, one that has unexpected turns, accidental encounters and challenges. Furthermore, the narratives of individuals are the narratives of relationships with other humans, beings, places, and environments. This insistence on wholeness is compatible with the multimedia emphasis of many of the artists interviewed.

Just as many First Nations languages are verb- rather than noun-oriented (as Sadie Buck observed), their music is often action-oriented, offering new possibilities for being a Native American woman, sometimes by finding contemporary means of reinforcing historically rooted traditions and values, sometimes by playing—tricksterlike—with various identities of modernity (be they diva, rock star, historian, activist or environmentalist), sometimes by insisting on the in-betweeness of living among different cultural worlds. But at the same time, the work of this important group of artists reframes 'experience' by storying the world in terms of specific places, people they have met, humorous events and also "sharp edges" they have encountered. At the same time, it would be unfair to say that they resist *a priori* and bounded concepts of culture or community to the same extent as many Euro-American feminists or postmodernists. Their music insists both on their individuality and on an array of solidarities.

Notes

1   One indication of the activity of Native American women singers is the steady growth of applications to the Aboriginal Women's Voices Project in Banff, Alberta. Project director Sadie Buck told me that, while she had to search hard to find 12 participants for the first year of workshops in 1995, 68 applications for 12 places were received in 1998.

2   There are a growing number of published interviews: with Maggie Paul and Elin James in *Sound of the Drum* (1990) with five Shoshone women in Vander's *Songprints* (1988), with Buffy Ste. Marie as well as her male colleagues John Trudell and Litefoot in E.K. Caldwell's *Dreaming the Dawn: Conversations with Native Artists and Activists* (1999), and with a number of elders in Kulchyski et al., *In the Words of Elders: Aboriginal Cultures in Transition* (1999), Miller and Chuchryk (1996), and Keeling (1989). One ethnomusicological anthology (Keeling, 1989) provides an introduction to women's traditional musical roles and practices in different parts of North America. Several monographs by ethnomusicologists focus on the musical practices of Native American women; these include Frisbie (1993 [1967]), Vander (1988), and Giglio (1994).

3   Comparisons with mainstream artists are inevitable in media reviews and casual conversation. For instance, Lucie Idlout has been described as the ani di franco of the north, Mishi Donovan has been related to Sarah McLachlan in the quiet emotional intensity of her message, and so on.

4   See, for example, Gunn Allen (1986) and Leacock (1980), the former more reliant on oral historical and the latter on documentary evidence.

5　A good introduction to the traditional musical roles of First Nations women may be found in the CD booklet written by Rayna Green and Howard Bass for *Heartbeat: Voices of First Nations Women* (Smithsonian Folkways 1995).

6　Furthermore, as Plains Cree Métis historian Emma La Roque has noted: "it should not be assumed, even in those original societies that were structured along matriarchal lines, that matriarchies necessarily prevented men from oppressing women" (1996:14).

7　Hungry Wolf has described this for the Plains Blood and Ojibwe people (1996:78). Benton has described the gift of the Ojibwe dance drum to a woman (see Diamond et al 1994:34-38).

8　Interview published in *Sound of the Drum* (1988:13).

9　*Slash* (Penticton, BC: Theytus Books, 1985).

10　This tragic event concerned Mohawk resistance to the sale of land, part of which was an ancient burial ground, to a developer. Mohawk warriors and allies from other First Nations confronted the Canadian army in 1990. The saga has been documented by Abenaki filmmaker Alanis Obomsawin in her award winning documentary *Kanesatake*, and several other short films focusing on participants in the struggle.

11　Her writing often straddles the boundary between prose and poetry. Among her publications are two 'chapbooks', several award-winning anthologies such as *She Had Some Horses* (1983), *In Mad Love and War* (1990), and *The Woman Who Fell From the Sky* (1994), as well as the edited anthology of writing by Native American women, *Reinventing the Enemy's Language* (1997).

12　Vice versa, high profile playwrights including Tomson Highway and Shirley Cheechoo are also accomplished musicians.

13　Initially funded by the W.K. Kellogg Foundation in 1996 (http://www.cradleboard.org/main/html).

14　Buffy's contribution to the Native American community, however, is multi-faceted. She has facilitated recognition of Native American music in many ways, including being one of the initiators and advocates for the Juno Award for the Best Music of Aboriginal Canada in 1994. Her community work as well as her artistry have been honoured, including induction into the Juno Awards Aboriginal Hall of Fame in 1997.

15　Direct claims of a proud identity include songs such as Susan Aglukark's *O Siem*, Fara's *Pretty Brown*, or Melanie Chartrand's *I Am Métis*. Celebrations of local places in songs such as Marg Raynor's *Giant's Tomb or Midsummer Isle*, Aglukark's *Pond Inlet*, Ste. Marie's *Cripple Creek* or Youngblood's *Moaning Cavern* also reinforce local pride. Other ways of supporting the community include administrative support for artists. As a Board member at the American Indian Community House in New York, Soni Moreno influences the programming of Native artists, singers, dancers and writers in what she describes as "a community of many nations."

16　Once again, Buffy Ste. Marie was the pioneer in this regard with songs such as *The Incest Song* and *Babe in Arms* (concerning wife abuse).

17　These songs predated Bill C-31 whereby Canadian Native women married to non-Native men regained their status.

18　The achievements of many of the women who responded with such modest generosity are considerable. Pura Fe's success on Broadway and the New York jazz scene (with the Mercer Ellington Orchestra, for instance), or Harjo's Lifetime Achievement Award from the Native

Roots Music 373

Beverley Diamond. Native American Contemporary: The Women • **35**

Writers Circle of the Americas, and the New Mexico Governor's Award for Excellence in the Arts in 1997 are often cited. *In Mad Love and War,* and *The Woman Who Fell From the Sky* have received book awards. At the first Native American Music Awards (1998), Buffy Ste. Marie was named the Best Pop Artist, Joanne Shenandoah named Best Female artist and her album *All Spirits Sing* the best children's album. Shenandoah also received the 1997 Native American Record of the Year Award from the Association for Independent Music INDIE Award committee in 1997, Mishi Donovan was awarded a Juno for the Best Music of Aboriginal Canada in 1997, Joanne Shenandoah and Joy Harjo (an 8-time NAMA finalist) have each received a First Americans in the Arts and Outstanding Musical Achievement Award in 1993 and 1998, respectively. Jani Lauzon, The Six Nations Women Singers, and the participants on the *Hearts of the Nation* album have been nominees for Junos and/or Canadian Aboriginal Music Awards. Manitoba songwriter and producer Laura Vinson and Vancouver Métis singer-songwriter Fara received Canadian Aboriginal Music Awards in 1999. Buffy Ste. Marie's extensive record of achievement include an award as Best International Artist in France for *Coincidence and Likely Stories*; her song *Up Where We Belong* as adapted for the film track of *An Officer and a Gentleman*, received an Academy Award in 1982. Her high profile collaborations with Janis Joplin, Barbra Streisand, Elvis Presley and others are highlighted in several biographical sketches. See also footnote 13.

19 Several of her Inuit colleagues do make use of the traditional sounds and styles that Idlout avoids, but they too defy expectations by unusual juxtapositions and arrangements. Throat singing, for instance, a musical genre which is generally a women's genre, and one which has attracted the attention of southerners interested in extended vocal techniques, is juxtaposed by Tudjaat with a popular song, representing their double vision, simultaneously past and present. Anita Issaluk accompanies throat singing with guitar, adapting the tradition to the resources of the present. Idlout also does these vocal games, on occasion, in live performances such as one at the Vancouver Folk Music Festival in 1998.

20 *Aboriginal Voices* magazine has presented different perspectives on these issues in three recent volumes (5/2, 6/2, 6/4). The latter parodies what its author sees as stereotypic identity making by First Nations artists themselves.

21 See, for example, Mohanty et al (1991) and Narayan (1997).

22 In 1996, women outnumbered men on Top-40 charts across North America. Dickerson (1998) documents the impressive rise to the top of women in popular music and presents "Top 20 Album Charts" for the years from 1986 to 1997. Two women with aboriginal roots are represented on those charts: Rita Coolidge and Shania Twain.

References

Bourdeau-Waboose, Jan
    1995   "Roots & Fame: The Challenges Facing Susan Aglukark." *Aboriginal Voices* 2(2):14-6.

Caldwell, E. K. compiler
    1999   *Dreaming the Dawn. Conversations with Native Artists and Activists.* Lincoln: University of Nebraska Press.

Cronk, M. Sam, compiler
    1990   *Sound of the Drum.* Brantford: Woodland Cultural Centre.

36 • *the world of music 44 (1) - 2002*

Cruikshank, Julie in collaboration with Angela Sidney, Kitty Smith, and Annie Ned
    1990   *Life Lived Like a Story.* Lincoln: University of Nebraska Press and Vancouver: Univer-
            sity of British Columbia Press.

Diamond, Beverley et al
    1994   *Visions of Sound: Sound-Producing Instruments in Native Communities of Northeast-
            ern America.* Chicago: University of Chicago Press and Waterloo, Ontario: Wilfrid
            Laurier University Press.

Dickerson, James
    1998   *Women on Top: The Quiet Revolution That's Rocking The American Music Industry.*
            New York: Billboard.

Edut, Ophira
    1999   "Techno.fem: Buffy' New Gigabyte." *Ms* 9(5):86-8.

Frisbie, Charlotte Johnson
    1993   [1967] *Kinaaldá. A Study of the Navaho Girl's Puberty Ceremony.* Salt Lake City: Uni-
            versity of Utah Press.

Giglio, Virginia
    1994   *Southern Cheyenne Women's Songs.* Norman: University of Oklahoma Press.

Gunn Allen, Paula
    1986   *The Sacred Hoop. Producing the Feminine in American Indian Traditions.* Boston:
            Beacon Press.

Hall, Stuart
    1999   "Culture, Community, Nation." In *Representing the Nation: A Reader.* David Boswell
            and Jessica Evans, eds. London: Routledge, 33-44.

Harjo, Joy and Gloria Bird eds.
    1997   *Reinventing the Enemy's Language: Contemporary Native Women's Writings of North
            America.* New York: W. W. Norton.

Keeling, Richard ed.
    1989   *Women in North American Indian Music: Six Essays.* The Society for Ethnomusicolo-
            gy, Inc. Special Series No. 6. Bloomington: Society for Ethnomusicology.

Kulchyski, Peter et al eds.
    1999   *In the Words of Elders. Aboriginal Cultures in Transition.* Toronto: University of Tor-
            onto Press.

La Fromboise, Teresa et al
    1994   "Changing and Diverse Roles of Women in American Indian Cultures." In *Native
            American Resurgence and Renewal: A Reader and Bibliography.* Robert N. Wells, Jr.
            ed. Mutchen, N.J.: Scarecrow.

La Roque, Emma
    1996   "The Colonization of a Native Woman Scholar." In *Women of the First Nations: Pow-
            er, Wisdom, and Strength.* Christine Miller and Patricia Chuchryk, eds. Winnipeg: Uni-
            versity of Manitoba Press.

Leacock, Eleanor
    1980   "Montagnais Women and the Jesuit Program for Colonization." In *Women and Coloni-
            zation. Anthropological Perspectives.* Mona Etienne and Eleanor Leacock, eds. New
            York: Praeger.

Roots Music   375

Beverley Diamond. Native American Contemporary: The Women • **37**

Martin, Kallen
    1996   "Pura Fe and Native American Jazz." *Aboriginal Voices* 3(2):13.

McConnell, Andrew
    1996   "Joanne Shenandoah." *Aboriginal Voices* 3(2):12.

McMaster, Gerald
    1999   "Towards an Aboriginal Art History." In *Native American Art in the Twentieth Centu-
            ry*. W. Jackson Rushing III, ed. London: Routledge, 81-96.

Miller, Christine and Patricia Chuchryk, eds.
    1996   *Women of the First Nations: Power, Wisdom, and Strength*. Winnipeg: University of
            Manitoba Press.

Mohanty, Chandra et al eds.
    1991   *Third-World Women and the Politics of Feminism*. Bloomington: Indiana University
            Press.

Narayan, Uma
    1997   *Dislocating Cultures: Identities, Traditions And Third-World Feminism*. New York:
            Routledge.

Peterson, Richard
    1998   "Songs from the Wood Thrush (Ulali)." *Aboriginal Voices* 5(4):30-3.

Scott, Joan
    1992   "Experience." In *Feminists Theorize the Political*. Judith Butler and Joan W. Scott, eds.
            New York: Routledge, 22-40.

Seesequasis, Paul
    1995   "Joy Harjo: In Mad Love & War." *Aboriginal Voices* 2(2):49-51.

Stawarz, Jean
    1994 "Buffy Sainte-Marie. Songs of Conscience." *The Runner* 1(3):26-39.

Vander, Judith
    1988   *Songprints: The Musical Experience of Five Shoshone Women*. Urbana: University of
            Illinois Press.

Vizenor, Gerald
    1999   [1994] *Manifest Manners. Narratives on Postindian Survivance*. Lincoln: University
            of Nebraska Press.

Wright-McLeod, Brian
    1996   "Bury My Heart. A Brief History of Resistance and Protest in Contemporary Native
            Music." *Aboriginal Voices* 3(2): 36-9, 49.

Discography

Selected Anthologies

Children of the World: A Compilation of Some of Native Canada's Best Music
    1995   Group Concept Music PPF4 2023.

Heartbeat. Voices of First Nations Women
    1995   Washington: Smithsonian Folkways. SF CD40415.

38 • *the world of music 44 (1) - 2002*

Heartbeat 2: More Voices of First Nations Women
    1996   Washington: Smithsonian Folkways. SF CD40445.

Hearts of the Nations
    1997   Aboriginal Women's Voices in the Studio. Banff Centre for the Arts / Sweetgrass.
            AWV/Banff 97.

The Inuit Artist World Showcase
    1995   Inukjuak: Inukshuk Productions.

Till the Bars Break
    n.d.   Irresistable Mayan Revolutionary/Cargo Records. IMR014.

Weaving the Strands. Music by Contemporary Native American Women
    1998   Red Feather Music RF 3001.

Solo or Group Albums

Aglukark, Susan
    1995   *This Child*, EMI Canada E 4 7241 8 32075 4 1.

Burch, Sharon
    1993   *Yazzie Girl*, Canyon CR534.

Burch, Sharon
    1999   *Colours of My Heart*, Canyon CR536.

Chartrand, Melanie
    n.d.   *Colorblind*. Winnipeg: Sunshine Records SSCT 4291.

Donovan, Mishi
    1996   *The Spirit Within*. Winnipeg: Sunshine Records, SSCT 4258.

Donovan, Mishi
    2000   *Journey Home*. Winnipeg: Arbor Records, AR-11192.

Fara (Palmer)
    1997   *This is My World*, Blackmoon Records, Burnaby, BC.

Fara (Palmer)
    1999   *Pretty Brown*. n.p.: New Hayden Music Corporation, NHMC 1717.

Harjo, Joy
    n.d.   *Furious Light*. Poet's Audio Centre.

Harjo, Joy
    1994   *In Mad Love and War*. Wesleyan University Press (book and cassette).

Harjo, Joy
    1996   *Letter from the End of the 20th Century*, Silver Wave SD/SC 914.

Issaluk, Anita
    1999   *Songs for the Northern Heart*, Arroyo Music. PBM 307.

Lauzon, Jani
    1994   *Blue Voice, New Voice* Toronto: Ra Records, RR0113.

Lauzon, Jani
    1998   *Thirst*, Toronto: Ra Records, RR0115.

Pura Fe
    1995   *Caution to the Wind*. Shanachie/Cachet 5013.

Robertson, Robbie
    1994   *Music for the Native Americans*. Capitol CA 7243 8 28295 4 6.

Robertson, Robbie
    1998   *Contact from the Underworld of Redboy*. Capitol 7243 8 54243 2 8.

Sainte-Marie, Buffy
    1970   *The Best of Buffy Sainte-Marie,* Two Volumes. Vanguard CVSD 3/4.

Sainte-Marie, Buffy
    1992   *Coincidence and Likely Stories*. Capitol 21920.

Sainte-Marie, Buffy
    1996   *Up Where We Belong*. EMI Canada E4 35059.

Seventh Fire
    1994   *The Cheque is in the Mail*. Sioux Lookout, Ontario: First Nations Music Y4 7 7621
            10016 6 7.

Shenandoah, Joanne
    1996   *Matriarch*, Silver Wave SD 916.

Shenandoah, Joanne
    1998   *Orenda*, With Lawrence Laughing. Silver Wave SD 918.

Six Nations Women Singers (Sadie Buck, Betsy Buck, Charlene Bomberry, Pat Hess, Janice G.
Martin, Jaynane Burning)
    1996   *We Will All Sing. Edwadrenodo:nyo*, SOAR 175-CD.

Starr, Arigon
    1997   *Meet the Diva*. West Hollywood: Wacky Productions Unlimited WPU 41225-2.

Trejo, Judy (with Delgadina Gonzalez and Christina Gonzalez)
    1997   *Circle Dance Songs of the Paiute and Shoshone*. Phoenix, AZ: Canyon Records CR
            6283.

Ulali (Pura Fe – Tuscarora; Soni Moreno –– Apache, Yaqui; Jennifer Kreisberg – Tuscarora)
    1994   *Mahk Jchi*, Hartford, CT: Original Vision Records.

Wayquay
    1997   *Tribal Grind*, Global Beat. 9B10202.

Youngblood, Mary
    1998   *The Offering*, Silver Wave SD 917.

Youngblood, Mary
    1999   *Heart of the World*, Silver Wave SD 921.

[17]

The jukebox of history: narratives of loss and desire in the discourse of country music

AARON A. FOX

Introduction

Is country music for real? This question haunts country's detractors, critics, fans and analysts, as it haunts all students of popular culture. Country music is only an extreme example of the instability, contradiction and ironic reflexivity characteristic of popular cultural forms in general in postmodern, capitalist society. It seems impossible to locate an 'authentic' country music text, performance or context, one which represents the 'real' life of a 'real' community without alienated nostalgia, false consciousness or kitschy commodification. On the other hand, country remains more overtly loyal to the experience, desires and language of a particular class and culture than almost any other major popular musical genre. A unique, if elusive core of 'authenticity' tantalises country's supporters and infuriates its critics, but attempts to separate the true from the false in country music, whether at the level of text, context or performance, are bound to fail. Country resists all such attempts; it incorporates and combines the true and the false into a poetic which is explicitly deconstructive of the ideology which these categories encode.

Simon Frith has reminded us that 'music can not *be* true or false, it can only refer to *conventions* of truth or falsity' (1988, p. 100). I am concerned in this article with the discursive structures and interpretive practices which comprise these conventions of 'authenticity', through the intertwining of 'the true' and 'the false', in country music, and with the implications of these conventions for a critical understanding of popular culture. These structures and practices are marked in the texts and contexts of country music by signs which are created and transformed through strategies of intertextuality, elaboration, intensification and inversion. Through these strategies, the categories of 'the true' and 'the false' are set into a complex, indeterminate motion.

In the resulting confusion, nothing is what it seems to be. Solid 'objects' become speaking 'subjects', and heartbroken 'subjects' consume themselves as commodified 'objects'. 'Natural' ideological meanings and codes are denaturalised, only to be renaturalised and appropriated to other codes and ideologies. Ostensible signs of 'the true' and 'the false' are inverted and conflated. Through this semiotic hysteresis, country music enacts, reproduces and criticises the contradictory conditions of its own production as an aesthetic commodity in capitalist society. This article tracks this subversive and playful, yet also contaminated and compromised, self-deconstruction through the discourses of country music.

54   *Aaron A. Fox*

Metanarratives of Loss and Desire

Country's deconstructive semiotic play occurs both *in* its sung narratives and *on* a narratively structured cultural and psychological terrain. The narratives of country songs emerge in the interstices of two competing, yet interdependent, cultural *metanarratives*, which I will call the metanarratives of Loss and Desire. These metanarratives are powerful and diffuse cultural 'stories' which make sense of and reproduce social and psychological experience in capitalist society. They organise and produce, and are in turn reproduced by, country music's textual narratives, performance conventions, and its contexts of production and consumption.

Each of these metanarratives can be read as an inversion of the other, and each depends for its salience upon a representation of the other. The metanarrative of Desire makes people and feelings into reified objects to be bought, sold, used up and replaced. This narrative is enacted through the very practice of consuming music as a commodity, and it is explicitly and implicitly re-told in many song texts. According to this objectifying story, the old and worn out is quickly forgotten, and replaced by the shiny and brand new. The narrative subject is constituted publicly as a consumer of an endless stream of desired objects.

The metanarrative of Loss resists this equation of subjective fulfilment with the consumption of objects and inverts the terms of the metanarrative of Desire.[1] Whereas the metanarrative of Desire makes feelings and people into 'things', the metanarrative of Loss turns 'things' into speaking, feelingful presences. According to this story, country music is consumed not as a disposable commodity, but in a profoundly historical mode which re-values the old and the worn out, and which is unable to forget the past. This inability to forget, which is the potential obverse of any commodified relation, becomes a thematic obsession in country music. This 'subjectified' mode of *self*-consumption is a poetic archaeology of the piled up memories which constitute the subject in the poetics of country music.

These interdependent yet opposed metanarratives of Loss and Desire are intertwined at every level of country's poetics. They permeate and connect the levels of performance, text and context. This intertwining begins with the basic linguistic practices which constitute 'country' as a unified discourse: writing, performing and listening to songs.

Writing and singing: the poetics of de- and re-naturalisation

Country's division of labour between songwriters and song-speakers (i.e. performers) conforms to Derrida's well known analysis of the relation between writing and speech (or between text and voice) in general, under what he calls the 'metaphysics of presence' (Derrida 1978). The country songwriter takes as her object language which is ideologically marked by its origins in the realm of 'everyday' and 'ordinary' discourse, and transforms this overtly plain language into something which is marked as a 'poetic' text, but which retains overt connections to the realm of 'ordinary' life.[2] This effect de-naturalises the everyday (or ideological) way of using the language which it objectifies, in which the conventionality of linguistic signification is effectively transparent, or 'natural' to its users.[3]

Country poetically distils the wide range of everyday language, drawn largely from working-class social contexts, into a generically limited taxonomy of situations and ideas, by using simplified (especially clichéd) language, precise mimetic effects of place and time, and the importation of 'actual' social discourse, in the form of reported or oblique speech and in intertextual quotations from other songs and genres. This 'poetic' effect calls attention to the rules of language *itself* – it has a 'metalingual thrust' (Mannheim 1986) – and it calls attention to the conceptual and ideological order those rules express (Jakobson 1981). The semantic closure which gives ordinary discourse its 'natural' or ideological character is opened to an awareness of the rules governing the 'language games' of ordinary speech and social life. The song*writer*, in other (Derridean) words, creates a powerful 'absence' of 'natural' meaning. This in turn creates a *desire* for a re-established 'presence' of meaning to fill the absent space. This is precisely the general effect Derrida associates with writing in relation to speech.

The basic operation performed by the country music *singer* on this poetic text responds to this desire-creating absence by *recovering* or 'renaturalising' part of the lost conversational 'naturalness' of this denaturalised language. The singer, in other words, creates a 'presence' to restore what the songwriter has opened to consciousness *as* an 'absence' of ordinary sense.[4]

The result of this is a double transformation of language at the levels of text *and* performance. On the one hand, relatively 'private' ordinary speech is heard in extraordinary poetic configurations which reveal its structural conventionality and expose its ideological assumptions. On the other hand, a highly marked 'public' mode of communication in capitalist society, namely, singing as consumable entertainment, is heard to strain for the ideological naturalness of 'ordinary' private speech.

This recovered presence and naturalness of country performance is in part a musical effect of volume, timbre and ornament. For example, the centrality of the voice in country recording (it is always foregrounded in the mix and lyrics are always intelligible), has been a consistent feature of the genre throughout its history. The voice must be as audible and as easy to understand as it would be in ordinary, private conversation, where the emphasis is on its semantic content. Likewise, vocal *quality* in country singing has typically been both aesthetically distinctive *and* 'imperfect'. The nasal, rough, timbrally distinct and/or accented voices of most great country singers are at once unique and ordinary, an effect which spins a story about both the uniqueness (denaturalisation) and the ordinariness (renaturalisation) of the figure of the singer. The use of a highly ornamented vocal style, including such effects as yodelling in early country music, and the elaborate turns and shakes in the singing of modern stars such as Reba McEntire and Randy Travis, marks the poeticised use of language. But this is balanced by the use of a 'talking' delivery, in 'talking songs' (e.g. George Kent's 'Hello, I'm a jukebox', discussed below), 'talking' verses inserted in songs before a final chorus (e.g. the double last verses in the George Jones/Tammy Wynette duet 'Southern California'), spoken opening lines, or spoken last lines or words.

This play of denaturalising and renaturalising effects is basic to the poetics of *live* as well as recorded performance in country music. For example, after denaturalising themselves through a marked form of fancy dress, highly stylised stage movements, and other familiar trappings of the distanced, aesthetic experience of staged musical performance, country musicians partially renaturalise the marked distinction between the stage and the dance floor by breaking the performative 'frame' which separates them from their fans. Songs are frequently introduced with stories which relate them to the singer's biography, which is presented as an exaggerated version of a biography common to the singer and their audience. Songs are thus explicitly claimed to be about 'the real lives of real people'.[5] Singers speak directly to members of the audience, often in extended dialogues which are audible to the entire audience, becoming part of the show. Members of the band are typically introduced by naming their home town and state, establishing their credentials as 'ordinary' people from 'ordinary' places. Live performance too is thus *both* a highly marked, denaturalised activity *and* an icon of 'natural', unmarked speech communication between 'ordinary' people.

The initial denaturalisation of everyday language in country song*writing*, by contrast, is a textual effect (although it is realised through performance), created by an extreme *elaboration* and *intensification* of 'ordinary' ways of speaking. This can be seen in the dense, pervasive use of puns, clichés, and word-play in country songwriting:

> In your arms I found the passion I thought
> had died
> When I looked into your eyes, girl, I found
> myself.
> And when I first kissed your lips, girl, I
> felt so light,
> I've got to **hand it to you**, girl, you're
> something else
> But on the **other hand**, there's a golden
> band
> To remind me of someone who would not
> understand.
> **On one hand**, I could stay, and be your
> lovin' man
> But the reason I must go, is on **the other
> hand** . . .
> (Randy Travis (Overstreet & Schlitz 1986))

In addition to the triple pun marked in bold type (itself distilled out of an obsessively anatomical and so denaturalising attention to the poetic scene), this song illustrates the poetics of the cliché which is ubiquitous in country music. Here, a highly naturalised unit of language is used ironically, both as the source of the triple pun ('on the other hand') and also to structure an apparently 'sincere' discourse (the man's 'lines') which turns out to be patently ironic and false in the context of the overall narrative. The cliché, in other words, is a naturalised usage in everyday language which is denaturalised by placement in an ironic poetic context, by being taken literally where its everyday use is metaphoric, and by sheer elaboration into an absurdly long string of further clichés.

This operation of denaturalisation also depends upon the generically restricted subject-matter of country narratives. In country music, intensely 'private' and 'inarticulate' (an alignment which is 'natural' in capitalist society) linguistic contexts (stories of cheating, divorce, lost love, family and home, and economic failure) are *inverted* to become intensely *public*, poetic, and articulate expressions. As Webb Pierce put it, to write a hit country song, 'you sing about the things that [people] think about most, but don't talk about' (Horstman 1986, p. 145). Sometimes, however (luckily for students of discourse), people *do* try to talk about these things publicly:

Caller: Well, we had just moved to a new area, and we had a – he was about two and a half –

and she just was working, she went to work for this person . . . and, ah, I guess our communication wasn't the best that it could be, and found that, ah, they hit it off quite well, she being, uh, . . . an extrovert, and, and ah, my, my personality is more the introvert, it just kinda progressed from there into, uh, uh, an affair, and uh, and then she started pulling back cuz, he was ma. . ., uh, married, and um, uh, but was, you know, quote unquote, in an 'unhappy relationship' type situation . . . it just keeps eating at me.
Host: Do you, in fact, in your secret heart of hearts, sit back and say, 'yes, *I* was partially responsible for this?'
Caller: I would be, yeah, very open to the fact that, uh, I wasn't meeting her needs as far as, uh, just communicating . . .[6]

The self-conscious 'inarticulateness' of this narrative, taken from a call-in radio show which offers psychological counselling, is typical of the way such stories are told on talk-radio. Admittedly, this is not a natural, private context: my point is that such contexts are extremely well hidden and even rare. The caller attests to this when he tells the host that he cannot bring himself to tell this story to his wife, exactly inverting the presentation of such discourse in country music, where such themes, addressed *to* the spouse, are ubiquitous, and, of course, highly public. But my comparison is justified, because this is an anonymous and unedited public context, compared to the publicly 'authored' and polished presentation of country performances of similar narratives.

The caller's narrative exemplifies the 'raw material' for country's transformation of ordinary, private, inarticulate speech. The story is told in shorthand notations. For example, we know that 'he was about two and a half' refers to the strain a child places on a marriage where both parents hold jobs. The caller couches his description of the narrative's characters in typological terms, 'she being an extrovert', and he being more of '*the* introvert'. He also draws on the linguistic resource of 'quoting' (by using a metalinguistic marker, 'quote, unquote') the common cultural story, which permeates country music, of an unhappy relationship justifying adultery. His wife's affair is 'eating at him', a theme which country elaborates as a 'consumption of self' through memories (see below). Later in the call, it is revealed that the affair in question took place thirteen *years* ago: the caller is stuck in memories, recalling the 'timeless' character of country's narratives of loss (Stewart n.d.).

All of these features of the 'natural' discourse surrounding the intense, inarticulate and private 'feelings' of an alienated subjectivity are linguistic resources for country music's poetic transformation of everyday speech. But country 'cheatin'' songs convert this inarticulateness into an intensely articulate expression, an ironic, articulate rumination *on* inarticulateness itself:

> When tears come down like fallin' rain
> You'll toss around and call my name
> You'll walk the floor, the way I do
> Your cheatin' heart will tell on you.
> (Hank Williams (Williams 1952))

Like the caller's narrative, Hank Williams uses shorthand notations to illustrate the poetic scene (here, metonymy and metaphor). Likewise, country constructs metalinguistic descriptions, or 'quote . . . unquotes', such as Hank Williams' intertextual use of 'You'll Walk the Floor', which, since Ernest Tubb's 1941 hit 'Walking the Floor Over You' (itself a denaturalisation of a cliché), has been what country's victims of love-gone-bad have routinely done. But the talk-show caller is obsessed with converting 'feelings' into a fair partitioning of blame and a plan for the future, conforming to the modality of psychology's 'rational' discourse on subjectivity. Country, by contrast, converts blame and the loss of a clear future into the narrative impetus to profoundly 'irrational' *feeling*, construct-ing a backwards-looking, self-consuming subjectivity. Country's narrative charac-ters are also *types* of people – cheaters, honky-tonk angels, long-suffering wives, etc. – who are expected to behave in certain ways, but unlike the caller's 'types', country's characters cannot change. The atemporality of the caller's narrative – an event that happened thirteen years ago, but could have happened yesterday for all the telling indicates – is echoed in country's endless agony, its narrative motion 'back into the years', rather than forward into future possibilities. But, again, unlike the caller's narrative, country music's narratives are not set in a discourse of 'rational' meta-commentary. There is no voice of reason to interrupt and say 'get on with your life, it happened thirteen years ago', as the host of the talk-show eventu-ally will do. Country's stories are poetic narratives in which the immersion in feeling itself is the *raison d'être*, and in which the poetic subject *is* simply a self-consuming pile of memories.

This analysis conveys the complex transformations which country music's denaturalising writing effects on the 'ordinary' languages of private desire and public rationality. But, again, this transformation is itself inverted by the perform-ance conventions which renaturalise this initially denaturalising movement, 'talk-ing' these meanings back into the realm of the personal and the private, distilling the public, poetic expression back down into a one-to-one talk, addressed to the individual listener as a bar-room *confidant*.

The result of this operation on everyday language is the opening of an ironic discursive space, where an intersection of two ways of using language, the 'public' and 'private' languages of capitalist society, can occur. The 'authentic' language of emotion is contrasted with the 'false' language of the market, transforming each in the direction of the other. This effect, which makes public discourse conform to private feelings and private feelings conform to public language and presentation, is exemplified by Reba McEntire's 'Have I got a Deal for You':

> Well you look like the kind, who's got an
>   eye for a bargain,
> the kind of guy who likes to shop around.
> Well I've got me this old heart that I'm a
>   puttin' on the market,
> and I'll make you a deal that you can't
>   turn down.
> Have I got a deal for you, a heart that's
>   almost like brand new.
> And I'll let it go so cheap, you'll think you
>   stole it before you're through,
> Have I got a deal for you! . . .
>   (Reba McEntire (Heeney & Leap 1985))

This mixture of the registers of public and private speech (such as advertising and romance) often plays with registers which are *already* mixed in everyday discourse, as in 'One Woman Man', where George Jones alternates between a low-pitched, cajoling, salesman's purr and a forceful, excited, high-pitched shout as he 'pitches' himself to a woman:

Narratives of loss and desire in the discourse of country music 59

> [*low voice, low-pitched, cajoling*]
> Won't you let me baby justa kinda stick
>   around!
> I'll always love ya honey, and I'll never let
>   you down!
> [*loud voice, high-pitched, entreating*]
> I'll never love another, even if I can!
> Come to me baby, I'm a one-woman man!
>   (George Jones (Franks & Horton 1988))

Both of these timbral and semantic registers index generic registral conventions of ordinary discourse – private confidence and public declaration – *and* conventions of advertising which themselves derive from and confuse the meanings of these conventions of 'ordinary' speech, so that we have learned not to trust the screaming huckster or the salesman who seems overly 'friendly'.

The register-mixing in these songs is further inflected with irony by a confusion of discursive positions. The relationship between the 'I' and 'You' (for instance, in 'Have I got a Deal for You', but also as discursive positions generally), oscillates between the 'aesthetic' (these are characters in a story) and 'ordinary' commercial uses of language (the singer is pitching his or her product to the listener, and has become, themself, the object of desire). This tension operates at the level of performance and at the level of the poetic narrative itself. Again, each use partially transforms the other. The narrative is the ostensible commodity on display and for sale, and yet its very narrativity, by convention, transforms the economic exchange of story-for-labour (the consumption of pop music as a commodity) into an 'aesthetic experience', because this is poetically, contextually and performatively marked as an 'aesthetic' narrative, rather than as a 'real', private conversation *or* a 'real' public advertising pitch.

What is crucial here is that these transformations (of poetic and ordinary language, of private feeling and public consumption, of real experience and fantasy, and of narrative as 'commodity' versus narrative as 'aesthetic experience') are never finally completed. The opposed terms (as signs) in each opposition are mutually constituting, just as the very concept of 'entertainment', exemplified by the social activity of consuming popular music, is constituted as a sign under capitalism as a mode of experience dialectically engaged with the sign of 'work'. Country poetically sustains narrative-generating *tensions* between these signs.

The tension between work and *fulfilled* private desire can easily be sustained in country narrative. This tension, of course, is precisely the 'story' of the genre, 'advertising', which is drawn into country's code-mixing discourse, and this story is the site of what I have been calling country's articulation of the 'metanarrative of Desire'. Some country songs narrate this ideological resolution explicitly, as when Keith Whitley sings:

> My boss is the boss's son
> and that makes for a real long day.
> And when that day is finally done
> I'm facing forty-thousand cars on the
>   interstate.
> Feelin' lower than a well-digger's shoes
> knee-deep in a mess of blues,

> but those blues just fade away
> when I hear my baby say . . .
> 'It ain't nothin' a little bit of love won't fix' . . .
>   (Keith Whitley (Haselden 1989))

In contrast to the blatant poetic marker of class consciousness in the first line, this song's subtle and implied resolution to the tension between work and desire is 'a little bit of love'. The use of 'fix' to describe the effect indexes the extent to which this story equates fulfilment with consumption, in this case, of a service to restore a worn-down spirit, itself equated with an *object* (shoes), mimetically renaturalised, as reported speech in direct discourse (introduced by 'When I hear my baby say . . .').

There are other examples where the nature of such 'fulfilment' (through consumption) is even more extreme. Love is no longer even a humanly provided service, as it is in 'It Ain't Nothin' '. It has become instead an object, a reified thing-in-itself to be owned and consumed, and a pure commodity. In Eddy Raven's 'Joe Knows How to Live', for example, the trapped 'family man' at the factory enviously admires his co-worker Joe, for his weekend leisure pursuits (travelling to Mexico with a girlfriend). Again, using the renaturalising mimetic technique of reported speech in direct discourse to make the fulfilment of desire ('women are like money') at once both a 'natural' resolution (for 'Joe') and an unattainable *object* of the narrator's own desire, 'Joe' is quoted as saying:

> He said: 'Women are made to love, money
>   is made to spend,
> Life is something, buddy, you will never
>   live again.'
> *[and the narrator returns to comment]*
> Well I've got to admit it, Joe knows how to
>   live.
>   (Eddy Raven (Barnes, Seals and Lyle 1986))

This emergent dialectic of constantly re-created desire extends even into the context for this story, which is 'Monday morning at the factory gates', suggesting that Joe's hedonism is checked by a worker's routine in the end. There is still one more transformation to these poetic oscillations of work and fulfilment: the song *itself* is consumed as a leisure product which must be purchased by the kind of work it appears to critique. This spiral of narrative transformations and self-reproducing desires is inscribed in the very act of consuming a popular musical 'product' which narratively treats desire as capable of being fulfilled through the consumption of commodities such as popular songs and Mexican vacations.

But this constantly fulfilled and re-created desire is only a part of country's meta-story. The possibility of private fulfilment through the consumption of objects of desire, which sustains the metanarrative of Desire, creates its own 'other', an underside of private failure, of desire unfulfilled, which is doubly shameful when it shares an ideological and linguistic formation with stories of desire *fulfilled*, as it does in country music. This underside is where country creates an alternative to the metanarrative of Desire: the metanarrative of Loss, of 'tradition', of nostalgia, of historical consciousness, and of the low-down 'structure of feeling' (Williams 1977) motivating country's famous poetics of 'descent' and 'lament' (Steward n.d.). Again, I emphasise that this narrative is engaged *with* the metanarrative of Desire. It *depends* for its poetic resonance on the hegemony of that narrative. The two stories need each other: the metanarrative of Loss depends on the possibility of unfulfilled desire, while the metanarrative of Desire depends on the naturalisation of an otherwise contradictory and alienating experience of private fulfilment through public consumption which generates further desire for new commodities.

The poetic representation of the metanarrative of Loss also involves trans-formations of everyday language. But these transformations, while they share a linguistic space with their other, pivot in a different metaphorical and historical direction from the metanarrative of Desire. Where this latter narrative looks forward to a fulfilment – to getting home to be 'fixed' (Keith Whitley), or to the realisation of a 'fantasy', as in Reba McEntire's 'Lookin' for a New Love Story' – narratives of Loss, as Stewart shows (n.d.), start at the end of a conventional story of failure and look *backwards*, obsessing on 'what might have been'.

The narrative task here becomes the reconstruction of the past through an 'archaeology' of highly objectified 'memories'. These memories are a double bind, establishing the same kind of productive linguistic tension as the mixing-up of the languages of love and advertising in 'Have I got a Deal for You' and 'One Woman Man'. The 'memories' are *themselves* objects of desire, but they are constructed as both eminently attainable and profoundly unsatisfying. The act of consuming objects of desire is hypostatised into the act of *forgetting*, in effect, a never-ending 'consumption' of the remembering subject. The narrative motion, which appears to have stopped at the end of a story of frustrated desire (Stewart n.d.), goes into historical reverse. The existing state of things is transformed by an archaeology of the past. The *climax* of the narrative structure comes at 'the bottom' of the remem-brance and the bottle, and resolves into a physical space filled with material markers of the past, such as pictures, letters and furniture.[7]

Just as with narratives of Desire, narratives of Loss must poeticise everyday language and effect the oscillation and mutual transformation of the 'marked' and the 'natural' described at length above. The narrative 'operator' is *still* the force of desire, still a linguistic articulation between the wanting and the wanted or the private and the public. The linguistic medium of this tension, as I argued above, is the movement from ordinary to poetic language in writing (denaturalisation) and part-way back again in performance (renaturalisation). Country music achieves this movement in the metanarrative of Loss in part by reifying a certain *kind* of desire as perpetually unfulfilled – 'private' desire, the same kind which is 'fulfilled' (only to be re-created) by consumption in the competing narrative of Desire.

The transformations in the direction of articulateness and 'public' discourse which country's poetics perform on what are 'naturally' (ideologically) intensely private and inarticulately expressed feelings are as important to the narrative of Loss as they are to the narrative of Desire. It is the very 'private' nature of these sad stories that denaturalises *publicly* performed narratives of unfulfilled desire, pre-cisely *because* they are profoundly 'unnatural' in a 'public' context.

While country performers denaturalise these stories simply by performing them (intertwining this effect with the renaturalising effects of performance), country writers also denaturalise these 'private' feelings at the level of content. Songwriters must *transform* the narrative of Desire into a narrative of Loss by making the painful feelings and memories *themselves* into ironic objects of desire, objects which are both frustratingly attainable and maddeningly unforgettable.

This transformation at the level of content is effected by *inverting* the poetics of the competing metanarrative. For example, where narratives of fulfilled desire convert *feelings* into goods and services, the narrative of Loss converts *objects* into signs of intense feeling, or even into subjects. And just as the metanarrative of Desire makes the discourse of country music *itself* into a model of its narrative conversions of 'feelings' into 'objects' (by modelling the conversion of 'aesthetic experiences' into 'leisure purchases'), the most powerful *de*-objectifications in the narrative of Loss also involve country music's history, its old songs, and icons of its commercial mediation, such as radios and jukeboxes.

An example of this is the use of the jukebox as a poetic 'operator' which introduces textual and melodic fragments of earlier country songs into an ongoing narrative. At one level, songs on a jukebox are 'objects' mediated by another 'object', in a pure example of the consumption of music as a fetishized commodity: cash is exchanged for songs. Here, a relation between producers and consumers of music is represented as a relation between concrete things, namely, particular songs in a matrix of other songs, all made equivalent by the principle of exchange-value. The value of songs is represented as an accumulation of cash; in order to stay on the jukebox, a song must earn its rent.

The *poetic* use of the 'jukebox' in country music *inverts* this archetypal example of alienation, commodity fetishism, and the loss of history, into a historically self-conscious assertion of control over the process of mediation.[8] It transforms commodities (old, 'disposable' songs, in terms of the market), into powerfully concentrated *feelings*, which literally reach out from the past, 'furnishing' the space of desire in the present with dense intertextual references:

> There's a fool in the mirror, lookin' back
>   across the bar,
> Reflections of woman, whose world just
>   fell apart.
> Now the life we built together, and the
>   'golden rings' are gone,
> And 'it's whiskey versus memories', and it
>   looks like 'the race is on'.
> I've got Jones on the Jukebox, and you on
>   my mind,
> I'm slowly goin' crazy, a quarter at a time.
> 'He stopped lovin' her today', oh, but I'm
>   'still doin' time',
> I've got Jones on the jukebox, and you on
>   my mind.
> (Becky Hobbs, 'Jones on the Jukebox'
> (Vickery, Hobbs and Goodman 1983))[9]

The words marked by quotation marks are intertextual references to songs made famous by George Jones (who is, of course, the 'Jones' of the song's title). These references are more than just inert quotes; they stand mimetically for both the physical space (in a bar, with these songs playing on the jukebox) and the *content* of the 'private' feelings of the subject articulated, however publicly and poetically through songs.[10] The parallelism of 'jukebox' and 'mind' confuses the two entities, creating an intertextual and objectified (i.e. consumable) subjectivity.[11]

At the 'bottom' of this backward- and downward-moving narrative, the jukebox is completely de-objectified, transformed from a thing into a speaking *subject* which has absorbed the voice of the 'private' subject into its public poetic. An example is George Kent's 'Hello, I'm a Jukebox', which is a spoken dialogue with a drinking man's voice imputed rather than heard, over a distantly heard song which comes forward in the mix between spoken verses (a hyper-mimetic version of the jukebox effect). This layering of voices – the unheard questions of the drinking man, the spoken answers of the jukebox, and the constantly playing 'song' in the background of the 'actual' song – dramatises the conversion of the jukebox from a mere 'object' which mediates commodities, into a collapsed pile of public expression and private feeling. 'Consuming' a song like this enacts an ironic 'consumption' of the self:

> (Song in background: Diana Duke singing
> 'Tonight the Jukebox Plays for Me') Spoken:
> Hello, I'm a jukebox. No, you're not
> losin' your mind. You see, we just never
> say anything, except at a very special
> time. And I know this is a special time
> for you, mister. But why don't you sit
> down and have your drink. Oh, I know,
> you didn't come in here for talking – you
> came in here to think . . .
>   (George Kent (Hall 1969))

This transforming of objects into feelings and voices has other 'operators', from the ubiquitous radios and telephones, to (more recently) answering machines, all the way up to whole houses full of 'things':

> I hear the ticking of the clock
> It seems to beg me stop
> Each picture on the wall seemed to cry
> And that old rusty gate,
> I can hear it beg me wait
> While the curtain in the window waved
> goodbye . . .
> (Ray Price, 'Curtain in the Window' (Ross 1958))

This poetics of object/subject transformation, this 'furnishing' of a subjectivity with 'speaking objects', inverts the mode of consumption modelled by the metanarrative of Desire, and enacted by the production, mediation and consumption of country music as a commodity. Both poetics depend upon an ironic space opened up by the discourse's metalinguistic play of 'the natural' and 'the constructed', the 'writerly', and 'performative' operations of naturalisation, denaturalisation, and renaturalisation, and the metanarrative, mutually transforming slippage between public and private, between things and feelings, between fulfillment and loss, and between forgetting the past and being stuck in it.

The poetics of mediation and the textuality of 'contexts'

Just as the material conditions for the production, mediation and consumption of country's narratives are poetically metaphorised and interpreted in 'texts', these conditions are themselves *poetically* constructed, and are inflected with the same complex tensions of metanarrative meanings. At the level of mediation, however, the contradictions which I have argued are inscribed at the level of language itself become even more explicitly practical contradictions. Country's deconstructive poetic, I have just argued, undermines the notion of an 'authentic' *text*. Now I wish to argue that there is no 'authentic' interpretive *context* either. In other words, I disagree with theories of popular culture which make a distinction between 'authentic' and 'inauthentic' *readings* of texts, (and not just between 'texts' *per se*). The 'texts' of popular idioms are produced, mediated, and consumed in social *contexts* charged with the same essential contradictions which are demonstrably inseparable at the level of texts themselves.[12]

This claim has serious implications for cultural criticism. From a perspective that retains the notion of 'authentic' contexts, mass-mediation tends to be seen as a reified, constraining 'structure', an absolute limit to cultural 'resistance'. One position in this structure is occupied by 'consumers', or 'the public', an object-position which can only be expressed through the exchange of alienated labour for alienating 'entertainment'. The *producer* in this dialogue is restricted equally by the same structure: her product must pay its rent and generate surplus value to exist. If one retains a notion of an 'authentic' account of the social structure as a standard against which critical 'penetrations' (Willis 1981) of this structure are to be judged, the options for cultural 'resistance' (that is, for 'authentic' uses of popular culture) are drastically limited to *refusal* (to buy or sell) and/or *marginalisation*.

The notion of 'authenticity' as resistance characterised by this refusal and marginalisation is confined as a possibility to a society's 'disenfranchised' and to its 'avant-gardes' (Connor 1989, pp. 56-7). This is authentic resistance only if one accepts the (capitalist) fiction of a market in which individuals and groups are 'free' to participate (or not). It is the retention of this notion of the 'authenticity of the margins' as a critical standard for 'resistance' which reproduces the ideology of artistic 'autonomy' from the market and everyday life under capitalism, and the concomitant critique of popular culture's complicity with capital (compared to 'folk' and 'high' art). In fact, however, discourses at the 'margins' of the market are ripe for appropriation (to the 'aesthetic' function) precisely *because* marginality becomes a pre-requisite for 'authentic' critique.

Country music suggests another way of imagining discursive resistance, one which explores the contradictions embedded in this notion of the 'authentic'. This resistance takes the form of a historical self-construction and consciousness, a 'back-talking'[13] of authority which speaks through the terms and paradigms of dominant discourses (in capitalist society, this means the market), using signs held in common across class, gender and ethnic boundaries, and which systematically turns these discourses inside out and upside down.

I have been arguing that country music's poetic *does* systematically invert (i.e. denaturalise) the linguistic and ideological categories of capitalism. But I have also argued that this denaturalising poetic is *always* and *simultaneously* partially renaturalised. It cannot escape the linguistic and material conditions of its production, mediation and reception, but nor does it pretend that such 'escape' is an effective possibility under present conditions. Its 'resistance' will not conform to any paradigm of 'authenticity', and will not be reified and separated from the range of concrete, ongoing interpretive and economic practices and contexts surrounding and permeating country music's 'texts'.

An example of this play of contexts is the distinction between AM and FM country music radio, a distinction that is at once technological, economic and ideological.[14] The importance of radio in the history of country music is unique among American popular musics (Gaillard 1978, pp. 15 ff.). Country's commercial youth occurred during the Depression era. As incomes and record sales fell, radio supplied a burgeoning audience with 'free' music (another capitalist fiction, of course) in the form of 'barn dances' and variety shows (see Malone 1985, pp. 31-235, for a detailed history). This established radio advertising as a crucial part of country music's economy (and poetics), and the early radio era established a precedent for the local, audience-specific and audience-responsive programming which continues to characterise AM country radio to this day.

The rise of FM radio technology, stereo and multi-track recording, and the expansion of the country music industry (in competition with rock and other 'youth' musics) which began in the late 1950s and has continued, with dips and surges, to the present day, were all implicated in a cleavage between two socially and technologically marked contexts for the reception of country music. Part of this distinction is, in a sense, an effect of the technology itself (although this must be located ultimately in the social uses of technology). In particular, the aesthetics of 'production quality', that is, of mediation which approaches the sound of 'real' or 'live' music, are served best by FM radio, which can broadcast in stereo and which produces a more 'accurate', less distorted and wider-frequency broadcast signal than AM radio.[15]

The technologies of stereo and multi-track recording, and more recently of 'MIDI' digital recording, have become essential to the production of most popular music since the late 1960s. The 'producer', the person whose job it is to give a record its identifiable 'sound', which is the means of distinguishing one pop music 'sign' from another (Frith 1988), has become more important than the singer, songwriter or instrumentalist in the economy of popular music.

Country music moved more slowly than rock and pop to embrace these new techno-ideologies, for a variety of interesting reasons, but they are now dominant in country music as well. Whether pursuing younger audiences (with 'youth' as an ideological and marketing category rather than a chronological description) or following a technological, 'evolutionary' logic, country songs, while still emphasising words and melody to a greater degree than most other popular musics, have shifted to an ever greater emphasis on 'beat' and 'sound', the operative aesthetic categories of rock and pop. And, of course, country has had its share of 'superstar' producers ever since the days of Chet Atkins and the 'Nashville Sound', which might be called the beginning of the rise of the 'technological aesthetic' in country music (Jensen 1984).

Most new country music recordings now sound more 'live' than older recordings, in terms of the ideological construction of 'liveness' as 'good' (i.e. 'authentic') sound, discussed by Frith (1988, pp. 20-2). This is right in step with the post-modern move to make 'sound' the measure of 'language', converting even language into a simulacrum of itself. But for this effect of sonic 'hyperrealism' to work, country must be heard in a technologically sophisticated mediation. FM radio meets this requirement, playing mostly compact discs (the absence of records' surface noise removing a previous scratchy marker of mediation), broadcasting in stereo, and playing multiple songs 'in a row' (to use the radio lingo), without disc jockey talk-over or advertising. This heightens the contrast between DJ and advertising 'talk' and country's new hyperreal sound.

AM radio, on the other hand, even when it plays the same country songs as

FM, necessarily obscures their digital sonic gloss, thinning out the deep bass and booming bass drum on new recordings, and, of course, eliminating the stereo effect which gives recorded music 'depth' and 'liveness'. The most remarkable transformation of all is the effect on the singing voice, which loses its timbral richness and blend, and stands out sharply from the instrumental accompaniment. This pushes words and melody to the aural foreground, to stand or fall on their poetic and melodic merits, and tends to favour the 'traditional' country vocal timbre and technique (nasal, broad, 'imperfect'), which, as I argued above, mark the performer as both 'unique' and 'ordinary'. The differences between the interpretive frames appropriate to AM or FM radio means that songs which are effective on FM radio may fail to work on AM radio, and vice versa.

Adding to this, and of course, bound up with this 'technological' distinction between AM and FM 'sound', AM country radio is far more 'talk' oriented, usually using a one-song-at-a-time format, with a DJ who speaks between songs, or even over their beginnings and endings. Advertising is packed in with songs in a more heterogeneous mix than on FM country radio, where you will most often hear a dense block of music (four to twelve songs), followed by an equally dense block of advertisements. AM radio DJs, both because they talk more and because of their constituency, are 'personalities', often using distinctly marked voices and regional accents (telling the same story about their 'ordinariness' as they do for singers), talking about music, politics and sports, spinning a general commentary on the world, and 'back-talking' commercials. For example, when Don Bowman, a disc jockey on the KVET-AM station in Austin, Texas, hears a sententious advertisement for a bank ask rhetorically 'Why do you bank where you do?', he back-talks the advertisement with the phrase 'I don't *know*', in a rich and cynical drawl which implies '*and* I don't care'. FM radio DJs talk less, typically speak in unaccented and uniformly modulated and pitched voices, and very rarely break the 'frame' of their performance with meta-performative gestures such as Bowman's 'back-talking'.

The AM/FM distinction is especially marked in terms of formats. FM radio uses the 'playlist' approach to country programming, familiar from most rock and pop stations, in which a fixed list of songs is played over and over, mixing up a majority of current hits from the *Billboard* country singles chart with smaller numbers of newly released singles, and very few 'oldies' (usually 'classic' songs from major artists). The size of this playlist rarely exceeds thirty-five songs (Ross 1988), meaning that it repeats in cycles every six to eight hours, depending on the time of day and the number of advertising and news breaks. The incremental changes made in a playlist rarely exceed more than three or four songs per week.

AM radio marketing and programme directors employ a different strategy. AM country music stations *will* play current hits, of course, but typically will mix these with an older set of songs which, however, are *not* necessarily 'classics', but rather 'worn-out' songs that have slipped off the FM playlists and off the *Billboard* charts. Often, AM DJs will make a point of playing requests for 'obscure' recordings, which rarely have 'classic' status.

Another feature of AM country radio is its constituent-specific programming. FM stations tend to be high-powered and engaged in a direct competition with pop and rock stations for top positions in the 'Arbitron' ratings which measure total listenership in a market at a particular time, and which bear directly on the price and amount of advertising a station runs. This gives FM radio stations an incentive to advertise themselves on TV and billboards, and to approach programming as an exercise in increasing popularity across *all* potential segments of the market. AM stations, on the other hand, often cater to specific, long-term constituencies, a core of 'regular' listeners for whom the AM ethos is part of a (usually occupational) ritual, giving these stations an incentive to please these particular regular listeners in order to keep them. For example, listener call-ins on AM stations tend to feature 'regular' callers, known by their first names, whose calls are often taken live, as opposed to the FM convention of repeatedly playing back recordings of several of the day's calls, often using calls from contest winners, whose testimonials 'prove' the reality and generosity of the contests which have now become a major means of radio-station marketing in the USA, on the theory that listeners will listen longer to a particular station (and so through commercials and other 'talk') if the station spaces 'chances to win' throughout the broadcast day.

AM radio addresses a regular and often specific set of listeners: rush hour commuters, early-morning service workers or, in rural areas, early-rising farmers, and overnight truck drivers. A 'direct address' is built in to the discourse of AM radio: requests are typically honoured and their source acknowledged, traffic or weather updates are geared toward specific interests (road conditions on trucking shows, morning ploughing weather on rural stations, etc.); and the advertising is often specifically targeted to constituencies, compared with the more broad-based advertisements on FM radio.

An illustration of an AM format which fits this description is the late-night, 'trucker' radio show, of which there are several nationally syndicated examples in the USA (Malone 1985, p. 320). These shows are broadcast nationwide from midnight into the early morning hours. They mix precise national traffic, weather and road condition reports, with extensive DJ patter before each song, recorded country humour, advice for truckers on mechanical, legal and financial issues, advertisements for every imaginable remedy for back pain and haemorrhoids, for truck stops all over the country, and for motor oils, truck dealers and truckers' legal aid services. Along with all of this, there is, of course, a steady stream of country music.

But *what* kind of country music? First, these shows claim to play an 'all request' format. Songs are often played following a live call from a trucker, often identified by his C.B. radio 'handle', who chats with the DJ (who is, of course, a 'personality') and then requests a song. Otherwise, nearly every song is introduced with an attribution of request which is precisely detailed and usually uses occupational jargon, e.g. 'This [song] is for everybody from old buddy Ken Long checking in from T-Town heading to Cincinatti, running with Excel transportation out of Wichita, Kansas'.

Of particular interest is the kind of music which is requested and played. First, almost *nothing* newer than about three years old is played, with rare exceptions; one almost never hears the current hits that are the staple of FM radio. Second, the songs that *are* played are distinguished, for the most part, by their 'obscurity' and lack of 'classic' status, regardless of their age. The bulk of the requests are for the obscure 'B-sides' from country music's 'historical jukebox', not for the 'classic', older hits which sometimes find their way onto the playlists of FM country stations.

The 'jukebox' effect described above as a poetic, 'textual' device marking an intertextual re-presentation of old songs and old feelings can be seen in the case of this 'trucker radio' to operate at the 'contextual' level of mediation. The space of the present is filled with constructed 'obscure' signs of the past, in a backwards narrative movement and in a thin, nasal 'AM' voice which back-talks the shiny, new and hyperreal-sounding objects of consumer desire which are across the dial on the FM stations. The choice of AM country radio therefore appears to be an insider's 'authentic', ideological gesture of resistance to the 'narrative of Desire'.

But this ideologically constructed nostalgic preference for yesterday's (rare, obscure, under-appreciated) wine is, none the less, intertwined with its 'other', the ideology of musical 'product' (as music is referred to by members of the country music business). The resistant discourse of 'AM country' speaks through and inverts the languages of the discourse it resists, such as the ideology of 'classic' country music (the 'A-sides' of the 'jukebox of history') which informs FM radio's programming of old songs in the margins of an otherwise unrelenting commitment to The New.

There is no stopping the dialectic of naturalisation, denaturalisation, and renaturalisation, not even long enough to locate an 'authentic' moment of resistance. Indeed, this notion of recycling and revaluing yesterday's 'trash', this *very* gesture of resistance which characterises apparently 'authentic' uses of country music such as AM radio, is equally susceptible to renaturalisation. Country's cycle of poetic transformations can easily accommodate the 'authenticity' of historical consciousness into its dialectic.

An example of this is the so-called 'New Traditional' movement which has been the major stylistic current in country music since the early 1980s. Its practitioners and celebrators posit a reified 'traditional' discourse, variously located between the 1940s and the early 1970s, which is said to have been eclipsed during the late 1970s by 'commercial', or 'crossover' (i.e. 'inauthentic') country. The value of this 'tradition' lies in its very historical distance and 'authentic' or 'classic' status. Yet the resurrection of this 'authentic' discourse relies upon the most contemporary means of production and mediation, and is constructed aesthetically in some of the same terms as the 'false' and 'commercial' country music of the 1970s which it claims to supplant. The re-emergence of 'traditional' song genres and (digitally processed) 'acoustic' instrumentation is accompanied by an emphasis on 'technology', 'production', 'beat' and 'sound' which is thoroughly up-to-date and parallels the contradictory logic of similar 'back to basics' moves in other popular genres in recent years. This construction is then marketed as 'new, improved tradition' (Gleason 1988), and fear is expressed by radio programme directors of a 'traditional product glut' (Ross 1988), phrases which perfectly capture the oxymoronic *irony* and perpetual instability of 'authenticity' in the discourse of country music.

A fascinating recent example of this postmodern intertwining of signs of the 'Traditional' ('authentic') and signs of the 'New' ('false') is Hank Williams, Junior's 'duet' recording of 'There's a Tear in My Beer' (written and originally recorded by Hank Williams, Senior, but never released), and the accompanying video in which Hank Junior appears to perform with (the image and voice of) his long-dead father. The song quickly rose up the *Billboard* country singles chart, a thoroughly denaturalised retrieval of an 'authentically' obscure B-side (the significance of using a previously unreleased, or 'newly re-discovered' song), and the first, denaturalising stage in country's poetic operation.

Meanwhile, Hank Williams, *Senior*'s 'classic' (and once shunned as 'inauthentic') recordings are being advertised in boxed sets, with 'the original surface noise intact' (as a late-night TV ad puts it), or in 'original undubbed mono', as Polydor's complete reissue series proudly declares on each jacket, recapturing the ideological category of AM radio's scratchy, voice-centered sound for the market. These are coded statements of authenticity. They renaturalise the numerous 'inauthentic' recordings of Hank Williams, Senior which have been sold on late-night television for the last twenty years with claims of having been 'cleaned up' or 're-mastered in stereo' and/or 'modernised' or 'sweetened' with added strings and choirs. This process culminates in Hank, *Junior's*'s 'Tear in My Beer' video, in which the bearded, long-haired son appears to dance and interact with a forty-year-old image of the father whom he barely knew, against a recording which has been digitally stripped of its original, Drifting Cowboys backing and all of its authenticating 'surface noise', and which has had this replaced by a new studio recording of the instrumental tracks by Nashville musicians, playing, however, in an 'authentic' classic idiom.

Conclusion: culture and criticism beyond 'authenticity'

Will the 'real' Hank Williams please stand up? My point is that he *cannot* stand up without falling off. Country music will not stop spinning long enough for a critic (or a fan, artist or record company executive) to grab something 'authentic' and step off the merry-go-round. At the risk of critical vertigo, country *compels* a reading which asks not 'where's the "real" thing here?' but rather asks what these complex practices are saying about the 'real' itself. As an engaged, 'back-talking' commodity in an economy of representations, country calls into question all definitions of the 'authentic' – whether applied to texts, contexts, readers or interpretations – and drowns them out in its cackling, carnivalesque laughter and in its oceans of beer and tears. Country interrogates *all* 'authenticities', submitting them to trial-by-irony, before regaining its performative balance. Country resists the market by engaging with it completely, only to sell out its 'resistance' as 'tradition'. Country explores and dramatises its own conditions of (im)possibility as an 'aesthetic commodity' under the postmodern (ill-) logic of late capitalist culture. Finally, country's poetic self-deconstruction challenges students and critics of popular culture to examine their own critical practice for its ideological assumptions about 'the true' and 'the false', and to imagine a move beyond 'authenticity'.

Acknowledgements

Thanks especially to Katie Stewart for her ideas and support, and to Barbara Hampton, Steven Feld, Simon Frith, Joli Jensen, Mari Keefe, Frank Magne, fellow students at Texas and my 'country' friends at Ann's Other Place, Lockhart, Texas. I appreciate the permission to quote lyrics granted by various songwriters and publishers, and the help of Misha Hunke at BMI in Nashville. I am grateful for financial support from The Mellon Fellowships in the Humanities and The University of Texas at Austin.

Endnotes

1 Of course, it is possible to see Loss as the primary narrative and Desire as its inversion. Following the Marxist tradition, I read Loss as a resistant response to capitalist society's fetishism of the commodity, but the specifically capitalist form of commodity fetishism could be

read just as easily as a debasement of the rich and magical relation to 'objects' implied in the narrative I am calling 'Loss', a kind of relation which is found in non-capitalist societies as well as in dominated subcultures within capitalist societies.

2 As Stewart notes (n.d.), citing numerous examples in Horstman (1986), the paradigmatic 'story behind the song' in country music is almost unfailingly a fragment of 'overheard' ordinary language use, a phrase extracted from 'real life' and made to speak poetically.

3 I am referring to the 'poetic' function as defined by Jakobson (1960) as an 'orientation to the "message" itself' and as a projection of paradigmatic relations onto the syntagmatic plane which reveals the conceptual structure underlying 'ordinary', non-poetic uses of language (1981).

4 The country song*writer* is, typically, an anonymous, 'absent' figure, while the singer is a larger-than-life 'presence'. This division of labour between songwriters and performers has persisted in country despite the rise of ('authentic') singer-songwriters in other popular genres.

5 It is important to understand that this 'reflection' of 'the real lives of real people' is a specific, renaturalising ideological *effect* located within a poetic which in other aspects *subverts* this effect. The error of taking country song texts as naïve, direct, unmediated 'ethnographic data' about the culture of the social groups that listen to country music is common in the tradition of sociological writing about country music.

6 The use of [. . .] in this example marks a pause, not an elision.

7 Some of the finest current songs in this genre are sung by Randy Travis, who seems to have a preference for songs which make a detailed, literally 'archaeological' catalogue of these historical markers, e.g. 'Diggin' Up Bones', 'No Place Like Home', 'Old 8 by 10' and '1982'.

8 This is not to say that there are not 'real' uses of jukeboxes which enact this poetic of de-objectification. I am preparing an ethnographic study of a country music beer-joint which will

demonstrate the assertion that the 'poetic' is an approach to 'reality', and not just a feature of texts (Jakobson 1960).

9 Becky Hobbs' sung performance (quoted here) differs from the published text for this song; interestingly, the original (published) version contains even more song title quotations than the recorded version. The move from 'writing' to 'performance' is here explicitly marked by a reduction in poetic denaturalisation through word play.

10 Another well known example of this technique of transformation is 'It wasn't God who made Honky Tonk Angels', Kitty Wells' famous 'answer' to Hank Thompson's 'The Wild Side of Life'. Here Thompson's original song is heard and replied to, 'as I sit here tonight, the jukebox playing/ that song about the wild side of life', (Miller 1952).

11 This consumption of an 'objectified subjectivity' made up of piled-up memories is also marked by the poetic use of an ironic distance from the 'self' in the line, 'there's a fool in the mirror/ lookin' back across the bar'. The use of the image of a 'mirror' is a classic device for introducing the split, self-consuming subject in country songs.

12 Indeed, the 'text/context' distinction is *itself* a conventional reading which critics have naturalised as 'authentic'. At least for country music, so-called 'contexts' are charged with 'textualised' meanings, and 'texts' are 'contexts' for many kinds of concrete social practices.

13 My use of the term 'back-talking' as a broad metaphor for the kind of 'resistance' practice I am describing marks my deep indebtedness to Stewart's work, which develops the metaphor of 'back-talk' into a theory of resistance (see Stewart 1990).

14 The AM/FM choice is *profoundly* ideological: a country musician who read a draft of this article told me, 'there ain't no such goddamn thing as "FM country music".'

15 The capacity for stereo broadcast has been developed only recently for AM radio, and is not yet reflected widely in the programming of AM radio stations or in the home-electronics market.

References

Connor, S. 1989. *Postmodernist culture* (London)

Derrida, J. 1978. *Writing and Difference* (Chicago)

Frith, S. 1988. *Music for Pleasure: Essays in the Sociology of Pop* (London)

Gaillard, F. 1978. *Watermelon Wine: The Spirit of Country Music* (New York)

Gleason, H. 1988. 'Beyond labels: marketers search for fresh ways to promote new, improved country', *Billboard*, 15 October, p. C-6.

Horstman, D. 1986. *Sing Your Heart Out, Country Boy* (Nashville)

Jakobson, R. 1960. 'Concluding statement: linguistics and poetics' in *Style in Language*, ed. T. A. Sebeok (Cambridge)

   1981. 'Poetry of grammar and grammar of poetry', in *Selected Writings III* (The Hague), pp. 87-97 (orig. 1960)

Jensen, J. 1984. 'Creating the Nashville sound: a case-study in commercial culture production', unpublished Ph.D. thesis, University of Illinois

Malone, B. 1985. *Country Music U.S.A.: A Fifty Year History* (2nd ed.) (Austin)

Mannheim, B. 1986. 'Popular song & popular grammar, poetry & metalanguage', *Word*, 37 (1-2), pp. 45-75

Ross, S. 1988. 'Crowded country airwaves: radio, records uneasily share new prosperity; new artist door begins to close', *Billboard*, 15 October, p. C-6

Stewart, K. n.d. 'The narrative poetics of American "country" lament: a re-presentation of country music's lost love and Appalachia's litanies of the dead' (manuscript)

   1990. 'Backtalking the wilderness: "Appalachian" engenderings', in *Uncertain Terms: Negotiating Gender in American Culture*, eds. Faye Ginsburg and Anne Tsing (Boston)

Williams, R. 1977. *Marxism and Literature* (Oxford)

Willis, P. 1981. *Learning to Labor* (New York)

Songs Quoted/Permissions

(Alphabetical by first-listed writer)

72   *Aaron A. Fox*

[18]

Searching for Rockordion: The Changing Image of the Accordion in America

MARION S. JACOBSON

> For the mod youngster who digs the rock, folk and Mersey beat of the swinging '60s, a Combo 'Cordion called Tiger is stalking the scene. You're the swinger with Tiger Combo. Combo 'Cordion is excitement.[1]

These words written by Faithe Deffner, publicist for her family's accordion manufacturing firm, may have been aimed at selling accordions to teenagers. But they revealed a harsh reality accordion players had to acknowledge—the latent lack of excitement about their instrument and, more alarmingly, the decline of the values it represented. Indeed, to the white, middle-class players and entrepreneurs who promoted and taught the instrument, the piano accordion had once represented the possibility of cultural elevation and success. By the mid-1960s, however, the popular music landscape was changing: the accordion (and the community that supported it) was no longer central. Although devotees of the accordion knew that the success of rock had tarnished the popularity of their favorite instrument, this advertisement held out the hope that rock could be revamped into something that mainstream Americans could accept.

The Tiger Combo accordion was offered to the public very briefly in the 1960s, along with other "improved" instruments, as part of a long-standing effort to raise the accordion's stature. The Tiger Combo's significance rests upon departing from the familiar strategy of promoting the accordion as a way to introduce the public to classical music and

Marion Jacobson is assistant professor of Music and Humanities at Albany College of Pharmacy and Health Sciences. She has published articles in *Jewish Folklore and Ethnography* and in two edited volumes: *American Klezmer: Roots and Offshoots* (University of California Press, 2002) and *Chorus and Community* (University of Illinois Press, 2006).

redirect its interest in folk music toward classical technique and written arrangements. Most buyers of the accordion between 1933 and 1963 came from working- and middle-class families who enjoyed classical music, but did not have a great deal of formal musical education or disposable income. Many families even relied on door-to-door accordion salesmen for their children's musical education.[2] With time came prestige and a steadier income stream. In turn manufacturers could produce both larger and more powerful accordions with higher price tags, as well as more affordable models.

To analyze the attempts to improve and popularize the accordion puts several issues into focus: the changing social status of these instruments and people's relationships to them, and how these reflect ideas of opportunity, legitimacy, and marginality that developed in American culture at mid-century. In these ideas we can see the significance of the piano accordion's "rise and fall (and rise)" in America.

Accordion as Technology: Discourses of Opportunity

The modern accordion, a type of free-reed instrument, can be traced back to the early nineteenth century when the Austrian inventor Cyril Demian patented the device known as *akkordeon*.

> It has bellows fixed to it, in such a way that it can easily be carried, and therefore traveling visitors to the country will appreciate the instrument. It is possible to perform marches, arias, melodies, even by an amateur of music with little practice, and to play the loveliest and most pleasant chords of 3, 4, 5 etc. voices after instruction.[3]

The earliest accordions (all European, from the 1830s and 1840s, and known as "Demians") were hardly more than palm-sized, resembling a harmonica with bellows more than the modern full-sized accordion, which can weigh up to thirty-five pounds. Demian's patent prescribes his *akkordeon* as a substitute orchestral instrument for use by solo travelers in the country for the purpose of playing "marches, polkas, and waltzes," assuming that such a thing would be adequate should it be impossible to bring a "real" musical instrument on the journey. Convenient and innovative, the accordion could mechanically reproduce sounds of the orchestra at will. And that was its chief virtue.

For its first 100 years the accordion developed through an evolving series of patents that attested to the difficulties involved in improving its sound quality, portability, and ease of playing. Many unusual and one-of-a-kind designs appeared. A few early German and Austrian models displayed at A World of Accordions Museum in Superior, Wisconsin, are even equipped with bells attached to the outside. The most significant innovation was the chromatic accordion. In 1850, in Vienna, F. Walther rearranged the reeds of a three-row diatonic accordion to play a forty-six-note, fully chromatic scale. Unlike the diatonic buttons of previous accordions, each button of this accordion played the same note regardless of the bellows' direction. Walther's chromatic keyboard layout became the system out of which the piano accordion grew.[4]

From 1850 onward the accordion underwent much experimentation, all of it requiring increasingly complex physical construction.[5] The advocates of the accordion were committed to the idea of innovation and providing evidence of the instrument's technical improvements. As the demand for the accordion grew, the industry responded with cheaper, more efficient production in plastics and seemingly infinite variations on keyboard design, number of reeds, and tonal quality.

Players quickly came to believe that Italy produced the "finest" accordions. This belief stemmed from the development of a major accordion production center in Castelfidardo in Italy's March region in the late nineteenth century and the dramatic and profitable success of pioneering accordion producers and importers such as Dallape, Soprani, Guerrini (Enrico and Paolo) Serenelli. Later, in the 1940s and 1950s, these accordion industry captains displayed their newfound wealth and their domination of the industry—particularly in the United States—by building mansions on Castelfidardo's main thoroughfare, renamed "Dollar Street." The dramatically visible success of these ventures moved the accordion in new and profitable directions that the early entrepreneurs could never have imagined. By 1953 the piano accordion was a top-selling musical instrument.[6]

By then a typical accordion-marketing strategy in America was to promote the instrument as an efficient, technologically advanced product of American ingenuity. Hundreds of different kinds of reeds and switching devices (for shifting registers or playing multiple tones) were patented. Of course, most of this innovation was taking place on the inside of the instrument, involving subtle changes in the reeds and tongues, too complex for the ordinary consumer to understand. So advertisers had to refer to other more familiar technologies. ("Television may be around the corner," reads an ad for the Butti accordion, "but the Butti Television Grand is here.")[7] Clocks and cars appeared alongside accordions in Excelsior ads. New designs suggested that the mechanical qualities of accordions were becoming fetishized. Switches and screws were no longer concealed on the outside. The cases became sleek, consistently black and white with a minimum of decorative imagery. As the accordion acquired the more uniform appearance of a piano, it gained a potential for more efficient design, cheaper materials, and more profitability. One of the unintended effects of this mini-industrial revolution of the piano accordion was the virtual disappearance of the button accordion from the market. In the 1920s, the U.S. distributors' catalogs had designated two categories of accordions:

the "Viennese style" (button accordions) and "Italian style" (the piano accordion). By 1938 the national designations disappeared, and the "accordions" seen in advertisements were virtually all piano accordions.[8]

For the better part of the twentieth century, Americans eagerly supported the hegemony of the piano accordion. The ease of mass-producing and marketing a single model such as the piano accordion pushed down prices and opened the door for competing brands and models, allowing families an almost overwhelming number of choices. As the industry peaked in the 1920s, over 100 firms operated in Castelfidardo, producing accordions mainly for export to the United States. By 1950 over 100 accordion firms based in Castelfidardo were producing 250,000 instruments, mainly for export, and 95 percent of all accordions purchased in the United States were exported from Italy.[9] During the war years, when Italy slowed production while the demand for accordions rose in the United States, new American accordion factories attempted to fill the gap. The Italo-American Company made twenty-five accordions a week in Chicago during its peak years of business between the late 1930s and the 1950s.[10] Manufacturers took advantage of new celluloid materials and plastics technologies to manufacture accordions more cheaply and efficiently. Plastic cases were molded in simpler designs. As the influence of vaudeville died out in 1930, so did vaudevillian-style accordions equipped with rhinestones and elaborate mother-of-pearl ornamentation designed to catch the lights onstage.

The new look of the accordion helped to emphasize, at least visually, the "technological" aspects of the accordion that the manufacturers wanted to sell to their customers. Accordion companies promoted their products as the fruits of American technology, compatible with the ideal suburban lifestyle. Italian manufacturers competed with one another to develop the most efficient switching devices, the most attractive grilles, and the lightest construction. The delicate nature of accordion reeds and their tendency to rust in humid weather also prompted innovations: "Acmaloy Reeds," for example, were "unconditionally guaranteed" while "Directone reeds" promised "tremendous carrying power." Superlatives abound in advertisers' descriptions of these newer Italian-made accordions: The Finest. The Most Exquisite. Master Craftsmanship. Thrilling. The Best. The Best and Nothing but the Best. The Greatest Development in Accordion History.

But the innovations of accordions would have meant nothing unless the instruments were affordable. An entry-level accordion such as those made by Acme could be purchased in the Sears, Roebuck or J. C. Penney Catalog in the range of $50 to $100.[11] Retailers sent accordion salesmen/teachers door to door, selling accordion-and-lesson packages, often on the installment plan. As the new plastics technologies and new mass-production techniques enabled companies to manufacture smaller-sized, less expensive instruments, new markets were sought after: women and children. A Soprani accordion advertisement showing a young woman playing a stylish pearl-white accordion promises that the new Ampliphonic Midget Grand is "Light as a Fiddle," "Simply Irresistible . . . and easy to play for recreation, enjoyment, and profit." A Coronet accordion advertisement (see fig. 1) displays the slender profile of "Miss Jean Donnelly, America's Accordion Queen" next to a "Slim Line Accordion." This model, aimed at women players, offered "inches less bulk and the creation of a new totally feminine appearance." Women could also buy Coronet accordions in "lovely colors, with high style." Families were encouraged to buy accordions for their children to ensure their musical and moral development. "No gift more precious, no instrument more appealing," urges a display ad for the accordion in *The Etude* magazine in the 1930s. "The future of your children is in your hands. For the sake of their happiness, be sure it includes the wholesome influence of [an] Accordion."[12] Americans became familiar with the idea of the accordion as an entry-level musical instrument, one appropriate for families on a budget.

One might date the birth of the "accordion movement" to 1938, the year that witnessed three important events in the life of the accordion: the completed transition to the manufacture of accordions in plastics;[13]

Figure 1. A 1950s Coronet "Accordion Queen" advertisement emphasizing the instrument's "high style"—and offering a free nineteen-jewel watch with purchase.

the founding of the American Accordionists Association (AAA); and the introduction of Pietro Diero's "advice column" for accordionists in *The Etude*, a magazine devoted mainly to teachers of piano and stringed instruments. In the early 1940s a writer for *Accordion World* could celebrate the accordion as piano's triumphant successor:

> Being a complete instrument in itself it has no equal as an entertaining medium in the home, outdoors, or wherever people gather to enjoy good fellowship. During the past 15 years or so the accordion has risen to the top of the field as a best seller in the musical instrument market. At present it threatens to replace the piano as the medium through which Junior or little sister are initiated to the delights and sometimes pains of a musical education. Even grandpa and grandma are taking to it like a duck to water.[14]

More leisure time and affluence in the postwar decades gave Americans more disposable income and more opportunity to purchase and learn to play musical instruments.[15] In addition, many American GIs who had heard accordions in France and Germany were bringing the instruments home and learning to play them. The increasing numbers of makes and models available made the task of selecting an accordion increasingly bewildering. There was such a large increase of interest in the accordion that critics noted, at different points, an "accordion shortage," an "accordion teacher shortage," and the "need for accordionists in jazz orchestras."[16] It was truly an era worthy not only of the name "Golden Age of the Accordion," but "Golden Age of Musicmaking" among middle-class American families, who drew on the potential of the accordion to revitalize their musical talents and energies and expand their cultural opportunities (see fig. 2).[17]

Discourses of Legitimacy

As the accordion expanded its reach into mainstream middle-class American culture before World War II, its role in American culture was contested. The accordion became a subject of debate and dialogue among a community of experts teachers and performers who presented themselves as "guardians" of the accordion with the instrument's best interests at heart (if not necessarily those of the everyday musicians). The expert accordion community's primary goal was to earn for the accordion the legitimacy they believed it needed and deserved within the Western classical tradition. These experts intended to remain at the forefront of the accordion phenomenon not primarily by producing or selling accordions, but by arranging music, making recordings, playing accordion on the radio, writing method books, and opening accordion schools and studios. An abundance of documentation on proper accordion playing by accordion

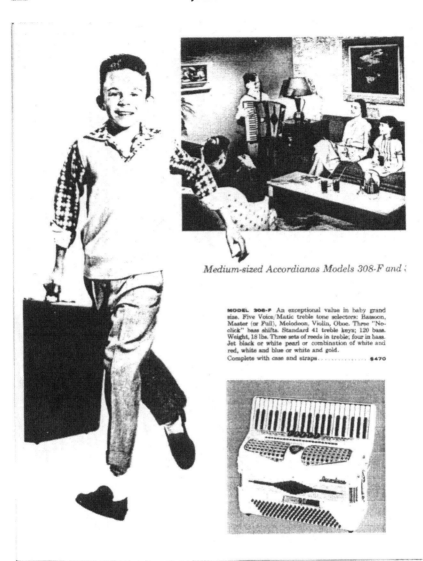

Medium-sized Accordianas Models 308-F and ;

MODEL 308-F An exceptional value in baby grand size. Five Voice/Matic treble tone selectors: Bassoon, Master (or Full), Melodeon, Violin, Oboe. Three "No-click" bass shifts. Standard 41 treble keys; 120 bass. Weight, 18 lbs. Three sets of reeds in treble; four in bass. Jet black or white pearl or combination of white and red, white and blue or white and gold.
Complete with case and straps $470

Figure 2. A ca.-1960 Accordiana advertisement depicting the accordion's role in an orderly, well-groomed, middle-class family.

teachers writing and publishing how-to guides and treatises on the accordion suggests that a small, confined "accordion world" or "accordion appreciation movement" developed in the 1930s. This was a unique off-shoot of the "musical appreciation movement" originating in England and America in the 1900s, a loosely organized effort of music teachers and critics aimed at improving the public's taste in music through the study of the classics, and distributing their methods through such democratic institutions as choral societies and the school system.[18] Luminaries of the vaudeville world such as Guido Deiro (1886–1950) and concert artist-composers, such as Guido's brother Pietro Deiro (1888–1954) were instrumental in popularizing the piano accordion in the United States in the early 1900s, establishing a link between this relatively new instrument and the great tradition of art music in Europe.[19]

Among the "gateways" to better music appreciation that advocates of this movement discussed and debated in the 1930s was the study of the accordion undertaken in conjunction with study of the "laws of music" in musicianship classes in school.[20] *The Musical Times* debated the accordion's influence on mass taste and its potential to inspire players of "mediocre" music to make better choices in the future. Notes one critical observer of the "accordion movement" in England in 1936:

> I know it is perfectly easy for "superior" people to sneer at this, and I am the first to admit that it is not the most perfect gateway towards an appreciation of classical music, but I do submit that, as a direct result of the advent of the accordion in this country, thousands of people (1) have learned to read music fluently, (2) have acquired a knowledge of elementary theory and harmony and (3) have begun to enjoy good music, and have made an acquaintance (superficial, perhaps, but still an acquaintance) with some of the masterpieces of the great composers.[21]

In a 1948 article in *Accordion World* one author reflects a romantic-populist slant as he describes the accordion as a "musical flower whose tonal fragrance is permeating deep into the heart of people."[22] However, accordion advocates had an agenda—and it was more than reaching people's hearts. They expressed certainty that the popular folk music commonly associated with the accordion would ultimately fade and give way to a new genre: accordion music for the concert hall.

Advocates of the accordion looked to the manufacturers for evidence that the instruments could be made orchestra-ready. They needed to be built for speed (that is, with various improvements made in the action of the keyboard) and configured in a way that would allow the player to perform classics from the standard repertoire, with adequate tones in the bass (button) side of the accordion and easy access to the register shifts. As the accordion's self-appointed guardians pointed out, the instrument deserved the same opportunities the piano, flute, and other instruments enjoyed because it had trod the same well-worn path of struggle and triumph. As *Accordion World* magazine explained in 1947,

> The early beginning of the piano's existence can be likened to that of the accordion, in the respect that until recently the accordion strug-

gled along with practically no music that could raise it to a place of eminence in the realm of the finer instruments. The accordion has broken the shackles that have long made it a stepchild among the great instruments and has, at last, come into its own. It takes its place among the higher instruments.[23]

But for the accordion to truly deserve a place among the "higher" instruments, it could not be merely a portable, convenient, and cheaper version of the piano. It needed to legitimize itself through a new series of improvements that would enable it to claim a place among classical instruments. One alleged improvement that became the subject of debate was the "Stradella" system, the accordion's now-standard arrangement of bass notes arranged in a "circle of fifths pattern," with single notes (in vertical stacks of perfect fifths) lined up with their major, minor, seventh, and diminished chords along each horizontal row of buttons on the left hand side of the accordion. (Almost all method books for accordion assume that the player uses this system.) But accordion makers have been known to experiment with 140, 160, and even 220 basses, and some players (such as Guido Deiro, who made his fame with a 132-bass accordion) preferred to have more basses available.[24] Once the layout of the "standard" piano accordion became widely recognized, some players expressed concern that their instrument would cease to develop and improve. Willard Palmer, a noted teacher of the accordion and developer of a series of method books, wondered why players should be satisfied with the Stradella system: "The reason why the accordion can never reach the heights that many wishful thinkers among accordion enthusiasts dream about . . . lie(s) mainly in the bass side of the instrument where the shortcomings are so tremendous that the greatest genius could not overcome them in attempting to interpret great music." Another concert accordionist wrote, "the bass side of the instrument is a stumbling block to the true and conscientious artist [but] is a boon to the mediocre performer for [it] enable[s] him to play certain forms of hackneyed and inferior music with greatest of ease and a minimum of effort."[25] Since the Stradella bass system was designed as a shortcut system for easily reaching I, IV and V chords in the common major keys (C, F, and G being easiest) and this chord-bass patterns is used in many traditional waltzes and polkas, as well as rock 'n' roll and blues, we can easily interpret his statement to mean that he feared that the accordion would discourage players from moving on to "better" music. In *Accordion World* magazine, an "Open Letter to Accordion Manufacturers" stated the serious accordionist's need for a larger bass keyboard, with an additional two octaves of usable range for the left hand, so that "all of Bach's organ works will be possible for the accordion."[26]

In order to be a "fine" instrument worthy of the classics, some felt, the accordion needed not just a larger range of notes but better tone. The new "multishift" accordion, developed in the early 1940s, was equipped with four sets of reeds (one set of high, two sets of medium and one set of low reeds) that were set in various combinations to imitate the sounds of string and woodwind instruments from the Western symphony orchestra, after which the switches were named: Violin, Clarinet, Piccolo, Oboe, and Bassoon. In the 1940s, a number of accordion companies designed and perfected the "free bass" accordion system, based on the chromatic scale, freeing interested players from the circle of fifths. The free-bass system developed by John Serry featured dual keyboards for the left hand and incorporated two sets of reeds tuned in octaves, providing a range of tones exceeding three and a half octaves. These were designed for independent access for the thumb and the remaining fingers of the performer's left hand. The free-bass system was (and still is) seen as a liberating and elevating force in the accordion.[27] Noted one defender of the accordion as a vehicle for musical appreciation in the 1930s, "the tonal quality is improving so much so that in some of the larger instruments it is really exquisite."[28]

In the three decades before, during, and after the Second World War, accordion players created an unprecedented range of opportunities aimed at expanding the pedagogy and repertoire for their instrument, which had not traditionally been part of the symphony orchestra, and broadening the sensibilities of the accordion-playing public. The Italian emigrants not only imported and distributed the brand-name accordions from Castelfidardo, but also opened the earliest music schools dedicated to the teaching of accordion in San Francisco, New York City's Little Italy, Detroit, Newark, and Philadelphia. Because the accordion was not taught in conservatories and only a handful of colleges and universities offered the accordion major, these accordion schools aimed to combine the study of the instrument with comprehensive traditional Western musical training. The Neupauer Conservatory, a "Professional School of Accordion" in Philadelphia, advertised a "full-time program leading to diploma in performance, teaching, arranging and composition." (A 1964 issue of *Accordion Horizons* from the mid-1960s lists classified ads for two dozen accordion schools, including two locations for the Joe Biviano School of Music in Connecticut and Manhattan and an "exclusive accordion camp" in Augusta, Georgia.)[29] Such schools established graded accordion ensembles for their students, so that accordion orchestra and band concerts were an established feature of American communal musical life in the late 1930s. Massed concerts featuring multiple groups and thousands of players were a regular feature of Chicago and New York City cultural life in the 1940s and 1950s. Since the major newspapers sent their music critics to cover these events, particularly when they involved large numbers of players in major venues like Carnegie Hall, the accordion bands became one of the most visible expressions of the "accordion phenomenon" in America through the early 1960s.

With the establishment of the American Accordionists Association (AAA) and the Accordion Teachers Guild (ATG) in 1938, top teachers and players banded together to become a unified presence in the accordion world, and they were (and in some cases still are) identified with making authoritative decisions in accordion pedagogy, repertoire, and instrument design. The notable accordionist and pedagogue Anthony Galla-Rini (b. 1904), who began his career as part of an accordion-playing vaudeville act with his father, has been seen as an important influence on the accordion, rescuing the instrument from its low status as a vaudeville instrument to higher status as a vehicle for classical music:

> The objectives that Anthony wished to stress in his career were: (1) to teach the accordion as a professionally-recognized instrument, (2) to exploit the full potential of the accordion, to (3) compose and arrange music and (4) to promote the accordion in the concert field where he felt it truly belonged.[30]

Given the numerous "learn to play accordion by mail" pitches and the appeals to piano teachers to teach the accordion as a profitable sideline, it is easy to understand why some pedagogues were concerned about establishing a pedagogy for the instrument.[31] Galla-Rini developed one of the earliest accordion method books and wrote two concertos for accordion and symphony. He developed the first system of notation that revealed the pitches in the five sets of reeds in the left-hand keyboard. The information he provided was used by accordion manufacturers in standardizing the reed arrangement for the left hand. Method books and pedagogical writings developed for the accordion focused on overcoming the limits of the instruments, and teachers of the accordion celebrated its unique properties, with method-book topics such as "mastering the bellows shake." Willard Palmer speculated on the unfairness of the accordion not attaining the "highbrow" status of instruments such as flute or piano in modern symphony orchestras. "Can a piano sustain tones, make a melody sing, and breathe with life?" he asked. He argued that truly devoted accordionists should become eloquent spokespeople for their instruments.

> We need never to apologize to anyone. . . . I'm proud to call myself an accordionist. The fact that our instrument is a newcomer to the world of serious music offers us a challenge to be real pioneers in providing for it a needed library of solos, concertos, etc., probing the secrets of new techniques and demanding improvements in the construction of the instrument. We are the people who must guarantee that its development be as rapid as possible, and who must see to it

that it is properly and quickly recognized by the best of musicians
as an instrument worthy of the best of music.[32]

As Palmer and his fellow "classicizers" of the accordion pointed out,
the accordion was only as good as the repertoire written for it. Warned
one teacher of the accordion, "good musical taste having been of a de-
plorably low standard in the past . . . such banalities as 'Sharpshooters
March' and 'Beer Barrel Polka' should not be played in public, nor given
as lesson assignments."[33] The learned exponents of "accordion culture"
saw it as their mission to provide students and teachers of the accordion
with appropriate literature—transcriptions of the classics, and "original"
works for accordion by nonaccordionist composers. To encourage nonaccordionist composers to write for the accordion, the AAA established
a commissioning committee headed by the legendary accordion advocate Elsie M. Bennett (1918–2005). Bennett spent the better part of her
career lobbying for distinguished American composers to write for the
accordion. The AAA also sponsored significant concerts in major venues
such as New York City's Carnegie Hall, where the accordion was first
featured in 1947, when accordionist Toralf Tollefifson presented Pietro
Deiro's Accordion Concerto in E.[34]

One could argue, that these tropes centering on "elevating" the accordion through "improvements" and developments in the classical
repertoire betray an aggressively exclusionary strategy. As in the American theater and the mainstream classical music world, the development
in the accordion world of what Lawrence Levine and other scholars
would recognize as a "highbrow" culture drew attention to the importance of classical models and privileged them over the "lowbrow" or
the transplanted folk musics of Europe. The attempts to create a "classical" music culture around the accordion could easily be dismissed
as the by-products of a cultural "inferiority complex," which led to
imitation and transcription rather than innovation. The accordion appeared to reinforce the hierarchies among "highbrow/middlebrow/
lowbrow" cultures. I would argue, however, that the accordion staged
border crossings from its very origins. As we have seen in Demian's
patent, the modern accordion emerged at the crossroads between European "elite" and folk cultures. The vernacular styles of many musical
communities, especially Italians and Italian Americans, tempered its
repertoire and performance. As the arbiters of the accordion looked
down upon and ignored a wide range of popular music that Italians
produced, they could not ignore the fact that their countrymen in the
United States (together with Poles, Slavs, Latinos, and other immigrant
ethnic groups in America) continued to produce and enjoy their own
music. The discourse of "legitimacy"—how to make the accordion belong in high culture—was also a conversation about marginality.

Discourses of Marginality

The values of the "accordion world" intertwined with issues of ethnicity and class. For example, the success story of the accordion in America is one particularly charged with significance for Italians and Italian Americans. As we have seen, accordions made in Italy were the most prized for their aesthetic appeal and their reed quality. The terms "Italian craftsmanship" and "made in Italy" frequently appeared in accordion ads, and most professional players expressed a preference for Italian-made accordions.[35] The Italians led the accordion field both in Europe, where they continued to manufacture the most desirable instruments for the world market, and in the Americas, where they sought new markets for the instrument in ever widening circles of classical, jazz, as well as Cajun, conjunto and tejano players.[36]

Some Italian immigrants who introduced the accordion to America became celebrities—Guido Deiro attained notoriety not only as a vaudeville star but by marrying Mae West. Italian accordion virtuosi and teachers such as the Deiros remained at the forefront of the accordion phenomenon not only by producing and selling accordions, but by arranging music, making recordings, playing accordion on the radio, writing method books, and—joining the great wave of other Italian, Jewish, and Irish immigrants to the United States prior to 1924—opening the first music schools and studios in the United States. Our foregoing observations about choices made by accordion teachers in the effort to "legitimize" their instrument suggests that certain "traditional Italian" styles, practices, and even a whole category of accordions were abandoned or deliberately excluded from their efforts. When the factories of Castelfidardo singled out one type of accordion to mass produce and distribute globally, it was not the button diatonic accordion (widely used in Italian and European folk styles), but the piano accordion, a pan-European instrument valued for its ability to play a range of styles. When teachers of the accordion selected popular Italian songs to arrange for their students, or present onstage, these songs were "dressed up" for the concert stage (along with other types of national folk musics and styles) as part of their effort to elevate the accordion's prestige. Pietro Deiro and his fellow teachers and concerts brought well-varnished, highly entertaining, and written-down (never improvised, as in traditional folk practice) versions of Italian songs to their listeners and students, such as "Tarantella Napolitana," "Return to Sorrento," "Mari Mari," and arrangements of Italian opera arias, alongside polkas, tangos, pasodobles, and foxtrots, which they also arranged in a similar style. One finds this repertoire not only in written arrangements played on concert stages and competitions, but in the working repertoire of the Italian cabaret accordionists active in the 1930s, 1940s, and 1950s, some of whom were seen as highly influential as teachers and performers in the accordion world.[37] These performances, highlighting opera arias and standards of the European classical repertoire, as well as a Central and Northern Italian folk repertoire, elide distinctions between "classical" versus "folk repertoires, and "highbrow" versus "lowbrow" traditions.

At the same time that the "accordion world" enabled a cosmopolitan expression of Italian-ness on the sidelines of highbrow accordion culture, it also encouraged awareness of a diversity of accordion-based ethnic and popular musical styles developing in the commercial music field at the time. Beginning in the late 1920s, accordion-based dance music played by Tejanos (Texan Mexicans), conjunto, and even mariachi had considerable local and regional success, soon to be exploited by record labels in much the same manner that the "race record" phenomenon exploited an interest in African American folk music. Emigrating from Italy to Houston in 1963, a young entrepreneur named John Gabbanelli cornered the market for accordions made by his family firm in Castelfidardo by catering to Tejano and Cajun players. A variety of Gabbanelli accordion models (piano accordions and button diatonics) featured the three colors of the Mexican flag.[38]

At the same time that the accordion world privileged the classics, it enabled social interactions among players of differing styles and backgrounds. In the late 1930s, opportunities to play jazz in club dates attracted both amateur and professional accordionists. A 1938 article in *Accordion World* urged players, "Why not add some AMERICAN MUSIC to your repertoire?"[38] In a 1941 advice column for accordionists, Pietro Deiro considered the earning potential of "jazz orchestra and radio" accordionists and urged players to learn "modern rhythms" for these types of jobs, as well as for their engagements at hotel dining rooms, private parties, lodge affairs, and church banquets.[40] The accordion and the "accordion professional" that Deiro describes mediated a variety of musical repertoires, styles, and musical worlds.

In 1947 a young Italian American butcher's son named Dick Contino appeared on the *Ed Sullivan Show* with a vigorous performance of "Lady of Spain," a cosmopolitan foxtrot from the repertoire of Myron Floren, a regular on Lawrence Welk's show.[41] Although Contino presented a seductive "teen idol" image, his virtuosic accordion style and technique seemed consistent with the accordion world's ideals. These representations allowed the accordion world to "filter" the influences of "ethnic" or "foreign" and popular music, at least for the moment. It presented a compromise between the more highbrow tastes of the accordion old guard and the emerging popular sensibilities of the mass audience.

Beginning in the 1950s, the commercial success of rock 'n' roll and indications of changing popular tastes sent more ominous signals to the members of the accordion world. In 1954 Bill Haley and the Comets recorded "Rock Around the Clock," arguably the first rock-'n'-roll hit and the moment of rock 'n' roll's arrival on the international scene.[42] But the original formation of Haley's group, the Saddlemen, featured an accordion.[43] As a country swing band, that group seemed to prefigure the ability of accordion to "transition" to the rock band, or at least open up new professional opportunities in teen styles. In the 1958 film *The Girl Can't Help It*, an obscure rock band known as The Three Chuckles, featuring accordion player Teddy Randazzo, makes an appearance. The handsome profile and athletic style of Dick Contino is evident in Randazzo's performance. He is not only agile in the backbend, wielding twenty-five pounds of metal and celluloid on his chest (although this does not appear to be a full-sized 120-bass accordion), he also appears radiantly confident of his rock idol image. There was, for the present, at least some evidence to suggest that an accordion-playing rock star would soon appear on the scene.

The accordion industry, at least in the 1960s, appeared to cater to rock musicians and fans by producing a variety of compact, easily portable, and inexpensive *accordion-derived* instruments. The Chicago Musical Instrument Company made and marketed a series of electronic organs in the United States. That company also introduced a new instrument called the Cordovox, an accordion wired to an organ generator. While demonstrating this instrument to his customers at a Pasadena music store, a young musician named John R. West was tapped to be the keyboard player for Gary Lewis and the Playboys (see fig. 3), who in the mid-1960s would regularly make the Top Ten list. When the band appeared on *Hullaballoo*, a teen dance show, West's Cordovox appeared to be snapped shut. He was simply playing electronically without moving the bellows, and the resulting sound was a tinny, faint organ-like timbre, never evoking the rich texture of the accordion reeds. (The emcee interviewing the band made a remark about the lazy accordion player.)

The Playboys' former producer, Snuff Garrett, later spoke about the use of the accordion in this band (and other rock bands of the period). "The accordion was really for novelty effect," he said. "In the industry we called it a 'color' instrument, like the autoharp or the whistle sounds we used. The accordion could really cut through the band. I was always trying to 'hide' John's sound." Garrett's aim, as he explained, was for the guitar sound to predominate in the band. "I have a lot of respect for what Lawrence Welk did," said Garrett, "but there was no way the accordion could touch the guitar . . . or even the keyboard."

One factor that may have impeded the accordion's use in rock 'n' roll was its ubiquity, particularly on radio and television. Because the accordion had been used so much in dance and pop orchestras for shows in the 1950s, its sound may have become relegated in the public's mind to music that was featureless "background" music with hardly a personality of its own—particularly not one that would appeal to youth.[44]

Searching for Rockordion   231

Figure 3. A detail from the front cover of Gary Lewis and the Playboys' first album, *This Diamond Ring* (1965), showing John R. West playing his Cordovox with the group on the *Ed Sullivan Show* earlier that year.

The accordion became associated, like the dance bands in which it appeared, with staid "establishment music." And, of course, there was the *Lawrence Welk Show*, which, during its national run on ABC from 1955 to 1971, displayed the accordion week after week in its most stereotypical (and traditional ethnic) commercial forms.

One factor in the accordion's disappearance from the popular music mainstream may have been its weight and size. Not every piano accordion had 41 treble keys and 120 bass keys. But classical teachers would have discouraged their students from buying smaller instruments, because they lacked the full keyboard and a full array of register shifts that were indicated in arrangements of classical music for accordion. Moreover, one can easily understand why, in a tight and competitive market, accordion dealers would have steered customers toward larger instruments, which were more expensive and profitable. In the accordion distributors' catalogs from the 1930s, 1940s and 1950s, only piano accordions, and then only full-sized (41-treble and 120-bass) ones, appear with any regularity.

Yet we know from unofficial accounts that full-sized accordions could hurt players' self-images, not just their lower backs. I recently spoke with players who grew up playing the accordion in the 1950s and 1960s about how they perceived the possibility of playing rock 'n' roll as accordionists. Most of them stopped playing the accordion and switched to other electric keyboard instruments such as the Hammond organ (introduced in 1936), which was "much better for banging out staccato chords."[45] They perceived the accordion as "old school" and outmoded and the associations with ethnic and folk music as unwelcome baggage. Hans Stucki, an Ohio-born accordionist-turned-keyboardist for The Angry, recalled, "I wanted to play 'real rock and roll music'—enough already with the Swiss . . . the Gospel, the accordion contests."[46] Another player who was accomplished at the accordion and grew up in the "competition scene" discusses the impact of popular music trends in his choice to abandon the accordion:

> As the Beatles and similar groups consumed our imaginations in 1964, I gave up the accordion. I never saw a group with an accordion at the time—not as I recall, anyway—not even Gary Lewis and the Playboys, whom I liked very much via airplay, but don't remember seeing on television. It was only sometime after their heyday that I learned they had had an accordion player (or Cordovox?) in their group. I was aware, however, of the thin, reedy Farfisa organ sound so popular among garage bands of those same years. And I liked it. But I don't think I ever consciously connected it with the accordion sound that apparently fueled it in the first place. When I was about 12 I got a guitar for Christmas. Nothing could stop me from practicing. The guitar was it for me.[47]

A number of former accordion players I interviewed, all of whom happened to be male, indicated that the instrument made them uncomfortable with their onstage profile. "The accordion had the wrong image. It made you look fat or pregnant. It wasn't much help in getting the girls, which is what rock music was all about anyway."[48] Indeed, there is plenty of anecdotal evidence from the 1960s—and abundant images of slim, trim Beatles and Rolling Stones toting featherweight Fenders—that suggests many players of the accordion experienced a disjuncture between their chosen instrument and the commercial interests and values behind their new favorite music. The question, then, is what did the accordion industry do in response to the need to "include" the accordion in the mainstream world of rock?

Discourses of Inclusion

In 1955 Americans bought 120,000 accordions (a figure comparable to the sale of all the brass instruments purchased by public schools). By 1958 the total number of accordions sold dropped to 92,000. What must have seemed particularly alarming, especially to music dealers who were members of the National Association of Music Merchants (and would have tracked such information in the annual reports), was the steady rise in guitar sales: 250,000 in 1955 to 700,000 in 1963. But we find no mention of this trend, nor the dramatic arrival of "Beatlemania," as noted in the major media. In 1964 there is no evidence of a response to what must have seemed like a miserable year when guitar sales topped one million and accordion sales dropped down to 50,000, half the figure reported for the console organ. In Castelfidardo seventeen accordion factories closed down between 1960 and 1963.[49]

Searching back issues of *Accordion World* magazine for any official response to the rock 'n' roll phenomenon or the Beatles, I found no mention of either, only a handful of articles by teachers urging students to adhere to their studies of classical repertoire and technique. However, one alarmist accordion teacher in 1957 noted the dangerous influences of rock 'n' roll:

> A careful analysis reveals that Rock 'n' Roll has a hypnotic influence on its participants while on the dance floor and is the germ of nervous energy and unrest led by hopped-up rhythm and doped-up music resulting in gang warfare, riots, broken furniture and broken limbs, plus crime and rape of every nature and description known to our law enforcement authorities.[50]

The proposal for "Keeping Rock 'n' Roll under Control" was twofold: (a) stronger policing at dances and (b) steering accordion students toward "correct" choices in popular songs to play.

> A pupil with a family "jive" background after six or eight weeks can begin to be prepared for "Old Smokey," "Whatever Will Be Will Be," and "Love Me Tender." Then as he advances in ability, he can be introduced to simplified arrangements of "Neapolitan Nights," or "O Sole Mio" or semi-classics with a definite melodic appeal.[51]

The best way to appreciate the accordion world's dramatic hostility and indifference to rock is to compare its reception of rock with that of *Guitar World* magazine, which merged with *Accordion World* magazine in 1958 to form *Accordion and Guitar World*. While the guitar section (in the front of the magazine) urged readers to "embrace rock, become a hep teacher and watch your popularity grow," the accordion half remained silent on the issue.[52] Accordion enthusiasts hoped that rock 'n' roll would only be a passing fad that would eventually lead students back to the classics. As Elsie Bennett, the accordion advocate put it, "One of the finest examples of growth and change has been the development of the accordion from a 'popular' fun instrument to the status of a standard 'serious' instrument in orchestra or band and of a solo instrument worthy of the greatest musical talent."[53] It is difficult to tell how many accordionists shared Bennett's optimism and how many were more inclined to agree with an anguished comment from a distinguished accordion maker: "*that* music trend put a bullet hole through the accordion!" Either way, few felt empowered to take action.[54]

As the organized voice of the accordion world was keeping watch over the repertoire and technique of accordion students, one accordion company hatched a unique plan. Deffner had been in the accordion business since 1934 and had been doing more than 30 percent of the U.S. volume in accordions. One of their companies, Pancordion, maker of instruments for Myron Floren and Lawrence Welk, designed the Tiger Combo accordion and had it built in Italy. But Deffner also owned the Titano accordion line, and because the two accordion firms had exclusive dealer franchises in the United States and dealt with accordion schools, Titano made a version of the Tiger Combo for Titano dealers, called the 'Combo Cordion.[55] (As both were similarly conceived and presented as the "Rockordion" in advertising, I will refer to both as Tiger accordions.) The Tiger was equipped with two regular sets of reeds and a microphone hookup for amplification. Neither the size nor the technology of this accordion was unique but some of its design features were. Made to break the mold of uniform black-and-white accordions, the Tiger was sprayed with a multicoat color finish and lacquered in a choice of three Fiat colors: Fire, Sun, and Blue Moon. Enhancing the visual impact of the glossy auto paint was a slanted keyboard—to allow the audience to see the accordion player's "flying fingers." Calling attention to the action on the keyboard was the reverse color scheme: white "black notes" and black natural keys. What most distinguished the Tiger from other acoustic and electric accordions was an extra set of reeds, tuned a fifth above, that were intended to be used to perform the current popular music: "a quint reed activated on three of the instrument's six treble registers, providing piercing lead or swinging chords in the audio colors which are presently flipping teen age [sic] record fans."[56]

If Deffner's press release for the Tiger failed to send the message that this was not Lawrence Welk's accordion, Deffner's "Make the Scene with Tiger" ad campaign did (see fig. 4). The ads, which appeared in *Accordion World* in the mid-1960s, show a line drawing of four young men clad in Beatles-style slim pants, with the accordionist playing lead. The Tiger—that is, the "Rockordion"—was available at $150, including a colorful carrying case.[57]

Following the last known 1967 advertisement (see fig. 5), we lack documentation on the fate of the Tiger accordion. What were the intentions of the Deffners? Would there be more such instruments? An American Idol–style star search? Of recordings and radio broadcasts, there seem to be none. What were their intentions for "Rockordion"? Was this simply an attention-getting label, or a grand plan to transform the accordion into a "rockordion," a leading instrument of the American rock band? One issue that has surfaced among players commenting on the Tiger years later was the peculiarity of playing with the quint reeds. The addition of the fifth added a dense chordal texture that seemed out of touch with rock music. "When you played 'Love Is Blue' using simple thirds, the quint

Searching for Rockordion   235

Figure 4. Original artwork for a late-1960s advertisement for the
Tiger Combo 'Cordion, showing the instrument (with reverse key
colors) in an imaginary rock band.

reeds automatically formed block chords. Great for Elvis's late ballad
style, but not rock 'n' roll."[58]

Tigers simply appear to evaporate after a brief moment on the scene,
much the way Dick Contino himself did when he was drafted to serve
in the Korean conflict in 1952.[59] Willard Palmer, who worked with Faithe
and Ernest Deffner, was best known to his public (and remembered in his
obituary by Deffner) as the founder of the accordion program at University
of Houston and the coauthor of the ten-volume Palmer Method for Accordion, developed in partnership with Bill Hughes.[60] If Palmer was ever seen
in public promoting the Tiger, the record does not show it. Palmer was in

Figure 5. This advertisement for a Combo 'Cordion, trying to promote the accordion's suitability for rock music, appeared in *Hullabaloo* 2, no. 6 (October 1967): 10—on the reverse side of a page on the Monterey Pop Festival.

his forties—an elder statesmen where rock is concerned—at the time the Tiger was introduced. Both Palmer and Ernest Deffner are deceased, and there is no information on Deffner's website about the Tiger. Elsewhere, echoing Bennett's view of popular music, Deffner attributed the failure of the Tiger to the short-sightedness of accordion teachers. "The program didn't succeed because accordion teachers saw rock as a passing fad. They disliked the music and refused to teach it to their students."[61]

Ultimately the Tiger accordion, developed as an inexpensive, entry-level instrument, failed to receive the backing of its own constituency.

Ralph Stricker, who was involved in developing electronic accordions in the 1960s and 1970s, notes the Tiger could not be seen by professional players as a "serious" instrument: its 72-bass keyboard did not have the range and its reeds did not have the quality expected from a "professional" instrument.[62] By 1965 the accordion itself was in the midst of what many perceived to be a terminal state of decline within the general music scene—as becomes clear from accounts in the mass media and impressions from former players. Notes one writer, "It was in the early 1960s, with the rise of rock 'n' roll that Western teenagers came to view the squeezebox as the embodiment of everything that was hackneyed, dorky and terminally kitsch about their parents' culture."[63]

Beyond the Tiger: Discourses of Inclusion into the 2000s

The "disappearance" or "failure" of the accordion in the rock era cannot be explained only by changing tastes, but through changing attitudes toward ethnicity and class in the United States. To borrow a coinage from Ien Ang, the accordion locates a "fundamental uneasiness in our condition of togetherness-in-difference."[64] Picking up the accordion could either signify the idea of multicultural inclusiveness or an internalized xenophobia underlying discourses about immigrants and their musical traditions. "If you grew up in an Eastern European, working-class family, you had a greater chance of playing an accordion than if you were from an upper-middle income family," writes Len Wallace, an accordionist and social activist. "If you grew up striving to become upwardly mobile, it meant that you ditched your accordion and picked up something else to play."[65] Guy Klucevsec, who grew up playing accordion in a Slovenian-American milieu, notes that "in the 1960s and 1970s it was out; it was the most unhip instrument you could be playing." As an experimental composer and performer making an effort to avoid playing ethnic music in the early days of his career in the new music scene, Klucevsec was occasionally hired to play "Italian" or "ethnic"-sounding music on television commercials. "When they need something that sounded really square, they would use an accordion," he recalls. "I once did a commercial for Polly-O mozzarella cheese. They used me to do the music for their competitor's cheese, which was hard and dry and tasted bad."[66]

If "cheesy" ethnic music played on the accordion was one indication that the accordion movement had run its course, parody and covers were another. In 1979 a California teenager named Al Yankovic brought his accordion into the bathroom across the hall from a local radio station and recorded "My Bologna," a parody of the Knack's hit single, "My Sharona." Yankovic may never have intended to make it as a classical accordionist, although his parents had invested in years of lessons at a local music studio. But after the "My Bologna" single was played on

Dr. Demento's radio show, Yankovic discovered that he could make a career of spoofing rock 'n' roll hits on the accordion.[67] No wonder, then, that in the 1980s, members of the San Francisco–based band Those Darn Accordions developed a "plan" to "rehabilitate" the accordion's image. "Roving gangs of accordion-wielding marauders would descend upon unsuspecting diners in the city's posh restaurants, barrel through the front door playing demented versions of 'Lady of Spain' and back out again before anyone could respond with rotten tomatoes," reported the *Santa Cruz Sentinel*.[68] In the early 1990s, Toronto native Dominic Amatucci, who had abandoned his childhood accordion for soccer, one day decided that "he had to record the entire Beatles catalog on the accordion." This effort resulted in his present band, the Accordion Beatles. The band's mission is not parodic, though; rather, it is a conventional rock tribute band with an unconventional instrumentation. Amatucci claims that his aim is to exploit the accordion as a one-man orchestra to capture the rich textures of the Beatles' music.[69] Yet, like Yankovic, the Accordion Beatles calls attention to the accordion's post-rock-'n'-roll vulnerability. Parodies and tributes can serve as woeful reminders that the accordion had reached its weary end game.

A real-life hero of the contemporary American accordion scene, and a prophet of the accordion's return, is William Schimmel. Schimmel grew up playing accordion in a working-class German American family in Philadelphia, and he found his family's ethnic folk music more enjoyable than the Beethoven and Clementi transcriptions he played in accordion recitals. "My uncles would arrive with their accordions and all hell would break loose: dancing, eating, drinking, cigar smoking, poker-playing— real fun!"[70] But when Schimmel arrived at the Juilliard School of Music, he found no "place" for the accordion in the conservatory system. Hence he decided to concentrate on piano and composition. In the early 1980s Schimmel heard Astor Piazzolla's New Tango Quintet, whose second tour of the United States included a phenomenally successful concert in Central Park in 1987.[71] Notes Schimmel, "the tango is reminiscent of romantic failure and existential despair. The tango expects all of that but the trick is that you go down and out, but you do it in style. It's the ultimate 'screw you.'"[72] Schimmel's efforts to transcribe Argentine tangos for the piano accordion and his efforts to distill the essence of what he heard as the "Argentine counterpart to the blues," resulted in the Tango Project, a trio whose renditions of tango music (originals and traditional tunes) were featured in films such as *Scent of a Woman*, *True Lies*, and the HBO series *Sex and the City*. His credentials in the accordion world (he graduated from the Neupauer Conservatory's accordion program), his technique and stature as a Juilliard-trained classical composer have earned him the support and guardianship of the American Accordionists Association.

Some of Schimmel's most significant collaborations have been with mainstream pop/rock artists such as Tom Waits and Sting, thereby helping to integrate the accordion, finally, into the world of rock 'n' roll—if not as a soloist's instrument at the front of the band, but a valued part of a band's texture. At the same time, Schimmel actively teaches and promotes the accordion, not to mention composing many new works for the instrument. His collaborations with symphony orchestras and theater productions have made him a visible and respected contributor to New York's contemporary musical scene. In his introductory remarks for the Accordion Seminar he founded in 1994, he describes the "built-in ironic duality of the accordion," which is both "hip and square, beautiful and ugly."[73]

Around the time that Schimmel's work became more widely known and emulated in the new music scene in New York City, the global world music industry created a special slot for the accordion in a list that includes Cajun, Zydeco, polka, klezmer, Tex-Mex, and conjunto. As noted in the literature on the "folk revival" phenomenon in America, these musical styles came to the fore in the late 1970s and early 1980s as a reflection of a shift in sensibility among children of assimilated American parents who struggled to identify their own voices and experiences through those of heartfelt, passionate performances of ethnic music.[74] Some of the most notable exponents of these musical traditions have been accordionists: Buckwheat Zydeco, Rockin' Dopsie, Clifton Chenier, Flaco Jimenez, Nathan Abshire, and David Hidalgo of Los Lobos. Their skills as improvisers (not to mention their skill and savvy in appealing to rock-'n'-roll and blues fans) have cultivated the image of the independent, spontaneous, and authentic "folk musician" par excellence. The links of these traditional forms to contemporary rock have, by association, highlighted the use of the accordion as the "people's instrument." In the albums of Sheryl Crow, John Mellencamp, Paul Simon, Billy Joel, and Bruce Springsteen, one finds contributions by backing accordionists. Listening to the heartfelt and understated accompaniments by accordionist Charlie Giordano on Springsteen's *Sessions* album—particularly on "We Shall Overcome"—suggests earlier connections between the accordion and the protest movements of earlier eras, in which the instrument was sometimes played at rallies and demonstrations—and was famously celebrated for its role in these.[75] As John Berger romantically put it in a *Granta* magazine article in 1986, "The accordion was made for life on this earth, the left hand marking the bass and the heartbeats, the arms and shoulders laboring to make breath, and the right hand fingering for hopes."[76]

Few contemporary bands have made a clearer connection between the accordion and the idea of the "people's music" than Brave Combo, a self-described "polka band with a mission." Brave Combo created a niche for high energy, fast-paced, "ethnic-eclectic" music centering on the accordion: polka versions of Jimi Hendrix's "Purple Haze" and the Rolling Stones' "I Can't Get No Satisfaction" played as a cumbia. The world they evoke through their motto, "peace through polka," and their references to Surrealist art and marching band traditions,[77] provide a dreamy, utopian vision of American pop culture as a patchwork of different styles and traditions filtered down through the accordion and fused into a wacky musical melting pot to be savored by all. Like Weird Al's parodies, their performances chip away at the homogeneous sameness of rock music, but their idealistic mission is to reveal the diversity and richness at the source of American culture. "Our directive is to break down people's perceptions about what's cool in music. Our deal is to shake up people's ideas about what they label hip, or right or wrong."[78] Brave Combo's work highlights the accordion as an "instrument from below" animated by the range of disparate identities that symbolizes the development of American culture.

Few events highlight the renewed "populist" dimension of the accordion more than large public gatherings of players and fans. Since the early 1990s, a half-dozen organized accordion festivals have devoted themselves to "reviving the accordion from dormancy."[79] Such events are outgrowths of the traditional outdoor accordion band concert and competition showcase, and the "accordion picnics" such as those that took place in San Francisco of the 1930s.[80] The Cotati festival, held near Guido Deiro's home in Northern California, focuses on younger musicians and local and emerging bands with an ethnic twist (Aztex, Polkacide and the Mad Maggies), and even featured seventy-six-year-old Dick Contino at its 2006 event. One of the best publicized performances at Cotati is a round-robin performance of "Lady of Spain" bringing members of the audience onstage to perform the "sacred anthem of all accordionists" in the "people's key of C," followed by the "Beer Barrel Polka."[81] Some players learn the song the night before the performance, if they can play accordion at all.[82] Its impact, like that of Brave Combo's music, comes from the juxtaposition of the commonplace with the "completely unexpected."[83] Like the accordion "old guard" that collaborated behind the scenes to stave off encroaching disorder and chaos from the world of rock, the accordionists of Cotati gather in public, in broad daylight, to present their own vision of inclusive, eclectic mayhem.

Conclusion

The meanings embedded in the story of America's fascination with the accordion are numerous. In the 1930s–1950s, the idea of legitimacy, paired with the various formulas for technological improvement of the instrument, encouraged a wide range of discourses and uses of the accordion.

For the "guardian contingent" and their middle-class patrons, classical music was the proper medium for the accordion, because the mechanisms for classical transmission were already in place, owing to the efforts of the musical appreciation movement. Organized networks of local entrepreneurs promoting an ideology of self-improvement and cultural elevation delivered musical instruction, music appreciation, wholesome entertainment, and moral guidance for the whole family directly to the customer's doorstep.

Though inclusiveness was part of the vision promoted by the accordion guardian contingent—and a justification for its legitimacy—a problem emerged from the contradictions in its alleged pluralistic ideal. The piano accordion could appeal to immigrant parents of Eastern European and Italian descent, who were familiar with the instrument as part of their folk traditions. Yet, if they were taught to play their own folk music at all, it was in written-out arrangements rather than in the spontaneous, improvised, traditional style. This type of repertoire was mass-produced in uniform arrangements for accordion bands and competitions, which encouraged their students to play primarily classical music transcribed or arranged for the accordion. Accordion teachers tended to focus on how the repertoire functioned in recitals and competitions, rather than the local cultural (folk) traditions underpinning the repertoire.

Players who came of age during the 1960s and 1970s could detect a coercive element in their accordion teachers' pedagogy—rejecting, through their ultimate rejection of the accordion, the idea of the homogenized, wholesome, and white Christian American family. As one former player notes,

> teaching a kid to play the accordion in the 1960s had less to do with preserving regional music styles than it did with keeping them out of the clutches of Jimi Hendrix, LSD and those no good Thayer kids across the street. So . . . an accordion would be one means to keeping me on the path to my mother's idealized version of myself—cleancut, God-fearing, and well versed in the subtle and oh-so-unhip vagaries of polkas and bouncy spirituals . . . the contraption made me feel like a small blond butterball donkey, a beast of musical burden.[84]

Despite this protective mother's best efforts, it was the bland and faceless image of accordions and accordion playing that made young players all the more vulnerable to the incursion of Jimi Hendrix. Rock 'n' roll presented sartorial images that were too tantalizingly different from and contradictory to those promoted in accordion club circles. Encouraged by the accordion's perfectability, its potential to be "versatile," and its appeal to new markets, the Tiger tried to link "accordion" and "cool." The "Rockordion" can be seen as an ironically failed response to rock and only a half-hearted effort to impose some order on the perceived chaos of rock. To be sure, the Rockordion was a vision of musical hybridity that was never realized, only hinted at in the Tiger advertisements. Indeed, the guardians of the accordion had unwittingly produced a hierarchy of the accordion that was later replicated by the mainstream music world when it "excluded" the accordion from the rock band—and relegated it to a tool for kitsch, parody, and cheesy ethnic music.

The accordion finally did what Faithe Deffner always hoped it would do: re-emerge, though much later and on much different terms. A flourishing of traditional folk styles neglected by the accordion world—Cajun, polka, klezmer, and Tex-Mex—emerged with it, coexisting with tributes and parodies in the repertoires of groups like Accordion Beatles, Those Darn Accordions, and Brave Combo. It may have come as a surprise to Deffner and the developers of accordion technology that the accordions that became most prevalent in the public eye were not high-class piano accordions, but the traditional accordions specific to ethnic and folk traditions, such as the Cajun button accordion and the bandoneon. When piano accordions appeared in rock bands in the 1980s, they were rarely the expensive variety, but smaller and more compact models—some of them played in deliberately understated, unpretentious fashion.[85] What the accordion guardian contingent envisioned as "the instrument of tomorrow" seemed to be part of an interest in the past and a desire for the more "authentic" and "folksy" sound produced by harmonicas, acoustic guitars, and acoustic accordions.

The resurgence of the accordion—driven by so-called roots music and aimed at a white, urban audience—challenged the white middle-class community that had previously presented itself as the accordion's guardians. (The absence of the American Accordionists Association from the forefront of discourse around the accordion today is notable—although they do lend their sponsorship to Schimmel's unconventional Accordion Seminars at the Tenri Institute in New York City.) While the story of the accordion in America is still unfolding, the idea of the accordion as "hip" or "cool" is worth exploring further. The nature of the accordion's "core values" perpetuated something of the aspirations associated with the middle-class pursuit of success and status in America (legitimacy). Ironically, the accordion also provided a model of exclusion (marginality) as teachers steered their students away from traditional and popular musics and toward classical performances in competitions and concerts. "Peace through polka" is Brave Combo's amusing quip, but the idea of mutual acceptance has always weighed heavily in the accordion world, both for the guardian contingent and later revivalists. The accordionists of the 1930s aimed, in their own way, to erase prejudice and encourage respect for difference, even if some of their methods now seem misguided. Their vision, while it privileged classical music as *the* shining example of what this one instrument could do for all Americans, promoted a vision of cultural diversity. The accordion can be highbrow, lowbrow; classical, or popular; it can be a product of exquisite craftsmanship or "the people's instrument"; it can deviate from all of the above. Ultimately, by sounding the themes of hybridity and multiculturalism, the accordion champions a unique vision of inclusivity.

ACKNOWLEDGMENTS

This article is based on research carried out at the New York Public Library's Research Division and World of Accordions Museum in Superior, Wis. A Discovery Grant from the Albany College of Pharmacy generously supported my research and travel to Wisconsin in the summer of 2005. I am also extremely grateful to accordion experts Faithe Deffner and Helmi Harrington for their collegial support and willingness to share valuable insights, as well as for their wonderful collections of instruments and documents.

An early version of this paper was presented in 2003 at the forty-eighth annual meeting of the Society for Ethnomusicology in Miami, Florida. My warmest thanks to Kenneth J. Blume, Tom Hilliard, and Elizabeth L. Wollman for their comments on earlier drafts of this paper, and especially to Michael Hicks, the current editor of *American Music*, who went out of his way to provide invaluable insights and sources on the accordion's checkered history in the field of rock 'n' roll.

NOTES

1. "Tiger Combo 'Cordion Introduced," undated press release provided by Ernest Deffner Affiliates, Long Island City, New York. I wish to thank Ms. Deffner, author of the above press release, for making available materials from the company's archive, and for her willingness to share information relevant to this paper.

2. Many players describe an early encounter with a door-to-door salesman as pivotal in development their early interest in the accordion. As a recent Wikipedia article on "Weird Al" Yankovic notes, an instrument salesman traveling through Lynwood, California, offered the Yankovic family accordion lessons at a local studio. http://en.wikipedia.org/wiki/%22Weird_Al%22_Yankovic#Early_life, accessed June 1, 2007.

3. Demians' accordion patent, May 23, 1829, translated by Karl and Martin Weyde. The Classical Free-Reed: A Short History of Free-Reed Instruments in Classical Music. Accessed Aug. 10, 2006, from http://www.ksanti.net/free-reed/history/demian.html.

4. Helmi Harrington, "Accordion Chronology," unpublished manuscript in the collection of the World of Accordions Museum, Superior, Wisconsin.

5. Since the 1600s, the regions of Central and Northern Italy have made and exported objects of beauty for worldwide consumption, as well as the skilled labor force needed to produce and sell them—as recent studies of Lucchese businessmen and Piedmontese stone-cutters have shown (see, e.g., Gloria Nardino, *Che bella figura! The Power of Performance in an Italian Ladies' Club in Chicago* (New York: State University of New York Press, 1999). Courtly patronage of the arts and the difficulty of farming as an occupation in these rocky, mountainous areas were factors in the development of industry, as well as foreign domination and the nineteenth-century unification movement. Castelfidardo first made Italian history by being the site of an definitive battle in which the Piedmontese defeated the pontifical army (backing France's Bourbon dynasty), putting an end to foreign domination of Italy. The accordion was seen as a key to Italy's modernization, as it was the first (hand-made) item to be mass produced and exported on a large scale. By improving the accordion and

making it commercially viable abroad, Italian accordion "moguls" could contribute to the
broader project of demonstrating Italy's economic power and cultural significance to the
wider world. See Beniamino Bugliacchi, "Castelfidardo: International Centre of Accordion
Production in Italy." http://www.accordions.com/index/his/his_it.shtml, accessed June
1, 2007. These family-owned companies were and, in some cases, still are creating the most
highly prized accordions, valued for their reed quality, their handling, and their ability to
produce a powerful sound without the excess weight.

6. Bugliolacchi, "Castelfidardo."

7. Personal collection of the author.

8. Information from accordion distributor's catalogs in the 1920s and 1930s provided
courtesy of Tony Arambery of the National Association of Music Merchants.

9. From accordion distributor's catalogs courtesy of Tony Arambery.

10. Personal communication with Anne Romagnoli, who inherited the company from
her father, Joseph Romagnoli, July 15, 2006.

11. The World of Accordions displays a number of accordion advertisements from mail-
order catalogs in its collection of documents.

12. Soprani display ad, *The Etude* (October 1939): 669; Coronet accordion advertisement,
c. 1960, from the collection of the author; "No Gift More Precious" (display ad, brand name
illegible), *The Etude* (July 1939): 129.

13. Helmi Harrington, curator, interview with author, World of Accordions museum,
Superior, Wis., June 10, 2005.

14. John Serry, "What's Wrong with the Accordion?" *Accordion World* (January 1947): 8.

15. George Rood, "It's Upbeat, Swinging, and Profitable," *New York Times*, June 21, 1965,
18.

16. Pietro Deiro, "The Game of Teaching," *The Etude* (March 1939): 139; Rood, "It's Upbeat,
Swinging, and Profitable."

17. The idea of an accordion "Golden Age" is explored in Ronald Flynn's compilation
of biographies, memoirs, and reflections from the first and second generation of notable
accordionists and teachers in the United States. Flynn's work focuses mainly on the Ital-
ian-American accordion community of San Francisco. See Ronald Flynn et al., eds., *The
Golden Age of the Accordion* (Schertz, Tex.: Flynn Publications, 1984).

18. Addressing American and British music educators, Percy A. Scholes outlines the
agenda for improving "what the public knows" about music in "Musical Appreciation!
An Appeal to Our Music Critics," *Musical Times*, July 1, 1931, 613–16.

19. Born in Italy in 1886, Pietro went to New York two years after his brother, who had
made a success in vaudeville, arrived. Pietro's transcriptions of classical music, and his
arrangements of Italian opera folksongs, whether he played them solo or with orchestral
accompaniment, helped to "elevate" the accordion from its marginal status to the level of
classical music. His approach was consistent with other teacher-composers, such as Charles
Nunzio, Charles Magnante, Willard Palmer, and numerous accordion artists from Europe
who used popular folksongs as the basis for creating a great accordion repertoire. For a
discussion of the Deiro brothers' careers, see Henri Doktorski, "The Classical Squeezebox: A
Short History of the Accordion in Classical Music," *Musical Performance* 4 (2001): 136–46.

20. Ibid, 616. The piano is the only instrument mentioned as suitable for this purpose.

21. D. E. Tobias, "The Piano-Accordion," *The Musical Times* 36 (September 1936): 834.

22. Hilding Bergquist, "A Symphonic Seat for the Accordion," *Accordion World* (1948):
19.

23. "Accordion Going Places." *Accordion World* 47 (June 1947): 18. Available at www.
ksanti.net/free-reed/essays/accordiongoingplaces.html, accessed July 14, 2007.

24. Few Americans had seen a piano accordion, much less one as elaborate as Guido's,
until Deiro appeared on the vaudeville stage in 1910. For a discussion of Deiro's accordion,
as well as his musical arrangements and recordings, see Henri Doktorski, "Guido Deiro's

Polca Variata," http://guidodeiro.com/sheetmusic/polcaessay1.html, accessed June 1, 2007.

25. Willard Palmer, "Should Accordionists Play Bach?" *Accordion World* (1949): 17, 18.

26. Ibid. Noted the author of a Wikipedia article on John Serry, one of the creators of the free-bass system, this design freed the artist from a fixed chord structure which character-ized Stradella Bass system and facilitated the performance of classical compositions. "John Serry, Sr.," www.en.wikipedia.org/wiki/john_serry_sr, accessed July 14, 2007.

27. "John Serry, Sr."

28. Eustace Pett, "The Piano Accordion," *The Musical Times* (August 1936): 740.

29. Classified advertisement, *Accordion Horizons*, December 1964, 38.

30. Flynn et al., eds., *Golden Age of the Accordion*, 84.

31. *The Etude* (March 1940): 238. Pietro Deiro's "Accordion Department" advice columns for accordionists in the 1930s and 1940s, occasionally reminds piano teachers who may be reading this column that teaching the accordion can provide a reliable second income source.

32. Willard Palmer, "What's Right with Our Instrument?" *Accordion World* (February 1947). Available at www.ksanti.net/free-reed-essays/palmer.html.

33. Anthony Galla-Rini, "The Accordion in the Serious Field of Music," *Musical Mer-chandise Magazine* (1948): 1.

34. The American Accordionist Association Newsletter (Spring 2006) has an impressive list of composers commissioned by the AAA, among them Virgil Thomson, Otto Luen-ing, and William Grant Still. According to Robert Young McMahan's account in the same newsletter, Bennett was planning to approach Igor Stravinsky on a New York City street, but either she lost her nerve or he was in a hurry to catch a taxicab (see p. 16).

35. William Schimmel, "Excelsior! The Best and Nothing but the Best." *Free-Reed Journal* 4 (2002): 59–69.

36. Harrington interview.

37. Marion S. Jacobson, "The Valtaro Musette Tradition and the 'Other' Italians," *Worlds of Music* (forthcoming).

38. Julius V. Tupa, "The Gabbanelli Story: The History of Gabbanelli Accordions," in, Flynn et al., eds. *Golden Age of the Accordion*, 315–20. [see n. 30]

39. "Add Some AMERICAN Music to Your Repertoire." *Accordion World* (June 1938): 14.

40. Pietro Deiro, "Choosing an Accordion Career," *The Etude* (1941): 639.

41. Bob Bove, *Accordion Man: Dick Contino* (Tallahassee, Fla.: Father and Son Press, 1994), 47.

42. Paul Friedlander, *Rock 'n' Roll: A Social History* (Boulder, Colo.: Westwood Press, 1997), 29.

43. Reebee Garafalo, *Rockin' Out: Popular Music in the USA* (Upper Saddle River, N.J.: Pearson-Prentice-Hall, 2005).

44. George Nelson describes this phenomenon convincingly in *Where Did Our Love Go? The Rise and Fall of the Motown Sound* (New York: St. Martin's Press, 1985).

45. Jerry Trecroce, email correspondence with author, Sep. 2, 2003.

46. "The Angry: Canton, Ohio, 1962–1966," My First Band, www.myfirstband.com/FirstBandAngry.html, accessed Feb. 16, 2007.

47. Michael Hicks, personal communication with author, Feb. 16, 2007.

48. William Schimmel, interview with author, June 15, 2003.

49. National Association of Music Merchants, "US Musical Instrument Sales 1909–1965." Thanks to Tony Arambery, research director of NAMM, for providing this information.

50. Bill Bullock, "Keep Rock 'n' Roll Under Control," *Accordion World* (January 1957): 5.

51. "So You Lost a Student?" *Accordion World* (June 1956): 8.

52. Ralph Dougal, "How I Changed to Rock 'n' Roll." *Accordion and Guitar World* (October 1962): 10.

53. Elsie Bennett, "Commissioning Music for the Accordion," *Accordion Horizons* (1962): 43.

54. Rebecca R. Turco, "Accordions Do Rock 'n' Roll as Well as Lawrence Welk," *Menomenee Falls News*, February 1996, accessed at www.baldoni.com/Family_History.html, accessed July 14, 2007.

55. Faithe Deffner, email correspondence with author, Sept. 17, 2003.

56. "Introducing the Tiger Combo 'Cordion," press release from Deffner Associates, undated. (possibly 1965), 1, 2. From the collection of the author.

57. Ibid., 2.

58. Alan Polivka, email correspondence with author, Sept. 11, 2003.

59. Bove, *Accordion Man*, 41.

60. Faithe Deffner, "In Memory of Dr. Willard ('Bill') Palmer," *Free-Reed Journal* (July 1996); republished in the *Free-Reed Journal* and available at www.ksanti.net/free-reed/essays/palmerbio.html, accessed July 14, 2007.

61. "Celebrity Interview" with Faithe Deffner, http://www.accordions.com/interviews/deffner/index.shtml, accessed July 14, 2007.

62. Ralph Stricker, personal communication with author, Jan. 15, 2007.

63. Delfin Vigil, "Squeeze Play," *San Francisco Examiner*, June 4, 2006, first arts page.

64. Ien Ang, *On Not Speaking Chinese: Living Between Asia and the West* (New York: Routledge, 2001), 198.

65. Len Wallace, "Accordion: The People's Instrument," *Broadside, the National Topical Song Magazine* (1988), available at http://worldaccordion.tripod.com/, accessed April 2, 2007.

66. Richard Guilliatt, "The Main Squeeze," *Sydney Morning Herald*, Feb. 28, 1998, available at www.accordions.com/index/art/main_squeeze.shtml, accessed April 2, 2007.

67. "Weird Al," *Permanent Record*, http://php.indiana.edu/~jbmorris/FAQ/al.booklet, accessed April 2, 2007.

68. Wallace Baine, "Those Darn Accordions Revive a Ridiculed Instrument," *Santa Cruz Sentinel*, Feb. 3, 2005, www.santacruzsentinel.com/archive/2005/February/03/style/stories/04style.htm, accessed July 14, 2007.

69. Domenic's Accordion Beatles Page, http://www.fab-4.com/, accessed April 2, 2007.

70. William Schimmel, interview with author, June 17, 2003. Schimmel's reflections on his development as an accordionist, as well as information on the accordions and memorabilia he collects, can be found on his blog, www.billschimmel.com.

71. William Schimmel, interview with author, June 21, 2003.

72. Sarah Chan, "The Tango Project Is the Ultimate Screw You," *University of Alberta Gateway*, vol. 4 (March 17, 2005), available at http://www.gateway.ualberta.ca/view.php?aid=4201, accessed July 14, 2007.

73. Allan Kozinn, "New Works for a Square but Hip Instrument," *New York Times*, Sept. 5, 1994, first arts page.

74. See, for example, Robert Cantwell, *When We Were Good: The Folk Revival* (Cambridge: Harvard University Press, 1996); Ron Ayerman and Andrew Jamison, *Music and Social Movements: The Folk Revival in the United States* (Cambridge: Cambridge University Press, 1998).

75. For example, the famous photo of Agnes (Sis) Cunningham playing the accordion at a UCAPA rally in the 1940s.

76. John Berger, "The Accordion Player," *Granta 18: The Snap Revolution*, March 1, 1986.

77. Their song "Breakfast in Fur" is a reference to Meret Oppenheim's famous 1938 painting of a fur teacup and spoon.

78. Brave Combo artists' profile, available at http://www.brave.com/bo/profile/, accessed July 14, 2007.

79. Richard Busack, "Accordion Manifesto! Time to Talk Tough about the Accordion,"

Metroactive, available at http://www.metroactive.com/papers/sonoma/08.21.03/accordions-0334.html, accessed April 2, 2007.

80. A photograph of 10,000 participants at the Pezzolo Accordion Festival in San Francisco in 1936 appears in Flynn, *Golden Age of the Accordion*, 8.

81. Vigil, "Squeeze Play."

82. A video of the Menlo Park, N.J., "Accordion Invasion" demonstrates a similar phenomenon, hundreds of players gathering to declare (somewhat mockingly) "Lady of Spain" their "anthem," http://www.youtube.com/watch?v=h2QOnxbRiYU, accessed July 14, 2007.

83. FAQ file on Brave Combo, accessed April 1, 2007 at http://www.brave.com/bo/faq/.

84. "My Dark Accordion Past," Sept. 10, 2006, www.rankinblog.com/2006/09/index, accessed July 14, 2007.

85. Charlie Giordano plays a 48-bass Hohner model in the Seeger Sessions band.

[19]

From *Ranchero* to *Jaitōn:*
Ethnicity and Class in Texas-Mexican Music
(Two Styles in the Form of a Pair)*

Manuel Peña

T he purpose of this essay is to provide an interpretive summary of certain musical developments among Texas-Mexicans, or *tejanos.*† It is
the result of several years of fieldwork research related to two popular musical styles that were forged by tejano musicians during and after World War
II. The styles are known as *orquesta tejana,* or simply orquesta, and
norteño. Among tejanos the latter is more commonly referred to as *conjunto,* and that is the label that will be used here. I should point out that each
style, though intricately related to the other, actually merits its own study.[1]
Nonetheless, the relationship between the two types of music presents a
challenging subject for interpretation, not only to students of musical culture, but to social scientists generally. It is in response to that challenge that
this work was conceived.

The essay focuses mainly on the period 1935–1965, with particular emphasis on the decade or so after the war. Additionally, my primary interest
is to explain the dynamics that sustained the conjunto-orquesta relationship, particularly the series of contrasts the two musics came to articulate
and, indeed, embody: working vs. middle class,[2] ethnic resistance vs. cultural assimilation, continuity vs. change, and folk vs. "sophisticated."
Moreover, underlying these contrasts, or oppositions, was what I propose
to be the key factor operating in the emergence of both conjunto and orquesta—namely, the shift in tejano society from a Mexicanized, rural, folk,
and proletarian group to a class-differentiated, urban, and increasingly
Americanized and literate population.

In two earlier works (Peña, 1981; in press) devoted mainly to conjunto,
I noted two questions that are raised in considering the emergence of this
folk style among Texas-Mexicans. Since these questions (and their answers)
impinge directly on the emergence of orquesta as well, they are worth recalling here. The first question had to do with the musical evolution of the con-

---

*The subtitle was inspired by Gilbert Chase's "Two Lectures in the Form of a Pair."
†For the sake of convenience, Spanish terms like tejano, orquesta, etc., which are used
repeatedly throughout the text, will be italicized only the first time they appear.

junto, i.e., how such a style could crystalize so rapidly into a mature artistic form. The second dealt with the social and cultural significance of the music: the *timing* of the style's appearance and development, and, specifically, why a well-defined style should emerge among this particular group of people at this precise moment in their history (1935–1960). The problem of conjunto's emergence holds as well for orquesta, since, in a doubly remarkable accident of history, at the very same time that the former was establishing itself as a formidable artistic expression, the latter was likewise coming into its own.

Thus, keeping in mind the contrasts mentioned above—and by way of moving to resolve the question of the orquesta-conjunto nexus—I want to advance two hypotheses on the relationship between the two musics. The remainder of the essay will be devoted to an explanation of the two hypotheses. First, I propose that at the historical level the two musics unfolded within a framework of emerging class difference and conflict among Texas-Mexicans, and that as such they have signified an intrinsic class dialectic working itself out within Texas-Mexican society. My second hypothesis is linked to the first, but builds on a more "synchronic" base, as it were. That is, it posits orquesta and conjunto as symbolic projections of a Texas-Mexican social structure that was solid enough to survive both the disruptive effects of interethnic contact with American society and the fragmentation introduced by class differences. To put it another way, from a synchronic ("structural") perspective the two styles should be considered dual expressions of a unitary musico-symbolic whole that emerged out of the conflict between an ethnic tejano culture and a dominant, often hostile Anglo-American social order.

Before proceeding with the discussion of Texas-Mexican music, I want to bring up two observations on style that bear on the thrust of this work. First, while there are not many ethnomusicological studies that focus on the dynamics involved in style-formation, at least one sociologist of music has addressed the need for an approach that makes "intelligible for us why a certain style may have emerged in the social and cultural structure of a given period, and thus clarify the sociological pre-requisites and conditions involved" (Serauky, quoted in Etzkorn, 1973:9). A similar line of thought is pursued by James Ackerman, who proposes that the creative impulse out of which new styles spring may be thought of as "a class of related solutions to a problem—or responses to a problem" (1962:228). Following Ackerman's notion, I propose that the changes wrought by World War II and its aftermath posed a challenge to Texas-Mexican society that demanded solutions to a number of problems. Artistic expression offered one solution, and, as we shall see, stylistic developments in conjunto and orquesta suggest themselves as specific examples.

Distinguishable stylistic elements coalesced first around the accordion ensemble that Texas-Mexicans forged between 1935 and 1960. The orquesta tejana, whose instrumentation was a simplified version of the big American dance band, began to acquire its unique qualities after the war. Groping for direction at first, both conjunto and orquesta had gained coherent and expressive forms by the mid-1950s. By this time each ensemble had gravitated toward its respective social context: conjunto toward the mass of proletarian workers, orquesta toward a small but growing and influential middle class.

Nonetheless, despite their social and musical differences, and in line with the hypotheses set forth earlier, the two ensembles and their musical styles are best described as tending to diverge at the level of class (or, at least, occupational) consciousness, but to converge at the level of ethnic consciousness. This is to say that in modern Texas-Mexican society musical culture has not been strictly determined by socioeconomic factors; rather, ethnic conflict has played a critical role as well. In any case the tendency to converge, both stylistically and socially, was much stronger after the mid-1960s, a result of the closer alignment (for reasons to be explored later) of orquesta with the musical preferences of the working class. In the decade immediately following the war, however, the tension between convergence and divergence was much more pronounced, a state of affairs that reflected the inevitable contradictions that Texas-Mexican society faced as a consequence of the contrasts noted earlier, especially the contrast between cultural assimilation and ethnic resistance.

CONJUNTO: "A folk music, of the people"
I have documented the development of conjunto music in a forthcoming work (Peña, in press), and will therefore limit the discussion here to a few remarks about its emergence and the critical link that exists between it and orquesta. Briefly, the development of conjunto music was, in every sense of the concept, a folk phenomenon. As one orquesta musician observed (personal interview), "La música de conjunto es una música vernácula, del pueblo" ("Conjunto music is a folk music, of the people"). Without exception, its contributors had two characteristics in common: they were totally or for the most part illiterate, and they belonged to a proletarian class. In short, conjunto musicians were members of a society that was characterized by strong folk elements: a deep oral tradition, a lack of socioeconomic differentiation, a collective sense of ethnic identity, and a relative isolation from other groups (Paredes, 1958:9ff.).

By the 1930s, however, when the modern conjunto first began to take shape, the tejanos' participation in an expanding American political economy had begun the irreversible erosion of their traditional culture. The modern conjunto thus emerged at a critical moment in Texas-Mexican history, when many of the folk traditions were beginning to yield to the pressures of social change. Grounded in those traditions, the conjunto became a strong musical symbol for the folk, working-class Texas-Mexicans, a symbol, moreover, that was part of a larger response to the challenges of a new era. I shall have more to say about this later.

One other observation should be made about the conjunto and its relationship to earlier folk music practices. Its rapid standardization, which resulted in a highly uniform style with fixed relationships between the component instruments, undeniably set it apart from its predecessors. Nonetheless, certain continuities did persist. To begin with, the conjunto's principal member, the diatonic button accordion, had been a part of Texas-Mexican music since the 1880s, at least, although prior to World War II the one and two-row models were the rule, rather than the three-row model commonly used today (Peña, in press).

The early accordion (and the ad hoc ensembles that were built around it) shared another important attribute with the modern conjunto: Historically, accordion music in northern Mexico and South Texas has been firmly linked to folk, working-class elements of norteño society, both in Mexico and in Texas. The "respectable" class of Mexicans, meanwhile—as well as the Anglo-Americans—have looked with disfavor upon the instrument and the celebrations traditionally associated with it. For example, an early report in the San Antonio Express (August 20, 1880), referred to the dances where accordion music was often featured as "a great curse to the country." "The respectable class of Mexicans," the report concludes, "do not attend them." Until recently this harsh attitude was shared by middle-class or upwardly mobile tejanos. Arnaldo Ramírez, head of Falcon, the largest Mexican American record company today, and a man intimately familiar with Texas-Mexican music, summed up the attitude of "society" tejanos succinctly: "A la gente de sociedad," he said, "mencionar el acordeón era mentarles la madre" ("To people of 'society' to mention the accordion was to call their mother a name") (personal interview).

Two other factors that have remained more or less constant during the accordion's history among Texas-Mexicans are related to performance context and repertory. Both the early accordion and the modern conjunto have relied heavily on the dance—weddings and other domestic celebrations before World War II and public, paid-admission dances (as well as domestic celebrations) since the war. Repertorially, the changes that occurred after the war as part of the conjunto's emergence involved a streamlining of genre selection, more than anything else. That is, in addition to the *huapango tamaulipeco,* genres derived from 19th century instrumental salon music—the polka, redowa, mazurka, and schottische—were the mainstays of the early accordionists. After the war only the polka and the *huapango* retained a strong presence, though the former was superceded by the *cancion ranchera,* the latter performed for the most part in tempo di polka. As one musician explained, "La canción ranchera es una polka, pero cantada" ("The *canción ranchera* is a polka, only sung" [i.e., with lyrics added]).[3] Since the war only two genres have gained an appreciable presence in the conjunto's basic repertory—a *ranchero* version of the Mexican bolero, introduced in the late 1940s, and the Colombian *cumbia,* introduced in the mid-1960s.

Having stated the case for the continuities in the history of accordion music among Texas-Mexicans, I turn now to some important discontinuities. First, of course, is the matter of style, especially ensemble style, for it is here that the modern conjunto differs radically from earlier accordion music. To begin with, playing technique changed drastically during the mid-1930s (see below); moreover, until the 1920s the accordion was for the most part an instrument played solo (see, e.g., the San Antonio Express, June 18, 1881). Its incorporation into an ensemble should thus be considered a major break from past tradition. There is evidence, however, that as early as the 1890s the accordion had been randomly combined with sundry instruments, especially the *tambora de rancho* ("ranch drum").[4] The latter was a makeshift instrument that made use of homemade materials—goatskin heads, mallets, and drumsticks—as well as manufactured parts (metal rims, old parade drum carcasses). Moreover, in the late 19th century the *bajo sexto,* an instrument which evidently made its way to South Texas from the *bajío* region in Mexico (Martín Macías, personal interview), also began to come into use with the accordion. The *bajo* is a bass guitar with twelve strings in six double courses; it is ordinarily played with a plectrum. By the 1920s the accordion-*bajo sexto* duet was quite common, as was, indeed, the inclusion of the *tambora* (see Arhoolie Records, *Border Music* series, vol. 4).

Yet, despite the fact that the accordion-*bajo sexto-tambora* ensemble contained all the elements for at least a rudimentary *norteño* style, no stylistic uniformity existed, of the kind that involves set relationships between instruments. In fact, prior to the 1930s the above combination was not in any way standardized. Other instruments were often featured with the accordion, in particular the clarinet (*Border Music* series, vol. 4).[5] Thus, the early accordion ensembles, such as they were, should be considered improvisational in nature. It was not until the 1930s, when the accordion and *bajo sexto* became the anchors for a more permanent ensemble, that the stage was set for the formation of a new and lasting norteño style. Coincident with this development was the disappearance of the ad hoc accordion groups of an earlier day. It is my contention, of course, that one major reason why no uniform ensemble, with its own style, emerged sooner was the lack of a strong socioesthetic impulse, of the type that World War II engendered.

The mid-1930s, then, marks the juncture when the modern conjunto first emerged. The history of the ensemble and its style can be divided into two phases. The first is represented by those musicians who established themselves before the war—"los músicos viejos," as accordionist Narciso Martínez called them. The second phase belongs to "la nueva generación," under whose direction the music reached stylistic maturity.

Of the many musicians who contributed to the creation of the emergent style, three first-generation accordionists stand out in a retrospective assessment. These are Narciso Martínez (unanimously called "el primero"), Pedro Ayala, and Santiago Jiménez. The first two were born in 1911, in Mexico, the latter in 1913, in San Antonio. All three, however, shared the same socio-economic background: they descended from poor, farmworking families, and all had to work in menial jobs to support themselves, despite the fact that as recording artists they were in great demand for dance performances.

The importance of these three performers lies in the contributions that each made to the emerging ensemble and its style. Martínez is an especially pivotal figure, because from the beginning of his commercial career (1935), he was the first to exploit the capabilities of the right-hand, or "treble," side of the button accordion. In so doing, he initiated a radical departure from the earlier technique that the Mexicans shared with the Germans: He virtually stopped using the left-hand bass/accompaniment elements, leaving the rhythmic and chordal accompaniment to the very capable Santiago Almeida, one of the best of the early *bajo sexto* players. Jiménez deserves recognition because he was the first (in 1936) to make regular use of the contrabass (known among Mexicans as the *tololoche),* while Ayala fashioned a style in the years immediately following the war that adumbrated strongly the changes that the new generation of musicians was about to introduce.

The second generation of musicians included a number of outstanding performers, accordionists in particular, but, again, three of the latter may be acknowledged in this brief sketch. In the order of their rise to prominence, they are: Valerio Longoria, Tony de la Rosa, and Paulino Bernal. Longoria's accomplishments are many, but among the most notable is his introduction in 1947 of two vocal genres into the conjunto—the *canción ranchera* and the bolero (the latter, again, considerably simplified, or "rancheroized"). His most important contribution, however, was his enlistment of the modern drum set, in 1949. The drums had been in use in orquestas for some time, but conjuntos had generally avoided them because they were considered "too noisy" for the accordion and *bajo sexto* (Pedro Ayala, Tony de la Rosa, personal interviews).

Longoria's experiment soon caught on, however, and with the addition of the drums the modern conjunto's development was almost complete. By the early 1950s the ensemble was essentially in place, except that the contrabass, which had never been widely adopted for dance performances, was still confined to the recording studio. In the mid-1950s, however, in response to the shift toward complete amplification of the music (a significant development in itself), the electric bass not only replaced the *tololoche* in the studio, but became a regular member in what has since become the standard four-man ensemble: accordion, *bajo sexto,* drums, and electric bass.

Tony de la Rosa is known for his superb polkas, which featured an extremely staccato style on the accordion and a considerably slower tempo than hitherto common (see *Border Music* series, vol. 13). This style was deemed to be admirably suited to *el tacuachito,* a new polka dance that had recently been introduced in the working-class dance halls of San Antonio, and de la Rosa consequently became very influential with younger accordionists. He became so popular, in fact, that he was one of the first conjunto musicians to rely solely on his music for economic support. By 1952 he was criss-crossing the state of Texas in pursuit of what one orquesta leader called the "taco circuit" — large public dances that attracted thousands of cottonpickers who followed the seasonal harvest.

This brings us, finally, to the last and most famous exponent of conjunto music during its formative years — Paulino Bernal. El Conjunto Bernal is generally recognized as the "greatest of all time," as one orquesta musician described it. The group draws the praise of other musicians (and laymen) because, first, it was able to synthesize the stylistic elements that had been coalescing around the accordion ensemble since Martínez's initial emphasis on the treble end. Second, Bernal succeeded in attracting the best musicians available in the tradition, an accomplishment that enabled the group to bring the kind of finesse to the music that was unmatched before or after. Lastly, El Conjunto Bernal launched several innovations of its own — for example, the introduction of three-part vocalizations (1958) and the chromatic accordion (1964). In fact, in the mid-1960s two such accordions were featured. In sum, El Conjunto Bernal represented the apex of the conjunto tradition; no other group since then has been able to duplicate its innovative spirit.

Indeed, since the experiments of Paulino Bernal the music has remained virtually static, especially with respect to its most unique and characteristic genre — the *canción ranchera* in polka tempo. The question, of course, is why conjunto suddenly reached such a stylistic deadend. In other words, how could a vital, unfolding tradition do such a drastic about face after El Conjunto Bernal, became so rigidly conservative? My own interpretation is based on the crucial connection between music as an artistic expression and the social context that sustains it. However, I will postpone the question of conjunto's resistance to further change—indeed, to its emergence in the first place—for later. For now I want only to reiterate that the cultural strategies of a class, transposed to the esthetic realm, were the driving force behind the rise to prominence of this unique Texas-Mexican style.

Now I want to turn to orquesta and trace its own emergence vis-a-vis the conjunto.

ORQUESTA MUSIC: Squeezed Between Ranchero and "High Class"

Although the modern orquesta tejana was originally patterned after the American swing bands of the 1930s and '40s, it did have important precursors, both in Texas-Mexican and Mexican music. In fact, the orquesta tejana had not one but two predecessors, one of which was principally a string (violin), the other a wind (clarinet, trumpet, etc.) ensemble. The development of early Texas-Mexican orquestas (or orquesta-like groups), especially prior to the 1920s, remains to be investigated. Based on my own research, however, I can say that such orquestas did exist, and that, moreover, in many instances, particularly among the workers, the organization of the two types of ensemble remained highly diffuse, in terms of instrumentation and stylistic development.[6] More often than not, depending on the availability of often scarce instruments and musicians, among working-class folk the two types of instrument were actually combined to form makeshift orquestas. Under the patronage of a small middle class, however, better organized orquestas apparently operated, especially in urban areas such as San Antonio and El Paso (Strachwitz, 1975).

A noteworthy variant of the Texas-Mexican string orquesta was the so-called *orquesta típica,* modeled after the Mexican orquestas of the same name that sprung up in Mexico in the late 19th century (Baqueiro Foster, 1964:546; Geijerstam, 1976:83–84). The latter, in turn, were bourgeois versions of the rural, folk *típicas* that had existed among the Mexican proletarians throughout the 19th century (Mayer Serra, 1941:116ff; Baqueiro Foster, 1964:532). The bourgeois típicas were the product of the romantic nationalism that swept through Mexico after the expulsion of the French, when, according to historians Meyer and Sherman, "Self-esteem replaced the sense of shame of the introspective diagnoses of the past" (1979:466). In short, orquestas típicas symbolized the upper classes' attempts to invoke *lo mexicano* by appropriating selected elements of the true típicas of proletarian origin— especially those elements (e.g., stylized charro costumes) that evoked the simplicity of an idyllic, rural *(ranchero)* life. Thus, as Baqueiro Foster observed of the first officially designated típica: "We must speak, of course, of the founding of the Orquesta Típica Mexicana [as] a monument of musical nationalism in Mexico" (1964:546).

Judging from Baqueiro Foster's statement, it is evident that orquestas típicas were made to order for the kind of romantic nationalism, or *costumbrismo,* that the Mexican bourgeoisie was imbued with in the late 19th century. But, as Behague has noted, "popular [folk] music had to be clothed [in genteel "garb"] to make it presentable to concert audiences" (1979:100). Orquestas típicas were perfect examples of this. Ultimately, however, the contradiction between the romantic ideology these orquestas gave voice to and the unavoidable reality of class cleavage could not be reconciled. The seeds for the ambivalence of *lo ranchero,* a concept linked to *lo mexicano* (discussed below) and critical for understanding the formation of Texas-Mexican orquestas, were being sown in the Conservatorio Nacional de Música, where the first típica was founded in 1884. Half a century later, the modern mariachi and the orquesta tejana would emerge as the principal heirs to that contradiction.

In Texas, meanwhile, orquesta-like ensembles of sundry types, including the típica variety, were in abundance by the early 20th century, as is evidenced by the frequent reference to them in various sources (Peña, in press) — for example, an enthusiastic report on the founding of a "Nueva Típica Mexicana en Houston" in the March 6, 1930 edition of Excelsior, Mexico City's largest newspaper. Again, among the working class these orquestas were of an ad hoc, improvisational nature, since that is how they were found as late as the 1930s (cf. note 6 above). As mentioned, under the patronage of merchants, professionals and other groups of financial means, a few well organized orquestas did exist (Strachwitz, 1975). A variety of orquestas, then, some consisting of string, others of wind instruments (and some combinations) continued to operate in Texas until the 1930s, when they were finally supplanted by the conjunto, which emerged as the preferred ensemble among the common workers, and by the modern orquesta, which began to take hold among the more "respectable" (i.e., upwardly-mobile) segments of tejano society.

It was thus in the 1930s that more permanent and better organized wind orquestas — the new type, modeled after the American big bands — began to appear with increasing frequency. On the basis of informants' reports and the course that orquesta music subsequently took, it is clear that the new orquestas articulated the strategies of a nascent group of Texas-Mexicans, usually upwardly-mobile, who wanted to distance themselves from the mass of proletarian workers, and who desired at the same time to imitate the lifestyle of middle-class America. Highly symbolic of this desire, in my estimation, was the demand for American music, which was generously represented in the orquesta repertories (Beto Villa, Reymundo Treviño, personal interviews). Indicative of the sentiments that underlay the preference for things American, including music, are the words of a middle-class Texas-Mexican of the time: "We have American ways and think like Americans.

We have not been able to convince some [American] people that there is a difference between us [and the old Mexicans] (Taylor, 1934:245; brackets Taylor's).

By the mid-1930s several well established orquestas were playing in cities like San Antonio, Corpus Christi, Kingsville and in the Rio Grande Valley. These were the immediate predecessors of the modern orquesta tejana, as it came to be known by the 1950s. The man who more than anyone else was responsible for the creation of an orquesta tejana style began his professional career in the early 1930s. It was in 1932 that Beto Villa, Narciso Martínez's counterpart in the orquesta tradition, organized his first group. Since culturally and socioeconomically he belonged to the new middle class, and since his name became synonymous with orquesta music in Texas, it is worth discussion his life and career at some length.[7]

Villa was born in 1915, but unlike Narciso Martínez and the other early accordionists, he was fortunate enough to remain in school until he was 17. This is a critical fact about Villa's life, because his educational accomplishments were the exception rather than the rule for the Mexicans of his time, and also because Villa's musical experience in high school had a profound influence on his subsequent career. One more point about Villa's early life should be noted, and that is the fact that he was able to stay in school as long as he did because of his family's economic stability. His father was a prosperous tailor, as well as a musician of some note, having learned his art in Monterrey, a city in northern Mexico that until recently enjoyed special prestige among Texas-Mexicans as a center of musical culture (see Peña, in press).

It is interesting that the first group Villa organized was known as "The Sonny Boys." Although the members were all Mexican high school students, the band emulated the style of the American swing bands then in fashion—Benny Goodman, the Dorsey brothers, and others. It is important to note, however, that Villa was exposed to Mexican music too, since he also played with his father's group, as well as others active in the Falfurrias area, where Villa was born and raised. Through these the young saxophonist became familiar with Mexican or Mexicanized styles and genres, which ranged from salon music to Latin pieces such as the *danzón* and bolero.

Villa's opportunity to enter the commercial recording market came in 1946, at almost the same time that the first Mexican-American recording companies appeared on the scene. Indeed, *Ideal* Records, for a time the most active of these early companies, owed much of its initial success to the popularity of Villa's own music. Yet, Villa's commercial debut was inauspicious at best. For one thing, by 1946 the "father" of modern orquesta tejana seems to have postponed his pursuit of an American musical ideal. Instead, in his first recordings Villa opted for the ranchero sound then associated with conjunto music. That is, he restricted himself mostly to the polkas and waltzes that had become a part of Texas-Mexican folk music since the late 19th century. More than that, however, the "folklorization" (or "rancheroization," we might say) of Villa's music points to the likelihood that Villa realized that only by adopting a ranchero style would he be able to reach a wide audience. But this is not surprising, since in 1946, at least three quarters of the Mexicans in Texas were members of a working class that subscribed overwhelmingly to the ranchero music, that conjuntos and the Mexican mariachi had so thoroughly popularized.

In any case, when Villa approached Ideal, Paco Betancourt, one of the owners objected because he felt the band was not "professional" enough. It was a minimal orquesta, consisting of alto saxophone, trumpet, piano-accordion, and a rhythm section of electric guitar, contrabass, and drums. Consonant with its ranchero orientation, the group featured simple melodies, with unsophisticated harmonies. Indeed, it was the generally unpolished sound of the orquesta that prompted Betancourt to object. In the end, however, Villa prevailed, and at his own expense Ideal released two 78 RPM sides: "Porque te ries," a *vals,* and "Las Delicias Polka." According to Armando Marroquín, Ideal's other owner, here is what happened:

> So then the record came out — Boy! About a month after Betancourt started distributing it, he called me and said, "Say, tell him to record some more." They were asking for it in bunches. It was like a conjunto; it wasn't even an orquesta yet . . . There were only five or six — real small, ranchero-like (personal interview, my translation).

With this first recording, Villa's position in Texas-Mexican music was assured; but Marroquín's statement on the group's ranchero quality and its similarity to the conjunto is provocative. It confirms the link between orquesta and conjunto, a link made possible by the ranchero sound that all conjuntos shared and that many orquestas, including that of Beto Villa, were beginning to incorporate into their repertories. This brings up an important point: I propose that it was the ranchero sound complex that served as the common denominator between the two ensembles, although in other critical features they did differ — and sharply, both in style and social acceptance. We may be certain that Villa never lost sight of the ranchero, ethnic origins of his music. This is clearly demonstrated, for example, in his willingness to collaborate with none other than Narciso Martínez on several recordings. Especially fruitful was their recording of "Rosita Vals," an immensely popular tune whose success Ideal was never able to duplicate.

Yet, it soon became obvious that, despite his successes with Martínez, Villa was hardly interested in becoming permanently associated with conjunto music. In fact, by 1949 he had decided on a drastic change. First, he weeded out the "folk" musicians — those who had no formal training — from his fledgling orquesta. Raymundo Treviño, a long-time associate of Villa's, recalled what happened: "Those of us who could not read music—we were fired" (personal interview). Second, as is evident from the post-1949 recordings, he began to deemphasize the ranchero sound (though not to abandon it altogether) in favor of more cosmopolitan styles that would amalgamate American, Mexican, and more generalized Latin genres. In short, Villa was ready to return to his first love—the big American band sound, though he aimed to retain a Latin flavor as well, including the indispensable ranchero style. But above all, I believe that Villa was striving for a combination of styles that would mediate the contradictions between the ethnic nature of his audience, which was inescapably tied to the ranchero roots that conjunto epitomized, and the class aspirations of that same audience—aspirations that aimed at cutting all links with conjunto music and the "low-class" life it symbolized.

As I indicated earlier, the concept of *lo ranchero* has been firmly linked historically to the ideology of romantic nationalism, or *mexicanismo*. I would like now to offer a few explanatory remarks about its symbolic significance, in order to see what light it might shed on the subject under discussion. To grasp the concept's significance in tejano (as well as Mexican) culture, we need, first, to understand that the bulk of Mexican society has traditionally been folk and agrarian, and only in recent times has it moved forward with "modernization" (Cumberland, 1968). Second, ever since romantic nationalism first made its appearance in Mexico (after the expulsion of the French), it has been endemic among Mexicans, manifesting itself in numerous facets of national life. Particularly germane for this discussion is the heavy commercialization since the 1930s of some of the symbols of that nationalism, as capitalists began to convert them into profitable mass commodities, principally through radio and film. It was, in fact, in the 1930s that the ranchero label was first attached to the Mexican *canción* (Garrido, 1974:70). Moreover, it is evident that such labeling was a conscious effort by commercial promoters to capitalize on the ideology of romantic nationalism (cf. Saragoza, 1983).

The symbols I refer to belong to the vast collective consciousness that is Mexico's cultural heritage, symbols that have been selectively chosen for exaltation as representative of the glory of Mexico's history and culture. A number of these symbols have long enjoyed currency—for example, the Virgin of Guadalupe and the familiar Aztec warrior—but two encompass the concept of lo ranchero especially well, although they have become somewhat stereotyped. These are the *charro/vaquero* figure, which symbolizes the arrogant manliness (machismo) of the Mexican male, and the person of the *campesino,* which signifies the humble but perseverant spirit of that same Mexican.

These last two have been singled out for intensive exploitation in both music and film (often simultaneously) since the 1930s (Saragoza, 1983). As a result of this commercial exposure, the twin symbols of the charro and campesino have succeeded admirably in imparting to the concept of lo ranchero its visual substance. The one's dauntless machismo and penchant for action coexists with the other's stoicism and humility, which actually border on inertia and diffidence. But this juxtaposition creates tension, as the two symbols, representing opposite qualities, pull in different directions. In fact, they threaten the integrity of the concept itself. But this is precisely what Victor Turner has suggested about "root metaphors" (1974), which our symbols clearly are. Attached to concepts that are "linked analogically to the basic problems of an epoch" (Turner, 1974:26), they are subject to great ambiguity and contradiction. Such is the case with lo ranchero and its symbols, especially among Mexicans in the United States, where the contradictions are painfully apparent.

On this side of the border the ambiguities attached to lo ranchero are compounded by the pressures for assimilation and conformity. For example, to espouse lo ranchero, as many Chicanos do through their advocacy of *música ranchera,* is to overvalue their Mexican "roots": to ennoble the culture of pastoral, agrarian life, which is presumed unspoiled by social snobbery. Yet, this mystified vision can quickly turn into disillusion when jarred by the reality of modern life, especially in the United States, where the campesino (the sleeping man with the wide-brimmed sombrero) is a stereotype for fatalism and laziness. Thus, to the "progressive" Mexican-American the negative side of lo ranchero is never completely hidden. It lies ready to spring into consciousness to transform nostalgia into rejection, for the romanticized rancho also happens to harbor the *arrancherado*—the "low-class," coarse, excessively Mexicanized peon who cannot possibly appreciate the subtleties of modern, civilized life. There is an apt folk expression that captures the acculturated Mexican-American's indignation: "Mexico, recoge a tu gente." An appeal is made in this well-worn refrain for Mexico to reclaim its vagabonds, who are a source of embarrassment to the "respectable" Mexican-American.

Yet, despite the paradox, if there is one encompassing musical symbol among Texas-Mexicans, it is that conveyed by música ranchera (as is true among Mexicans generally, for that matter). A sound that spans several styles, música ranchera compresses a wide range of feelings and attitudes into a single esthetic moment. People immediately recognize a ranchero sound, whether it be interpreted by a conjunto, orquesta, or any other group, although it is true that some types of ensemble are considered more "naturally" ranchero than others—for example, the conjunto and the mariachi. But invariably, the music stirs vaguely defined but deeply experienced feelings of *mexicanismo*—or, in other words, romantic nationalism.

Thus, *ranchera* music has always been an integral part of Texas-Mexican musical consciousness, even among the upwardly-mobile urbanites. That fact was never lost on Beto Villa and other orquesta musicians. Consequently, even in the immediate post-war years, a ranchero style was cultivated by all but the most Americanized (i.e., culturally assimilated) orquestas. As one orquesta musician put it, "I think we have always included rancheras because it goes back to our ancestors and the type of music they liked and we listened to when we were little." And, as Armando Marroquín observed in discussing Beto Villa's popularity: "What helped Beto Villa was that he had everything—ranchero and 'high class.' "

But the negative side of lo ranchero was not lost on orquestas either, and it helps explain why orquesta musicians were so caught up in what one of them called "lo moderno"—the modern, which on closer examination turns out to be a code phrase for the assimilation of middle-class elements, not only from American bands, but from similarly situated groups in Mexico. Thus, in comparing conjunto and orquesta music, one prominent musician observed that while conjunto was the music of the farmworker, "the so-called upper crust demanded big bands and sophisticated music"—i.e., foxtrots, boleros, etc.

However, the orquesta tejana was also powerfully affected by developments in conjunto music, and it was never able to free itself completely from the latter's influence. Indeed, one of the problems we face in analyzing orquesta as a cultural expression is its extreme stylistic fluctuations—its many faces, as it were. To a far greater extent than any of the other musics that influenced it, orquesta tejana has always been a multi-dimensional musical expression, as even a cursory listening of the recordings made since the 1940s will reveal. Marroquín's comments on Beto Villa's oscillation between ranchero and "high class" should make it clear that, unlike conjunto, which adhered to a strongly homogeneous style, orquesta encompassed a broad spectrum of styles, only one of which, properly speaking, stamped the "tejana" label on it.

Thus, most orquestas attempted to amalgamate any number of disparate types of music, including those associated with the big American dance bands (e.g., foxtrots, swings, etc.), Mexican and Latin American dance bands (boleros, danzones, mambos), and, of course, the ranchero, regional style of the conjunto. Within this spectrum of styles and genres there were some orquestas—particularly the most culturally assimilated and middle-class oriented—that emphasized cosmopolitan music. They played, in the words of working class tejanos, "música mas *jaitona* ("more high-toned music"). However, the most commercially popular were those that, like Beto Villa's, succeeded in accommodating both the ranchero and the "sophisticated," or "high class."

Villa's success encouraged a spate of imitators, though, again, some pursued a more cosmopolitan style than others. Among the more "jaitón" orquestas was that of Balde González, the blind singer-pianist from Victoria, Texas. A highly acclaimed performer in the early 1950s, González, much more than Villa, attempted to project a smooth, sophisticated sound, one that blended American foxtrots with romantic boleros. In fact, a measure of González's assimilation of American musical ideas (tempered, nonetheless, by the limitations of his ethnic background) was his habit of adapting Mexican vocals to American rhythms, especially the foxtrot.

A more ranchero approach was taken by González's most popular successor in the rapidly expanding orquesta music market — singer-saxophonist Isidro López, from Corpus Christi. Born in 1933, López learned to play alto saxophone and clarinet in high school, as many other orquesta musicians did. In the meantime he was gaining experience by playing with various local groups. A significant development in López's career was his association with Narciso Martínez. For a time in the early 1950s he accompanied the latter on some of his tours around the state. This experience convinced López (as he pointed out to me), that at bottom, there has never been much difference between orquesta and conjunto. However, López also played for Balde González shortly before he organized his own orquesta (in 1955), and that association did leave its influence on his subsequent style.

In any case, although Isidro López clearly belongs in the orquesta tradition, he was acutely aware that the future of orquesta tejana music lay with the traditional working class, and its strong affiliation with the norteño variety of Mexican culture. Thus, although he did incorporate a variety of styles, López nevertheless leaned heavily toward the ranchero sound — one that he claims combined elements from both conjunto and mariachi. He labelled it *texachi,* López's own neologism, derived from the terms "Texas" and "mariachi." The synthesis worked; adapting the canción ranchera to the idiosyncrasies of the orquesta, López surpassed all his competitors in public appeal from the mid 1950s until 1965, when two new orquestas entered the picture: Little Joe (Hernández) and the Latinaires, and Sunny (Ozuna) and the Sunliners.

In a retrospective assessment it is clear the Isidro López was the man most responsible for setting in motion the final shift of orquesta music toward that of conjunto. However, that shift did not proceed in an uninterrupted sweep — an indication of the conflicting currents that determined the course of orquesta music. Thus, Little Joe, who most personifies the next phase of orquesta tejana, and Sunny Ozuna, who also ranks among the leading personalities, began their careers in pursuit of the exploding rock and roll market of the late 1950s. Like many of the younger — and usually better educated — tejano musicians, Little Joe and Sunny were caught up in the rock and roll wave that swept the United States at the end of the 1950s. This was a time when, according to one orquesta musician, "mexicano wasn't in" — when young musicians shunned not only conjunto but even the music of a Beto Villa and an Isidro López. They preferred to emulate American rock and roll groups. Little Joe and Sunny were no exceptions.

Clearly, what was taking place among the Mexicans in Texas was the inexorable assimilation of American culture, as Richard Garcia so cogently demonstrates in his essay, "The Mexican American Mind: A Product of the 1930s" (1983). The post-Depression babies — the first generation of Mexicans to enjoy a measurable upgrading in their education — were responding to the pressures of cultural assimilation, even if the barriers that effectively prevented them from complete integration into American society (i.e., through "primary" associations achievable principally through intermarriage) remained firmly in place. With cultural assimilation came a desire to adopt the lifestyles of American mass society. What Rubel observed, about upwardly-mobile tejanos in South Texas who had fought in World War II and Korea, certainly applied to an increasing number of tejanos born after the Depression. These also aspired "toward life goals which include[d] social equality with Anglos" (Rubel, 1966:12). They felt entitled to "clean" occupations, "high school and college education, and possession of such other status markers as automobiles, refrigerators, television sets . . . (ibid.)." In short, they demanded the amenities of middle-class citizenship. Lastly, among the symbols that signified upward mobility was music — specifically music that approximated the ideal of mainstream American life.

Thus — to discuss his rise to prominence first — Little Joe's first recording was a rock tune with the title of "Safari." This was followed by a number of sporadic efforts throughout Little Joe's career (and that of his brother, Johnny) to break into the "top forty" music charts. That proved to be an impossible task, and by 1965, perhaps discouraged by his failure, Little Joe finally decided to try his fortune in the tejano music circuit. He signed on with Sarape Records, a small label from Dallas, which produced an album titled "Amor Bonito" in 1965. It was a phenomenal success, catapulting Little Joe and the Latinaires into the forefront of orquesta tejana music. As trumpetist Tony Guerrero, who later was to become a mainstay in Little Joe's orquesta, recalled (personal interview), "I was in California when I heard about this new band out of Texas that was called Little Joe and the Latinaires, and a promoter told me, 'These guys are kicking Isidro López's ass all over the place.' "

Of the utmost significance, however, was the sound Little Joe had fashioned. It was thoroughly ranchero, down to the familiar duet-singing, in parallel thirds, that became the hallmark of Little Joe and his brother Johnny. Clearly, "Amor Bonito" signalled Little Joe's newfound interest in tejano music, but more than that, it marked the revival of ranchero music among the younger generation of Texas-Mexicans. In short, Little Joe's new style symbolized the final step in the "rancheroization" of orquesta music. Thereafter, despite orquestas' conspicuous forays into non-ranchero music (e.g., the always popular Mexican bolero), the staple genre, now played in what became *the* typical tejano style, was the canción ranchera, sung solo or duet and backed by increasingly standardized obbligatos from the horn section. This was, of course, the very same canción, set to the tempo di polka (and sometimes waltz) that had earlier become the hallmark of the conjunto style. After 1965, then, with the exception of a few local jaitón orquestas, the convergence of orquesta and conjunto was all but an accomplished fact.

Sunny Ozuna deserves our attention because, first, for a fleeting instant in 1963 the former carhop did manage to break into the "top 40 charts" with a rhythm and blues tune titled "Talk to Me." It was, however, a short-lived glory, as Ozuna quickly faded from the pop music scene. Second, although Ozuna soon discovered that his only real alternative was to pursue a career in the orquesta tejana field, to this day, as his manager once revealed to me, Sunny and the Sunliners have always tried to "cater to a more middle-class crowd" — that is, to those tejanos who think themselves as being a cut above the common workers. Like many other orquestas, Ozuna has done this by consciously maintaining a delicate balance between ranchero and "high class" (to recall Marroquín's statements about Beto Villa). Ozuna has been successful: like Little Joe he has maintained a visible presence in tejano music since the mid-1960s.

As the comments of Ozuna's manager indicate — and as I have tried to make clear — there have been two discernible (and contradicting) trends in orquesta tejana music since its inception. One is obviously ranchero and heavily influenced by the conjunto style. The other is difficult to classify neatly, since it has always aimed at amalgamating a number of disparate styles. We may, however, label it collectively (as I have done) as "sophisticated," "cosmopolitan," or "modern." Or, we may follow the native, working class usage and call it "high class" or "jaitón" — terms that I heard many times while growing up in Texas in the 1950s. In either case, some orquestas have not hesitated to shift back and forth between ranchero and jaitón. Moreover, the consensus among initiated layperson and musicians is that the distinguishing characteristic between ranchero and non-ranchero is harmonic complexity and, to a lesser extent, genre selection.

For example, a canción set in tempo di polka and arranged with relatively simple harmony — say, a I-IV-V-I (e.g., C-F-G^7-C) chord progression — is unequivocally ranchera, especially if, as is often the case, certain preestablished obbligato licks are used, as in the following phrase with the eighth-sixteenth-note figure:

On the other hand, the same canción may be substantially transformed by elaborating on the harmony: adding seventh and altered chords (e.g., Cmaj⁷-Fmaj⁷-G⁻⁹-C⁶⁺⁹), alternating keys, introducing syncopation, etc. The resulting sound would then be considered "sophisticated," rather than ranchero, depending on the degree of complexity. In sum, the more harmonic and rhythmic complexity introduced, the more "modern" the style is judged to be. Conversely, the simpler the harmony, rhythm, and obbligato backgrounds, the more a piece falls in the ranchero category.

The first of the ranchero orquestas was undoubtedly that of Isidro López, followed by those of Augustín Ramírez, Freddie Martínez, and Joe Bravo, to name three of the most popular to this day. On other other hand, orquestas such as Sunny and the Sunliners, Latin Breed, and Jimmy Edward's have chosen to deemphasize the ranchero mode, incorporating more diverse genres, including rhythm and blues and a host of others derived from Afro-Hispanic traditions (e.g., *salsa*). At the same time even when they perform the canción ranchera, the latter groups are easily distinguishable from the former by their use of the "sophisticated" elements I listed above.

One more point needs to be brought out in connection with the stylistic variation within orquestas tejanas. Since the mid-1960s, when the bulk of them committed themselves to working class audiences, they have had to limit their range of musical expression, insofar as they have become sensitive to the dictates of their new constituency (not to mention their economic survival). This means that experimentally minded orquestas must thread a thin needle, indeed. For if they exceed the stylistic limits imposed on them by working class tastes, then they threaten to dissolve the slender threads that link them to tejano musical culture. This they cannot afford to do, since, as one orquesta musician put it, "We can't afford to experiment too much anymore. The orquesta crowd is getting smaller and smaller. We're squeezed in between the conjuntos and American music." Indeed, some conjunto musicians have predicted, with more than a trace of satisfaction, the imminent demise of orquesta music.

Predictions notwithstanding, orquesta is anything but dead. On the contrary, while it has faced adverse times, it has continued to hold its own through the years. In fact, beginning in the early 1970s the orquesta tejana witnessed a major resurgence and burst of innovation that has been unrivalled before or after. It is probably not premature, then, to label the 1970s as the "golden age" of orquesta tejana music. With the appearance in 1973 of an album by Little Joe y la Familia (the Latinaires renamed), titled "Para la Gente," an active new phase was ushered in. A score of productions by other orquestas followed in quick succession, each attempting to match La Familia's rather daring experiments, which included the addition of violins (sometimes a melotron), dense harmonies, and a constant assault on the basic polka beat of the canción ranchera. The experiments worked commercially, I think, because in the midst of the experimentation the basic ranchero sound was preserved.

More importantly, however, the experiments worked because orquestas had gained substantial support among a generation of high school and college students who were growing up in the shadow of the Chicano power movement and who were at that time reexamining their whole ethnic identity. These students were ripe for artistic expressions that reflected their newfound pride in things Chicano. Orquestas capitalized on this ethnic revivalism, of course. Indeed, they were themselves caught up in it. Little Joe's decision to change the name of his group from Latinaires to La Familia (in 1970) is a perfect case in point. Clearly, as Little Joe has many times demonstrated, this was a political decision (cf. Patoski, 1978), intended to identify his group with the tide of Chicanismo that was surging among the younger generation. With this aim in mind, what better label to link himself with the Chicano Movement than the strongly evocative "La Familia"? Lastly, it is evident that much more than conjunto music (which perhaps smacked too much of the cotton sack), orquesta admirably fulfilled the esthetic preferences of the young Chicanos.[8]

Since about 1978 orquesta music has witnessed considerable stylistic retrenchment, as well as a decline—though *not* a demise—in its popularity. But, as one orquesta musician put it, "Conjunto music has its epochs, we have ours. We'll come back." Renamed *La Onda Chicana* ("The Chicano Wave"), it has held its ground into the 1980s, thanks largely to the efforts of the indefatigable Little Joe Hernández.

An Interpretive Summary

Now that I have traced the evolution of conjunto and orquesta, I would like to add a few comments on the social and cultural variables that were present at the inception of these two styles, and the possible relationship between these and the emergence of the two ensembles.

First, as a number of researchers have observed (e.g., Landolt, 1976; Foley, et al., 1977), tejano society experienced important—if not dramatic—socioeconomic changes during World War II. Indeed, the war ought to be considered a threshold for Texas-Mexican society. This was a period when the process of urbanization was greatly accelerated, when the native born for the first time outnumbered the immigrants, and when tejanos began to be absorbed into the American political economy in occupations that offered some upward mobility. In addition, thousands of young men fought in the war, and they returned to civilian society with a new sense of purpose that contributed to the redefinition of citizenship, not only for them but for many other Mexican-Americans as well.[9] In sum, these tejanos demanded—with some success—equal treatment in housing, education, employment, and so forth. But success had its ramifications for the structure of tejano society. Among other things, homogeneity of class gave way to differentiation, and its attendant distinctions (e.g., "clean" vs. "dirty" occupations). In short, the war changed the makeup of tejano society in an irrevocable way, presenting it with a set of challenges it had never before faced.

Perhaps the most far-reaching consequence of the changed nature of Texas-Mexican society was the increasing disparity in cultural assimilation between the middle and working classes, a disparity that was reflected in the undeclared rift that developed between them. For example, even the old ethnic solidarity was called into question by upwardly mobile tejanos who were caught up in the assimilation of American middle class ideology (cf. Rubel's quote above; Taylor, 1934; Madsen, 1964). It is important to note, however, that despite the internal changes in tejano society that emerged during World War II, the formidable ethnic boundary that separated tejano and Anglo remained, posing a nearly insurmountable obstacle against the complete structural (i.e., marital) assimilation of tejanos into Anglo-American society.

It was against this backdrop of *internal* socioeconomic differentiation and *external* ethnic segregation that orquesta and conjunto were cast. Here it is worth recalling James Ackerman's comments on style formation as a response to the challenges of an age. These remarks are eminently applicable to the emergence of conjunto and orquesta. For what tejano society witnessed was a fundamental shakeup of its infrastructural composition, along with a high degree of social upheaval. In my estimation, this social upheaval could not be negotiated without profound cultural dislocation. This dislocation, expressible in terms of social uncertainty and conflict, necessitated solutions. This is where conjunto and orquesta fulfilled their design: they were cultural solutions to infrastructurally generated problems.

In the case of conjunto, we can explain its emergence in this way: In the face of an unsympathetic middle class that saw the working class (both native and immigrant) as an impediment to the acceptance of Mexicans into American society because of its alleged "backwardness," the less acculturated workers felt obligated to respond in kind and to elaborate cultural strategies in their defense. These strategies were intended to defend and also legitimize working class existence and cultural sovereignty. Thus, if upwardly-mobile tejanos were critical of working class lifestyles, then the latter countered with its own ridicule. Middle-class oriented people were considered *agringados* (gringoized Mexicans), or worse, *agabachados,* an even more caustic epithet for Mexicans who were seen by traditional (usually) working class people as snobs who pretended to be what they were not. Worst, in so doing they not only demeaned themselves, but also committed the contemptible act of denying their true cultural heritage—their *mexicanismo.*

Thus, working class tejanos, convinced that only they and their kind were true *mexicanos,* clung ever more tenaciously to their culture. "Soy puro mexicano" ("I am a real Mexican") was a popular phrase that working class tejanos certainly subscribed to. I suggest that underlying the working class's displeasure with *agringado* tejanos was its unarticulated conviction that the latter aimed to undermine long-standing Mexican traditions that all tejanos were heir to (not without reason; cf. Taylor, 1934), and that they had a duty to defend (see Limon, 1977 on *agringado* joking). It mattered not that many of those traditions were being seriously eroded by American cultural hegemony, or that many were in fact yielding to social change. To the working class they were immutable and imparted continuity to their threatened system of cultural values.

As I have suggested previously (Peña, in press), it was out of this clash between change and continuity, between cultural assimilation and ethnic resistance, and between middle and working class ideology that conjunto music derived its cultural energy and symbolic power. By balancing innovation with tradition—by being subjected to changes strictly at the hands of working-class artists—conjunto music, as a symbolic expression, negotiated through esthetic means the conflicts and uncertainties that its constituency was experiencing in the socioeconomic sphere. In sum, the creation of this unique artistic expression was a symbolic solution to the conflicts I have outlined. Lastly, once the original conflict between proletarians and their middle class antagonists was mediated musically—that is, once conjunto music was seen as consummated—further innovation came to a halt. In short, as an esthetically satisfying expression, reflective of working class sentiments, conjunto music was considered "perfected" by its practitioners. Thus, new accretions, such as the introduction of the piano-accordion, for example, were seen as superfluous and detracting from the singular beauty of the music.

A similar case can be made for orquesta. Just as the stylistic maturation of conjunto signified a working class response to the challenges posed against it by the changing conditions of its existence, so did orquesta likewise correspond to the Texas-Mexican middle class's search for an appropriate expressive (artistic) response to its own emergence as an ideological bloc in tejano society. On the one hand, orquesta — at least in its first phase, up until 1965 — was clearly an alternative mode of artistic expression to conjunto. That much was made abundantly clear by the testimonies of the numerous musicians and others I had contact with during my research. Lack of space prohibits introducing all of the comments elicited — including the many I heard as a young orquesta musician in the late 1950s and early '60s. The statements of Moy and Delia Pineda, two veteran orquesta musicians, perhaps sum up the relationship between orquesta and the middle class — even today, when orquesta and conjunto are so much closer in form and substance. The following is an excerpt from a conversation I had with them:

> Peña: Do conjunto and orquesta cater to the same people?
> M. Pineda: No they're both different. La gente que le gusta la orquesta (people who like orquesta), they like something a little more sophisticated.
> Peña: Well, do you think class might have something to do with it?
> M. Pineda: There you go . . .
> D. Pineda: Yes, definitely.

Yet, the unavoidable reality of interethnic conflict and the subordination of Mexicans generally (Barrera, 1979) — especially before the civil rights gains of the 1960s — made middle class status for Texas-Mexicans a rather precarious proposition. Quite simply, the upwardly-mobile tejanos were caught on the horns of a dilemma. On the one hand they aspired to be American, though Anglo society did not welcome them into its midst.[10] On the other hand, a retreat to the cultural position of the traditional proletarian class was out of the question, because the middle class's ideology, which was shaped, paradoxically, by American middle class institutions such as the schools, clashed at many points with the ethnic culture of traditional tejano society. The middle class's position can be summed up succinctly: socially and culturally it lived in a state of contradiction.

Musically, this state of contradiction was mediated — and reflected — by orquesta's extreme variations in style. For the sake of analysis, these variations may be reduced conceptually to simple bi-musicality, with American styles on one side and Latin ones on the other. Moreover, the bi-musicality was an extension of middle class tejanos' increasing biculturalism, a biculturalism that straddled the interethnic boundary between Mexican and Anglo life experiences (see Paredes, 1968, on bicultural conflict in joking behavior). Beyond bi-musicality there was also pervasive bilingualism and ambiguous attitudes about family, religion, and traditions generally — all a commentary on the contradictory position of the middle class. (Ambiguity crept into working class life as well, but with far less unsettling results.) In short, the upwardly-mobile tejano was caught in a bicultural bind that promoted considerable social stress. I suggest that the stylistic flip-flopping orquestas engaged in—their struggle to mediate the differences between the Mexican and traditional vs. the American and "modern"—was a manifestation of that stress.

In summary, orquesta music represented a symbolic response by the middle class to the challenge of socioeconomic disparity and the pressures of cultural assimilation. As I have pointed out, this challenge was fraught with contradictions that were reflected in the music itself. Given these contradictions, middle class tejanos in time came to respond with what was probably the only alternative available to them. Thus, preaching assimilation but frustrated in their attempts to gain full acceptance in the Anglo's world, they betrayed their own ideology by reverting to ethnic resistance. The musico-symbolic dimensions of this contradiction were clearly illustrated by Moy Pineda. Speaking of certain "élite" dances he played for, Pineda commented that

> . . . they want to show off by getting a big orchestra, and they have their daughters presented to society. It's supposed to be very exclusive. They want that big band, and we got those fancy tuxedoes; but the music—the first hour we do, man, special arrangements ["Stardust," "Misty," etc.]—and nobody's dancing. But about an hour—I take off with "Los Laureles," "El Abandonado" [ranchera tunes]. Ching! *Everybody* gets on the dance floor . . . When they start drinking they go back to the roots.

In such ways have the bulk of middle class tejanos attempted historically to validate their existence—by embracing selected aspects of American culture, while out of necessity retaining many of their antecedent symbols. As Pineda's statements attest, the middle class Texas-Mexican has historically been bicultural, but not so much by choice as by default. And, in this betwixt-and-between position that the middle class has found itself, orquesta music has played its unique role, by negotiating the contradiction between a frustrated assimilation on the one hand and a persistent ethnic allegiance on the other. The musical solution has been: aspire for the jaitón, but keep the ranchero at hand.

POSTSCRIPT: Two Styles in the Form of a Pair

As I have pointed out, since the 1960s orquesta and conjunto have been on a strongly convergent course (with the exception of a few local, jaitón orquestas that cater chiefly to the middle class). Among the reasons that can be cited, the surrender of many tejanos to the attraction of American popular culture stands out as one of the most salient. This is especially true of those tejanos who are upwardly-mobile and educated. Orquesta has thus had to turn to a new clientele, which nowadays is drawn mostly from the working class and other segments which are motivated by ethnic sentiments and who find the music appealing.

In a current assessment of the two musics, one easily notes the similarity between orquesta and conjunto, though inevitable differences remain: obviously a wind ensemble can never duplicate the sound of the accordion. Moreover, as I mentioned earlier, some of the more "modern" orquestas have maintained a dialogue with other types of music, including American jazz, rock, and even country, as well as Afro-Hispanic. By doing so, these orquestas have kept open new horizons at the other end of the orquesta spectrum. On the other hand, groups like that of Roberto Pulido y los Clásicos have managed to achieve a creditable synthesis by combining two saxophones with the accordion, thereby creating a hybrid orquesta-conjunto sound.

Thus, by the late 1970s it was possible for American journalists to lump conjunto and orquesta into one rubric, that of *música tejana* (cf. George, 1978; Patoski, 1978). This classification was basically correct. Today, the similarities between the two musics are readily acknowledged by most performers in either tradition. As Narciso Martínez perceptively observed when I asked him about the present state of conjunto and orquesta: "Ahorita está muy cerquita una cosa de la otra" ("Right now one thing is pretty close to the other"). It is also recognized in an offhand way by the people themselves, who often refer to the two styles as "música tejana." That is why it is possible to speak of conjunto and orquesta as twin forms, or—to paraphrase Eric Satie—two styles in the form of a pair.

Biographical Data

Manuel Peña has a Ph.D in anthropology (folklore and ethnomusicology) from the University of Texas at Austin. He did his fieldwork in Texas, investigating Texas-Mexican music, particularly the development of two musical styles among Texas-Mexicans—*orquesta tejana,* or simply *orquesta,* and *conjunto,* otherwise known as *norteno.* A native of Texas, Peña is currently an associate professor at California State University, Fresno.

Footnotes

1. A preliminary assessment of conjunto music may be found in Peña, 1981. A more thorough sociohistorical analysis may be found in Peña (in press).

2. As used here, the terms "working class" (also "proletarians") and "middle class" have a specific meaning, derived in part from the writings of Eric O. Wright (1976) and Nicos Poulantzas (1973). Briefly stated, my conception of class is based on structural considerations: The working class is that sector which has no controlling access to the means of production, nor does it have any control over the labor power of others. It has only its own labor power to sell. Narrowly defined, the middle class shares attributes with both the capitalist (bourgeoisie) and the worker (e.g., managers, who may not own a share of the means of production but who do control the labor power of others). However, in delineating the tejano middle class, I have also included the "labor aristocracy"—mainly white collar workers—because ideologically they behaved much like the true middle class. This was a critical factor in the orquesta-conjunto nexus.

3. According to one conjunto musician's estimate, 80% of the modern conjuntos' repertory consists of *canciones rancheras,* mostly played as *corridas,* i.e., in polka rhythm and tempo. The *cancion* is occasionally performed in ¾ time *(valseada)* or, even less frequently, in 6/8 time. On the other hand, prior to WW II conjuntos almost never performed vocal music. The reasons for this restriction had to do with social conventions. A combination of instrumental *and* vocal music was associated in the public mind with the disreputable atmosphere of the *cantina.* Thus, although accordion groups played in *cantinas* frequently, for "decent," that is, domestic, celebrations they were strictly prohibited from singing. The social upheaval ushered in by the war changed all that (see Peña, in press).

4. One source of information on early accordion-*tambora* pairings is my father, who was born in 1895 and who clearly recalled the impression the two instruments made on him when he first noticed them around the turn of the century. He was raised in Salineño, a village on the Texas-Mexican border. Another source is the San Antonio Express, which occasionally featured articles on tejano dances where reference is made to the accordion and, in one, to the "beating of drums," though the label *tambora de rancho* is not specifically used (see June 18, 1881; August 3, 1890).

5. The LP cited is of course not the only source that illustrates the diffuse nature of accordion music to the 1920s. Chris Strachwitz of Arhoolie Records, has in his possession over 100 '78s that document the variety of early accordion music, at least as far back as the 1920s. To my knowledge no commercial recordings of accordion music were made prior to that period.

6. Thanks to Tom Kreneck of the Houston Public Library, I have recently come upon a wealth of photographs that date from as early as 1915 and that document this very point. The wild assortment of instruments found in these photographs is a graphic testimony to the variety of ensembles to be found in early Texas-Mexican society. Judging from the condition of the instruments and the musicians' dress, it is obvious that many of these were of working-class origin.

7. This biographical sketch is derived in part from an interview that Linda Fregoso held with Villa in 1980. I owe a special debt of gratitude to her for allowing me to share her information.

8. During three years that I spent at the University of Texas at Austin (1977–1980), the Texas Union used to turn the tavern over to Chicano students every Thursday for "Chicano Night." Music for dancing was provided by a "disco" jockey. True to their designation, the events featured mostly "Chicano" music. More specifically, in accordance with what was a tacit consensus that a genuinely Chicano atmosphere prevail, orquesta tejana music was offered, *de rigueur.* In all the times that I attended Chicano Night I do not recall hearing any conjunto music.

9. Cf. Grebler, Moore, and Guzman: "In our initial interviews throughout the Southwest, Mexican-Americans in the 30- to 50-year age class again and again referred to the new horizons opened up by the war itself and by postwar educational benefits . . . Service abroad exposed Mexican-Americans to other peoples and cultures . . . Thus, many Mexican-American veterans returned with a new sense of opportunities" (1970:201).

10. This brings to mind the words of an Americanized Texas-Mexican friend who had been brought up on the Anglo side of our town in South Texas, and who, as a high school student, began to gravitate toward Mexican social circles and to reexamine his ethnic allegiance. In a poignant recognition of his dilemma, he once told me, "I don't know where I belong anymore, but I can't ride the fence much longer." He eventually married a Mexican-American woman.

References

Ackerman, James S.
  1962   "A Theory of Style." *The Journal of Aesthetics and Art Criticism* 20:227–237.
Barrera, Mario
  1979   *Race and Class in the Southwest.* Notre Dame: University of Notre Dame Press.

Baqueiro Foster, Geronimo
   1964   *La musica en el periodo independiente.* Mexico, D.F.: Instituto Nacional de Bellas
           Artes.
Behague, Gerard
   1979   *Music in Latin America: An Introduction.* Englewood Cliffs: Prentice Hall.
Cumberland, Charles C.
   1968   *Mexico: The Struggle for Modernity.* London: Oxford University Press.
Etzkorn, K. Peter
   1973   *Music and Society: The Later Writings of Paul Honigsheim.* New York: John Wiley
           and Sons.
Foley, Douglas, et al.
   1977   *From Peones to Politicos: Ethnic Relations in a South Texas Town.* Austin: Center
           for Mexican American Studies.
Garcia, Richard A.
   1983   "The Mexican American Mind: A Product of the 1930s." In *History, Culture and
           Society: Chicano Studies in the 1980s,* Mario T. Garcia, et al., eds. Ypsilanti, Mich.:
           Bilingual Press, 67-93.
Garrido, Juan
   1974   *Historia de la musica popular en Mexico.* Mexico, D.F.: Editorial Contemporanees.
Geijerstam, Claes af
   1976   *Popular Music in Mexico.* Albuquerque: University of New Mexico Press.
George, Marjorie
   1978   "That Good Old Tejano Music." *Southwest Airlines Magazine (Jan.)* 32-37.
Grebler, Leo, Joan Moore, and Ralph C. Guzman
   1970   *The Mexican-American People: The Nation's Second Largest Minority.* New York:
           The Free Press.
Landolt, Robert G.
   1976   *The Mexican-American Workers of San Antonio, Texas.* New York: Arno Press.
Limon, Jose
   1977   "*Agringado* Joking in Texas-Mexican Society: Folklore and Differential Identity."
           In *New Directions in Chicano Scholarship,* Ricardo Romo and Raymund Paredes,
           eds. La Jolla: U.C. San Diego, 33-50.
Madsen, William
   1964   *The Mexican-Americans of South Texas.* New York: Holt, Rinehart and Winston.
Mayer-Serra, Otto
   1941   *Panorama de la musica mexicana.* Mexico, D.F.: Fondo de Cultura Economica.
Meyer, Michael C., and William L. Sherman
   1979   *The Course of Mexican History.* New York: Oxford University Press.
Paredes, Americo
   1958   "*With His Pistol in His Hand.*" Austin: University of Texas Press.
   1968   "Folk Medicine and the Intercultural Jest." In *Spanish Speaking People in the
           United States,* June Helm, ed. Seattle: University of Washington, 104.119.
Patoski, Joe Nick
   1978   "Little Joe." *Texas Monthly* (May): 134-137; 211-214.
Peña, Manuel
   1981   "The Emergence of Conjunto Music, 1935-1955." In *"And Other Neighborly
           Names:" Social Process and Cultural Image in Texas Folklore,* Richard Bauman and
           Roger Abrahams, eds. Austin: University of Texas Press, 280-299.
           The Texas-Mexican Conjunto: History of a Working-Class Music. Austin: Universi-
           ty of Texas Press (in press).
Poulantzas, Nicos
   1973   "On Social Classes," *New Left Review* 78:27-54.
Rubel, Arthur
   1966   *Across the Tracks: Mexican Americans in a Texas City.* Austin: University of Texas
           Press.

Saragoza, Alex
    1983   "Mexican Cinema in the United States, 1940–1952." In *History, Culture, and Society: Chicano Studies in the 1980s,* Mario T. Garcia, et al., eds. Ypsilanti, Mich.: Bilingual Press, 108–124.
Strachwitz, Chris
    1975   Jacket notes in *Texas-Mexican Border Music,* vol. 4, Berkeley: Arhoolie Records.
Taylor, Paul
    1934   *An American-Mexican Frontier.* Chapel Hill: University of Carolina Press.
Turner, Victor
    1974   *Dramas, Fields, and Metaphors.* Ithaca: Cornell University Press.
Wright, Eric O.
    1976   "Class Boundaries in Advanced Capitalist Societies." *New Left Review* 98:3–41.

[20]

Encounter with "The Others from Within": The Case of Gypsy Musicians in Former Yugoslavia

Svanibor Pettan

Abstract

This essay is composed of four thematic circles. The first circle provides an introduction to the issue of "Otherness" in folk music research in the territories of what was the Socialist Federal Republic of Yugoslavia. The second circle points to the features of "Otherness" associated with Gypsy musicians and presents some research approaches to their music and musicianship. The third circle focuses on Gypsy musicians in Kosovo and presents one specific approach to the question of their musical taste. The fourth circle concerns the issue of representation based on the humanitarian project Kosovo Roma.

Gypsy musicians' perception of their own music directly contradicted the values advocated by folk music researchers, thus their musicianship was often subjected to negative interpretations. It is much closer to the holistic perspective advocated by an anthropologically conceived ethnomusicology. Gaining insight into the musicianship of these "Others from within" has the potential to overcome the nationally determined scope of research in the territories of former Yugoslavia and lead to a broader look at the musical practices within the given territories.

1. "The Others" in the View of Folk Music Researchers

The subject of folk music research in central and southeastern Europe very often concerns folk music of the researcher's country and/or ethnic group. Researcher's interest in most cases is limited to the older and regionally distinctive part of peasant repertoire. Fieldwork is considered the basis for collecting, transcribing, analyzing, classifying, documenting, and publishing. Extensive fieldwork that focuses on musical products, is fairly characteristic. Musical training is required, most often within musicology departments. The aim of folk music research is to care for a particular music, which researchers interpret as particularly valuable for the national identity.[1]

Such a description of folk music research partly refers to the past, partly remains valid in present circumstances, is influenced to various extents in various places by modern ethnomusicological concepts and approaches. Researchers in central and southeastern Europe, therefore, have different opinions about the scope of ethnomusicology, its methods, and aims. Some consider folk music research and ethnomusicology synonymous (e.g. Kumer 1977), yet others recognize a variety in terms of research subjects (folk music, folklore music, traditional music, or simply music) and approaches (connections of *music* and *culture*; Ceribašić 1998).

Ethnomusicologists in the former Yugoslavia studied—almost as a rule—folk music of their own territory. Due to ideological constraints and personal views, for some this territory covered an area as wide as Yugoslavia, yet the majority preferred to limit their scholarly efforts for the most part to their own territorial-political unit within Yugoslavia (a republic or autonomous province), and to their own ethnic and/or linguistic group. The first South-Slav ethnomusicologist prior to the establishment of Yugoslavia, Franjo Kuhač (1834-1911), himself a Croat, was influenced by the vision of political unification of South Slavs. Therefore, he found appropriate to make clear that "Everywhere I say *Croatian people, Croatian music, Croatian tradition* I mean also *Serbian people, Serbian music, Serbian tradition,* because Croats and Serbs share one language and one folk music, though with some local specific features" (Kuhač 1909:3). His "Others" were non-Slavs—Hungarians, Germans, and Italians. By analyzing all these different folk musics he intended to make clear which features were autochthonous Croatian ones and which influences came from foreigners.[2]

The next important Croatian ethnomusicologist, Božidar Širola, wrote on the eve of World War II, that "the greatest influence on Croatian folk melodies came from the Middle East. (...) In Croatian folk music it is most evident in Bosnian and Herzegovinian folk songs, and mostly in the songs of Muslim population." (1940:156) In concordance with ideological concepts in his immediate surroundings at that time, Širola thought of the Muslim population in Bosnia and Herzegovina as of ethnic Croats. In the same chapter "Foreign influences on Croatian folk melody" in his book, he mentions Czech researcher Ludvik Kuba's entirely positive opinion on Oriental influences in Croatian, Serbian, and Bulgarian melodies. In contrast to German and Italian influences, Oriental influences amalgamated well with the Croatian basis (comp. Širola 1940:158-159).

Yugoslav authorities were determined to reduce substantial cultural boundaries related to the differences between Habsburg and Ottoman heritage[3] and to the firm ethnic, religious, and linguistic identities within the country. Folk music researchers did not participate in this politically motivated program.[4] Typically, research was conducted within the republic or province of a researcher and/or within a researcher's own ethnic and/or linguistic group. For instance, until recently ethnomusicologists from Slovenia showed almost exclusively interest in folk music of ethnic Slovenes within the so called Slovene ethnic territory that includes parts of the neighboring countries of Austria, Hungary, and Italy, at the same time showing little or no interest at all in folk music of minority groups within Slovenia. In a book on folk music in Kosovo, one Serbian researcher disregarded songs in languages other than his own (Vasiljević 1950), while in an encyclopedic entry on music in Kosovo

Roots Music   *461*

Svanibor Pettan. Encounter with "The Others from Within" • **121**

Fig. 1: Non-traditional costumes selected by members of a popular amplified Gypsy ensemble from western Kosovo for cassette cover. 1985. Photo: Studio Nimi.

an ethnic Albanian researcher considered only Albanian music (in Kovačević 1984). The approach was different in Bosnia-Herzegovina where researchers, at least partly due to the absence of one dominant ethnic group and linguistic boundaries, considered cross-ethnic research.

Regular annual meetings of Yugoslav folklorists served as a forum at which individual scholars presented the results of their investigations in "their" units to the colleagues from the other parts of the country. Folk music of the entire Yugoslavia was considered only at the university-level education in ethnomusicology;[5] for special projects such as the symposium *The Folk Arts of Yugoslavia* in Pittsburgh (Kolar 1976),[6] the *Informative Bulletin with Bibliography*—on achievements in ethnomusicology, ethnoorganology and ethnochoreology in Yugoslavia—(e.g. Bezić 1989), and the concert in Belgrade, which served as a basis for the creation of the LP record *Yugoslavia. Traditional Folk Music* (Dević 1978);[7] also, further more, for individually conceived projects such as pentatonicism in Yugoslavia (Hrovatin 1958), Yugoslav folk dance zones (Ivančan 1964), styles of Yugoslav folk music (Bezić 1981), and Yugoslav folk music instruments (Gojković 1989).

The emphasis on "Us" did not leave much space for the study of "Others," i.e., "inside" (e.g. musics of minorities) or "outside" (e.g. musics of the world). The motives underlining (until recently) the almost exclusive interest in "our" folk music can be represented by the following four characteristic sentences. They were extracted from my personal contacts with researchers and checked at a conference in Sarajevo in 2000 that succeeded in bringing together several ethnomusicologists from the territories of what was Yugoslavia.[8]

1."The question of our folk music is the question of our national roots." This sentence points to the concept of a national mission claimed by researchers and to the conviction that a scholarly contribution is valuable only if it refers to the researcher's national framework.

2. "Who will do the research in our country if not ourselves." This sentence can be understood as an expression of fear that the job will not be done without the efforts of domestic researchers.

3. "A researcher is always greater authority for 'own' than for 'foreign' music." One could certainly interpret this sentence as an expression of fear from misrepresentation in the studies of foreign researchers.

4. "Folk music is dying out." This points to the notion that the fast disappearing folk music must be recorded before it is too late. Consequently, the work on products is often given priority over the study of processes.[9]

Fig. 2: Folklore
ensemble Malesori from
Gjonaj (Kosovo)
composed of ethnic
Albanian dancers and
Gypsy musicians
performs at the 23rd
International Folklore
Festival in Zagreb
(Croatia). 1988.
Photo: Svanibor Pettan.

These four sentences are still used not only to affirm the study of "Us," but also to discourage studying the "Others." Other characteristic sentences have the same connotations: "Folk music in some parts of national territory is insufficiently explored," "There is a shortage of researchers," "It is hard, if not impossible, to get involved with a 'foreign' culture to a sufficient extent," "Research elsewhere is more demanding in financial terms," and "Who has the authority to supervise a thesis on the music of the 'Others.'" In spite of these notions, including potential supervisors' fear of incompetence due to research of only "Us", the introduction of new subjects, approaches, and aims already has, to various extents, increased the number of ethnomusicologists within the given territories. Alternatives to paying tribute to national culture became possible and researchers found themselves in a position to test scholarly concepts and methodologies on material that was not necessarily determined by national ideologies. This essay considers Gypsy musicians—widely seen as the extreme "Others," not somewhere far away, but among "Us"—within the framework of nationally determined research traditions.

Roots Music 463

Svanibor Pettan. Encounter with "The Others from Within" • **123**

2.   Gypsy Musicians as "the Others"

When Gypsy and non-Gypsy "folklore ensembles" performed at the same public events in the territories of former Yugoslavia, the striking differences between their approaches were often raising discussions among researchers and other professionals. Non-Gypsy repertoire, instrumentation, dress and dancing were in most cases related to concepts such as rural, old (old-fashioned), belonging to a given ethnic (national) group, and (in many instances) to a given region. Gypsies, however, seemed to prefer urban, new (modern), international and regional, the latter in a much broader sense. Members of a non-Gypsy folklore ensemble looked alike and acted in a uniform way, while members of a Gypsy ensemble used to emphasize their individual features, as in dress and dance movements (cf. Fig. 4,3). Common denominator for Gypsies in all former Yugoslav territories was a tendency to present themselves as modern musicians, capable and willing, only to a certain extent, to adapt to stage performances organized by non-Gypsies. In the annual concert series of amateur folklore ensembles from the Zagreb area in Croatia in the 1990s Gypsies were usually placed in the concert reserved for minorities. In a sharp contrast to Ukrainians, for instance, who emphasized *bandura* and some other traditional instruments, Gypsies rather used a synthesizer. Ukrainians presented traditional Ukrainian songs and stylized traditional Ukrainian dances in stylized and uniform Ukrainian costumes. Gypsies presented songs currently beloved by their community[10] and a variety of currently beloved dances in stylized costumes with individualistic features. Only the Gypsy audience participated actively in the concert by clapping, singing, and shouting, although exclusively during Gypsy performances.[11]

   The four characteristic sentences discussed earlier in the context of folk music research can easily be applied to folklore ensembles. Equally shared by folk music researchers and folklore ensembles alike is the importance assigned to national roots, sense of obligation to consider "Our" folk music, notion of being qualified to deal with "Our" folk music only, and the wish to prevent disappearance of this music. This perhaps accounts for negative statements on Gypsy musicianship expressed by some scholars from the position of folk music research. For instance, the ethnologist, Tihomir Đorđević, who conducted research in the early 20th century stated that Gypsies in Serbia failed to preserve any of their own music, but corrupted and "gypsycized" adopted Serbian music (Đorđević 1984[1910]:39). A later account claimed that "it has been found that they corrupt not only national music of various countries, but also new music, for instance, jazz." (Gojković 1977:48).

   Different attitudes advocated by the younger generation of ethnomusicologists resulted in a variety of approaches and led to entirely different conclusions. Some ethnomusicologists participated in music making with the Gypsies (Kertész-Wilkinson 2000), others compared several Gypsy versions of a Gypsy tune (Hemetek 1999) and a non-Gypsy tune (Pettan 1992), or Gypsy and non-Gypsy practices such as the *folklore* and folk revival movements in Hungary (Kovalcsik 2000). In concordance with Mat Salo's Barthian-inspired opinion that "'Gypsy' does not refer to an ethnic

group, but to a set of groups tentatively considered as related to one another (...)"
(1979:95), research was directed on the one hand towards individual groups within a
given territory and on the other hand (to a lesser extent) towards possible common
features among various groups. Particularly useful was the interdisciplinary comparative research in Austria's five Gypsy communities (e.g. Halwachs, Heinschink, and
Fennesz-Juhasz 2000), where it even helped to increase Gypsy's political position
(Hemetek 2000).[12]

Although a universal definition of Gypsy music is not feasible, "there is, nevertheless, music which gypsies feel to be their own, though it varies from country to
country" (Sárosi 1980:865). Max Peter Baumann extracted two contrasting styles of
performance within a broad international framework: slow melodies in free rhythm
(*uzun hava, lassu, loke gila, cante jondo*) and dance songs in strict rhythm (*kırık hava, friska, kelimaske gila, cante festero*; Baumann 2000). In Hungary, Russia, and
Spain certain forms of Gypsy music became "national music, veritable emblems of
the country" (Silverman 2000:270). The intention of Gypsy musicians to become acceptable as specialists not only to members of their own group in ethnic terms, but to
the entire multi-ethnic setting within the given territory is particularly relevant. It can
be related to the concept of a modern multicultural state rather than to the concept of
a nation-state. A given region then can be interpreted as a setting for intercultural
musical encounter rather than as a place of ethnically clean musical culture.

The encounter of different concepts naturally requires negotiations. Negotiations
between Gypsy musicians and their audiences may encompass a variety of issues
such as repertoire, instrumentation, dress, manner of performance, and, nevertheless,
price.[13] Negotiability of these issues suggests that Gypsy musicians have a broad
base for music making, broader in comparison to non-Gypsy musicians, which
makes them attractive to a variety of audiences. In Kosovo they were able to accommodate any audience with its own music, music of other Kosovo communities, and
various music from outside the province. Familiarity with such a broad repertoire enabled some Gypsies to participate as musicians even in customs related to annual and

*Fig. 3: Performance of a
folklore ensemble
composed of the Gypsies
at the Festival of Kosovo
Folklore in Gllogovc /
Glogovac. 1986.
Photo: Svanibor Pettan.*

Roots Music   *465*

Svanibor Pettan. Encounter with "The Others from Within" • **125**

life cycles of other communities, thus gradually becoming the sole keepers of non-Gypsy customs.[14] The ability to sing in several languages and to play certain instruments was another of their advantages.[15] Thus, they were willing to wear traditional costumes of the given non-Gypsy group for non-Gypsy celebrations or stage performances which made them look like ethnic Albanians, ethnic Turks, or ethnic Muslims (cf. F_ig. 2). They were also regarded as musical masters expected to create merry and festive moods by improvising praising lyrics about guests gathered at a given celebration, by virtuoso instrumental improvisations, by theatrical gestures, and by playing to the ear of a guest thus inducing a heightened state of mind.[16]

Fig. 4: Performance of a folklore ensemble composed of ethnic Albanians at the Festival of Kosovo Folklore in Gllogovc / Glogovac. 1987.
Photo: Svanibor Pettan.

I witnessed several negotiations between Gypsy musicians and their hosts in Kosovo. At one occasion in 1990, a Gypsy musician proved to me that—despite political tension between ethnic Albanians and ethnic Serbs—he was able to perform a Serbian tune in an Albanian wedding without any negative consequences. Some other time, a Gypsy musician's arguments in favor to use a more "modern" saxophone instead of an "old fashioned" clarinet did not convince the non-Gypsy hosts, who valued clarinet as a more suitable instrument for the given occasion. Some other changes were imposed without direct negotiations, such as the replacement of hi-hat and snare drum with the *indijanke* pair of bongos within the standard drum set (cf. Fig. 1).

3.   An Approach to Gypsy Musicians in Kosovo

The basic notion of my studies of Gypsy music in Kosovo (1989-1991) was to look at any music considered by Gypsy musicians (cf. Silverman 1981). The research was conceived in five concentric circles. The first circle encompassed the Gypsy community in which I conducted in-depth research, the second encompassed other Gypsy communities in the city of Prizren , the third encompassed Gypsies elsewhere in Ko-sovo, the fourth encompassed Gypsies in other parts of what was Yugoslavia, and the fifth encompassed Gypsies in the entire world. About 60% of my informants within the first three circles were Arlija, sedentary Gypsies, Muslims, whose mother tongue was Romani, and for whom music in most cases served as a secondary source of in-come.[17]

In order to gain insight into the aesthetic system of Gypsy musicians encom-passed by the first three circles I prepared a tape with forty-five musical examples, lasting up to thirty seconds each, and played it to my informants. Listening to the re-cordings served as a tool to inspire my informants to talk about performers and mu-sics. The examples were grouped into two sections: Gypsy music and Non-Gypsy music.[18] In both sections there were examples from Kosovo and from outside the province. I was specifically interested in what music they liked or disliked. If music belonged to some specific ethnic, religious, or local group, would their attitudes to-wards this group affect their musical taste? If they liked or disliked some kinds of music or specific tunes, what were their criteria for evaluation? The overview of opinions in this chapter follows the order of musical examples on the tape.

3.1 Gypsy music from Kosovo

Although the shawm-and-drum ensembles were most common among Gypsies, sev-eral of my informants, including some of the most respected shawm players, did not like these instruments. For instance, one of the best shawm players in a town in southern Kosovo said, "I always preferred clarinet, but this instrument [shawm] brings more money." Gypsy musicians who performed in amplified ensembles dis-liked shawm-and-drum ensembles for similar reasons: "We perform for hours, while they [shawm and drum players] perform for only half an hour for walking a child[19] and earn tips which are sometimes higher than ours."

Songs to frame drum accompaniment were associated primarily with women and, in spite of serving as a source for repertories of male musicians, they were not much appreciated by male Gypsy musicians.[20] Leaders of amplified ensembles from Kosovo were generally appreciated and the names of some of them were known throughout the province. Most of my informants were able to identify at least two of them from listening to my examples.

In some cases, opinion about the origin or personal characteristics of the perform-ers affected judgements about the music. One of the informants, asked about a partic-ular musician, said: "He is a *Gabelj*;[21] we do not like such music [his music]" or "He would not come to the wedding for which he was hired if somebody else would pay him more; do not ask me to talk about such a bad person."

Most informants agreed that Nehat Gaši (1948-1991) was the most successful Gypsy musician born in Kosovo. He was one of the first Gypsy musicians in the province who introduced amplified accordion, made the first commercial recordings

Roots Music 467

Svanibor Pettan. Encounter with "The Others from Within" • **127**

and composed many songs in Romani. His songs were included in the repertories of many Gypsy musicians in Kosovo. Most opinions about him bordered on uncritical admiration: "He was the king of Gypsy music." However, some musicians were critical about him saying that he was a "good singer and excellent composer, but weak as accordion player" and that he "lacked variety, his songs were all in Romani and in the same style."

Other commercially successful Gypsy performers from Kosovo such as Ramuš Ramuši and Šemo Ibrahimi were remembered and appreciated for the distinctive, modern styles they developed in the 1970s. Ibrahimi was credited with the introduction of the "Indian style," inspired by Indian film music, but his songs were not performed any more by other Gypsy musicians.

3.2 Gypsy music from other parts of former Yugoslavia

Of all Gypsy musicians from former Yugoslavia outside of Kosovo, Esma Redžepova from Macedonia was appreciated the most. She represented the older style of singing, influenced by Turkish music, with much ornamentation. Redžepova's songs were considered stylistically akin to Gypsy songs from Kosovo. They were especially appreciated by those Gypsies of Kosovo who spoke the same dialect of Romani as Redžepova, and by Gypsies from the older generation. Since she was not featured in the media at the time, most of her songs were not even known to younger Gypsy musicians in Kosovo.

Muharem Serbezovski, a Macedonian Gypsy singer, representing a style somewhat similar to that of Redžepova, was appreciated for his singing skills but strongly condemned for his practice of presenting borrowed Turkish tunes as his own.

Šaban Bajramović, a well-known Gypsy singer from Serbia, was appreciated in Kosovo for his skills as a singer. Arlija Gypsy musicians criticized him for performing songs heavily influenced by Serbian music and not much appreciated by them. In contrast, his singing delighted Gurbet Gypsy musicians, whose style was more closely related to the Serbian.

The commercially successful Gypsy virtuoso on several aerophones, Ferus Mustafov from Macedonia, was admired in Kosovo. A respected Gypsy musician from a town in western Kosovo, himself playing in Albanian style, said about Mustafov: "Ferus is the best. He plays many instruments. A good musician has to play several languages [sic], and Ferus does so." Mustafov's compositions, although stylistically different from Kosovo musics, became part of Kosovo Gypsy repertories.

Gypsy brass bands, characteristic of Serbian tradition, were appreciated mainly in those areas of Kosovo which were in close proximity to southern Serbia.[22] Elsewhere in the province they were not favored.

Gypsy musics from other regions of the former Yugoslavia were not appreciated in Kosovo.[23] The example of shawm-and-drum music from Bosnia and Herzegovina, which resembled archaic polyphonic vocal music from the Dinaric mountains, was among the most disliked examples.

Informants were indifferent to music performed by Gypsy *tamburica* [long-necked lute] players from Vojvodina and Croatia, but the Croatian example was considered more appealing because of the faster tempo and inclusion of the drum. Improvisation on dulcimer by the respected Gypsy musician from Slovenia, Miška Baranja, was considered good, but not particularly appealing.

3.3   Gypsy music from the areas outside of the former Yugoslavia

Next I played Gypsy music from Bulgaria, Turkey, Russia, Hungary, France, and Spain. Most of my informants expressed appreciation for technically demanding and stylistically mixed music performed by the clarinetist, Ivo Papasov, and his amplified ensemble from Bulgaria. They compared his playing to that of Ferus Mustafov of Macedonia. The famous clarinetist and nightclub musician from Turkey, Mustafa Kandıralı, has for years been the idol of most clarinet players in Kosovo. His recordings circulated among Kosovo Gypsies, and all my informants admired his manner of playing.

Russian Gypsy music in general was not appreciated, mainly for its "lack of rhythm." Although cassettes with this kind of music, even performed by the ensembles from Serbia (Odjila) and Bosnia and Herzegovina (Sar e Roma) were available in stores in Kosovo, Gypsies did not buy them.

Next, I referred to the two principal song types practiced by Vlach Gypsies in Hungary, the slow songs (*loki gili*) and dance songs (*khelimaski gili*).[24] My informants in Kosovo were unfamiliar with these song types and did not appreciate the excerpt of a dance song which I played for them. One would think of attributes like "fast, aggressive and full of rhythm" with which a keyboard player from a town in central Kosovo characterized "good music," as accurate to describe Gypsy performance of the Hungarian genre czardas. Nonetheless, Gypsies in Kosovo considered it "foreign to Kosovo style."

Only a few Gypsy musicians in Kosovo heard about the Gypsy guitarist, Django Reinhardt, who is remembered as one of the finest jazz musicians of all times. His music did not particularly appeal to any of my informants.

Music performed by the popular Franco-Spanish ensemble, Gypsy Kings, was appreciated by the young generation of Kosovo musicians for its strong rhythm and modern instrumentation.

3.4   Non-Gypsy music from Kosovo

Most Gypsy musicians I interviewed disliked Albanian village music because of its harsh vocal quality and accompaniment on the much-disliked long necked lutes

Roots Music 469

Svanibor Pettan. Encounter with "The Others from Within" • **129**

(*çifteli, sharki*). Albanian urban music shares some features with Turkish music and most Gypsy musicians liked it and performed it on regular basis.

Serbian urban songs and fast dances were appreciated. But in the 1990s Serbs did not ask Gypsies native to Kosovo to perform at their feasts and because of the tense political situation Gypsies have almost stopped playing Serbian music.

Gypsy musicians in Kosovo appreciated Turkish music, but they did not like it performed on the long-necked lute, *saz*. If amplified sazes were used in an ensemble, they tolerated them.

Narrative songs of Kosovo's ethnic Muslims, performed by a male singer accompanied by a long-necked lute, *tambura*, were disliked.

3.5 Non-Gypsy music from outside of Kosovo

Gypsy musicians from Kosovo considered epic songs accompanied by bowed lute characteristic of Montenegrins. They strongly disliked this kind of music, calling it "boring" and "repetitive," and pointing to the lyrics that were irrelevant for them.

The vocal polyphonic peasant genres, particularly the *ganga* of Bosnia and Herzegovina were strongly disliked. So was the singing to the accompaniment of the *sopela* shawm from the Istrian peninsula in Croatia.

The folk-pop music of Serbia and Bosnia and Herzegovina, called *novokompono-vana narodna muzika* in the literature, was appreciated and performed. My informants pointed to its appealing melodies, prominent rhythm, singing style (especially the ornamented Bosnian style), and the amplified sound quality.

Slovenian polka was found to be "lively, but not appropriate for Kosovo audiences."

I selected four examples from the repertoire of Western art music: excerpts from *Toccata and Fugue in D Minor* (Johann Sebastian Bach), *La Traviata* (Giuseppe Verdi), *The Blue Danube* (Johann Strauss) and *The Rite of Spring* (Igor Stravinsky). Of them the Strauss waltz was liked the best. A clarinet player from southern Kosovo offered this comment on the Bach example: "Like a prayer in church, like a bone with no meat;" on Verdi: "This is opera; not for me. But the singer evidently finished school. She is not like our singers;" on Strauss: "We rarely perform this rhythm. The music is fine, I like it;" and on Stravinsky: "No, by no means."

Middle-aged musicians who had been exposed to jazz on the radio in the past appreciated it to a limited extent. The particular example of swing that I played for my informants was described as "old-fashioned." Most informants disliked rock, while younger musicians appreciated rap, as a fashionable genre. Gypsy musicians in Kosovo performed neither of these genres.

Non-Western music was represented by examples from Turkey, Egypt, India, China-Taiwan, Indonesia, Puerto Rico, and Tanzania. The Turkish example of the fashionable *arabesk* genre was highly appreciated by all informants, even the performer was instantly recognized. Egyptian shawm-and-drum music and Indian snake-charmer music were considered akin to Gypsy musics in Kosovo.[25] The example of Indian classical music was instantly recognized as Indian because of its specific sound quality. Many informants pointed out that this was the music from the country of their ancestors. Music for Chinese zither *zheng* was considered boring, and the timbre of the instrument not appealing at all. Balinese gamelan music inspired the following comment: "No melody, no rhythm, no taste, only metal." Both Puerto Rican *salsa* and sub-Saharan African drumming were appreciated for their emphasis on rhythm.

The experiment has shown that the Gypsy musicians from Kosovo preferred above all Turkish and Western influenced urban music from the Balkans. This included a variety of genres, regardless of ethnic and religious affiliation of the performers. The evaluation of a piece of music, in some cases, depended on personal characteristics of the performer, if known. However, the most important criteria for evaluation were musical features of a tune, performance medium, and the appropriateness of the music to be performed in a local setting. Musical features especially appreciated by the Gypsy musicians were lively and strong rhythm, even without clear melody (Tanzania), smooth timbre (unlike old Balkan voice quality and Balinese gamelan), virtuosity, and improvisation.

4.   The Issue of Representation

My visit to Kosovo in late 1999—eight years after the wars which have marked the end of the Socialist Federal Republic of Yugoslavia and which had prevented me from continuing research over there—made me aware of the desperate situation of the Gypsies in Kosovo. Gypsies became silenced victims of the Albanian-Serbian conflict in which the great majority of them did not want to participate. The logic was simple: there was nothing for them to gain, regardless of the final outcome of the conflict. Many were forced to leave their homes in Kosovo in the course of the 1990s, while those who remained lived in fear for their lives. The question that entered my mind was how to help them? The decision to create a humanitarian CD-ROM based on my fieldwork materials was made soon afterwards. This document of a musical life that does not exist any more aims, in the short term, to raise money to support Gypsies' physical and cultural survival in Kosovo and, in the long term, to make the legacy of Gypsy musicians from Kosovo widely known, a part of common knowledge. This legacy, not imposed "from above," may serve as a powerful metaphor of coexistence and the alternative to the present segmentation into ethnic cells.

It was the first-hand experience with Kosovo Gypsy musicians that made me abandon the purist paradigm of folk music research as inappropriate for my work on this project. The examples on the CD-ROM point to acculturation and other processes in which music is not seen as a "frozen" product, but rather as a living and ever-changing organism. The examples reflect rural and urban, old (old fashioned) and new (modern), as well as own and foreign in both ethnic and territorial terms, howev-

Roots Music 471

Svanibor Pettan. Encounter with "The Others from Within" • **131**

er, not as mutually exclusive categories. Incorporation of all these intertwined aspects was essential to the definition of Gypsy musicianship in Kosovo.

This brings in the question of representation. Due to lost contacts through the succession of wars in the territories of former Yugoslavia, I was simply not in a position to ask for the opinion of my former informants. The selection is very diverse, in concordance with the sentence that I heard from several Gypsy musicians in Kosovo: "We are the best musicians, because we are universal and international." It covers a wide range of music performed for Gypsy and non-Gypsy audiences, these being differentiated by ethnic, religious, linguistic, regional, generational and gender-related identities. The examples are divided into four thematic blocks: Musical instruments and ensembles; Gypsies for Gypsies; Connections with non-Gypsy traditions and topics; and Openness and creativity.

In the first thematic block shawm-and-drum players accompany horse races organized by ethnic Muslims, female frame drum players sing in Albanian at a Gypsy female celebration, a brass band plays a Turkish tune at a wedding organized by ethnic Croats, an urban *čalgija* ensemble performs instrumentally a song shared by Serbs and (ethnic) Muslims, while a modern amplified ensemble introduces dance music in the context of a Gypsy circumcision feast.

The second thematic block brings a lament in Romani, followed by a dervish tune, sung by Gypsy children in Arabic. The performance of a given community's "anthem" is characterized by the singer's spontaneous switch from Romani to Turkish. Female-style Gypsy music performed by men in a private domain (singing to frame drum accompaniment) and public domain (singing to amplified ensemble accompaniment) shows how the principal Kosovo Gypsy genre at the time of my research, the *talava*, was brought to widespread popularity. Yet another example documents the performance of a celebrated Gypsy musician from outside of Kosovo, whose presence in a local wedding was expected to increase the respect for the given family.

The third thematic block starts with music performed on a double-stringed plucked lute, which is otherwise not appreciated by the majority of Gypsies in Kosovo. A female song medley, recorded at a Gypsy circumcision feast, features songs that spontaneously follow one another in Albanian, Serbian, and in the dialect of the local (ethnic) Muslims. The next example features a Gypsy clarinetist in an ensemble composed of ethnic Turks and dominated by the sound of Turkish amplified long-necked lutes. Performance of an Indian film tune at a Kosovo wedding was characteristic of Gypsy musicians only and to some extent reflected the awareness of their Indian "roots." A step further is the performance of a song in Romani about the American TV series Dynasty, which points to the switch in preferences from East to West and from the "old" cinema to the more modern and easier accessible medium — television.

The fourth thematic block is composed of two contrasting versions of Lambada, the first being performed on "traditional" shawms-and-drums, the latter on "modern" synthesizer. Why *Lambada*? For obvious reasons, folk music researchers do not find

132 • *the world of music 43 (2+3) - 2001*

themselves in a position to trace the "original" version of a tune according to which the other versions are made. *Lambada*—based on the tune *Llorando se fue* composed by the brothers Gonzalo and Ulises Hermosa and popularized by the ensemble Kaoma—provided me with such an opportunity thanks to its frequent broadcasting. Kaoma's video spot enabled many Gypsy and non-Gypsy musicians in Kosovo to include it in their repertoires. The two audio examples and ten video excerpts point to creative adaptation of this tune for local multi-ethnic consumption.

5. Conclusion

Gypsies are widely perceived by non-Gypsies as the eternal "Others". On the one hand they are looked down upon as individuals as well as an imagined community, on the other hand they are appreciated because of their skills, particularly, of those related to music making. Seen from the positions advocated by folk music researchers this ambivalence made them look like a specific, particularly emphasized case of anomaly. Dispersed all over the world, having no nation-state of their own, and even lacking a strong sense of belonging to a national (Gypsy) body, Gypsies seem to personify conditions that are as far as possible removed from conditions a folk music researcher would wish for his or her own ethnic group. Gypsy musicians do not perform one "Gypsy folk music" and even do not necessarily distinguish between own and adopted music.[26] The criteria for their acceptance of any tune may vary—from a positive aesthetic response to a notion of its market value among the audiences—but the notion "we have to appreciate this tune because it is 'our' folk tune," is not of primary relevance to them. Their interest may be in who is singing, in what he or she says, and how well it is said, irrespective of the tune's origin (cf. Kertész-Wilkinson 1992:132, Pettan 1996a:56).

A sense of responsibility for own national roots on the one hand and open-mindedness towards the "Others" on the other correspond with the paradigms advocated by folk music researchers and folklore ensembles on the one hand and with those of modern ethnomusicologists and Gypsy ensembles on the other. From the point of view of folk music researchers, Gypsies' and ethnomusicologists' interest in "music wherever whenever" is seen as threat to the legitimacy and exclusivity of their concepts.[27] Some other relevant distinctions include: national vs. global framework, self-sufficiency vs. openness, interest in the survival of products vs. interest in processes such as acculturation, globalization, and identity construction, and the characteristic "we" pattern that is above any individuality vs. the "I" pattern that points to the sense of individuality of musician and researcher alike.

Results of the test, presented in the third part of this essay, point to Gypsy musicians' clear notions on what music is acceptable for them and what music is not, and why is it so. Performing certain music can be a subject of negotiation, but there are also musics that Gypsy musicians simply do not want to perform. In any case, ethnic origin of a music is not considered a criterion suitable for deciding on its adoption and performance for any audience, including the Gypsies themselves.

Such an attitude supports the evidence that members of any ethnic group usually do not impose ethnic limits on their musical practices. They perform neither exclusively the music created within their own community in ethnic terms, nor exclusively rural, old (old-fashioned) and local music. It is the folk music researchers who focused their scholarly attention on this particular segment of music, thus projecting a partial and therefore distorted image of the totality. Ethnomusicological approaches advocated in this essay, based on the fieldwork experience of Gypsy musicians as "the Others from within", call for the broadening of the scope of ethnomusicological research "at home."

Notes

1 "That other folk songs in other languages might also be common in these regions simply did not matter for scholarly geography, for they were not relevant to the argument being made." (Bohlman 1996:xix)

2 He also researched Oriental influences on Croatian music. There he expressed the conviction that the Ottoman Turks were just mediators who brought Arabic traits to Europe (Kuhač 1899).

3 Both were seen in negative light as being imposed by foreigners.

4 In order "to avoid proclaiming meaningless socialist dogma, scholars were often constrained to ignore some connections that actually existed between and among cultures." (A. Petrović 1997:57)

5 Folk songs from the republics and autonomous provinces were printed in textbooks for all levels.

6 Yugoslav scholars were asked to prepare papers on specific topics covering the whole Yugoslav territory. For instance, the Serbian scholar Radmila Petrović reported on folk music, Bosnian Cvjetko Rihtman on folk music instruments, Slovenian Zmaga Kumer on folk ballads, and Macedonian Blaže Ristovski on oral lyric poetry.

7 Montenegro, Slovenia, and the Kosovo province were not included.

8 *Muzika u društvu* (Music in Society). The conference papers were published soon afterwards (Čavlović 2001).

9 The second out of four approaches to the problem of purpose in ethnomusicology according to Merriam, given the inevitability of change, "cannot be the only aim of ethnomusicology." (Merriam 1964:8-10)

10 Not necessarily of Gypsy origin, but either instrumentally or in a translation to Romani or some other tongue used within the community.

11 This comparison is based on an annual staged event that in succession features non-Gypsies and Gypsies. It is, however, true that the majority of Gypsy musicians, for a variety of reasons, prefer to perform in an entirely different context—at weddings (this opinion is shared by the famous Gypsy musician from Bulgaria, Ivo Papasov, see Buchanan 1996:208). According to

my own experience, the distinction between *narodna muzika* (folk music) and *svatbarska muzika* (wedding music), as developed by Timothy Rice for Bulgaria (Rice 1996, see also Pejčeva 1999), is applicable to the southeastern part of what was Yugoslavia.

12 These groups are: Burgenland-Roma, Sinti, Lovara, Kalderash, and Arlije.

13 Radmila Petrović described the innovative role of Gypsy musicians in the domains of repertoire and performance media in her study on acculturation of folk music in southeastern Yugoslavia (R. Petrović 1974:157).

14 Examples for Kosovo extend from Gypsy performances of non-Gypsy ritual songs (e.g. Lazarević-Golemović 1954) all the way to the instrumental accompaniment for horse races and free-style wrestling, organized by non-Gypsies. The examples from Hungary (Vekerdi 1976), Bulgaria and Romania (Kertész-Wilkinson 2001) point to the same tendency.

15 Gypsies in Kosovo played exclusively or predominantly the *zurla* shawm, *tupan* double-headed cylindrical drum, *grnata* clarinet, *saksafon* saxophone and *cümbüş* fretless banjo.

16 "In many societies Gypsy musicians help to induce heightened states of mind in their audiences, such as *kefi* in Greece, *duende* in Spain or Hungarian *mulatas* (merry-making or 'merry-making with tears'), echoed in the Vlach Gypsy concept of *voja kerel*, a sacred 'liminal' state that combines joy, sorrow, consolation, extreme happiness and peace" (Kertész-Wilkinson 2001:618).

17 Due to the unfavorable circumstances for Gypsies in Kosovo at the time of creating this essay and in concordance with the practice of some other authors (e.g. Sutherland 1975, Subhi Hanna 1982), the names of specific locations and informants are not indicated.

18 The term "Gypsy music" referred to any music performed by Gypsies, regardless of its origin. Consequently, "non-Gypsy music" referred to the variety of musics performed by any ethnic group other than Gypsies.

19 "Walking a child" is a phrase that referred to the public exposure of a boy who was going to be circumcised. It was customary among Muslims in Kosovo to invite guests and musicians to celebrate the circumcision event. In cities, an amplified ensemble performed for dance. At some point during the feast, shawm and drum players arrived. The dance stopped and the attention of the audience became focused on the richly dressed boy sitting on the shoulders of a walking relative who toured the hall. Soon afterwards shawm and drum players were free to leave with big tips.

20 The mainstream Kosovo Gypsy genre of the 1990s, the *talava*, was rooted in female repertoire (for a detailed presentation of *talava* see Pettan 1996b).

21 *Gabelj* is a pejorative term that was used in Kosovo by sedentary Gypsies for nomadic Gypsies.

22 Here I refer to Kosovo and southern Serbia as culturally distinct entities. Southern Serbia with its centers in Niš, Leskovac and Vranje, was known for Gypsy brass-bands.

23 A major celebration of Kosovo Gypsies living in Croatia or Slovenia would require Gypsy musicians from Kosovo. Musicians from Croatia or Slovenia, themselves members of other Gypsy communities, were not considered appropriate at all.

24 "These songs, which occur only with gypsies and can therefore justifiably be called gypsy folksongs, can be distinguished from the songs of other peoples on the basis of certain characteristics of style." (Sárosi 1978:24-5)

25 Both were performed by players to whom people in Egypt and India referred to as "gypsies."

26 "Neither one worldwide nor one pan-European Rom music exists, despite an emerging awareness of ethnic unity." (Silverman 2000:271) "The music that professional Rom musicians play
for their own people may or may not differ from the music they play for others." (ibid:270)

27 According to Ankica Petrović, some "senior scholars were ready, even in the late 1980s, to
term contemporary Western approaches as 'decadent' or 'bourgeois ethnomusicology' in order
to protect their own doctrine." (A. Petrović 1997:58)

References

Baumann, Max Peter
  2000 "'Wir gehen die Wege ohne Grenzen...' – Zur Musik der Roma und Sinti." In *Music,
        Language, and Literature of the Roma and Sinti*. Max Peter Baumann, ed. Berlin:
        VWB, 167-177.

Bezić, Jerko
  1981 "Stilovi folklorne glazbe u Jugoslaviji." *Zvuk* 3:33-50.

Bezić, Jerko (ed.)
  1989 *Etnomuzikologija, etnoorganologija i etnokoreologija u SFR Jugoslaviji 1988. / Eth-
        nomusicology, Ethnoorganology and Ethnochoreology in SFR Yugoslavia in 1988*.
        Zagreb: Zavod za istraživanje folklora.

Bohlman, Philip
  1996 *Central European Folk Music. An Annotated Bibliography of Sources in German*. New
        York: Garland Publishing.

Buchanan, Donna
  1996 "Wedding Musicians, Political Transition, and National Consciousness in Bulgaria."
        In *Returning Culture. Musical Changes in Central and Eastern Europe*. Mark Slobin,
        ed. Durham: Duke University Press, 200-230.

Ceribašić, Naila
  1998 "Ethnomusicology and Ethnochoreology at the Institute during the Nineties." *Narodna
        umjetnost* 35/1:53-71.

Čavlović, Ivan (ed.)
  2001 *Muzika u društvu*. Sarajevo: Muzikološko društvo BiH and Muzička akademija u Sara-
        jevu.

Dević, Dragoslav
  1978 *Yugoslavia. Traditional Folk Music—Narodna muzička tradicija* (LP 22-2570). Beo-
        grad: RTB.

Đorđević, Tihomir
  1984 [1910] "Cigani i muzika u Srbiji." *Naš narodni život* 7:32-40.

Gojković, Andijana
  1977 "Romi u muzičkom životu naših naroda." *Zvuk* 3:45-50.
  1989 *Narodni muzički instrumenti*. Beograd: Vuk Karadžić.

Halwachs, Dieter, Mozes Heinschink, and Christiane Fennesz-Juhasz
  2000 "Kontinuität und Wandel. Der Stellenwert von Sprache und Musik bei Roma und Sinti
        in Österreich." In *Music, Language, and Literature of the Roma and Sinti*. Max Peter
        Baumann, ed. Berlin: VWB, 99-154.

136 • *the world of music 43 (2+3) - 2001*

Hemetek, Ursula
  1999   "Gelem, gelem, lungone dromesa – I Went a Long Way. The Anthem of the Gypsies, a
          People Without Country or Homeland." In *Glazba, folklor i kultura / Music, Folklore,
          and Culture*. Naila Ceribašić and Grozdana Marošević, eds. Zagreb: IEF – HMD, 323-
          330.
  2000   "Ando Drom – Auf dem Weg. Die Rolle der traditionellen Musik im Prozess der poli-
          tischen Anerkennung der Roma in Österreich." In *Music, Language, and Literature of
          the Roma and Sinti*. Max Peter Baumann, ed. Berlin: VWB, 371-392.

Hrovatin, Radoslav
  1958   "Pentatonika u Jugoslaviji." *Rad 10. kongresa SUFJ*: 269-275.

Ivančan, Ivan
  1964   "Geografska podjela narodnih plesova u Jugoslaviji." *Narodna umjetnost* 3:17-38.

Kertész-Wilkinson, Irén
  1992   "Genuine and Adopted Songs in the Vlach Gypsy Repertoire: a Controversy Re-exam-
          ined." *British Journal of Ethnomusicology* 1:111-133.
  2000   "Bi-musicality and the Hungarian Vlach Gypsies. Learning to Sing and Dance as an
          Ethnomusicological Research Tool." In *Music, Language, and Literature of the Roma
          and Sinti*. Max Peter Baumann, ed. Berlin: VWB, 361-370.
  2001   "'Gypsy' Music." In *The New Grove Dictionary of Music and Musicians*, Vol. 10.
          Stanley Sadie, ed. London: Macmillan Publishers, 613-620.

Kolar, Walter (ed.)
  1976   *The Folk Arts of Yugoslavia*. Pittsburgh: DUTIFA.

Kovačević, Krešimir (ed.)
  1984   *Leksikon jugoslavenske muzike*. Zagreb: Jugoslavenski leksikografski zavod "Miroslav
          Krleža."

Kovalcsik, Katalin
  2000   "The Gypsy Folklore Movement in Hungary." Paper presented at the intercongression-
          al symposium The Past in the Present, Budapest.

Kuhač, Franjo
  1899   "Das türkische Element in der Volksmusik der Croaten, Serben und Bulgaren." (Sepa-
          rat-Abdruck aus *Wissenschaftliche Mittheilungen aus Bosnien und der Hercegovina*,
          VI. Band). Wien: Carl Gerold's Sohn.
  1909   *Osobine narodne glazbe naročito Hrvatske*. Zagreb: Dionička tiskara.

Kumer, Zmaga
  1977   *Etnomuzikologija*. Ljubljana: Filozofska fakulteta Univerze v Ljubljani.

Lazarević-Golemović, Jovanka
  1953-4 "Lazarice u Prizrenskom Podgoru." *Glasnik Etnografskog instituta Srpske akademije
          nauka* 2-3:557-563.

Merriam, Alan P.
  1964   *The Anthropology of Music*. Evanston: Northwestern University Press.

Petrović, Ankica
  1997   "The Status of Traditional Music in Eastern Europe." In *Folklore and Traditional Mu-
          sic in the Former Soviet Union and Eastern Europe*. James Porter, ed. Los Angeles:
          Department of Ethnomusicology, UCLA, 49-59.

Roots Music 477

Svanibor Pettan. Encounter with "The Others from Within" • **137**

Petrović, Radmila

1974   "Narodna muzika istočne Jugoslavije—proces akulturacije." *Zvuk* 2:155-60.

Pettan, Svanibor

1992   "'Lambada' in Kosovo. A Profile of Gypsy Creativity." *Journal of the Gypsy Lore Society* 5/2:117-130.

1996a   "Gypsies, Music, and Politics in the Balkans. A Case Study from Kosovo." *The World of Music* 38/1:33-61.

1996b   "Selling Music. Rom Musicians and the Music Market in Kosovo." In *Echo der Vielfalt. Traditionelle Musik von Minderheiten-ethnischen Gruppen = Echoes of Diversity. Traditional Music of Ethnic Groups-Minorities.* Ursula Hemetek, ed. Wien: Böhlau Verlag, 233-245.

Rice, Timothy

1996   "The Dialectic of Economics and Aesthetics in Bulgarian Music." In *Returning Culture. Musical Changes in Central and Eastern Europe.* Mark Slobin, ed. Durham: Duke University Press, 176-199.

Salo, Matt

1979   "Gypsy Ethnicity: Implications of Native Categories and Interaction for Ethnic Classification." *Ethnicity* 6:73-96.

Sárosi, Bálint

1980   "Gypsy Music." In *The New Grove Dictionary of Music and Musicians*, Vol. 7. Stanley Sadie, ed. London: Macmillan Press, 864-870.

Silverman, Carol

1981   "Gypsy Ethnicity and the Social Contexts of Music." Paper presented at 76th Annual Meeting of the American Anthropological Association, Houston, IL.

2000   "Rom (Gypsy) Music." In *The Garland Encyclopedia of World Music*, Vol. 8. Timothy Rice, ed. New York: Garland Publishing, 270-293.

Subhi Hanna, Nabil

1982   *Ghagar of Sett Guiranha: A Study of a Gypsy Community in Egypt.* Cairo: American University in Cairo.

Sutherland, Anne

1975   *Gypsies: The Hidden Americans.* New York: The Free Press.

Širola, Božidar

1940   *Hrvatska narodna glazba.* Zagreb: Matica Hrvatska.

Vasiljević, Miodrag

1950   *Jugoslovenski muzički folklor I. Narodne melodije koje se pevaju na Kosmetu.* Beograd: Prosveta.

Vekerdi, Jószef

1976   "The Gypsy's Role in the Preservation of Non-Gypsy Folklore." *Journal of the Gypsy Lore Society* 4/1(2):79-86.

[21]

The Whole and the Sum of the Parts, or, How Cookie and the Cupcakes Told the Story of Apache History in San Carlos

DAVID SAMUELS

On the San Carlos Apache Reservation in southeastern Arizona, popular music circulates as a means of constructing statements of indigenous Apache identity in the community. The sense of Apache identity depends at least as much on engagement with, and revoicing of, "dominant" cultural expressions as it does on the persistence of the traditional forms associated with cultural heritage. In this article I trace out some of the aesthetic tropes that recur in these contemporary expressions of identity, arguing that it is a sense of shared history, rather than one of shared culture, that informs identity in this community. I also argue that the theoretical productivity of the concept of hybridity, if anything, is its potential for guiding researchers to foreground the strategic creation of utterances rather than assuming the explanatory power of cultural provenance in a philological sense.

ON SAN CARLOS APACHE VETERANS DAY, 1995, the Pacers got a gig playing for the tribal cattle association outside their office building after the big parade.[1] We spent the afternoon and evening switching off, five songs at a time, with an all-veteran chicken scratch band from Sells, a punk band from San Carlos, and a man from Sacaton who sang country songs to a karaoke accompaniment. As we played, I noticed Big Bell, who had been the lead singer of a group called the Dominoes 30 years ago, dancing across the parking lot. After every song, people in the crowd shouted for "Mathilda," as they had all afternoon, as they did every time we played. Most of the band members had grown tired of the song. I, on the other hand, had developed an intellectual curiosity about and attachment to "Mathilda," this 35-year-old song that has retained so much evocative power in the San Carlos Reservation community.

The impetus for the analysis that follows grows out of this distinction between my intellectual distance from "Mathilda" and Big Bell's feelingful, embodied response—a response that was repeated, with variation, over and over by different actors in different contexts during the course of my stay in San Carlos. "Mathilda" has circulated through San Carlos and Bylas for more than three decades, and people's responses to it are

David Samuels *is Assistant Professor of Linguistic Anthropology at the University of Massachusetts at Amherst* steeped in those communities' histories and the multiple ways in which the song is woven into people's personal experiences and social memories.

One such person—both in the sense that he was personally affected by the song and that his life personally affected the lives of many others who continue to fondly nurture his memory in their experiences of the song—was Theodore Kindelay, better known as Sluggo. He passed away more than ten years ago, but in spite of that, Sluggo remains a very important presence in the communities of the reservation. He is very important because he sang rock and roll. People say Sluggo was the best rock singer the reservation ever produced. Sluggo sounded like Rod Stewart, said one. Sluggo sounded like Smokey Robinson, another said. Pat, the Pacers's lead guitarist, told me that Sluggo had the right voice for every type of song. To this day, when one of the songs he was known for comes on the radio—say, "Slip Away," "Sail Away," or "I'm Your Puppet"—people remember him.[2] Sluggo influenced two generations of popular musicians in the community—all the members of the Pacers were in a band with Sluggo at one time or another. He is fondly remembered as someone who might have "made it," if only things had been a little different. Before he died, Sluggo tape recorded at least a portion of his life story. His family allowed me to make a copy of one of those cassettes, which covered the period from about 1956, when he was sent to the Franciscan St. John's school in Sells, Arizona, to 1965, when he went to the Bureau of Indian Affairs (BIA) boarding school in Stewart, Nevada. At the beginning of the tape, Sluggo talks about his discomfort when he first came home to Bylas in 1963 and met his relatives again after so many years away: "The first evening I came home, I was really homesick. Where? St. John's. There was no running water in the house, no electricity, no TV, radio, or anything like that. I quickly got over that, but some of my cousins came over to check me out and I felt out of place, since I couldn't talk Apache."

As the summer wore on, Sluggo became more comfortable in the community. It was rock and roll that eased the way:

> But that summer was a whole change in my life. First starting out, my cousin Carl had a band known as the Cyclones. Every evening they would practice at Andrew Juan's house, and we the peons would stand around outside smoking cigarettes, checking out the music. That went on mostly every evening. The songs they usually played I learned by listening to them were "Mathilda," "Just Because," "Breaking Up Is Hard to Do," and "Hello Josephine." That's how my singing began.
>
> One afternoon, cousin Carl and Andrew were practicing up on a couple of chords, that [sic] they were taking out their Silvertone amps and Silvertone guitars. We hung around them until I asked them, "Do you want me to sing 'Breaking Up Is Hard to Do' for you?"
>
> "Do you know it?" they asked. I said, "Sure!"

On another tape that I have, from 1981, Sluggo is sitting in for Philip Cassadore on the Apache Hour radio program on KIKO-AM, clearly having learned enough Apache in the intervening years to deejay a program, read advertisements, and announce requests.

466   Journal of American Folklore 112 (1999)

Warp and Weft

In this article I want to talk a little about how things become part of a community, about how material that arguably comes from "the outside" is woven into the fabric of everyday life, taking on deeply contextualized symbolic meanings. In doing so, I also want to make an argument about how the concept of hybridity interrogates the ways in which we naturalize cultural distinctions. What does it mean to say "hybridity" rather than "syncretism," "modification," "culture transfer," "incorporative integration," or some other such term? If the term *hybridity* merely offers, to mangle a metaphor, old wine in a new bottle, then why not simply keep one of these other terms?

I think the term can denote changes both in the world and in our approaches to it. In brief, I sense two shifts. First, the older terms tend to concentrate on conjunctions. An approach to the syncretism between American Indian and American popular musics, for instance, might emphasize the productive use of such shared features as vocables, pentatonicism, and drums. In contrast, hybridity foregrounds combinations of *disjunctions*. For instance, Deborah Kapchan describes linguistic hybridity as "the mixing of formally noncompatible genres and registers" (1996:4), and, from a descriptive point of view, it is this noncompatibility that distinguishes hybridity from syncretism's attention to the mixing of compatible materials (see Herskovits 1938; Waterman 1952).

Second, the earlier terms tend to foreground the idea of systemic encounters—"African music" with "Western music" and so forth. This is wholly in keeping with anthropologists' approach to aesthetics in general at the time. The approach is compatible with, for example, Maquet's sense that, because aesthetics is about the individual encounter with a work of art, anthropology has had little to say to that because the discipline does not operate at that level (1979); or with Geertz's notion of art as a "cultural system" (1983:94–120). I would argue that by contrast the term *hybridity* indicates a shift in focus onto the utterance. This shift foregrounds the notion of discourse (as the cultural poetics of particular contextualized utterances) rather than language (as the system of lexicon and syntax). It thus can lend itself more readily and generally to contemporary questions of agency, maneuver, and tactics in the constitution of social reality.[3]

To put this another way, in an increasingly global and translocal world, what distinguishes hybridity as an analytical concept ought to be how it can help us to understand the richness and density of radically local experience. By focusing on the utterance, I would hope that the concept of hybridity would bring us closer to experience, by shifting our focus away from systems and institutions as such and more clearly onto how people experience systems and institutions and how power works in and through socialized individuals.[4]

Too often, though, it seems to me, we fall back on a mode of analysis of hybrid expressions which we might call "philological," one that is overly archaeological and genealogical in form. While particular expressions are the data of such an analysis, its purpose is dedicated to untangling strands in order to clearly place their points of origin. When we speak about music, for instance, we have a tendency to explain styles by formulating their genealogical "roots." Reggae is ska plus Rastafarian mysticism; ska is mento plus American rock 'n' roll; mento is rhumba-shaded rhythm plus European chord structure; American rock 'n' roll is blues plus country western (see Davis and Simon 1977; Lipsitz 1994; White 1991). Such an analysis of hybrid forms can celebrate the creativity of bricolage but cannot locate the creative spark of style.[5] Not that this creative spark is easy to locate in any event, but my sense is that the notion of hybridity, by training our attention on particular situated utterances, forces us to grapple with strategic practices by disallowing the cover of "cultural systems" as a fallback explanation.[6]

The philological observation, accurate though it may be, is predicated on a concept of history that essentializes the indexical relations between knowable groups of people and expressive practices. But the sedimentation of the passage of time also breaks apart these indexical relationships. Indeed, part of the political transformation at stake in hybrid utterances is to challenge and interrogate the naturalized authority of those indexical relations (Kapchan 1996). To presuppose that the attribution of historical origins should take precedence in the analysis of hybrid utterances helps to create an alienating discourse, reinforcing the outside perspective of the researcher (see Stewart 1991). For in order to objectively know that something belongs "historically" to either one group or another, it is necessary to place oneself outside both groups to observe the flow between them. What the concept of hybridity ought to do for us, I think, is force us closer to the ground.

Them and Us

Let me offer here an example of what I mean by the alienating perspective in the analysis of hybrid expressions. One means of creating hybrid expressions in San Carlos, of embedding a second voice within an utterance, is by code switching song texts.[7] For example, the melodic contours of traditional Apache songs involve short, reiterative melodic phrases. Singers often comment on this melodic style by replacing a song's Apache-language text with reiterative English texts, such as the days of the week or the alphabet:

One afternoon, I was driving with a friend out to his mother's house, and in the middle of our conversation he broke into song:

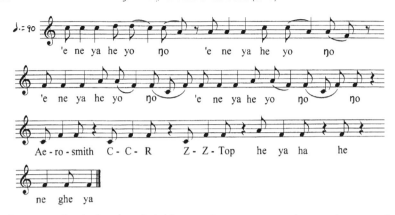

One way of analyzing these hybrid expressions—an extremely tempting way—is to maintain that there is an inside and an outside, that one part of the expression—vocables and melodic form—comes from inside "Apache culture" whereas another part—English language and rock band names (Aerosmith, Creedence Clearwater Revival [CCR], ZZ Top)—comes from outside, from the dominant "white culture." The hybrid utterance is then the produced effect of the history of the political domination of the Apache community, an expression of the encroachment of "white culture" on "Apache culture." A number of issues appear to flow naturally from this analytical perspective. One group of questions centers on the sources of the various materials used in the construction of the expression: where do different things come from?

In this sense, I could say that "Mathilda" and "Just Because" and ZZ Top and CCR emanate from a sort of New Orleans bayou center of rock, a center that spread across Louisiana and Texas and through the southwest into southern California during the 1950s and early 1960s (see Bernard 1996). I could talk about the dispersal of particular songs geographically into the community. "Mathilda," for instance, was originally recorded by a New Orleans–based group called Cookie and the Cupcakes. The song was a minor hit, rising as high as number 48 on the Billboard charts in 1959. Despite this somewhat limited status, the song was intensely influential throughout the southwest. It has been covered by Roosevelt Nettles, by The Fabulous Thunderbirds, and by Freddy Fender. For its part, "Just Because" was originally recorded by New Orleans–born Lloyd Price, best known for "Stagger Lee," which spent a month at number one in 1959.

A second set of questions centers around the intentionality of speakers and performers: why are these particular elements arranged in this particular way? As for my friend's playful song, there the poetic choices are constrained somewhat by the melodic resources at hand: we needed a collection of three-syllable phrases in which the second syllable is unstressed. B. B. King, Megadeth, Motley Crüe, and Johnny Cash fit; Deep Purple, Merle Haggard, and Van Halen do not. Given those constraints, though, there are any number of bands and performers, popular in San Carlos, that could have been chosen. So we return to the local importance of a particular style of rock music, popular in the southwestern regional corridor extending from New Orleans across

Texas into the Southwest, in his selection of ZZ Top, from El Paso, and CCR, which certainly cultivated a "bayou" image despite being from the San Francisco Bay area.

And all of this is "real"; I do not mean to deny the importance or the truth-value of this sort of analysis.[8] What is unclear to me, in the context of these expressions that draw on arguably mixed resources, is how explanatory that philological approach is or what exactly it explains. If the inevitable analytical response to hybrid expressions is to dissect them into their constituent parts, then we unduly alienate our analysis from the object being analyzed. These hybrid expressions are not comments about what it means to be "Apache" in the context of "U.S. culture." [9] They are comments about what it means to experience life in San Carlos. An analysis that stops at the incongruity of certain juxtapositions stops short of that experience. If I hold out any hope for "hybridity" as a concept, it is that it might rescue us from what Baudrillard has called "the hysteria of causality" (1988:189), the rationalist insistence that history is explanation (see also White 1987; Young 1990).

Then and Now

What would it mean to take hybridity as a more radical challenge to the ways in which culture contact and culture change have been figured in the history of anthropology? to say, in effect, that "Mathilda," "Just Because," "Breaking Up Is Hard to Do," and "Hello Josephine" are Apache songs and that Aerosmith, CCR, and ZZ Top are Apache bands? to not worry so much about where these things come from and instead concentrate on how they take on deeply felt symbolic meaning for communities? To my thinking, it would mean backgrounding the explanatory force of "culture" (in its sense of "heritage," what we might call culture$_1$) in the constitution of contemporary identities and in turn foregrounding the explanatory force of "culture" (in its sense of "everyday practice," what we might call culture$_2$).[10] That is, by shifting our attention from the persistence of cultural$_1$ forms to the everyday circulation of cultural$_2$ forms, we ground our sense of the community in the entangled and indeterminate practice of everyday life. If we are able to accomplish this, I think, we must move from an exterior analytical place, where we witness things moving "into" and "out of," to an interior place, where we can witness things circulating "around" and "through." This gets us nearer the heart of the matter in San Carlos, where the everyday circulation of cultural$_2$ forms is accounted for by appealing not necessarily to a shared heritage or culture$_1$ but, rather, to a shared history of engagement and encounter with a wide array of cultural$_2$ forms.[11]

The Centrality of History on the Reservation

In the community of San Carlos, history is ubiquitous. It is in the land and the way people respond to the land. It is in the way people talk about their lives and experiences. To begin with, everyone knows something of the history of the community. As you drive around with people, they point out the bluff where the frame of an old covered wagon still stands, the canyon where old cavalrymen are buried. They might take you to the graded bed where the railroad tracks ran before Coolidge Dam was built. Everyone knows the old Military Trail leading to Fort Apache. And everyone seems to have a story about where the real boundary of the reservation is.

But if history is ubiquitous and pervasive, it is also disjointed and fragmented. These episodes and bits of knowledge do not find coherence by being drawn together into a chronological statement of events. History here is not about chronology. It is about feeling, the feeling of belonging in a place, knowing that your presence in a place is justified. That feeling is cultivated in San Carlos in cameo moments of aesthetic pleasure, whereby complex and divergent elements are superimposed and linked in instants that are often as short-lived as they are poignant. In these moments, present, past, self, other, knowledge, and feeling coalesce in a richly layered image of historical meaning.

History, then, is a premier modality of aesthetic pleasure and judgment in San Carlos. The backward look, through space and time, is an important and desired effect of aesthetic expression. All sorts of expressive endeavors are judged to be particularly successful if this transportation occurs. One friend described his pleasure at a ceremony he attended by commenting that, as he and his wife lay in their verandah at night, as he listened to the gentle breeze and a very light rain began to fall, his thought was, "Wow, this is what it was like back then." "Back then" is an open, indeterminate, enigmatic time, to which one can go, given the proper invitation.

One of the desired effects of musical expression in San Carlos, then, is to transport the listener backward, into other times and other places. Given the history involved, and the sense of loss and longing that often accompanies it, it is unsurprising, perhaps, that an old Apache song or traditional ceremony can create that kind of feeling for the past in a listener. This feeling is embodied in an Apache interjection: *héla*! It is when something reminds speakers of a time or place that they miss or that they thought had been lost. And this is one of the things that people expect a good song to do.

But this sense runs both deeper and broader than "traditional Apache music." A good song is one that allows listeners to imagine the way things used to be. A traditional song can do that, certainly. But so can an old rock and roll song. Most adults seem to have a collection of old 45s and cassette tapes, and many compile them into personal collections that they carry around, ready to play on any available car stereo. These songs remind people of other times and places, of friends and relatives long gone, of days at the Lutheran Mission school in East Fork or the BIA boarding school at Stewart or Riverside. These memories easily flow into historical imagination because—at least for people of a certain age—to remember school days is to remember a political relationship with the three Great White Fathers of assimilation: government, Christianity, and education. To remember the 1950s is to remember the 1850s—it is a very slippery slope.

I do not think, though, that it is necessarily the age of a song that gives it this transportative power. Rather, it is the emotional and feelingful responses it evokes in a listener. Mediation plays an important role here in its capacity for repetition. The recurrence of a song on the radio, on the jukebox at Curley's, played on a boom box or by a band at a party, allows a building up and layering of experiences and feelings. Repetition brings these times, places, and people back into the apprehension of the listener, so that what once was is again: "Héla! Alchesay Hall!"; "Héla! Sluggo used to sing that." This layering of people, places, events, and music is the thickening of experience, the knowledge of what it means, how it feels, to be from San Carlos. This thickening becomes historical consciousness; for more accurate than saying that music triggers memory is to say that music triggers the imagination. The feelingful layering of indexicality and iconicity leads one to say, as my friend said to himself at the ceremony, "Wow, this is what it was like back then," in this sense: "If I exchanged places with someone from 'back then,' we would both be having the same feeling that I'm having now." One Bob Marley song—of course, Bob Marley—reminds a friend of mine of Old San Carlos.[12] "Never been there, never saw it, never lived there," he said. Yet and still, the song puts him in mind of those days and of hard times.

I also want to emphasize the particular power of music in the constitution and evocation of this historical consciousness. Music's involvement here is visceral, trigger-ing potent and deeply and immediately felt body memories and sensibilities. One can contrast the participatory consciousness (see Keil and Feld 1994) evoked by music, for instance, to the type of historical consciousness one might get from looking at old photographs. One friend of mine told me about sitting in his Spanish class at Globe High School in the late 1960s. He was leafing through a library book that contained old photographs of Apaches. The class was supposed to be learning a Spanish song that day:

> [I stopped to look at] a picture of those guys being herded toward Old San Carlos from—they were walking, Geronimo and his group, and soldiers on horseback, and then they were, you could see the dust, it was like in a wash. And I still remember how that song goes, [sings] "quando caliente el sol, da da da da da da," it was a mellow song, and it gave me a melancholy feeling over me, and I *felt* for those people.

The music—not an Apache song by any means—allowed him to enter into the photograph he had been looking at and experience that world—not to imagine what they felt, or to understand what they felt, but to feel what they felt.

One 12-year-old girl told me that she, like many people in San Carlos, liked to think about "the history, my culture, the way it was, the way it *is*." And there are songs—Mariah Carey's "Hero," Guns 'n' Roses's "November Rain," the whole of Bob Marley's *The Legend*—that put her in that frame of mind, for, when Indians were going through hard times, she said, from *reading* history you get the idea that the Indians would have lost faith. "But," she said, "when you put that song on top of it, it makes it seem like they *would* have faith, if they had that *song*"—that song would have helped them.

Conclusion: Rock and Roll

Veterans Day, 1995, the Pacers got a gig playing for the cattle association after the big parade. As we played, I noticed Big Bell dancing across the parking lot. He rocked and jittered to the beat, shimmying and shaking to the bottom-heavy pulse laid down by our drummer. Someone once told me that Kane plays "Hawaii Five-O style," and as he thundered through yet another roll around the tom-toms, Big Bell seemed to quiver with every note, allowing the sound to possess him.

472 *Journal of American Folklore* 112 (1999)

With a voice like Aaron Neville, Big Bell used to be the backbone of the Dominoes, an important band in the early 1960s in San Carlos. Big Bell's cousin, Ernie Lee, had passed away a year earlier, and his family made sure that the obituary in the local paper included that he "played guitar and sang" for the Dominoes (*San Carlos Apache Moccasin* 1995:2). Like the Rebels, the Dreamers, and the Statics, the Dominoes were big in their day, playing regularly at the new armory and the Little Maverick in Safford. These days, when prompted to sing, Big Bell often offered up "Come Go with Me," the Dell Vikings's hit from 1957. A lot of people who were not there at the time would probably be surprised to learn that he had been a mainstay of the band era in San Carlos. But those who were there remember it.

People in the crowd were shouting for "Mathilda," as they had all afternoon, as they did every time the Pacers played. Most of the band members had grown tired of the song, as one might expect they would after playing it three times a night, every time the band performed publicly. One of the band members once described his attitude toward the song, saying, "Well, they want to hear 'Mathilda,' so I figure let 'em choke on 'Mathilda' if it makes them happy." On the other hand, I had developed an intellectual curiosity about this 35-year-old song, this minor hit that Sluggo sang, this song that has retained so much evocative power. So a few months earlier Marshall had decided—both to take advantage of my interest and to allay the boredom of the rest of the band—that he would have me sing the song, even though I did not know more than half the words. "Don't worry," he said. "No one really knows the words." So once again we launched into "Mathilda." And there in front of me was Big Bell, standing a couple of yards away from me, facing me with his arms outstretched, his back arched, a look of beatific release on his upturned face, singing along, leaning into every note with all his heart. *He* knew all the words. I am transfixed, still, by our co-performance. He felt the song so thoroughly, and as I sang, I could see that "Mathilda" possessed him fully, as he possessed it. So completely did it pulsate through every fiber of his being—who am I to say that this is somebody else's music?

Notes

A version of this article was originally presented at the conference "Theorizing the Hybrid" at the University of Texas at Austin, 22–24 March 1996. My thanks go to Deborah Kapchan and Pauline Turner Strong for inviting me to present at that conference and for reading earlier drafts of the article. I also wish to thank Andrew Causey, Keila Diehl, Steven Feld, David Henderson, and Susan Lepselter for their helpful comments on earlier drafts. This manuscript was completed during an Institute of American Cultures postdoctoral fellowship in the American Indian Studies Center at UCLA, and I thank the center for that time. To Big Bell, Marshall, Kane, Pat, the Pacers, and a number of others who preferred to remain anonymous I give my thanks for allowing me to make them characters in this story and for reading earlier versions of it. To the Kindelay family, I give my thanks for allowing me to use portions of Sluggo's autobiography. All errors and omissions are my own.

[1] From August 1994 to February 1996, I lived in a trailer in the Seven Mile Wash district of San Carlos, supported by grants from the National Science Foundation, the Wenner-Gren Foundation, and the Jacobs Fund for Native American Research. I carried out ethnographic fieldwork with rock and country musicians in the communities of San Carlos and Bylas. The Pacers, also known as the Country Pacers, were the best-known band in the community, and I had the privilege of playing guitar with them during the 17 months of my research.

[2]"Slip Away" was recorded by Clarence Carter and released in 1968 (Atlantic 2508), reaching as high as number six on the Billboard Hot 100; "Sail Away" was released by Creedence Clearwater Revival in 1972, on the album *Mardi Gras* (Fantasy F-9404). If it was ever released as a single, it never made the top 40; "I'm Your Puppet," recorded by James and Bobby Purify in 1966 (Bell 648), also reached number six on the Billboard charts (Whitburn 1987).

[3]Conceptually, of course, this means that the referent for "hybridity" is as much the observer as the observed. Preference for the term denotes an approach to cultural phenomena that owes a certain allegiance to Bakhtin (1981, 1984, 1986) and a more open and unbounded notion of "culture" in general, as well as a renewed consideration of the place of expressive culture in the constitution of everyday life (Appadurai 1990; Gupta and Ferguson 1992; Hannerz 1987; Keil and Feld 1994; Stewart 1996).

[4]A number of people working in the areas of language socialization and bilingualism have taken a similar approach. See Kulick 1992, Schieffelin 1990, Schieffelin and Ochs 1986, Urciuoli 1996, Zentella 1997.

[5]I would argue that some of the blame for this type of analysis lies with the ascendance of cultural studies and its somewhat problematic acceptance of the transparency of commercial market categories.

[6]This does not mean that there is nothing "systematic" about "culture." It is a question of where to focus one's attention.

[7]It should be clear by now that, according to my reading, code switching is a hybrid, not a syncretic, practice. Indeed it is interesting to note in this context that one of the earlier uses of the term *hybrid* appears in ethnomusicologist Willard Rhodes's discussion of American Indian songs with English words (1963).

[8]An analogous problem revolves around the phenomenon of linguistic change and loan words. Some Western Apache words, such as *beso* for "money" or *silaada* for "soldier," are recognized by native Apache speakers as loans from Spanish (*peso* and *soldado*, respectively). This transparency is not always the case, however. There are, for instance, two words in Apache that might be translated as "God"—*bik'ehgoihinań* and *yusń*. These two terms live side by side, much in the way that *elohim* and *yahweh* appear in the Old Testament. Although *bik'ehgoihinań* is unquestionably an Apachean form (meaning something along the lines of "the living being responsible for life"), linguists have argued that *yusń* is a borrowing of the Spanish *dios*, with an animating postpositional enclitic *-n*. Native speakers of Apache, however, disagree, arguing that *yusń* is derived from *yigołsįh* ("he or she knows it"), with the postpositional *-n*, and thus has a meaning close to "omniscient" or "all knowing." This etymology does not disprove the linguists' observations, but it opens up a field of inquiry that these observations, which dismiss such native notions as being mere "folk etymology," cannot address (Alleyne 1996).

[9]Or they are so at only one level of objective analysis.

[10]Clearly this by no means exhausts the multiple meanings and uses attributed to the term *culture*. However, I believe it does, in fact, cover a wide range of the uses to which the word has been put in discussions of ethnic or cultural identity.

[11]One reviewer suggested that this resonated with the old "folklore in" versus "folklore of" debate. Put in those terms, my sense of the matter is that there is no "folklore of" unless it is also "folklore in." An account of the persistence of a cultural₁ form in a new context—even assuming the persistence of the form—must take account of that new context, as was pointed out by Kirshenblatt-Gimblett (1975).

[12]The song is "Johnny Was," from *Rastaman Vibration* (Island/Tuff Gong ILPS 9383 [1976]). The importance of Bob Marley in contemporary San Carlos will have to be the subject of another—much longer—article.

References Cited

Alleyne, Mervin. 1996. Models of Language Mixture: The Creole Case. Paper presented at the conference "Theorizing the Hybrid," University of Texas at Austin, March 22–24.

Appadurai, Arjun. 1990. Disjuncture and Difference in the Global Culture Economy. *Public Culture* 2(2):1–24.

Bakhtin, Mikhail. 1981. *The Dialogic Imagination: Four Essays*, ed. Michael Holquist and Caryl Emerson; translated by Caryl Emerson. Austin: University of Texas Press.

——————. 1984. *Problems of Dostoevsky's Poetics*, ed. and translated by Caryl Emerson. Minneapolis: University of Minnesota Press.

474 *Journal of American Folklore* 112 (1999)

_____. 1986. *Speech Genres and Other Late Essays,* ed. Caryl Emerson and Michael Holquist; translated by Vern W. McGee. Austin: University of Texas Press.

Baudrillard, Jean. 1988. *Selected Writings,* ed. Mark Poster. Stanford, CA: Stanford University Press.

Bernard, Shane K. 1996. *Swamp Pop: Cajun and Creole Rhythm and Blues.* Jackson: University Press of Mississippi.

Davis, Stephen, and Peter Simon. 1977. *Reggae Bloodlines: In Search of the Music and Culture of Jamaica.* New York: Anchor Books.

Geertz, Clifford. 1983. *Local Knowledge: Further Essays in Interpretive Anthropology.* New York: Basic Books.

Gupta, Akhil, and James Ferguson. 1992. Beyond "Culture": Space, Identity, and the Politics of Difference. *Cultural Anthropology* 7:6–23.

Hannerz, Ulf. 1987. The World in Creolization. *Africa* 57(4):546–559.

Herskovits, Melville. 1938. *Acculturation: The Study of Culture Contact.* New York: J. J. Augustin.

Kapchan, Deborah. 1996. *Gender on the Market.* Philadelphia: University of Pennsylvania Press.

Keil, Charles, and Steven Feld. 1994. *Music Grooves.* Chicago: University of Chicago Press.

Kirshenblatt-Gimblett, Barbara. 1975. A Parable in Context: A Social Interactional Analysis of Storytelling Performance. In *Folklore: Performance and Communication,* ed. Dan Ben-Amos and Kenneth S. Goldstein, pp. 105–130. The Hague: Mouton.

Kulick, Don. 1992. *Language Shift and Cultural Reproduction: Socialization, Self, and Syncretism in a Papua New Guinean Village.* New York: Cambridge University Press.

Lipsitz, George. 1994. *Dangerous Crossroads: Popular Music, Postmodernism, and the Poetics of Place.* London: Verso.

Maquet, Jacques. 1979. *Introduction to Aesthetic Anthropology.* Malibu, Calif.: Undena Publications.

Rhodes, Willard. 1963. North American Indian Music in Transition: A Study of Songs with English Words as an Index of Acculturation. *Journal of the International Folk Music Council* 15:9–14.

San Carlos Apache Moccasin. 1995. Ernie Lee. *San Carlos Apache Moccasin,* January 3: 2.

Schieffelin, Bambi B. 1990. *The Give and Take of Everyday Life: Language Socialization of Kaluli Children.* New York: Cambridge University Press.

Schieffelin, Bambi B., and Elinor Ochs, eds. 1986. *Language Socialization across Cultures.* New York: Cambridge University Press.

Stewart, Kathleen. 1991. On the Politics of Cultural Theory: A Case for "Contaminated" Critique. *Social Research* 58:395–412.

_____. 1996. *A Space on the Side of the Road: Cultural Poetics in an "Other" America.* Princeton, N.J.: Princeton University Press.

Urciuoli, Bonnie. 1996. *Exposing Prejudice: Puerto Rican Experiences of Language, Race, and Class.* Boulder, Colo.: Westview Press.

Waterman, Richard. 1952. African Influence on the Music of the Americas. In *Acculturation in the Americas,* ed. Sol Tax, pp. 207–218. Proceedings of the 29th International Congress of Americanists, vol. 2. Chicago: University of Chicago Press.

Whitburn, Joel. 1987. *The Billboard Book of Top 40 Hits: Fascinating Trivia and Complete Chart Data about the Artists and Their Songs—1955 to the Present,* 3rd edition. New York: Billboard Publications, Inc.

White, Hayden V. 1987. *The Content of the Form: Narrative Discourse and Historical Representation.* Baltimore: Johns Hopkins University Press.

White, Timothy. 1991. *Catch a Fire: The Life of Bob Marley.* New York: Henry Holt and Co.

Young, Robert. 1990. *White Mythologies: Writing History and the West.* London and New York: Routledge.

Zentella, Ana Celia. 1997. *Growing Up Bilingual: Puerto Rican Children in New York.* Malden, Mass.: Blackwell.

Name Index